MW00591077

AGE
OF
EMPIRES
IV

Introduction

Welcome to the official Companion Book for Age of Empires IV!

We chose to call this a companion book—rather than a game guide or, as Craig Mullins suggested, "a true nerd book"—because the sheer variety of things it's filled with made calling it anything else feel a little bit misleading. While it does fill the role of a guide to the game, a lot of the space on the following pages is dedicated to concept artwork and to commentary from the game's developers at Relic and World's Edge. Putting together a book that requires input from across every discipline and level of the development team while they're all hard at work finishing and balancing the game is no easy task. The result is something that we think can both enrich the experience of playing the game and act as a time capsule of where the game and the many people involved in its development stood in late 2021, as Age of Empires IV neared its long-awaited release.

We'd like to thank the people at World's Edge and Relic who helped make this book possible. These people really do care to a remarkable degree about this game and franchise. In fact, if you're someone who's excited to hold this book in their hands, you can direct a large portion of your thanks to Noble Smith—his absolutely genuine passion for art books is a major reason why this book happened at all. He, along with Han Randhawa and Savannah Harrison, pushed this book to the finish line and helped us make it something unique. We wanted to make a book that would have a lot of value for fans of the series, but perhaps more importantly, might bring new players deeper into the game and the series it belongs to. Ultimately, we hope this book helps players to find their feet in a complex, fast-paced competitive game and gives them an appreciation of exactly what it took to bring it all to life.

—The Future Press Team

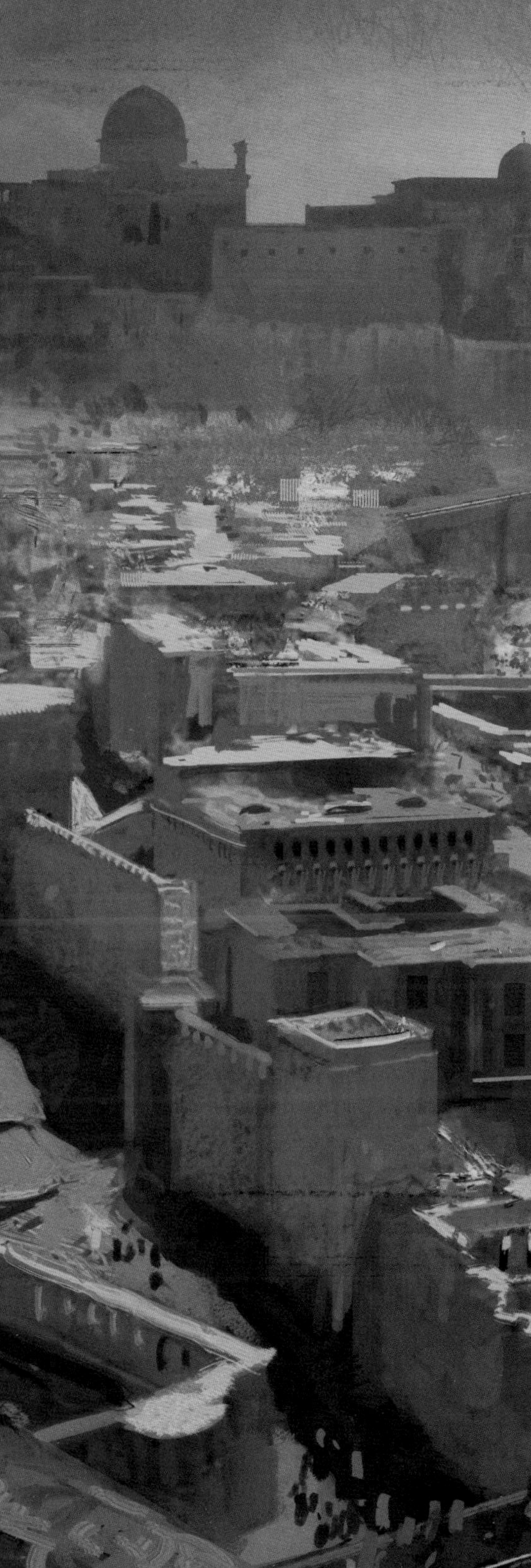

I remember the first time I played Age of Empires. I was working at Westwood Studios on the Command & Conquer series, and we'd heard of this new Real Time Strategy game that was focused on history. "History? No, that can't be right. Really? History is dead, isn't it? Why go there?"

My (naive) perspective in 1997 (I'd spent ~4 years in the games industry at that point) was that games needed something flashy and catchy to attract players, and history couldn't be that! While I'd certainly enjoyed history in school, likely because I had some very engaging and passionate teachers, I never thought of it as fertile ground for an RTS. So, I approached the game with a measure of skepticism, certainly.

After spending time with it, I came to two conclusions: First, I really needed to adjust my perspectives on what could appeal to players, and second how bloody clever it was to make a game that centered on human history. While it wasn't our modern world, which is where my head was in making games at the time, it was about us—humanity's past: the people and cultures that through their actions shaped the modern world. It was immediately understandable and relatable in a way that every other game couldn't just expect people would understand; all the steps needed to explain technology and progress just melted away, because we were dealing with people and human events and endeavors that everyone could relate to. It all just clicked. Brilliant!

Over the years, I've played all the Age games as they released, spending the most time playing co-op "comp stomps" in Age II with friends and partners. It was always fun to jump into the delightful mix of city building, economy, campaigns, and combat that defined the Age experience and carved its own space with a unique blend of features and pacing. I always had fun with the games in all the ways I'd play them; there's nothing but good memories surrounding them for me.

When I was approached in 2016 with the ask "What would a new Age of Empires game want to be?" I was honored that I could contribute to this storied franchise. Trying to find the best mix of respecting the heritage of Age of Empires while also modernizing with Age of Empires IV is an ongoing challenge that myself and all of the incredibly talented people on the development teams will continue to work on well into the future.

What I've come to appreciate about Age of Empires is how much the game series has meant to so many people around the world, and in all the different ways it has done so. As just one of many people that have contributed to the legacy of Age of Empires, I couldn't be more humbled by the various responses the series has received—for over 20 years!—tfrom all the fans from around the world, each coming to Age with such vastly different perspectives and identities, yet all finding common ground within these games that so effectively unite players and lovers of history.

One thing I've taken to heart in working on Age is that we need to represent each person (or culture's) stories accurately and with passion. This book is a celebration of that journey we've undertaken in developing Age of Empires IV, with all of you in mind as we went. Our goal was to make sure we found gameplay in the uniqueness of each Civilization, captured their artistry and flair in the art direction and design, and celebrated these cultures and their roles in history.

We hope you find the journey in these pages as delightful and fascinating as we at World's Edge and Relic Entertainment did when undertaking it.

—Adam Isgreen
Franchise Creative Director, World's Edge

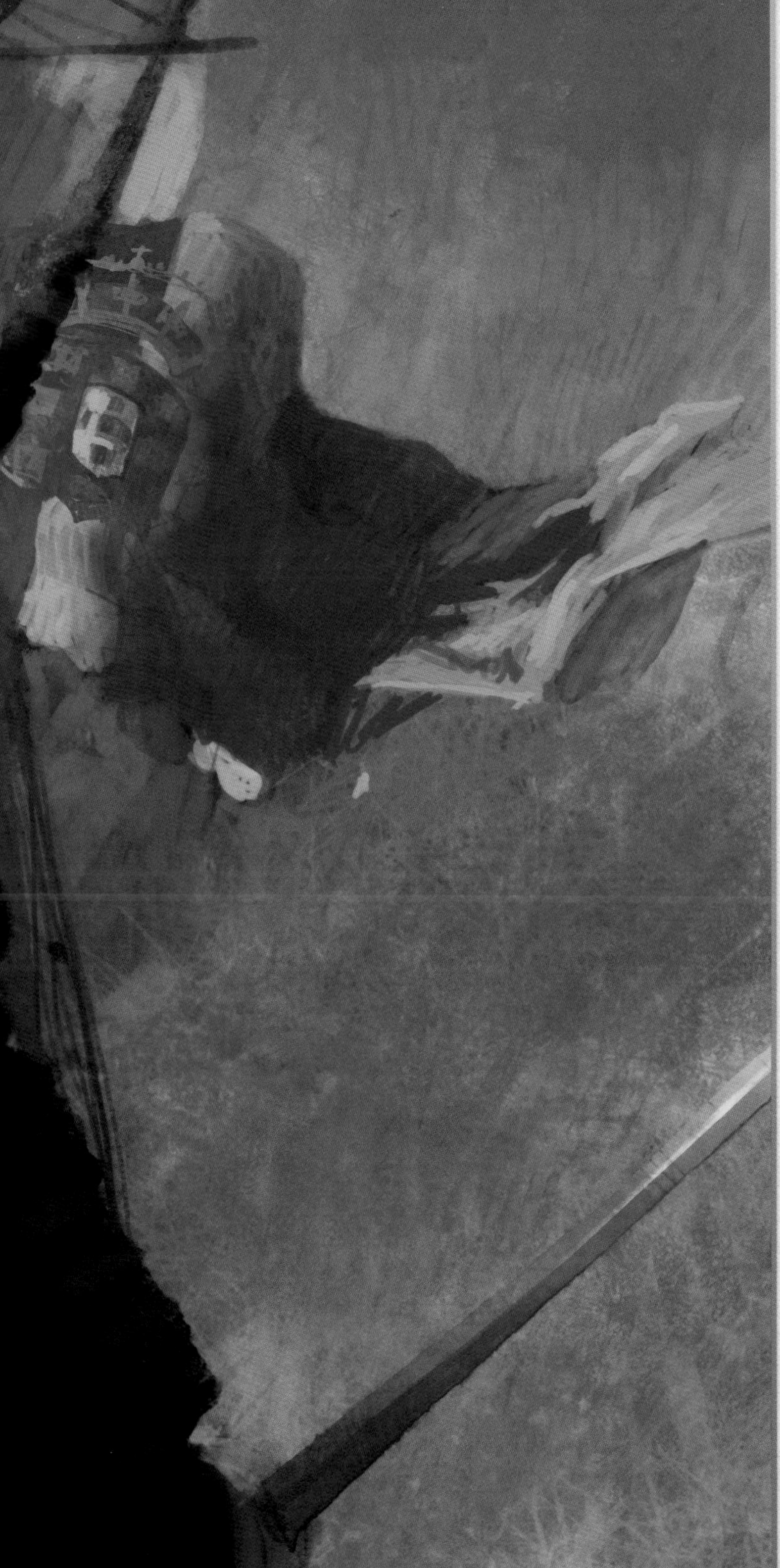

Table of Contents

Preface

Wow. It's here. Almost seven years ago, a producer from Microsoft called a studio manager in Vancouver and asked, 'Do you like Age of Empires?' And now, you're holding the Age of Empires IV Companion Book, full of the imagery and creativity and passion that has also gone into the award-winning game. The journey has been long, and beautiful, and scary, and difficult, and so rewarding. Age fans have been with us every step of the way, so, congratulations! You are all game developers now.

We here at World's Edge have been asked, 'Why Age? And why now?' There are some prosaic reasons: computers finally have the power to do more of what made Age great in the first place, real-time strategy is ripe for a renaissance, most of the world is connected in a way that makes it possible to reach a truly global audience. But the real reason is that we got to choose. We've all been Age fans and players from the beginning, and every person on this team has dreamed of bringing Age back for the modern era for a long time. Every moment is a moment in history; this is OUR shared moment. Go make history yours.

– Shannon Loftis
VP, Studio Manager, World's Edge

About the Data

Age of Empires IV is a competitive game that Relic and World's Edge will continue to tweak in the interest of balance long after its initial release. This means that some of the data in this book is subject to change after publication and is likely to become less accurate over time. Knowing this, we feel that including it all is still important for the community and for new players, both as an accurate starting point and as a complete picture of the game's balance upon release.

Principal Designer, Narrative Lead

Philippe Boulle

What is your role on the project, and what does your day-to-day work consist of?
I'm the Narrative Lead, which means I'm responsible for all the storytelling elements in the game. This can mean setting up cameras and voice over in missions, writing and reviewing videos with our partners, recording speech in studio, and more. And of course, working with my great team of other narrative designers.

What are your favorite game/s of all time?
Hard to name just one. My RTS love goes all the way back to *Dune II*. Favorite game of the last generation was probably *Horizon Zero Dawn*.

Favourite non-Age of Empires RTS game/s?
The original *Company of Heroes.*

How much time do you spend playing games outside of work?
I tend to go through cycles, with some periods where outside work time is taken up by family and "real life" and others when I am diving deep into a game that's become an obsession. Hades is the most recent of the former category. That and my weekly tabletop roleplaying, of course.

What's your general playstyle in RTS games?
I'm a classic turtle, looking to take my time and build defences. I mostly play campaigns, taking my time with the content.

Which is your favorite civilization in AoE IV, and why?
I love the Mongols and their mobility, along with the amazing history they represent.

Which are your favorite units in AoE IV, and why?
I love the French Monk for the amazing put-upon delivery of "Wololo!" from the voice actor. Makes me smile every time.

What feature of the game are you most excited for players to try out?
I'm definitely looking forward to people seeing the beautiful cinematics that highlight the history in the campaign.

Design Director

Christopher Rubyor

What is your role on the project, and what does your day-to-day work consist of?
My current role for Age of Empires IV is Design Director. At a high level, my focus is ensuring our design vision and goals are being achieved throughout the course of development. From a more tactical day-to-day point of view, I work closely with our internal/external partners attending daily stand-ups and a variety of design-related meetings to provide oversight and ensure feature/content implementation is on track. I also serve as a subject matter expert and RTS guru for both our internal and external Age teams.

What are your favorite game/s of all time?
This is an amazingly difficult question that spans decades of gaming across of variety of platforms. Here are a couple that have influenced my desire to create compelling RTS games.

1. Chess—I would play chess for hours with my dad. The simplicity of the pieces and their unique function matched with a simple battlefield (chess board) make for a truly elegant strategy experience.
2. *Herzog Zwei* for the Sega Genesis—I would play this game for hours learning every map and nuance of the AI. There was a lot of depth to the design; a hybrid between tower defense and RTS. My friends and I spent many weekends battling split screen.
3. *Star Control II*—Shooter combat, galactic exploration, resource management, and saving the Earth, what is there not to love?
4. *Dune II: The Building of a Dynasty*—Brought my love for strategy games to a whole new level. I was in 12th grade when Dune II was released. After playing through the campaigns, I remember telling my parents that I'm going to build a game like this one day. I never would have thought one year later from that conversation I would be working for the company (Westwood Studios) that created it.

How much time do you spend playing games outside of work?
Varies week to week. Sometimes I'll spend 12+ hours playing games or none at all. When I'm not playing, I'll work on my own games in Unity, which tends to eat a huge chunk of time.

What's your general playstyle in RTS games?
Rush! Strike First. Strike Hard. No Mercy!

Which is your favorite civilization in AoE IV, and why?
I enjoy playing the Mongols. They start with max popcap, their Ovoo automatically collects stone, and all their structures are mobile. This adds a lot of efficiency to their playstyle.

Which are your favorite units in AoE IV, and why?
There are so many units to choose from! But the staple of my battle groups usually includes the following: Battering Ram—these are not only good at breaking down walls but offer some good hit and run gameplay against lighter structures. Monk—these units are incredibly powerful in Age IV. Unlike past Age games, a Monk holding a Relic gives the player an area of effect conversion ability, no more single target. So, players can convert large groups of enemy units to fight for them. This can turn the tide of any battle, but it is difficult to execute due to the vulnerability of the Monk unit. Mongol Khan—this unit functions as a leader/hero that can inspire units in proximity via several abilities. In addition, the Khan grows in strength with each new Age the player achieves.

What feature of the game are you most excited for players to try out?
I'm really excited about the campaign mode that's been developed for Age IV. The team has done an amazing job of blending history and RTS to create a truly rich and highly compelling experience.

Principal Artist, Art Director

Zach Schläppi

What is your role on the project, and what does your day-to-day work consist of?

My role on Age IV is Art Director. Depending on the phase of the project, I'm typically either establishing the high-level direction, collaborating with the team to guide the visual direction of the game, reviewing concepts and asset, and/or mentoring developers—also known as, "my calendar is full of meetings!"

Have you worked on any previous Age of Empire games?

I have not. My background started in lighting and compositing for feature animation, but I transitioned to game development because the future of lighting in game development looked brighter. I worked primarily in open-world first and third person shooters on console with some mobile and eSport development along the way. My focus has been on refreshing franchises, so naturally I was very excited at the opportunity to work on Age of Empires IV.

What are your favorite game/s of all time?

I have three favorite games that I often think about throughout my career: *Shadow of the Colossus*—they did such a great job instilling these creatures with awe. I wanted to be with them, not kill them. *Uncharted II* was the first time I played a game where the visuals matched the majesty that I felt with Miyazaki's work in *Spirited Away*. The third game is *Red Dead Redemption*—the world was so well realised; I could live out any moment from my most favorite Peckinpah Western.

Favourite non-Age of Empires RTS game/s?

My first experience with RTS was when I worked at Electronic Arts Los Angele—they merged with Westwood Studios and so *Command & Conquer* and *Lord of the Rings: Battle for Middle Earth* was in the building. I wasn't aware of RTS until they handed out *LotR:BFME*. I took it home. I admit, it took a while for me to understand how to play RTS, but I found my fun and played Gondor because I likened it to the Middle Ages. Yet, I was inexplicably ignorant of Age of Empires at the time! Years later I discovered *Company of Heroes* after wondering what my colleagues were playing after work. I was instantly pulled in by the World War II setting, modified RTS mechanics, and it looked and sounded beautiful. This is probably my favorite—given the graphics and tone of gameplay. Must have made an impression on me, as I joined the company. Imagine my joy upon realizing I would be working on an Age of Empires title that takes place in the Middle Ages—the very game I unknowingly have been wanting to play for years!

How much time do you spend playing games outside of work?

I hate validating the marketing data I read about, but now that I am married, with young children in tow—my time budget for video games has shrunk from long format sprawling open world games to mobile and short FPS bouts.

Which is your favorite civilization in AoE IV, and why?

All the civs have some great elements I love, whether it's the nest of bees for the Chinese, the elephant units for the Delhi Sultanate or the Long Bow for the English. Overall, I really love the look of the French civ and the visual sumptuousness of the Abbasids.

Which are your favorite units in AoE IV, and why?

Any of the gunpowder units. If only because after hearing almost an hour of gameplay—such a palette cleanser to hear gun and cannon fire above the din of trebuchets and wololos.

What feature of the game are you most excited for players to try out?

I'm really curious to see how stealth woods is received by the general community. It changes the way scouts are used and introduces an extra dimension to the battlefield.

Franchise Narrative Director

Noble Smith

What is your role on the project, and what does your day-to-day work consist of?

I am the keeper of the historical canon and overseer of all franchise storytelling.

Have you worked on any previous Age of Empire games?

Age I: DE; Age II: DE; Age III: DE and all DLC.

What are your favorite game/s of all time?

The *Diablo* franchise; *Portal*; *The Legend of Zelda: Breath of the Wild*.

Favourite non-Age of Empires RTS game/s?

Warcraft; *Company of Heroes*.

How much time do you spend playing games outside of work?

Not as much as I'd like to.

What's your general playstyle in RTS games?

Turtle master.

Which is your favorite civilization in AoE IV, and why?

This would have to be the Delhi Sultanate because the Tower War Elephants are so cool; but I love the designs for all the units (even the villagers), the architecture and the Persian language & music.

Which are your favorite units in AoE IV, and why?

Elite English Longbowmen (for range); HRE Landsknecht (for melee); French Lancers (speed); Delhi Sultanate War Elephants (the tanks of our game); and Rus Streltsy (for their devastating firepower against armored units).

What feature of the game are you most excited for players to try out?

Shooting from walls. Fighting on walls. Using siege towers to invade the top of a wall. Basically…walls.

Franchise Creative Director

Adam Isgreen

What is your role on the project, and what does your day-to-day work consist of?

I'm World's Edge's studio creative director, so I oversee the creative elements of our projects to ensure they delight our customers from all over the world. I oversee the design, audio, art, and narrative elements of our games and look to how we combine them all to create a great experience for our different games and audiences.

Have you worked on any previous Age of Empire games?

I worked on the DE versions of Age I, II, and III from the creative direction angle.

What are your favorite game/s of all time?

I've played just about every game genre and every PC/console that was mass produced since the Atari 2600 originally launched. I love all genres and all types of games. Favorites include *The Secret of Monkey Island, X-COM, Star Control II, Killer Instinct, Castlevania: SotN, Terraria*, the *Panzer Dragoon* series, *Jet Set Radio, Dragon Quest* series, *Persona 4 Golden, Horizon Zero Dawn, Forza Horizon* series, *Sega Rally, CONTROL*... that's just a taste.

Favorite non-Age of Empires RTS game/s?

The *C&C* series, specifically *Red Alert* and *Red Alert II*. I was at Westwood Studios for years and was one of the key people that created the RA universe. It's hard not to love it!

How much time do you spend playing games outside of work?

30+ hours a week, either weeknights or weekends, but I game almost every day if I can.

What's your general playstyle in RTS games?

Really this depends on the civilization, but I tend to gravitate towards those that use fewer number of units but have interesting technological advantages or unique elements to them that rely on cool tech options.

Which is your favorite civilization in AoE IV, and why?

The Delhi Sultanate is my current favourite because elephants. And tech. =)

Which are your favorite units in AoE IV, and why?

Elephants for the power and strategies the two types bring to the battles. I also tend to like special units like the Landsknechts of the HRE

What feature of the game are you most excited for players to try out?

The campaigns and our new approach to storytelling and history for an RTS. We've never done anything like this before and I'm looking forward to hearing what players think of it!

Senior Designer, Balance Lead

Eric Wrobel

What is your role on the project, and what does your day-to-day work consist of?

Making sure the game is perfectly balanced.

What are your favorite game/s of all time?

I have a number of them! Specifically, Action RPG would be *Diablo II*, and really if you are playing an action RPG if it doesn't start with "*Diablo*" and end with a number, you are doing it wrong. City-building games always have a fond place in my heart. *Caesar III* hit a nice balance between economic development and military conflict. For Grand Strategy games it's has to be Sid Meyer all the way! All six *Civilization* games were fantastic... Even when a spearman sunk my battleship in *Civilization I*!

Favorite non-Age of Empires RTS game/s?

Warcraft III for innovating with heroes, items, and upkeep mechanics. *Starcraft II* campaign blending of gameplay mechanics, story, and progression. *Lord of the Rings: Battle for Middle-earth II* for the cavalry-trampling mechanic.

How much time do you spend playing games outside of work?

It's too embarrassing to check the thousands and thousands of hours on my Steam account! And then there's also all the time spent watching people streaming games. Oh, I play boardgames too... and hockey is technically a game. Let's just settle on: "Games are big part of my life"!

What's your general playstyle in RTS games?

I tend to follow this tried-and-true method when playing RTS Games:

1. Out-think my enemy with unit counters
2. Know where they want to position their army before they do
3. Out-micro the enemy and run them around the map
4. Forget to macro while I'm doing these things and lose because I have thousands of unspent resources
5. Queue up for another match

Which is your favorite civilization in AoE IV, and why?

LOVE asymmetric design standouts like the Mongols - They get a hero unit and can't build walls or keeps! I enjoy playing the Chinese for their speedy construction and dynasty system full of special bonuses and extra landmarks! The Rus because for them wolves are [...] full of gold!

Which are your favorite units in AoE IV, and why?

Everything gunpowder because the look and feel is so powerful. I also enjoy using the Mangudai, being able to move and shoot is a super fun micro tool. Also, the Ram construction in the field, so thematically appropriate for a middle ages game. And +1 to Abbasid for building Mangonel in the field!

What feature of the game are you most excited for players to try out?

Being able to play 1000s of ladder games with each one feeling unique because of random maps, asymmetric civs, and landmark choices.

Principle Designer, Narrative

Lauren Wood

What is your role on the project, and what does your day-to-day work consist of?

Narrative design is a really broad role, encompassing a wide variety of work from blue-sky conceptualising to writing to bug fixing. On this project, my main work areas were historical research throughout the project; writing, editing and directing large portions of the narrator's voice over; writing any narrative text that appears on screen (unlockable historical articles, mission briefings, etc.); reviewing documentary edits from the film production crew; implementing and testing voice over in the missions and fixing bugs in the script.

What are your favorite game/s of all time?

I love a good narrative-led game with lots of puzzles. There are so many good ones, but I especially liked *Portal, Immortals: Fenyx Rising, Hellblade: Senua's Sacrifice, Ico* and *The Legend of Zelda: Ocarina of Time.*

How much time do you spend playing games outside of work?

If there's a game I'm really into, I'll play for probably a couple of hours a night.

What's your general playstyle in RTS games?

I am a relatively inexperienced RTS player, so I tend to go super defensive. Walls everywhere, big investment in economy and upgrades, and I never go on the attack until my army is good and ready!

Which is your favorite civilization in AoE IV, and why?

There are so many to experience, but I particularly like the nomadic ability of the Mongols. Being able to pack up your production and relocate to a better spot is amazingly freeing! It takes away the stress of wondering if you picked the right location to build your base. Out of resources? Just move!

Which are your favorite units in AoE IV, and why?

Tactically, I tend to go heavy on the archers as I like to pick the enemy off from a distance. I especially like being able to deploy palings. From a historical perspective, it's great to have civ-specific units in there like the Mongol Mangudai Horse Archers and the more unusual units like the Abbasid Camel Archers and the Delhi War Elephants. I enjoy the spectacle of seeing them in action!

What feature of the game are you most excited for players to try out?

Having been immersed in the production of all the narrative content on this game, I am excited to see how the campaign is received. We're treading new ground with our documentary-style narrative content, and the films turned out spectacularly well. I hope people enjoy them and maybe learn something too!

Senior Designer, Narrative

Kristina Wiik

What is your role on the project, and what does your day-to-day work consist of?

My role on the project as Narrative Designer has me doing a little bit of everything! I do a lot of writing for the Mission content but I'm also in charge of implementing this content and making sure it all sounds good in the game. I work closely with the mission designers to make sure the narrative is serving the mission's intent and vice versa—it's a collaborative effort! I also script events and ensure camera sequences all look good, so I get a nice balance of creative and technical work.

Have you worked on any previous Age of Empire games?

Nope, this is my first one and I'm really excited about it!

What are your favorite game/s of all time?

The Witcher III, AoE II, *Rimworld, Myst, Hearthstone, Silent Hill II, Shadow of the Colossus, Warcraft III, Counter Strike 1.6*—I'm going to stop myself here and try not to keep adding to the list…

How much time do you spend playing games outside of work?

Probably too much. I really enjoy discovering new titles and giving them their due. I try to play a lot of different genres—I think there's so much room for games to influence each other and it's important to keep a broad perspective as a designer.

What's your general playstyle in RTS games?

If left to my own devices, I'll almost always turtle and play defensively. It's been interesting challenging myself to explore new playstyles when working on Age of Empires IV. Specifically, it's fun surprising my opponent by playing more aggressively; because a lot of my co-workers knew me as a turtle player early on, I've been able to catch folks unaware here and there and disrupt them in ways they didn't expect. It's been fun!

Which is your favorite civilization in AoE IV, and why?

I definitely enjoy playing the Mongols, especially when I'm going for an aggressive start: early cavalry can be devastating in the opening beats of a game. Additionally, the Mongols' ability to pack up production and rotate around the map with their resources can be a huge relief in the later game, both in terms of freeing up resources and cognitive load for me as a player.

Which are your favorite units in AoE IV, and why?

I am partial to the Nest of Bees—who doesn't like fireworks?!

What feature of the game are you most excited for players to try out?

I'm biased as a Campaign designer, but I am very excited for players to get their hands on the missions. I think the way we intertwine the systems of our game with the history of our

...chise History

AGE OF EMPIRES
15th October 1997

AGE OF EMPIRES: THE RISE OF ROME
31st October 1998

AGE OF EMPIRES II
30th September 1999

AGE OF EMPIRES II: THE CONQUERORS
25th August 2000

AGE OF EMPIRES II: THE AGE OF KINGS (PS2)
October/November 2001

AGE OF MYTHOLOGY
30th October 2002

AGE OF MYTHOLOGY: THE TITANS
30th September 2003

AGE OF EMPIRES III
18th October 2005

AGE OF EMPIRES II: THE AGE OF KINGS (DS)
14th February 2006

AGE OF EMPIRES III: THE WARCHIEFS
17th October 2006

AGE OF EMPIRES III: THE ASIAN DYNASTIES
23rd October 2007

AGE OF EMPIRES
(NINTENDO DS) MYTHOLOGIES
24th November 2008

AGE OF EMPIRES ONLINE
16th August 2011

1997

Age of Empires

- *Covers Stone Age and Antiquity*
- *Had a campaign exclusive to its trial version (Reign of the Hittites)*
- *Has the most cheat units available in the entire franchise*
- *One of, if not the first Real Time Strategy game that covers a historical period*

1998

Age of Empires: The Rise of Rome

- *Expansion for Age of Empires*
- *Strong focus on the Roman Empire*
- *Introduced unit queue*
- *Had a campaign exclusive to its trial version (First Punic War)*

1999

Age of Empires II

- *Set in the Middle Ages*
- *Campaigns focus on Europe, Asia and Africa*
- *Introduced*
  - *Formations (Line, Box, Staggered, Flanked)*
  - *Stances (Aggressive, Defensive, Stand Ground, No Attack)*
  - *Gates*
  - *Markets with the option to buy and sell resources*
  - *New population limit for Single-player: 200*
  - *Game mode: Regicide Players will be defeated if their king will be killed*

2000

Age of Empires II: The Conquerors

- *Expansion for Age of Empires II*
- *Campaigns focus on Conquerors*
  - *"Battles of the Conquerors" - a selection of long scenarios, focusing on historic events such as Hastings (1066) or Agincourt (1415)*
- *The Saxon Revolt*
  - *Hidden bonus scenario included on the CD*
  - *Made by Andreas Marscheider, Winner of Microsoft's Charlemagne Scenario Contest in 2000*
- *Despite not being Conquerors, the Koreans were added because Microsoft wanted to compete with Starcraft in South Korea*

2001

Age of Empires II: The Age of Kings (PS2)

- *Port of Age of Empires II without its add-on*
  - *Ported by Konami*
  - *The port uses the stats from The Conquerors, which means that Town Centers cost both Wood and Stone*
- *One of the few PS2 games that were shipped on CD instead of DVD*
- *Released in Europe and Japan*

2002

Age of Mythology

- *First 3D title in the AoE franchise*
- *Mixes ancient history with mythology*
- *Three civilizations in the base game*
- *The Golden Gift*
  - *Originally an add-on campaign, available to download for free on Microsoft's website*
  - *Later bundled with Extended Edition*

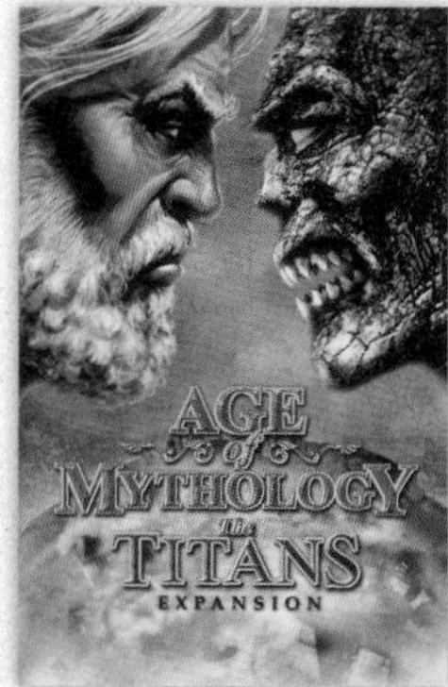

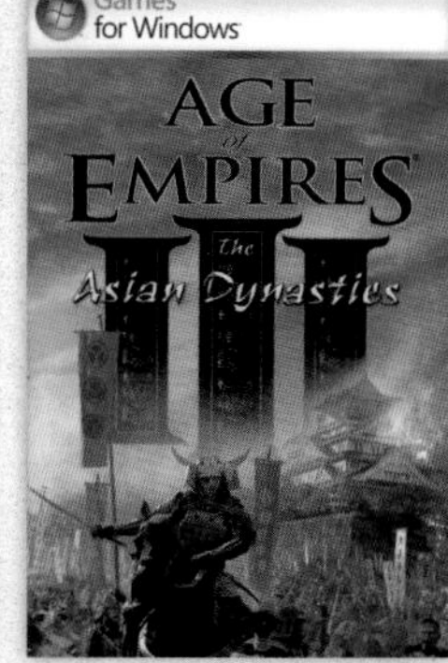

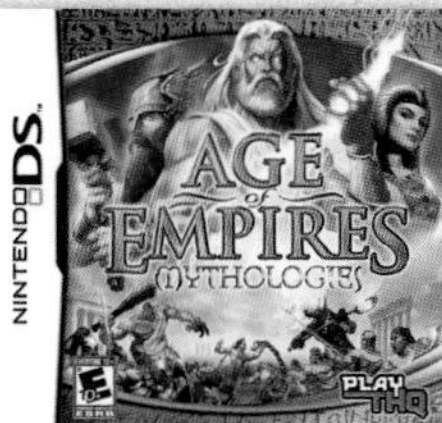

2003

Age of Mythology: The Titans

- Expansion for Age of Mythology
- Introduces "auto queue"
  - Infinite unit creation as long as you have enough resources
- Introduces
  - 5th Age: Titan Age
  - Titans Godlike creatures with powerful abilities

2005

Age of Empires III

- Covers Colonial Period in America
- New features:
  - Shipments (cards you can send from your home city that grant resources, stronger versions of buildings or units)
  - Treasures (resources that are guarded by wild animals or units on the map)
  - Physics simulation and damage
- The campaigns mix history with some fictional elements

2006

Age of Empires II: The Age of Kings (DS)

- Nintendo DS port
- Turn-based strategy with grid-based movement
- Advance to the next Age through researching

Age of Empires III: The Warchiefs

- Expansion for Age of Empires III
- Adds native American tribes (Sioux and Iroquois) and Aztecs as playable civilizations to the game
- New gameplay mechanic: Revolution
  - Instead of advancing to the fifth and final Age (Imperial Age), European countries can revolt from their home states
  - Through this, players can choose from different countries they can turn into (e.g. British turn into United States)

2007

Age of Empires III: The Asian Dynasties

- Expansion for Age of Empires III
- Adds 3 Asian civs to the game (India, China, Japan)
- New skirmish maps in Asia
- Base for the "Wars of Liberty" mod
  - Fan-made expansion that adds even more civilizations (e.g. Australia & Serbia) and maps to the game

2008

Age of Empires Mythologies (Nintendo DS)

- Turn-based strategy with grid-based movement
- Less faithful to historical authenticity of mythologies than the PC original
- Uses cut content from PC version

2011

Age of Empires Online

- Free to Play game
- Set in Antiquity
- Civilizations are upgraded through completing quests
- Servers closed on 1st July 2014

Craig Mullins, AoE III: DE Key Art *"The Chinese characters in the center left are from the original work I did for Age of Empires III back in 2006-7. Everything else was painted especially for this. There's a lot of work that went into the right side of this, especially the Discovery ship and the Tahitians going out on the boats. All of that was painted just for this composition."*

2013

Age of Empires II HD

- HD port of Age of Empires II: The Age of Kings and its addon The Conquerors
- Minor improvements
  - Smoother fog of war
  - New fire effect
  - 16:9 support
  - 60 FPS

Age of Empires II HD: The Forgotten

- First official expansion since The Conquerors, was originally the Forgotten Empires mod, released in 2012
- New game modes & features
  - Capture the Relic
    AoE's counterpart to the highly popular Capture the Flag mode
  - Treaty
    Peace time at the beginning of a game
- 5 new civilizations (Italians, Slavs, Magyars, Inca, Indians)
- 6 new campaigns + one collection of "Battles of the Forgotten"

2014

Age of Mythology: Extended Edition

- HD remaster of Age of Mythology and its expansion
- Improved visuals including a day-night cycle
- Available on Steam

Age of Empires: Castle Siege (Mobile)

- F2P Mobile game
- Mixture of real-time strategy and Tower Defense
- Servers closed on 13th May 2019

2015

Age of Empires II HD: The African Kingdoms

- Second official expansion for HD Edition
- 4 new civilizations (Malians, Ethiopians, Berbers, Portuguese)
- 4 new campaigns
- New game mode: Sudden Death
  - Players will be defeated if they lose their only Town Center available

Age of Empires: World Domination (Mobile)

- F2P Mobile game
- Servers closed in November 2016

2016

Age of Mythology: Tale of the Dragon

- Expansion for Age of Mythology: Extended Edition
- New content
  - Chinese civilization
  - Three new gods
  - AoE II-like monk unit

Age of Empires II: Rise of the Rajas

- Last official expansion for the HD Edition
- 4 new civilizations (Malay, Burmese, Khmer, Vietnamese)
- 4 new campaigns
- New general units:
  - Imperial Skirmisher
  - Battle Elephant

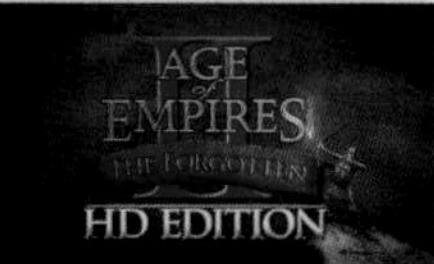

2018

Age of Empires Definitive Edition

- Was originally intended to be released in October 2017 (20th Anniversary of AoE)
- 4K Remaster of original + Rise of Rome
  - Improved visuals: buildings collapse when destroyed
  - Original soundtrack rearranged by orchestra
- Changes to campaigns
- Reign of the Hittites: First two scenarios removed as they were similar to the tutorial
- Certain missions renamed and reworked
  - Most notable change: "Coming of the Huns" from the Imperium Romanum campaign (mirrored version of AoE II's "The Catalaunian Fields" from the Attila campaign)
- Classic mode
  - Original graphics, sound effects and music with new UI
  - Only available in Singleplayer

2019

Age of Empires II Definitive Edition

- 4K Remaster of Age of Empires II and all official content
  - Improved visuals: buildings collapse when destroyed
  - Original soundtrack rearranged by orchestra
    Includes tracks previously exclusive to AoE II's demo and beta versions
- Includes new expansion: The Last Khans
- Originally planned as a DLC for the HD Edition
- Total civilization count: 35 (without DLCs)
- 200 hours of singleplayer content with campaigns
- Each campaign has been recreated and is now fully voiced
- "El Dorado" campaign has been replaced by an Inca campaign
- New game Modes
  - Empire Wars
    The game starts in Feudal Age with an already running economy
    Default game mode for Red Bull Wololo
  - Battle Royale
    Patched in with Anniversary Patch in November 2020

Craig Mullins, AoE II: DE Key Art

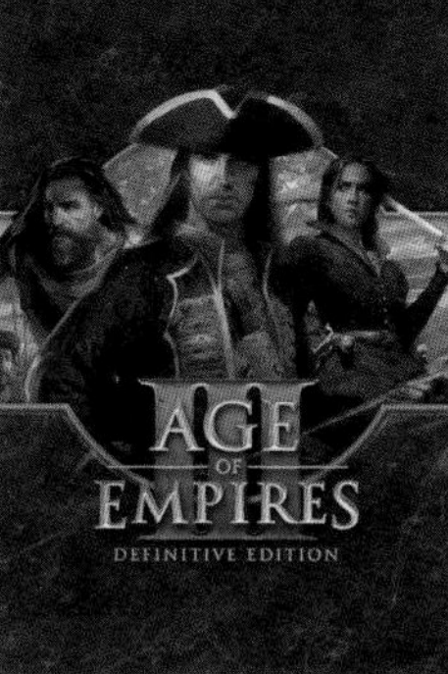

2020

Age of Empires III Definitive Edition

- *4K remaster of Age of Empires III and all official released content*
- *2 new civilizations: Inca and Sweden*
- *Changes to some of the game's terminology*
- *Reworked campaigns from The Warchiefs*
- *13th April 2021: Release of US Civilization, unlockable via 50 challenge event or as a paid DLC*
  - *Each challenge is named after a US state*

2021

Age of Empires II Definitive Edition: Lords of the West

- *2 new civilisations: Burgundians and Sicilians*
- *3 new campaigns introduced*
  - *Edward Longshanks (Britons)*
  - *The Grand Dukes of the West (Burgundians)*
  - *The Hautevilles (Sicilians)*
- *New unique units*
  - *Coustillier (Burgundian unique cavalry unit which can charge it's attack)*
  - *Flemish Militia (Burgundian unique infantry unit)*
  - *Serjeant (Sicilian unique infantry unit which can construct Donjons)*

Age of Empires III Definitive Edition: The African Royals

- *2 new civilizations: Ethiopia and Hausa*
- *3 new Historical Battles: Battle of the Three Kings, Fall of the Hausa and The Era of the Princes*

Age of Empires II Definitive Edition: Dawn of the Dukes

- *Released in August 2021*
- *Set in Eastern Europe*
- *Two new civilizations: Bohemians and Poles*

Age of Empires IV

- *Set in Middle Ages*
- *Gameplay mixes elements from of AoEII and III*
- *Campaigns in documentary style*
- *Released October 28th 2021*

2013

AGE OF EMPIRES II HD
9th April 2013

AGE OF EMPIRES II HD: THE FORGOTTEN
7th November 2013

2014

AGE OF MYTHOLOGY: EXTENDED EDITION
8th May 2014

AGE OF EMPIRES CASTLE SIEGE (MOBILE)
18th September 2014

2015

AGE OF EMPIRES II HD: THE AFRICAN KINGDOMS
5th November 2015

AGE OF EMPIRES: WORLD DOMINATION (MOBILE
December 2015

2016

AGE OF MYTHOLOGY: TALE OF THE DRAGON
28th January 2016

AGE OF EMPIRES II: RISE OF THE RAJAS
19th December 2016

2018

AGE OF EMPIRES DEFINITIVE EDITION
19th February 2018

2019

AGE OF EMPIRES II DEFINITIVE EDITION
14th November 2019

2020

AGE OF EMPIRES III DEFINITIVE EDITION
15th October 2020

2021

AGE OF EMPIRES II DEFINITIVE EDITION: LORDS OF THE WEST
26th January 2021

AGE OF EMPIRES III DEFINITIVE EDITION: THE AFRICAN ROYALS
2nd August 2021

AGE OF EMPIRES II DEFINITIVE EDITION: DAWN OF THE DUKES
10th August 2021

AGE OF EMPIRES IV
28th October 2021

CHAPTER

A New Age Begins!

Age of Empires is a franchise with a long, storied history and a deeply passionate community. For those new to the series, there's a lot to take in, so we've structured this chapter as a primer to ease you in to Age of Empires IV as smoothly as possible. For seasoned fans of the series, this chapter will let you quickly see what's new and different—from the basic mechanics to the map selection and playing against the A.I.—and it's all interspersed with developer commentary and concept artwork.

An Introduction to Competitive Age of Empires

As with many long-running competitive franchises, Age of Empires is thriving in the era of esports. Major organizations and sponsors are helping to bring the game to an increasingly large audience. It wasn't always this way, though; the AoE competitive scene started out small. It was, for many years, funded, organized, and administered entirely by its passionate fan base, who have been playing and enjoying the series since 1997. It wasn't until the early 2010s, with the rapid increase in the popularity of streaming services such as Twitch and YouTube, that community tournaments began to be broadcast to thousands of viewers. In more recent years, the series' combination of fast-paced action, limitless strategic options, and increasing accessibility gained the attention of sponsors who began enthusiastically supporting the competitive scene through prize pool contributions, media coverage, and tournament hosting.

ESports, in which multiplayer video games are played competitively in front of spectators, typically by professional gamers, has grown alongside the franchise over the past decade, to become an industry now valued at over one billion U.S. dollars. While games such as League of Legends, Defence of the Ancients 2 and Counter Strike: Global Offensive currently dominate the worldwide esports scene, the Age of Empires franchise continues to gain the attention of viewers, players, and sponsors around the world. For anyone picking up the series for the first time, a large and dedicated worldwide community of players awaits them—whether you want to play and learn the game for fun, or reach for the highest competitive levels, you'll find an abundance of players online eager to play and teach.

Contributors to this Book

In addition to the developers at Relic and World's Edge providing help and commentary, a few players from the AoE Community Council have provided significant contributions to this book. The Community Council is an initiative that had began several years prior to AoE IV's release, and involves the developers selecting a group of players from the community—from competitive to more casual, based on their contribution to the community—to play early versions of Age of Empires IV and provide feedback on various parts of the game. This crucial feedback helps to make ensure that the overall community's desires are incorporated and considered during development.

These are the Community Council members that worked on this book:

Clemensor	Maggy @205Maggy
Floos @FloosWorld	LilTrouble @LilTrouble__

Stuart Ng
Farming Mood Image
Concept Artwork

Designing Excitement

"The Age of Empires IV dev team was forged by esports—competing in, watching, and casting them. We love esports. Our number one priority has actually not been towards this target, but simply towards making the best game possible. The great thing about esports is that the ingredients for an exciting game to play also make for an exciting game to watch! Clearly visualized mechanics, easy to understand gameplay, random maps, cinematic presentation, asymmetric factions, and deep strategic decision making. We didn't set out to make an esport, but will be enjoyed by esports fans if that's what they want."

—Eric Wrobel
Senior Designer, Balance Lead, Relic

Ongoing Feedback

"Community feedback has played an essential role in Age of Empires IV's development from a very early stage. At several points in production we have sent a focused build of the game out to a small but growing group of players that make up what we call the Community Council. The team engages in discussion with and collects feedback from the council, which is then collated and reviewed. In many cases the feedback we receive is clear enough that we're able to translate it directly into action and can ready the changes in preparation for the next build. In others, we may have to find compromises that address feedback while respecting technological and production constraints—the realities of game development!

When Age of Empires IV is released to the world, we will have a much larger council providing us with feedback—that is, everyone. We'll be keeping a close eye on our forums and social channels to understand what the community's top priority items are and we'll be monitoring our telemetry to see how players engage with Age of Empires IV. Understanding both of those streams of data will help us prioritize which features, bugs, and improvements we should be spending our time on."

—Michael Conkin
Senior Designer, Ritual & Retention Lead, Relic

Series Growth

Age of Empires is often described as a "classic" series yet its ability to adapt and grow with the changing interests and demands of players is undoubtedly one of the reasons the game has remained relevant and popular. The number of active players of each of the Definitive Editions has grown steadily, and tournament prize pools have increased accordingly in recent years. Peak viewership for Age of Empires II:DE has reached new heights in the past year, with a total of over 38 million hours watched. The chart here shows peak active players for games in the franchise according to SteamDB.

Game	Peak Active Players (Steam)
Age of Empires:DE	2,705 (Nov '19)
Age of Empires II:HD	27,618 (Feb '20)
Age of Empires II:DE	38,725 (Dec '20)
Age of Empires III:DE	18,142 (Oct '20)

Mods

One of the greatest strengths of the Age of Empires franchise is the ability for players to modify—or "mod"—the games. The inclusion of the "Scenario Editor" with the original Age of Empires game, and most further entries in the series, created the opportunity for fans of the game to leave their own mark on the franchise. It also brought with it a unique opportunity to boost the competitive tournament scene via new scenarios, new game-modes, and especially new maps. The result is an ever-changing environment which benefits players and viewers in a way few other competitive series can boast: map pools and event themes remain fresh and captivating and competitive players embrace tournaments with unusual, mod-based rules. In 2021 alone, Age of Empires II: Definitive Edition has included fan-made maps in its official map pool, namely Four Lakes (a variant of Hidden Cup's "Cross" map), and the infamous Michi map.

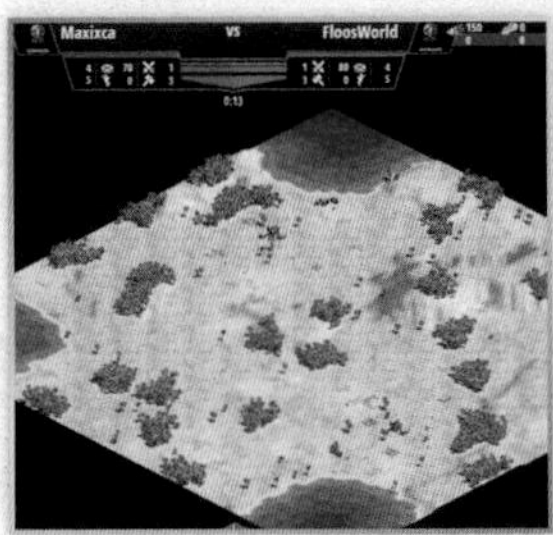

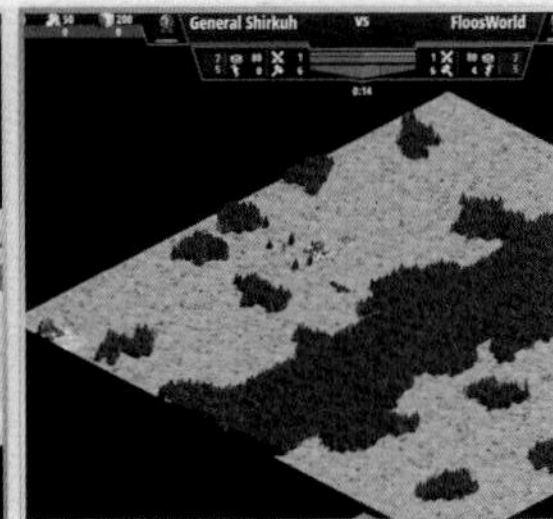

Here's a list of key mods and custom game modes throughout the series:

Age of Empires I

UPatch HD

- *Mod for the original release of Age of Empires 1.*
- *Adds support for modern resolutions up to 4K.*
- *Minor balance changes.*
- *In-built mod selector.*

5th Legacy

- *Mod for pre-Definitive Edition Age of Empires 1.*
- *Adds 30+ new civilizations to the game (e.g. Huns, Celts, Trojans).*
- ***New unit:** Scout, a villager-like unit that automatically walks over the map.*
- *Upgrade preview. The UI now gives you hints on which upgrades you can research with your civilization.*
- *Compatible with UPatch HD.*

Age of Empires II

Forgotten Empires

- ***Mod for Age of Empires II:** The Conquerors.*
- *Generally considered to be one of the most important mods for the franchise.*
- *Was later officially ported to HD Edition as its first DLC.*

Portuguese Civ Mod

- ***Mod for Age of Empires II:** The Conquerors.*
- ***Adds 5th Age:** Renaissance.*
- ***Adds 5th Resource:** Experience.*
- ***New Buildings and fortifications:** Trade Workshop, Tavern, Sea Walls, Sea Towers.*
- ***Wonder Power:** An additional bonus for your civilization once your wonder has been built.*
- ***Dodgeball:** A custom game mode for Age of Empires II: The Conquerors upwards. All players are Mongols and have a Bombard Cannon. The goal is to eliminate all opponents' Bombard Cannons.*
- ***Forrest Nothing:** Custom map for Age of Empires II: The Conquerors upwards. Popularized by T90, all players' bases are surrounded by trees.*

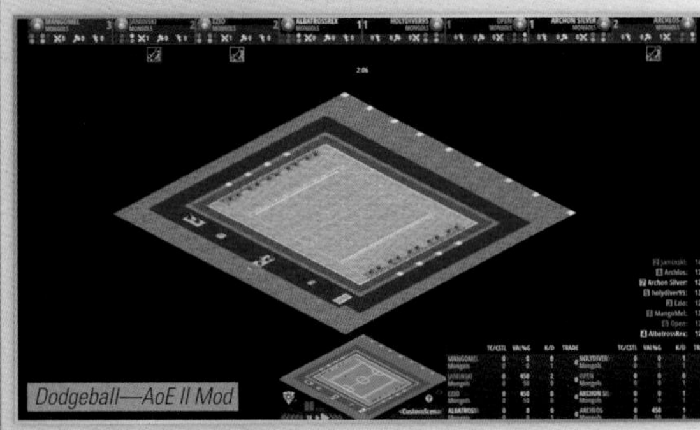
Dodgeball—AoE II Mod

Age of Empires III

Wars of Liberty

- ***Mod for Age of Empires III:** The Asian Dynasties.*
- *28 civilizations, including Australians, Serbians, Tupi and Greeks.*
- *New maps such as New Zealand, Australia, Black Forrest or even the moon.*
- *Villagers can put down fire. Fire can spread and be put out.*
- ***New building:** Safehouse. Spies are trained here and work differently from the original game. They can be only seen by your explorer and spies. They plant bombs, perform stealthy kills and can detonate buildings.*

Notable Names

There have been many notable players whose skill and strategy have helped to push the competitive scene forward over the years as it steadily morphed from groups of smaller communities into a full blown esport. Here we'll spotlight just a few from each of the main franchise games.

Age of Empires

Chim Sè Đi Nắng

Known by the nickname "Sparrow Go Sunshine", Chim Sè Đi Nắng is an idol amongst Vietnamese *Age of Empires* players. Having started playing the game at around 12 years old, the "Sun Sparrow" accumulated over 1.2 million followers on social media, and in 2019 was the number one streamer on the *Facebook Gaming* streaming platform. In-game, he is ruthless, but outside of the battlefield Chim Sè Đi Nắng is a humble, approachable man who helps organise professional esports events for the thriving Vietnamese *Age of Empires VNS_Cool*community. In a television appearance, he said that "being able to balance between live streaming, playing games and daily life is also a bit difficult, but thanks to the support of the fans, I will continue with the path that I have chosen."

Age of Empires II

Ørjan "'TheViper'" Larsen

Born in Norway and currently residing in Germany, TheViper is considered by many to be the best Age of Empires player in the world. His achievements are extensive, winning Hidden Cup 1, 2 and 3, Nili's Apartment Cup 1 and 3, King of the Desert 1 and 2, Death Match World Cup 3 and 4, just to name a few. Across his competitive career to date, TheViper has won over $140k U.S. dollars, and his game knowledge, alongside his macro, micro, and decision making skills has earned him the title of "Greatest Of All Time," as voted by fellow AoEII professional players on the community portal Aoezone.net.

Darko 'DauT' Dautovic

Born in Serbia in 1985, DauT is fondly referred to as "The Lord" within the community and has been active in the competitive scene since 2002. DauT might not have the fastest APM and might sometimes attempt risky castle drops, but ultimately he is a player who has certainly made his mark in the competitive scene. Like his teammate TheViper, DauT also has an impressive record of tournament results in both 1v1 and Team Game events, including winning RedBull Wololo 3 in 2021, taking his overall winnings to over $90k U.S. dollars.

Designer, Maps Lead

Nick Taylor

What is your role on the project, and what does your day-to-day work consist of?

I'm a designer on the procedural maps team, so I work on the components that make up our multiplayer maps and environments. My day-to-day includes things like balancing where and how many of each resource spawns on a given map, tweaking the terrain generation settings (for example tuning the width of a river, or upping the chance of a mountain to spawn on a particular map) and working with the art team to create our biomes by procedurally placing all of our textures, plants and rocks in the correct places.

What are your favorite game/s of all time?

Always tricky to narrow down! If I had to pick only a few, I'd include things like *Pokemon Yellow*, *Halo: Combat Evolved*, *Skyrim*, and *Metroid Prime*, all of which managed to capture a fantastic sense of exploration of their respective worlds. I've logged an embarrassing amount of time in *Skyrim*.

Favorite non-Age of Empires RTS game/s?

I'll give a big shout out to the Star Wars conversion of Age II, *Galactic Battlegrounds*, which I played to death as a kid! I played a ton of *Halo Wars* in its heyday too, but my comfort RTS that I always go back to is *Star Wars Empire at War*. Warping in with your huge fleet of Star Destroyers is still one of the coolest things you can do in any RTS.

What's your general playstyle in RTS games?

It totally depends on the game—I mained Zerg in *StarCraft*, so I'm no stranger to getting in a quick rush victory, but in Age of Empires IV, I've found I enjoy a more turtle playstyle. Maybe it's because I stare at the maps all day and I love envisioning how I can best set up my walls and defences, but I find building up my hopefully impregnable defense and having it tested to be super fun and compelling.

Which is your favorite civilization in AoE IV, and why?

I love playing the HRE—getting to build the Prelate in the Dark Age to manually boost my economy feels so interesting and different, then having them available to go and gather up as many relics as I can as soon as I hit Castle Age is a really fun sub-objective in every match. The music with the monk chanting is also just so so good!

Which are your favorite units in AoE IV, and why?

I really love all our gunpowder units, seeing a line of cannons blast through a wall with all the smoke effects is super satisfying, and having a row of culverins up on a hill sniping high value targets of an oncoming army really makes defending fun to watch and play.

Stuart Ng
Chinese Civilization Mood Image
Concept Artwork

Hamzah 'Hera' El-Baher.

Known for his impressive speed and micro, Hera made his mark as a top competitor in 2018 at the age of just 19. Since then, Canada's top player has evolved from a pure micro-oriented, aggressive player, into a mature and complete one, mastering all varieties of maps and facets of the game. While he remains one of the fastest players in the world, Hera now prefers relying on his macro to win games more reliably. Hera's style is characterized by his ability at expending his economy, even under heavy pressure, confidently defending and winning in the late game thanks to his unit control, raiding, and general macro play.

Age of Empires III

Haitch

Also known as "Hazza", Haitch is a young and friendly British player, caster and streamer. Only a few years ago Haitch was considered a "rising talent," and true to expectations he now claims the rank of Major General. Haitch is a master of the Russian civilization, yet his knowledge of other civilizations, his micro-management skills, and his mechanical execution places him among the best. Having won multiple invitational events, Haitch recently claimed his first Championship title when he beat Mitoe in the finals of the 2020 Winter Championship. He has been extremely successful across multiple game modes. particularly in the past two years, and perhaps the best is yet to come.

Kaiserklein

Frenchman Kaiserklein's Age of Empires III persona is considered legendary within the community, with extremely accurate micro-management, extensive game knowledge, and an impressive accumulation of competitive results. The winner of innumerable weekend tournaments, both seasons of the ESOC Grand Tour, the original Time2Micro tournament, the ESOC WarChiefs Classic 2 and a top finisher in every Seasonal Major since 2017, Kaiserklein has an exceptional track record. Favouring the German and French civilizations, Kaiserklein has been described by fellow AoEIII players as the "fearless French fanatic."

Samwise12

Samwise12 is one the most experienced players currently playing AoEIII:DE and has continuously performed at the highest level since the game's earliest years. Hailing from England, Samwise12 is known as a master of the French civilisation and has a unique build order named after him—the Samwise Build—which dominated the early meta. He has also achieved the highest ever recorded online ranked power rating of Level 53 Field Marshall. Samwise12's early honours include winning the Hope Tourney 1, NerVe Clan 1v1 and placing 2nd in the Hope Tourney 2 before taking a break from the game. On his return to the scene with the creation of ESOC (Ensemble Studios Online Community), Samwise won the $1,000 2015 Summer Seasonal tournament and has continued to play the game at an exceptional level, becoming a much-loved and well respected member of the community.

Notable Events

As with notable players, the long history of the Age of Empires franchise has produced many legendary esports events. These three tourneys have been highlighted as they each showcase a different game mode.

Age of Empires II

Hidden Cup

Undoubtedly the largest ongoing tournament in the professional Age of Empires II scene, the Hidden Cup series adds an element of mystery to the game. Players are given a pseudonym to play under, so viewers and casters don't know who is who, and the players themselves don't know who they're playing against, making preparation and planning more difficult. Hosted by T90, Hidden Cup has been held four times, with the Hidden Cup IV prize pool reaching over $87,000 U.S. dollars, and the finals between Hera (John the Fearless) and JorDan (Admiral Yi Sun-shin) peaking at over 76,000 viewers.

RedBull Wololo

With the new game mode of Empire Wars—introduced one year after Definitive Edition's release—the RedBull Wololo series has so far hosted four online events, with the top Age of Empires II professional players competing in fast-paced 1v1 battles that begin in the Feudal Age as opposed to the standard Dark Age. In RedBull Wololo, each player's economy is

ESOC Global Championship 2021 RO8 (Age of Empires III)

already established, with a set number of villagers, economy buildings, as well as a barracks and a blacksmith, so they can immediately jump into the action. In the most recent event, Wololo V: Enthrone, hosted at Heidelberg Castle in Germany, the finals came down to an epic seven-game showdown between Liereyy and TheViper, with TheViper taking the win 4-3 to claim the 'Enthroned' title and the impressive Trebuchet Trophy.

Death Match World Cup

Death Match World Cup 4 is the largest, most competitive Death Match (DM) tournament of recent years. Featuring a fast-paced and thrilling game mode, this tournament not only showcased the most popular DM settings as played on the ladder, but also featured a mixture of never before seen settings in any prior DM event. 32 players battled through two action-packed weeks of DM to grab a slice of the DM community-funded $10,000 prize pool and coveted title of King of DM. The finals between TheViper and TheCode brought in over 12,000 viewers.

Age of Empires III

World Cyber Games (2008)

In 2008, the World Cyber Games (WCG) was synonymous with the term 'esports', and Age of Empires III was young with a thriving online community. The tournament took place in Cologne, Germany, and all participants were flown out to take part in the LAN event. Two titans of Age of the Empires III scene went up against each other in the finals: iamgrunt, a secretive Korean player who was known for his incredibly high win rate and his unwillingness to share his strategies, and h2o, the U.S. underdog. The finals were a brief best-of-three, with both players playing the Japanese civilisation. Despite his underdog status, h2o was victorious in a short but epic 2-1 series.

New World Championship (2019)

In 2019, the New World Championship breathed new life into the competitive scene of Age of Empires III. The tournament was stacked with the very best of a small, but loyal community. A series of qualifiers reduced the player-pool down to eight of the best players, who were then flown to England, where they took part in a LAN event in Manchester. LordRaphael faced off against diarouga in a best-of-nine final that lasted a total of seven games before diarouga was crowned victorious. His victory cemented him as one of the great minds of the game, with his ability to out-think his opponents being a notable point of his play-style.

AoEIII Global Championship (2021)

The Global Championship was the first major tournament for the Definitive Edition of Age of Empires III. The tournament had a total prize pool of $5,000, making it the largest since the 2008 World Cyber Games. The tournament came at a time when the Age of Empires III community was experiencing a resurgence in player-base, having reached a new peak after the release of the United States civilisation The tournament featured an amazing best-of-seven finals showdown between favorites Haitch and Mitoe, which ended in a 5-2 victory for Haitch.

Teams and Organizations

Since the emergence of the competitive Age of Empires scenes across each game, players have formed and developed their own clans and teams. As the popularity of tournaments expanded, more teams were created and the status of some teams rose above the rest. *TyRanT* was an early Age of Empires II team formed in 2011 by two of the best players of the time, TheViper and DauT. From 2011 to 2018 many other top players joined the team, including RiuT, BacT, F1Re, Jibda, slam, and TaToH. Other prestigious and popular teams in AoEII included Suomi (2015) consisting of Finnish players, Aftermath (2016), and Heresy (2018).

Outside of the player-formed teams, the first esports organisation that entered the Age of Empires competitive scene was *Team Secret*, in July of 2018. Five of the players from team *TyRanT* joined the team.

Another large impact on the relationship between Age of Empires and the esports industry was with the forming of *Escape Gaming*. This esports organisation, lead by Zak 'ZeroEmpires' Robinson, was unique in the Age of Empires scene, as its competitions and reach spanned across all three main titles in the Age franchise. While Escape Gaming didn't form a professional Age of Empires team as it did in *Dota 2*, Escape did host competitive events from their headquarters in Manchester, U.K. When Escape Gaming closed in 2017, the efforts of Zak and his team lead the way for other esports organisations to follow. *Team Secret* was the first to show serious interest in Age of Empires II, considered a "low risk' esport" at the time, and a win-win for both parties as more eyes would be on the game, and the organisation was investing in a classic game that was rapidly growing.

From the perspective of the AoE community, the involvement of Team Secret lent the series more legitimacy as an esport—having such an established and prestigious esports organisation involved meant that more were likely to follow. In recent years, organisations such as Tempo Storm, Red-Bull, and GamerLegion have seen the potential and value in the Age of Empires competitive scene and have enthusiastically joined the scene.

Looking Ahead

"We've been playtesting this game for thousands of hours and we'll still log in to play on the weekends just for fun! AoE IV will have all the features in place to support competitive play, but it's up to the players to decide how seriously they want to take it. There is probably an appetite for competition from long-time fans of the franchise, especially around discovering new strategies. One of our goals with balance is to lay the groundwork and continue to update the game so that it can be fun, challenging, and competitive for those players."

—Zak "ZeroEmpires" Robinson
Senior Designer, Balance, Relic

An Introduction to Systems & Mechanics

Welcome to Age of Empires and the Real Time Strategy (RTS) genre! Whether this is your first RTS game or you're a seasoned player, Age of Empires IV is for everyone, and this chapter will ease you into the game. It includes an introduction to the nuances of the RTS genre, how Age of Empires is unique in its playstyle, and offers player's a guide for getting started.

Age of Empires is a game that is considered by many in its community to be "easy to learn but hard to master". RTS games require you to think on the spot and react quickly to ever-changing situations, which means that "time" is the most valuable resource. Due to the fast-paced nature of RTS games, it's impossible to focus on all tasks at once. Instead, you must prioritize your focus on different elements of game-play, such as economic balance, military production, map exploration, and army control. Knowing when to focus on what, however, can be difficult to learn. It's also important to realize that speed is not everything, and sometimes players with lower APM (Actions Per Minute) can win games due to their decision-making and strategy choices.

Execution and output in real-time always play a major role in RTS games, and can even overcome the rock-paper-scissor nature of unit counters. For example, you might think that if your opponent makes Spearmen and you make Archers, you should win. But that doesn't hold true if your opponent is outproducing you because their economy is better, and they end up with 50 units compared to your five. To put it succinctly: a really well-executed but unideal strategy will often outperform a superior but poorly executed strategy.

Execution

As you become increasingly more confident with the nature of the RTS-specific rules and requirements, the next step towards mastery is execution. Execution of these game elements is a broad concept, but is achieved through a combination of general game knowledge (e.g. what bonuses your civilization can make use of, which units counter which, etc.), multitasking (e.g. managing your economy and military at the same time and prioritizing different focus areas in-game), and creating the muscle memory to perform these tasks faster and more accurately. A big part of this will be learning to use the many keyboard shortcuts available to perform different actions with units and buildings. This is a much faster method than clicking on the icons, and allows you to focus on the action rather than having to take your eyes off the field.

One of the main appeals of the Age of Empires series is the variety of strategic options available. The wide range of variables, such as different civilizations, maps, military units, economic strategies, technology options, and general tactics, results in games that are always different and require strategic thinking. You have complete creative control over the strategies you execute when playing, and the flexibility to adapt as the game plays out. Adding an extra layer on top of the other strategic choices are the different civilizations, each with their own strengths and weakness that will impact both your overall strategy, and the moment-to-moment tactics you employ.

Game Modes

One of the reasons the Age of Empires franchise has been so beloved for such a long time is that it's a game that offers something for everyone. There are many different ways in which to play Age of Empires IV, and here we'll go over each of them.

You'll notice that some technologies, buildings, and stats can vary significantly between Campaigns and the Skirmish or Multiplayer modes. The game itself will mostly stay the same, but you'll need to adapt to these differences accordingly. All of the stat tables for the units and buildings presented throughout our book are primarily based on Skirmish/Multiplayer balance.

Single Player: Art of War

The Art of War missions are a collection of missions designed to introduce new players to different Age of Empires gameplay elements. Each mission has a distinct theme and set of objectives, with the goal being to complete them as quickly or efficiently as possible to earn either a bronze, silver, or gold award. These missions are great to use as benchmarks for the progress of your skills, as while you're playing, practicing, and improving, you'll be able to succeed in the Art of War missions faster and more efficiently.

Many Art of War missions are timed, which means they're also a good tool for veteran players to use for sharpening or perfecting their skills by attempting to get the fastest times possible.

Single Player: Campaign

The Campaigns allow you to immerse yourself in history by diving into the rich narratives of four distinct campaign scenarios; **The Normans**, **The Hundred Years War**, **The Mongol Empire**, and **The Rise of Moscow**. Campaigns can be played at various difficulty levels; Story, Easy, Intermediate, or Hard, so regardless of your skill level they'll offer exciting gameplay that allows you to grow as a player while you progress through them.

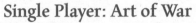

Senior Designer, Balance

Zak "ZeroEmpires" Robinson

What is your role on the project, and what does your day-to-day work consist of?
I'm officially a Balance designer. We play the game, do a lot of analysis, and then implement changes. We iterate quite quickly, so we get the opportunity to see things developing right in front of us. I also advise on a lot of other game areas with input about player expectations and how changes will impact how the game is played.

Have you worked on any previous Age of Empire games?
I playtested the AoE II Forgotten Empires fan expansion and later the African Kingdoms expansions. I also hosted and produced many tournaments and events for AoE II between 2011 and 2019.

What are your favorite game/s of all time?
Age of Empires II, *Team Fortress 2*, *CS:GO*, Boardgames (*Terraforming Mars*, *Tzolkin*, *Great Western Trail*, etc.)

How much time do you spend playing games outside of work?
Too much time—I play most days.

What's your general playstyle in RTS games?
Boomer—lots of villagers to form a huge economy and then flood units.

Which is your favorite civilization in AoE IV, and why?
I love the Chinese because of their defensive playstyle with the opportunity to boom well. Progressing through the dynasties and unlocking the unique dynasty units is also really fun!

Which are your favorite units in AoE IV, and why?
Landsknechte are awesome, they are extremely squishy but pack an absolute punch. It's so satisfying to charge at low HP units and just wipe them out.

What feature of the game are you most excited for players to try out?
The Aging up mechanics with choosing between a different landmark each time. It opens the door to many different combinations and strategies.

Campaign and Skirmish Stats

"Campaign and Skirmish split off, balance wise, so that ongoing balance work won't destabilize Campaigns as we move forward into launch and beyond. The Campaigns are maintained by a separate team and difficulty levels are determined based on the balance of the Campaign data. Balance testers do play and give feedback to the Campaign team to help with setting difficulty levels."

—Zak "ZeroEmpires" Robinson
Senior Designer, Balance, Relic

The campaigns will let you experience history from a new perspective, while teaching you about basic game mechanics.

As you journey through the campaigns you'll not only participate in famous historical battles and meet key figures from history, you'll also learn more about them through augmented reality videos that place the historical action over the modern-day locations. In Age of Empires IV, the focus on accurate and informative historical education is also taken to the next level with the inclusion of the Hands on History videos that are unlocked as a reward for the completion of missions. These documentary-style videos take you even deeper into different aspects of historical life. A full guide to all of the Campaign missions begins on P.314.

Single Player: Skirmish

Another popular single-player game mode is the 'Skirmish', in which you can customize a number of lobby settings to create a game suited to your preferences. There are many options for customization in the Skirmish mode, such as choosing from one of the many maps, changing the size of that map or the visual style of the biome it features, and numerous settings for the number of A.I. players, difficulty, and many more. To find out more about all of the options found in this mode, please head to P.53.

Multiplayer: Co-op VS A.I.

This mode is very similar to Skirmish, with the main difference being the ability to team up with other players to battle the A.I. opponents. Here you can test potential team compositions between different civilizations to find synergies that work well for you and your teammates, as well as working on co-op timings for different strategies. Being in sync with your co-op partner is a big part of co-op play, and knowing which of you will focus on economy and who will do the rushing ahead of time will save you a lot of problems.

Multiplayer: VS Players

Online battles against other human players are where you'll face the ultimate test of the skills and knowledge you've developed when playing through the other modes. You can choose to participate in either solo 1v1 battles or team games with up to four players per team. Just click the Search for Game button to automatically find a match that meets your specifications. In the Multiplayer mode you'll also find options to search for custom games that have been set up by other players, or even observe matches between players that are currently in progress. If you're trying to get better at the game, observing other players to see what they do and when they do it can be a very useful tool, especially if you're observing highly skilled players.

Player Profiles & Unlockable Customizations

From the Main Menu you can click on your profile icon to access your player profile. In here you'll see a number of stats and a list of your recent accomplishments based on what you've done in the game. By completing various actions in the game—such as completing Mastery tasks, or finishing Campaigns—you can also unlock a number of different cosmetic items to customize the look of your profile. Your profile portrait and coat of arms are visible to all other players, and you'll see theirs either by looking at their profile or at the start of a match, and players can even select a monument to display at their Town Center in Skirmish and Multiplayer matches. A well-crafted profile can tell you a lot about a player's likes and accomplishments, so it's worth browsing through the different menus to see what's available and how to get it, so you can craft your perfect profile.

Where to Begin?

While it's important to note that you can play Age of Empires however you prefer, and experience the different modes in any order. If you're starting from scratch and aiming to improve, we've come up with a simple progression order that you can follow to naturally advance through the modes.

1. **Play the Art of War Missions:** You can progress through these missions at your own pace and will be guided through the objectives one at a time. The Art of War missions not only explain how to do something, but also why it's important, making them the perfect jumping-off point for new players.

2. **Try the Campaigns (P.314):** The Normans campaign provides new players with a great introduction to gameplay mechanics, while telling the story of William of Normandy's quest into the Kingdom of England, and the events that followed. Each subsequent campaign offers more of a challenge than the previous one, both in terms of mission design and the complexity of the civilization you'll be in control of when playing it, allowing you to improve your skills as you play through them.

3. **Set up a Skirmish Game vs the A.I. (P.53):** There are multiple A.I. difficulty levels to choose from so you can find one that matches your ability, and play on a map that suits your playstyle (e.g. Dry Arabia for an open and aggressive map, Black Forest for a more closed and defensive map or Warring Islands for naval warfare). This is a good place to learn how to operate on your own without set mission objectives to guide you, and it's where you'll really start to develop your own playstyle.

4. **Dive into Multiplayer (P.53):** You can then take your skills into the multiplayer modes, either in a solo match against another human player, team games against human players or team up with people to battle against multiple A.I. opponents. Be aware, playing against other humans is quite different from playing the A.I.. Humans are thinking and reacting on the go just as you are, making mistakes and adapting just as you are, and have unique strengths and weaknesses depending on who you play.

5. **Gain Perspective:** Remember that Age of Empires IV is a game for everyone, regardless of experience or ability; your main goal should be to have fun progressing at your own pace and remember, with every game lost there's a lesson to learn, and an opportunity to improve next time!

Age of Empires Terminology

Over the course of the franchise's history the community has developed, or incorporated from the RTS genre in general, a number of phrases and terms that are used as shorthand when talking about certain mechanics or situations. Throughout this book we have used some of these terms where they're most applicable to convey the mechanics by the simplest means. If you're new to the franchise or the community, it's worth taking a bit of time to familiarize yourself with these terms so that when interacting with other players, or reading through this book, you have a full understanding of what's being discussed.

Lexicon	
To Raid	Attacking the enemy's Villagers or base while they are undefended.
To Idle Yours or Another Player's Economy	Having Villagers that are not working in any capacity, or making somebody else's Villagers idle through raids.
To Boom	To focus on economic development with little to no military or defense.
All-In	This is the antithesis of Booming, with no/minimal investment into economic development, all resources going into military, and then an aggressive playstyle to end the game quickly.
To House/get Housed	Not being able to produce units due to not having enough houses.
To be Pop Capped	Hitting the population capacity (200/200)
To Rush	Attacking early in the game with military units. e.g. Longbowmen-rush: An early attack with Longbowmen.
Fast Castle	Going to Age III as fast as possible by skipping Age II, building one Landmark straight after the other.

Economy 101

Building an empire, regardless of how you intend on using it in the game, is going to take a lot of resources, which is why understanding all of the various types of resources in the game and how to use them is one of the most important things to learn. In Age of Empires there are four gatherable resources: Food, Wood, Gold, and Stone. Each of these can be gathered from different sources, and each source provides different amounts; the one thing they all have in common, however, is that all of them can be gathered by the humble Villager unit.

The rate at which your Villagers will gather a resource can be augmented through various technologies and the abilities of other units, and there are some civilization-specific traits that can have an effect. There's an upper limit of 100,000 of each resource that you can hold, but just hoarding resources won't get you very far, so unless you're saving up for something specific, you should be using them as quickly as they come in. To keep up with that demand, it's important to be as efficient as possible with your resource gathering—always try to have the drop-off location for a resource as close to the source as possible, to minimize Villager walking time.

Hunting and Herding

Animals can be killed by both Villagers and military units without any penalty, which makes killing the more powerful animals, such as the Boar, a lot easier. Dead animals do not decay in Age of Empires IV, which allows for a more flexible approach for your Food gathering Villagers. Sheep can be herded, which means they will follow a Scout that gets close enough to it, allowing you to lead them to specific locations. Once one is following you, it will take on your team's color and can no longer be taken by an opposing player.

*With the **Survival Techniques** technology your Villagers will not only carry more hunted meat, but they will also gather it faster.*

Be careful when hunting a Boar. Unless you have some significant upgrades for your Villagers, or are very brave, only ever approach them with large groups of units.

In Another Age...

Hunting and herding animals is a crucial part of resource collection in the early stages of all Age of Empires games, as they are among the fastest means of acquiring Food. In previous Age of Empires games, animals had to be killed by Villagers, otherwise you'd lose the ability to gather Food from it. Dead animals also decayed over time, simulated in-game by a constant loss of 1 Food every few seconds, which is why having enough Villagers ready and good Mill placement was vital to ensuring you lost as little Food as possible. Since Age of Empires II, certain animals such as Sheep and Turkey could be herded, and previously, it was also possible for other players to "steal" the animals you were herding by getting closer to them than you were.

Resource Details		Amount per Instance	Gather Rate (resource/second)
Sheep	Food	250	0.75
Berries	Food	250*	0.66
Farms	Food	120**	0.75
Deer	Food	350	0.825
Boar	Food	2000	0.9
Shoreline Fish	Food	1000	1 (Villagers)
Shoreline Fish	Food	1000	0.9 (Fishing Ship)
Deep Water Fish	Food	2000	1.275
Trees/Wood	Wood	150	0.75
Small/Large Gold Vein	Gold	4000/8000	0.75
Small/Large Stone Outcropping	Stone	1500/3000	0.75

*Can be increased to 500 with the Delhi Sultanate and Abbasid Dynasty if a Mill is built nearby
**Regenerates over time

Respecting Faiths

Reflecting pork being haram, or forbidden, in the Islamic faith, the Abbasid Dynasty and the Delhi Sultanate in Age of Empires IV cannot hunt boar for food. You must hunt deer or harvest berries—which will provide a bonus of increased food if you construct a Mill near its bushes and convert them into an Orchard.

Resource Details

"One of the smallest changes which can have the largest effect is modifying the gather rate of resources. Everything is connected to a player's economy – the resources available to you determine what decisions you can and can't make, and your need for a specific resource shapes how you designate your villagers or which tech path you are more likely to take."

—Zak "ZeroEmpires" Robinson
Senior Designer, Balance, Relic

Food

Drop-off Locations	
Town Center	All
Dock	All
Mill	All - Mon/Rus
Granary	Chi
Ger	Mon
Hunting Cabin	Rus
King's Palace	Eng
Palace of Swabia	HRE
Steppe Redoubt	Mon
High Trade House	Rus

Primary Uses

- *Producing Units*
- *Building Landmarks*
- *Researching Technology*

There are seven different types of Food source in the game, and on all standard maps, you'll usually have multiple different sources of Food available at any given time. Sheep and Berries are the sources you'll typically find closest to your initial Town Center. Sheep can be hunted by any unit, and their carcass will remain on the ground for Villagers to gather Food from, while Berries can just be picked straight from the bush whenever you find them. Both of these are good sources of Food early on due to their proximity to your starting location, which makes it less likely that your Villagers will come into contact with enemy units.

Slightly further out you'll typically start to see Deer, and if you're on a map with water, Shorline Fish. Deer are usually found in groups and have a faster gathering rate than both Sheep and Berries, which makes them a very tempting source of Food, especially if you build a Mill or similar building close by to minimize Villager travel time. If you have the option, however, Shorline Fish should always be one of your first choices for Food due to the speed at which they can be gathered. Shorline Fish can also be gathered by Fishing Ships, and while they might be your only option on some maps, because the Wood required to build them is quite significant at the start of a game, you're much better off using Villagers if possible.

Fishing Ships truly shine on maps with deeper waters, where you can find Deep Water Fish. These fish can only be gathered by Fishing Ships, and while that means a large investment of Wood to construct both the ships and a Dock, the speed at which Deep Water Fish can be gathered means they're too lucrative to pass up.

Instead of killing Sheep wherever you find them, use a Scout to herd them and bring them closer to a drop-off location first—this will make your Food gathering more efficient.

To make your Farmers more efficient and keep them safe, you should build all your Farms around Town Centers and Mills.

Senior Designer, UX Lead

Euphemia Wong

What is your role on the project, and what does your day-to-day work consist of?

As the UX Lead, I act as the link between game design and UX/UI. I communicate the vision, requirements and collaborate on designs that lead to UX/UI team output and deliverables. My day-to-day work depends on the stage of the project. Earlier in the project there's a lot more requirements-gathering and design work involved, whereas later in the project, it is more about supporting the team during implementation and prioritizing work.

What are your favorite game/s of all time?

Bishi Bashi, *Wangan Midnight Maximum Tune*, *Final Fantasy VIII*, *Heroes of the Storm*, and *Overcooked*.

Which is your favorite civilization in AoE IV, and why?

My favorite civ in AoE IV is the Mongols because they are just so different from all the other civs. Being able to move structures around makes it feel so dynamic and changes the game.

Which are your favorite units in AoE IV, and why?

Elephants. Because elephants are just super cool, just look at the way they move! Gentle giants to you, devastating to your opponents!

What feature of the game are you most excited for players to try out?

Sacred Victory. The design and implementation ended up being quite complex so I'm looking forward to seeing players try it out!

Sustainable Farming

The finite sources of Food, by their nature, will eventually start to run out. If you don't want your production to slow down as the game progresses, you'll eventually need to transition to a more sustainable Food income, and that's where Farms come in. Farms are the most reliable Food source in the game, and the only one that continuously regenerates so that you can keep gathering from it. There are a number of technologies, units, and buildings that can further increase the effectiveness of Farms, and having a large number of them is one of the primary means of having a late-game booming economy.

Professional Scouts

Once the **Professional Scouts** technology has been researched, your Scout is able to carry carcasses back to your Town Center (or another drop-off location), and they'll also deal a whopping +200% extra damage to animals. That extra damage can come in very handy if you want to attempt to hunt the most fearsome animal in the game: the Boar. Boar contain 2000 Food, which is a significant amount that can last you a while, but they're also a serious threat, and you should never attack them with Villagers or single Scouts under normal circumstances. It should be noted, however, that, while playing as the Islamic Delhi Sultanate and Abbasid Dynasty, you can kill Boar, but meat cannot be gathered from them.

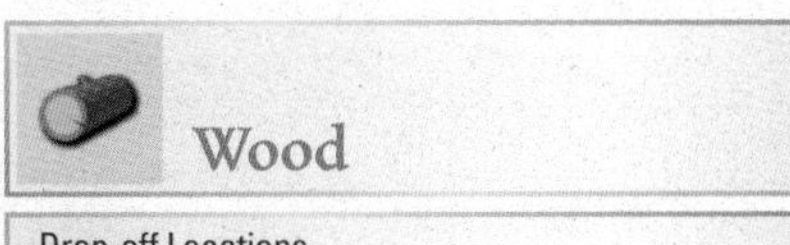

Wood

Drop-off Locations	
Town Center	All
Lumber Camp	All - Mon
Ger	Mon
King's Palace	Eng
Palace of Swabia	HRE
Steppe Redoubt	Mon

Primary Uses
- *Producing Units*
- *Constructing Buildings & Fortifications*

Wood is arguably the most important resource in the game, because of the number of different things that require it—everything from a single Spearman to some of the largest buildings require some amount of it. Unlike other resources that can be gathered immediately, to start gathering Wood your Villagers must first cut down a tree. All trees can be felled, and with upgrades researched primarily at a Lumber Camp, your Villagers can chop trees down faster, and gather the Wood more efficiently.

A potential strategy to keep in mind is denying your opponent access to woodlines. In most cases, your opponent will have many Villagers felling trees along the woodlines on their side of the map, and if you can deny access to those trees by building an Outpost or placing ranged infantry nearby, then you can disrupt their Wood income. To defend yourself against this tactic, it's recommended that you stick to woodlines either behind your starting position, or as far away from your opponent as possible. If you'll be in one area for a while, you can also build your own Outpost nearby to gain extended vision around the area, giving you advance warning if your opponent does try to make a move on your Villagers.

Until you upgrade the speed at which you can chop down trees, it's important not to move your Wood gathering Villagers around a lot, because you'll waste a lot of time cutting down trees that could be spent gathering Wood.

Gold

Drop-off Locations	
Town Center	All
Mining Camp	All - Mon
Ger	Mon
King's Palace	Eng
Palace of Swabia	HRE
Steppe Redoubt	Mon

Primary Uses
- *Producing Powerful Units*
- *Building Landmarks*
- *Researching Technology*

Gold is a highly coveted and precious resource in Age of Empires IV. Not only is it required to build Landmarks and advance through the Ages, but you'll also need it for nearly all technologies and upgrades found in the game, as well as for producing some of the strongest units. Unlike Food and Wood, Gold can often be hard to come by, and it's usually found in more contested areas of the map.

Because of their scarcity, it's important to scout around the map to find multiple Gold Veins—this way, when one runs dry, you already know where to send your Villagers to next. Once you've found a Gold Vein, your Villagers can begin mining and gathering it like any other resource, and to making dropping it off quicker, you should always build a Mining Camp as close to the Gold Vein as possible. As Gold Veins are quite large in size, many Villagers are able to mine from them simultaneously, which can be both a blessing and a curse. Using many Villagers will allow you to gather the Gold quickly, but that also presents a high-value target for your opponent; if the Gold Vein is in an exposed area, it's important to keep those vulnerable parts of your operation as safe as possible with some defensive units.

Unlike with many other resources, your Villagers won't automatically transition to another source once the Gold Vein has run dry, which means there's the potential for a lot of idle Villagers if you don't keep an eye on them. When all of the Gold Veins have been mined, Traders and trade routes will become your main source of Gold income.

Stuart Ng
Exploration for Stone/Gold Deposits
Concept Sketch

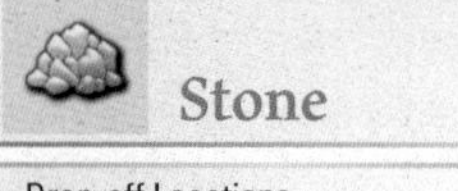

Stone

Drop-off Locations		
Town Center		All
Mining Camp		All - Mon
Ger		Mon
King's Palace		Eng
Palace of Swabia		HRE
Steppe Redoubt		Mon

Primary Uses

Constructing Buildings & Fortifications

Stone is by far the scarcest resource in Age of Empires IV, even more so than Gold, but how you acquire it is very similar. Like Gold Veins, you can find Stone Outcroppings around the map that can be mined by your Villagers to gather the Stone, and then dropped off at a nearby Mining Camp. The amount of Stone you require is typically based on your playstyle, but you'll nearly always want some to build additional Town Centers with when you reach the Feudal Age to increase your Villager production capacity. Outside of that, it's primarily used for defensive fortifications such as Stone Walls and Towers, deadly Keeps, and their weapon emplacements. You'll typically find Stone Outcroppings in the same kind of contested areas as Gold Veins, which means that the same risks and precautions should be taken when attempting to mine it.

The Mongol Ovoo

Mongols are the only civilization that are unable to traditionally mine for Stone, but that doesn't mean they can't obtain it. The Mongols have a unique building called an Ovoo, and it can only be built on top of Stone Outcroppings. Once placed, it will automatically start siphoning off the Stone and depositing it into your resource bank periodically.

Although they can't build any defensive fortifications with that Stone, the Mongol use for it is arguably more important, and if used correctly, one of their biggest strengths. Any buildings placed next to an Ovoo will have access to improved versions of their functionality that require Stone. For example, at a production building you'll be able to produce two units in the time it would normally take to produce one, and research buildings can research improved versions of technologies with even greater benefits.

Trades, Tributes & Markets

Market Rates		
Buy Increment	+4 Gold	A S D
Sell Decrement	-2 Gold	Z X C
Wood/Food Starting Buy Price	130 Gold	
Stone Starting Buy Price	170 Gold	
Wood/Food Starting Sell Price	70 Gold	
Stone Starting Sell Price	90 Gold	
Wood/Food Min Price	14 Gold	
Stone Min Price	58 Gold	
Max Price	1000 Gold	
Normalization Rate	30s per Increment	

Markets are a crucial part of managing and growing your economy, and learning how and when to use them efficiently is the final piece of the economic puzzle. Once a Market is built, you're able to use Gold to purchase any of the other three resources in increments of 100. Being the savvy business they are, however, the more you purchase, the more the Market will charge you, with the price increasing at every increment you purchase. Similarly, if you have an abundance of the other resources, you can also sell any of them for Gold, with the amount you receive going down for each increment of 100 sold.

These price fluctuations are based on each resource individually, so if you've only been buying Stone and the price has skyrocketed, your Wood and Food prices will still be at their base levels. The value of a resource will start to normalize when you're not trading on it, and it takes 30s for the cost to normalize by one increment. So if you purchased 1000 Stone, that's 10 increments, meaning it would take 300s for the price to fully normalize. It's because of how much the prices can fluctuate when you're buying and selling a resource that Markets should be used in moderation. If you have far too much of a resource and are not concerned with how much you're getting, then, of course, trade as much as you like, but in general, it's best to trade in small amounts periodically, or in emergency situations where you need Gold or one of the other resources extremely quickly.

Trade Routes

Another functionality of Markets is to produce Traders, specialized units that can be sent on expeditions to either neutral Trade Posts, or the Markets of other allied players in team games, to establish a trade route. With each successful roundtrip your Traders will return with a bounty of Gold, the amount of which will vary based on the length of the trip: the longer the trip, the more Gold you'll bring in. The size of the map you're playing on also has an influence on this, because the return rate on a trade route of equal length on different-sized maps will get you different amounts. For example, on a Micro size map, you'll get roughly four Gold per trade over a distance of 10 tiles, and 55 Gold per trade if there are 50 tiles between both of the Markets. If you then move to a Small map, that same 50 tile trade would only net you 39 Gold. The type of building you trade with also has an impact on the amount of Gold you'll bring back, with the riskier neutral Trade Posts providing 20% more Gold than the safer option of an allied player's Market.

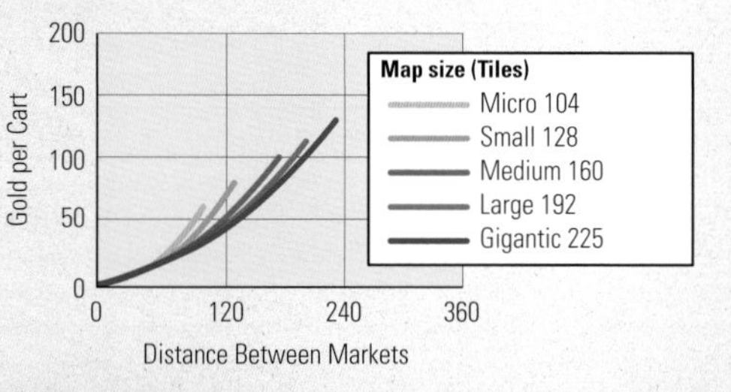

Remember: A longer Trade route will yield a greater profit, but will also be more difficult to defend.

Paying Tribute to Allies

In Team Games, Markets fill a special role because they enable you to trade resources to other allied players, albeit at a cost. Once a Market has been placed, you'll find the "Players & Tribute" button in the top right corner of your UI; if you click it, it will bring up a list of players in your game, and you can then select one of them to send a Tribute to. Like normal trades at a Market, Tributes can be of any resource in increments of 100, but since you're not buying and selling for Gold, the Market will instead charge you a 30% handling fee, paid in the resource you're sending as Tribute. So, if you want to send 100 Wood to another player in Tribute, it will cost you 130 Wood to do so.

Like all Market functions, this is not something that you'll use all of the time, but there will be times when it can absolutely benefit you or another member of your team that desperately needs a resource, which can end up saving the game. Also, depending on your team composition, player's roles, and the location of resources on a map, you might decide it's best for some players to focus on specific resources more than others, and then you can use this system to share them amongst the team.

The Tribute system is just a click away whenever a teammate is in need.

Unit Production Breakdown

With all of your newfound economic knowledge now in hand, this table will show how best to put it to use for efficient production. Here we'll let you know exactly how many Villagers you'll need gathering each resource to continuously produce a unit, and how many Villagers in total that adds up to. What this means is that with the number of Villagers indicated, you can gather the resources required to cover the cost of a unit within the time it takes to produce that unit, allowing for constant production with no downtime.

These values are taken according to base gathering rates and without any economy upgrades—so you'll know what you're working with from the very start of a game—and they are rounded to the nearest whole number to account for any slight inefficiencies. Once you start upgrading your economy or making use of unique civilization traits, then the number of Villagers needed will naturally go down.

Unit Production

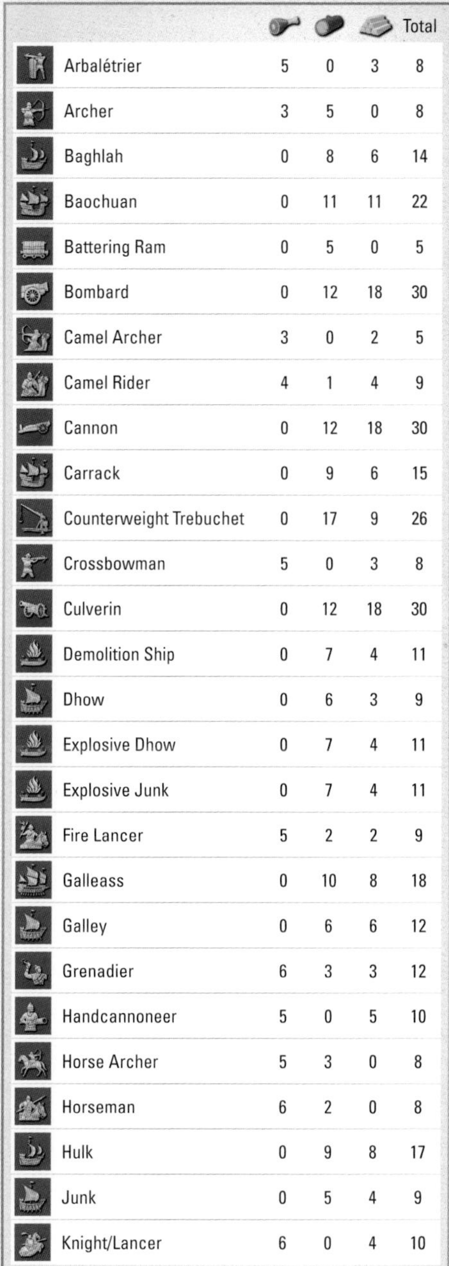

Unit				Total
Arbalétrier	5	0	3	8
Archer	3	5	0	8
Baghlah	0	8	6	14
Baochuan	0	11	11	22
Battering Ram	0	5	0	5
Bombard	0	12	18	30
Camel Archer	3	0	2	5
Camel Rider	4	1	4	9
Cannon	0	12	18	30
Carrack	0	9	6	15
Counterweight Trebuchet	0	17	9	26
Crossbowman	5	0	3	8
Culverin	0	12	18	30
Demolition Ship	0	7	4	11
Dhow	0	6	3	9
Explosive Dhow	0	7	4	11
Explosive Junk	0	7	4	11
Fire Lancer	5	2	2	9
Galleass	0	10	8	18
Galley	0	6	6	12
Grenadier	6	3	3	12
Handcannoneer	5	0	5	10
Horse Archer	5	3	0	8
Horseman	6	2	0	8
Hulk	0	9	8	17
Junk	0	5	4	9
Knight/Lancer	6	0	4	10

Unit				Total
Landsknecht	4	0	6	10
Light Junk	0	5	4	9
Lodya Attack Ship	0	5	3	8
Lodya Demolition Ship	0	7	4	11
Longbowman	4	5	0	9
Man-at-Arms	6	0	2	8
Mangonel	0	14	7	21
Mangudai	6	0	2	8
Monk/Imam/Scholar/ Shaman	0	0	5	2
Nest of Bees	0	10	10	20
Palace Guard	6	0	2	8
Prelate	0	0	9	9
Ribauldequin	0	12	18	30
Royal Knight	6	0	4	10
Scout	4	0	0	4
Spearman	6	2	0	8
Springald	0	9	9	18
Streltsy	4	0	4	8
Tower War Elephant	9	0	14	23
Traction Trebuchet	0	14	5	19
Trader	0	3	3	6
Trade Ship	0	7	3	10
Villager	4	0	0	4
War Elephant	14	0	9	23
War Junk	0	9	7	16
Warrior Monk	2	0	6	8
Xebec	0	11	7	18
Zhuge Nu	4	2	2	8

Unit Management

Now that you've learned everything you need to know about gathering the resources to build your army, in this section we'll take some time to go over how you can control and understand your units. Becoming familiar with all of the tools available to you when controlling your army, or knowing the strengths and weaknesses of a unit just by quickly glancing at the stat icons, is all part of the journey of improving at the game.

Unit Stats

The first things you should familiarize yourself with are the various stats that each of the units in the game can have, along with the icons that represent them. While outside of a competitive match you have plenty of time to mouse over individual stats and icons to see what each of them do, in the heat of a match against another player, that can cost you crucial time. The ultimate goal should be to become familiar enough with every unit that you know all of their stats without having to look at them, but while you're learning, it can help to quickly select an opponent's unit to inspect it; cutting that time down by learning what the icons represent is a good first step in that direction.

Unit Stats

Stat	Description
Health	The amount of health a unit/building has; as it takes damage, this value is depleted, and when it reach 0 the unit or building is dead/destroyed.
Armor	Represents of the total armor a unit or building has, based on a combination of the two separate armor types it poses.
Stat Markers	These markers can be found alongside the health and armor values, and serve as a quick visual reference for the overall health or armor of the unit/building. Looking at this should give you a good general idea of those values, without having to look at the specific numbers.
Melee Armor	Represents the amount of melee armor a unit has; the higher the number, the less melee damage taken.
Ranged Armor	Represents the amount of ranged armor a unit/building has; the higher the number, the less ranged damage taken.
Fire Armor	Represents the amount of fire armor a unit/building has; the higher the number, the less fire damage taken from enemy incendiary attacks.
Attack	Represents the amount of melee attack damage a unit is capable of inflicting
Ranged Attack	Represents the amount of ranged attack damage a unit is capable of inflicting
Incendiary Attack	Represents the amount of incendiary attack damage a unit is capable of inflicting. Most melee units will automatically switch to using Torches as an incendiary attack when attacking buildings.
Siege Attack	Represents the amount of siege attack damage a unit is capable of inflicting, and is exclusively used by siege engines.
Movement Speed	Shows you how many tiles a unit can move across in a second; the higher the number, the faster they are.

Upgrade technologies found at the Blacksmith and University can improve the stats and fighting abilities of your units significantly, and the combat advantage gained from them is something you should always take advantage of.

Attack Speed

Although it doesn't have an icon in the unit/building stats, Attack Speed is extremely important to pay attention to. This value will let you know how frequently a unit, emplacement, or building is capable of attacking, and is one of the best indicators of their full offensive capabilities. It's all well and good if something has an extremely high attack value, but it if only fires once every 10 minutes, its total damage output would be a lot lower than something that does half as much damage, but attacks three times as fast. Thankfully, in Age of Empires IV, everything has an attack speed that's measured in seconds not minutes, but you'll still need to take into account the attack damage, and speed when comparing units to see which one actually deals more damage over a given period of time.

Sometimes a bigger damage number will work in your favor over faster attacks, such as if you have a group of three units, and you know all it takes is a single attack from each of them to defeat your opponent's unit. In that scenario, it doesn't matter that much how slow the subsequent attack is, because the unit you're attacking would be dead. Generally speaking, the longer a fight goes on, or the lower the damage value, the more attacks you'll need to complete, and the more important attack speed becomes.

Damage & Armor

When it comes to attack and defense values, the main thing to remember is that there is a direct relationship between the two. So if a unit has a melee attack rating of four, and it attacks another unit with a melee defense rating of four, the defending unit will lose no health. It's also important to remember that the units you encounter may not always have their default values, because there are numerous technologies in the game that can augment both of these stats; never assume that you have enough units to defeat an enemy unit in a single hit without checking first.

Macro & Micro Control

Age of Empires IV is a game that plays out over two different scales of management: the macro, and the micro. Macro control is the big picture; economy balance, map control, game plan, adaptability, and unit production. These things are developed across the whole game, and small macro decisions, such as building a Lumber Camp closer to a woodline for optimal efficiency, can add up to having a big impact across the approximate thirty minutes or more that each game takes. Good macro control is developed over time as your overall game knowledge improves and you build up a sense of the timings for things in a match.

Micro control is when your attention is given to smaller moments in the game. This can include moving individual units in your army to avoid incoming attacks from an enemy siege engine, quickly getting your Villagers to safety from a raid, or trying to finish off specific enemy units with less health, to name a few. Micro control is best improved through manual practice in games; it's only through repetition that you'll develop both the necessary physical muscles, and muscle memory to raise your overall APM (Actions per Minute), which is one of the main components of effective micro control.

You should aim to have a balance between your macro and micro gameplay, alternating between each of them at appropriate times. A skill seen in great players is that they know when to focus on which element of the game. Although it should be noted that good macro play will generally beat good micro play; micro can win you battles, but macro tends to win the war. Of course, if your macro play is already pretty good, then as your micro play becomes better over time, the more battles you'll win, and it will only get easier to win the war.

Attack Move

Default Key: [A]

If you're unsure about what's between you and your destination, you should always use the Attack Move command when telling your units to move, so that they'll attack any enemy units or buildings they encounter along the way. The main thing to remember with this command is that, unlike the normal move command, which is triggered by right-clicking on a location, you actually left-click to initiate an Attack Move after selecting the command.

Stand Ground

Default Key: [V]

Under normal circumstances, as soon as one of your units spots an enemy unit, or is attacked, it will move out to attack, and then if that enemy unit starts to retreat, your unit will follow it to try to finish it off. Depending on the skill level of your opponent, or the type of scenario you're trying to set up, that behavior can potentially put your units in a lot more danger.

Skilled opponents might attack one of your units in the hopes of getting it to follow them back to an ambush they've set up, or similarly, you might be looking to set up your own ambush, and having your units leave a Stealth forest prematurely could ruin your timing. The Stand Ground command can be used to avoid all of these scenarios because, when toggled on, your units will only attack an enemy unit if it is directly within their attack range, and they will not pursue enemy units.

You still have full manual control even with Stand Ground on, so you don't need to worry about turning it off when you're about to launch your ambush.

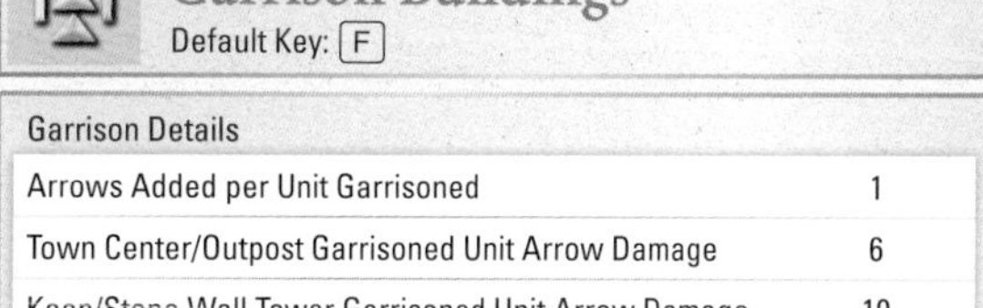

Garrison Buildings

Default Key: [F]

Garrison Details	
Arrows Added per Unit Garrisoned	1
Town Center/Outpost Garrisoned Unit Arrow Damage	6
Keep/Stone Wall Tower Garrisoned Unit Arrow Damage	10

Defensive fortifications are an important part of keeping your base—or any important area—secure, but sometimes they need some additional help to repel a group of incoming attackers, and that's where Garrisoning comes in. Any infantry unit can be garrisoned inside an applicable building, and there are two ways of doing it. You can either select the unit, click the garrison command icon (or press the keyboard shortcut key), and then left-click on the target building, or after selecting the unit, if you mouse over the target building the cursor will automatically change to a garrison icon, and then you can right-click to garrison the unit, bypassing the need to manually select the garrison command.

The amount of damage dealt by the arrows fired by garrisoned units is fixed, so it doesn't matter which unit type you garrison, they'll always be doing the full amount of damage. This can be an important fact to remember, because you'll get more offensive benefit from garrisoning a unit the weaker it is in open combat. The number of available garrison slots, however, does vary between buildings, and this is the main reason why it's such an effective tactic to garrison nearby Villagers into buildings such as Town Centers or Keeps that have a lot of garrison slots; this will greatly increase your defensive capabilities, without having to commit any additional military units.

You'll know you can garrison units inside a building because, when you left-click on it, you'll see the number of filled and potential garrison slots available directly above it.

Ungarrison Buildings

You can have units that are garrisoned inside a building leave their post at any time simply by clicking on the building, and then selecting the ungarrison command, at which point they'll leave the building and stand at the ready nearby.

Seek Shelter
Return To Work

Villagers have a unique garrison ability that can be used in an emergency if they come under attack from an enemy raid. If you select one or a group of Villagers you'll see the **Seek Shelter** button among the available commands, and if you click it, all of the selected Villagers will quickly run to the nearest building that they can garrison and automatically get inside. Then, once the danger has passed, instead of ungarrisoning normally, use the **Return to Work** command and all of those Villagers will get right back to work exactly where they left off.

Control Groups

Default Keys

Forming a Group .... CTRL + [1-9]
Add Units to Existing Group: .... Shift + [1-9]
Focus Camera on a Specific Group: ... Double Tap Group Number Key

While a regular Age of Empires IV game typically starts with only six Villagers and a Scout, towards the end you can be managing up to 200 units! With that level of chaos, it can be hard to control your military while managing your economy at the same time. One of the main methods of bringing some order to this chaos is through the use of Control Groups.

A Control Group can be formed from either a single unit or numerous units, and it can include as many different types of unit as you want. When you have your group composition in mind, drag a selection box over them all, and then simply hold CTRL and press one of the [1-9] keys to form the group. As with many of the game's other commands, you can change the required keys in the Controls part of the Settings menu if you prefer to use different keys.

Once a group has been created, you can then use other keyboard commands to quickly select it again at any time, or focus the camera on it from anywhere on the map. When a group is selected, you can see the units within it in the info panel to the right of your resources in the HUD; and if the group has multiple unit types, each will have its own icon, and clicking on it will select all units of that type within the group. Alternatively, pressing the TAB key will also cycle through each of the unit types within a group. This functionality allows you to give orders to individual unit types within a group made up of multiple types.

If you combine multiple unit types in one Control Group, such as Archers with Knights, keep in mind that the group will move at the pace of the slowest unit in it. If you're trying to time attacks carefully, this can actually be a very good thing, because it ensures all of your units will arrive at the same time, whereas if they weren't in a Control Group, they would move at their own pace and their arrival would be staggered. This does only count for military units, however; Villagers will always move at their own pace, even when in a Control Group with other units.

Each Control Group will also appear as an icon on the side of your screen that shows you the group number and the total number of units within it; clicking this icon will also select the group.

The recommended method of using Control Groups for military application is to have each different unit type in a separate group. For example, in this situation, you could have the Longbowmen on Group 1, Spearmen on Group 2, Siege units on Group 3, and the forward Villagers on Group 5 to easily distinguish them from your military units and avoid sending them into battle.

You can also assign buildings to a Control Group, which makes it very easy to access them quickly from any point on the map, in case you need to produce units or research technology from them at a moment's notice. Another advanced functionality is the ability to assign units to multiple Control Groups, which allows you to have one big Control Group for your entire army, and then subgroups within it for the individual unit types.

Formations

An extension of Control Groups are Formations, which are used to align your units into specific arrangements on the field, each of which provide different strategic benefits. By default, all of your units will assume the standard formation when they move together, which has them form up in multiple short rows, each of the other three formations has to be manually selected.

Line Formation

Default Key: [Z]

As the name suggests, the Line Formation puts all of your selected units into a single long line. This formation can be useful when you're trying to guard a wide pass on a map, or fully encircle a group of attacking enemy units. Depending on your tactics, it can be an especially useful formation for ranged units, because by spreading them out you're able to force them to target more enemy units at once, rather than all shooting the same target.

Wedge Formation

Default Key: [X]

The Wedge Formation is primarily used when you want to have a spearhead of units at the front to break through the enemy lines, while other units move in behind them safely. Cavalry charges with infantry behind them are one of the best uses of this formation. It's also useful if you want to maintain a buffer of units in front of the one you're trying to defend, such as keeping infantry in front of a siege engine to protect it while it attacks.

Staggered Formation

Default Key: [C]

If your opponent is using a lot of siege units, then you should strongly consider putting your units into the Staggered Formation. In this formation, your units will be a lot more spread out, which can significantly lessen the effectiveness of siege attacks, because it will be a lot harder for them to hit multiple units at a time.

Charge Attacks

Charge Attack Details		Min. Distance	Max Distance	Duration	Cooldown	Damage
Basic	Spearman, Man-at-Arms, Horseman, Landsknecht	2 Tiles	5 Tiles	5s	10s	Normal
Heavy	Knight/Lancer	2 Tiles	10 Tiles	7s	15s	+50% Bonus Damage on Hit
Elephant	War Elephant	2 Tiles	10 Tiles	7s	20s	+100% Bonus Damage on Hit

Torches

Torch Damage	Damage				Counter Bonus	Bonus Against	Range	Speed
	I	II	III	IV				
Fire Lancers	N/A	N/A	45	45	10	Siege	1.00	2.00s
Villagers	5	5	5	5	10	Siege	1.00	2.00s
All Other Melee Units	10	13	16	20	10	Siege	1.00	2.00s

A well timed charge can devastate the enemy's lines.

Slower units can have difficulty creating enough separation to attempt a second Charge Attack once they're already in combat, but that's not the case with cavalry. The combination of fast movement speed and the large amount of bonus damage that Knights/Lancers possess makes multiple charge attack attempts not only viable, but a potentially deadly tactic.

All cavalry units, and some melee infantry, have the ability to automatically initiate a charge attack when they're first closing in to attack an enemy unit, either when following the Attack Move command, or if you manually give an attack command. When initiated, the unit will get a movement speed increase as they charge towards the target, and the charge itself will continue until either the duration expires, or contact is made with the enemy units. The hit delivered at the end of a charge attack will also typically have greater range than the unit's standard attack, and with some units, it can also deal more damage, making it a very powerful tool to keep in mind during battles.

Because it takes some time to build up the moment for a Charge Attack, there's a minimum distance at which you need to be before one can be initiated, and similarly, units can only keep the increased pace up for so long, so there's a maximum distance they can charge. A short rest period is also needed after a successful charge, so you'll need to be patient before trying to initiate a follow-up charge.

If you try to initiate an attack on either a building or siege engine with a melee unit, you'll notice that it will put away its normal weapon and pull out a flaming torch to attack with. Torches are more effective than normal weapons against those targets because they tend to lack Fire Armor; unlike normal unit damage, however, Torch damage is fixed and, for all units other than Villagers, is based on the Age your civilization is currently in, with each successive Age increasing the amount of Torch damage your units can inflict.

In Another Age...

A building on fire was purely a visual indicator that it had sustained a lot of damage in previous Age of Empires games. If you're a returning player to the franchise, this change to the system is something you need to constantly be mindful of so that our previous game knowledge doesn't end up costing you a lot of buildings.

Once a building has sustained a critical amount of damage from any source it will catch fire and start to burn, causing it to continuously lose its remaining health over time until it's destroyed. The only way to put out a burning building is to have a Villager repair it, so if you're under siege, make sure to have some Villagers nearby for emergency repairs, and always prioritize burning buildings to avoid unnecessary losses.
Burning buildings are easily identifiable because they'll have a bright red glowing flame symbol above their health bar, making it very easy for you to see where you need to send your Villagers, even in the heat of battle.

Special Abilities

Certain units like the Longbowman, the Khan, or Leader units in the campaigns have special abilities that can make them excel in various situations when they're used correctly. They can be activated by either clicking the icon or pressing the corresponding key of the ability you want to use, after which it will immediately activate. Special abilities can be anything from a healing aura that restores the health of nearby units, to offensive buffs that increase the lethality of your units in combat.

All special abilities have a cooldown period after activation before you can use them again. You need to consider where and when to use them to get the most out of them, because mistiming an activation can mean the difference between victory and defeat. When deciding whether or not you want to add a unit to your army composition, it's important to take these abilities into account; even if a unit has relatively low stats, if it's capable of buffing a significant amount of other units it can still be extremely valuable.

Special abilities can turn battles in your favor that you would otherwise lose. Timing and using them correctly is crucial for success.

Balancing Special Abilities

"We use active abilities sparingly because of the additional complexity and overhead that they add for the player. For that reason, abilities are often situational or have long cooldowns so that it's less of an absolute requirement to use them and more of a strategic decision. Take Palings for example, they take a long time to set up and are only useful for protecting from cavalry charges. This means that players are using them before a battle starts and only in situations against cavalry, limiting the scope of the ability and making it more manageable.

Active abilities are also only on one unit at most per civ in skirmish mode, this helps players to keep track of which units need special attention."

—Zak "ZeroEmpires" Robinson
Senior Designer, Balance, Relic

Siege Engines & Gunpowder Artillery

In addition to infantry and cavalry units, you'll also gain access to various machines of war as you play, and these are some of the most powerful and deadly units in the game. These units come in many different varieties—with some like the anti-siege unit, Culverin having very specific functions—but generally speaking, their role is to inflict a lot of damage to a target, which in most cases tends to be either buildings or groups of units.

The difference between non-gunpowder siege units and gunpowder ones is usually the arc the projectiles take after firing; non-gunpowder siege units tend to fire in high parabolic arcs, allowing you to fire over walls or buildings, whereas gunpowder siege units tend to have a more direct trajectory and are only able to hit targets in front of them. Siege attacks also have the distinction of being the only attack type capable of destroying Stone Walls, so while your other attacks might be able to destroy Stone Wall Gates and Towers, they won't be able to destroy the actual walls themselves.

While these machines are engineering marvels, all of this devastating power does come at a cost of both movement speed, and maneuverability. Most siege engines lack the stability to fire from their packed-up travel configuration, so once you select a target they need to unpack into a more stable firing position. Similarly, after firing, if you then want to move your siege engine again, it will need time to tear down back into its traveling mode. The extra time for both setting up and tearing down is something you always need to keep in mind when trying to launch an attack or retreat from incoming enemies. It's always recommended to have some other units nearby to protect your siege engines during that vulnerable period.

If you hold down the right mouse button when you right-click to have a siege engine move to a location, you'll be able to bring up the targeting markers for its attacks while it's still moving into place. This lets you line up your trajectory while moving into position, and as a bonus, when you release the right mouse button the siege engine will automatically set up if required, saving you valuable time if you're using the siege engine for defense.

Attack Ground

Default Key: G

Most siege units have the unique ability to initiate attacks without having to target an enemy unit or structure, and you can do that via the Attack Ground command. After selecting the Attack Ground command you'll see the icon for it next to your normal cursor, and then if you right-click anywhere in the environment the siege unit will start bombarding that area. This command can come in very handy if you want to preemptively defend an area against potential attacks, or deny your opponent access to a specific location on the map, such as a Sacred Site.

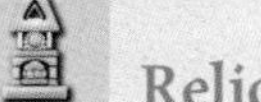

Relics

Relics are a rare item that can be found randomly on any map, and under normal circumstances, they can only be picked up by religious units after you reach the Castle Age. Once picked up, Relics can serve a number of different functions from Converting enemy units so that they fight for your side, or you can garrison them inside religious buildings to start generating Gold over time. Due to the high demand for Gold as the game progresses and natural sources run out, this persistent means of acquiring it can be very beneficial to your late-game economy. If you research the **Tithe Barns** technology from a religious building, each Relic garrisoned inside one will also generate +30 Food, Wood, and Stone every minute, on top of the Gold, making them an even more enticing prize.

The Holy Roman Empire has the unique ability to garrison Relics inside Docks and defensive fortifications giving them a large boost to their stats, or in the case of the Dock, increasing the attack speed of your entire navy.

Conversion

Default Key: [T]

Conversion Radius	5 Tiles
Conversion Time	6s
Cooldown*	120s

*Cooldown time is separate for each Relic, and only comes into effect after a successful Conversion

Conversion is a very powerful Relic ability that can absolutely turn the tide of a battle when used at the right time. Any religious unit that's holding a Relic is capable of attempting to Convert enemy units by activating the Convert command, after which you'll see a circular indicator around your religious unit. Any enemy units that you manage to keep within this radius will be Converted after six seconds, at which time they'll join your forces and you can command them just like they're one of your units. Conversion has no time limit, so once you Convert a unit it will be yours for the remainder of the match.

While it can be useful against an enemy army of any composition, Convert attempts are generally best saved for when you spot high-value targets amongst your opponent's units. It's a risk bringing your religious unit to the front lines of a battle to get into range for a Convert attempt, so you want to ensure that you provide a sufficient protection detail, and that the payoff is worth that risk. Even if the attempt fails because the enemy units moved out of range, it can still be a useful tactic because by forcing most units to move you take away their ability to attack, giving your forces the advantage.

Faith Conversion

Default Key: [W]

When playing as the Abbasid Dynasty, if you research the **Faith** technology from the **Culture Wing** of the **House of Wisdom** you can gain access to a different Conversion method. Through the addition of Faith, the Imams of the Abbasid Dynasty do not need to hold a Relic in order to use the Convert command. However, this method of Conversion can only be used on a single enemy unit, rather than a group, and it has a cooldown period of 60s on both a successful and unsuccessful Conversion attempt.

Balancing Conversion

"One of the more interesting anecdotes that I can speak to is how the conversion ability came about. Early on in the project there were a lot of buildings, units, and abilities in place that hearkened back to previous entries in the franchise. Notably absent though, was the Monk conversion ability. Monk gameplay mostly centered around healing units, which was even accompanied by a soft "Wololo" as a nod to their predecessors. Healing was fun, but I missed the feeling of smugness I got from stealing my opponent's units!

Around the same time, we were trying to nail down Sacred Victory and the role of Relics in Age of Empires IV. It occurred to me that there might be a way to make Relics more interesting while also reviving the iconic "Wololo," so I spent an afternoon prototyping a crude version of a religious unit area-of-effect conversion ability. The idea was to create a bombastic moment of tension that would be fun to execute, dodge, and spectate. Of course, the power of an area-of-effect eclipsed the individual unit conversion of the past. To account for that the religious unit would need to be holding a Relic, which also increased the Relic's value and provided a choice to the player: Return the Relic to a Monastery for late-game Gold or take it on the offensive.

My thanks go out to the amazing Balance team, who tuned the religious unit's speed, visibility, conversion radius, and a bunch of other variables to help retain the ability's power without breaking the game. As a mechanic, conversion can be divisive because while it feels amazing to steal units it feels proportionally awful to lose them. Nevertheless, after a couple of playtests the ability resonated—Sometimes in the form of screams around the office."

—Michael Conkin
Senior Designer, Ritual & Retention Lead, Relic

Stuart Ng
Mood Imagery
Concept Sketches

Unit Counters

At its core, the Age of Empires IV combat system is a game of rock, paper, scissors, where each military unit has strengths and weaknesses against other military units in the game. These unit counters can have a large impact on the outcome of battles; if you fight your opponent with equally sized armies, and your army is primarily made up of units that counter the ones in your opponent's army, you're almost guaranteed to reign victorious. The strategic significance of these match-ups should never be underestimated.

Unit counters are often referred to in one of two ways: hard counters, and soft (tactical) counters. A hard counter is when a unit has a significant combat advantage, often in the form of a large amount of bonus damage, against another unit of similar resource and population cost. A basic, and classic, example of this is the triangle of Archers being a hard counter to Spearmen, Spearmen being a hard counter to Horsemen, and Horsemen being a hard counter against Archers.

Soft (tactical) counters tend to be a bit less clear cut and come with more caveats. Generally, rather than using bonus damage like a hard counter, you would instead leverage economic or production factors to gain an advantage. For example, Crossbowmen inflict bonus damage against heavily armored units, but this does not mean that they will outright counter Heavy Melee Cavalry. Only if the Crossbowmen outnumber them by a significant margin, or have backup from other units, will the Crossbowmen come out on top. Crossbowmen being a tactical counter in this situation is supported by their cheaper cost and production time, allowing you to field a lot more of them than your opponent could heavy melee cavalry units in the same amount of time.

Archers are considered soft counters to Crossbowmen primarily because of their significantly cheaper production cost and faster production time, but the additional range of the Archers and slow reload of the Crossbowmen are also factors to consider.

There are more match-ups and edge-case scenarios in Age of Empires IV than could ever be covered in a single table, but the one we've provided here is designed to give you a foundation for how the different types of counters work. You can then take this foundation into matches with you and apply the knowledge to different situations and build up your own internal database of counters. Just as important as knowing which units counter which, is knowing which units you shouldn't use against certain other ones, because sending in a group of units against a group that counters them is a guaranteed path to defeat.

Unit Counters

If Attacked By...	...Counter With	Avoid Using
Arbalétrier	Light Melee Cavalry/Siege	Melee Infantry, Small groups of Heavy units
Archer	Cavalry/Siege Units	Spearman
Battering Ram	Melee Units	Ranged Infantry
Bombard	Melee Units	Ranged Infantry
Camel Archer	Heavy Melee Cavalry	Melee Infantry
Camel Rider	Melee Infantry	Cavalry
Cannon	Melee Units	Ranged Infantry
Counterweight Trebuchet	Melee Units/Culverin	Ranged Infantry
Crossbowman	Light Melee Cavalry/Siege Units	Melee Infantry, Small groups of Heavy Units
Culverin	Melee Units	Siege Units
Fire Lancer	Spearman	Light Ranged Infantry
Grenadier	Cavalry	Light Infantry
Handcannoner	Light Melee Cavary/Siege	Melee Infantry
Horse Archer	Heavy Melee Cavalry	Infantry
Horseman	Spearman, Heavy Melee units, Camels	Archers
Knight/Lancer	Spearman, Camels	Ranged Infantry, Siege

If Attacked By...	...Counter With	Avoid Using
Landsknecht	Ranged Units	Light Infantry/Cavalry
Longbowman	Heavy Melee Cavalry/Siege	Infantry
Man-at-Arms	Crossbowman/Gunpowder Infantry	Archer, Spearman, Horseman
Mangonel	Melee Cavalry/Springald/Culverin	Ranged units/Infantry
Mangudai	Heavy Melee Cavalry	Infantry
Nest of Bees	Melee Cavalry/Culverin	Ranged units/Infantry
Palace Guard	Crossbowmen/Gunpowder Infantry	Archer, Spearman, Horseman
Ribauldequin	Cavalry/Culverin	Infantry
Royal Knight	Spearman, Camels	Light Ranged Units
Spearman	Ranged Units	Cavalry
Springald	Melee Units/Culverin	Siege Units
Streltsy	Siege Units	Heavy Melee Infantry
Tower War Elephant	Spearman	Other Melee Units
Traction Trebuchet	Melee Units/Springald/Culverin	Ranged Units
War Elephant	Spearman	Other Melee Units
Zhuge Nu	Light Ranged Units	Melee units

It is important to produce an army composition that covers the weaknesses of its units. Melee cavalry paired with ranged infantry units lets you counter melee infantry and any siege engines looking to counter your ranged infantry.

The Foundation of Balance

"When the balance process kicked off, it was important to ensure that the foundational Rock/Paper/Scissors counters such as Spearman vs. Cavalry were in place. These concepts are ingrained into the franchise and critical to player familiarity. Once the foundational RPS elements were seeded, the teams' focus shifted to ensuring the civilizations in AoE IV felt unique during tactical play. This meant going beyond simple data changes (health, damage) and adding in a deeper layer of asymmetry not found in the other Age games. The balance team spent many months tuning the various unique units, structures, upgrades and technologies to the theme and playstyle of each civilization.

At launch we believe players both new and old will be delighted by what Age IV has in store for them. Like the Definitive Editions, Age IV will continue to be supported with updates and improvements to ensure a high-quality experience for years to come."

—Christopher Rubyor
Design Director, World's Edge

1

Environments & Buildings

Equally as important as the units you use are the buildings that produce them and the environment you use them in, both of which feature a number of abilities and functionality that will greatly improve your gameplay if you keep them in mind. Many of these features are new to the Age of Empires franchise, so even if you're a returning player you're sure to learn something new here.

Sacred Sites

Sacred Sites, like neutral Trade Posts, are places on the map through which you can gain access to an alternate stream of Gold revenue. These sites are positioned randomly on the map at the start of each game, so you'll need to explore your surroundings if you want to find them. The white glow on the ground around them is the easiest thing to look for. Once you know the location of a Sacred Site, you'll need to wait until you reach the Castle Age before you can actually do anything with it, because you're going to need a religious unit.

If you bring any religious unit to a Sacred Site from Age III onwards you'll immediately start to capture the site once you enter it. This capture process is indicated by a progress bar underneath the Sacred Site nameplate, which slowly fills over time for as long as your religious unit is on the site. When the bar is full, the capture of the site will be complete and the white glow will change to match the color of your team, at which time it will also start generating Gold periodically at a rate of 100 Gold per minute.

After capturing a Sacred Site you do not need to keep your religious unit on it anymore in order to keep receiving the Gold, but that doesn't mean it's an entirely secure revenue stream. If any enemy unit, not just an enemy religious unit, steps onto the Sacred Site they'll start neutralizing your control over it, and if the progress bar empties, the site will return back to a neutral state. The enemy would still need to bring in a religious unit of their own to capture the Sacred Site, but the fact that they can negate your control of it without one does make it a bit harder to keep control over one.

The amount of Gold they generate is significantly less than you can get through trading, but it can still help offset the cost of some units or technologies while you're playing. The main thing that makes them so attractive is that, after you capture them, you can leave them completely unattended and don't have to risk any units if you don't want to. If you know enemy units are in the area, however, knowing the likelihood that they'll try and neutralize the site if they find it means that they can be effective places to use as bait for an ambush.

Although the Delhi Sultanate can produce religious units in Age I, under normal circumstances if you move them onto a Sacred Site they won't start to capture it until you reach Age III. They can, however, research the Sanctity technology at a Mosque to allow them to capture them earlier.

Stealth Forests

Stealth Forests are a new type of terrain feature to the Age of Empires series, and they bring with them a lot of new tactical opportunities. A Stealth Forest is typically found near patches of normal forest and they're easily identifiable by the dead or dying trees that they're made up of, and the patches of brown dying grass at the base of those trees.

If you move units inside of a Stealth Forest they'll immediately take on a soft glow in your team's color and your units will start to whisper instead of talking normally. With smaller groups of units, it's very easy to tell if they're all within a Stealth Forest area, but with larger groups, you might need to rely on the glow.

When a unit is inside a Stealth Forest it will be rendered completely invisible to most enemy units, while your units retain all of their normal sight capabilities. This enables you to launch unexpected attacks on hapless enemy units passing by or allow your melee infantry to get close to ranged units to attack them without having to take significant damage as they approach. If you're moving units around the map, or just out exploring, you should always be careful when moving past a Stealth Forest, because you never know just what might be lurking inside.

Only the keen eyes of a Scout are able to penetrate the foliage of a Stealth Forest and reveal what's hidden within it, which is just another reason why it's s important to always bring one with you when moving units around the map.

Stealth Forest Counters

"One of my favorite new features is Stealth Forests. They allow players to set up ambushes, hide strategic buildings or gain intelligence in new ways. We've also seen entire armies pass right by each other without knowing it! So tense! Of course, we built counters into this new element, so scout units now have a late-game power in that they can see clearly into stealth forests, making them key in preventing ambushes. Building outposts in stealth forests also gives you normal line of sight. I love that we've even got unique unit whisper responses when they're inside stealth forests too! And of course, being an Age game, you can harvest these forests just like normal ones, so if you've got a stealth forest patch near your base... you may want to chop that down as soon as possible to prevent the enemy from ambushing you from it!"

—**Adam Isgreen**
Franchise Creative Director, World's Edge

Line of Sight & Elevation

On most maps in the game, you'll encounter some form of elevation change, either from a hill, mountain, cliff, or valley, and the higher your units or buildings are, the further they're able to see. This site range increase rises gradually the higher you get (and at different rates for different units), but the highest the increase can go is three tiles above the unit or building's base range. Claiming an elevated position will provide you with a lot of additional map awareness by allowing you to spot enemy units sooner, which makes keeping map control easier.

Units or buildings that already have a long sight range on flat ground can become even better spotters by simply moving them to the top of a hill, and no other building exemplifies this better than the Outpost. For ranged units and buildings with attacks, the difference between their attack range and sight range is usually quite small, but Outposts have a significantly larger sight range, so putting one on top of a hill will just make the best early warning building even better. The sight ranges provided in this table are based on units being on flat terrain, so to work out their maximum increase, simply add three tiles.

Line of Sight Ranges

		Sight Range in Tiles
Military	Melee Infantry	6
Military	Regular Buildings	4
Military	Melee Cavalry	4
Military	Archer	6
Military	Longbowman	8
Military	Crossbowman	7
Military	Handcannoneer	5
Military	Horse Archer	5.5
Military	Tower Elephant	6
Military	Camel Archer	6.5
Siege	Mangonel	10
Siege	Ribauldequin	7
Siege	Counterweight Trebuchet	17
Siege	Traction Trebuchet	14
Siege	Springald	11
Siege	Cannon	11
Siege	Culverin	13
Siege	Bombard	11
Building	Keep	10
Building	Outpost	14.76
Building	Town Center	10
Building	Stone Wall Tower	10

Walls

The one thing that walls had in common in all of the previous Age of Empires games is that they were considered a solid object like any other building and no unit could walk on or over them.

Age of Empires IV changes that paradigm. By building either a Stone Wall Tower or Gate on a section of wall you'll notice that an additional small doorway is placed at the bottom of the wall near it, and through that door, any infantry unit can gain access to the top of the Stone Wall. Similarly, Siege Towers can be constructed in the field by infantry units after learning the **Siege Engineering** technology at the Blacksmith, allowing you to transport your troops to the top of an enemy Stone Wall. When taken together, both of these new mechanics can lead to pitched battles on the top of Stone Walls, creating a new dynamic fighting arena for players to explore.

Units on top of Stone Walls receive different elevation bonuses than those at the top of hills, and those come in the form of a two tile attack range increase, and a damage reduction of 66%. Combined, both of those bonuses make any group of ranged units atop Stone Walls a force to be reckoned with.

In Another Age...

Walls have been an essential part of building up a good defense or slowing the enemy down so that you can prepare a counterattack, throughout the entirety of the Age of Empires franchise. In Age of Empires I, there was only the Stone Wall, and before you build it, you had to research specific technologies at the Granary. Although you could build the wall itself in three different sizes, there were no gates, so if you wanted to leave an opening to walk through you had to improvise by constructing a cheap building such as a House in the middle of it.

Age of Empires II introduced the Palisade Wall, which only cost 2 Wood and could be constructed as early as the Dark Age. Stone Walls become available once you reached the Feudal Age. Gates that automatically opened and closed to allow friendly units to pass through were also introduced, which led to situations where an enemy unit could follow a friendly one into your base through the gate. Age of Empires III, from the Exploration Age onwards, you can construct Wooden Walls, which are later upgraded to Stone Walls via the Bastion technology in the Fortress Age. Unlike Age of Empires II, Gates would never let enemy units through them, much to the joy of many a forgetful player.

Buildings & Construction

Like most previous installments in the Age of Empires franchise, buildings in this game are placed within a grid-based tile system, and any construction is always done by your Villagers. When you click on a building in a Villager's menu, an outline of that building will appear around your cursor and the building grid will become visible on the ground; the tiles colored white within the grid indicate the space that will be occupied by the selected building.

Trying to construct a building on uneven terrain is no problem for the Villagers in this game, and they'll automatically level the ground for you, even if the building is on the side of a hill. As an added bonus, they'll also landscape the grounds within a one tile radius of a building, creating pathways and other picturesque arrangements.

A new feature of the building process in Age of Empires IV is the ability to assign your Villagers to build multiple of a single building type at once. After selecting your desired building from the Villager's menu, if you then hold down the Shift key while you left-click to place the building, you can keep clicking multiple times to place subsequent buildings around the initial one. Your Villagers will then automatically construct all of the buildings in order, without you having to do anything else. Using this method you can greatly speed up the placement process of multiple instances of the same building near each other, such as when you want to increase your population capacity and need to construct a group of Houses.

It should also be noted that the game will always leave a gap between buildings where units can pass through, even if you build them right next to each other. The only buildings which allow you to block off an area are the Stone and Palisade Walls. Another thing to be aware of is that if you try to place a building in an area that's occupied by an animal, Villagers will simply stand patiently nearby until the animal moves out of the way before starting construction.

Most civilizations also have buildings that can provide bonuses to other units or buildings that are within their influence of aura range. Influence typically refers to a unique system for a civilization and the radius adheres to the in-game tile grid. Aura's on the other hand are circular and their benefits are more general. While most of the time the size of the influence range is fixed, some buildings—such as the Holy Roman Empire's Town Center—can extend it. The actual benefits provided are as varied as the buildings themselves, and can be anything from attack buffs to healing, or even new abilities such as the Emergency Repair system from the Holy Roman Empire's Town Center.

Rally Points

The perfect location for a production building might not always be the perfect place for the units it produces to await further orders, and that's when you'll want to make use of the Rally Point functionality. After selecting any production building, if you right-click anywhere on the map you'll see a golden flag appear on the map briefly; that location will be designated as the Rally Point for the selected building. From that point onwards, any units you produce from that building will automatically walk to the Rally Point on their own.

There are a lot of different tactical applications for this system, for both the military and economic sides of your empire. For example, setting a Rally Point from your Town Center will allow you to have new Villagers you produce walk straight to the area you want them to gather resources from. You can use Archery Range Rally Points to automatically position ranged infantry on top of Stone Walls, or if you have a forward base near your opponent, set a Rally Point right in the middle of your assault so that your reinforcements get straight into the battle.

If you have multiple of the same type of production building near each other, you can double left-click on one of them to select them all, and then when you right-click on the map you'll place a Rally Point for all of them in the same location.

Putting a rally point close to a battle can help swing things in your favor by having reinforcements go directly where they're needed. Be careful with this, however, because if it looks like you'll lose the battle, you'll need to move the Rally Point back to a more secure location to avoid sending units straight to their death.

 Landmarks & Aging Up

Default Key: [T]

Advancing through the Ages is something that has always been an important aspect of Age of Empires because doing so grants access to increasingly stronger units, buildings, and technologies. In Age of Empires I and II, you advanced to the next Age by collecting enough resources and constructing two buildings of the current age. In Age of Mythology and Age of Empires III, this was changed to picking between different gods or politicians once the required amount of resources had been gathered.

Similar to the Age of Empires III: The Asian Dynasties expansion, Age of Empires IV uses a series of iconic Landmark buildings with each civilization to advance through the Ages. In the Feudal, Dark, and Castle Ages with most civilizations, you'll have to pick from one of two different Landmarks to advance the Age, with each subsequent set of Landmarks costing an increasing amount of resources. Each Landmark building also usually comes with unique functionality or properties, so you'll need to pick whichever one is best for the strategy you're currently using. The Abbasid Dynasty stands apart from this system, because they have a single Landmark building, to which they construct additional wings to advance the Age.

Like most buildings, Landmarks have to be constructed by Villagers, and due to their lengthy construction times, you're going to want to assign a decently sized group of them to the job. In addition to the small progress bar that appears at the construction site, when you start work on a Landmark you'll have a much larger progress bar prominently displayed under the Age indicator at the top of the UI, which shows you the number of Villagers currently working on constructing the Landmark.

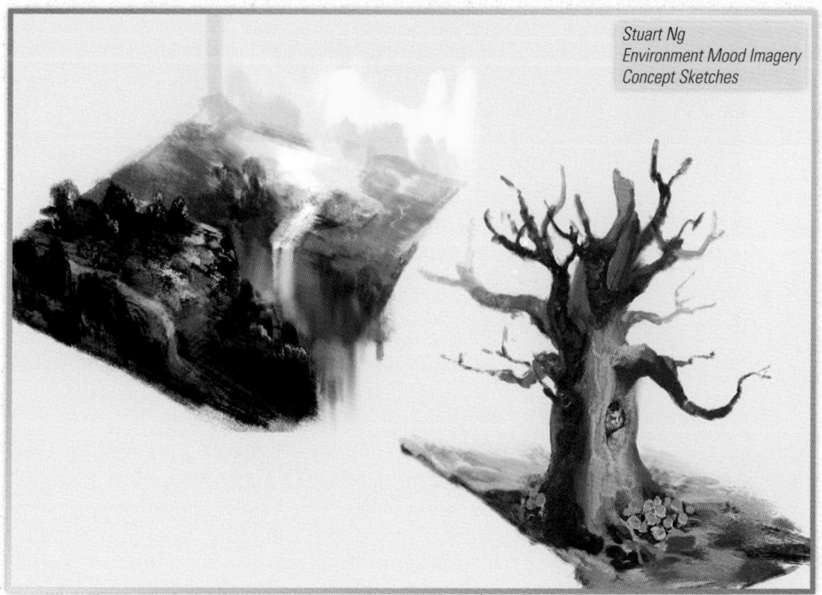

Stuart Ng
Environment Mood Imagery
Concept Sketches

Franchise Art Director

Han Randhawa

What is your role on the project, and what does your day-to-day work consist of?

As Art director, I work on anything visual or art related in-game, as well as external facing marketing. I work with our amazing team to bring visual consistency and further develop the AoE brand with our external partner Art Directors, their art teams and external OS art teams. I do many creative collaborations, paintovers, and help solve unique visual challenges. The role entails more than just quality of visuals and brand building, it's also visual storytelling and developing visual languages for the future of AoE as an IP.

Have you worked on any previous Age of Empire games?

I've worked on every one of the "Definitive Editions" re-releases From AoE: DE, AoE II: DE to AoE III: DE. These we call "Legacy" titles, and we have Melinda Rose our ace Senior Artist/Lead Artist, who covers those games, while I primarily have eyes on AoE IV.

What are your favorite game/s of all time?

Oh, please can I include *Darksiders 1* & *2*? Even though its cheating because I was Art Director on those games? I have deep fondness for what we created there with the Vigil Games team. I also love the *Batman Arkham* series—they did an amazing job of allowing you to inhabit the character of Batman. My all-time favorite & most joyful memory is of *Streets of Rage* for Sega Megadrive (Genesis in the U.S.). It was the SFX & Music that really grabbed me about that game.

How much time do you spend playing games outside of work?

As much as humanly possible. I have two kids who play huge amounts of *Halo* & *Destiny*, so I also watch a lot of games being played, it's much easier for me to cognitively break down art style and visuals in playthroughs and see how art is successful as a piece of visual design for players, as well as having a beautiful style. You can learn much about breaking down visuals by watching folks play—how players make choices, how the game feeds back via visuals, tracking their delights and frustrations.

Which are your favorite units in AoE IV, and why?

The English Longbowmen are ace—I simply love the palings system for archers. However, visually, I think the elephants from the Delhi Sultanate are so cool and they look fantastic when attacking a castle wall, just their presence is immense.

What feature of the game are you most excited for players to try out?

I hope folks will be excited by getting units on walls and attacking those with siege weapons. I'm also excited for folks to see the "Hands on History" videos that Noble [Smith] worked on with Relic and Lion TV. This is an unprecedented amount of high quality and unique footage and work for fans of history to consume! I

Principal Audio Designer, Audio Director

Bryan Rennie

What is your role on the project, and what does your day-to-day work consist of?

I'm the Audio Director for Relic on Age of Empires IV. The cool part of my job is my day to day can change drastically depending on where we're at in the project. I could be out in the field recording sound effects, which might include big explosions or rare weapons, or I might be in a studio working with musicians on the soundtrack. There will also be times where I'm working with actors and sitting in on dialog recording sessions.

What are your favorite game/s of all time?

I'm going to go old school with *Super Mario Bros.* It hit me at the right time as a kid and I just loved that game. It was the first game I played on the NES, which blew me away coming from a Coleco Vision system. The levels were amazing. It was fun to explore and find secret rooms and shortcuts and share those with your friends. Then there's the music score.... So iconic.

How much time do you spend playing games outside of work?

Not as much as I should, but probably between 3-6 hours a week. I find it hard to put aside the developer in me when playing games and be objective enough to just enjoy the experience.

Which is your favorite civilization in AoE IV, and why?

I think it would have to be the Chinese. Their units and weapon types set them apart from all the other civs. The tax collection, the Guandao melee weapon that the Man-at-Arms units carry, and the Nest of Bees cannon give the Chinese a really unique look and playstyle. The speech and music really define the identity of the Chinese and Zach's team has done a wonderful job making the buildings and units look great.

Which are your favorite units in AoE IV, and why?

For me there are two, the Holy Roman Empire Landsknecht unit and the Chinese Nest of Bees. The Landsknechte have this deadly melee weapon that Nick Bedell created a great impact sound for that makes them feel really powerful. It's really satisfying when they charge in with a jumping attack and land a devastating blow. The Nest of Bees' visuals and sound effects are similar to fireworks, which is done so well that it's one of my favorite things that happens in the game.

What feature of the game are you most excited for players to try out?

I would have to say the wall combat. With the stone walls being walkable by units and increasing the distance ranged units are effective create some really great possibilities for gameplay. Also, the visual and audio spectacle of walls being attacked by siege units is just a really great moment in the game. Leonardo Barragan, who did the sound design on the destruction, did such a good job of making destruction really impactful and satisfying to the player. It feels great to finally take down the walls and break through and equally devastating to be on the receiving end of that.

Technological Upgrades

At many buildings in the game, you're able to spend resources in order to learn various technologies that can improve a number of different aspects of your empire. These technologies are often found in buildings that are directly related to the technology subject (such as learning how to improve your gathering rate at a Mill, or improving the armor of your military ships at a Dock), but sometimes, as in the case of a Blacksmith or University/Madrasa, entire buildings are dedicated solely to technology.

The impact of a given technology also varies, with some individual technologies conveying strong bonuses on their own, while others have multiple tiers that provide you with increasing levels of benefit as you progress through them. Nearly all of these technologies require Gold to research, and when you consider how many there are, and the accumulative effect they can have on both your military and economy when you start researching a lot of them, you start to see why Gold is such a highly coveted resource. Learning when to start researching the different technologies, and how to leverage them in regards to your strategy, is another facet of Age of Empires gameplay that you'll develop over time as you become more experienced.

Upgrading your units will also result in a visual change. Pay attention to these details to quickly judge the upgrades and strength of your opponent's army.

The table presented on the following pages will give you an overview of every technology available in the game, presented in alphabetical order to make them easy for you to find. Through this table you'll be able to familiarize yourself with and compare all of the potential upgrades for the different civilizations and units to better leverage their strengths or weakness to your advantage.

Technology Overview

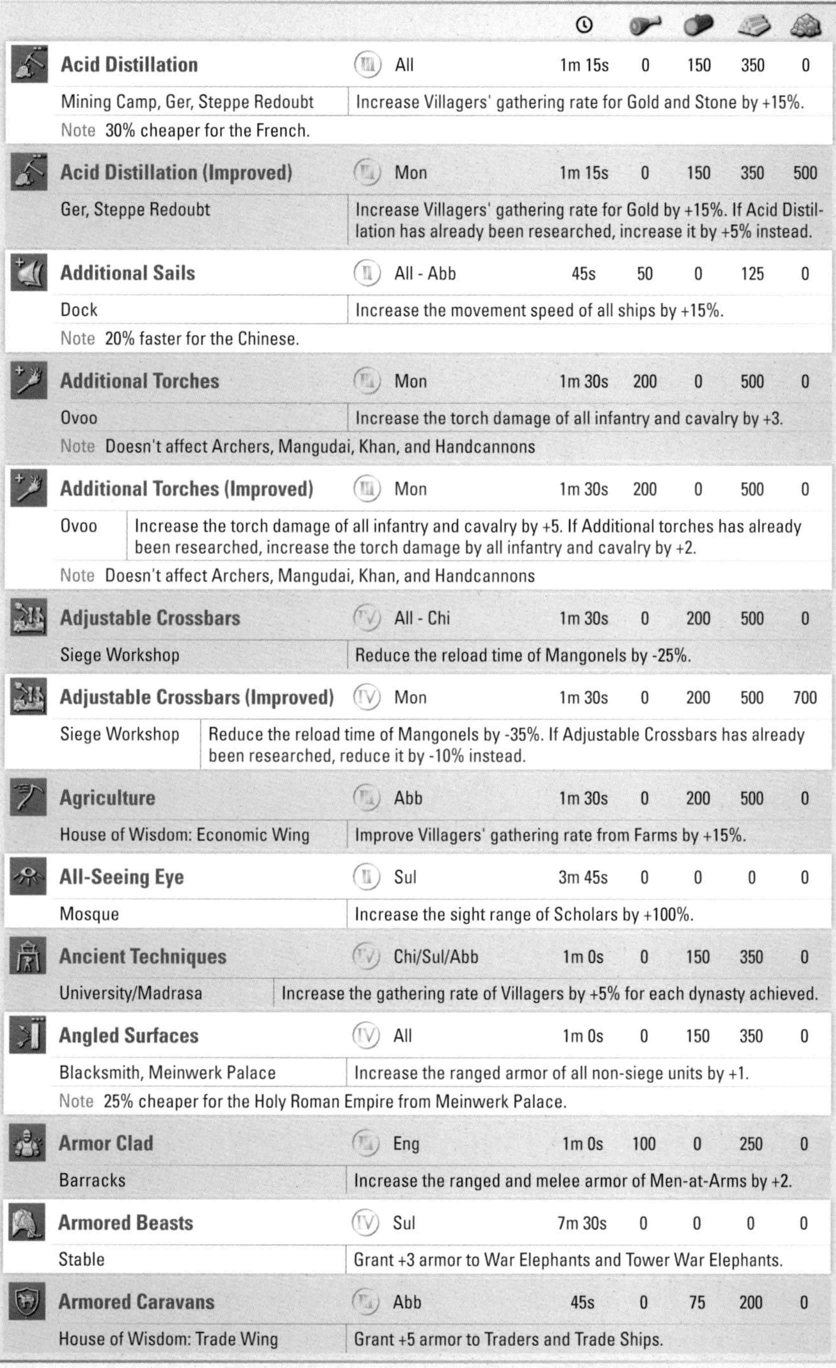

Technology	Age	Civilization	Time	Food	Wood	Gold	Stone	Researched at	Effect	Note
Acid Distillation	III	All	1m 15s	0	150	350	0	Mining Camp, Ger, Steppe Redoubt	Increase Villagers' gathering rate for Gold and Stone by +15%.	30% cheaper for the French.
Acid Distillation (Improved)	II	Mon	1m 15s	0	150	350	500	Ger, Steppe Redoubt	Increase Villagers' gathering rate for Gold by +15%. If Acid Distillation has already been researched, increase it by +5% instead.	
Additional Sails	II	All - Abb	45s	50	0	125	0	Dock	Increase the movement speed of all ships by +15%.	20% faster for the Chinese.
Additional Torches	II	Mon	1m 30s	200	0	500	0	Ovoo	Increase the torch damage of all infantry and cavalry by +3.	Doesn't affect Archers, Mangudai, Khan, and Handcannons
Additional Torches (Improved)	III	Mon	1m 30s	200	0	500	0	Ovoo	Increase the torch damage of all infantry and cavalry by +5. If Additional torches has already been researched, increase the torch damage by all infantry and cavalry by +2.	Doesn't affect Archers, Mangudai, Khan, and Handcannons
Adjustable Crossbars	IV	All - Chi	1m 30s	0	200	500	0	Siege Workshop	Reduce the reload time of Mangonels by -25%.	
Adjustable Crossbars (Improved)	IV	Mon	1m 30s	0	200	500	700	Siege Workshop	Reduce the reload time of Mangonels by -35%. If Adjustable Crossbars has already been researched, reduce it by -10% instead.	
Agriculture	II	Abb	1m 30s	0	200	500	0	House of Wisdom: Economic Wing	Improve Villagers' gathering rate from Farms by +15%.	
All-Seeing Eye	II	Sul	3m 45s	0	0	0	0	Mosque	Increase the sight range of Scholars by +100%.	
Ancient Techniques	IV	Chi/Sul/Abb	1m 0s	0	150	350	0	University/Madrasa	Increase the gathering rate of Villagers by +5% for each dynasty achieved.	
Angled Surfaces	IV	All	1m 0s	0	150	350	0	Blacksmith, Meinwerk Palace	Increase the ranged armor of all non-siege units by +1.	25% cheaper for the Holy Roman Empire from Meinwerk Palace.
Armor Clad	II	Eng	1m 0s	100	0	250	0	Barracks	Increase the ranged and melee armor of Men-at-Arms by +2.	
Armored Beasts	IV	Sul	7m 30s	0	0	0	0	Stable	Grant +3 armor to War Elephants and Tower War Elephants.	
Armored Caravans	II	Abb	45s	0	75	200	0	House of Wisdom: Trade Wing	Grant +5 armor to Traders and Trade Ships.	

Technology	Age	Civilization	Time	Food	Wood	Gold	Stone	Researched at	Effect	Note
Armored Hull	III	All - Chi/Mon	1m 0s	150	0	250	0	Dock	Increase the armor of all military ships by +2.	
Arrow Volley	IV	Eng	1m 0s	0	150	350	0	Archery Range, Council Hall	Longbowmen gain Arrow Volley, an activated ability that increases Longbowmen attack speed by +70%.	50% faster research time at the Council Hall.
Arrowslits	II	All - Chi	30s	0	0	25	50	Outpost/Wooden Fortress	Adds defensive arrowslits to this structure. For Outposts only one weapon emplacement can be added.	25% cheaper for the Holy Roman Empire.
Balanced Projectiles	II	All	1m 0s	0	100	250	0	Blacksmith, Meinwerk Palace	Increase the ranged damage of all non-siege units and buildings by +1.	25% cheaper for the Holy Roman Empire from the Meinwerk Palace.
Balanced Projectiles (Improved)	III	Mon	1m 0s	50	0	300	350	Arsenal	Increases the ranged damage of all non-siege units and buildings by +2. If Balanced Projectiles has already been researched, increase it by +1 instead.	Campaign only.
Banded Arms	IV	Rus	45s	0	100	225	0	High Armory	Increase the range of Springalds by +1.5 tiles.	
Battle Hardened	IV	Chi	1m 0s	150	0	350	0	Barracks	Increase the health of Palace Guards by +30.	
Benediction	II	HRE	45s	0	75	200	0	Monastery	Inspired Villagers construct +15% faster.	
Biology	IV	All-Fre	1m 30s	300	0	700	0	University/Madrasa, Blacksmith	Increase the health of all cavalry by +20%.	Researched at a Blacksmith by the Mongols only.
Biology (Improved)	IV	Mon	1m 30s	300	0	700	1000	Blacksmith	Increase the health of all cavalry by +30%. If Biology has already been researched, increase it by +10% instead.	
Blessing Duration	III	Rus	45s	75	0	200	0	Monastery, Abbey of Trinity	Increase the duration of Saint's Blessing by +10 seconds.	
Bloomery	I	All	1m 0s	50	0	125	0	Blacksmith, Meinwerk Palace	Increase the melee damage of all non-siege units by +1.	25% cheaper for the Holy Roman Empire from the Meinwerk Palace. Free for the French.
Boiling Oil	III	All-Mon	1m 0s	0	0	250	100	Keep, The White Tower, Elzbach Palace, Berkshire Palace, Red Palace, Spasskaya Tower	Towers and Keeps gain a boiling oil attack against nearby units that deals 30 damage.	25% cheaper for the Holy Roman Empire from the Meinwerk Palace. Free for the French.

Technology	Age	Civilization	Time	Food	Wood	Gold	Stone
Boot Camp	IV	Abb	1m 30s	300	0	700	0
House of Wisdom: Military Wing	Increase the health of all infantry by +15%.						
Boyar's Fortitude	III	Rus	1m 30s	200	0	500	0
Stable	Increase the health of Rus cavalry by +20.						
Camel Barding	IV	Abb	1m 30s	300	0	700	0
House of Wisdom	Increase the armor of camel units by +2.						
Camel Handling	III	Abb	30s	75	0	200	0
House of Wisdom	Increase movement speed of camel units by +15%.						
Camel Rider Shields	III	Abb	1m 30s	300	0	700	0
House of Wisdom: Military Wing	Grant Camel Riders shields, improving their melee armor by +3.						
Camel Support	I	Abb	1m 0s	50	0	125	0
House of Wisdom: Military Wing	Camels increase the armor of nearby infantry by +1.						
Cannon Emplacement	IV	All - Rus	1m 0s	0	0	75	300
Outpost, Keep, The White Tower, Berkshire Palace, Red Palace, Elzbach Palace	Add a defensive cannon emplacement to this structure. For Outposts only one weapon emplacement can be added.						
Note 25% cheaper for the Holy Roman Empire.							
Cantled Saddles	III	Fre	45s	75	0	200	0
Stable, School of Cavalry, Royal Institute	Increase Royal Knights' bonus damage after a charge by +10.						
Note 20% cheaper from the Royal Institute.							
Castle Turret	I	Rus	30s	0	0	0	75
Wooden Fortress	Increase the damage of arrows fired from this Wooden Fortress by +2.						
Castle Watch	I	Rus	30s	0	0	0	100
Wooden Fortress	Increase the sight range of this Wooden Fortress by +6 tiles.						
Cedar Hulls	IV	Rus	1m 30s	300	0	700	0
Dock	Increase Lodya Attack Ship health by +200 and increase ranged armor by +1.						
Chaser Cannons	IV	All - Rus	1m 30s	300	0	700	0
Dock	Increase the weapon range of Warships by +1 tile.						
Note 20% faster for the Chinese.							
Chemistry	IV	All	1m 30s	300	0	700	0
University/Madrasa, Blacksmith	Increase the damage of gunpowder units by +20%						
Note Researched at a Blacksmith by the Mongols only. Chinese unlock this technology for free upon reaching Age IV.							

Technology	Age	Civilization	Time	Food	Wood	Gold	Stone
Chivalry	II	Fre	1m 0s	0	50	125	0
Stable, School of Cavalry, Royal Institute	Royal Knights regenerate +1 health every 1 seconds when out of combat.						
Note 20% cheaper from the Royal Institute.							
Clinker Construction	III	Rus	1m 0s	200	0	500	0
Dock	Increase Lodya Attack Ship health by +200.						
Composite Bows	IV	Abb	1m 30s	0	300	700	0
House of Wisdom	Reduce the reload time of Archers by -25%.						
Corned Gunpowder	IV	Eng/Mon	1m 30s	175	0	800	0
Arsenal	Increases damage of ranged units by +20%.						
Note Campaign only.							
Corned Gunpowder (Improved)	IV	Mon	1m 30s	175	0	800	975
Arsenal	Increases damage of ranged units by +30%. If Corned Gunpowder has already been researched, increase it by +10% instead.						
Note Campaign only.							
Court Architects	IV	All - Mon	1m 30s	0	0	700	300
University/Madrasa	Increase the health of all buildings by +30%.						
Crannequins	IV	All	1m 30s	175	0	800	0
Arsenal	Improve the reload speed of Crossbowmen by +30%.						
Note Campaign only.							
Crannequins (Improved)	IV	Mon	1m 30s	175	0	800	975
Arsenal	Improve the reload speed of Crossbowmen by +40%. If Crannequins has already been researched, increase reload speed by +10% instead.						
Note Campaign only.							
Crossbow Stirrups	IV	Fre	1m 30s	300	0	700	0
Archery Range, Royal Institute	Reduce the reload speed of Arbalétriers by -25%.						
Note 20% cheaper from the Royal Institute.							
Crosscut Saw	IV	All	1m 15s	300	0	700	0
Lumber Camp, Ger, Steppe Redoubt	Increase Villagers' gathering rate for Wood by +15%.						
Note 30% cheaper for the French.							
Crosscut Saw (Improved)	IV	Mon	1m 15s	300	0	700	1000
Ger, Steppe Redoubt	Increase Villagers' gathering rate for Wood by +20%. If Crosscut Saw has already been researched, increase it by +5% instead.						
Cupellation	IV	All	1m 15s	0	300	700	0
Mining Camp, Ger, Steppe Redoubt	Increase Villagers' gathering rate for Gold and Stone by +15%.						
Note 30% cheaper for the French.							

Technology	Age	Civilization	Time	Food	Wood	Gold	Stone	Researched at	Effect	Note
Cupellation (Improved)	IV	Mon	1m 15s	0	300	700	1000	Ger, Steppe Redoubt	Increase Villagers' gathering rate for Gold by +20%. If Cupellation has already been researched, increase it by +5% instead.	
Damascus Steel	IV	All	1m 0s	150	0	350	0	Blacksmith, Meinwerk Palace	Increase the melee damage of all non-siege units by +1.	25% cheaper for the Holy Roman Empire from the Meinwerk Palace. Free for the French.
Decarbonization	III	All	1m 0s	100	0	250	0	Blacksmith, Meinwerk Palace	Increase the melee damage of all non-siege units by +1.	25% cheaper for the Holy Roman Empire from the Meinwerk Palace. Free for the French.
Devoutness	III	HRE	1m 0s	100	0	250	0	Monastery	Inspired Villagers gather resources +10% faster.	
Double Broadax	II	All	1m 15s	75	0	175	0	Lumber Camp, Ger, Steppe Redoubt	Increase Villagers' gathering rate for Wood by +15%.	30% cheaper for the French.
Double Broadax (Improved)	II	Mon	1m 15s	75	0	175	250	Ger, Steppe Redoubt	Increase Villagers' gathering rate for Wood by +20%. If Double Broadax has already been researched, increase it by +5% instead.	
Double Time	IV	Rus	45s	100	0	225	0	Archery Range	Streltsy gain the Double Time ability, which increases their movement speed by +30% and speeds up their Static Deployment time by +50% for 10 seconds.	
Drift Nets	III	All	1m 15s	150	0	350	0	Dock	Increase the gathering rate of Fishing Ships by +15% and their carry capacity by +20.	20% faster for the Chinese.
Efficient Production	I	Sul	3m 45s	0	0	0	0	Mosque	Allow Scholars to garrison in military buildings, boosting production speed by +100%.	
Elite Army Tactics	IV	All	1m 30s	300	0	700	0	University/Madrasa, Blacksmith	Increase the health of all melee infantry by +10% and their damage by +10%.	Researched at a Blacksmith by the Mongols only.
Elite Army Tactics (Improved)	IV	Mon	1m 30s	300	0	700	1000	Blacksmith	Increase the health of all melee infantry by +15% and their damage by +15%. If Elite Army Tactics has already been researched, increase health and damage by +5% instead.	
Enclosures	IV	Eng	1m 0s	0	150	350	0	Mill	Each Farm Enclosure being worked on by a Villager generates +1 Gold every 3.5 seconds.	
Enlistment Incentives	IV	Fre	1m 0s	150	0	350	0	Keep, Royal Institute, Red Palace	Improves the French influence by reducing unit costs by a further -10%.	20% cheaper from the Royal Institute.
Explosives	IV	All	1m 0s	150	0	350	0	Dock	Increase the damage of Incendiary Ships by +40%.	20% faster for the Chinese.
Extended Lines	II	All	1m 15s	75	0	175	0	Dock	Increase the gathering rate of Fishing Ships by +20% and their carry capacity by +10.	20% faster for the Chinese.
Extra Ballista	III	All - Rus/Sul/Abb	1m 0s	150	0	250	0	Dock	Adds a swivel ballista to Attack Ships. Swivel ballistae can fire in any direction and deal +15 damage.	20% faster for the Chinese.
Extra Hammocks	III	Chi	49s	100	0	250	0	Dock	Junks of the Archer Ship type gain additional crew, allowing them to fire two more arrows in each volley.	
Extra Materials	II	Chi	45s	0	0	200	75	Keep	Stone Wall Towers and Outposts repair nearby damaged Stone Walls. A single section is repaired at a time for +20 health per second.	
Faith	IV	Abb	1m 0s	150	0	350	0	House of Wisdom: Culture Wing	Imams can convert units without holding a Relic, but can only target a single unit.	
Fertilization	III	All	1m 15s	0	150	350	0	Mill, Ger, Hunting Cabin, Steppe Redoubt	Increase Villagers' gathering rate for Food by +15%.	30% cheaper for the French.
Fertilization (Improved)	III	Mon	1m 15s	0	150	350	500	Ger, Steppe Redoubt	Increase Villagers' gathering rate for Food by +20%. If Fertilization has already been researched, increase it by +5% instead.	
Fine Tuned Guns	IV	Rus	1m 0s	150	0	350	0	High Armory	Reduce reload time of Bombards by -25%.	
Fire Stations	II	HRE	45s	50	0	125	0	Dock	Increase the repair rate of Docks by +100%.	
Fitted Leatherwork	II	All	1m 0s	50	0	125	0	Blacksmith, Meinwerk Palace	Increase the melee armor of all non-siege units by +1.	25% cheaper for the Holy Roman Empire from the Meinwerk Palace.

Technology	Civilization	Time	Food	Wood	Gold	Stone	Building	Effect	Note
Forced March	Sul	3m 45s	0	0	0	0	Blacksmith	Infantry units gain the Forced March ability. This ability makes them move +100% faster for 10 seconds, but they cannot attack while it is active.	
Forestry	All	45s	25	0	50	0	Lumber Camp, Ger, Steppe Redoubt	Double the rate at which Villagers chop down trees.	30% cheaper for the French.
Forestry (Improved)	Mon	45s	25	0	50	75	Ger, Steppe Redoubt	Villagers fell trees in a single chop.	
Fortify Outpost	All - Mon/Rus	30s	0	0	0	100	Outpost	Add +1000 health and +5 fire armor to this Outpost.	
Fresh Foodstuffs	Abb	1m 0s	50	0	125	0	House of Wisdom: Economic Wing	Reduce the cost to produce Villagers by -50%.	
Gambesons	Fre	45s	0	100	250	0	Archery Range, Royal Institute	Increase Arbalétrier melee armor by +5.	20% cheaper from the Royal Institute.
Geometry	All - Mon	1m 30s	0	300	700	0	University/Madrasa	Increase the damage of Rams and Trebuchets by +30%.	
Grand Bazaar	Abb	1m 30s	300	0	700	0	House of Wisdom: Trade Wing	Traders also return with a secondary resource. This resource is +25% of the base Gold value and is set at the market.	
Greased Axles	All	1m 0s	0	150	350	0	Siege Workshop, Astronomical Clocktower	Increase the movement speed of siege engines by +20%.	
Greased Axles (Improved)	Mon	1m 0s	0	150	350	500	Siege Workshop	Increase the movement speed of siege engines by +30%. If Greased Axles has already been researched, increase it by +10% instead.	
Handcannon Slits	Chi	30s	0	0	25	50	Outpost	Add defensive handcannon slits to this structure. Only one weapon emplacement can be added.	
Hearty Rations	Sul	5m 0s	0	0	0	0	House of Learning	Increase the carrying capacity of Villagers by +5.	
Heavy Maces	HRE	1m 0s	100	0	250	0	Barracks, Burgrave Palace	Men-at-Arms wield maces, increasing their bonus damage against heavy targets by +6.	
Herbal Medicine	All	1m 0s	0	0	350	0	Monastery, Mosque, Prayer Tent, Abbey of the Trinity	Increase the healing rate of religious units by +100%.	The Delhi Sultanate can research this in Age I.
Herbal Medicine (Improved)	Mon	1m 0s	0	0	350	350	Prayer Tent	Increase the healing rate of religious units by +150%. If Herbal Medicine has already been researched, increase it by +50% instead.	
Honed Blades	Sul	7m 30s	0	0	0	0	House of Learning	Increase the melee damage of Men-at-Arms and Knights by +3.	
Horticulture	All	1m 15s	0	75	175	0	Mill, Ger, Hunting Cabin, Steppe Redoubt	Increase Villagers' gathering rate for Food by +15%.	30% cheaper for the French.
Horticulture (Improved)	Mon	1m 15s	0	75	175	250	Ger, Steppe Redoubt	Increase Villagers' gathering rate for Food by +20%. If Horticulture has already been researched, increase it by +5% instead.	
Imperial Examinations	Chi	1m 0s	50	0	125	0	Imperial Academy	Increase the maximum amount of Gold carried by Imperial Officials from 20 to 40.	
Improved Blessing	Rus	45s	0	0	275	0	Abbey of the Trinity	Improve the damage granted by Saint's Blessing by +1.	
Improved Processing	Abb	1m 30s	0	300	700	0	House of Wisdom: Economic Wing	Villagers drop off +8% more resources.	
Incendiary Arrows	All	1m 30s	0	300	700	0	University/Madrasa, Blacksmith	Increase the damage of ranged units and buildings by +20%. Does not apply to gunpowder units.	Researched at a Blacksmith by the Mongols only.
Inspired Warriors	HRE	1m 0s	100	0	250	0	Monastery	Prelates can inspire military units, improving their armor by +1 and damage by +15%.	
Insulated Helm	All	1m 0s	100	0	250	0	Blacksmith, Meinwerk Palace	Increase the melee armor of all non-siege units by +1.	25% cheaper for the Holy Roman Empire from the Meinwerk Palace.
Iron Undermesh	All	1m 0s	0	50	125	0	Blacksmith, Meinwerk Palace	Increase the ranged armor of all non-siege units by +1.	25% cheaper for the Holy Roman Empire from the Meinwerk Palace.
Knight Sabers	Rus	1m 0s	150	0	350	0	Stable	Increase the melee damage of Knights by +4.	
Long Guns	Fre	1m 0s	100	0	250	0	Dock	Increase the damage of naval cannons by +10%.	
Lookout Towers	Sul	5m 0s	0	0	0	0	House of Learning	Increase the sight range of Outposts by +50%.	

Technology	Age	Civ	Time	Food	Wood	Gold	Stone	Building	Effect	Note
Lumber Preservation	III	All	1m 15s	150	0	350	0	Lumber Camp, Ger, Steppe Redoubt	Increase Villagers' gathering rate for Wood by +15%.	30% cheaper for the French.
Lumber Preservation (Improved)	III	Mon	1m 15s	150	0	350	500	Ger, Steppe Redoubt	Increase Villagers' gathering rate for Wood by +20%. If Lumber Preservation has already been researched, increase it by +5% instead.	
Marching Drills	II	HRE	1m 30s	100	0	250	0	Blacksmith, Meinwerk Palace	Increase the movement speed of infantry by +10%.	25% cheaper for the Holy Roman Empire from the Meinwerk Palace.
Master Smiths	IV	All	1m 0s	150	0	350	0	Blacksmith, Meinwerk Palace	Increase the melee armor of all non-siege units by +1.	25% cheaper for the Holy Roman Empire from the Meinwerk Palace.
Medical Centers	III	Abb	1m 0s	100	0	250	0	House of Wisdom: Culture Wing	Keeps heal nearby units for +2 health every 1 second.	
Military Academy	III	All	1m 0s	0	100	250	0	Blacksmith, Meinwerk Palace	Reduce the time it takes to produce infantry, cavalry, siege, and transport units at buildings by -25%. Does not affect religious units or other support units.	25% cheaper for the Holy Roman Empire from the Meinwerk Palace.
Military Academy (Improved)	III	Mon	1m 0s	0	100	250	400	Blacksmith	Reduce the time it takes to produce infantry, cavalry, siege, and transport units at buildings by -35%. Does not affect Scouts, religious units, or other support units. If Military Academy has already been researched, reduce the time by -10% instead.	
Monastic Shrines	IV		45s	0	100	225	0	Prayer Tent	Monasteries allow Imrpoved Production in their districts even without an Ovoo.	
Mounted Precision	IV	Rus	1m 30s	100	0	250	0	Archery Range	Increase the weapon range of Horse Archers by +2.	
Navigator Lookout	III	All	1m 0s	75	0	200	0	Dock	Increase the sight range of military ships by +2 and their weapon range by +1.	20% faster for the Chinese.
Network of Citadels	III	Eng	45s	0	0	200	75	Keep, The White Tower, Berkshire Palace	Increase the Network of Castles attack speed bonus from 25% to 50%.	
Patchwork Repairs	I	Sul	5m 0s	0	0	0	0	Dock	Increase the repair rate of Fishing Ships by +100%.	
Phalanx	II	Abb	1m 0s	50	0	125	0	House of Wisdom	Increase the attack range of Spearmen by +100%.	
Piety	IV	All	45s	0	0	325	0	Monastery,Mosque, Prayer Tent, Abbey of the Trinity	Increase the health of religious units by +40.	The Delhi Sultanate can research this in Age I.
Piety (Improved)	IV	Mon	45s	0	0	325	325	Prayer Tent	Increase the health of religious units by +60. If Piety has already been researched, increase it by +20 instead.	
Piracy	II	Mon	1m 0s	100	0	250	0	Dock	Gain +50 Wood and +50 Gold when sinking an enemy ship.	
Platecutter Point	IV	All	1m 0s	0	150	350	0	Blacksmith, Meinwerk Palace	Increase the ranged damage of all non-siege units and buildings by +1.	25% cheaper for the Holy Roman Empire from the Meinwerk Palace.
Prescision Cross-Breeding	IV	All	1m 15s	0	300	700	0	Mill, Ger, Hunting Cabin, Steppe Redoubt	Increase Villagers' gathering rate for Food by +15%.	30% cheaper for the French.
Precision Cross-Breeding (Imp.)	IV	Mon	1m 15s	0	300	700	1000	Ger, Steppe Redoubt	Increase Villagers' gathering rate for Food by +20%. If Precision Cross-Breeding has already been researched, increase it by +5% instead.	
Preservation of Knowledge	II	Abb	1m 0s	0	50	125	0	House of Wisdom: Culture Wing	Reduce the cost of all technology by -30%.	
Professional Scouts	I	All	45s	0	25	75	0	Mill, Ger, Hunting Cabin, Steppe Redoubt	Scouts gain the ability to carry animal carcasses and +200% damage against wild animals.	30% cheaper for the French.
Professional Scouts (Improved)	II	Mon	1m 0s	0	50	125	175	Ger, Steppe Redoubt	Scouts gain the ability to carry animal carcasses, +300% ranged damage against wild animals. If Professional Scouts has already been researched, increase ranged damage against wild animals by +100%.	
Pyrotechnics	IV	Chi	1m 30s	150	150	700	0	Siege Workshop, Astronomical Clocktower	Increase the range of gunpowder units by +20%.	
Raid Bounty	II	Mon	1m 30s	100	0	250	0	Ovoo	Increase raid income for igniting a building to 100 Food and Gold.	
Raid Bounty (Improved)	II	Mon	1m 30s	100	0	250	350	Ovoo	Increase raid income for igniting a building to 125 Food, Wood and Gold. If Raid bounty has already been researched, increase the raid income for igniting a building by 25 Food, Wood, and Gold	

Technology	Age	Civilization	Time	Food	Wood	Gold	Stone	Building	Effect
Reinforced Defenses	IV	HRE	1m 0s	0	0	250	100	Keep, Elzbach Palace	Increase the health of walls, towers, and gates by +40%.
Reinforced Foundations	II	Sul	2m 5s	0	0	0	0	House of Learning	Houses and Town Centers grant an additional +5 maximum Population.
Reload Drills	IV	Chi	1m 30s	0	300	700	0	Siege Workshop, Astronomical Clocktower	Reduce the reload time of Bombards by -33%.
Reusable Barrels	IV	Chi	1m 0s	0	150	350	0	Siege Workshop, Astronomical Clocktower	Reduce the cost of Nest of Bees by -25%.
Riveted Chain Mail	IV	HRE	1m 0s	150	0	350	0	Barracks, Burgrave Palace	Increase the melee armor of Spearmen by +3.
Roller Shutter Triggers	IV	All	1m 0s	0	150	350	0	Siege Workshop, Astronomical Clocktower	Increase the weapon range of Springalds by +2 tiles and reduce their reload time by -25%.
Roller Shutter Triggers (Imp.)	IV	Mon	1m 0s	0	150	350	500	Siege Workshop	Increase the weapon range of Springalds by +3 tiles and reduce their reload time by -35%. If Roller Shutter Triggers has already been researched, increase their weapon range by +1 and reduce reload time by -10% instead.
Royal Bloodlines	IV	Fre	1m 30s	300	0	700	0	University, Royal Institute	Increase the health of all cavalry by +35%. Note 20% cheaper from the Royal Institute.
Saint's Reach	III	Rus	45s	0	0	275	0	Abbey of the Trinity	Increase the range of Saint's Blessing by +3 tiles.
Sanctity	I	Sul	5m 0s	0	0	0	0	Mosque	Allow Scholars to capture Sacred Sites before the Castle Age (III). Sacred Sites generate +100% more Gold.
Setup Camp	II	Eng	45s	25	0	75	0	Archery Range, Council Hall	Longbowmen gain the ability to Setup Camp, which heals them for +1 health every 1 seconds. Note 50% faster research time at the Council Hall.
Shattering Projectiles	IV	Eng	1m 30s	0	300	700	0	Siege Workshop	Trebuchet projectiles shatter on impact, increasing their area of effect.
Shipwrights	II	Eng	45s	50	0	125	0	Dock	Reduce the cost of ships by -10%.
Siege Elephant	IV	Sul	5m 0s	0	0	0	0	Archery Range	Upgrade Tower War Elephants to have Elite Crossbowmen as riders instead of Archers.
Siege Engineering	II	All - Abb	1m 0s	0	50	125	0	Blacksmith, Meinwerk Palace	Melee and ranged infantry can construct Siege Towers and Battering Rams in the field. Note 25% cheaper for the Holy Roman Empire from the Meinwerk Palace.
Siege Engineering (Improved)	II	Mon	1m 0s	0	50	125	175	Blacksmith	Melee and ranged infantry can construct Siege Towers and Battering Rams in the field. Improved Siege Engineering allows for the construction of Mangonels, Springalds and Trebuchets as well.
Siege Crew Training	IV	Rus	45s	100	0	225	0	High Armory	Setup and teardown speed of Trebuchets and Mangonels is instant.
Siege Works	IV	All	1m 0s	0	150	350	0	Siege Workshop, Astronomical Clocktower	Increase the health of siege engines by +20% and their ranged armor by +3.
Siege Works (Improved)	IV	Mon	1m 0s	0	150	350	500	Siege Workshop	Increase health of siege engines by +30% and their ranged armor by +4. If Siege Works has already been researched, siege engines gain an additional +10% health and ranged armor by +1 instead.
Siha Bow Limbs	II	Mon	45s	0	75	200	0	Archery Range	Increase the ranged damage of Mangudai and the Khan by +1.
Siha Bow Limbs (Improved)	III	Mon	45s	0	75	200	275	Archery Range	Increase the ranged damage of Mangudai and the Khan by +2. If Siha Bow Limbs has already been research, increase the ranged damage of Mangudai and the Khan by +1 instead.
Silk Bowstrings	II	All	1m 0s	50	0	450	0	Arsenal	Archers gain +2 tile attack range. Note Campaign only.
Silk Bowstrings (Improved)	III	Mon	1m 0s	50	0	450	500	Arsenal	Archers gain +10 tile attack range. If Silk bowstrings has already been learned, gain +8 tile attack range instead. Note Campaign only.
Slate and Stone Construction	II	HRE	1m 0s	0	0	250	100	Keep, Elzbach Palace	All buildings gain +5 fire armor.
Slow-Burning Defenses	IV	Sul	3m 45s	0	0	0	0	Keep	Increase the fire armor of Stone Wall Towers, Keeps, and Outposts by +10.
Specialized Pick	II	All	1m 15s	0	75	175	0	Mining Camp, Ger, Steppe Redoubt	Increase Villagers' gathering rate for Gold and Stone by +15%. Note 30% cheaper for the French.

Senior Community Manager

Eliot Hong

What is your role on the project, and what does your day-to-day work consist of?

I am the Community Lead, spearheading the Community Team for Age of Empires IV. I work closely with our dev team, our publishing team at World's Edge, and the Age of Empires community to make sure we're engaging and listening throughout development and post-launch. My day-to-day consists of listening to what the community is talking about and syncing that with our dev team's goals in making Age of Empires IV.

What are your favorite game/s of all time?

My favorite game of all time is *Super Mario RPG*—it's the first game I completed on the first console I ever owned from start to finish, and I try to play it at least once a year.

Favorite non-Age of Empires RTS game/s?

It'll have to be the original *StarCraft*—I played it so much, along with *WarCraft III*. My first RTS game ever though was *Command & Conquer.*

How much time do you spend playing games outside of work?

I usually play 3-4 hours a night, and primarily play on my PC, with the occasional Switch game here and there.

What's your general playstyle in RTS games?

My general style is to get my economy established ASAP and get early control of the map, and then do raids until I can get a sizeable army to take out my opponents. I tend to play aggressively and prefer that over turtling.

Which is your favorite civilization in AoE IV, and why?

My favorite civilization is the Delhi Sultanate—once my base is established I am able to then control the pace of the game via tech advantage and War Elephants, which allows me to push while sieging my opponents!

Which are your favorite units in AoE IV, and why?

My favorite unit in the game is the Nest of Bees—I love the visual effects it has and the area-of-effect damage. It's an effective unit to clear clumps of units and allow me to push through my opponent's army. Plus, the sound effects from firing its weapons—just wait until you experience it!

What feature of the game are you most excited for players to try out?

I'm excited for players to get into the campaign and unlock all the Hands on History content we created. There's a deep breadth of history that was curated from a global team to make available for players to dive into.

Technology	Age	Civ	Time	Food	Wood	Gold	Stone	Researched at	Effect
Specialized Pick (Improved)	II	Mon	1m 15s	0	75	175	250	Ger, Steppe Redoubt	Increase Villagers' gathering rate for Gold by +15%. If Specialized Pick has already been researched, increase it by +5% instead.
Spice Roads	II	Abb	1m 30s	0	100	250	0	House of Wisdom: Trade Wing	Increase Gold income from Traders by +30%.
Springald Emplacement	III	All - Rus	30s	0	0	50	125	Outpost, Wooden Fortress, Keep, The White Tower, Berkshire Palace, Red Palace, Elzbach Palace, Kremlin	Add a defensive springald emplacement to this structure. For Outposts only one weapon emplacement can be added. Note: 25% cheaper for the Holy Roman Empire.
Steeled Arrow	II	All	1m 0s	0	50	125	0	Blacksmith, Meinwerk Palace	Increase the ranged damage of all non-siege units and buildings by +1. Note: 25% cheaper for the Holy Roman Empire from the Meinwerk Palace.
Stone Bounty	IV	Mon	45s	100	0	225	0	Ovoo	Add +75 Stone to the raid income for igniting a building.
Stone Bounty (Improved)	IV	Mon	45s	100	0	225	325	Ovoo	Add +125 Stone to the raid income for igniting a building. If Stone Bounty has already been researched, add +50 Stone to the raid income for igniting a building.
Stone Commerce	IV	Mon	1m 0s	150	0	350	0	Market, The Silver Tree	Having 9 or more active Traders causes them to supply Stone as well as Gold.
Stone Commerce (Improved)	IV	Mon	1m 0s	150	0	350	500	Market, The Silver Tree	Having 9 or more active Traders causes them to supply and inceased amount of Stone as well as Gold.
Superior Mobility	I	Mon	45s	0	25	75	0	Ovoo	Packed buildings move and pack/unpack +50% faster.
Survival Techniques	I	All	1m 15s	0	50	100	0	Mill, Ger, Hunting Cabin, Steppe Redoubt	Increase Villagers' hunted meat carry capacity by +15 and hunted meat gather rate by +10%. Note: 30% cheaper for the French.
Survival Techniques (Improved)	I	Mon	1m 15s	0	50	100	150	Ger, Steppe Redoubt	Increase Villager's Hunted meat carry capacity by +25, hunted meat gather rate by +20%. If Survival Techniques has already been researched, increase carry capacity by +10 and hunted meat gather rate by +10% instead.
Swiftness	III	Sul	7m 30s	0	0	0	0	Mosque	Increases the movement speed of Scholars by +50%.
Teak Masts	II	Abb	1m 0s	100	0	250	0	Dock	Increase Dhow health by +100.

1

Principal Artist, Presentation Lead

Barry McDougall

What is your role on the project, and what does your day-to-day work consist of?
I've had a great opportunity to work on many parts of the game but mostly I've been working on video and game capture production. I am excited to have our fans play the game, the campaign and witness all the amazing content we've produced for Age of Empires IV.

What are your favorite game/s of all time?
Wow! That's a lot of games to pick from. I have fond memories of *Street Fighter II*, *Resident Evil 4*, *Uncharted: Drake's Fortune*, *Heroes of the Storm*, and currently playing *Runeterra*.

Favorite non-Age of Empires RTS games?
Big fan of the *Dawn of War* franchise.

How much time do you spend playing games outside of work?
A couple of hours a week. Though I prefer to be off the computer so I put my hobby time towards miniature table-top strategy games.

What's your general playstyle in RTS games?
I'm fairly defensive and like to turtle up in my games. This is why when I play Age of Empires IV, I like playing the Mongols as they have a very different playstyle from my norm.

Which is your favorite civilization in AoE IV, and why?
The Delhi Sultanate is one of my favorites, I really dig the architecture and, of course, they have the big hitters—War Elephants!

Which are your favorite units in AoE IV, and why?
The Mangudai are super fun—kiting enemy units with the Mongol horse archers is always gratifying.

What feature of the game are you most excited for players to try out?
I'm most excited for players to get into the narrative campaign and see history unfold.

Technology	Civ	Time	Food	Wood	Gold	Stone	Researched at	Effect	Note
Textiles	All	20s	50	0	100	0	Town Center, King's Palace, Palace of Swabia	Increase Villagers' health by +25.	Research time is faster for the French with each subsequent Age.
Tithe Barns	All	1m 0s	0	0	500	0	Monastery, Mosque, Prayer Tent, Abbey of the Trinity	Relics placed in a Monastery provide an income of +30 Food, +30 Wood, and +30 Stone every minute.	The Mongol version only provides +20 to each resource.
Tithe Barns (Improved)	Mon	1m 0s	0	0	500	500	Prayer Tent	Relics placed in a Monastery provide an income of +20 Food, +20 Wood, and +20 Stone every minute.	This is in addition to the +20 of each from the normal version of the technology, bringing the total to +40.
Tranquil Venue	Sul	3m 45s	0	0	0	0	House of Learning	Mosques restore +1 health to nearby friendly units every second.	
Two-Handed Weapons	HRE	1m 0s	100	0	250	0	Barracks, Burgrave Palace	Men-at-Arms wield two-handed weapons, increasing their damage by +6.	
Village Fortresses	Sul	5m 0s	0	0	0	0	Keep	Keeps act like Town Centers, including unit production, population capacity, and technology.	
Wandering Town	Rus	45s	100	0	225	0	High Armory	Ram damage increased by +100%.	
Wedge Rivets	All	1m 0s	0	100	250	0	Blacksmith, Meinwerk Palace	Increase the ranged armor of all non-siege units by +1.	25% cheaper for the Holy Roman Empire from the Meinwerk Palace.
Wheelbarrow	All	1m 30s	0	50	150	0	Mill, Ger, Hunting Cabin, Steppe Redoubt	Incease the carry capacity of Villagers by +5 and their movement speed by +15%.	30% cheaper for the French.
Wheelbarrow (Improved)	Mon	1m 30s	0	50	150	200	Ger, Steppe Redoubt	Incease the carry capacity of Villagers by +7 and their movement speed by +15%. If Wheelbarrow has already been researched, increase carry capacity by +2 instead.	
Whistling Arrows	Mon	1m 0s	100	0	250	0	Ovoo	Increase the Khan's Signal Arrow duration by +5 seconds and range by +2 tiles.	
Whistling Arrows (Improved)	Mon	1m 0s	100	0	250	350	Ovoo	Increase the Khan's Signal Arrow duration by +7 seconds and range by +3 tiles. If Whislting Arrows has already been researched, increase the Khan's Signal Arrow duration by +2 seconds and range by +1 tile.	
Yam Network	Mon	1m 0s	0	100	250	0	Outpost	Yam speed aura applies to all units instead of just Traders and cavalry units.	
Zeal	Sul	7m 30s	0	0	0	0	Mosque	Units healed by Scholars gain +50% attack speed for 3 seconds.	

An Introduction to Skirmish/PvP

If you're looking to feel the thrill of battle long after you've survived The Siege of Rochester or broke through the Blockade at Lumen Shan in the Campaign scenarios, then you'll find it within the arena of Skirmish/PvP. The unpredictability of your opponents in these modes keeps every game feeling fresh; these are the crucibles within which legends are born, and only the most skilled players will leave their mark on history!

Game & Map Setup

The first choice you need to make when setting up a game is what type you want to play, and what win conditions you want active. In Age of Empires IV, there are three main win conditions for Skirmish/PvP matches, and in the Standard game type, you have the ability to enable one, two, or all three of them for any given match. The choice of win condition is one of the most important that you have to make when setting up a match, because single win conditions will ultimately dictate the focus of the players in the match and lead to very different playstyles. Multiple active win conditions on the other hand tend to make matches more freeform and flexible, and figuring out which one your opponent is working towards is another aspect of the game that you have to learn with time and experience.

Game Type	
Standard	This is the most common game type you'll encounter; it has the greatest flexibility, and allows for a variety of match options and win conditions.
None/Sandbox	Play without any win conditions. The only way for a player to lose in this mode is for them to resign from the game, and the player left after all of the others resign is the winner. This is the ideal game mode to test build orders, unit capabilities, and whatever else you want. It also lends itself to just enjoying building your empire to see how your beautiful city unfolds.

Win Conditions	
Landmarks	This win condition has a simple objective: the destruction of all enemy Landmarks. Once all Landmarks have been destroyed, the enemy will automatically resign and victory is yours. Be careful, as Landmarks can be reconstructed!
Sacred Sites	Throughout the map, there are certain spots that are referred to as a "Sacred Site". These are special places that periodically generate Gold for the player that holds it, and they can be only captured by a religious unit. For this win condition you'll need to capture and hold all Sacred Sites on the map for 10 minutes, with the number of sites depending on the map
Wonder	Wonders are a building that becomes available for construction once you reach the Imperial Age, and if this win condition is active you'll need to build one, and then defend it for 15 minutes to be declared victorious.

Starting Resources

You can choose between two different amounts of starting resources: Standard and High. The Standard amount has you start with minimal resources, requiring you to incorporate economy building into your game plan during the match. High, on the other hand, has you start with much larger amounts of resources, allowing you to focus more on the military and technology sides of gameplay. As the name implies, Standard is the setting that's active in most matches, because it means players have to account for all aspects of the game, whereas High is generally used for specific types of custom matches that focus more on construction and production.

Amounts	Food	Wood	Gold	Stone
Standard	200	150	100	0
High	+9999	+9999	+9999	+9999

Starting Age

Depending on what you want available to players as soon as the match begins, you can choose to start a match in either Age I, Age II, Age III, or Age IV. When starting in one of the later Ages, however, you will not automatically inherit the technologies from the previous Ages—you still have to research everything. While you do get immediate access to all of the buildings in your selected Age, you don't have the option to construct or use Landmarks from the earlier Ages. For civilizations such as the Chinese that rely on Landmarks to move through their Dynasties, the choice of starting Age can have a significant impact on their capabilities.

Stuart Ng
Mood Imagery
Concept Sketches

1

Map State

Lastly, you can choose the level of information that each player has available at the start of a match. Through these options, you can tailor how much of an effect the fog of war and the visibility of your opponent's movements and actions will have on a match. The more revealed map states are not commonly used in most competitive games, but for practicing against the A.I. or another person, having more information available can help you with learning timings and routes that opponents are likely to take, and can be invaluable.

Map State	
Concealed	This is the normal state of the map, with full fog of war in effect, meaning you'll need to rely on units to reveal the terrain and features.
Explored	There is no fog of war present, allowing you to see the basic layout of the map and the location of resources, but not the location or movement of your opponent's forces.
Revealed	Similar to explored, but the map now also shows the location of your opponent's buildings and units.

Map Setup

After setting up the rules of the match, you'll then need to decide which map to play on, how many players will be involved (either A.I. or human opponents), and how it looks. To help you better decide, this section will go over the different rules for how resource amounts and location are determind, along with a number of other topics.

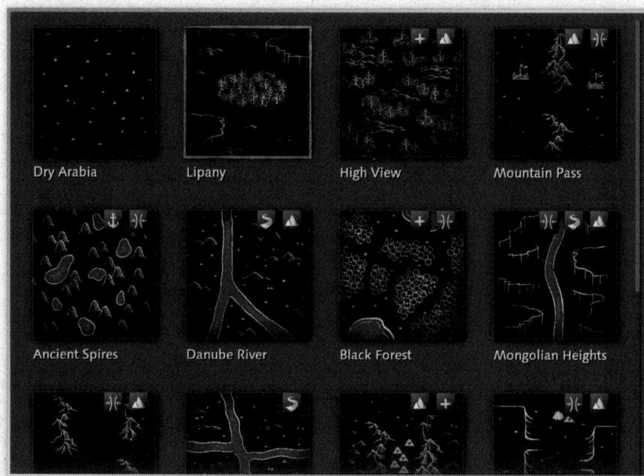

Before a custom game you have a variety of setting and maps to choose from

Senior Designer, Ritual & Retention Lead

Michael Conkin

What is your role on the project, and what does your day-to-day work consist of?

I am the lead designer for the core game mode and a team called Ritual & Retention, which focuses on the social, progression, and multiplayer experience in Age IV. The features that we build are designed to teach players the complexities of the game and each Civilization. There are so many interesting mechanics to discover, and we think that helping players master them is the first step towards creating an engaging and competitive multiplayer environment.

My day-to-day work varied wildly based on the stage of the project. In the early days much of my time was dedicated to writing design documentation and collaborating with other designers, programmers, and artists to plan out the features that we wanted to build. Then, we entered a period of prototyping where I would spend most of my days scripting the core game mode experiences, including win conditions and the Art of War challenges. Lately, I am focused on bug fixing and preparing for launch and live operations.

What are your favorite game/s of all time?

There are too many to name, but I will credit the games that always seem to be top of mind when this question is asked. In no particular order, *The Legend of Zelda: Breath of the Wild* redefined what it meant to explore an open world for me. I have logged more hours in *CounterStrike* than I care to reveal (more recently I have deep-dived into *Valorant*, but credit goes to the OG). *Metal Gear Solid II* and the recent *Hitman* stand out for me in the under-serviced stealth genre. Of course, I would be remiss not to also mention Age II for the countless number of LAN sessions it spawned in my earlier years.

Favourite non-Age of Empires RTS game/s?

Is *Age of Mythology* cheating? *Command & Conquer: Red Alert* was a staple growing up. In recent years I really enjoyed my time with *Homeworld: Deserts of Kharak* and, while not a traditional RTS, *Stellaris*.

How much time do you spend playing games outside of work?

I have periods of feast and famine but when I really sink my teeth into a game, I would guess I play for an average of 10 hours a week.

What's your general playstyle in RTS games?

I tend to not to be overly aggressive and enjoy building a massive, well-defended empire in Age games. In recent playtests I often race to construct the first Wonder and brace myself for the coming onslaught of attacks with a front-line of archers on walls and a maze of outposts inside them.

Which is your favorite civilization in AoE IV, and why?

My favourite civilization that I may never master are the Mongols. I aspire to migrate around the map and establish a network of outposts that facilitate hit-and-run raiding with my Khan-inspired horsemen. Until I can pull that off, you will find me hiding behind my English stone walls.

Which are your favorite units in AoE IV, and why?

I love the changes made to the Scout. Using them to hunt and carry back food is very satisfying and their ability to see through stealth forests keeps them relevant in the late game. The award for coolest utility goes to the Mongol Khan (hard to argue with the deployable scouting falcon). It's also hard to ignore the bombastic spectacle and destruction of the Chinese Nest of Bees.

What feature of the game are you most excited for players to try out?

I am excited to see how players react to and utilize the Monk's new conversion ability. I think it is going to make for some exciting shifts in competitive matches.

Resource Distribution

Crafted Maps differ from normally generated maps in that their resources and cliffs always spawn in the same locations.

Classic Land Local Resource Distribution

Wood	Sheep	Deer	Berries	Boar
Forest 1	Starting Sheep	Close Deer	Close Berries	Close Boar
Range Band: 11.25 - 12.5 Tiles	Quantity: 2x1 Range Band: 7.5 - 8.75 Tiles	Quantity: 1x7 Range Band: Accessible	Quantity: 1x6 Range Band: 9.5 - 10.5 Tiles	None
Forest 2	Mid Sheep	Far Deer	Mid Berries	
Range Band: 16.25 - 17.5 Tiles	Quantity: 2x1 Range Band: 15 - 17.5 Tiles	Quantity: 1x7 Range Band: 37.5 - 40 Tiles	Quantity: 1x6 Range Band: 21.25 - 22.5 Tiles	
Forest 3	Far Sheep			
Range Band: 30 - 32.5 Tiles	Quantity: 2x1 Range Band: 22.5 - 25 Tiles			

Classic Island Local Resource Distribution

Wood	Sheep	Deer	Berries	Boar	Shorline Fish
Forest 1	Starting Sheep	Close Deer	Close Berries	Close Boar	Shorline Fish
Range Band: 11.25 - 12.5 Tiles	Quantity: 2x1 Range Band: 7.5 - 8.75 Tiles	Quantity: 1x7 Range Band: Accessible	Quantity: 1x6 Range Band: Accessible	Quantity: 1x1 Range Band: Accessible	Quantity: 6 Range Band: Accessible
Forest 2	Mid Sheep	Far Deer	Mid Berries		
Range Band: 12.5 - 15 Tiles	Quantity: 2x1 Range Band: 15 - 17.5 Tiles	None	None		
Forest 3	Far Sheep		Far Berries		
Range Band: Accessible	None		None		

Contested Zone Resource Distribution

Map Size	No. of Players	Map Type	Small Gold	Large Gold	Small Stone	Large Stone	Small Boar	Large Sheep
Micro	2	Classic Land	1	2	1	--	2	2
		Classic Island	--	2	--	--	--	--
Small	4	Classic Land	2	3	2	--	3	4
		Classic Island	--	3	1	--	--	--
Medium	4	Classic Land	2	4	3	--	4	6
		Classic Island	--	4	1	--	--	--
Large	6	Classic Land	3	5	4	--	5	6
		Classic Island	--	5	2	--	--	--
Gigantic	8	Classic Land	4	6	4	1	6	8
		Classic Island	--	6	2	--	--	--

Range Band: The Rough Range Within Which the Resource can be Found**

Quantity: The Amount and Arrangement of the Resource. For Example, 2x1 is Two Separate Instances of One Resource, Meaning One Resource Will be Generated in Two Separate Locations. Whereas 1x7 Means That All Seven Resources Will Appear in the Same Location.

To decide how resources are created and distributed on a map when the match begins, the game looks at two different parts: the local zone, and the contested zone. The local zone is considered the area surrounding the initial starting point of a player, and the contested zone is parts of the map that are equally accessible to all players. The local zone around a player will always have the same amount of resources in it on any given map, regardless of the map size or how many players are in the match, whereas the resources within the contested zone will vary based on the map size. The number of resource locations that are generated through this system are totally independent of your starting resource selection in the game setup section.

The exact resources that you find within a player's local zone will vary, with different ones being available on land maps or island maps; we've included those distinctions in our breakdown of the maps later in the section. Those resources are typically what you'll need to get your base and economy up and running at the start of games, and then as you move out into the more dangerous contested zone, you'll start to encounter the resources you need for more powerful units and buildings.

Biome

The biome selection allows you to radically change the visual style of a map, giving you some added variety to how a map feels, or letting you thematically adjust the setting of a specific match or battle you want to take part in. It's important to note, however, that this change is purely cosmetic, and maps will still retain the key geographical features that you like about them.

Team Starting Locations

This setting is one of the most important to consider if you're playing in a match involving teams of more than one player. It allows you to choose to either have starting locations be totally random, or have teammates spawn together. Random locations can lead to very uneven games where one player can end up having to face off against multiple nearby opponents, but it can be a nice way to mix things up once in a while. As the name suggests, having teams spawn together means that players on a team will always start near each other, which, for teams of three or more, means that you'll have two players on the outer flanks, and one or two sandwiched in the middle; these middle players are commonly referred to as "pocket players". Even when you select to have teams spawn together, the starting position of any given player within that team spawn area is still randomized.

> **Map Seed**
>
> If you find a particular combination of map, biome, or geographical features that you like on a map, pull up the menu and you'll find the Map Seed above the other menu options. This combination of letters and numbers can then be entered on the Map Setup page to replay that exact same map.

European Temperate

Representation of the Typical European Grassland

Taiga Summer

Based on the Deep Woods that Dominate Northern Europe and much of Russia

Taiga Winter

A Version of Taiga that Represents the Period of Snow Melt in Early Spring

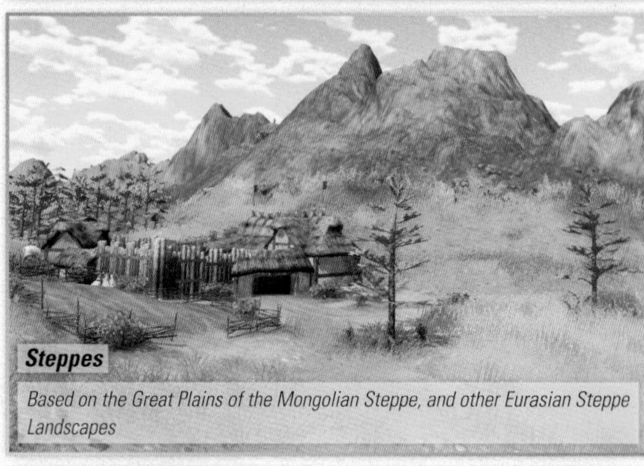

Steppes

Based on the Great Plains of the Mongolian Steppe, and other Eurasian Steppe Landscapes

Gobi Desert

Based on the Gobi Desert Straddling Modern-Day Northern China and Southern Mongolia

Asian Temperate

Representation of a Typical Forest from Eastern China

Chalk Downs

Based on the Coasts of England and France, Featuring the Chalk-White Cliffs and Dirt

Asian Subtropical

Representation of the Lush Subtropical Forests Found in China, Stretching Across Asia Towards India

Map Features

In the top right-hand corner of the icon for most maps, you'll find one or more smaller icons that are used to let you know about the specific geographical or economical features of a map. If you haven't seen a map before and are unsure how it will play, these icons can help you make a more informed choice to ensure that you get a map that will play to the style of game you're looking for.

Map Features		Sight Range in Tiles
+	More Resources	Features More of one Particular Resource Than Usual
▲	Elevation	Features Terrain Where Shifts in Elevation Provide Natural Advantages
)(	Choke Point	Features Narrow Contested Pathways That are Important to Secure
⚓	Naval	Features Large Bodies of Water That Require Ships to Travel Over
S	River	Features a River That Winds Through the Terrain

Designing for Player Fantasy

"When sitting down to design a map, often I like to think about player fantasy. It doesn't have to be a universal fantasy, but for a particular type of player, I'd ask myself what their ideal type of map layout would be for a given fantasy they would want to act out through our game. For turtle players, who just love defending their choke points and owning their fortress, what would be better than a map where everyone starts on a cliff with limited access points and lots of resources to fight over? That's where Hill and Dale came from, and it was made exactly for those players whose love of the game comes from great sieges and intense defending.

In other cases, it could be for the player who loves exploring, and that's the sort of foundational feeling that I hope gets evoked when playing Archipelago, with the potential for many small islands that could hold resources, relics, sacred sites, and more. Some maps push and stress our sandbox in unique ways, like Highview with its extensive stealth forests, made for players who love sneaking around and ambushing their opponents; some are meant to provide unique team game settings, like Warring Islands. My hope is that no matter what type of player you are, you end up finding a map that really gels with the way you love to play."

—Nick Taylor
Designer, Maps Lead, Relic

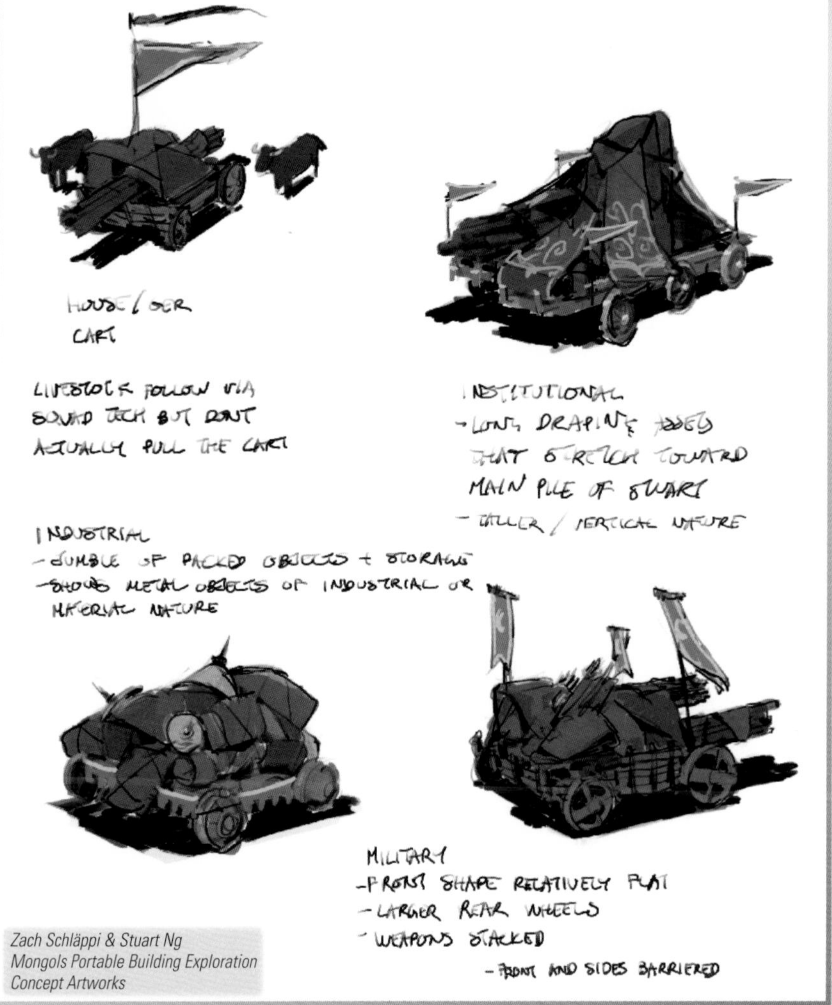

Zach Schläppi & Stuart Ng
Mongols Portable Building Exploration
Concept Artworks

Stuart Ng
Mood Imagery
Concept Artworks

Fields of Battle

Now that you've learned about all of the options and rules for how things are generated on maps, it's time to go over each individual map. In this section, we'll provide you with the classifications for each map so that you know how resources are generated on it, as well as some other key details and information about the main features of the map or the playstyles that it's suited for. We've also grouped maps up into general categories to better discuss aspects of gameplay that are relevant for them, but these groups are not found within the game.

Open Land Maps

Open land maps are characterized by small-to-mid-sized forests, with large open spaces between them. These maps invite an aggressive approach to gameplay, because the open areas provide multiple approach routes for your opponent, making defensive play—especially if you factor in the costs involved in walling yourself off over such large areas—more difficult. Unless you put your opponent on the back foot defensively, you'll very often have to prioritize which areas of your base to secure first, and whether to use military units or fortifications, which is what makes defending on these maps so hard.

To ensure continuous Villager production at the start of a match, you'll need to assign four of your starting Villagers to gather Food from Sheep close to your Town Center. While those Villagers travel to and start gathering Food from the Sheep have your other two Villagers build a House. Next, have those two Villagers build a Lumber Camp near a forest to start gathering Wood, alongside any newly produced Villagers. Between two and four additional Villagers on Wood is a good start, but the exact number will vary based on your given strategy. If you want to reach Age II quickly, then have your next two Villagers start gathering Gold.

Building your first Landmark will require a large surplus of Food, so after assigning two Villagers to Gold, have all of the subsequent ones gather Food. Look for groups of Deer or Berry patches and set up a Mill nearby. As soon as you have the necessary resources, have four or five of your Food gathering Villagers construct your Landmark, while ensuring that you keep up Villager production. After this, your Villager distribution should shift based on whatever plan and strategy you're attempting to employ.

Community Map Feedback

"We worked with a group of hardcore Age of Empires fans for much of development, the Community Council, and we would regularly ask them about maps and map features every time we sent them a build of the game. Lots of balancing decisions and design direction was gleaned from these discussions, and topics like mountain height and placement of sacred sites on some maps were changed as a direct result of this collaboration."

—Nick Taylor
Designer, Maps Lead, Relic

Dry Arabia

An open map based on the classic Age of Empires Arabia map.

Dry Arabia is a very open map, with only a few hills and Stealth Forest areas dotted around. These Stealth Forests are key tactical spots that can be used to surprise enemy armies that happen to walk past. There are plenty of resources out in the contested zones, and without any geographical features to provide cover or restrict movement, those areas will see even more combat and be harder to defend. If your opponent is focusing a lot on resource locations, then be sure to take advantage of the neutral Trade Post on either side of the map for a secondary revenue stream.

Resource Spawn	Sacred Sites	Position
Classic Land	3	Within contested zone

High View

A hilly map where Stealth Forests permeate the lowlands.

High View puts player's starting positions atop small hills, with patches of Stealth Forest dividing them, and compared to Dry Arabia, there are more forested areas. Scouts will be important for safely moving around on this map, because it can be difficult to track enemy units through all of the Stealth Forests otherwise.

Resource Spawn	Resource Distribution	Sacred Sites	Position
Custom Classic Land	Some of the outer resources like secondary Gold Veins and Deer are brought slightly closer to player starting positions	3	Two in corners, one in center, all along a diagonal line

King of the Hill

Fight for the resources in the center of the map!

King of the Hill is probably the most open and aggressive map in this group, with only a small amount of Wood and other resources around your initial base. The center of this map is dominated by a huge hill, on top of which you'll find the majority of the Stone, Gold and Food gathering locations. With so many resources in play at one location on the map, it's inevitable that conflict will occur there, and victory on this map will often go to the player than can maintain control of the hill the longest.

Resource Spawn	Resource Distribution	Sacred Sites	Position
Custom Classic Land	Smaller forests than Classic Land	1	On top of the central hill

Dry Arabia Asian Suptropical

High View Taiga Winter

King of the Hill Chalk Downs

Lipany

Several cliffs are all that separate players from the rest of this relatively open map.

Lipany is very similar to Dry Arabia and plays in much the same way. The main difference is that the cliffs around the map put extra emphasis on careful unit placement, because of the additional line of sight that units on top of those cliffs will have.

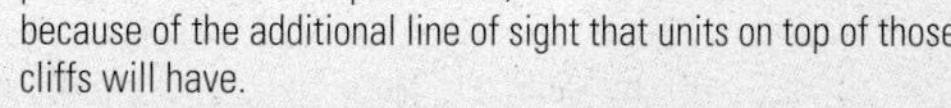

Resource Spawn	Sacred Sites	Position
Classic Land	3	Within contested zone

Closed Land Maps

Closed land maps are characterized by only having one or two narrow paths that lead to your base, along with large, impassable forests and mountains. The prominence of such geographic features naturally lends these maps to a more defensive playstyle. Because you only have a few approaches to be concerned about, walling up your base is much easier on these maps.

Your goal in Age I should be to make additional Town Centers as soon as you reach Age II, so that you can mass-produce Villagers, and given the expense of Town Centers, you should start saving towards the required resources straight away. Other than a couple of Villagers to get the required amount for your Age II Landmark, you shouldn't assign many Villagers to Gold, and instead of helping to build up your Food surplus, newly produced Villagers should start gathering Stone or Wood. The number of Villagers you assign to Stone and Wood will depend on how many additional Town Centers you want to construct, with each one requiring roughly three Villagers on Stone and six on Wood.

Once construction of your Landmark has begun, put two or three additional Villagers onto Gold so that you can start researching economic technologies as early as possible. Depending on how the match is progressing, you'll want to leave most of the Villagers you had gathering Stone and Wood on those resources, so that later in the game you can add either more Town Centers or some defensive fortifications based on your needs. Do not forget to add Farms gradually as well, however, to ensure that you have a sufficient and sustainable Food source within your walls.

Lipany European Temperate

Stuart Ng
Environment Type Exploration
Concept Artworks

Senior Concept Artist

Stuart Ng

What is your role on the project, and what does your day-to-day work consist of?
I'm a senior concept artist on Age of Empires IV, and my job was to develop the visual look of the game by helping to design the characters, buildings, ships, and environments.

Have you worked on any previous Age of Empire games?
Nope I haven't, but I grew up playing Age I and II in my younger years.

What are your favorite game/s of all time?
Monster Hunter. And more *Monster Hunter*.

Favorite non-Age of Empires RTS game/s?
I was very obsessed with all the *Starcraft* and *Warcraft* games. So much so that I created my own total conversion for *Starcraft* I back in the day. It made a big splash in the Korean community.

How much time do you spend playing games outside of work?
Every responsible chance I get, I'm playing something every night. Did I mention *Monster Hunter*?

What's your general playstyle in RTS games?
I like to try everything I can depending on my opponent, mood, and faction choice. But having fun is my most important goal.

Which is your favorite civilization in AoE IV, and why?
I really like the Mongols as they were the most different when working on the game. The aesthetics of their buildings, and how much historical significance they had during the centuries which Age 4 takes place in; it's incredible.

Which are your favorite units in AoE IV, and why?
I really like the villagers of any one of the Age IV factions. They're the true backbone of the game and totally under-appreciated!

What feature of the game are you most excited for players to try out?
I'm excited for players to experience the uniqueness that each of the different Age 4 factions has to offer. We took a lot of care in considering the cultural differences, technological achievements, and historical context for each faction.

Altai

A rugged, mountainous area that creates many choke points.

In 1v1 matches, Altai is more akin to an open than a closed map, with a large, open—albeit hilly—stretch of land between both players, and a mountainous area behind them. In team games, allied players will start very close to each other, which will make it easier to combine your forces when defending. The valley behind the mountainous area behind the starting positions can generally only be accessed via a narrow valley, which makes it a prime, easily defensible area to establish a satellite base. Both of these factors combined makes this a great map for more defensive and economic-based approaches early in the match. Just make sure to stop your opponents ganging up on you or one of your allies before you can get established!

Resource Spawn	Resource Distribution	Sacred Sites	Position
Custom Classic Land	Deer are positioned closer to player starting positions	3	One in the center, two at mirrored positions in the outer valleys

Black Forest

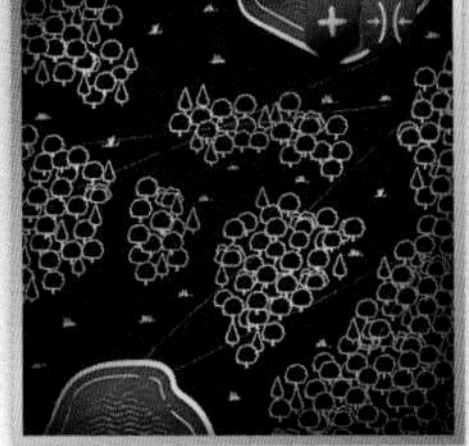

Dense woods makes this map difficult to traverse.

Black Forest is probably the most defense-orientated map in this group, and with only one or two narrow pathways leading to each starting location, successfully walling yourself in will be very easy. Each starting area also features a small pond containing shoreline Fish behind it, making early economic development quite similar to a water map in that you're encouraged to build a Dock early in games to speed up gathering the fish. Without the additional threat of enemy naval units, however, you can concentrate fully on developing your economy. The narrow paths of this map do not mean that you'll be immune to any kind of aggression from your opponent, they just make it harder for attacks to succeed because enemy units will be forced through narrow choke points that you can easily defend.

Resource Spawn	Resource Distribution	Sacred Sites	Position
Custom Classic Land	Deer and Sheep are placed closer to Town Centers, small deposits are replaced by large deposits, and more single trees.	0	--

French Pass

Concentrated Gold sources lie in the valley in the center of the map.

French Pass is somewhat of a defensive map, but it also requires speed. Large reserves of Gold sit in the middle of the map, but mountain ranges stand between player starting positions and that Gold. Having to travel around the mountains makes aggressive rush distances much longer, and since approach routes are limited, defense is relatively easy early on, when small raids will be relatively ineffective. Military will become more of a focus as the match progresses, and to fund it you'll need to come out from behind your walls to get the Gold; whichever player can secure the Gold first, is likely to be the victor.

Resource Spawn	Sacred Sites	Position
Classic Land	2	One at each end of the mountain pass

Altai Asian Subtropical

Black Forest Chalk Down

Hill and Dale

Players can either start on a defensive hill or in a resource-abundant valley.

On this map, players will usually start on a defensive hill, with the standard starting resources on that same hill. Each hill has three paths leading up to it from the dale below, which should make defending your hill early in games relatively easy. As the game progresses, you'll need to venture down into the dale and combat other players for control over the bounty of resources, Sacred Sites, and Trade Posts that sit within it.

Resource Spawn	Resource Distribution	Sacred Sites	Position
Custom Classic Land	Some of the outer resources like secondary Gold Veins and Deer are brought slightly closer to player starting positions	3	Within contested zone

Mountain Pass

A mountain range with narrow passes cuts through the center of the map.

On Mountain Pass, a huge mountain range in the middle divides the map into two halves, with only one path leading to the other side. This not only makes for very long rush distances for your units, but nearly all combat on this map will be focused around a single, small chokepoint. Viable strategies include taking control over the chokepoint with early aggressive play, or sitting back and playing defensively to build up a superior army to claim it later. Getting greedy and overcommitting during aggressive play on this map is especially dangerous, however, and can easily result in a loss.

Resource Spawn	Resource Distribution	Sacred Sites	Position
Custom Classic Land	Some of the outer resources like secondary Gold Veins and Deer are brought slightly closer to player starting positions	2	One on each side of the mountain range

1

French Pass Taiga Winter

Hill and Dale Gobi Desert

Mountain Pass Taiga Summer

River Maps

The defining geographical features of river maps are a large landmass divided by one or more rivers that can only be crossed by either bridges or fords depending on the map generation. Starting out on these maps is only slightly different than open land maps, because there are no Deep Water Fish, and gathering Shorline Fish early in the game is risky.

Throughout a match on these maps, it's crucially important to control the river crossings; if you control the rivers, you'll generally control the flow of the game, as well as access to neutral Trade Posts and Sacred Sites. Of course, some out-of-the-box thinking can help you get around such control if you're on the receiving end of it. While there's not a heavy emphasis on naval units on these maps, they can still be used quite effectively. A few ships in key places can help in both securing and breaking through any river crossing defenses, and the narrow confines make Demolition Ships especially potent in these scenarios Similarly, sneaking a Villager across a river early on in a match to establish a forward military base near your opponent to keep the fighting on their side of the river can be an effective tactic.

Mongolian Heights

A maze of plateaus and valleys is bisected by a river in this spiritual successor to Age of Empires II's Mongolia.

Each player/team will spawn on one of the two landmasses created by the river that runs through this map, so the river crossing again will be a highly contested area. The plateaus and valleys can make unit movement take a bit longer than usual, and can offer some slight offensive or defensive possibilities, but otherwise should not greatly influence how you play.

Resource Spawn	Sacred Sites	Position
Classic Land	2	Near the outer fords on opposite sides of the river

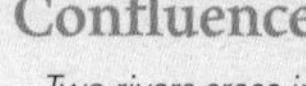

Confluence

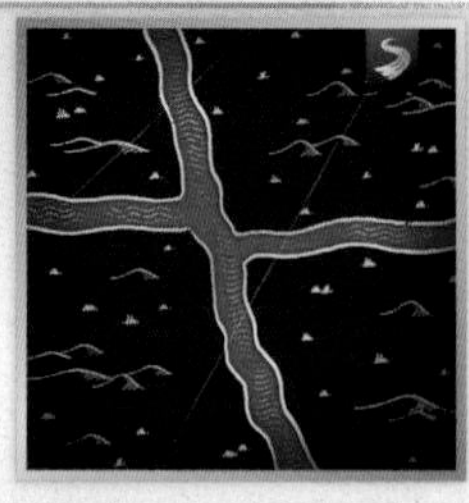

Two rivers cross in the center of the map.

The rivers on this map split the land into exactly four quadrants, so in 1v1 matches, most of the fighting will take place in the two neutral quadrants, and in team games, the river crossings between quadrants will be the most contested areas. Transport Ships will play an important role on this map, because they'll enable you to move between the landmasses without having to rely on normal river crossings, and a well-timed flanking attack will often be the decisive strike on this map.

Resource Spawn	Sacred Sites	Position
Classic Land	4	One in each quadrant created by the intersecting rivers

Danube River

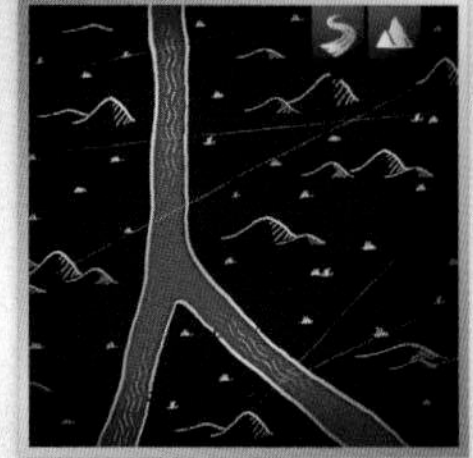

A river is nestled among gently rolling hills.

This map will be generated in one of two different ways: The mighty Danube will either split the map directly in half or the river will split, creating three landmasses. Each player/team will occupy one of the landmasses, so if the map was split into three, the final section would be unoccupied. In the instances of an unoccupied landmass, you'll often be able to find additional resources on it, but it's random as to which one you'll find there.

Resource Spawn	Sacred Sites	Position
Classic Land	3	Within contested zone

Confluence Taiga Summer

Danube River European Temperate

Mongolian Heights Steppes

Map Iteration

"Factoring in competitive play was one of our biggest tools in balancing the maps overall. We worked closely with our Balance team to create competitive ladder maps, and they gave us lots of valuable feedback. One example that comes to mind was the initial implementation of the openings of the mountain ranges on Altai. At first, the locations of the openings along the ridge were random, but this led to some matches where one player had much more access to the resources and trade posts on the outer edges of that map, due to both openings randomly spawning on that player's side of the map. When sitting down with the Balance team, they were able to give concrete examples of how much that accessible part of the map was able to swing a match in one player's favor. We changed the openings to be mirrored, giving equal access to both sides.

It's also important to note that while our goal is to have all maps be competitive in high-level play, we designed some maps more with crazy fun in mind than competition. King of the Hill is a good example of this, as we see it as a map that is fantastic for crazy eight player free for all matches but won't be the competitive players' first choice for the ladder, and that's totally okay. We want to have maps that serve many purposes."

—Nick Taylor
Designer, Maps Lead, Relic

Lake Maps

Lake maps pose some interesting questions to players, and there are a lot of tactical considerations to take into account during matches. On each of these maps, you'll find one or more lakes, and the fish in and around them is such a good source of Food that you'll often have to fight other players for control of them. There's enough land that you can also choose to ignore the lakes entirely, and instead play these maps the same as any normal open land map. This is where the primary choice on these maps comes into play. If you ignore your opponent for too long and they're reaping the benefits of the extra resources from all the fish, then you'll eventually fall behind significantly, which could lead to you being overwhelmed as the match progresses.

However, trying to build a Dock on these maps as early as you would on a water map brings its own series of problems. Firstly, you have to actually find the lake, and then you have to send Villagers to an exposed position to build the Dock and start gathering the fish, and protecting them can be difficult. You also need to keep in mind that if you invest heavily into naval units, it can be easy for your opponent to defeat you with a land attack early in matches because the Wood required for investing into your navy economy can just as easily be used by your opponent to build up their land military. Figuring out which of when to take any of these actions will need to be weighed on a per match basis.

Ancient Spires Asian Temperate

Ancient Spires

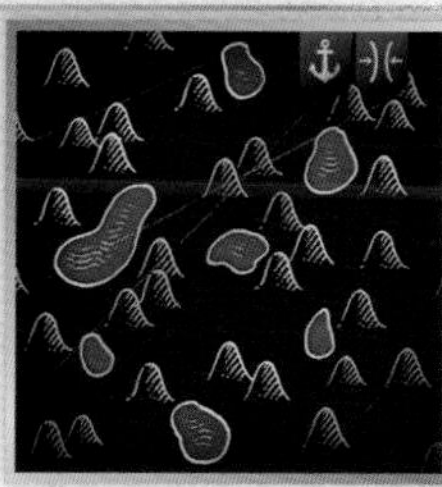

Tall rock spires cover the land, creating interesting paths through the terrain.

This map features numerous tall rock spires and lakes, all of which will add a lot of time to navigate around whenever you need to move your units across the map, which is something you'll need to take into consideration when launching an attack. The lakes all have Shorline Fish on their banks, although the amount of them will vary greatly depending on the size of the lake. Although these fish can be a great source of Food, because there are so many lakes, and they're so spread out, trying to defend Villagers are multiple locations like this is nearly impossible, and using naval units would cost too much both in terms of resources and population capacity. The only exception to this is if there's one particularly large lake with a lot of resources; some investment into naval military can be useful for both resource and map control in general on these lakes.

Resource Spawn	Sacred Sites	Position
Classic Land	3	Within contested zone

Stuart Ng
Environment Type Exploration Concept Artworks

1

Boulder Bay Chalk Downs

Boulder Bay

A deep ocean inlet divides the map into two, with a single narrow pass.

Although there's a direct land connection between all players on this map, the majority of it is dominated by the large central deep water bay. Because of the land connection, however, this map plays more like a lake map than a water map where you traditionally fight between islands. The vast ocean makes both land and naval routes to your opponent's base quite lengthy, although the naval option is usually the quicker of the two. The shape of the bay also naturally leads to narrow sections of land, and these are prime locations to try and establish a defensive foothold to repel land attacks. Given the number of resources and more direct access to your opponent's base, however, it's on the water where much of the combat on this map will take place, so you'll need to invest sufficiently into naval units.

Resource Spawn	Resource Distribution	Sacred Sites	Position
Custom Classic Land	Replaces the small Classic Land deposits with large deposits to help facilitate both land and naval unit production	2	One on the small island in the bay, the other on the mainland at the end of the inlet

Nagari Asian Temperat

Nagari

Lakes rest among a pair of easily defensible mountain ranges.

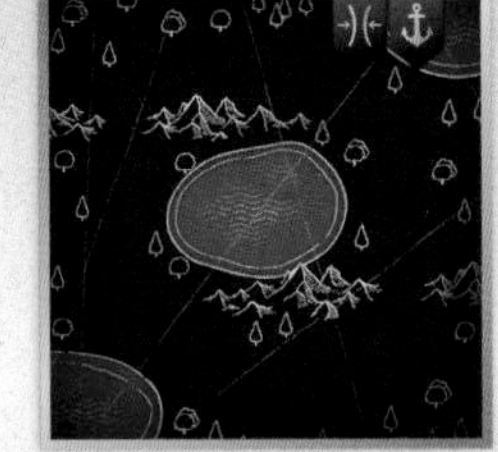

The large central lake on this map is home to some highly lucrative Deep Water Fish, which can a great opportunity to get an economic advantage over your opponent if you're willing to take the risk in trying to secure the area with some naval units. It's not the only body of water on the map, however, and you'll typically find smaller ponds on either side of the map that have some shoreline Fish, which will typically be much safer to gather. The mountain ranges on either side of the lake mean that you'll typically only have to defend against attacks coming from the flanks, and since there's a direct path to your opponent's base, you can ignore the lake altogether and focus on purely land-based economy and military units.

Resource Spawn	Sacred Sites	Position
Classic Land	2	One on each site of the central lake

Incentivizing Naval Play

"We wanted to encourage players to invest in naval units since water is a unique feature found only on some maps. It's intended to be a pleasant surprise that players can exploit to their advantage. To achieve this, fish gather faster than other food sources and boats are stronger than land units. This makes fighting over a pond in the middle of the map a key tactical point. When players find water in the corner of the map it creates an exciting opportunity to gain advantage over the enemy."

*—**Eric Wrobel***
Senior Designer, Balance Lead, Relic

Creating Random Maps

"Random maps was one of those non-negotiable things for us that really sets AoE apart from other RTS games. If things are completely random one player is likely going to have an advantage over the other. We spent a lot of time working on exactly how random things should be. A gold mine can spawn anywhere in a 360 degree arc around your base, but both players should have equal walking distances."

*—**Eric Wrobel***
Senior Designer, Balance Lead, Relic

Water Maps

On these maps, every player starts on their own island, and is separated from other players by an ocean. Between each of the islands that house a player you'll find neutral islands with important resources, or even a Trade Post for your Trade Ships to make use of; controlling these neutral Islands will often be the key to victory on water maps. A Dock is almost mandatory on these maps and should be built as early as possible. Not only does the Dock facilitate efficient gathering of Shorline Fish in the early Ages,, but you'll want the infrastructure already in place to start producing military naval units as soon as possible.

As soon as you've established a Lumber Camp and have 150 Wood, task your Villagers that have been gathering Food from Sheep to build a Dock, and then switch to gathering Food from Shorline Fish to take advantage of the faster gather times. Lumber is in high demand on these maps, so all of your next Villagers should go straight to gathering it to facilitate the production of Fishing Ships, which will be your primary method of Food acquisition.

The only way to circumvent naval warfare being the determining gameplay on these maps is to play as if you were on a land map, and then use Transport Ships to carry your land military to your opponent's island. This kind of play is extremely risky, however, and if you don't kill your opponent in your initial attack you'll be so far behind economically that it will be almost impossible to come back from.

Archipelago Steppes

Warring Islands European Temperate

Stuart Ng
Gold Deposit Exploration
Concept Artwork

Archipelago

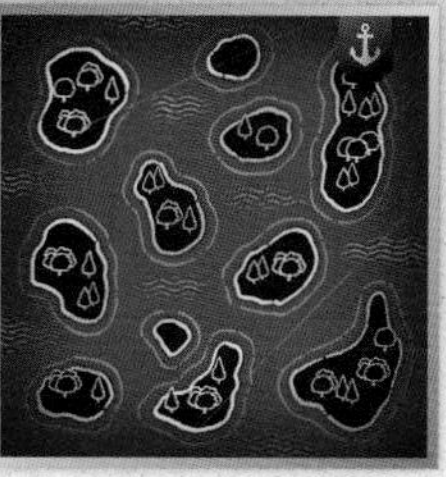

A group of small islands in the middle of a large ocean.

The small islands that make up the Archipelago map are among the smallest land masses in the game, making land-based combat all but impossible. Each player will start on their own small island, and there will be numerous other small islands dotted around the map where you'll find an array of resources, Sacred Sites, and Trades Posts. Resources can be hard to come by on this map, so scouting far and scouting early to find the most lucrative neutral islands will be a big part of play on this map.

The starting islands for each player are small enough that an enemy fleet of ships can completely surround them, all while retaining the ability to hit most of your buildings from the water. This makes a land-based defense almost impossible to pull off, so you're much better off investing the large majority of your resources into naval units, both for protecting your Fishing Ships, and for defending your coastline.

Resource Spawn	Sacred Sites	Position
Classic Island	2	Placed on neutral islands

Warring Islands

Teams spawn together on islands.

The islands of the Warring Islands map are significantly larger than those of Archipelago and they're mainly situated around the edge of the map. Each player/team spawns on their own large island with plenty of starting resources, and there'll be two other smaller islands in the middle, where you'll find neutral resources and features that you'll need to battle your opponent for.

In 1v1 games, your starting island is large enough that the edges of it go off the map, making it impossible for your enemy to surround with naval units although. Ships with longer attack ranges will still be able to hit most of your buildings from the angles that are available, however. On larger versions of the map with more players, each player will spawn on their own island. Naval military units are still your best bet for offense and defense on this map, but because the angles are a lot more limited, you can concentrate all of your defenses on the exposed side of your island and let that be the arena for all of your combat.

Resource Spawn	Sacred Sites	Position
Classic Island	2	One on each of the central Islands

Battling A.I. Opponents

Testing your skills and build orders against A.I. opponents can provide a valuable learning experience. The A.I. has several difficulty settings, and if you choose to play against multiple A.I. opponents, you can even select the difficulty for each of them individually, allowing you to tailor a match to your liking and make it enjoyable, regardless of your skill level.

In this section, we'll go through each of the different difficulty settings, what you can expect from them in terms of how games will play out, and provide you with a build order that works with every civilization against even the toughest A.I. opponent. Obviously, we can't account for every map type, so since it's the most common type, we've opted to gear the build order towards play on an open land map, like the much-loved "Dry Arabia".

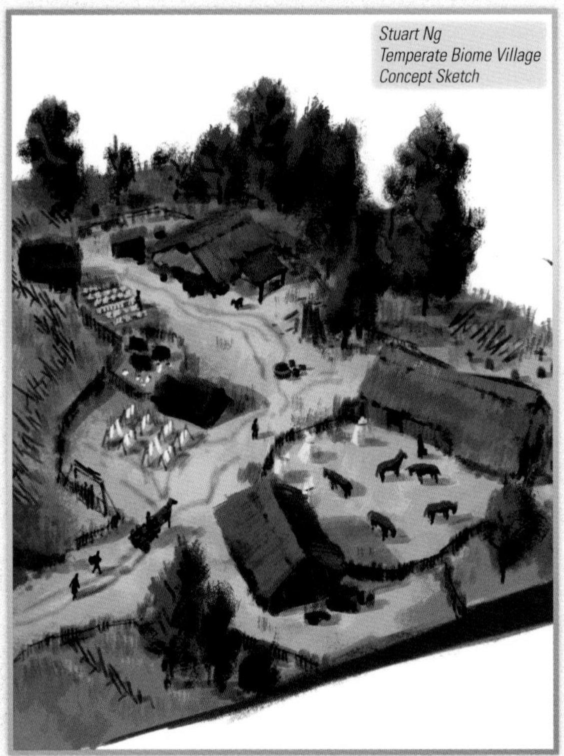

Stuart Ng
Temperate Biome Village
Concept Sketch

Difficulty Settings

Easy A.I.

The Easy A.I. is where players either new to Age of Empires, or RTS games in general, should start their journey. Learning how to build a strong economy during the start of a match, or a large army towards the late game, are skills that will carry your forward towards the higher difficulties, and this setting is perfectly suited to developing them.

Easy A.I. Behavior

- *Very slow empire building*
- *Economy defined by late uptimes and long travel distances for working Villagers*
- *Military production is slow and minimal*
- *Attacks are infrequent and light*

General Tips for Beginners:

1. Keep producing Villagers until late in the Castle Age or early Imperial Age. In doing this, however, it's important not to make your production queue too long at any given time, because that will tie up a lot of your Food that could be used for other things while the Villagers in queue are being produced. You'll want to queue up a few units at a time, and then periodically add to the queue to ensure constant production.

2. When in Castle Age, build up to four additional Town Centers and produce Villagers out of them all until you have 80 to 90 working Villagers. Try to use your hotkeys to cycle through the Town Centers and quickly add Villagers to the production queue. These Villagers will form the basis of a strong economy, which you'll need in order to produce a powerful army in the Imperial Age.

3. Another priority in the Feudal Age is to build some defenses. Place military production buildings like a Barracks, Archery Range, or a Stable near the outskirts of your base and start producing units from them. A small army of 6 to 15 units will be able to defend against possible raiding groups from the A.I. on this difficulty.

Intermediate A.I.

The Intermediate A.I. is overall a lot more efficient, faster, and harder-hitting than the Easy A.I., and this is a good setting to play on if you have some experience with RTS games, or progress to when your skill level is outpacing the Easy A.I.. Be prepared to get attacked relatively early and frequently in games, and to have the A.I. set up increasing amounts of defenses around its base as the game goes on. This is a good difficulty on which to practice early-game aggressive play on, because the A.I. is relatively slow at setting up defenses, which rewards you for your speed.

Intermediate A.I. Behavior

- *Moderate speed empire building*
- *Average uptimes and travel distances for Villagers leads to a slightly more efficient economy*
- *Military production is moderate, with additional base defenses*
- *Attacks will come earlier in the match and are comprised of more units*

Hard A.I.

The Hard A.I. is a serious step up from its Intermediate counterpart, and should only be selected if you're a seasoned RTS game player. You'll need to be quick with your timing on a lot of actions, and this is the first difficulty setting where you'll really need to start doing a lot of multitasking and making use of shortcut keys. Attacks from the A.I. will be varied and ferocious, so establishing a solid defense will be an important factor in defeating it. Just be careful not to play too defensively, because this A.I. can severely punish you with both great economic and military strength the longer a match progresses.

Hard A.I. Behavior

- *Fast empire building*
- *Efficient economic growth*
- *Military production is fast and constant, with much earlier and stronger defenses*
- *Attacks will come early and frequently during the entire match, with multiple simultaneous groups that employ a variety of timings and strategies*

Hardest A.I.

This difficulty offers the highest level of A.I. challenge in the game, and is the closest you'll come to facing off against a relatively skilled human opponent. As such, it's only recommended for players that have a lot of experience with high difficulty settings in RTS games, or players that want a serious challenge. The A.I. on this difficulty is very quick with its economic growth, and will typically reach Age II before you do. Thankfully, however, on this setting, the A.I. tends to take its time to build up its forces a bit more, so you'll rarely see attacks during Age I.

There are still some inefficiencies in the approach the A.I. takes with its economy (such as not placing drop-off buildings near their resources, and not always gathering the closest resources,) which means that if you are doing things as efficiently as possible, you should be able to outpace its economy, provided you're also doing them fast enough.

Later in the match, this A.I. will also build walls far out from its base in an attempt to gain map control, and it will place resource drop-off buildings around the map to secure additional resources; try to exploit both of these things to gain the advantage, and you should have the ultimate goal of trying to defeat it before it can reach Age IV. If you let the match reach that point without having first made a dent in its economy, you'll end up facing a tremendous force that will be hard to take down.

Hardest A.I. Behavior

- *Fastest empire building*
- *Very efficient economic growth*
- *Military production is fast, varied, and efficient*
- *Attacks feature larger and more diverse groups of enemies that take multiple different approaches and feature a large number of different units*

Stuart Ng
Delhi Sultantate Battle
Concept Artwork

Executive Producer

Michael Mann

What is your role on the project, and what does your day-to-day work consist of?

As the Executive Producer, my roles varies day to day from setting priorities, to evangelizing the game internally and externally, empowering the teams & studios, removing roadblocks, and brainstorming what is next. The best part of day is getting time to play the game.

Have you worked on any previous Age of Empire games?

I have played Age of Empires for years, however, my onboarding to the franchise was on Age of Empires: Rise of the Rajas, and working with Forgotten Empires and SkyBox Labs. Bert, Ryan, and Alex of Forgotten Empires & the Age Community were excellent in mentoring me into the franchise and sharing their wealth of knowledge.

What are your favorite game/s of all time?

Very tough question to answer as there have been so many games that have touched my life at different phases. The arcade was heaven to me in my youth. I remember playing hours of *King's Quest* in my childhood and my parents would set a timer for how long I could play. It was one those white egg timer looking things that would tick, it drove me crazy, and it may be the reason why I don't eat eggs today. Then there was *Utopia*, *Sub Hunt* for the Intellivision that consumed years. I have been fortunate enough to enjoy a range of amazing titles through generation of standups, consoles and PC that have touched my life.

What's your general playstyle in RTS games?

When I start playing a new RTS game I tend to be a base builder (turtle) to start and transition my game experience. As of late I have been focusing on early raiding to try to get an edge. I have some success; however, I need to work more on my micro.

Which is your favorite civilization in AoE IV, and why?

I don't really have a favorite civ, however, my recent focus has been on the Delhi Sultanate. Working on my build order and trying to maximize their technology advantage with the Scholars. The mighty War Elephants are impressive visually as well as powerful melee unit.

Which are your favorite units in AoE IV, and why?

One of the more spectacular units in game is the Nest of Bees as it's a visually stunning and powerful siege weapon. It's fireworks shooting out of a cannon. The one unit that gets overlooked is the Villager. The Villagers are so multifunctional, hardworking and they just do—go chop a forest down or mine for gold and they just perform.

What feature of the game are you most excited for players to try out?

I'm really excited for our players to try out the Asymmetrical civilizations as is one the key innovations in Age of Empires IV. It brings such diversity,depth and strategy to the game and franchise.

Audio Director

Todd Masten

What is your role on the project, and what does your day-to-day work consist of?

I am the Audio Director at World's Edge and I oversee every sound that goes into the Age of Empires franchise. Day-to-day my job consists of approving assets provided by the development team and providing feedback and guidance.

Have you worked on any previous Age of Empire games?

I've worked on Age of Empires Definitive Edition, Age of Empires II: Definitive Edition, Age of Empires III: Definitive Edition, along with all accompanying expansions for the DE titles.

What are your favorite game/s of all time?

My favorite game of all time would have to be *Everquest*. This title reinforced in-game roles that required social interaction and teamwork to achieve your true potential. I don't have the time I once had for MMOs, but titles like *Everquest* opened up gaming to an entirely new audience.

How much time do you spend playing games outside of work?

I've had a particularly busy past few years, so my gaming time has been curtailed considerably. I do get in a few hours a week when I can manage to catch a break. I tend to spend more time on console lately, with some minimal time on my Steam/Windows libraries.

What's your general playstyle in RTS games?

I turtle. I like to jump out quickly and build defensive fortifications and thwart early attacks and rushes while slowly building a giant army in an attempt to crush my enemies.

Which is your favorite civilization in AoE IV, and why?

I personally like the Mongol civilization. Aside from being a stark departure from standard AoE civilizations, the VO and music turned out particularly well and I enjoy the nomadic quality of my town centers.

Which are your favorite units in AoE IV, and why?

The Nest of Bees and the Siege Tower really stand out to me. I enjoy the chaos caused by unleashing my nests and unloading my siege towers to initiate wall combat always brings a smile to my face.

What feature of the game are you most excited for players to try out?

The series has never had a nomadic civilization, so I am very curious to see what players do with the Mongols civilization. There are some ingenious ways to play the Mongols and I cannot wait to see what other creative options players come up with.

Build Order and Guidance

This Build Order was developed to give you a clear and simple path to both improving as a player, and for beating the A.I. at even the Hardest difficulty setting on a standard open land map. To ensure the minimal amount of economic or military bonuses, this build order was tested using the Holy Roman Empire without making use of either their Prelates or Landmark abilities. If you were to take advantage of unique civilizations bonuses with any civilization, that will only make things easier for you.

This build order is not meant to be set in stone; the goal is that once you become familiar with the general principles we've employed here, that you'll formulate your own build orders to suit the specific strategies that you want to use with the different civilizations. Similarly, the time markers are being used to show you the timings of doing different tasks relatively efficiently, and don't need to be followed exactly. Obviously, the higher the difficulty you're playing on, the faster you'll need to be, so this gives you something to work towards.

Some practice will be required to get your timing right for both your economy and when attacking the opponent, so if you're inexperienced, you shouldn't expect to get it right first try. The most important thing to focus on is trying to minimize idle time in all aspects of the game, meaning your Villagers should always be doing something, and your production buildings should always be producing units or researching something.

The A.I. chooses different approaches with different civilizations, meaning you might need to adjust it based on which one you're facing. For example, with the Rus the A.I. is generally more defensive and produces fewer units early than with Chinese or English, who are generally harder to tackle head-on.

Warning: *This build order can work against human players, but it's certainly far from ideal for that kind of match. You'll need to further refine and tailor it to your needs when playing against other people.*

General Build Order Tips

- *Scouting at the start is vital to ensure success: you'll need about 8 Sheep for a sufficient amount of Food, otherwise, you'll need to adjust your timings or production.*
- *Make new Lumber Camps whenever a new one fits between the forest and the old Lumber Camp to ensure efficiency.*
- *f you can keep up production well enough, the A.I. will likely not attack you, and if it does, you should have enough army to repel the attack.*
- *Do not forget Houses! You will need a total of 70 population space.*
- *Very few economic or military upgrades are needed, although they would be recommended normally and should be a part of your eventual personal build order.*
- *If you want to ensure an early victory you can also bring all of your Villagers to the fight.*
- *The army in this build order should be sufficient for victory, but that doesn't mean you should stop everything else. If you can multitask between the battle and your base, keep up unit production, rally newly produced Villagers to Gold, and then start building Farms because your Sheep will start running out, and you should have a surplus of Wood to build them. This would also be a good time to transition towards Age III.*

Civilization Specific Considerations

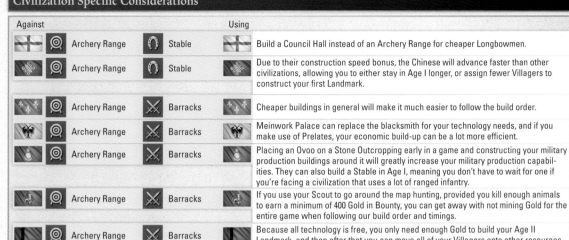

Against		Using
Archery Range	Stable	Build a Council Hall instead of an Archery Range for cheaper Longbowmen.
Archery Range	Stable	Due to their construction speed bonus, the Chinese will advance faster than other civilizations, allowing you to either stay in Age I longer, or assign fewer Villagers to construct your first Landmark.
Archery Range	Barracks	Cheaper buildings in general will make it much easier to follow the build order.
Archery Range	Barracks	Meinwork Palace can replace the blacksmith for your technology needs, and if you make use of Prelates, your economic build-up can be a lot more efficient.
Archery Range	Barracks	Placing an Ovoo on a Stone Outcropping early in a game and constructing your military production buildings around it will greatly increase your military production capabilities. They can also build a Stable in Age I, meaning you don't have to wait for one if you're facing a civilization that uses a lot of ranged infantry.
Archery Range	Barracks	If you use your Scout to go around the map hunting, provided you kill enough animals to earn a minimum of 400 Gold in Bounty, you can get away with not mining Gold for the entire game when following our build order and timings.
Archery Range	Barracks	Because all technology is free, you only need enough Gold to build your Age II Landmark, and then after that you can move all of your Villagers onto other resources. They do take longer to research, however, so you'll want to build the Blacksmith as soon as you enter Age II and start researching Siege Engineering straight away, along with Hardened Spearmen at the Barracks. The Tower of Victory is also a good choice of Age II Landmark because it will give a permanent attack speed increase to all units that pass through its aura.
Archery Range	Barracks	Build the House of Wisdom after building your first House, and start advancing to Age II as early as possible.

Build Order

Time (min)	Villager Number	Task	Notes
0:00	4	Sheep	Keep Sheep as close as possible to your Town Center
0:00	5&6	Wood	Place Lumber Camp adjacent to closest forest
0:20	7	Wood	– –
1:00	8&9	House and Gold	2 Villagers on Gold in total
1:40	10&11	Sheep	– –
3:20	12-16	Mill and Deer Build Age II Landmark	Choose the closest group of Deer and place a Mill in the middle of them Task 5 Food Villagers to build it. 3 from Sheep, 2 from Gold
3:40+	17+	Wood	From this point on rally all incoming Villagers to Wood
4:00	18	House and Barracks	Produce one Spearman while the Age II Landmark is being constructed
5:00	21	Reach Age II Build Archery Range (and Stable if applicable)	Use your two Gold Villagers to construct this building, and then retask them to Gold again. The other three Villagers should go back to Sheep
5:00+	21+	Research Hardened Spearman in the Barracks and start production of Spearmen/ Horsemen and Archers	With the economy balance you have, you should be able to continuously produce out of both military buildings and the Town Center at this point
8:00	30	Build a Blacksmith and research Siege Engineering	You should have roughly 9 Spearmen, 6 Horsemen and 9 Archers at this point
9:00	33	Move out with your army	Stop outside of the opponent's sight and use your Scout to locate your opponent's base
10:00	36	Build two Battering Rams	Do not forget Houses! Rams require 3 population space
10:00+	36+	Attack!	Focus on your opponent's Town Center with your Rams first, with you other units clearing a path for them

Early UI Designs

"In the early days of the project we did a ton of research and referenced past Age games and other RTS games to help come up with the first versions of the UI. As UX designers we have a whole toolkit of usability principles, design methods, and experience in design to point us in the right direction as we try to make things as intuitive and helpful as possible for the player. However, what's even more important in user-centred design is ensuring that we continue to conduct user testing along the way, as well as listening to feedback from the community. Using all of these insights to guide us as we continue to iterate and improve upon the designs is what's most important to our vision for the game's user experience."

—Euphemia Wong
Senior Designer, UX Lead, Relic

Early Main Menu Designs

CHAPTER

Cultural Enrichment

The eight civilizations in Age of Empires IV are each a finely crafted microcosm of their namesake culture, balanced on a knife edge to make the game's battles as epic and strategic as possible. This chapter showcases each Civilization in turn, breaking down their playstyles and strategies to give as clear as possible a picture of their place within the game's strategic whole.

English

TIME PERIOD REPRESENTED: 850 - 1555 CE EASE OF USE: ★★★

Overview

- *Great at Defending.*
- *Specializes in Melee and Ranged Infantry.*
- *Exceptional Farming Economy.*
- *Ideal for Beginners.*

Play with the English if you enjoy playing...

Assyrians or Hitties in **AoE 1**
Britons or Ethiopians in **AoE 2**
British in **AoE 3**

Starting Resources

200	150	100	0

Bonuses

- *Construct Farms for 50% Less Wood. Farms Near Mills Gather 15% Faster.*
- *Vanguard Man-at-Arms Available in the Dark Age (I).*
- *Stronger Villagers who Wield Short Bows.*
- *Town Centers, Outposts, Towers, and Keeps Provide the Network of Castles Bonus, Giving 25% Attack Speed to all Affected Units.*
- *Town Centers Fire Twice as Many Arrows.*
- *Military Ships Have +1 Range.*

The English are a great defensive civilization thanks to their Network of Castles system, which grants an attack speed increase to units close to specific defensive structures. Line the walls that connect those structures with their unique Longbowmen—with their longer attack range and special abilities—and you've got a recipe for a neigh impenetrable defense. The English are also exceptional farmers, with lower Farm costs and increased efficiency thanks to their Mills. They have very traditional gameplay that is similar to previous Age of Empires titles, making them a great choice to play when you're first getting into AoE IV. They'll feel familiar if you've played other titles in the franchise, and they're accessible enough that new players shouldn't feel overwhelmed by their options.

Unique Units

 Longbowman	Longer Range Archer that can Deploy Defensive Palings, Making them More Effective Against Cavalry	P.144

Strengths

The main strength of the English lies in their melee and ranged infantry. Men-at-Arms are already one of the most versatile melee units in the game, but the complimentary technologies available to the English elevate them to being among the most powerful. The English have a similar advantage in ranged infantry with their deadly Longbowman. The unique abilities of the Longbowman make them a viable unit choice in situations where normal Archers wouldn't stand a chance. This is most evident with their **Place Palings**, ability allowing them to stun incoming cavalry—the traditional ranged infantry counter—and if they do get hit, they can heal themselves with their **Setup Camp** ability.

Not only are their Farms cheaper to build, but their Mills boost the Food income of any Farm built around it; by planing your construction ahead of time you can ensure that no Farm is ever outside of a Mill's influence. Another unique ability of English Farms can be unlocked with the **Enclosures** technology, which enables Farms to generate Gold as long as a Villager is working at it, giving the English a reliable passive source of Gold income. The large radius of the Network of Castles also means that English Farms are a lot easier to defend than those of other civilizations, ensuring a very stable economy. One of the main buildings used as part of the Network of Castles is the Keep, and English Keeps have the unique functionality of being able to produce all military units, making it even easier to secure an area with them.

The Vanguard Man-at-Arms is a fearsome unit in the early stages of a game, so be sure to capitalize on them by sending out small raiding parties on your opponent, ideally before they can produce units that can effectively counter them.

Age I - Dark Age	Age II - Feudal Age	Age III - Castle Age	Age IV - Imperial Age
TOWN CENTER [P.234]			
Villager [P.137]; Scout [P.135]	Textiles [P.52]		
HOUSE [P.221]			
MILL [P.227]			
Survival Techniques [P. 51]; Wheelbarrow [P. 52]	Professional Scouts [P. 49]; Horticulture [P. 48]	Fertilization [P. 47]	Prescision Cross-Breeding [P.49]; Enclosures [P. 47]
LUMBER CAMP [P.223]			
Forestry [P. 48]	Double Broadax [P. 47]	Lumber Preservation [P.49]	Crosscut Saw [P. 46]
MINING CAMP [P.229]			
	Specialized Pick [P. 50]	Acid Distillation [P. 45]	Cupellation [P. 46]
FARM [P.216]			
BARRACKS [P.242]			
	Hardened Spearman [P.158]	Veteran Spearman [P.158]	Elite Spearman [P.158]
Vanguard Man-at-Arms [P.150]	Early Man-at-Arms [P.150]	Man-at-Arms [P.150]	Elite Man-at-Arms [P.150]
		Armor Clad [P. 45]	
DOCK [P.246]			
Fishing Boat [P.191]; Transport Ship [P.192]	Trade Ship [P.193]; Galley [P.202]	Hulk [P.200]; Demolition Ship [P.196]	Carrack [P.204]
	Shipwrights [P. 50]; Extended Lines [P. 47]	Drift Nets [P. 47]; Navigator Lookout [P. 49]	Chaser Cannons [P. 46]; Explosives [P. 47]
	Additional Sails [P. 45]	Armored Hull [P. 45]; Extra Ballista [P. 47]	
PALISADE WALL [P.272]			
PALISADE GATE [P.272]			
OUTPOST [P.270]			
	Arrowslits [P. 45]; Fortify Outpost [P. 48]	Springald Emplacement [P. 51]	Cannon Emplacement [P. 46]
COUNCIL HALL [P.275]			
	Setup Camp [P. 50]; Longbowman [P.144]	Veteran Longbowman [P.144]	Elite Longbowman [P.144]; Arrow Volley [P.45]
ABBEY OF KINGS [P.276]			
	TOWN CENTER [P.234]		
	Villager [P.137]; Scout [P.135]; Textiles [P.52]		
	MARKET [P.225]		
	Trader [P.136]		
	BLACKSMITH [P.260]		
	Bloomery [P. 45]	Decarbonization [P. 47]	Damascus Steel [P. 47]
	Steeled Arrow [P. 51]	Balanced Projectiles [P. 45]	Platecutter Point [P. 49]
	Fitted Leatherwork [P. 47]	Insulated Helm [P. 48]	Master Smiths [P. 49]
	Iron Undermesh [P. 48]	Wedge Rivets [P. 52]	Angled Surfaces [P. 45]
	Siege Engineering [P. 50]	Military Academy [P. 49]	
	BATTERING RAM [P.182]		
	SIEGE TOWER [P.188]		

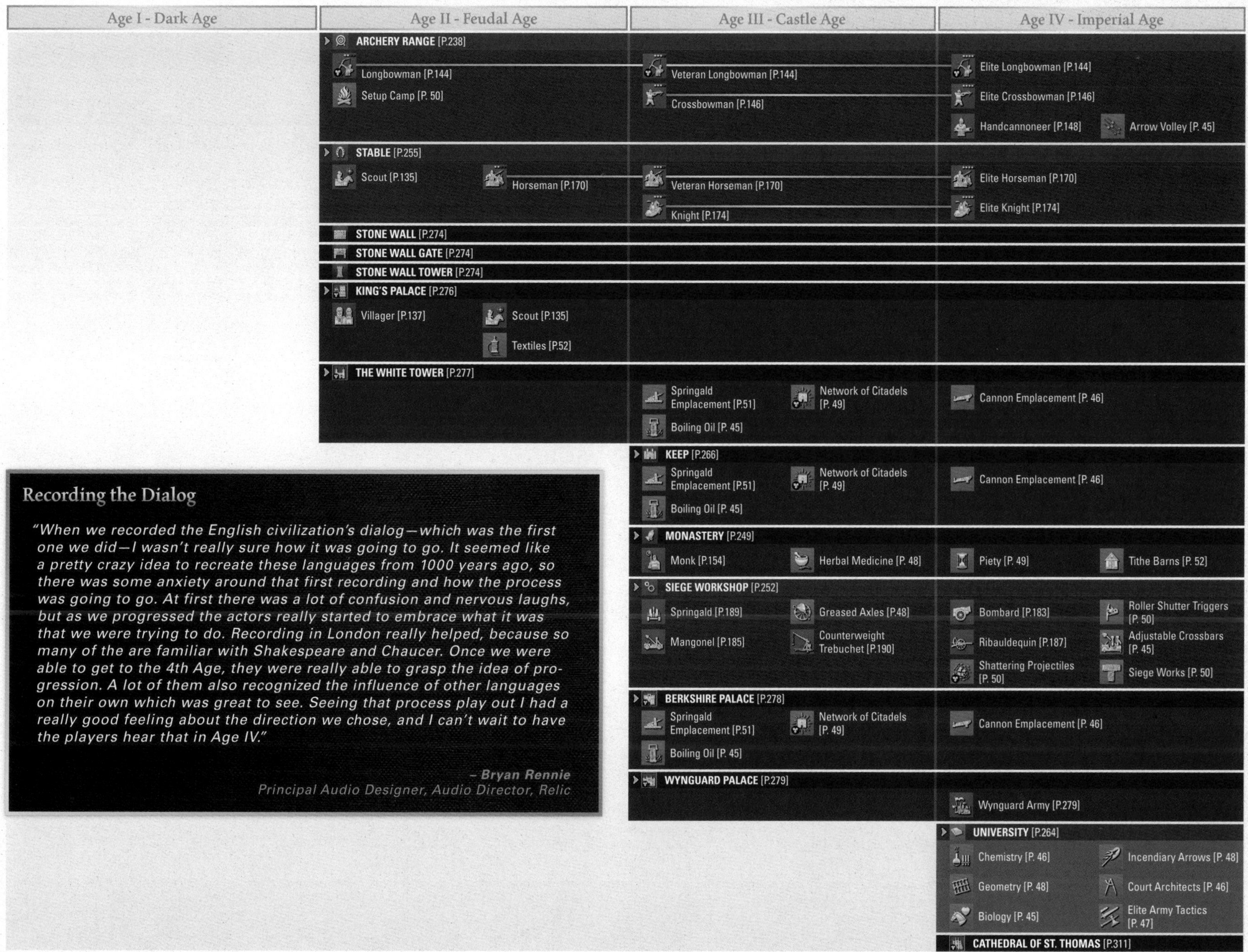

Age I - Dark Age
Age II - Feudal Age
Age III - Castle Age
Age IV - Imperial Age
ARCHERY RANGE [P.238]
Longbowman [P.144]
Setup Camp [P. 50]
Veteran Longbowman [P.144]
Crossbowman [P.146]
Elite Longbowman [P.144]
Elite Crossbowman [P.146]
Handcannoneer [P.148]
Arrow Volley [P. 45]
STABLE [P.255]
Scout [P.135]
Horseman [P.170]
Veteran Horseman [P.170]
Knight [P.174]
Elite Horseman [P.170]
Elite Knight [P.174]
STONE WALL [P.274]
STONE WALL GATE [P.274]
STONE WALL TOWER [P.274]
KING'S PALACE [P.276]
Villager [P.137]
Scout [P.135]
Textiles [P.52]
THE WHITE TOWER [P.277]
Springald Emplacement [P.51]
Network of Citadels [P. 49]
Boiling Oil [P. 45]
Cannon Emplacement [P. 46]
KEEP [P.266]
Springald Emplacement [P.51]
Network of Citadels [P. 49]
Boiling Oil [P. 45]
Cannon Emplacement [P. 46]
MONASTERY [P.249]
Monk [P.154]
Herbal Medicine [P. 48]
Piety [P. 49]
Tithe Barns [P. 52]
SIEGE WORKSHOP [P.252]
Springald [P.189]
Greased Axles [P.48]
Mangonel [P.185]
Counterweight Trebuchet [P.190]
Bombard [P.183]
Roller Shutter Triggers [P. 50]
Ribauldequin [P.187]
Adjustable Crossbars [P. 45]
Shattering Projectiles [P. 50]
Siege Works [P. 50]
BERKSHIRE PALACE [P.278]
Springald Emplacement [P.51]
Network of Citadels [P. 49]
Boiling Oil [P. 45]
Cannon Emplacement [P. 46]
WYNGUARD PALACE [P.279]
Wynguard Army [P.279]
UNIVERSITY [P.264]
Chemistry [P. 46]
Incendiary Arrows [P. 48]
Geometry [P. 48]
Court Architects [P. 46]
Biology [P. 45]
Elite Army Tactics [P. 47]
CATHEDRAL OF ST. THOMAS [P.311]

Recording the Dialog

"When we recorded the English civilization's dialog—which was the first one we did—I wasn't really sure how it was going to go. It seemed like a pretty crazy idea to recreate these languages from 1000 years ago, so there was some anxiety around that first recording and how the process was going to go. At first there was a lot of confusion and nervous laughs, but as we progressed the actors really started to embrace what it was that we were trying to do. Recording in London really helped, because so many of the are familiar with Shakespeare and Chaucer. Once we were able to get to the 4th Age, they were really able to grasp the idea of progression. A lot of them also recognized the influence of other languages on their own which was great to see. Seeing that process play out I had a really good feeling about the direction we chose, and I can't wait to have the players hear that in Age IV."

– Bryan Rennie
Principal Audio Designer, Audio Director, Relic

2

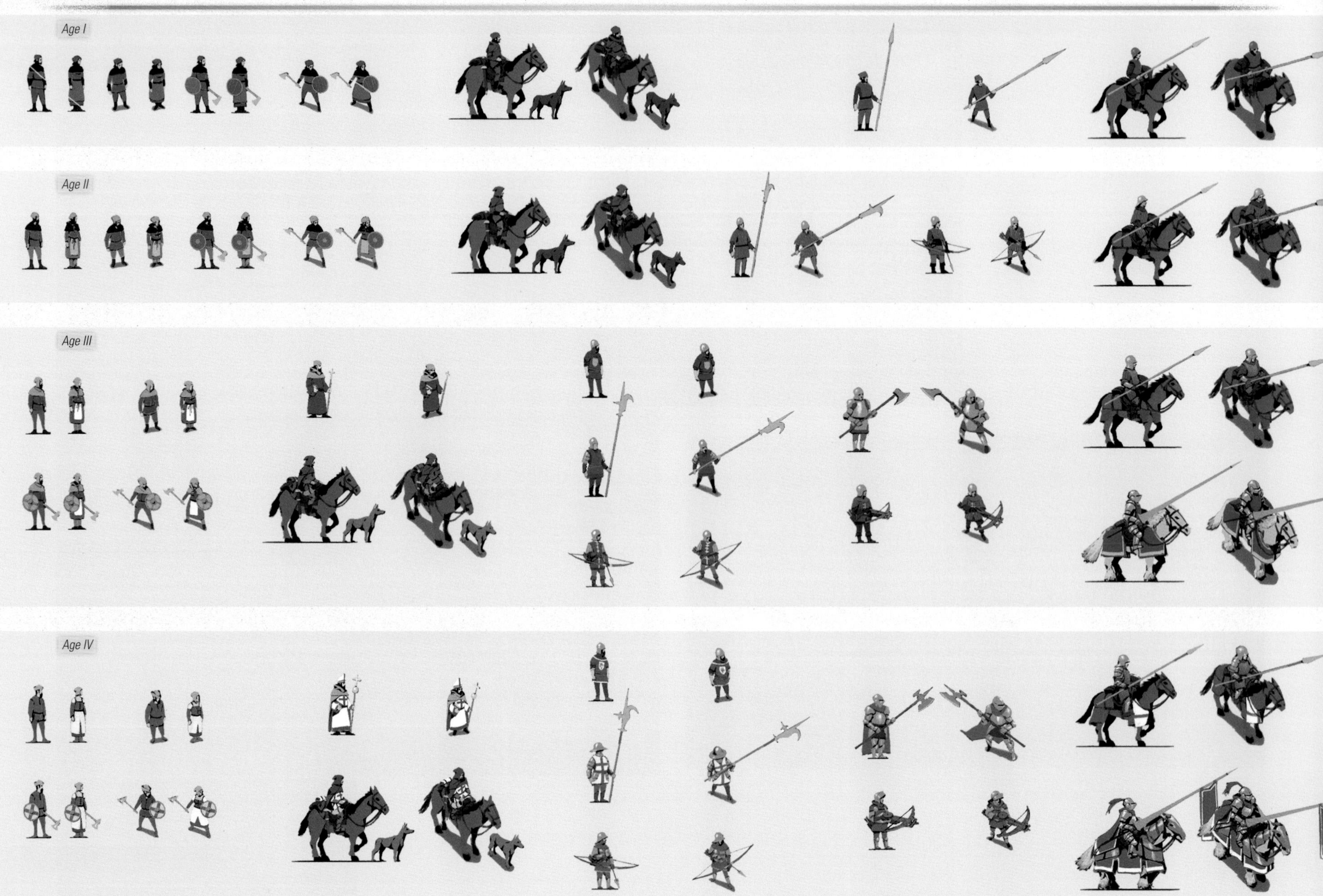
Age I
Age II
Age III
Age IV

Weaknesses

The English can struggle against armies comprised of very strong and sturdy units, especially if they've been solely relying upon their basic infantry units. Unless you take a balanced approach with them, they can have difficulties against the more powerful siege and cavalry units that are available later on, when it's population space rather than Gold that limits an army's capabilities.

Civilization Features

Network of Castles

The Network of Castles is essentially an alarm system that greatly boosts English defenses once certain buildings are in place. The alarm is a ringing bell that triggers the instant an enemy unit comes within the sight range of one of the compatible buildings. This provides you with additional situational awareness, because it can be heard even if you're looking at a different part of the map; if you build your base with this functionality in mind, you make it much more difficult for your opponent to hit you with a surprise attack.

Compatible Buildings	
Town Center	P.234
Outpost	P.270
Keep	P.266
Stone Wall Tower	P.274

An alarm is not the only benefit of the Network of Castles, however; any unit within the influence range of a compatible building when the alarm sounds will also receive a +25% increase to their attack speed. If you build a Keep, you can also research the **Network of Citadels** technology to increase that to +50%. Between the alarm, the attack speed bonus, and the range advantage of the Longbowman, it becomes apparent that playing defensively behind Stone Walls covered in Longbowmen can be a very effective strategy.

Keeps

English Keeps have the same defensive capabilities as the Keeps of other civilizations, but they also have the unique ability to produce every single type of military unit available to

Adding more to their early game defensive capabilities, English Town Centers fire twice as many arrows per volley compared to other civilizations, making them much better suited to protecting your Villagers before you get other defenses set up.

the English, including cavalry and siege engines. This ability makes using a Keep as the cornerstone of forward a base even more effective, because you won't have to build additional military production buildings, and can get straight to producing units.

Enclosures

The **Enclosures** technology can be researched from a Mill after you reach the Imperial Age, and it allows any Farm currently being worked on by a Villager to generate +1 Gold every 3.5 seconds. While that may not sound like a lot, when you consider how many Farms you can have towards the end of

*Placing all of your farms around Mills will greatly enhance your Food income, due to the **Island of Agriculture** bonus making them more efficient with each Age.*

longer games, you start to see how easily it adds up. Most civilizations have to rely on trade for Gold later in games, and while that is a lot more lucrative, it also carries some risk. Through this technology the English have a safe and predictable means of obtaining some supplementary Gold.

Villagers

The Villagers of most civilizations only use their bows for hunting animals, and will switch to a melee weapon whenever attacking an enemy unit. English Villagers, however, have a shortbow as well as their hunting bow, and they're not shy about using it against enemy units. While the combat prowess of a Villager is low, English Villagers can put up more of a fight due to being able to being able to attack much earlier. They still won't be able to stand up to groups of military units, but against weaker, or lone targets, a group of English Villagers can actually come out on top. This ability also invites some level of experimentation with aggressive strategies, using Villagers in conjunction with military units to help establish forward bases and fortifications near your opponent's position.

General Playstyle

The English can manage to keep their enemies on their toes while staying relatatively safe behind their walls, making their gameplay approach quite flexible and easier to handle than most other civilizations'. Their army may not be the most mobile—given that they trend more towards infantry—but the extra range of some of their units can make up for that and give them an edge in close battles. Taking key positions around the map, and then solidifying your presence there with the formidable defensive options that are available is key to winning as the English, and done correctly, can severely limit your opponent's options and expansion capabilities.

Dark Age (Age I)

The English are the only civilization that get access to heavy melee infantry during this Age, in the form of the Vanguard Man-at-Arms. The sturdiness of this unit compared to the Spearmen that most other civilizations can field allows you to be quite aggressive, because small groups of them can inflict quite a lot of damage to enemy units and buildings before being stopped. The extra sturdiness also helps in taking out enemy Villagers, because they can withstand more defensive arrow fire from Town Centers or Outposts.

The difficult part about incorporating Men-at-Arms into your Dark Age game plan is that you have to gather your resources and produce them quickly enough to hit your opponent before they can enter the Feudal Age and get access to stronger units. You need to deal quite a lot of damage to your opponent to make the investment worth it; time it poorly and you can end up behind when entering the Feudal Age, but done correctly, you can pull significantly ahead.

If you're planning on taking a more economic/defensive approach, then you should begin gathering Stone during the construction of your Landmark, using the Villagers that were on Gold. Then prioritize less Villagers on Food (but enough to maintain Villager production) and more on Wood. This way you should be able to start building additional Town Centers shortly after entering Age II.

Age Advancement

The Council Hall is the more flexible choice of Landmark here. In it you can produce Longbowmen at the equivalent rate of two Archery Ranges, and because Longbowmen are good on both offense or defense, that gives you a lot of options.

If you're planning on leaning heavily into defensive gameplay, then the healing powers of the Abbey of Kings might be the Landmark to pick. Its healing aura affects both yours and allied units, and if you build it close to a wall, it's easy to keep the ranged units manning them at full health.

Feudal Age (Age II)

The easiest path for aggressive play during this Age is to focus on Longbowmen from the **Council Hall**, because that will let you start production straight away. If you're going this route, only put a small number of Villagers on Gold (purely to pay for Longbowman upgrades), while the majority of your Villagers should be dedicated to Food and Wood to ensure continuous production of more Longbowmen and Villagers. Using this method you can amass a large group of Longbowmen in a very short period of time. Your opponent is likely to be producing cavalry units during this Age to counter your Longbowmen, and even though they can deploy palings, you should still building a Barracks and start producing Spearmen to help out with countering that cavalry.

With nine Longbowmen you can kill an enemy Villager in a single volley if they have no upgrades, so once you have that amount, use them as a raiding party to harass your opponent's Villagers during this Age.

Defensively, try to stay within safe distance of your Town Center(s), and start creating Farms as soon as the natural Food sources nearby start to run out, always making sure to place them within the influence range of a Mill. The extra Food income means you can put less Villagers on Food and still maintain a balanced economy, and it also lets you put Villagers to work gathering other resources that would have otherwise been gathering Food.

Age Advancement

The choice of Landmarks here is mainly dictated by whether or not you've already built an additional Town Center. If you haven't, then the King's Palace is a solid choice because it has all of the same abilities, and you're going to have to step up Villager production to keep up with the military needs of the next Age.

If you do already have another Town Center, or just want to really solidify a defensive position, then the White Tower might be more beneficial overall to you because it has the same capabilities as a formidable Keep.

Castle Age (Age III)

If you don't want to box yourself in with walls, consider using Keeps in strategic places instead, and then garrison units inside to maximise their effect.

In Age III you should be prepared to encounter strong siege weapons like Mangonels as your opponent tries to counter your large groups of infantry units. In anticipation of that, you should set up either a Stable or Siege Workshop and produce cavalry or Springalds to counter those Mangonels. If you've been producing Longbowmen and Men-at-Arms, this would be the time to use them to try and push your opponent and gain an advantage before they can overpower you with stronger units in the next Age.

If your big push doesn't manage to finish off your opponent, you should start preparing for the late game by building Stone Walls and Towers around key areas of your base, and man them with Longbowmen for some extra firepower. Keep some melee infantry or cavalry behind your walls so that you can send them out to deal with any siege units your enemy brings to bear. This level of defense can be hard for opponents to break through before they get access to the more powerful siege weapons of the Imperial Age.

Age Advancement

The Berkshire Palace is essentially a very strong Keep that has 50% extra attack range and fires double the amount of arrows per volley. It retains the unique ability to produce units like other English Keeps, so it's a good all-round choice for both offensive and defensive gameplay.

For a fraction of the cost they would normally be, the Wynguard Palace can produce a small batch of military units that includes a Trebuchet. If you're struggling with either resources or military production and strength, then **Wynguard Palace** gives you an option that can solve both problems.

Imperial Age (Age IV)

After you've reached the Imperial Age, you should research the **Enclosures** technology to start generating some additional Gold, since natural Gold should be starting to run dry by this time. This will allow you to upgrade the units you're focusing on. Your ideal army composition should be powerful siege units (Bombards/Trebuchets), that are protected by fully upgraded Longbowmen and Spearmen, with a force of cavalry (Knights/Horsemen) in the flanks to combat your opponent's siege units.

This is not a particularly mobile arrangement, which means you should play to the strengths of the English static defenses and advance slowly, fortifying as you go to entrench and secure your position. Placing your units and fortifications on top of hills will help with this due to the additional sight range—just be sure to position your Longbowmen and siege units in a way to best take advantage of it.

English Masteries

After the invasion of William the Conqueror, England would never be the same. It entered an era of accelerated progress, seeing the formation of modern-style governance, the construction of enduring castles, and the battlefield domination of its key weapon for centuries to come: the longbow.

- Profile Image [1]
- Text [2]
- Coat of Arms Pattern [3]
- Coat of Arms Sigil [4]
- Monument [5]

Mastery	Objective	Tip	XP	Rewards
Nice Try, Spy	Kill an enemy Scout in the Dark Age (I)	English Villagers can attack at range with longbows, and the English Town Center has increased defensive capabilities to stop enemy scouting in its tracks.	1000XP	English Farmer [1] Scorched Earth [2]
Assize of Arms	Produce 30 Longbowmen from the Council Hall in the Feudal Age (II)	The Council Hall Landmark produces Longbowmen. The Archery Range is not required.	1000XP	Royal Lion [4] Build and Control [2]
Test of Strength I	Win a 1v1 Custom or Skirmish match against the Easy A.I.	Defeat a single Easy A.I. opponent in a Custom or Skirmish match. Go to the Single Player screen to create a Skirmish match.	1000XP	Falconry for Status [2] Stone Tools [1]
Rally the People	Build the King's Palace and produce 10 Villagers from it in the Castle Age (III)	The King's Palace acts as a Town Center, giving the English another option for quick Villager production.	1000XP	Deer [1] The Cost of Stone [2]
Swift Harvest	Reach the Castle Age (III) with 16 Farms influenced by Mills	Farms placed directly around a Mill receive a bonus to harvest rate.	1000XP	Double Stripe Banner Pattern [3] The Assize of Arms [2]
Gather Round	Heal 10 Longbowmen with the Setup Camp Ability	Research Setup Camp in the Archery Range.	1000XP	Boom and Bust [2] Fish [1]
Test of Strength II	Win a 1v1 Custom or Skirmish match agains the Intermediate A.I.	Defeat a single Intermediate A.I. opponent in a Custom or Skirmish match. Go to the Single Player screen to create a Skirmish match.	1000XP	Lumberjack [5] A Traitor's Fate [2]
Keep Them Busy	Produce 20 units from Keeps	The English are uniquely able to produce units from Keeps.	1000XP	The Marketplace [2] Fure Arrow [1]
Raise the Alarm	Defeat 50 enemy units while affected by the Network of Castles	The Network of Castles provides a defensive advantage to the English, increasing their attack rate when near Outposts, Towers, Keeps, or Town Centers.	1000XP	Stag's Head [4] A Death of Indulgence [2]
Hail of Arrows	Defeat 20 enemies with Longbowmen affected by the Arrow Volley upgrade	Research Arrow Volley in the Archery Range. Fully upgraded Longbowmen are strong, but still require protection from melee attackers.	1000XP	Eleanor of Aquitaine [1] Projectile Horrors [2]
Test of Strength III	Win a 1v1 Custom or Skirmish match against the Hard A.I.	Defeat a single Hard A.I. opponent in a Custom or Skirmish match. Go to the Single Player screen to create a Skirmish match.	1000XP	Magna Carta [2] Bowman [5] English Longbowman [1]
Reap What You Sow	Accrue 5000 Gold from Enclosures	Research Improved Enclosures to gather Gold faster.	1000XP	Nicola de la Haie [1] The Longbows of Agincourt [2] Dual Fish [4]
For the Wyn	Produce 5 Wynguard Armies from the Wynguard Palace	The Wynguard Palace produces multiple units simultaneously.	1000XP	The 70-Year-Old-Knight [2] Jester [1]
From the Skies	Destroy 20 enemy units with Trebuchets affected by the Shattering Projectiles technology	Research Shattering Projectiles in the Keep. Trebuchets are susceptible to melee units – keep them guarded.	1000XP	William the Conqueror [1] Coin Clipping [2]
Test of Strength IV	Win a 1v1 Custom or Skirmish match against the Hardest A.I.	Defeat a single Hardest A.I. opponent in a Custom or Skirmish match. Go to the Single Player screen to create a Skirmish match.	1000XP	Eleanor of Castile [5] Trial by Ordeal [2] Oak Tree [4]

Chinese

TIME PERIOD REPRESENTED: 907 - 1644 CE EASE OF USE: ★ ★ ★

Overview

- *Perfect All-Rounder Civilization, Viable on any Map and Setting.*
- *Can Enter Different Dynasties that Provide Unique Buildings and Units.*
- *Specializes in Gunpowder and Siege Units.*
- *Exceptional at Adapting.*

Play with the Chinese if you enjoy playing...

Macedonians or Sumerians in **AoE 1**
Celts, Chinese, or Slavs in **AoE 2**
Chinese in **AoE 3**

Starting Resources

200	150	100	0

Bonuses

- *Villagers Construct Defenses 50% Faster and all Other Buildings 100% Faster.*
- *Chemistry Technology is Granted for Free When Advancing to the Imperial Age (IV).*
- *Docks Work 20% Faster.*

The Chinese are a multifaceted civilization, featuring a variety of unique units, buildings, technologies and systems that allow them to quickly change their direction and game plan, forcing the enemy to adapt or perish. Like other civilizations, advancing through the Ages requires the building of a Landmark, but the Chinese also have the option to build a second Landmark during each Age to unlock a Dynasty, giving access to another suite of beneficial effects. The increased construction speed of Chinese Villagers also makes gaining map control and actually building those Landmarks much faster and easier. If you enjoy expanding your territory and multitasking with different systems, the Chinese might just be the civilization for you.

Unique Units

Unit	Description	Page
Zhuge Nu	Repeater Crossbowman Effective vs Light Units	P.163
Fire Lancer	Light Cavalry Unit Effective vs Buildings	P.168
Grenadier	Throws Grenades Capable of Doing Area of Effect Damage	P.147
Nest of Bees	Fires a Barrage of Rockets, Doing Area of Effect Damage	P.186

Strengths

Flexibility and adaptability are undoubtedly the Chinese civilization's greatest strength. Due to their many unique units and expansive tech tree, they can adapt to almost anything the opponent can throw at them. Their mastery of gunpowder means that they don't have to spend time building a University and researching **Chemistry** upon entering Age IV. This means that all of their gunpowder units will get an automatic and immediate bump in power at the start of that Age.

At first, all of the possibilities and tactics they offer—combined with their unique mechanics—can be overwhelming for both new players and veterans alike, but dedicate some time to studying and mastering their abilities and the devastating fruits of your labor will soon become apparent. Regardless of which playstyle you gravitate towards, or what mode and map you're playing on, the well-rounded nature of the Chinese makes them a safe pick for any game.

Weaknesses

Their complexity and abundance of options really can make the Chinese overwhelming to use, especially if you've just started to play the game. You may find it beneficial to learn the basic mechanics of the game with more straightforward civilizations first, such as the English or French, and then progress to the Chinese once you're more familiar with things.

In terms of gameplay, the Chinese do not have any glaring weaknesses. It can be tricky to reach their full potential, however, because you effectively have to invest twice as many resources for every Age advancement if you want to unlock all of the associated Dynasty bonuses. Those investments need to be carefully judged on a per-game basis to ensure you're not falling behind your opponent in other ways.

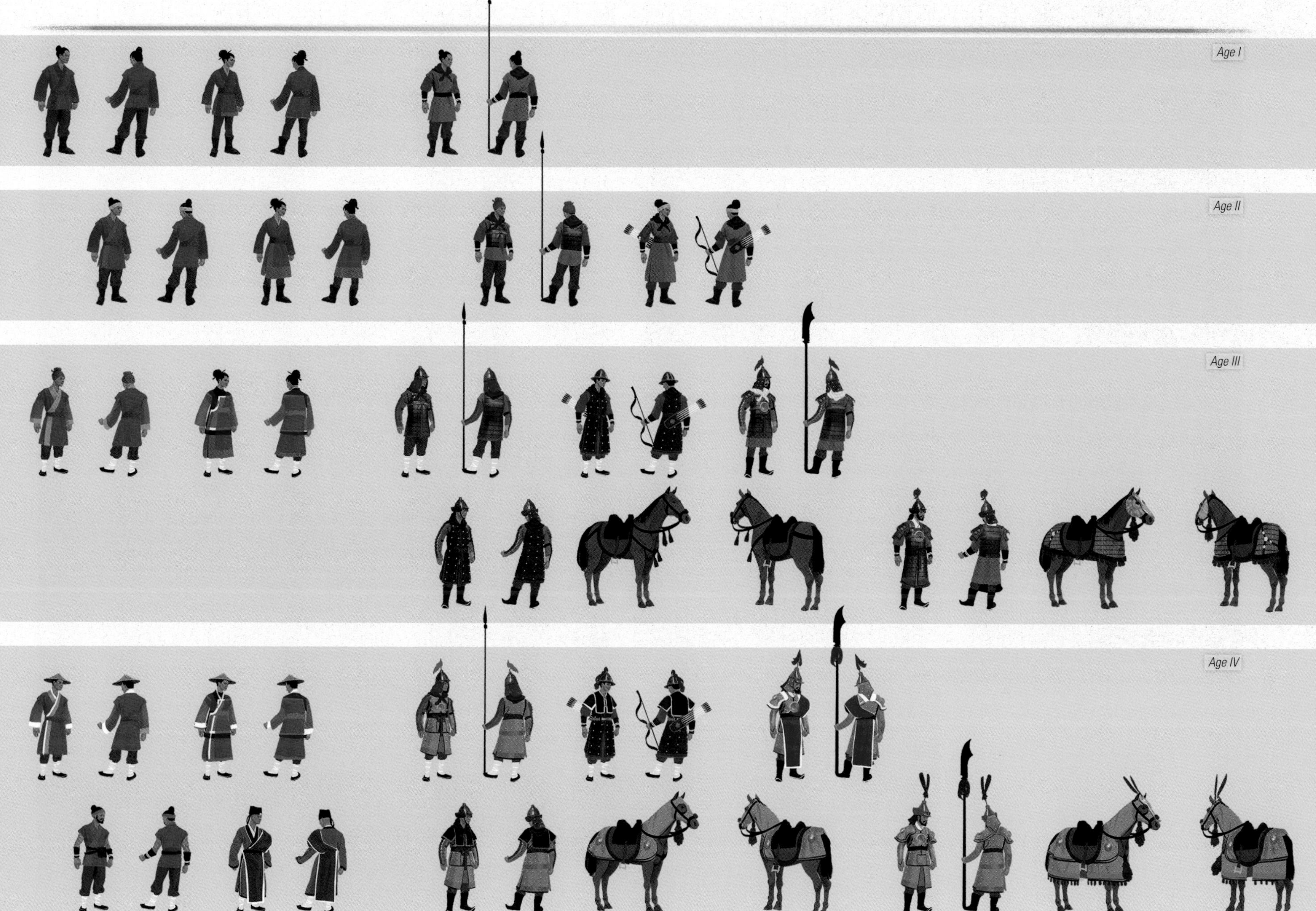
Age I
Age II
Age III
Age IV

	Age I - Dark Age	Age II - Feudal Age	Age III - Castle Age	Age IV - Imperial Age
TANG DYNASTY [P.82]				
TOWN CENTER [P.234]	Villager [P.137]; Imperial Official [P.134]; Scout [P.135]	Textiles [P.52]		
HOUSE [P.221]				
MILL [P.227]	Survival Techniques [P. 51]; Wheelbarrow [P. 52]	Professional Scouts [P. 49]; Horticulture [P. 48]	Fertilization [P. 47]	Prescision Cross-Breeding [P.49]
LUMBER CAMP [P.223]	Forestry [P. 48]	Double Broadax	Lumber Preservation [P. 49]	Crosscut Saw [P. 46]
MINING CAMP [P.229]		Specialized Pick [P. 50]	Acid Distillation [P. 45]	Cupellation [P. 46]
FARM [P.216]				
BARRACKS [P.242]	Spearman [P.158]	Hardened Spearman [P.158]	Veteran Spearman [P.158]; Palace Guard [P.150]	Elite Spearman [P.158]; Elite Palace Guard [P.150]; Battle Hardened [P. 45]
DOCK [P.246]	Fishing Boat [P.191]; Transport Ship [P.192]	Trade Ship [P.193]; Junk [P.202]; Extended Lines [P. 47]; Additional Sails [P. 45]	War Junk [P.202]; Explosive Junk [P.196]; Drift Nets [P. 47]; Extra Hammocks [P. 47]; Navigator Lookout [P. 49]; Extra Ballista [P. 47]	Baochuan [P.204]; Chaser Cannons [P. 46]; Explosives [P. 47]
PALISADE WALL [P.272]				
PALISADE GATE [P.272]				
OUTPOST [P.270]		Handcannon Slits [P. 48]; Fortify Outpost [P. 48]	Springald Emplacement [P. 51]	Cannon Emplacement [P. 46]
IMPERIAL ACADEMY [P.280]		Imperial Examinations [P. 48]		
BARBICAN OF THE SUN [P.280]				
SONG DYNASTY [P.82]		Village [P.237]		
TOWN CENTER [P.234]		Villager [P.137]; Scout [P.135]; Imperial Official [P.134]; Textiles [P.52]		
MARKET [P.225]		Trader		
BLACKSMITH [P.260]		Bloomery [P. 45]	Decarbonization [P. 47]	Damascus Steel [P. 47]
		Steeled Arrow [P. 51]	Balanced Projectiles [P. 45]	Platecutter Point [P. 49]
		Fitted Leatherwork [P. 47]	Insulated Helm [P. 48]	Master Smiths [P. 49]
		Iron Undermesh [P. 48]	Wedge Rivets [P. 52]	Angled Surfaces [P. 45]
		Siege Engineering [P. 50]	Military Academy [P. 49]	

Age I - Dark Age	Age II - Feudal Age	Age III - Castle Age	Age IV - Imperial Age
	BATTERING RAM [P.182]		
	SIEGE TOWER [P.188]		
	ARCHERY RANGE [P.238]		
	Archer [P.141]	Veteran Archer [P.141]	Elite Archer [P.141]
	Zhuge Nu [P.163]	Veteran Zhuge Nu [P.163]	Elite Zhuge Nu [P.163]
		Crossbowman [P.146]	Elite Crossbowman [P.146]
			Handcannoneer [P.148]; Grenadier [P.147]
	STABLE [P.255]		
	Scout [P.135]; Horseman [P.170]	Veteran Horseman [P.170]	Elite Horseman [P.170]
		Lancer [P.174]	Elite Lancer [P.174]
		Fire Lancer [P.168]	Elite Fire Lancer [P.168]
	STONE WALL [P.274]		
	STONE WALL GATE [P.274]		
	STONE WALL TOWER [P.274]		
	ASTRONOMICAL CLOCKTOWER [P.282]		
		Clocktower Springald [P.189]; Clocktower Counter-weight Trebuchet [P.190]; Clocktower Nest of Bees [P.186]	Clocktower Bombard [P.183]
	IMPERIAL PALACE [P.283]		
		YUAN DYNASTY [P.82]	
		Granary [P.219]	
		KEEP [P.266]	
		Springald Emplacement [P.51]; Extra Materials [P. 47]; Boiling Oil [P. 45]	Cannon Emplacement [P. 46]
		MONASTERY [P.249]	
		Monk [P.154]; Herbal Medicine [P. 48]	Piety [P. 49]; Tithe Barns [P. 52]
		SIEGE WORKSHOP [P.252]	
		Springald [P.189]; Greased Axles [P.48]; Nest of Bees [P.186]; Counterweight Trebuchet [P.190]	Bombard [P.183]; Reload Drills [P. 50]; Roller Shutter Triggers [P.50]; Reusable Barrels [P. 50]; Siege Works [P. 50]; Pyrotechnics [P. 49]
		GREAT WALL GATEHOUSE [P.285]	
		SPIRIT WAY [P.285]	
			MING DYNASTY [P.82]
			Pagoda [P.232]
			UNIVERSITY [P.264]
			Chemistry [P. 46]; Court Architects [P. 46]; Geometry [P. 48]; Ancient Techniques [P. 45]; Biology [P. 45]; Elite Army Tactics [P. 47]; Incendiary Arrows
			ENCLAVE OF THE EMPEROR [P.311]

The Chinese Playstyle

"I think my favorite civilization would have to be the Chinese. Their units and weapon types set them apart from all the other civs in Age of Empires IV. The Tax Collector unit, the Guandao melee weapon that the Man-at-Arms units carry, and the Nest of Bees cannon give the Chinese a really unique look and playstyle. The speech and music really define the identity of the Chinese and Zach Schläppi's team has done a wonderful job making the buildings and units look great. They're the type of civilization that if you invest the time learning to play with them you can really deal some damage."

– Bryan Rennie
Principal Audio Designer, Audio Director, Relic

Progressive Balancing

"Balance is challenging during development because so many systems are constantly changing or not working as intended. At one point we had melee units stacking up on each other and they could basically focus fire like they were archers but without overkilling. At one point no one could stop my four barracks spearman rush! Over time, you fix more and more issues and things keep getting tighter and more precise. Balance just comes at the end of the process—It's like using a small chisel on the hands once the main marble figure has been shaped."

– Eric Wrobel
Senior Designer, Balance Lead, Relic

Civilization Features

Dynasties

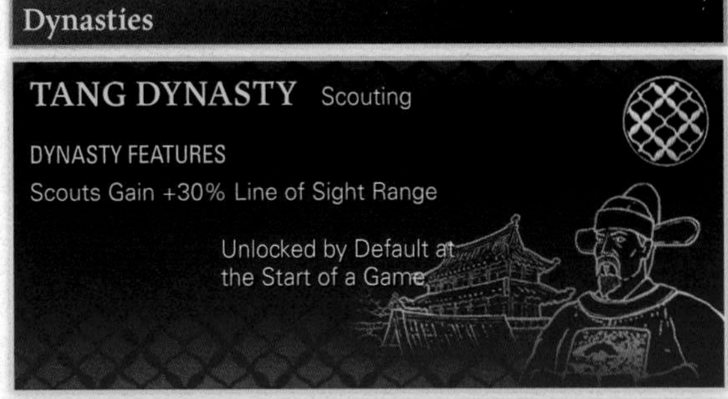

TANG DYNASTY Scouting
DYNASTY FEATURES
Scouts Gain +30% Line of Sight Range
Unlocked by Default at the Start of a Game

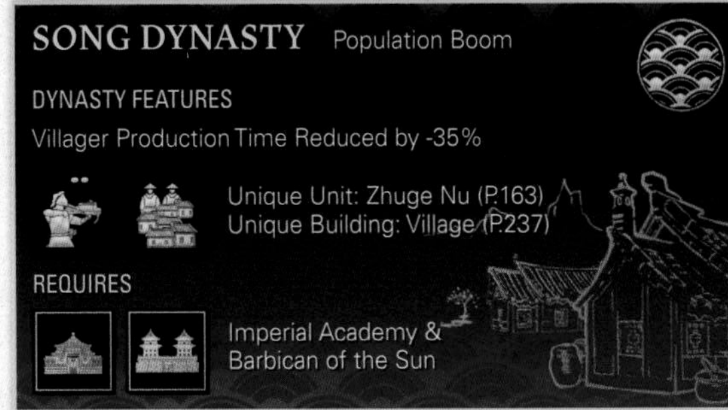

SONG DYNASTY Population Boom
DYNASTY FEATURES
Villager Production Time Reduced by -35%
Unique Unit: Zhuge Nu (P.163)
Unique Building: Village (P.237)
REQUIRES
Imperial Academy & Barbican of the Sun

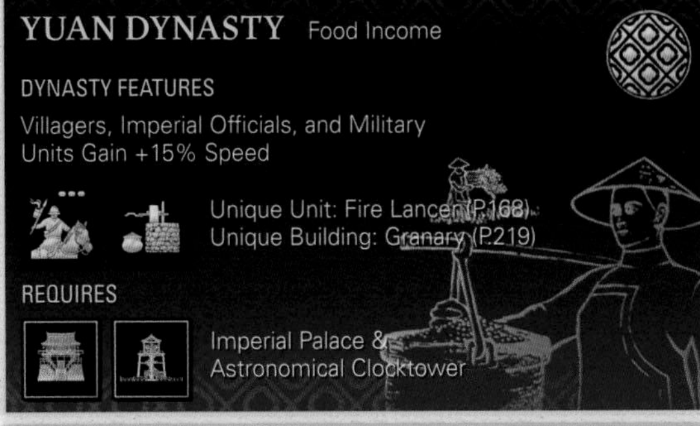

YUAN DYNASTY Food Income
DYNASTY FEATURES
Villagers, Imperial Officials, and Military Units Gain +15% Speed
Unique Unit: Fire Lancer (P.168)
Unique Building: Granary (P.219)
REQUIRES
Imperial Palace & Astronomical Clocktower

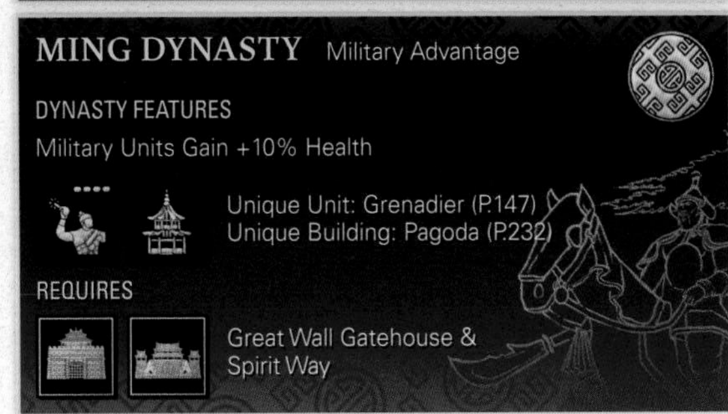

MING DYNASTY Military Advantage
DYNASTY FEATURES
Military Units Gain +10% Health
Unique Unit: Grenadier (P.147)
Unique Building: Pagoda (P.232)
REQUIRES
Great Wall Gatehouse & Spirit Way

When playing as the Chinese, you'll always start in the Tang Dynasty, and—as you advance through the Ages—you'll have the ability to build the other Landmark for each Age to unlock a new Dynasty. Unlike Ages, however, Dynasty progression is not linear, so if you're in Age III, you can unlock the Yuan Dynasty by building a second Age III Landmark, without needing to have previously unlocked the Song Dynasty. Similarly, if you're already in the Yuan Dynasty, building the second Age II Landmark will put you into the Song Dynasty. There's no way to go back to a previous Dynasty after moving to a new one, however, so you need to be sure that the benefits of a new Dynasty outweigh the loss of the features you'll leave behind.

Because you can choose when to build the second Landmark and unlock a particular Dynasty, you have a lot of flexibility with this system, and can pick whichever Dynasty is best suited to the situation at hand. The bonuses, units, and buildings that feature in each Dynasty are only available while you're in that Dynasty, so when you move to another one, you'll lose access to those from the previous one. This brings an element of risk to the system, because if you switch Dynasty without properly gauging the situation, you could lose access to something that would have helped counter an opponent's move. This can be offset somewhat towards the later stages of a game, where you can build the **Spirit Way** Landmark, which lets you produce units from any Dynasty that you've previously unlocked.

Another thing to consider is the decision to use Dynasties proactively or reactively. If you're more of a reactive player, then waiting to see what your opponent is doing before unlocking the best Dynasty to counter them is the way to go. For more proactive players, a solid strategy will involve planning ahead and building your economy and military around the Dynasty that will give you the most benefit when you unlock it.

Resource management also plays a key part in these decisions, because you could be sitting on a lot of resources to allow for quick Landmark production to enter a Dynasty, but those resources could be put to use for other military or economic gains. The ability to accurately judge when and how to best interact with the Dynasty system can only come through experience and game knowledge, and is just one of the reasons why the Chinese civilization is so complex to play.

Taxation System

Every time you produce a unit or research technology when playing as the Chinese, most of the buildings you do those things at will accumulate a tax in the form of Gold. Dedicated resource drop-off buildings also generate taxes every time a Villager drops off resources. The unique Chinese Imperial Official unit (produced from Town Centers) can then go around and collect those taxes and deposit them back at your Town Center to contribute to your total Gold. You can either have the Official collect and drop off the taxes automatically as they're generated, or you can do it manually if you want to save them up and deposit them in a lump sum.

Technology Details

Action	Gold Generated
Resource Drop-off	1* Gold
Unit Produced	4* Gold
Technology Researched	32* Gold

*Values are doubled if the building is within the influence range of an **Imperial Academy** Landmark

Imperial Officials can collect taxes from buildings within a 15 tile radius of their position, so you can spread them out around your base for maximum efficiency. After taxes have been collected from a building, there's a 30s cooldown period before they can be collected again.

Because you generate taxes based on productivity, the system favors a playstyle that involves either producing a lot of units or researching a lot of technology; the more you do, the more you earn. In general, Gold from taxes should be viewed as a supplementary income that you can use to offset the cost of some things, rather as a primary source of Gold.

By the nature of the system, you'll generate very little in taxes at the start of a game (when your production and research capabilities are low), but they'll become more and more lucrative as you progress. Given that resources are scarce at the start of games, and Imperial Officials are relatively expensive to produce, you'll benefit more from the production of Villagers rather than Imperial Officials early on. None of the taxes you generate go to waste—you can always collect them later when you have the resources to dedicate towards producing Imperial Officials.

General Playstyle

The Chinese approach is a game of adaptation and flexibility. Their wide range of technologies and units makes them hard to predict, so make use of that fact and weigh all of your options carefully. There are no set rules when playing as the Chinese—everything is possible—just make sure not to get choice paralysis, because inaction will nearly always lead to defeat. Generally speaking, however, it's during the Song Dynasty and the Castle Age that the Chinese really start to shine and pull away from other civilizations, so until you reach that point, it's best to keep a low profile.

Age Advancement

The **Imperial Academy** doubles the tax accumulation rate of buildings in its influence range. If you plan your base around it, and intend on either producing a lot of units or doing a lot of research, you can very quickly earn back the Gold it took to build and start turning a profit.

Alternatively, the **Barbican of the Sun** is a purely defensive structure, so if you want to defend an area, or you're getting attacked a lot, it can be a very safe choice.

Dark Age (Age I)

As with all other civilizations, you can send four of your starting Villagers to Sheep, and the other two to build a Lumber Camp and collect Wood. It can also be worth producing at least one Imperial Official to use their Supervise ability for either increased gathering rates or faster unit production, depending on your needs.

2

Chinese Masteries

From the engineering feat of the Great Wall to the finely tuned chemistry of gunpowder, China's mastery of warfare ensured centuries of unbroken dynastic rule. Its ingenious inventions were the awe of the Middle Ages, forever cementing China as one of the great forces of technological progress in human history.

Profile Image [1]
Text [2]
Coat of Arms Pattern [3]
Coat of Arms Sigil [4]
Monument [5]

Mastery	Requirement	Description	XP	Rewards
Building Blocks	Accrue 1500 resources and have a population of 15 before the Feudal Age (II)	An early focus on economy is important to any civilization.	1000XP	Chinese Scout [1] A Unique Architecture [2]
State Revenues	Collect 250 Gold in tax with an Imperial Official before the Castle Age (III)	Imperial Officials automatically collect taxes from economy buildings that are in use, such as Mills and Camps.	1000XP	Sickle [4] Paper Money [2]
Test of Strength I	Win a 1v1 Custom or Skirmish match against the Easy A.I.	Defeat a single Easy A.I. opponent in a Custom or Skirmish match. Go to the Single Player screen to create a Skirmish match.	1000XP	Mu Guiying [2] Zhuge Nu Repeater Crossbow [1]
A Storm of Bolts	Produce 20 Zhuge Nu and use them to defeat 30 enemies	Enter the Song Dynasty to be able to produce Zhuge Nu crossbowmen.	1000XP	Chinese Siege [1] Repeating Crossbow [2]
Expansion Villages	Construct 2 Villages and achieve a Population of 100 before the Castle Age (III)	Enter the Song Dynasty to access Villages. Villages significantly increase your population capacity.	1000XP	Chevron Banner Pattern [3] Town Planning [2]
Imperial Supervision	Supervise the production of 30 military units with an Official	The Supervise ability allows you to order an Official to supervise a military production building to increase its capabilities.	1000XP	Chinese Worker [1] Scholar-Officials [2]
Test of Strength II	Win a 1v1 Custom or Skirmish match against the Intermediate A.I.	Defeat a single Intermediate A.I. opponent in a Custom or Skirmish match. Go to the Single Player screen to create a Skirmish match.	1000XP	The Thirty-Six Stratagems [2] Provider [5]
Shared Wealth	Generate 500 Gold in tax at buildings affected by the Imperial Academy's increased tax revenue	Buildings producing units, researching technology, and ambiently adding income, such as the Pagoda, generate additional tax when near the Imperial Academy.	1000XP	Chinese Grenadier [1] A Prized Crop [2]
Path of the Spirit	Construct 6 buildings affected by the Spirit Way Landmark's reduced dynasty unit costs	Build Archery Ranges and Stables in close proximity to the Spirit Way to gain the reduced dynasty unit cost.	1000XP	Recurve Bow [4] A Legendary Blade [2]
Iron Cannons	Defeat 40 enemies with siege engines from the Astronomical Clocktower before you lose 20 of your Clocktower siege engines	The Astronomical Clocktower allows production of superior siege engines.	1000XP	Chinese Firelancer [1] Astronomical Clock [2]
Test of Strength III	Win a 1v1 Custom or Skirmish match against the Hard A.I.	Defeat a single Hard A.I. opponent in a Custom or Skirmish match. Go to the Single Player screen to create a Skirmish match.	1000XP	Chinese Gunpowder [1] Live Fire [2] Wu Zetian [5]
A Thunderous Onslaught	Defeat 50 enemies with infantry and cavalry units equipped with Gunpowder weapons	Many Chinese gunpowder units are also dynasty units.	1000XP	Empress Liu [1] The First Firearm [2] Star Sigil Frame [4]
Seven Stories	Generate 1500 of each resource type (Food, Wood, and Stone) from your Pagoda	Pagodas generate additional Food, Wood, and Stone when holding Relics.	1000XP	Nest of Bees [1] Pagoda Lore [2]
The Red Scarf	Achieve a Conquest Victory while in the Ming Dynasty	The Ming Dynasty increases military unit health.	1000XP	Emperor Hongwu [1] Defense By Flame [2]
Test of Strength IV	Win a 1v1 Custom or Skirmish match against the Hardest A.I.	Defeat a single Hardest A.I. opponent in a Custom or Skirmish match. Go to the Single Player screen to create a Skirmish match.	1000XP	The Child Emperor [2] Hand Cannon [4] Nest of Bees Monument

Due to the Chinese's faster construction speed you can either build your Age II Landmark with more Villagers than you normally would, giving you a big speed advantage, or build it with less, and construct it in the normal amount of time but come out ahead economically.

Feudal Age (Age II)

Because of how beneficial the Song Dynasty is for growing your economy, your main goal upon reaching this Age should be to get the resources required to build the second Landmark and enter it as soon as possible. The dramatic increase to both your economy and general development that you get from being in the Song Dynasty lets you be greedier than with other civilizations in terms of production and research, so you can afford to play somewhat passively and just react to what your opponent is doing. While you're building up, if they don't make a move and try to attack you, they'll just end up falling further behind.

Archers and/or Spearmen are a solid defensive choice, and you should invest in additional Imperial Officials now to start collecting the taxes you generate. Having multiple Imperial Officials now will also let you quickly pivot between rapid economic and military growth depending on which buildings you Supervise with them. If you really want to speed up your economic growth, this would be the time to build additional Town Centers to capitalize on the reduced Villager production time. If you're planning on unlocking other Dynasties, the groundwork you lay for your economy here will pay off greatly later on when constructing the additional Landmarks.

Age Advancement

The Astronomical Clocktower gives you access to siege engines as soon as you enter Age III, bypassing the need for a Siege Workshop. Whether you intend to use them offensively or defensively, rapidly producing siege engines straight away can give you a big advantage, especially when these Clocktower versions also have 50% more health than normal variants.

If you're using an aggressive playstyle with a lot of raiding, then the ability to reveal the location of your opponent's Villagers granted by the Imperial Palace will be extremely beneficial for planning your attacks.

Castle Age (Age III)

The Castle Age gives you access to a unique siege engine: the Nest of Bees. This powerful weapon can deal huge amounts of damage to enemy infantry, and because it can fire over walls, it's useful for both offense and defense. You also have the option to enter the Yuan Dynasty now, but given the associated high cost, you'll need to decide which is more beneficial: changing Dynasties, or advancing to the Imperial Age, because the costs are comparable.

If you choose to go the Dynasty route, you'll still need to consider the timing, because you'll lose the benefits of the Song Dynasty as soon as you change. Make sure your economy is in a place you're content with first, and that you've produced as many Zhuge Nu as you need. The biggest upside of the Yuan Dynasty is the Granary. This building greatly enhances the Food output of the Farms around it, and it will accumulate taxes every time Food is collected there. Farming is the main source of Food at this stage of the game, so if you focus your farming economy around the Granary, you can vastly improve your overall economic output.

Age Advancement

The Great Wall Gatehouse is a formidable defensive tool that can only be built on top of Stone Walls. If you've already established a solid defense with walls and units atop them, the extra health for those walls and damage bonus for nearby units granted by this Landmark can be excellent addition to that playstyle.

If, however, you want to focus on Dynasty-specific units as the core of your military, then the Spirit Way is the clear choice. This Landmark frees you from the constraints of the Dynasties, and allows you to produce units from any Dynasty you've previously unlocked.

Imperial Age (Age IV)

The Imperial Age comes with a great power spike for the Chinese early on, because they don't have to construct a University and research **Chemistry** to give all of their gunpowder units a +20% damage increase. If you start producing gunpowder units as soon as you enter this Age, it's worth bringing them into battle as soon as possible so that you can take advantage of the extra damage before your opponent also gains access to it.

If you don't manage to defeat your opponent in your initial push during this Age, then you can always fall back, re-consolidate, and prepare for the move to the Ming Dynasty. This is where all of the economic growth that you went through in the Song Dynasty pays off—you should be able to cover the costs of all the Landmarks without sacrificing so many resources that it leads to your defeat. The Chinese are at their peak military strength in the Ming Dynasty, thanks to the additional health granted to all military units, and the Grenadier unit, which is exceptional at dealing with groups of enemy units.

French

TIME PERIOD REPRESENTED: 840 - 1559 CE EASE OF USE: ★ ★ ★

Overview

- *Efficient and Flexible Economy.*
- *Exceptional Trading Abilities.*
- *Specialize in Melee Cavalry and Aggressive Gameplay.*
- *Great for Beginners.*

Starting Resources			
200	150	100	0

Play with the French if you enjoy playing...

Yamato in **AoE 1**
Franks or Berbers in **AoE 2**
French or Ottomans in **AoE 3**

Bonuses

- *Faster Villager and Scout Production per Age (10%, 15%, 20%, 20%).*
- *Economic Technology is 30% Cheaper.*
- *Resource Drop-off Buildings are 25 Wood Cheaper.*
- *Trade Posts are Revealed on the Minimap at the Start of the Game.*
- *Traders can Return any Resource to the Market.*
- *Trade Ships Return 20% More Gold.*
- *Melee Damage Technologies are Researched Automatically and for Free.*
- *Stables and Archery Ranges Within the Influence Range of a Keep Produce Units 25% Cheaper.*

While the English are a great entry point to the game if you favor defensive play, the French are a good first choice for new players that lean more towards aggressive play. Cavalry are a big part of French game play, especially their unique and formidable Royal Knights. As an aggressive civilization, they shine when attacking early with their strong Feudal Age cavalry that can move around the map fast, always looking for new enemy Villagers to attack. These cavalry units don't come cheap, however, which is why you'll need to take full advantage of all of the strong and efficient French economy that has a number of powerful bonuses to help keep up production. These unique bonuses in combination with their powerful units makes the French a very beginner friendly civilization.

Unique Units

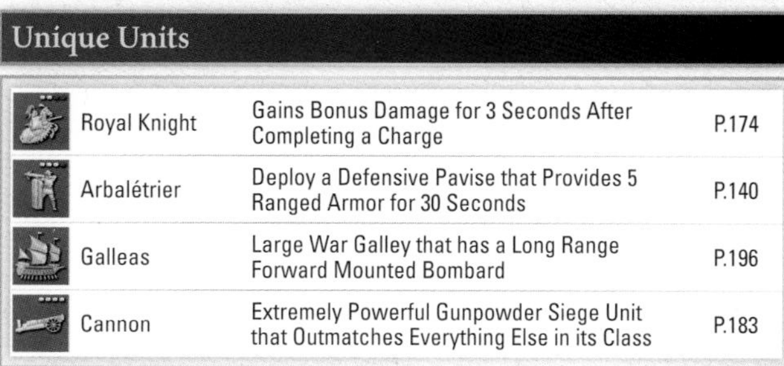

Unit	Description	Page
Royal Knight	Gains Bonus Damage for 3 Seconds After Completing a Charge	P.174
Arbalétrier	Deploy a Defensive Pavise that Provides 5 Ranged Armor for 30 Seconds	P.140
Galleas	Large War Galley that has a Long Range Forward Mounted Bombard	P.196
Cannon	Extremely Powerful Gunpowder Siege Unit that Outmatches Everything Else in its Class	P.183

Strengths

The two main strengths of the French are their flexible economy and powerful cavalry units. The French can produce their Villagers faster than most other civilizations, and their resource drop-off buildings are cheaper; combined, you have an economy that can grow very quickly and include all resources. To further bolster that, economic technologies are also cheaper to research, allowing you to further enhance whichever aspect of your economy is required for your given strategy.

And then there are the Royal Knights. Not only are they more powerful than normal heavy melee cavalry, but you also get access to them an Age earlier than most other civilizations get their equivalents. When you factor in the technologies that are available to strengthen them, and then start pairing them with the also very powerful Arbalétrier and Ribauldequin, the French can be almost impossible to stop without Camel or Elephant Units.

Weaknesses

The French are a well balanced civilization, and do not have any glaring weaknesses or shortcomings in their toolkit. The lack of any specialized mechanics does mean that some aspects of their playstyle don't quite reach the heights of some other civilizations, but this is offset by their ease of use. Even though they do have a strong economic foundation, you also can't escape the fact that their best military combinations are extremely expensive and slower to produce, so a skilled opponent can overwhelm them with mass produced cheaper units if they're not careful. Civilizations that have strong anti-cavalry tendencies such as the Abbasid Dynasty or Holy Roman Empire tend to fare better against the French, so choosing one of those is also a good option.

Age I - Dark Age	Age II - Feudal Age	Age III - Castle Age	Age IV - Imperial Age
TOWN CENTER [P.234]			
Villager [P.137]; Scout [P.135]	Textiles [P.52]		
HOUSE [P.221]			
MILL [P.227]			
Survival Techniques [P. 51]; Wheelbarrow [P. 52]	Professional Scouts [P. 49]; Horticulture [P. 48]	Fertilization [P. 47]	Prescision Cross-Breeding [P.49]
LUMBER CAMP [P.223]			
Forestry [P. 48]	Double Broadax [P. 47]	Lumber Preservation [P.49]	Crosscut Saw [P. 46]
MINING CAMP [P.229]			
	Specialized Pick [P. 50]	Acid Distillation [P. 45]	Cupellation [P. 46]
FARM [P.216]			
BARRACKS [P.242]			
Spearman [P.158]	Hardened Spearman [P.158]	Veteran Spearman [P.158]	Elite Spearman [P.158]
		Man-at-Arms [P.150]	Elite Man-at-Arms [P.150]
DOCK [P.246]			
Fishing Boat [P.191]; Transport Ship [P.192]	Trade Ship [P.193]; Hulk [P.200]	Galleass [P.195]; Demolition Ship [P.196]	Carrack [P.204]
	Extended Lines [P. 47]	Drift Nets [P. 47]	Chaser Cannons [P. 46]; Explosives [P. 47]
	Additional Sails [P. 45]	Long Guns [P. 48]; Navigator Lookout [P. 49]	
		Armored Hull [P. 45]; Extra Ballista [P. 47]	
PALISADE WALL [P.272]			
PALISADE GATE [P.272]			
OUTPOST [P.270]			
	Arrowslits [P. 45]; Fortify Outpost [P. 48]	Springald Emplacement [P. 51]	Cannon Emplacement [P. 46]
CHAMBER OF COMMERCE [P.286]			
	Trader [P.136]		
SCHOOL OF CAVALRY [P.286]			
	Scout [P.135]; Horseman [P.170]	Veteran Horseman [P.170]	Elite Horseman [P.170]
	Chivalry [P.46]; Royal Knight [P.174]	Veteran Royal Knight [P.174]	Elite Royal Knight [P.174]
		Cantled Saddles [P. 46]	
	TOWN CENTER [P.234]		
	Villager [P.137]; Scout [P.135]		
	Textiles [P.52]		
	MARKET [P.225]		
	Trader [P.136]		
	BLACKSMITH [P.260]		
	Bloomery [P. 45]	Decarbonization [P. 47]	Damascus Steel [P. 47]
	Steeled Arrow [P. 51]	Balanced Projectiles [P. 45]	Platecutter Point [P. 49]
	Fitted Leatherwork [P. 47]	Insulated Helm [P. 48]	Master Smith [P.49]

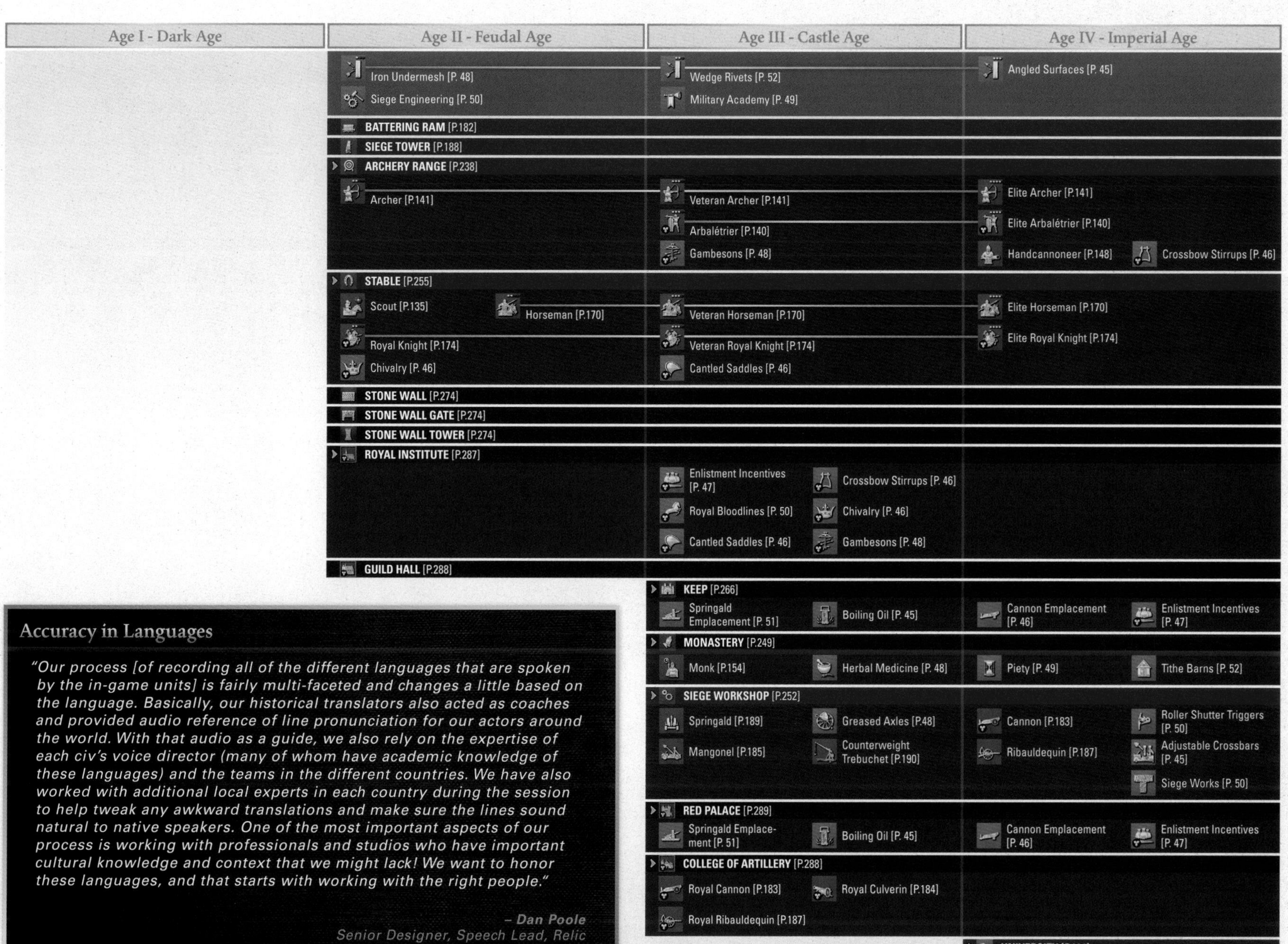

Accuracy in Languages

"Our process [of recording all of the different languages that are spoken by the in-game units] is fairly multi-faceted and changes a little based on the language. Basically, our historical translators also acted as coaches and provided audio reference of line pronunciation for our actors around the world. With that audio as a guide, we also rely on the expertise of each civ's voice director (many of whom have academic knowledge of these languages) and the teams in the different countries. We have also worked with additional local experts in each country during the session to help tweak any awkward translations and make sure the lines sound natural to native speakers. One of the most important aspects of our process is working with professionals and studios who have important cultural knowledge and context that we might lack! We want to honor these languages, and that starts with working with the right people."

– Dan Poole
Senior Designer, Speech Lead, Relic

Age I

Age II

Age III

Age IV

Civilization Features

Economy Bonuses

The French are an economic powerhouse. Their Town Centers can produce Villagers and Scouts faster as you progress through the Ages, which supports aggressive build orders and frees up resources that other civilizations must put towards additional Town Centers to keep up.

On top of that, the French economy can be quickly boosted due to economic technologies costing 30% less to research, and because melee damage technologies are researched for free, you don't have to worry about saving resources to spend on them. Because their technologies are so cheap, they should always be researched as soon as possible after you enter a new Age.

All resource drop-off buildings also cost 25 less Wood to build, so you can replace Lumber Camps even more frequently to ensure the fastest possible Wood acquisition. The resources you save through these reduced costs, in conjunction with the fast economic build-up, makes it easy to balance your economy, and the savings can then be put towards either growing your economy even further, or speeding up your military production.

French Markets

Markets also play a big part of French economic growth, more so than with most other civilizations. As the French, the location of all neutral Trade Posts is automatically revealed on the minimap at the start of every game, letting you know straight away where you need to explore to secure a trade route.

Even more importantly—unlike most Traders, which only return Gold—French Traders have the ability to manually pick which resource you want them to bring back, and you can switch that resource at any time. This means you can adjust the resource you bring as you move through the Ages based on your needs, and makes early game Markets beneficial to every playstyle, and not just ones that require Gold. As an additional benefit when you're playing on a water map, French Trade Ships return 20% additional Gold, making them even more lucrative.

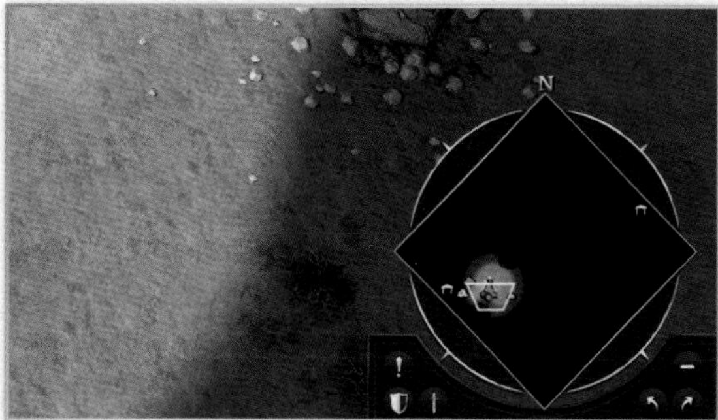

Once you become familiar with maps and how the locations of things are determined on them, having the Trade Posts revealed automatically can give you a big tactical advantage because it will give you a rough idea of where your opponent's base is.

Keep Influence

French Keeps have an area of influence around them that enables any Stable or Archery Range placed within it to produce units at a 25% reduced cost. Given the expense of French armies, the importance of this saving cannot be overstated. Even though a Keep is an expensive building, having at least one so that you can take advantage of the discount should always be a high priority.

Keeping that in mind, when planning your base you should ensure that your military production buildings are arranged in a way that lets you build a Keep near them as soon as you enter Age III. If you need to place that first Keep in a more defensive position, however, or you're looking to establish a forward base, then make sure to build any additional Stables and Archery Ranges near it later on when you need to expand production.

General Playstyle

As the French, you'll typically get into the action very early in games, with many of their Landmarks and bonuses guiding you towards aggressive play from the Feudal Age onwards. Early access to powerful heavy melee cavalry lets you build a fast and deadly army to raid your opponent with, and when you back them up with a booming economy, your goal should be to quickly overwhelm your opponent.

Dark Age (Age I)

This Age is relatively straightforward, because the French have no unique units or mechanics that require additional focus or production. Instead you'll be laying foundations that will begin reaping benefits in the next Age. Because so many options open up for the French in the Feudal Age, including even faster Villager production, you should aim to advance Ages as quickly as possible while building a stockpile of resources, even if it means sacrificing some unit production to do so. Remember that resource drop-off buildings being significantly cheaper means that you can put one less Villager on Wood than you would with other civilizations.

Age Advancement

The **Chamber of Commerce** has all the same functionality of a Market, saving you from having to build one, and it grants the added ability of making Traders or Trade Ships bring back +30% more resources. Couple this with the fact that you get +20% more resources from the neutral Trade Posts that are automatically revealed on your map, and you can see how this can lead to a lot of extra resources. Combined with the French's ability to select whichever resource they want Traders to bring back, this building lets you can tailor a large part of your economy around Trade before opponents even have their Market built.

The **School of Cavalry** fills the role of another building you'd be constructing straight away in Age II: the Stable. Early rushes with cavalry are a big part of the French playstyle, especially with their Royal Knights, and the special ability of this building to reduce the production time of all Stables (including this Landmark) by 20% will allow you to get them on the field and attacking your opponent even faster.

Feudal Age (Age II)

Feudal Age play will differ greatly for the French depending on which Landmark and playstyle you chose to go with. If you're going the aggressive route, the **School of Cavalry** in combination with one additional Stable will give you enough production capability to mount some early Feudal Age attacks. Make sure both buildings are always producing units, and if you start running low on resources, switch from Royal Knights to Horsemen.

With a small army of six cavalry units you can already start dealing a lot of damage to the outskirts of your opponent's base. After building that force up to between 12 and 15—and if possible, building a Blacksmith and researching the **Iron Undermesh** technology—you can even afford to bring your units into the heart of your opponent's base and fight near their Town Center for a short time. Pull your units back once you killed some enemy Villagers to minimize the damage they take, and if your opponent is using Spearmen to counter your cavalry, make use of the extra mobility cavalry has to evade them and attack other Villagers before they get too close. Alternatively, you could build an Archery Range and start bringing some Archers with you, but that would reduce your mobility.

Building a blacksmith as soon as possible in this Age is quite important for the French, because as soon as it's finished, you'll automatically learn the Bloomery technology for free thanks to their unique and powerful melee damage technologies.

With most civilizations, trading is not commonplace until the later stages, so it might seem like a very risky approach to go with the **Chamber of Commerce**. Given the unique French abilities to see neutral Trade Posts and to bring back whatever resource they want, it's a risk that can pay off greatly in this Age—and that pay-off just gets larger as you progress. You'll need to focus mainly on cheaper units rather than the fancy Royal Knights, because a lot of your Gold will need to go towards producing Traders; things will start off slow, but if you're in a safe position and can afford the investment, each Trader you add will bring you one step closer to your booming economy.

Age Advancement

The **Guild Hall** automatically generates 20 of any resource every 20 seconds, with that amount increasing by 20 every minute until you're getting 200 every 20 seconds. You can withdraw the resources at any time, but doing so will reset the generation rate back down to base levels. This Landmark adds another wrinkle to the unique French economy, because you can partially reduce the amount of Villagers gathering whatever resource you generate here. If you pair this with the ability of French Traders to bring back any resource, you have a lot of resources coming in without the need of Villagers, which means less potential targets for your opponents.

If you're involved in a lot of military action with Royal Knights and Arbalétrier, then the **Royal Institute** can be the better choice. It provides access to all of the unique French technologies, even ones from the Imperial Age, and most of them are geared towards improving those two units. Even if you aren't currently producing a lot of those units, if you plan on staying in the Castle Age for a long time then you probably will eventually, so this Landmark can still be of use to you.

Castle Age (Age III)

The Castle Age is when the military might of the French comes into full effect. If you've decided on an aggressive playstyle with the French, you should save up Stone and aim to build a Keep instead of additional Town Centers. Units produced from an Archery Range or Stable within the influence of a Keep are 20% cheaper, and if you picked the **Royal Institute** as your Landmark, you can already research **Enlistment Incentives** to increase that discount by an additional 10%. You don't want to miss this amazing discount, so try to place the Keep near as many of your existing Stables and Archery Ranges as possible. If you're planning on going this route, it's a good idea to have the placement of a Keep in mind when placing buildings during the Feudal Age, to make sure you leave enough space around them.

***Cantled Saddles** should be high on your priority list of technologies to research in this Age, because it will increase the bonus damage done after your Royal Knights charge by +10, which is a huge increase in damage.*

Even though a lot of your focus will be on cavalry, it's important not to overlook the other unique French units. In this Age you'll get access to the Arbalétrier, which has the ability to deploy a defensive pavise that grants an additional +5 ranged armor, and if you're on a water map, the deadly but expensive Galleass can outperform any other ship available at this time. Arbalétrier are best used to support your cavalry by drawing the fire of ranged units and countering anti-cavalry units like the Spearman, so that your cavalry can approach or flank unharmed. The French gain access to a lot of powerful units and technology in this Age, but all of them are expensive, which is why there's such a heavy emphasis on early economic growth.

Age Advancement

Although risky, if you're looking to establish a forward base close to your opponent, and plan on continuing to use cavalry and ranged infantry, then the **Red Palace** is an excellent choice. Not only does it have all of the normal Keep functionality—including the influence bonus to reduce unit production costs from Stables and Archery Ranges—but its offensive capabilities are significantly stronger than a normal Keep thanks to the arbalest attacks, which will make securing your base that much easier.

The **College of Artillery** grants you access to the Royal versions of the Cannon, Ribauldequin and Culverin—some of the most powerful siege engines in the game. This is a good choice of Landmark if you're already built up sufficient amounts of other types of units and are looking to produce some heavy-hitting units to finish your opponent off quickly.

Imperial Age (Age IV)

With their Royal artillery, and all of their unique technologies researched, the French can field one of the most powerful armies in the game during this Age. Your ideal combination would be a powerful group of Royal Knights, backed up by gunpowder siege/infantry or Arbalétriers. Any other unit types should be used in a supplementary way for quick side engagements to distract your opponent while your main army moves in.

If you've also invested some time into the French economic benefits and have a powerful economy behind you, this combination can be hard to overcome. Usually, the amount of powerful units would be restricted by resource costs, but the French economy can overcome that and keep up production.

In team games you can leave the fielding of other unit types to your allies and simply focus on putting together a powerful cavalry army, letting you take full advantage of their mobility and fighting prowess.

French Masteries

In the face of invasion, plague and revolt, medieval France paved a hard-won path from adversity to prosperity. Once a land of fragmented rule bound to a code of chivalry, a unified nation emerged, forged under the roar of cannon fire.

- Profile Image [1]
- Text [2]
- Coat of Arms Pattern [3]
- Coat of Arms Sigil [4]
- Monument [5]

Waste Not	Construct 4 resource drop-off buildings in the Dark Age (I)	Mills, Lumber Camps, and Mining Camps are considered resource drop-off buildings. The French can construct these at a reduced cost.	1000XP	French Coin [1] Cost of the Chevauchées [2]
Wheels of Burden	Research Horticulture, Double Broadaxe, and Specialized Pick before reaching Castle Age (III)	Research these technologies in the Mill, Lumber Camp, and Mining Camp, respectively. The French can research economic technologies at a lower cost – setting the stage for a prosperous economy.	1000XP	Sheaf of Wheat [4] The Jacquerie Revolt [2]
Test of Strength I	Win a 1v1 Custom or Skirmish match against the Easy A.I.	Defeat a single Easy A.I. opponent in a Custom or Skirmish match. Go to the Single Player screen to create a Skirmish match.	1000XP	The Black Death [2] Wold [1]
Horsing Around	Construct the School of Cavalry Landmark and then produce 20 cavalry units	The School of Cavalry gives a unit production speed bonus to all cavalry units produced in Stables or the Landmark itself.	1000XP	French Rider [1] Protection Money [2]
Clever Commerce	Accrue 2000 Food, Wood, orStone from Traders in the Feudal Age (II)	Unique to the French, Traders can trade for more than just Gold. Supplement your economy with resources that are hard to come by, or double down on stockpiling a resource you're going to need plenty of.	1000XP	Fleur-de-lis Banner Pattern [3] Black Monday [2]
In Shining Armor	Produce 40 Royal Knights from a Stable under the influence of a nearby Keep	Defeat a single Intermediate A.I. opponent in a Custom or Skirmish match. Go to the Single Player screen to create a Skirmish match.	1000XP	French Crossbow [1] A War of Treaties [2]
Test of Strength II	Win a 1v1 Custom or Skirmish match against the Intermediate A.I.	Research Crossbow Stirrups in the Archery Range. Pavise shields provide added protection against ranged attacks, making the Arbalétrier a great counter to other ranged units.	1000XP	A Dash for Glory [2] Sheperd [5]
Swift Bolts	Research Crossbow Stirrups and defeat 20 enemy units with Arbalétriers	The Red Palace Landmark functions as a Keep – including the ability to upgrade it with deadly weapons.	1000XP	French Armored Cavalry [1] A Battle of Bows [2]
Paint it Red	Construct the Red Palace Landmark and use it to kill 30 enemies in Castle Age (III)	The French are able to trade Gold for	1000XP	Fleur-de-lis [4] The Champagne Fairs [2]
Master Craftsmen	Accrue 2,000 Food, Wood, Gold, or Stone from the Guild Hall Landmark in the Castle Age (III)	other resources in the Guild Hall Landmark.	1000XP	French Lancer [1] Staying in the Saddle [2]
Test of Strength III	Win a 1v1 Custom or Skirmish match against the Hard A.I.	Defeat a single Hard A.I. opponent in a Custom or Skirmish match. Go to the Single Player screen to create a Skirmish match.	1000XP	French Blacksmith [1] King of Glass [2] Crossbowman and Pavise [5]
Fellowship	Win the match with a surviving army of 25 cavalry	The French have many cavalry-focused technologies to boost their survivability and damage. Choose the combination that best suits your playstyle.	1000XP	Blanche de Castile [1] The Pavise [2] Crossbow [4]
Military Warf	Kill 10 enemy units with Galleasses affected by the Armored Hull technology	The Galleass is a unique French ship armed with forward mounted bombards. This ship is vulnerable from the sides, but the Armored Hull technology can alleviate this.	1000XP	French Courtier [1] The Position of Honor [2]
With a Flourish	Achieve a Wonder victory while 20 Traders are active	Heavy defenses will be needed to keep your Wonder safe, all while more resources are trickling in.	1000XP	Jeanne D'Arc [1] The Bureau Brothers [2]
Test of Strength IV	Win a 1v1 Custom or Skirmish match against the Hardest A.I.	Defeat a single Hardest A.I. opponent in a Custom or Skirmish match. Go to the Single Player screen to create a Skirmish match.	1000XP	Pointed Dag Banner Shape [3] The Retrial of Jeanne D'Arc [2] Royal Knight [5]

Holy Roman Empire

TIME PERIOD REPRESENTED: 936 - 1517 CE EASE OF USE:  

Overview

- *Excellent Static Defenses.*
- *Specializes in Melee Infantry and Religious Units.*
- *Great for Enclosed Maps and Defensive Gameplay.*

Play with the Holy Roman Empire if you enjoy playing...

Romans, Choson or Shang in **AoE 1**
Byzantines, Goths, or Teutons in **AoE 2**
Germans in **AoE 3**

Starting Resources			
200	150	100	0

Bonuses

- *Prelate available in the Dark Age (I).*
- *Early Man-at-Arms Available in the Feudal Age (II).*
- *Villagers Have Increased Carry Capacity by +40%.*
- *Garrison Relics Inside of Outposts, Keeps, and Town Centers to Improve Their Sight Range, Weapon Range, Armor, and Damage.*
- *Docks can Garrison Relics, Increasing Attack Speed of all Ships by 5% per Relic (max 25%).*
- *Cost of Emplacements on Outposts, Wall Towers, and Keeps Reduced by 25%.*

As civilizations go, the Holy Roman Empire is a defensive powerhouse—their greatly reduced cost of emplacements on defensive buildings allows them to construct with impunity. This is backed up by a strong economy—boosted further by their unique Prelate unit's ability to inspire Villagers to work faster—and early access to Men-at-Arms to help defend Villagers from attacks, buying time to establish an early defensive perimeter.

The strength of their defense makes them relatively new-player friendly, because it's easier to fend off an opponent's early aggressive play. Since they have a couple of extra mechanics to juggle, however, they're slightly more complex and difficult to use than the similarly defensive-focused English. If you started with the English and enjoy defensive gameplay, then the Holy Roman Empire offers a natural progression from them once you're more familiar with the game.

Unique Units

	Unit	Description	Page
	Prelate	Provides Holy Inspiration to Villagers, Making Them Work 40% Faster for 30 Seconds	P.156
	Landsknecht	Light Infantry With a Large Two Handed Sword, Capable of Doing Significant Area Damage	P.149

Strengths

The Holy Roman Empire's biggest strengths are undeniably their defensive capabilities and melee infantry. In combination with their Prelates, you can use those attributes to fend off enemy attacks while advancing economically, and then launch a massive counterattack led by your Landsknechte. These melee infantry units are one of the best anti-infantry units in the game, and just a small group of them can successfully take on much larger enemy groups, either to clear a path to their siege units, or to stop infantry units from destroying your gates and towers. Even if your buildings do sustain some damage, thanks to the Emergency Repair system you can simply patch them back up. All of these things combined will make a well-established Holy Roman Empire defense very hard to crack.

Weaknesses

While not really a weakness, it does take some time to get used to efficiently using Prelates, because they require a lot of moving around to get the best out of them. This can make it hard for new players to use the Holy Roman Empire to their full potential, but they can still be very effective while learning and playing in a more basic way.

In terms of gameplay, the Holy Roman Empire can struggle somewhat against very mobile or powerful ranged armies—such as those employed by the Mongols—especially if drawn into combat in open territory or on large open maps. The Holy Roman Empire thrives on confined maps where it's difficult to move around and opponents can be forced through chokepoints. The best counter to that is to try to lure them out, either by cutting off their supplies or bombarding them from afar.

Age I
Age II
Age III
Age IV

	Age I - Dark Age	Age II - Feudal Age	Age III - Castle Age	Age IV - Imperial Age
TOWN CENTER [P.234]	Villager [P.137] Prelate [P.156] Scout [P.135]	Textiles [P. 52]		
HOUSE [P.221]				
MILL [P.227]	Survival Techniques [P. 51] Wheelbarrow [P. 52]	Professional Scouts [P. 49] Horticulture [P. 48]	Fertilization [P. 47]	Prescision Cross-Breeding [P.49]
LUMBER CAMP [P.223]	Forestry [P. 48]	Double Broadax [P. 47]	Lumber Preservation [P.49]	Crosscut Saw [P. 46]
MINING CAMP [P.229]		Specialized Pick [P. 50]	Acid Distillation [P. 45]	Cupellation [P. 46]
FARM [P.216]				
BARRACKS [P.242]	Spearman [P.158]	Hardened Spearman [P.158] Early Man-at-Arms [P.150]	Veteran Spearman [P.158] Man-at-Arms [P.150] Landsknecht [P.149] Heavy Maces [P. 48] Two-Handed Weapons [P. 52]	Elite Spearman [P.158] Elite Man-at-Arms [P.150] Elite Landsknecht [P.149] Riveted Chain Mail [P. 50]
DOCK [P.246]	Fishing Boat [P.191] Transport Ship [P.192]	Trade Ship [P.193] Galley [P.202] Extended Lines [P. 47] Fire Stations [P. 47] Additional Sails [P. 45]	Hulk [P.200] Demolition Ship [P.196] Drift Nets [P. 47] Navigator Lookout [P. 49] Extra Ballista [P. 47] Armored Hull [P. 45]	Carrack [P.204] Chaser Cannons [P. 46] Explosives [P. 47]
PALISADE WALL [P.272]				
PALISADE GATE [P.272]				
OUTPOST [P.270]		Arrowslits [P. 45] Fortify Outpost [P. 48]	Springald Emplacement [P. 51]	Cannon Emplacement [P. 46]
MEINWERK PALACE [P.290]		Bloomery [P. 45] Steeled Arrow [P. 51] Fitted Leatherwork [P. 47] Iron Undermesh [P. 48] Siege Engineering [P. 50] Marching Drills [P. 49]	Decarbonization [P. 47] Balanced Projectiles [P. 45] Insulated Helm [P. 48] Wedge Rivets [P. 52] Military Academy [P. 49]	Damascus Steel [P. 47] Platecutter Point [P. 49] Master Smiths [P. 49] Angled Surfaces [P. 45]
AACHEN CHAPEL [P.291]				
TOWN CENTER [P.234]		Villager [P.137] Scout [P.135] Prelate [P.156] Textiles [P.52]		
MARKET [P.225]		Trader [P.136]		
BLACKSMITH [P.260]		Bloomery [P. 45] Steeled Arrow [P. 51] Fitted Leatherwork [P. 47]	Decarbonization [P. 47] Balanced Projectiles [P. 45] Insulated Helm [P. 48]	Damascus Steel [P. 47] Platecutter Point [P. 49] Master Smith [P.49]

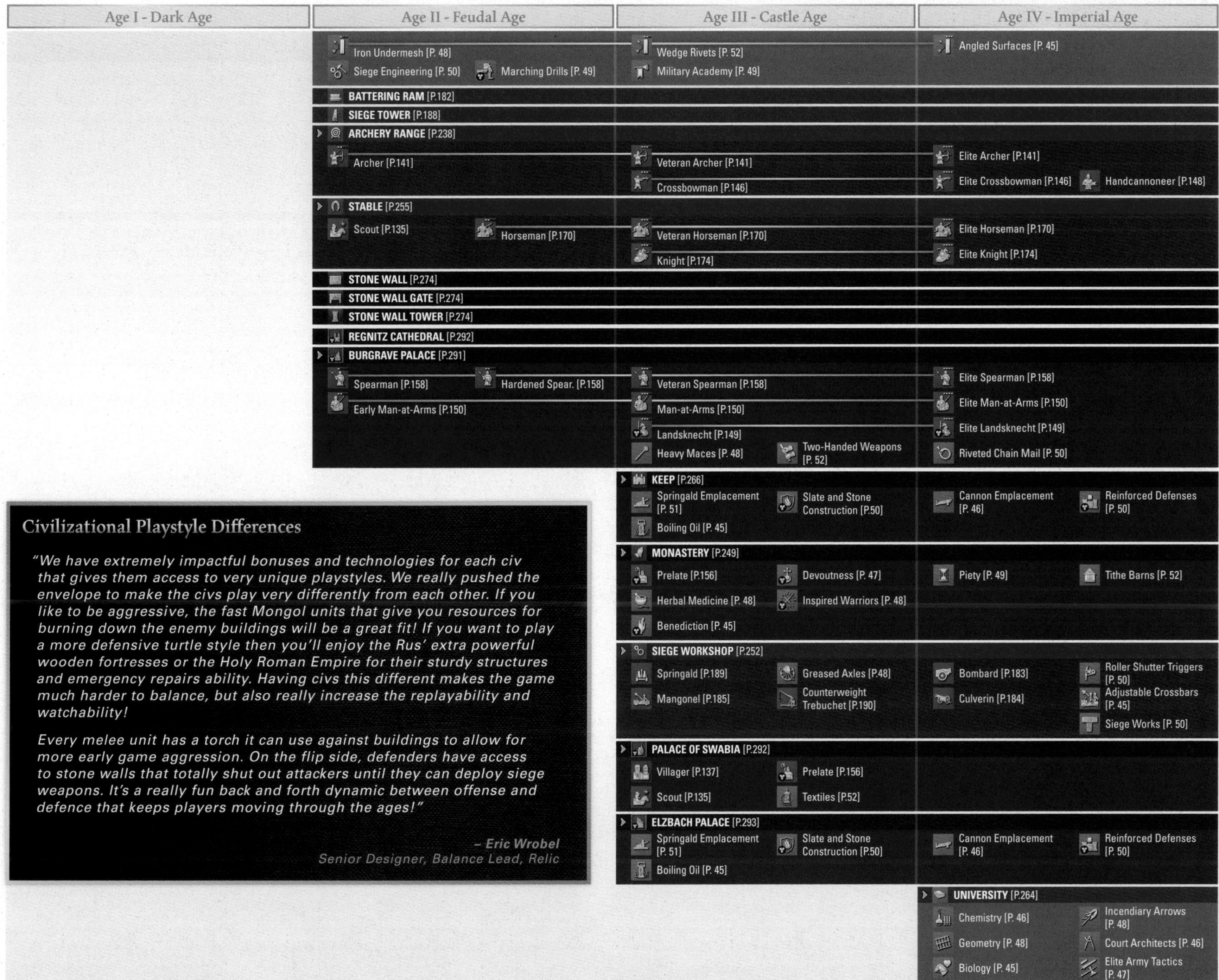

Civilizational Playstyle Differences

"We have extremely impactful bonuses and technologies for each civ that gives them access to very unique playstyles. We really pushed the envelope to make the civs play very differently from each other. If you like to be aggressive, the fast Mongol units that give you resources for burning down the enemy buildings will be a great fit! If you want to play a more defensive turtle style then you'll enjoy the Rus' extra powerful wooden fortresses or the Holy Roman Empire for their sturdy structures and emergency repairs ability. Having civs this different makes the game much harder to balance, but also really increase the replayability and watchability!

Every melee unit has a torch it can use against buildings to allow for more early game aggression. On the flip side, defenders have access to stone walls that totally shut out attackers until they can deploy siege weapons. It's a really fun back and forth dynamic between offense and defence that keeps players moving through the ages!"

– Eric Wrobel
Senior Designer, Balance Lead, Relic

2

Civilization Features

Prelates & Holy Inspiration

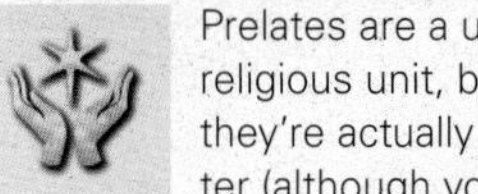

Prelates are a unique Holy Roman Empire religious unit, but unlike most religious units, they're actually produced from your Town Center (although you can also produce them from a Monastery in Age III), and are available from the start of the game. Through their **Holy Inspiration** ability, one Prelate can passively inspire up to 10 nearby Villagers. You can also manually select the ability if you want to use it to inspire a specific Villager. Once inspired, Villagers gather resources 40% faster, so if you spread out multiple Prelates between your different resource gathering areas, you can get a huge boost to your economic growth. When you reach the Castle Age you can increase this further with the **Devoutness** technology, which increases their gather rate by another +10%.

If you keep researching economic upgrades from the resource drop-off buildings as you progress through the Ages, and are using your Prelates wisely, the Holy Roman Empire's economic growth can ramp up very quickly, and can even surpass that of other civilizations. Micromanaging your Prelates to ensure that each one is always inspiring the maximum number of Villagers and that all of your Villagers are inspired is quite intensive, and one of the more technical and complicated aspects you'll need to learn when playing the Holy Roman Empire.

It's vitally important that you keep your vulnerable Prelates safe because losing one will hurt you more than losing a Villager. Not only do you lose the resources from producing it, but the 10 Villagers it was inspiring will work less efficiently.

Extra Carry Capacity

Going hand-in-hand with the Prelate's ability to increase the gathering rate of the Holy Roman Empire's Villagers, there's the civilization trait **Extra Carry Capacity** that increases their carry capacity by +40%. Used in conjunction with each other, Holy Roman Empire Villagers become some of the most efficient gatherers in the game, allowing you to either produce fewer Villagers and use the resources for other things, or keep your Villager production as normal and reap the benefits of a booming economy.

Relic Warfare

Relic Garrison Bonuses

Building	Bonus	Value
Outpost, Keep, Stone Wall Tower	Armor Increase	+50%
	Damage Increase	+35%
	Sight Range Increase	+25%
	Weapon Range Increase	+20%
Dock	Each Relic garrisoned increases the attack speed of all Ships by 5%, up to a maximum of 25%	

Prelates also play another key role for the Holy Roman Empire—collecting Relics. While Relics can be garrisoned in Monasteries like with any other civilization, they can also be placed inside defensive buildings to give them a huge boost in both offensive and defensive capabilities. Relics can also be placed in a Dock to increase the attack speed of all Ships, and if you have multiple Docks, the effect from garrisoning a Relic in each of them stacks for a massive overall increase.

Relics inside these buildings also retain all of their normal properties, so they'll still generate Gold. Given the more exposed placement of these buildings, however, and the fact that your opponent can see whether they house a Relic or not, you'll need to be ready for increased attacks on those buildings. It's also worth noting, however, that although you can produce Prelates at the start of the game in Age I, you can't actually pick up a Relic until Age III (or capture a Sacred Site). During the early Ages it's worth scouting around to locate Relics, so that you can easily claim them as soon as you enter Age III.

Emergency Repairs (V)

Influence Range Details	
Town Center	8 Tiles

What makes the buildings of the Holy Roman Empire so strong and ideal for defensive play is the influence bonus provided by their Town Centers. All buildings constructed within the large influence range of either the starting Town Center—or ones that are built later—will receive the **Emergency Repair** ability. Another feature of this unique influence range is that you can extended it. If you place a building on the outskirts of the Town Center's normal influence range, it will extend to encompass the whole building and an additional tile around it. Through this system, as long as you keep the influence range connected by placing your buildings near each other, you can effectively cover your entire base with just a single Town Center.

Any time a building with this ability takes damage, you can manually activate it to start an automatic repair process that does not require the attention of any Villagers. The building will repair at a rate of 150 health per second for 20 seconds, and even if you heal a building to full health, if it takes damage again before the duration runs out, it will automatically resume repairing. After using the ability there's a 45s cooldown period before you can use it again, so try and focus your defenses around buildings where the ability is on cooldown.

When planning your bases, keep the Emergency Repair ability in mind, and always try to place buildings in a way that keeps the expanding influence range of the Town Center connected to them.

Defensive Technologies

Building	Technology		Details
Keep Elzbach Palace	Slate and Stone Construction	III	All buildings Gain +5 Fire Armor
	Reinforced Defenses	IV	Increase the Health of Walls, Towers, and Gates by +40%
University	Court Architects	IV	Increase the Health of All Buildings by +30%

Upon reaching the Castle Age and building a Keep, the Holy Roman Empire start gaining access to defensive technologies that serve as the cherry on top of an already formidable array of defensive capabilities. The extra fire armor will help defend against attacks from melee units or incendiary arrows, giving you more time to react and use the Emergency Repair ability, and once you start increasing the health of everything, the survivability of your defensive structures goes through the roof.

Although all of these technologies are not a priority in every situation, they are great for defensive strategies in which you're trying to grow a booming economy from an enclosed position behind your walls. Taken in conjunction with buffs from garrisoned Relics, it can be hard for even the strongest of siege engines to break through the walls of the Holy Roman Empire.

*The **Elzbach Palace** Landmark contains two of the best defensive technologies in the game: **Slate and Stone Construction** and **Reinforced Defenses**.*

General Playstyle

The Holy Roman Empire is focused on strong defense and an economy backed up by religious units and melee infantry. They're not a particularly mobile civilization; instead, you'll be banking on strong static defenses to protect your growing economy and forcing your opponent to expend all of their resources trying to break through. When the time is right, you can then slowly advance on your opponent and crush them under the heel of your infantry. Due to their heavy use of Prelates and formidable fortifications, they also shine when the Sacred Sites victory condition is active.

Dark Age (Age I)

Much of the early game with the Holy Roman Empire should feel similar to other civilizations, because you do not yet have access to any of the main defensive structures. Prioritize arranging your base in such a way that every building is covered by the influence of your starting Town Center so they have access to the **Emergency Repair** ability; this ability alone can deny your opponent victories against your buildings if they launch early raids.

The next thing to consider is the timing for producing your first Prelates. The cost of a Prelate is quickly made up for by the increased efficiency of the Villagers they inspire, so it's worth putting a few of your starting Villagers on Gold earlier to make up for the cost of an early produced Prelate. Depending on your Villager production rate, your second Prelate should arrive around the time you're advancing to the next Age. If, however, your resources are spread out, you might want to add a second one earlier to cut down on the amount you have to move your first one around. This is especially important if you're playing defensively in the Feudal Age, because Stone Outcroppings are often a bit further away, and you'll need a lot of Stone for walls.

Once you're familiar with the game and are confident in your micromanagement skills, moving your first Prelate back-and-forth between the Villagers gathering from your starting Sheep and Wood will allow you to get the most benefit out of Holy Inspiration.

Age Advancement

Aachen Chapel is always a good choice of Landmark—the second Prelate you produce can be garrisoned inside of it to inspire all of the Villagers in its area of influence, saving you a lot of micromanagement time. Your first Prelate can then be used to inspire Villagers outside of that area.

The Meinwerk Palace Landmark is essentially a Blacksmith with a 25% discount on all of the technologies researched there. If you're thinking about pushing early in the Feudal Age using Early Men-at-Arms, the lower costs can make this a good choice to acquire upgrades sooner than your opponent.

Feudal Age (Age II)

If you're planning on attacking in this Age, take some time to first research **Marching Drills** at a Blacksmith. This technology makes all of your infantry units move 10% faster, which will give you a big advantage against your opponent's infantry; Archers won't be able to run away from your Early Men-at-Arms as easily, and your light infantry will easily catch them. This is a much safer approach that will minimize the damage you take while closing in. If you want to add an extra layer of defense, you can also research **Iron Undermesh**.

By making a small offensive push, you can stave off aggression from your opponent while you focus on your economy. If things start going well, you can switch to an all-out assault by researching **Siege Engineering** and commit to an attack with an army consisting of Early Men-at-Arms, Spearmen, and Battering Rams. The most important thing to remember is to only research those technologies if you're going to make use of them.

You can now begin to fortify your base by building Stone Walls around it with some Stone Wall Towers—just make sure they're within the influence range of your Town Center so that you can repair them if your opponent attacks. Once you have some more security, start growing your economy even more by switching to sustainable Food sources such as groups of Farms with a Mill and Prelate nearby.

Age Advancement

If you're planning on aggressively pushing your opponent during the Castle Age with powerful Landsknecht, then Burgrave Palace is best. It has the same capabilities as a Barracks, but with the unique ability to produce five units at once. You still have to pay the resource cost for all five, but the production time is that of one unit.

The choice to pick Regnitz Cathedral will depend entirely on how you intend on using the Relics you acquire. If you want them solely for the Gold generation, then the ability of this Landmark to house three of them, and generate Gold at a +200% rate can be extremely beneficial. If, however, you want to use Relics in your defensive buildings or a Dock, then you'll get little benefit from it.

A good mix of Melee Infantry units are at the core of the Holy Roman Empire's army and are a great offensive and defensive tool.

Castle Age (Age III)

Entering Age III you gain access to unique melee infantry technologies, and a powerful unique infantry unit, so this is the Age where the Holy Roman Empire's infantry can start to pull ahead of other civilizations. The Landsknecht attacks in a sweeping arc with their large swords, dealing damage over a small area; on their own, they can struggle against enemy ranged attacks, but if you get a group of them close to a group of enemy light infantry, they can be devastating.

You can also now research the **Heavy Maces** technology to increase the damage your Men-at-Arms deal to heavy targets, and **Two-Handed Weapons** to further increase their damage against all targets. If you've already built up an army during the Feudal Age, these additions can make it strong enough to start seriously pressuring your opponent.

On the defensive side, you also get some potentially big upgrades to play with during this Age. Your Prelates can finally pick up Relics, so if you've already scouted their locations, quickly secure them and bring them back to your base. Keeps become available, and they can add a lot of additional firepower to your defensive line, especially if you decide to garrison one of the Relics in them. You can also learn the final economic upgrades available at the resource drop-off buildings, allowing you to put the finishing touches on your economy. Then it's just a matter of sitting behind your walls while you build up your army and make your opponent spend resources trying to get in.

Age Advancement

If you're planning on producing the ultimate booming economy, then the Palace of Swabia can help you get the job done. Not only do you save resources when building it thanks to the -20% cost, but it can also produce Villagers cheaper and faster than any other building.

Elzbach Palace on the other hand is the ultimate defensive Holy Roman Empire building. It has all of the strengths of a normal Keep, but features an additional +50% health, and reduces the damage that nearby buildings take by 33%. Couple this with the defensive technologies available in the Imperial Age, and it's almost impossible to destroy this building.

If your base is getting attacked a lot, consider investing in the Slate and Stone technology from a Keep to give all of your buildings some additional fire armor.

Imperial Age (Age IV)

When playing as the Holy Roman Empire, it's easy to focus heavily on melee infantry in the previous Ages, but with all of the upgrades available to other civilizations in this Age, you should now start supporting them with some cavalry and siege units of your own. Prelates also provide you with a nice bonus in this Age. Due to the fact that your villagers are more productive, you can have fewer Villagers gathering resources overall, freeing up population space that you can fill with even more military units. This only works, however, if you've established a secure base; if a Prelate dies, you'll experience a huge drop-off in productivity.

If you've established a secure base by this point in the game, consider enhancing it further with some stronger weapon emplacements; combine those with the health and armor upgrades available in this Age, and you can present a very troublesome base for your opponent to assault. These defenses give you more time to react to aggression, and will make it easier to move out and attack your opponent thanks to the cover fire they provide. If it comes down to a base trade scenario, you will usually come out ahead if both players started on equal footing.

Given the strength of their defenses, the Holy Roman Empire excel in games where the Wonder Victory Condition is active, because your opponent will have an extremely tough time getting anywhere near it.

2

Holy Roman Empire Masteries

The Holy Roman Empire of the German Nation claimed to be the rightful successor to the ancient Roman Empire. Its emperors controlled central Europe with a stalwart army of hardened infantrymen, and aimed to capture the center of the Christian world itself: Rome.

- Profile Image [1]
- Text [2]
- Coat of Arms Pattern [3]
- Coat of Arms Sigil [4]
- Monument [5]

Mastery	Requirement	Description	XP	Rewards
Bestirred	Gather 500 resources with Villagers affected by Holy Inspiration in the Dark Age (I)	Use a Prelate to inspire Villagers with Holy Inspiration as they harvest resources.	1000XP	Scythe [1] Renovatio Imperii Romanorum [2]
Safety in Numbers	Construct 20 buildings within the range of influence of a Town Center	Buildings within the influence of Town Centers are more resistant to fire.	1000XP	Straight Swords [4] A Multitude of States [2]
Test of Strength I	Win a 1v1 Custom or Skirmish match against the Easy A.I.	Defeat a single Easy A.I. opponent in a Custom or Skirmish match. Go to the Single Player screen to create a Skirmish match.	1000XP	The Empress Matilda [2] Holy Roman Empire Shield [1]
Resupply	Defeat 15 enemy units with Men-At-Arms affected by the Two-Handed Weapons technology	Research the Two-Handed Weapons technology in the Barracks.	1000XP	Holy Roman Empire Citizen [1] A Fearsome Hedgehog [2]
Fleet of Foot	Research Marching Drills and produce a force of 30 infantry in the Castle Age (III)	Research Marching Drills at the Blacksmith.	1000XP	Single Stripe Banner Patter [3] The Edict of Salerno [2]
Ray of Hope	Research Herbal Medicine and produce 5 Prelates from the Monestery in the Castle Age (III)	Research Herbal Medicine in the Monastery.	1000XP	Mace [1] The Shifting Empire [2]
Test of Strength II	Win a 1v1 Custom or Skirmish match against the Intermediate A.I.	Defeat a single Intermediate A.I. opponent in a Custom or Skirmish match. Go to the Single Player screen to create a Skirmish match.	1000XP	Emperor of Falconry [2] Landsknecht [5]
Safeguard	Construct the Regnitz Cathedral, place a Relic within it, and accrue 3,000 Gold from it	Relics can be found on the map. Transport a Relic to the Regnitz Cathedral with a Prelate to accrue Gold.	1000XP	Holy Roman Empire Champion [1] A Fair Wage [2]
By a Landslide	Defeat 50 enemies with Landsknechte	The Landsknecht can be produced from the Barracks upon reaching the Castle Age (III).	1000XP	Sailing Ship [4] Cologne Cathedral [2]
Holy Tithes	Accrue 500 resources from Relics placed within Monasteries	Relics can be found all across the map. An optional technology, Tithe Barns, also provides additional resources when Relics are placed within Monasteries.	1000XP	Beguine Sister [1] Relics of the Holy Roman Empire [2]
Test of Strength III	Win a 1v1 Custom or Skirmish match against the Hard A.I.	Defeat a single Hard A.I. opponent in a Custom or Skirmish match. Go to the Single Player screen to create a Skirmish match.	1000XP	Holy Roman Empire Prelate [1] A Court of Science and Art [2] Holy Roman Empire Man-At-Arms [5]
Thou Shalt Not Pass	Construct the Elzbach Palace and then construct 3 Keeps within influence	The Elzbach Palace gives structures within the range of Influence increased defenses. Your Keeps will be much harder to destroy.	1000XP	Relic [1] The Walk to Canossa [2] Footman Maces [4]
Preach to the Choir	Convert 10 enemies with a Prelate	Prelates holding a Relic can use the Conversion ability, which has a chance to convert nearby enemies to the Holy Roman Empire.	1000XP	Landsknecht [1] The Crusades [2]
Wonderous	Research Reinforced Defenses and then achieve a Wonder victory	Research Reinforced Defenses in the Keep. With increased defenses you can defend your Wonder from your opponents.	1000XP	Charles V [1] A Fighting Style [2]
Test of Strength IV	Win a 1v1 Custom or Skirmish match against the Hardest A.I.	Defeat a single Hardest A.I. opponent in a Custom or Skirmish match. Go to the Single Player screen to create a Skirmish match.	1000XP	End of the Empire [2] Diamond Patter [3] Saint Cunigunde [5]

Mongols

TIME PERIOD REPRESENTED: 1000 - 1500 CE EASE OF USE: ★★★

Overview

- *Great on Open Maps.*
- *Suits an Aggressive Playstyle.*
- *Can Move Their Buildings, so are Highly Mobile.*
- *Specializes in Ranged Cavalry..*

Play with the Mongols if you enjoy playing...

Yamato in **AoE 1**
Huns or Mongols in **AoE 2**
Haudenosaunee,
Ottomans, or Swedes in **AoE 3**

Starting Resources

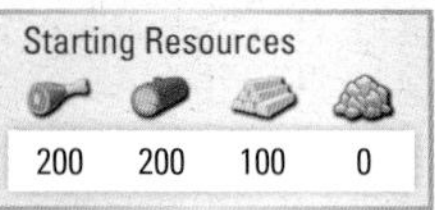

200	200	100	0

Bonuses

- *Plunder +50 Food and Gold by Igniting Enemy Buildings.*
- *Start with Maximum Population Limit and no Need for Houses.*
- *Early Horsemen in the Dark Age (I)*
- *Double Produce Units or Research Advanced Versions of Technologies Using Stone.*
- *Gain +10% Food, Wood, Gold, and Stone from Trade Routes with More Traders.*
- *Transport Ships Have +50% Health and Move +15% faster.*

The nomadic Mongols are set apart from other civilizations by their ability to pack up their buildings and relocate them to another place on the map. As the player, this allows for extreme flexibility—you can constantly reposition yourself around the map based on your current needs, be they looking for fresh resource deposits, or escaping enemy attacks. Mongols start with the maximum population capacity and have no need for static Houses, and their main source of Food comes from Sheep rather than Farms. The lack of population concerns coupled with early access to cavalry units, including the unique Mangudai, means they shine when mass producing units early in games for an aggressive playstyle, with an emphasis on raiding and burning down enemy buildings to plunder extra resources.

Unique Units

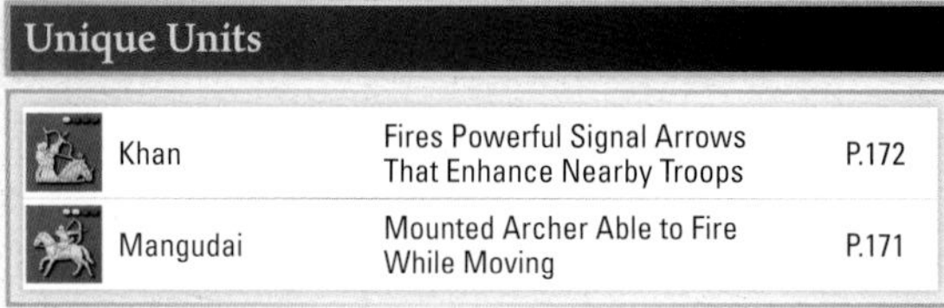

Unit	Description	Page
Khan	Fires Powerful Signal Arrows That Enhance Nearby Troops	P.172
Mangudai	Mounted Archer Able to Fire While Moving	P.171

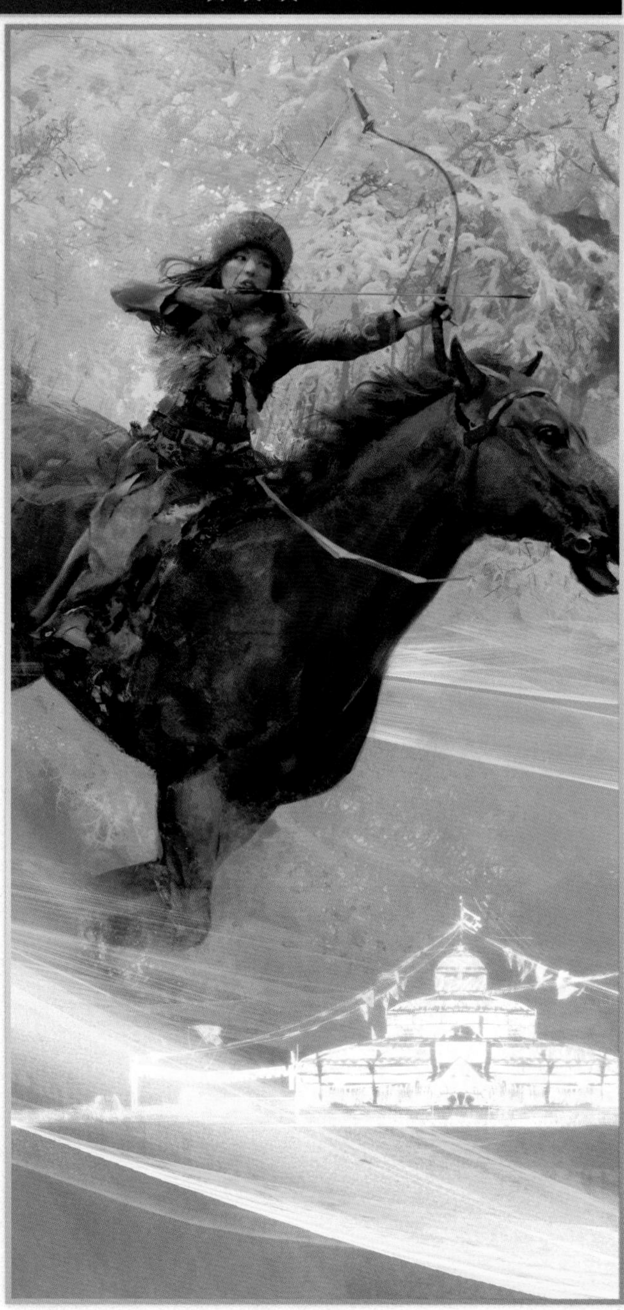

Strengths

The Mongol's strengths lie in their mobility and aggressiveness, so if you're a player who likes city building and strong static defenses, this civilization may not be the right one for you. Unlike other civilizations, the Mongols can build Stables straight away in Age I, from which they can produce the light cavalry Early Horseman. Having access to a cavalry unit that early in the game allows you to easily out maneuver the units of other civilizations, and is just one of the things that make the Mongols so formidable at employing fast paced and hard-hitting strategies.

The raiding capability of these early cavalry units is unmatched, and using them around the outskirts of your opponent's base to constantly harass them can be extremely effective. This will force the enemy to focus on your small raiding parties while you're still building up a huge main force back at your base. Usually, a good mix of melee and ranged cavalry—in combination with the Khan and all of the abilities they bring with them—can be very hard for opponents to deal with.

Technology and production speed are the other big advantages the Mongols have, thanks to all of the improvements they get access to when placing buildings within the influence range of an Ovoo. Not being able to build Stone fortifications means that the Mongols can dedicate all of their Stone towards improved technology or production, letting you easily outproduce other civilizations when playing as them. Couple that with the fast-paced raiding playstyle, and things can quickly snowball and become overwhelming for their opponents.

Weaknesses

The Mongols' main weakness is that they're terribly lacking in terms of static defensive fortifications. This makes them really bad at defending—if they get put on the back foot, it can be hard to recover. This all-or-nothing strategic leaning extends to their

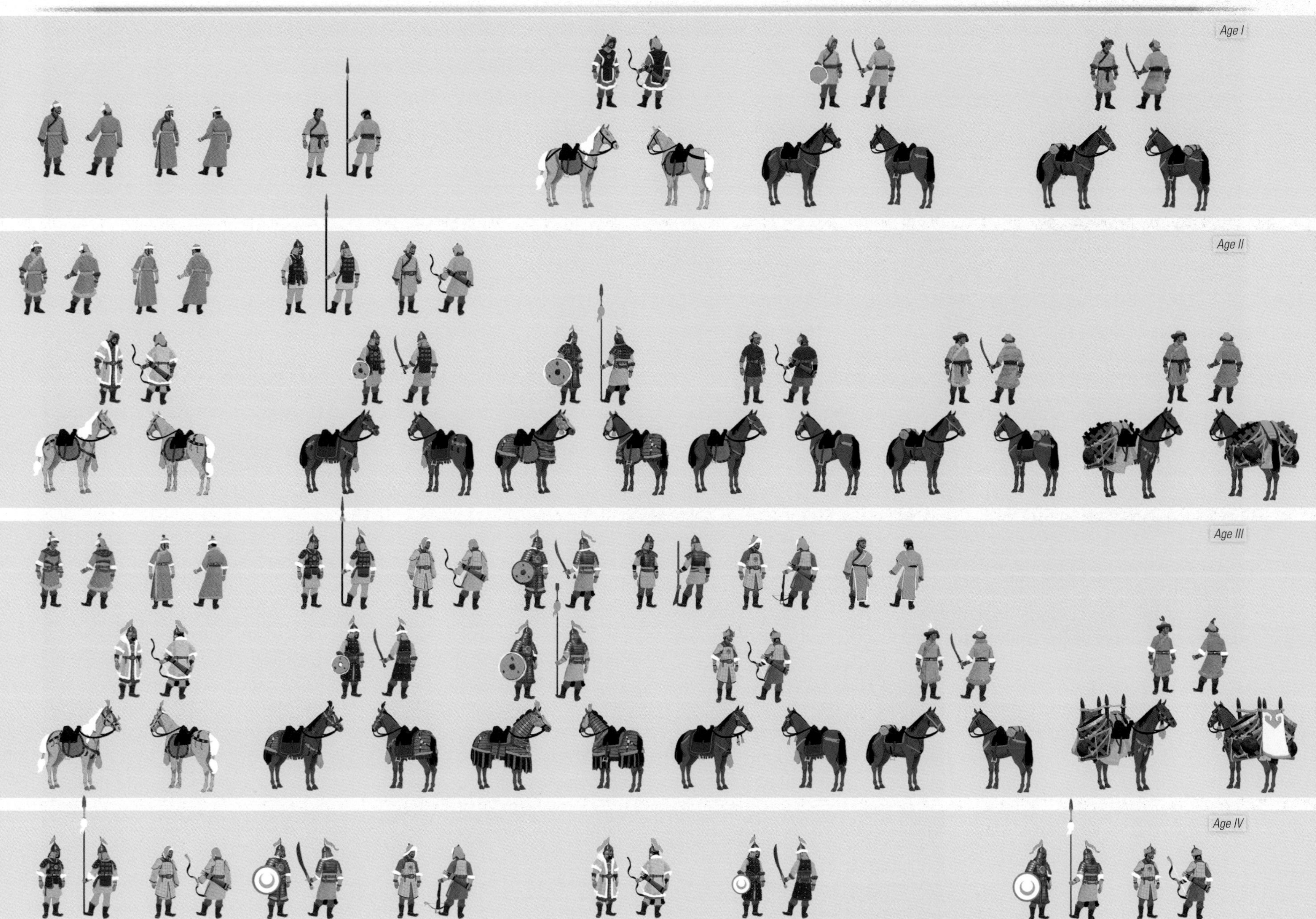
Age I
Age II
Age III
Age IV

Age I - Dark Age	Age II - Feudal Age	Age III - Castle Age	Age IV - Imperial Age
TOWN CENTER [P.234]			
Villager [P.137] Scout [P.135]	Textiles [P.52]		
GER [P.217]			
Forestry [P. 48] Wheelbarrow [P. 52]	Professional Scouts [P. 49] Horticulture [P. 48]	Fertilization [P. 47]	Prescision Cross-Breeding [P.49]
Survival Techniques [P. 51]	Double Broadax [P. 47]	Lumber Preservation [P.49]	Crosscut Saw [P. 46]
	Specialized Pick [P. 50]	Acid Distillation [P. 45]	Cupellation [P. 46]
OVOO [P.230]			
Superior Mobility [P. 51]	Whistling Arrows [P. 52] Raid Bounty [P. 49]	Additional Torches [P. 45]	Stone Bounty [P. 51]
BARRACKS [P.242]			
Spearman [P.158]	Hardened Spearman [P.158]	Veteran Spearman [P.158]	Elite Spearman [P.158]
		Man-at-Arms [P.150]	Elite Man-at-Arms [P.150]
STABLE [P.255]			
Scout [P.135] Early Horseman [P.170]	Horseman [P.170]	Veteran Horseman [P.170]	Elite Horseman [P.170]
		Lancer [P.174]	Elite Lancer [P.174]
DOCK [P.246]			
Fishing Boat [P.191] Transport Ship [P.192]	Trade Ship [P.193] Light Junk [P.202]	War Junk [P.202] Explosive Junk [P.196]	Baochuan [P.204]
	Extended Lines [P. 47]	Drift Nets [P. 47]	Chaser Cannons [P. 46] Explosives [P. 47]
	Piracy [P. 49] Additional Sails [P. 45]	Navigator Lookout [P. 49] Extra Ballista [P. 47]	
OUTPOST [P.270]			
	Arrowslits [P. 45]	Springald Emplace-ment [P. 51] Yam Network [P. 52]	Cannon Emplacement [P. 46]
DEER STONES [P.294]			
THE SILVER TREE [P.294]			
	Trader [P.136]		Stone Commerce [P. 51]
PASTURE [P.233]			
Herdable Sheep [P.233]			
	TOWN CENTER [P.234]		
	Villager [P.137] Scout [P.135] Textiles [P. 52]		
	MARKET [P.225]		
	Trader [P.136]		Stone Commerce [P. 51]
	BLACKSMITH [P.260]		
	Bloomery [P. 45]	Decarbonization [P. 47]	Damascus Steel [P. 47]
	Steeled Arrow [P. 51]	Balanced Projectiles [P. 45]	Platecutter Point [P. 49]
	Fitted Leatherwork [P. 47]	Insulated Helm [P. 48]	Master Smiths [P. 49] Biology [P. 45]
	Iron Undermesh [P. 48]	Wedge Rivets [P. 52]	Angled Surfaces [P. 45] Chemistry [P. 46]
	Siege Engineering [P. 50]	Military Academy [P. 49]	Incendiary Arrows [P. 48] Elite Army Tactics [P. 47]

Age I - Dark Age	Age II - Feudal Age	Age III - Castle Age	Age IV - Imperial Age
	BATTERING RAM [P.182]		
	SIEGE TOWER [P.188]		
	ARCHERY RANGE [P.238]		
	Archer [P.141]	Veteran Archer [P.141]	Elite Archer [P.141]
		Crossbowman [P.146]	Elite Crossbowman [P.146]; Handcannoneer [P.148]
	Mangudai [P.171]	Veteran Mangudai [P.171]	Elite Mangudai [P.171]
		Siha Bow Limbs [P. 50]	
	STABLE [P.255]		
	Scout [P.135]; Horseman [P.170]	Veteran Horseman [P.170]	Elite Horseman [P.170]
		Lancer [P.174]	Elite Lancer [P.174]
	KURULTAI [P.295]		
	STEPPE REDOUBT [P.296]		
	Horticulture [P. 48]	Fertilization [P. 47]	Prescision Cross-Breeding [P.49]
	Double Broadax [P. 47]	Lumber Preservation [P.49]	Crosscut Saw [P. 46]
	Specialized Pick [P. 50]	Acid Distillation [P. 45]	Cupellation [P. 46]
	Forestry [P. 48]; Survival Techniques [P. 51]		
	Wheelbarrow [P. 52]; Professional Scouts [P. 49]		
		PRAYER TENT [P.249]	
		Shaman [P.154]; Herbal Medicine [P. 48]	Piety [P. 49]; Monastic Shrines [P. 49]
			Tithe Barns [P. 52]
		SIEGE WORKSHOP [P.252]	
		Springald [P.189]; Greased Axles [P.48]	Bombard [P.183]; Roller Shutter Triggers [P. 50]
		Mangonel [P.185]; Traction Trebuchet [P.190]	Adjustable Crossbars [P. 45]
			Siege Works [P. 50]
		THE WHITE STUPA [P.297]	
		KHAGANATE PALACE [P.298]	
		Lancer [P.174]	Elite Lancer [P.174]
		Mangudai [P.171]; Veteran Mangudai [P.171]	Elite Mangudai [P.171]
		Early Horseman [P.170]; Horseman [P.170]	Veteran Horseman [P.170]; Elite Horseman [P.170]
			MONUMENT OF THE GREAT KHAN [P.311]

Mongol Siege Warfare

"One of the most terrifying situations I can imagine is being under siege. I recall researching the Battle of Xiangyang, portrayed in our game in the last three missions of the Mongol campaign. It struck me—and stuck with me—how terrifying it must have felt for the citizens of Xiangyang to be locked in the city with an army on their doorstep. Those who peeked over the walls would have seen a massive siege effort unfolding: numerous trebuchets, enemy forts surrounding the city, and an army of seasoned warriors.

As the Mongols choked the city by blocking the escape routes and cutting off supplies, famine would have taken hold in the city and fighting for resources would have been a daily struggle. It truly is one of the more terrifying situations I can imagine—no reprieve, no escape, and little hope of survival."

– Kristina Wiik
Senior Designer, Narrative, Relic

Authentic Instrumentation

"It was very important for the music to really "set the scene" for each of the Civilizations. As a result, each Civ's score is rooted firmly in the instrumentation and overall vibe of their culture. I placed great importance on as much differentiation between Civs as possible, which was predominantly achieved by a deep dive into each of the Civ's musical history and instrumentation, but also achieved by working with a team of five different composers, to allow for as much of a unique flavor between each of the eight Civs as possible."

– Lin Gardiner
Principal Designer, Music Lead, Relic

siege and naval units as well. Both are cheaper to produce or more agile than those of other civilizations, but they're significantly less powerful, so unless you overwhelm your opponent with sheer numbers of units, you're likely to come out on the losing end of battles, and then have to scramble to overproduce units before you can mount a comeback.

The comparatively low cost of their Traction Trebuchets does mean they can be produced faster upon reaching Age III, but you'll need to capitalize on that and push your opponent as soon as possible. That cost advantage starts to diminish as the more powerful but expensive units of other civilizations start to take the fields. For new players, the high mobility and speed of play with the Mongols can be a big weakness, because a hit-and-run playstyle demands a lot of attention and multi-tasking, something that is very difficult for new players to manage while learning other aspects of the game.

Civilization Features

A Nomadic Civilization

The Mongols always start as nomads, so at the beginning of a game your Town Center will be packed up and mobile rather than placed in a fixed position. This means you can move your Town Center and unpack it in the place most beneficial to your plan for the opening of the game. An ideal place will often be next to resources that you need in the early game, such as Berries, Wood or Gold.

Don't take too long deciding where to unpack your starting Town Center; location is important, but not at the cost of producing Villagers and falling behind your opponent.

Throughout the game it's good to stay true to the Mongols' nomadic playstyle, relocating your base to keep your opponent guessing as to its location, or if you need a new Stone Outcropping for your Ovoo. The main thing you need to keep in mind is that you need to keep open population space available, because while an unpacked building doesn't contribute to population capacity, a packed up building requires one space; if you're at 200/200 population you won't be able to move any of your buildings.

Ovoo

The Ovoo is one of the most important buildings the Mongols have access too, and it's not an understatement to say that, when used to its full extent, it forms the heart of the whole Mongol playstyle. Sacred Ovoos can only be constructed over a Stone Outcropping, and once there, they'll automatically start collecting those Stone deposits over time; this is the only means the Mongols have of gathering natural Stone because they cannot directly mine it.

The Ovoo also has another important feature: its ability to grant access to improved production or technology to any building placed within its influence range. For production buildings, you can pay some additional Stone to have that building produce two units at once, allowing for rapid growth in your military or economic power. Improved technologies also require Stone, and when learned, they provide additional benefits over the normal versions.

While you can unpack your starting Town Center anywhere at the start of a game, doing so next to a Stone Outcropping can be extremely beneficial, because once you've built an Ovoo on top and start gaining Stone, you'll be able to produce two Villagers at a time. It's important to note, however, that you can only have one Ovoo at a time, so you'll need to plan your base arrangement around it to ensure the maximum benefits. Luckily, if you need to rearrange things, you can just pack up your other buildings and move them around.

Because the Ovoo is the primary source of Stone for the Mongols, it's important to make sure that when an outcropping one is constructed on runs out of Stone, you find another Stone Outcropping to build a new one on. You'll even get a pop up on screen to let you know when an Ovoo has depleted a Stone Outcropping to let you know it's time to move.

Khanate

Instead of a Scout, Mongols start the game with a unique Khan unit that fills the role of a Scout, but comes with numerous additional benefits. The Khan has access to unique Signal Arrow abilities that can provide temporary buffs to the surrounding units, and—as you progress through the ages—you'll unlock new arrow types to increase your tactical options. They also have access to a Scouting Falcon that lets them maintain vision over an area, even after they've moved away, which is perfect for setting up ambushes. Another unique feature of the Khan is that if they fall in battle, another one will spawn at your Town Center for free after 120 seconds. The Town Center does have to be unpacked for the timer to start and the Khan to spawn, so if you're in the process of moving you'll have to either wait or stop where you are.

Trade and the Silk Road

Trading and the establishing of trade routes is another cornerstone of Mongol gameplay, and one that can be extremely lucrative if you put the time into setting it up. The Silk Road bonus automatically gets applied to any trades that you make with the prerequisite number of Traders, and when you get into higher numbers of Traders working along long trade routes, the extra resources can really start to add up.

Also playing into this is the **Yam Speed Aura** generated by Outposts. This increases the movement speed of any Traders that pass close to them, so if you establish a network of Outposts along your trade route, those additional returns will come in even faster. The **Silver Tree** Landmark that can be constructed to advance to Age II can also produce Traders cheaper and faster than a Market, allowing the Mongols to put their Traders to work faster and in greater numbers than other civilizations. If you have access to a safe trade route, with the **Silver Tree** you can setup an early game trade route and have your Villagers primarily gather Food and Wood, relying on Trade as your primary source of Gold.

Silk Road Bonus

Tier	# of Traders	Income	Example income per Trader
Default	1	Default	100 Gold
1	3	Amount of Gold plus 10% of that amount in Food	100 Gold + 10 Food
2	5	Amount of Gold plus 10% in Food and Wood	100 Gold + 10 Food + 10 Wood
3	7	Amount of Gold plus 10% in Food, Wood, and Gold	110 Gold + 10 Food + 10 Wood
4*	9+	Amount of Gold plus 10% in Food, Wood, Gold, and Stone	110 Gold + 10 Food + 10 Wood + 10 Stone

*Requires Stone Commerce Technology from the Market

Plundered Wealth

Plunder Values				
Default	50	0	50	0
With **Raid Bounty** Technology	100	0	100	0
With **Raid Bounty & Stone Bounty** Technology	100	0	100	75

Another factor in the Mongols' aggressive raiding playstyle is the way they benefit from setting enemy buildings ablaze. For every building you ignite as the Mongols you'll receive a bounty of resources, the amount of which can be further improved by researching specific technologies. It's important to make the distinction here between setting a building on fire and destroying it. Focusing on just setting buildings on fire not only gets you these resources, but they also serve as a distraction for your opponent, because they'll need to commit units and resources towards putting the fire out if they don't want to lose it. While they're busy doing that, you can be setting fire to other buildings, continuing to spread the chaos.

Pasturage

Further underlining their nomadic theme, Mongols do not construct Farms, since doing so would lock them into a location. Instead, the Mongols rely on Pastures that produce herdable Sheep that can be killed and used for a source of Food, just like other Sheep found in the wild. Pastures automatically generate Sheep over time (at an increased rate when placed near an Ovoo), and they stay within the confines of the Pasture so there's no additional herding to be done. Because you can have multiple Villagers working at a single Pasture, you also save a lot of space compared to Farms, resulting in even more freedom for your base layout. Like other Mongol buildings, Pastures can be packed up and moved to a new location whenever you want, and any Sheep at the Pasture can simply follow along behind it.

Great Dominion

Because the Mongols start out with maximum population capacity by default, they don't have to spend time and resources constructing Houses. This, in conjunction with Pastures, means you can build very efficient bases to get the most benefit out buildings with influence ranges such as the Ovoo. Or alternatively, you can get away with smaller, satellite-like Food gathering operations, because it's a lot harder for enemies to detect a couple of buildings than an entire farming operation.

The Yam Speed Aura & Outposts

Outposts play a special role for the Mongols. Not only are the they the only purely defensive structure that they can build, but they're also the gateway to the **Yam Speed Aura** buff. Any cavalry or Trader unit that passes within the vicinity of an Outpost will have their movement speed increased by 15% for 20s, and with the **Yam Network** technology, this effect can be extended to all unit types. Placed well, you can create a sort of highway for your units, enabling your cavalry to engage and disengage more quickly during raiding trips, or to speed up your Traders and make them more efficient.

General Playstyle

When playing as the Mongols, you'll usually want to choose a cavalry focused army composition, with Horsemen, Lancers, and Mangudai supported by your Khan's special abilities. Their early access to cavalry and ability to gain resources by setting enemy buildings alight results in a highly mobile army that excels at hit-and-run attacks.

Together with early Outposts to secure map control, these things allow you to play extremely aggressively as the Mongols in the hopes of striking your opponent while they're unprepared. In general, the biggest question a Mongol player has to ask themselves is not if they should strike, but when and where, only holding off aggression for brief moments to capitalize on the improved production granted by the Ovoo influence to rapidly bolster your numbers.

Dark Age (Age I)

After you set up your Town Center, the very next thing you should do is build your Ovoo on a suitable Stone Outcropping to start generating Stone, and give you access to the improved functionality of the buildings you place nearby. While the Ovoo is building, herd the first few nearby Sheep with your Khan and bring them to your Town Center—it's already time to start being the aggressor. Because of its ranged attacks, the Khan is perfectly suited to harass enemy Villagers during the early stages of the game. The goal here is to draw your opponent's attention, which will hopefully lead to Villager idle time on their end.

The Mongols have access to a Stable in Dark Age, allowing you to produce the Early Horsemen cavalry that you can use to form slightly larger raiding parties and increase the pressure on your opponent. Getting used to raiding with these small groups of cavalry units is an important part of learning to play as the Mongols, and the skills you learn here will carry over later in the game when you're working with larger groups. Until you're comfortable with an aggressive playstyle, producing a larger army early on can be very risky, because while you could pull ahead of your opponent, you could also fall far behind if things go poorly.

Because you can choose the location of your starting Town Center, you can pick the optimal position to allow for efficient gathering of more than one resource, meaning you should only need to build one additional Ger to cover whatever resource is furthest away. If that's Wood, make sure to pack up and move the Ger to a closer location as needed, rather than building a new one.

Age Advancement

The **Silver Tree** has all of the abilities of a Market, but produces Traders faster and cheaper than one. If you intend on setting up trade routes and want to start benefiting from them as early as possible, this would be the Landmark to pick.

Similar to an Outpost, **Deer Stones** will provide the Yam Speed Aura to any units within its area of influence, but it has the added benefit of granting the **Yam Network** technology to you as soon as it's completed. This Landmark should be considered a more defensive/offensive choice that you should put in a position to apply the **Yam Speed Aura** to your military units either for defending your base or going out on raids.

An early rush Horsemen can be considered successful if you force your opponent to produce Spearmen as a counter, or if you can idle their Villagers. The extra resources from burning a few buildings down at the same time doesn't hurt either.

Feudal Age (Age II)

In Age II, you can continue the aggressive theme with the Mongols by taking even more advantage of your improved production capabilities to quickly mass produce cheap units and apply pressure. While they're contending with the cheap units, start building up a more powerful army with Mangudai once you have enough Gold. You might not be able to fully finish off your opponent during this Age, but if you apply enough pressure with constant raids, you can severely weaken them.

Age Advancement

The **Kurultai** is another Landmark that can be very effectively used either offensively or defensively. When the Khan is near the building, all other units get healed and receive a damage buff, so if your opponent is pressuring you, it can help turn the tide defensively, or you can use it in a forward position to buff your raiding groups.

The **Steppe Redoubt** is an economic focused Landmark; it works the same as a Ger, but any Gold dropped off at it is increased by 50%. If you're struggling with Gold, or just need a lot of it for Lancers and Mangudai, placing this near your mining operation can help a lot.

The Feudal Age is when you should also start to think about where to place your Outposts around the map, with the goal of creating a network of them to apply the Yam Speed Aura to your units.

Castle Age (Age III)

The Castle Age is when the Mongols really start to shine. Now is the time to significantly ramp up production of your cavalry units and use them to launch hit-and-run attacks on your opponent from multiple directions simultaneously. Make full use of all of your Khan's abilities to buff your cavalry units as often as possible. Effective use of your Mangudai can be especially crippling for your opponent, because you can pick off enemy units while minimizing your losses, and then compound the damage by rushing in with superior numbers. If you notice your opponent start to weaken, quickly build a siege Workshop nearby and produce some Mangonels and Traction Trebuchets to support your army and put the final nail in the coffin.

Age Advancement

The **Khaganate** Landmark will make it easier to sustain a high number of cavalry units, because every 90 seconds it will spawn a small group of a random type. If you're a newer player or just struggling with production, this can be a solid choice to go for.

For more advanced warfare and strategies, the **White Stupa** will be more useful overall. It acts like an Ovoo, but it generates more Stone, and doesn't require being built on a Stone Outcropping. It also doesn't destroy your existing Ovoo; with all of the extra Stone and two buildings providing improved technology and production abilities, you gain a lot of possibilities.

Imperial Age (Age IV)

If you didn't finish off your opponent during the Castle Age, then you should try to do so as quickly as possible in the imperial Age, because the power of the Mongols start to trail off in this Age due to the more powerful siege units and static defenses that start coming into play. To keep up, you'll have to make use of your Ovoo to further improve your technologies and reduce the power gap as much as possible.

Ideally you should already have your Outposts placed around the map in such a manner that your whole trade route is affected by the **Yam Speed Aura**, and all of your units can quickly move around the map to places where they need to be. The extra speed will prove very useful for trying to find your opponent's weakpoints. As the Mongols, unless you enter this Age with the advantage, it can be an uphill battle to achieve victory, which is why the Castle Age is so important.

A horde of Lancers and Mangudai led by the Khan is the perfect composition for the Imperial Mongol army. Its speed and flexibility makes it hard for your enemies to keep up.

Mongol Masteries

Under the unifying rule of Genghis Khan, warring Mongolian tribes came together and forged the largest empire the world has ever known. What they lacked in resources, they made up for in cunning, skill, and efficiency. The Mongol Empire aimed for nothing less than world domination.

Profile Image [1]

Text [2]

Coat of Arms Pattern [3]

Coat of Arms Sigil [4]

Monument [5]

Mastery	Objective	Tip	XP	Rewards
Kettle and Smoke	Use the Improved Production ability to produce 6 Villagers before the Feudal Age (II)	Your Town Center must be within the influence of an Ovoo to access Improved Production for Villagers.	1000XP	Sheep [1] Leaving Home [2]
Superior Mobility	Defeat 5 enemies with cavalry before the Feudal Age (II)	The Mongols have the advantage of fast-moving cavalry available during the Dark Age (I).	1000XP	Gazing Sheep [4] The White Camel [2]
Test of Strength I	Win a 1v1 Custom or Skirmish match against the Easy A.I.	Defeat a single Easy A.I. opponent in a Custom or Skirmish match. Go to the Single Player screen to create a Skirmish match.	1000XP	Spill no Blood [2] Mongol Empress [1]
Vacant Steppes	Research Improved Husbandry, then gather 5,000 Food from Sheep	Building a Pasture within the influence of an Ovoo will spawn Sheep faster. Gaining an early Food advantage with well-placed Pastures can secure a stable economy.	1000XP	Mongol Traveler [1] The Joroo Gait [2]
Fire and Stone	Accrue 500 Stone by igniting enemy buildings	Researching Stone Bounty, found in the Ovoo, adds stone as a reward for raiding.	1000XP	Diamond Sigil Frame [4] Arrow Storm [2]
Burnt Offerings	Produce 40 cavalry units using improved production buildings influenced by an Ovoo	Buildings within the influence of an Ovoo can spend Stone on improved production items.Improved production produces two units instead of one.	1000XP	Mongol Cap [1] God Mountain [2]
Test of Strength II	Win a 1v1 Custom or Skirmish match against the Intermediate A.I.	Defeat a single Intermediate A.I. opponent in a Custom or Skirmish match. Go to the Single Player screen to create a Skirmish match.	1000XP	Feigned Retreat [2] Deer Stone [5]
The Silk Road	Construct the Silver Tree Landmark and 5 outposts. Gain the Yam speed aura 40 times with your Traders	Setting up Outposts along your trade route greatly increases the speed of your Traders.	1000XP	Mongol Footman [1] Pax Mongolica [2]
Gather Round	Construct the Kurultai and heal 500 health on your units via the Kurultai	When the Khan is near the Kurultai, other damaged units nearby will be healed.	1000XP	Rearing Horse [4] Sheep Dung [2]
Wolves and Rain	Research the Yam Network, then defeat 30 enemies with your troops unit affected by the Yam speed aura	Yam Network allows any friendly unit to be affected by the Yam speed aura.	1000XP	Signal Arrow [1] Ismail's Trebuchet [2]
Test of Strength III	Win a 1v1 Custom or Skirmish match against the Hard A.I.	Defeat a single Hard A.I. opponent in a Custom or Skirmish match. Go to the Single Player screen to create a Skirmish match.	1000XP	Mongol Horse Archer [1] The Wrestling Vest [2] Mongol Man-At-Arms [5]
Whistling Arrows	Defeat 50 enemies with units affected by the Khan's Signal Arrows. Do not lose your Khan during the match	Use the Mongol's speed and reach advantage to keep troops enhanced and the Khan alive.	1000XP	Khutulun [1] Firing From the Saddle [2] Checkered Banner Pattern [3]
The Heavy Load	Accrue 2,000 Stone using your Traders	Researching Stone Commerce and having 9 or more Traders active allows Traders to supply Stone.	1000XP	White Stupa [1] Hunting with Whistling Arrows [2]
Horn and Sinew	Research the Improved Shia Bow Limbs technology, then defeat 40 enemies with Mangudai, and achieve a Conquest Victory	The Improved Siha Bow Limbs technology is found in the Archery Range.	1000XP	Genghis Khan [1] Magic for War [2]
Test of Strength IV	Win a 1v1 Custom or Skirmish match against the Hardest A.I.	Defeat a single Hardest A.I. opponent in a Custom or Skirmish match. Go to the Single Player screen to create a Skirmish match.	1000XP	Falcon [4] Tender Flesh [2] Khatun [5]

Rus

TIME PERIOD REPRESENTED: 882 - 1547 CE EASE OF USE: ★ ★ ★

Overview

- *Specializes in the Hunting and Gathering of Natural Food Resources.*
- *Great at Taking Map Control.*
- *Formidable Heavy Melee Cavalry, Gunpowder Infantry and Religious Units.*

Starting Resources

Food	Wood	Gold	Stone
200	200	100	0

Play with the Rus if you enjoy playing...

Shang In AoE 1
Cumans in AoE 2
Russians in AoE 3

Bonuses

- *Generate Gold and Increase bounty When Killing Animals.*
- *Early Knight Available in the Feudal Age (II).*
- *Stronger Palisades with Twice as Much Health.*
- *Fishing Ships Don't Have to Return to a Dock to Drop off Food.*

The Rus' focus on wooden structures gives them a defensive advantage during the early stages of a game, with many of their strongest fortifications available early on. Because they can quickly fortify areas, they excel at setting up satellite bases to establish control over key areas of the map, denying opponents access to them.

This notion of satellite bases carries over to their unique bounty system, which encourages exploration and hunting; each kill adds to a bounty total, which affects the rate at which their Hunting Cabins generate Gold. Hunting Cabins need to be placed apart from each other to get the most Gold, and with Villagers gathering near each one, all it takes is a Lumber Camp and a Wooden Fortress to defend them and you have a mini-base; the interplay between these systems and buildings is one of the most crucial aspects of Rus gameplay.

Unique Units

Unit	Description	Page
Streltsy	Gunpowder Unit Which Gets Stronger When Stationary, has a High Melee Attack, and is Cheaper Than a Handcannoneer	P.161
Warrior Monk	Inspires Nearby Units When in Combat, Providing Bonus Armor and Damage	P.162
Lodya Ships	Can be Converted into any Type of Ship	P.198

Strengths

The most obvious strength of the Rus is their ability to passively generate a lot of Gold through their Hunting Cabins and bounty system. Because you can spread the Hunting Cabins out around the map, it's hard for opponents to find and destroy all of them, providing a relatively safe and non-centralized revenue stream. Their strong early wooden defenses also deter early raids, making it easier for you to establish your base and maintain the safety of your Villagers. Early access to heavy melee cavalry lets you begin raiding your opponent to try and cripple their economy while you continue to grow yours.

The safety you have in the early game lets you maintain a strong economy, and then once you reach the later stages of the game you can transfer that economic strength into military might, when their Knights and Streltsy can really shine. Their gameplay is somewhat similar to the English or French, but you have to play to their strengths even more so to get the most out of them.

The Rus are also have a strong naval economy early on, primarily because their Fishing Boats don't need to return a dock to drop-off Food, Not only does this save a lot of time, but it lets you be more flexible in which Fish you choose to harvest because you don't have to concern yourself with long trips back to the Dock.

Weaknesses

Rus players can often focus heavily on the bounty system and setting up hunting cabins early in games, and that can be used against them. If you use your own Scouts or small raiding groups to kill animals around the map and try to deny them prime Hunting Cabin placement areas, if they haven't put any Villagers on Gold, you can cripple their Gold income. There's also a learning curve to get used to in not being able to rely on Stone defenses later in the game. You have to get creative with your fortifications, come up with other ways to shore up your defense and resign yourself to the fact that, at the later stages of the game, your wooden defenses can be overcome by both melee and siege units.

Age I

Age II

Age III

Age IV

Age I - Dark Age	Age II - Feudal Age	Age III - Castle Age	Age IV - Imperial Age
TOWN CENTER [P.234]			
Villager [P.137] Scout [P.135]	Textiles [P.52]		
HOUSE [P.221]			
HUNTING CABIN [P.222]			
Scout [P.135] Wheelbarrow [P.52] Survival Techniques [P.51]	Professional Scouts [P.49] Horticulture [P.48]	Fertilization [P.47]	Prescision Cross-Breeding [P.49]
LUMBER CAMP [P.223]			
Forestry [P.48]	Double Broadax [P.47]	Lumber Preservation [P.49]	Crosscut Saw [P.46]
MINING CAMP [P.229]			
	Specialized Pick [P.50]	Acid Distillation [P.45]	Cupellation [P.46]
FARM [P.216]			
BARRACKS [P.242]			
Spearman [P.158]	Hardened Spearman [P.158]	Veteran Spearman [P.158] Man-at-Arms [P.150]	Elite Spearman [P.158] Elite Man-at-Arms [P.150]
DOCK [P.246]			
Lodya Fishing Boat [P.198] Lodya Transport Ship [P.198]	Lodya Trade Ship [P.198] Lodya Attack Ship [P.198] Extended Lines [P.47] Additional Sails [P.45]	Lodya Demolition Ship [P.196] Drift Nets [P.47] Navigator Lookout [P.49] Armored Hull [P.45] Clinker Constr. [P.46]	Cedar Hulls [P.46] Explosives [P.47]
FORTIFIED PALISADE WALL [P.272]			
FORTIFIED PALISADE GATE [P.272]			
WOODEN FORTRESS [P.270]			
Castle Turret [P.46] Castle Watch [P.46]	Arrowslits [P.45]	Springald Emplacement [P.51]	
KREMLIN [P.299]			
		Springald Emplacement [P.51]	
THE GOLDEN GATE [P.300]			
	TOWN CENTER [P.234]		
	Villager [P.137] Scout [P.135] Textiles [P.52]		
	MARKET [P.225]		
	Trader [P.136]		
	BLACKSMITH [P.260]		
	Bloomery [P.45] Steeled Arrow [P.51] Fitted Leatherwork [P.47] Iron Undermesh [P.48] Siege Engineering [P.50]	Decarbonization [P.47] Balanced Projectiles [P.45] Insulated Helm [P.48] Wedge Rivets [P.52] Military Academy [P.49]	Damascus Steel [P.47] Platecutter Point [P.49] Master Smiths [P.49] Angled Surfaces [P.45]

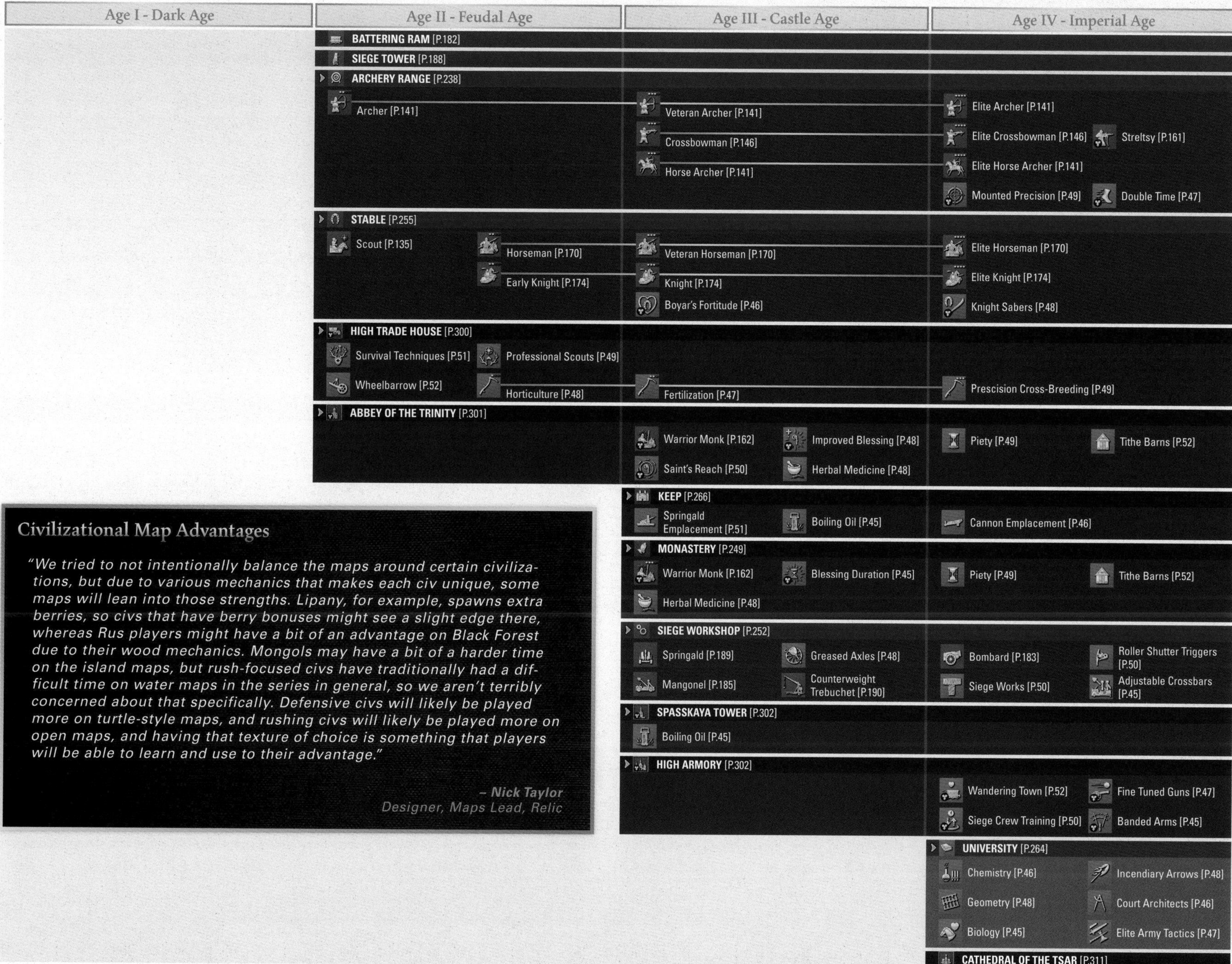

Civilizational Map Advantages

"We tried to not intentionally balance the maps around certain civilizations, but due to various mechanics that makes each civ unique, some maps will lean into those strengths. Lipany, for example, spawns extra berries, so civs that have berry bonuses might see a slight edge there, whereas Rus players might have a bit of an advantage on Black Forest due to their wood mechanics. Mongols may have a bit of a harder time on the island maps, but rush-focused civs have traditionally had a difficult time on water maps in the series in general, so we aren't terribly concerned about that specifically. Defensive civs will likely be played more on turtle-style maps, and rushing civs will likely be played more on open maps, and having that texture of choice is something that players will be able to learn and use to their advantage."

– Nick Taylor
Designer, Maps Lead, Relic

Civilization Features

Hunting Bounties

This system is the driving force that encourages you to explore as much of the map as possible with your Scout at the start of each game. Every animal that you kill will net you a bounty of Gold, and as your total adds up, you'll progress through the reward tiers. Not only does this significantly increase the gathering rate of your Villagers, but the Gold generation cycle for your Hunting Cabins gets a lot shorter, leading to more Gold income. Early in the game, the extra Gold from this system can allow you to advance to the next Age faster than other civilizations, and you can also get away with assigning fewer Villagers to gather Gold early on if you're confident in your hunting skills.

Rus bounty system

Tier	Gold Req.	Gathering Boost	Gold Gen. Cycle
1	100	+5% Villager Food Harvest Rate	27s
2	250	+10% Villager Food Harvest Rate	24s
3	500	+15% Villager Food Harvest Rate	18s

Gold bounty Values	
Sheep	+5
Deer	+10
Wolf	+25
Boar	+75

You can still get Gold from killing animals after reaching tier three of the bounty system, so it's worth continuing to have your Scout go around killing things for the extra income, especially during the early stages of the game.

Hunting Cabins

Rus Hunting Cabins are intrinsically linked to the bounty system, and learning how to use them together effectively is an important process for any new Rus player. Once placed, a Hunting Cabin will start passively generating Gold every 30 seconds, with the amount you get each cycle being determined by the number of trees near the cabin at the time of its construction. You get 0.45 Gold per tree, and you can safely cut down the trees after building the cabin because it locks the number in when the cabin is placed. As you progress through the tiers in the bounty system, each cycle will get shorter, netting you even more Gold.

You can't simply place all of your cabins in one location near a large number of trees, however, because if the aura of two cabins overlaps, no Gold will be generated. Hunting Cabins can also produce Scouts and serve as a drop-off locations, so as your Scouts hunt animals, you can assign Villagers to them to gather and return the Food left nearby.

It's only possible to generate a maximum of 250 Gold per cycle with your Hunting Cabins, so keep an eye on their info panel to see how much each one is generating, and stop building them once you have enough to hit that cap.

Wooden Fortifications

The Rus have access to a unique set of wooden fortifications that are significantly sturdier than those available to other civilizations. Fortified Palisade defenses have far more health than the normal versions, and while they're not immune to damage by melee units, they can withstand a lot more punishment before they crumble. This means your opponent will have to commit more units to break though, and you'll have additional time to react to attacks.

Continuing their theme of improving upon traditional wooden defenses, they've also taken the humble Outpost and turned it into a Wooden Fortress. These structures are one of the strongest early-game defensive buildings because they have more health and garrison spots than a normal Outpost. You can also increase the offensive capabilities of the Wooden Fortress early in games thanks to the **Castle Turret** and **Castle Watch** upgrades, which are available in Age I and only have a small cost in Stone. They also have an influence range, and any Lumber Camp or Town Center placed within it returns 20% more Wood, so if you're placing one near those buildings, it won't take long for you to recoup the cost.

A Transformative Navy

The Rus navy is rather unique. Their array of ships is similar to those of every other civilization, but every one of these ships is capable of turning into any other ship at a moment's notice. This makes them highly adaptable, allowing you to adapt to situations quickly. If your Fishing Ships are getting attacked, turn them into Attack Ships, or if you spot a target of opportunity, turn your Attack Ship into a Demolition Ship and blow it up—the possibilities are endless.

General Playstyle

Using the economic flexibility of the bounty system and Hunting Cabins, along with the strong early game defensive capabilities of the Wooden Fortress, your goal as the Rus should be to expand out from your base, establishing a presence over as much of the map as possible, as quickly as you can. This expansion and exploitation of natural resources is at the heart of Rus gameplay, and while it can be slow to build up, with time and effort you can turn them into a sprawling economic powerhouse that can trample opponents under the hooves of their powerful cavalry.

Dark Age (Age I)

Your primary goal in Age I should be progressing through the tiers of the bounty system, which means you'll need to do a lot of exploring and hunting with your Scout. Try to focus on Deer and Wolves, because Boar are too strong for your Scout to take on alone. Using this method you can often collect the Gold required for your Age II Landmark without having to put any of your Villagers to work mining it, allowing you to use them on other resources. This is quite a busy Age for the Rus, and you'll be required to do a lot of multitasking with different groups of units around the map if you don't want to fall behind your opponent.

The trail of bodies left behind by your Scout is ripe for harvesting by those Villagers, so now is the time to start your expansion. Look for a group of corpses that's also near some trees, and then send eight Villagers in total to that area to set up a small base—since that's how many you can fit into a Wooden Fortress. Have them build a Hunting Cabin and a Lumber Camp, and then split those Villagers between Food and Wood gathering. Try to set up multiple of these small bases around the map throughout the game and when you have the Wood, add a Wooden Fortress near each gathering operation to both increase your overall Wood income, and to provide some defensive capabilities. This opening Age is going to be Wood and Food intensive and requires most of your Villagers, which is why you'll need to be very proactive with your hunting to bring in the Gold.

Age Advancement

If you're focusing a lot of your resources on establishing smaller bases around the map, then you may have been neglecting the defense of your main base; the **Kremlin** can go some way to alleviating that problem. It's essentially a Wooden Fortress that comes fully loaded with nearly all of the technologies and upgrades already unlocked, so it's an early game defensive powerhouse.

The **Golden Gate** on the other hand is a purely economic Landmark. This Landmark is similar to a Market, but instead of trading as much as you want, it generates one unit of supplies every minute, and these supplies can be used to favorably complete one transaction—either buying or selling. If you're attempting a strategy that requires a lot of a specific resource, this Landmark can make things easier for you.

If an enemy does attack one of your satellite bases, quickly garrison your Villagers in the Wooden Fortress to fend them off.

Feudal Age (Age II)

Depending on the map and your opponent, you'll have to approach this Age either more defensively or more aggressively. Your Wood income should be sufficient to add a Wooden Fortress near every hunting and gathering base that you've established, allowing you to secure positions on the map that would normally be too risky to take. If you're on a map with a large number of forests and animals, this strategy is even more effective.

Because of the high Food income, your spread out base and powerful early cavalry you should build a Stable and start producing Horsemen as your main military unit, adding in Early Knights when Gold permits. Having cavalry on the field makes it much easier and faster to get reinforcements to one of your camps if it comes under attack. You can also use them to form raiding parties to attack your opponent's base, which has the added benefit of keeping them distracted and not searching for your smaller camps.

Early Knights are a great tool to reinforce attacked locations around the map. They are sturdy, mobile and can go on the offensive themselves.

The additional potential Food income from hunting should enable you to outproduce your opponent, as long as you're distributing your Villagers to take advantage of it. Using your Villagers in this way does take some getting used to, but the more you practice the more efficient you'll become at it. If you've built enough Hunting Cabins, you should have enough passive Gold generation to cover a decent amount of unit production, and if you're getting the maximum amount of Gold for them, it will only take a minute to generate the amount of Gold required for your next Landmark. If you want to start acquiring more upgrades, however, then now is the time to begin putting additional Villagers to work gathering Gold.

Age Advancement

The **High Trade House** is a perfect Landmark if you're looking to expand your economy. It behaves similar to a Hunting Cabin, but it generates a lot more Gold, and automatically spawns a Deer nearby periodically, making it a one-stop-shop for any number of your economic needs.

If you're looking to secure Relics quickly, or push your opponent during the Castle Age, then the cheaper Warrior Monk production and unique religious technologies provided by the **Abbey of Trinity** could be highly beneficial to you.

Castle Age (Age III)

Warrior Monks are one of the strongest military support units in the game, so from now on they should be a mainstay in all of your armies. Warrior Monks are not the only new cavalry unit the Rus get in this Age—there's also the addition of Horse Archers. If you were producing Horsemen and Knights in the previous Age, then it's worth switching to Horse Archers in this Age to round out your army as quickly as possible, counter the anti-cavalry Infantry of your opponent, and then transition back to a more balanced approach. Horse Archers should be used in much the same way as normal Archers, with the addition of superior mobility.

Add some powerful siege units to your cavalry army during the Castle Age to minimize the damage your army takes when attacking fortified positions.

Warrior Monks are a great addition for the Rus army and can be made right after reaching Age III through the ***Abbey of Trinity*** *Landmark.*

The Feudal and Dark Ages are the most intensive for the Rus, so if you've made it this far and your economy is nicely established, then it's time to focus on growing and upgrading your military. While most of the unique Rus upgrades are focused on their cavalry and more expensive units, it's important not to overlook basic units like Archers and Spearmen. These units are fast and cheap to produce, and can add a lot of value when mixed in with your more expensive units, especially if they're getting buffed by your Warrior Monks and used to counter specific enemy units.

Age Advancement

The **Spasskaya Tower** is great for solidifying the defense of a key area, or if you've managed to establish a forward base near your opponent, it can help secure your foothold there to maintain pressure. The fact that it comes fully loaded with all of the weapon emplacements of a Keep, and additional health, makes it a very safe choice regardless of how you intend on using it.

The **High Armory** allows you to produce siege units 20% cheaper from any Siege Workshop next to it, and it offers you a wide variety of unique siege engine related technologies. This is a good Landmark to pick if you need a lot of siege equipment to assault an entrenched opponent, or just want to improve the overall strength of your military.

Imperial Age (Age IV)

One of your first priorities in this Age should be to build a University and research **Chemistry** so that you can improve the attack of your Streltsy and make them the most powerful gunpowder infantry unit in the game. Streltsy are at their best when you can leave them stationary for a while—they'll build up their **Static Deployment** charges to increase their damage output—which makes them perfectly suited to defending an area. Their slow movement speed can make it awkward to time assaults when you're combining them with your cavalry, but if you can get them into position behind your melee cavalry and don't have to move them, they can inflict huge amounts of damage to your opponent's army.

This can be quite an expensive Age if you're producing a lot of Streltsy and Knights, and if the game is close, it'll be important to make sure your Gold-generating Hunting Cabins remain safe. While the Gold income from them alone is not enough to sustain your military production (Trade will still be your main source of Gold), it will certainly offset some of the costs. Using the Streltsy to guard them against attacks from small raiding groups can be quite effective, and you can keep using the cheaper Horse Archers as the ranged contingent of your main army.

Streltsy are the most powerful gunpowder unit in the game and are one of the go to units for the Rus in Age IV.

2

Rus Masteries

Hardened by devastating invasions, political instability, and long, bitter winters, the Rus were built for survival. Masters of hunting, trade, and wooden construction, they would rebuild their broken realm, as their leaders fought to birth a new empire under Moscow.

- Profile Image [1]
- Text [2]
- Coat of Arms Pattern [3]
- Coat of Arms Sigil [4]
- Monument [5]

Mastery	Requirement	Description	XP	Rewards
Hunting Grounds	Accumulate 50 bounty by hunting Sheep, Deer, or Boar in the Dark Age (I)	The Rus can achieve special bonuses and Gold by accruing bounty – which is gained by hunting animals in the wild. The rarer the animal, the higher the bounty. Boar are worth the most bounty, then Wolves, Deer, and lastly Sheep.	1000XP	Rus Forester [1] The Forest Provides [2]
Foresters	Construct 4 Lumber Camps within the range of influence of a Wooden Fortress	Villagers dropping off harvested Wood to a Lumber Camp within the influence of a Wooden Fortress receive additional Wood for their efforts.	1000XP	The Wolf Hunt [2] Rounded Banner Shape [3]
Test of Strength I	Win a 1v1 Custom or Skirmish match against the Easy A.I.	Defeat a single Easy A.I. opponent in a Custom or Skirmish match. Go to the Single Player screen to create a Skirmish match.	1000XP	Battle on the Ice [2] Boar [1]
On the Wild Side	Accrue 250 Gold from Hunting Cabins in the Dark Age (I)	Choose your placement for Hunting Cabins strategically. The farther into the wilderness – especially near wooded areas – the more Gold you will receive. Hunting Cabins are more effective when you have earned a high bounty total.	1000XP	Elena Glinskaya [1] The Fur Trade [2]
Birch Barricades	Construct 25 Fortified Palisade Walls with Villagers in the Dark Age (I)	The Rus' Palisade Walls are more effective than that of other civilizations.	1000XP	The Moscow Kremlin [2] Boar's Head [4]
Frontier Trading	Use the Golden Gate Landmark to make 5 traders in the Feudal Age (II)	The Rus can use the Golden Gate Landmark to trade resources.	1000XP	Rus Scout [1] A Crowded Winter [2]
Test of Strength II	Win a 1v1 Custom or Skirmish match against the Intermediate A.I.	Defeat a single Intermediate A.I. opponent in a Custom or Skirmish match. Go to the Single Player screen to create a Skirmish match.	1000XP	Rivals for the Throne [2] Forester [5]
Day and Knight	Defeat 15 enemies with Early Knights in the Feudal Age (II)	Rus gain access to Knights earlier than other civilizations – beat the rush with a rush of your own.	1000XP	Olga of Kiev [1] The Monk and the Mongol [2]
Divinity	Defeat 30 enemies with units affected by Saint's Blessing	Warrior Monks are fearsome fighters that do well in the center of battle. While fighting, Warrior Monks trigger Saint's Blessing – which improves the effectiveness of nearby combatants.	1000XP	Hand Ax [4] The Treading Square [2]
Mount the Attack	Research Boyar's Fortitude and Mounted Precision and then defeat 30 enemies with cavalry	Research Boyar's Fortitude and Mounted Precision in the Stables.	1000XP	Rus Horse Archer [1] Wandering Town [2]
Test of Strength III	Win a 1v1 Custom or Skirmish match against the Hard A.I.	Defeat a single Hard A.I. opponent in a Custom or Skirmish match. Go to the Single Player screen to create a Skirmish match.	1000XP	Rus Streltsy [1] The Reign of Elena [2] Streltsy [5]
Lay Siege	Research two upgrades from the High Armory and produce 20 siege engines in the Imperial Age (IV)	The High Armory contains unique technologies for Rus siege engines – which can strengthen your hold on the late game.	1000XP	Druzhina Knight [1] Rise and Fall of the Streltsy [2] Seal of Ivan
Black Powder	Research Double Time from the Archery Range and defeat 30 enemies with Streltsy	Research Double Time in the Archery Range.	1000XP	Rus Warrior Monk [1] The Boyars [2]
Ours is the Glory	Achieve a Sacred Victory with fully upgraded Warrior Monks	Construct the Abbey of the Trinity Landmark to gain access to unique Warrior Monk technologies – Saint's Reach and Improved Blessing. The Herbal Medicine, Piety, and Blessing Duration upgrades can be found in the Monastery as well.	1000XP	Ivan the Terrible [1] The Tsar and the Church [2]
Test of Strength IV	Win a 1v1 Custom or Skirmish match against the Hardest A.I.		1000XP	RightQuadrant Pattern [3] Fear and Control [2] Warrior Monk [5]

Delhi Sultanate

TIME PERIOD REPRESENTED: 879 - 1526 CE EASE OF USE: 

Overview

- *Weak in the Early Game, but Exceptional in the Late Game.*
- *Difficult to Master.*
- *Specializes in Powerful Elephant Units.*
- *Researches Technologies for Free, but at a Slower Rate.*

Play with the Delhi Sultanate if you enjoy playing...

Carthaginians or Persians in **AoE 1**
Malay, Byzantines, or Persians in **AoE 2**
Indians in **AoE 3**

Starting Resources

200	250	100	0

Bonuses

- *Gather from Berry Bushes 25% Faster but Cannot Gather From Boar.*
- *Scholar Available in the Dark Age (I).*
- *Infantry Units Able to Construct Defenses.*
- *Fishing Ships Equipped With an Archer.*

The Delhi Sultanate is a civilization that starts off relatively slowly and gradually builds in strength as the game progresses, until they become a late-game powerhouse. They have a unique way of researching technology: it requires no resource costs, but takes additional time to complete. In the spirit of collaborative learning, however, when multiple Scholars are garrisoned inside of a Mosque or Madrasa, they can reduce research time in nearby buildings. This unique approach to research and base building means that you'll need a lot of strategic forethought if you want to fully develop your empire. When your planning begins to bear fruit, though, you'll be rewarded with access to some of the most powerful land units in the game.

Unique Units

Unit	Description	Page
Scholar	When Garrisoned Inside of a Mosque, Scholars speed up Technology Research	P.157
War Elephant	High Health and Damage Unit With a Strong Siege Attack	P.179
Tower War Elephant	Imposing Ranged Unit That Can Fire While Moving and also has a Strong Siege Attack	P.178

Strengths

The Delhi Sultanate's strength doesn't become fully apparent until the later stages of a game. Their ability to research technology and upgrades without resource costs makes them less constrained by their economy, which results in a lot of flexibility. It does take some time to produce and garrison all of the required Scholars, and this is what makes the Delhi Sultanate get off to a slow start. Once this process gets going, however, it leads to an accumulative effect as they get exponentially stronger in each Age. The Delhi Sultanate can eventually field the mighty War Elephants, which are devastating and versatile units capable of dominating in combat. They also have a lot of technologies that enhance their overall defensive and economic capabilities, so they can be equally strong regardless of your preferred playstyle.

Weaknesses

Due to their slow research speed, the Delhi Sultanate will quickly fall behind other civilizations in terms of technology, meaning you'll often find yourself on the back foot during the early phases of the game. You'll have to play defensively and try to survive until all of the benefits from technologies and upgrades start to kick in. Being adaptable and having a lot of knowledge of the other civilizations' capabilities is crucial, making them a difficult civilization for new players to succeed with. If you're playing against the Delhi Sultanate, it's important to capitalize on their early game weakness by playing aggressively and trying to be as disruptive as possible to slow down their advancement.

Age I

Age II

Age III

Age IV

Building	Age I - Dark Age	Age II - Feudal Age	Age III - Castle Age	Age IV - Imperial Age
TOWN CENTER [P.234]	Villager [P.137] Scout [P.135]	Textiles [P.52]		
HOUSE [P.221]				
MOSQUE [P.249]	Scholar [P.157] Sanctity [P.50] Efficient Production [P.47] Herbal Medicine [P.48] Piety [P.49]	All-Seeing Eye [P.45]	Swiftness [P.51]	Zeal [P.52] Tithe Barns [P.52]
MILL [P.227]	Survival Techniques [P.51] Wheelbarrow [P.52]	Professional Scouts [P.49] Horticulture [P.48]	Fertilization [P.47]	Prescision Cross-Breeding [P.49]
LUMBER CAMP [P.223]	Forestry [P.48]	Double Broadax [P.47]	Lumber Preservation [P.49]	Crosscut Saw [P.46]
MINING CAMP [P.229]		Specialized Pick [P.50]	Acid Distillation [P.45]	Cupellation [P.46]
FARM [P.216]				
BARRACKS [P.242]	Spearman [P.158]	Hardened Spearman [P.158]	Veteran Spearman [P.158] Man-at-Arms [P.150]	Elite Spearman [P.158] Elite Man-at-Arms [P.150]
DOCK [P.246]	Fishing Boat [P.191] Transport Ship [P.192]	Trade Ship [P.193] Dhow [P.202] Extended Lines [P.47] Patchwork Repairs [P.49]	Baghlah [P.200] Explosive Dhow [P.202] Drift Nets [P.47] Navigator Lookout [P.49] Armored Hull [P.45]	Xebec [P.204] Chaser Cannons [P.46] Explosives [P.47]
PALISADE WALL [P.272]				
PALISADE GATE [P.272]				
OUTPOST [P.270]		Arrowslits [P.45] Fortify Outpost [P.48]	Springald Emplacement [P.51]	Cannon Emplacement [P.46]
TOWER OF VICTORY [P.303]				
DOME OF THE FAITH [P.304]	Scholar [P.157]			
TOWN CENTER [P.234]		Villager [P.137] Scout [P.135] Textiles [P.52]		
MARKET [P.225]		Trader [P.136]		
BLACKSMITH [P.260]		Bloomery [P.45] Steeled Arrow [P.51]	Decarbonization [P.47] Balanced Projectiles [P.45]	Damascus Steel [P.47] Platecutter Point [P.49]

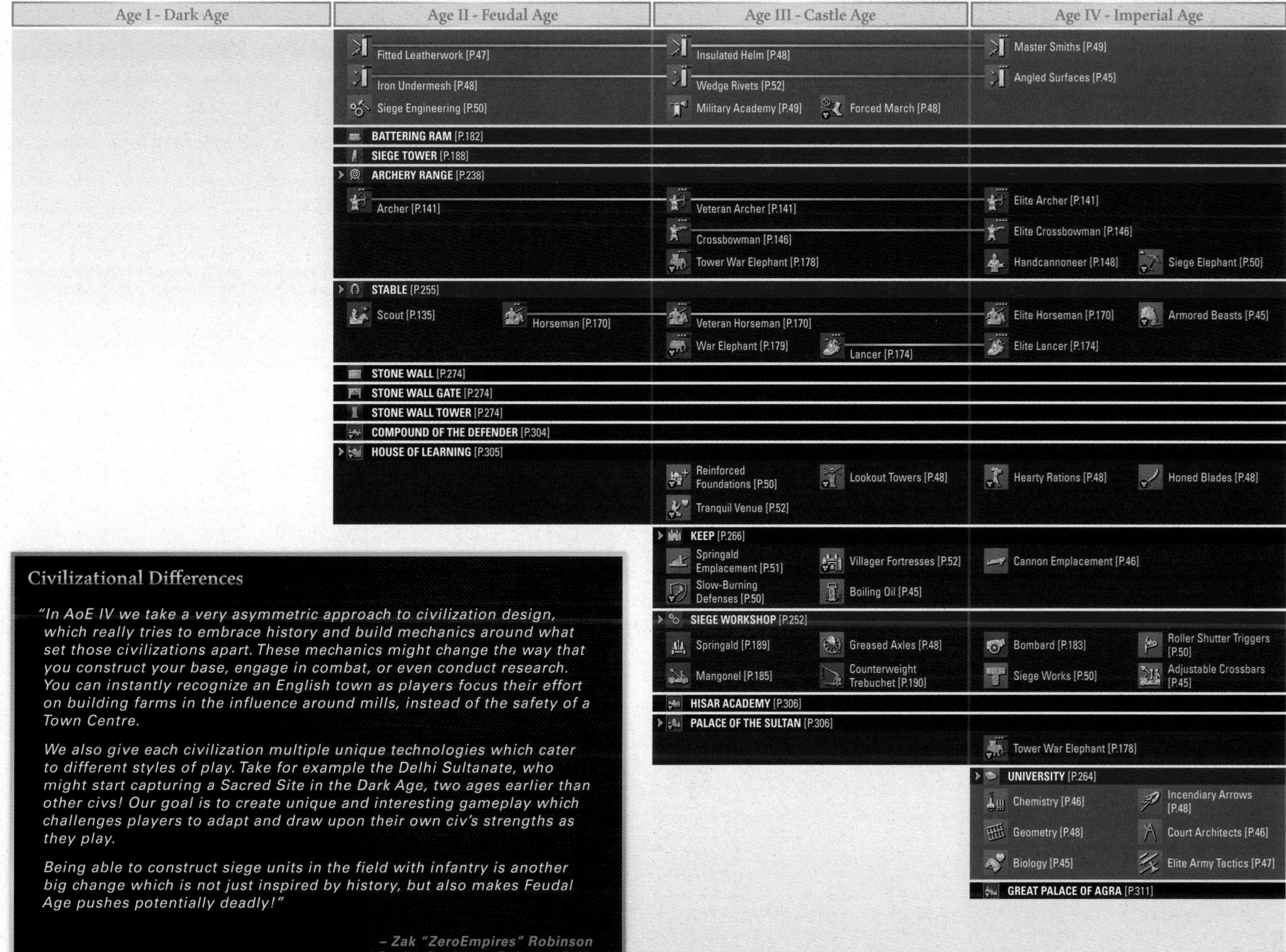

Civilizational Differences

"In AoE IV we take a very asymmetric approach to civilization design, which really tries to embrace history and build mechanics around what set those civilizations apart. These mechanics might change the way that you construct your base, engage in combat, or even conduct research. You can instantly recognize an English town as players focus their effort on building farms in the influence around mills, instead of the safety of a Town Centre.

We also give each civilization multiple unique technologies which cater to different styles of play. Take for example the Delhi Sultanate, who might start capturing a Sacred Site in the Dark Age, two ages earlier than other civs! Our goal is to create unique and interesting gameplay which challenges players to adapt and draw upon their own civ's strengths as they play.

Being able to construct siege units in the field with infantry is another big change which is not just inspired by history, but also makes Feudal Age pushes potentially deadly!"

– Zak "ZeroEmpires" Robinson
Senior Designer, Balance, Relic

Civilization Features

Scholarly Research

The Delhi Sultanate have the ability to freely research all technology and upgrades without having to pay any cost. However, the completion time of their research is significantly longer than that of other civilizations. It is possible to reduce that research time, but you'll need to take advantage of the unique interplay between Delhi Sultanate Scholars and some of their buildings to do so.

Unlike most civilizations, the Delhi Sultanate can construct their religious building—the Mosque—from the start of the game in Age I, and the first one built also comes with a free Scholar. Mosques also have a large area of influence around them, and you can garrison up to three Scholars in each one. Every Scholar garrisoned adds to your total global count, but each one garrisoned reduces the research time by slightly less than the previous one. Any building placed within the influence range of any Mosque can reap the full benefit of your total garrisoned Scholars. With the **Efficient Production** technology available at a Mosque, you can also enable your Scholars to garrison military buildings, speeding up their production time by 100%.

Later in the game when you get access to a Madrasa, it too can provide all of the same benefits as a Mosque. If you plan ahead and arrange your bases with this in mind, it's possible to have every building capable of researching something within this influence area so they can reap the benefits. Any technology you're interested in researching should be started immediately, regardless of how many Scholars you have, because the research time will automatically get reduced every time you garrison a new Scholar.

With nine Scholars garrisoned you can bring the research time in line with other civilizations, all while still being able to research them for free.

When you stop researching something as the Delhi Sultanate you'll retain any of the progress you made. This is indicated by a small progress bar at the bottom of the icon when you look at it in the building's menu. If you decide you need a different piece of technology from a building than the one you're currently researching there, this system allows you to stop that one, switch to a different technology, and then resume the one you were researching and pick up exactly where you left off. Investing in more Scholars, Mosques, and Madrasa and making full use of the Scholar research system is vital to the long-term prospects of the Delhi Sultanate in any game, and mastering it is a big part of learning to play as them.

Infantry Builders

Unlike other civilizations, the Delhi Sultanate's infantry units are able to construct Palisade Walls and Gates by default, and if you build the **Compound of the Defender** Age III Landmark, they'll also be able to build Stone Walls and Gates. Given their slow start in games, the ability to construct early-game defenses—without having to take Villagers away from precious resource gathering—is extremely important, and something you should always take advantage of. Later in games, this ability can also be used offensively to wall in opponents, or fortify strategic positions close to their base without needing to bring Villagers to the front lines.

Orchards

Usually, Berries are a slow source of Food income, with animals being a much-preferred early game Food. Delhi Sultanate Villagers, however, have developed special harvesting techniques that allow them to gather Berries 25% faster than Villagers of most other civilizations. This brings Berries almost to the level of Deer, and equal to Sheep in terms of Food income rate, although the **Survival Techniques** technology can further improve gathering rates from Deer. Building a Mill near Berry bushes will also increase their yield, turning them into Orchards.

Because you always start with a few Berry Bushes near your Town Center, they're a very safe option for Food. Normally you would have to choose between the safety of the Berries or the risky, but faster Food gathering from animals. As the Delhi Sultanate, you want to stay off your enemy's radar as much as possible, which makes hunting a risk; the increased gathering rate, and increased yield, means you can have the best of both worlds. Focusing on Berries in the early part of the game also saves you a lot of Wood that otherwise would have to go towards building Farms, but can now be used for other buildings or fortifications.

As the Delhi Sultanate, if you build a Mill near Berry Bushes they'll turn into Orchards that have twice as much available Food to gather.

Elephant Warfare

Being able to develop as a technological powerhouse would mean nothing if there were no units to take advantage of all of the upgrades, and in Tower War Elephants and War Elephants, the Delhi Sultanate have some of the most devastating. These powerful and noble creatures have been highly trained in the art of war, and on their own are capable of more destruction than most other units in the game. Each elephant is also manned by an infantry unit that can attack, making them even deadlier. This combination of attack types, in conjunction with their incredibly high health and defense, make elephant units an essential component of end game Delhi Sultanate gameplay.

Your already built Scholars can be used to heal wounded Elephant units, making them even more durable. Even on the battlefield Scholars are a really useful tool to sway the battle in your favor.

Contested Waters

While the Delhi Sultanate often favor defense and passivity during the early stages of the game, on water maps they have a unique opportunity for some early game aggression. Delhi Sultanate Fishing Ships are manned by an Archer, and thus are the only ship capable of attacking during Age I. Armed with this ability you can use your Fishing Ships to disrupt the Food income of your opponent by attacking their Fishing Ships, or even attacking their Villagers as they gather Shoreline Fish. Due to the fact that Docks can heal ships, you're unlikely to destroy any ships doing this, because your opponent will simply withdraw them, but with enough harassment, you can have a significant impact on their economy.

General Playstyle

Delhi Sultanate gameplay involves a lot of patience and careful planning, where each seemingly small move or building placement at the start of the game is all part of an elaborate scheme that will only become apparent to your opponent when it's too late for them to stop it. This slow-burn gameplay style requires careful weighing of options, aiming to strike a balance between projecting strength while building, but not being too greedy as to overextend yourself and expose your weaknesses. Once you finally have all of the pieces in place, you can unleash—seemingly out of nowhere—a deadly herd of elephants upon your opponent.

Dark Age (Age I)

Starting a game with the Delhi Sultanate following the same basic structure as other civilizations usually results in falling dangerously behind your opponent, so some key adjustments to your game plan are needed. Because Berries are a good, safe, source of Food for the Delhi Sultanate, building a Mill close to the nearby bushes so always be one of your first tasks.

Your next building should be a Lumber Camp as usual, but after that you should build a Mosque, ideally in a place where as many buildings as possible will benefit from its area of influence. As soon as it's placed, start researching technologies straight away in the order that best serves your strategy, because until you get more Scholars, the time required is going to be very long. You should usually stick with a single Scholar in this Age, because it's not worth delaying advancement to the Feudal Age just to produce an extra one. Similarly, the free research doesn't actually aid you a lot in this Age because there simply aren't enough technologies to research.

*The **Sanctity** technology available at the Mosque in the Dark Age should be one of the first things you start researching. With this technology, Delhi Sultanate Scholars can capture Sacred Sites from this Age onwards, rather than waiting until the Castle Age like other civilizations. Any you control will also generate +100% more Gold, which can help offset early game Scholar production costs.*

Age Advancement

Under nearly all circumstances, the **Dome of the Faith** Landmark will lead to faster progress towards a strong economy and military than the **Tower of Victory**, thanks to its ability to produce your essential Scholars for -50% less than a Mosque.

Any infantry unit that passes near the **Tower of Victory's** will have its attack speed permanently increased by 15%. In scenarios where you're playing very aggressively, or your opponent has you pinned back, this extra attack speed can be just the thing to gain an immediate advantage, and will still benefit you for the rest of the match.

2

Feudal Age (Age I)

Among of the first things you'll often have to do in this Age are building a Barracks and an Archery Range to begin producing a few infantry units to defend your base. You should then have them build walls around parts of your base, and begin upgrading to Hardened Spearmen straight away, since there's no cost. Your opponent likely knows that stopping the Delhi Sultanate early in the game is their best option, and this is the Age where you'll often have to start fending off their attacks. Remember that if you try to mirror the aggressive play of your opponent, you'll likely be at a disadvantage at this point of the game, so stay defensive and play within your means.

Given the number of potential technologies and upgrades that become available to you in this Age, this is when you should begin ramping up your research ability. Because you don't need to worry about research costs, nearly all of your Gold can go towards Scholar production. To speed that process up, start by building a second Mosque, making sure to place it near any buildings that are not within the influence range of your first Mosque. If you have the Wood, it's also worth building more than one Blacksmith so that you can research multiple upgrades simultaneously.

The difficulty here lies in weighing your options. Invest too much of your resources in technology and related buildings and you'll fall further behind with your military; invest too little, and your opponent will be knocking on your door with a full army by the time everything is researched. You need to pay attention to the flow of the game and try to gauge how your opponent is playing, and then invest your resources accordingly.

Age Advancement

As its name suggests, the **Compound of the Defender** is aimed squarely at defensive play. With it, infantry gain the ability to construct Stone Walls and Gates in addition to Palisades, and it also reduces the Stone cost of buildings and emplacements by 25%. If you need to buy yourself more time to grow your economy by further securing your base, then this Landmark can help.

The **House of Learning** is designed with the long game in mind, because it gives you access to five unique technologies that can be used to improve a number of different gameplay aspects—all you need to do is choose the order based on your needs.

Having your infantry build walls early in games allows you to still establish a defensive perimeter to keep you safe until you reach your full potential later on, while also freeing up your Villagers for more resource gathering.

Castle Age (Age III)

Arguably more so than with any other civilization, how you enter the Castle Age and deal with the situations within it can vary greatly based on the number of small choices you made along the way to get here. There is, however, one constant: you will gain access to War Elephants. With their tremendous cost, producing more than a few of them during this Age will prove difficult, especially if you don't want to delay entering the Imperial Age for a long time. You'll therefore need to support your elephant units with much cheaper infantry, as well as some Scholars to help keep them alive so you don't lose your iinvestment. To further aid elephant production, make sure you've researched Efficient Production from a Mosque so that you can garrison Scholars in your production buildings and reduce their production time. Three Mosques is a good number to aim for to ensure you're producing Scholars fast enough to ensure that upgrades and production is moving forward smoothly.

Elephants are extremely versatile, and can serve as both a powerful melee/ranged unit, and a siege weapon that's capable of tearing down Stone Walls and buildings. Just make sure to keep an eye on your population capacity, because each elephant takes up three population spaces.

To prepare for heavier production of elephants during the Imperial Age, you should spend a bit of time making sure your economy is set up to handle the strain. Aim for around 120+ Villagers in total; while that may sound like a lot, anything less and you won't be able to keep up with production, even with all of the economic technologies. If this means you need to produce a lot more Villagers, make sure to build additional Town Centers to speed that up. It's worth also building a Market now to establish a trade route for extra Gold income.

Age Advancement

The **Hisar Academy** is an interesting Landmark that has the potential to either change how your resource gathering Villagers are allocated, or how you much you engage with a Market. One Food is automatically generated every five seconds at this building, for every technology that has been researched. If you've been researching everything, this can add up to a lot of Food income, allowing you to either have fewer Villagers on Food, or sell some of that Food at a Market for additional Gold.

Similarly, the **Palace of the Sultan** can save you a lot of resources in the Imperial Age. This Landmark will automatically produce Tower War Elephants, the rate at which you can speed up by garrisoning Scholars inside. At its fastest with four garrisoned Scholars, it will produce one elephant every 1m 40s, which is only 40 seconds slower than at an Archery Range.

Imperial Age (Age IV)

If you decided to opt for the **Palace of the Sultan** Landmark, it can be beneficial to move some of your Scholars from other buildings to that one, so that you increase the rate at which it generates a Tower War Elephant. In this Age you now have access to a Madrasa, so build two or more of them (and produce more Scholars if you moved some to the Palace of the Sultan) to ensure that you research everything as quickly as possible.

Accumulating a large group of elephant units with a few siege engines—or a similar unit that's effective at taking down the Spearmen your opponent is likely to throw at your elephants—should be your primary goal at the start of this Age. If you manage to put together a decent-sized army, it will be almost impossible for your opponent to stop—especially given all of the upgrades you should have amassed—regardless of their defenses. One thing to be wary of, however, is your opponent's religious units; they should always be your primary target if you spot one. Elephant units are prime targets for Conversion, since their slow movement speed makes it difficult for them to escape the conversion ring. If your opponent gains control of some of your elephants, it can lead to a bad time for the rest of your units.

On the rare occasions that your opponent manages to stop your elephant units, the fact that your research capabilities should be running at full speed by this point means you should have no problem switching to other units. If the game has been close thus far, it's even worth preemptively researching all of your remaining upgrades and technologies once you've researched your primary ones, just so you're prepared and can react quickly if needed. This way your army will not only be more powerful than your opponent's, but also more flexible.

Even though they're very powerful, you should not rely solely on elephant units in Age IV. Supporting them with other units that counter the ones fielded by your opponent is vital for success.

Delhi Sultanate Masteries

Founded by a former slave boy, the Sultanate of Delhi rose to encompass almost the whole Indian subcontinent at the height of its rule. A melting pot of Hindu and Muslim cultures, it boasted elaborate architecture, world-renowned metal working, and the terrifying force of its thousands strong elephant corps.

- Profile Image [1]
- Text [2]
- Coat of Arms Pattern [3]
- Coat of Arms Sigil [4]
- Monument [5]

bounty of Berries	Increase the yield of 6 or more Berry Bushes before reaching the Feudal Age (II)	Constructing a Mill near Berry Bushes increases the amount of Food available.	1000XP	Delhi Sultanate Coin [1] Slave King [2]
Military Construction	Construct 10 Palisade Walls during the Dark Age (I) without using Villagers	Sultanate Infantry can build Palisade Walls.	1000XP	Squared Dag Banner Shape [3] Natural Defenses [2]
Test of Strength I	Win a 1v1 Custom or Skirmish match against the Easy A.I.	Defeat a single Easy A.I. opponent in a Custom or Skirmish match. Go to the Single Player screen to create a Skirmish match.	1000XP	Razia Sultana [2] Delhi Sultanate Villager [1]
An Economical Education	Spend no more than 500 Gold to produce 5 Scholars	Only scholars produced from the Dome of Faith count for completion.	1000XP	Delhi Sultanate Sword [1] Knowledge is Power [2]
A Valiant Victory	Defeat 40 enemies while affected by the Tower of Victory attack damage increase	Your infantry must pass near the Tower of Victory to gain this attack increase.	1000XP	Fight Fire With Fire [2] Crescent Moon [4]
The Science of Religion	Research 20 technologies in buildings influenced by Mosques or Madrasas	Research buildings must be within the influence distance of a garrisoned Mosque to get increased research speed.	1000XP	Delhi Sultanate Man-At-Arms [1] Domes of Power [2]
Test of Strength II	Win a 1v1 Custom or Skirmish match against the Intermediate A.I.	Defeat a single Intermediate A.I. opponent in a Custom or Skirmish match. Go to the Single Player screen to create a Skirmish match.	1000XP	A Thunderous Force [2] Anvil [5]
Military Management	Produce 20 military units from buildings you have garrisoned Scholars in	Research Efficient Production to be able to garrison a Scholar in military production buildings.	1000XP	Delhi Sultanate Healer [1] The Refugee Scholars [2]
Stone Construction	Use your military units to construct 1000 Stone's worth of structures	The Compound of the Defender grants Stone construction to Military Units.	1000XP	Curved Swords [4] Thwarting the Escalade Attack [2]
Protecting the Sword	Use Mosques to heal 1000 total health on your units	The Tranquil Venue technology allows Mosques to heal nearby units.	1000XP	Delhi Sultanate Cavalier [1] The Sharpest Blades [2]
Test of Strength III	Win a 1v1 Custom or Skirmish match against the Hard A.I.	Defeat a single Hard A.I. opponent in a Custom or Skirmish match. Go to the Single Player screen to create a Skirmish match.	1000XP	Delhi Sultanate Scholar [1] Fallen Giants [2] Scholar [5]
Military Economies	Produce 20 units from your Keeps	The Village Fortresses technology allows Keeps to produce Villagers and Scouts.	1000XP	War Elephant [1] The Prolific Poet [2] Spear [4]
Towering Threats	Construct the Palace of the Sultan, produce 10 elephants, and destroy 10 enemy buildings	The Elephants produced do not need to come from the Palace of the Sultan, however it does help.	1000XP	Razia Sultana [1] A Revered Beast [2]
Spreading the Word	Research Scholar Movement Speed and then achieve a Sacred Victory	Swiftness research is available at the Mosque.	1000XP	Mubarak [1] A Fertile Jewel [2]
Test of Strength IV	Win a 1v1 Custom or Skirmish match against the Hardest A.I.	Defeat a single Hardest A.I. opponent in a Custom or Skirmish match. Go to the Single Player screen to create a Skirmish match.	1000XP	Left Quadrant Banner Pattern [3] The Guns of Babur [2] Sultana and the Elephant [5]

Abbasid Dynasty

TIME PERIOD REPRESENTED: 750 - 1517 CE EASE OF USE: 

Overview

- *A Civilization of Counter Units, Especially Against Cavalry*
- *Can Enter the Golden Age, Allowing for Enhanced Development*
- *Specializes in the Research of Unique Technologies in their House of Wisdom*

Play with the Abbasid Dynasty if you enjoy playing...

Palmyrians or Cartaginians in AoE 1
Saracens in AoE 2
Indians in AoE 3

Starting Resources			
200	200	100	0

Bonuses

- *Gather from Berry Bushes 25% Faster but Cannot Gather From Boar.*
- *Infantry Units are Able to Construct Battering Rams, Siege Towers, Springalds, and Mangonels from Age I Onwards Without Researching Siege Engineering.*
- *Buildings Built Within the Influence Range of the House of Wisdom Gain +5 Fire Armor.*
- *Docks are 50% Cheaper.*

The Abbasid Dynasty is a civilization of counters, with a specialization in countering horse cavalry. They're at their best when you use game knowledge to anticipate what your opponent will do, or see what they're doing and quickly react to it. Unlike all other civilizations, the Abbasid Dynasty only have one main Landmark Building, and to advance through the Ages you have to choose one of four additional wings around it. Each wing focuses on a different aspect of gameplay, from your economy to military, so based on the circumstances of the game, you can build whichever one will suit you best at the time. As such, it can be difficult to adapt to this process if you're new to the game, but it's rewarding once you do.

Unique Units

	Camel Archer/Rider	Highly Mobile and Durable Units that Cause Nearby Enemy Cavalry Units to do Less Damage.	P.164

Strengths

The Abbasid Dynasty's greatest strength is their ability to cheaply and easily counter an opponent's strategies. They shine when played aggressively during the early stages of the game, thanks to their infantry's ability to construct Battering Rams without the need for any additional buildings or technology. If you use small groups of infantry for raiding parties, they can construct a ram anytime they encounter an enemy building or defensive structure to speed up its destruction.

This, in combination with the ability to improve your cheap infantry units—Spearmen or Archers, for example, through technologies at the **Military Wing**— means the Abbasid Dynasty pose a formidable early game threat to any other civilization. As you progress through the game, the different wings of the **House of Wisdom** allow you to be very flexible and unpredictable with your strategies, and you can easily adapt to whatever your opponent is doing.

Weaknesses

While the Abbasid Dynasty are very good at countering the strengths of other civilizations and taking the wind out of their opponent's sails, they do lack very strong and hard-to-counter units of their own. Their army is primarily based around cheap infantry units, and those can fall prey to strong siege engines later in the game, while their camel units are primarily for support, and do not fare so well when used as the main component of an army. This also means that the Abbasid Dynasty tend to fall off in terms of strength compared to other civilizations during the later portions of a game when the field is dominated by strong and expensive units.

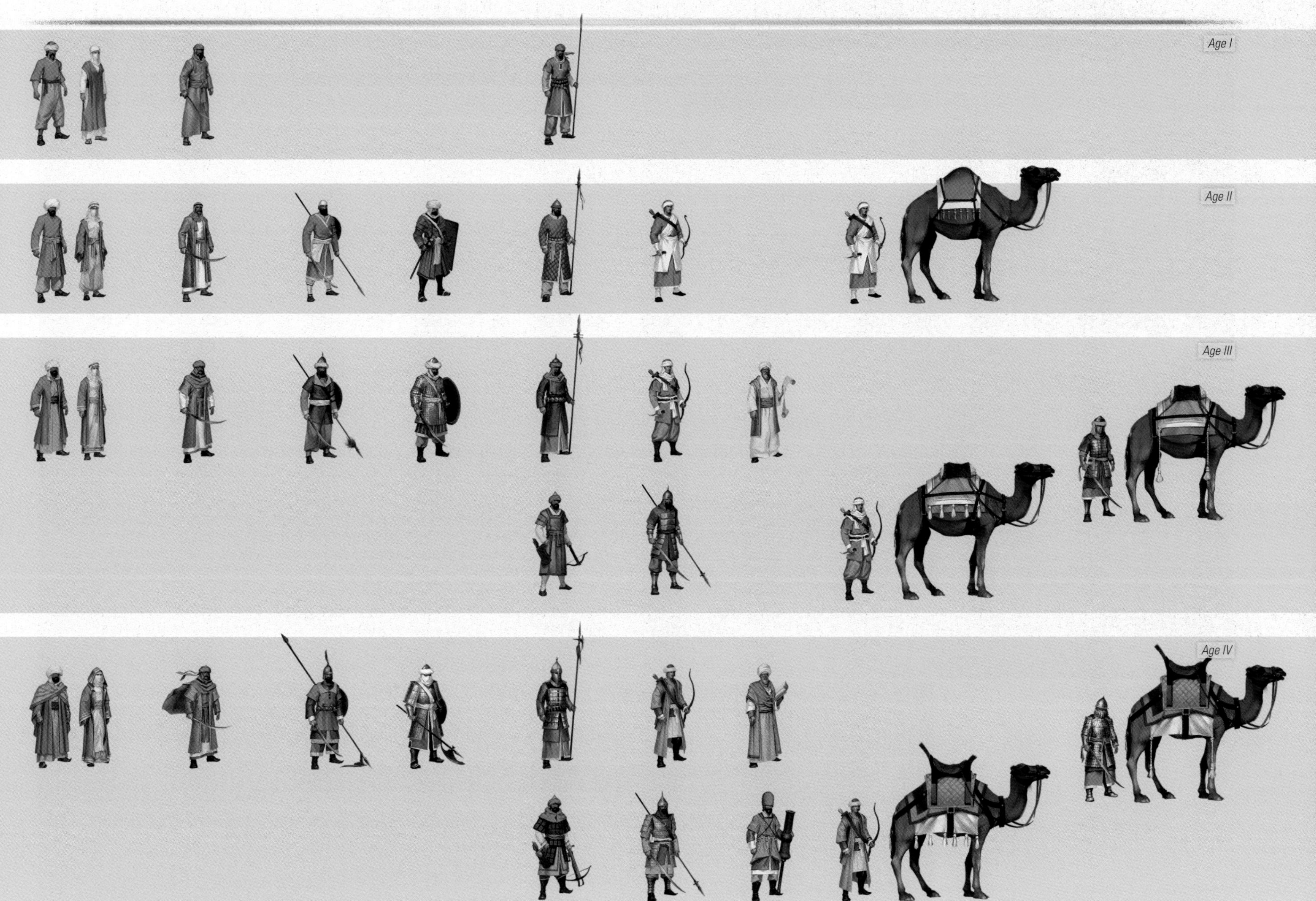
Age I
Age II
Age III
Age IV

Age I - Dark Age	Age II - Feudal Age	Age III - Castle Age	Age IV - Imperial Age
TOWN CENTER [P.234]			
Villager [P.137]; Scout [P.135]	Textiles [P.52]		
HOUSE [P.221]			
MILL [P.227]			
Survival Techniques [P.51]; Wheelbarrow [P.52]	Professional Scouts [P.49]; Horticulture [P.48]	Fertilization [P.47]	Prescision Cross-Breeding [P.49]
LUMBER CAMP [P.223]			
Forestry [P.48]	Double Broadax [P.47]	Lumber Preservation [P.49]	Crosscut Saw [P.46]
MINING CAMP [P.229]			
	Specialized Pick [P.50]	Acid Distillation [P.45]	Cupellation [P.46]
FARM [P.216]			
BARRACKS [P.242]			
Spearman [P.158]	Hardened Spearman [P.158]	Veteran Spearman [P.158]	Elite Spearman [P.158]
		Man-at-Arms [P.150]	Elite Man-at-Arms [P.150]
DOCK [P.246]			
Fishing Boat [P.191]; Transport Ship [P.192]	Trade Ship [P.193]; Dhow [P.202]	Baghlah [P.200]; Explosive Dhow [P.202]	Xebec [P.204]
	Extended Lines [P.47]	Drift Nets [P.47]	
	Teak Masts [P.51]	Navigator Lookout [P.49]; Armored Hull [P.45]	Chaser Cannons [P.46]; Explosives [P.47]
PALISADE WALL [P.272]			
PALISADE GATE [P.272]			
OUTPOST [P.270]			
	Arrowslits [P.45]; Fortify Outpost [P.48]	Springald Emplacement [P.51]	Cannon Emplacement [P.46]
HOUSE OF WISDOM [P.307]	Phalanx [P.49]	Camel Handling [P.46]	Camel Barding [P.46]; Composite Bows [P.46]
Culture Wing [P.309]	Preservation of Knowledge [P.49]	Medical Centers [P.49]	Faith [P.47]
Economic Wing [P.309]	Fresh Foodstuffs [P.48]	Agriculture [P.45]	Improved Processing [P.48]
Military Wing [P.310]	Camel Support [P.46]	Camel Rider Shields [P.46]	Boot Camp [P.46]
Trade Wing [P.310]	Spice Roads [P.51]	Armored Caravans [P.45]	Grand Bazaar [P.48]
	TOWN CENTER [P.234]		
	Villager [P.137]; Scout [P.135]; Textiles [P.52]		
	MARKET [P.225]		
	Trader [P.136]		
	BLACKSMITH [P.260]		
	Bloomery [P.45]	Decarbonization [P.47]	Damascus Steel [P.47]
	Steeled Arrow [P.51]	Balanced Projectiles [P.45]	Platecutter Point [P.49]
	Fitted Leatherwork [P.47]	Insulated Helm [P.48]	Master Smiths [P.49]

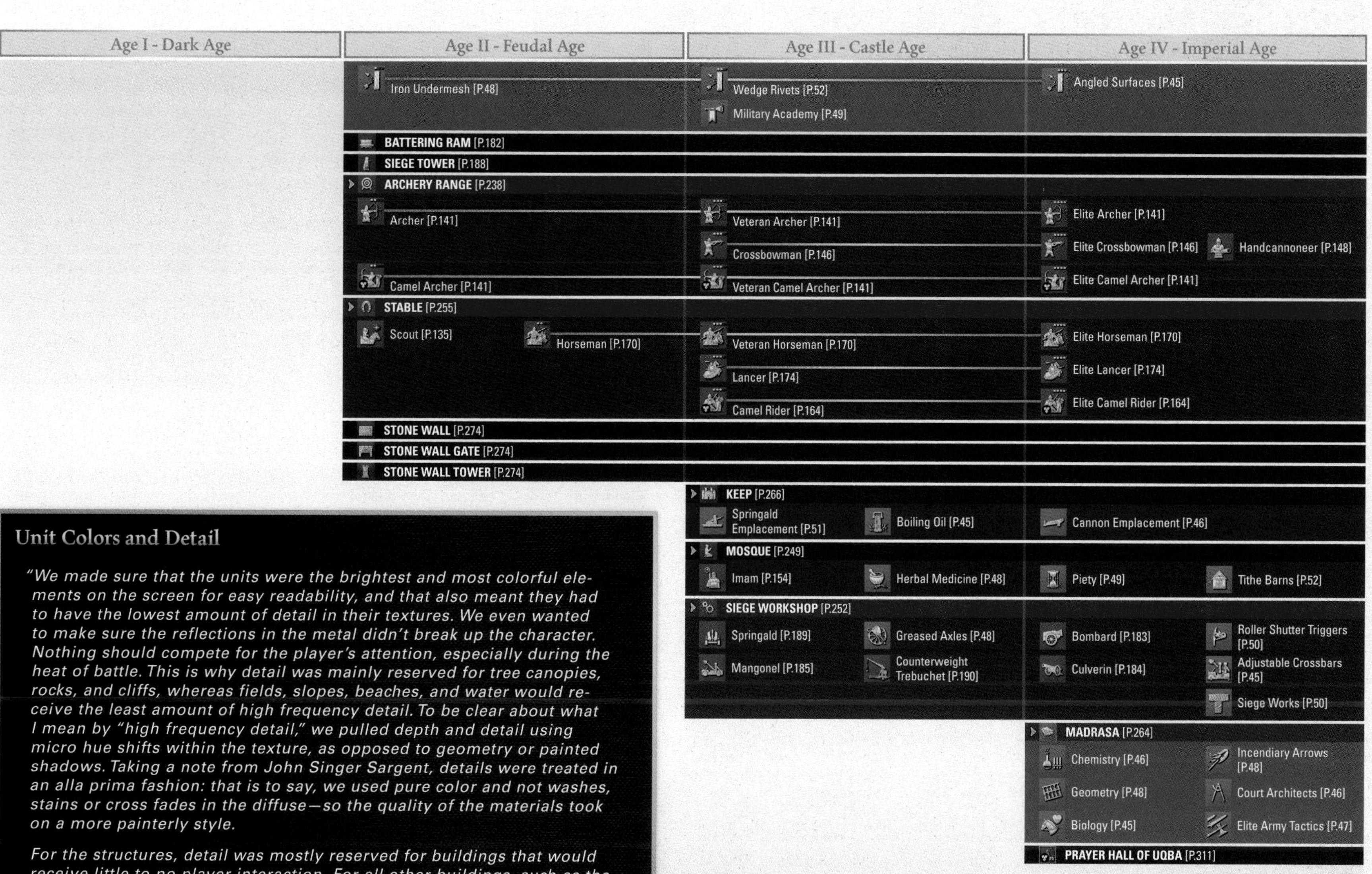

2

Unit Colors and Detail

"We made sure that the units were the brightest and most colorful elements on the screen for easy readability, and that also meant they had to have the lowest amount of detail in their textures. We even wanted to make sure the reflections in the metal didn't break up the character. Nothing should compete for the player's attention, especially during the heat of battle. This is why detail was mainly reserved for tree canopies, rocks, and cliffs, whereas fields, slopes, beaches, and water would receive the least amount of high frequency detail. To be clear about what I mean by "high frequency detail," we pulled depth and detail using micro hue shifts within the texture, as opposed to geometry or painted shadows. Taking a note from John Singer Sargent, details were treated in an alla prima fashion: that is to say, we used pure color and not washes, stains or cross fades in the diffuse—so the quality of the materials took on a more painterly style.

For the structures, detail was mostly reserved for buildings that would receive little to no player interaction. For all other buildings, such as the Town Center, research buildings, houses, etc., details were in the upper floors, eaves and ridge lines along the roof tops; parts that were away from overlapping units. Military buildings of all Ages followed the same simple layouts, whereas more unique or passive buildings would be more complex."

– Zach Schläppi
Principal Artist, Art Director, Relic

Civilization Features

House of Wisdom

The **House of Wisdom**—the only Landmark building available to the Abbasid Dynasty—starts off a humble building that's cheaply constructed by your Villagers in the Dark Age. By itself, it doesn't advance you to subsequent Ages, but once it's placed, you have the option to build additional wings onto the main building, and it's through those wings that you'll advance across Ages.

*Every wing added to the **House of Wisdom** increases the overall health of the building, to the point where once you have all four wings, it has one of the highest health pools in the game. It has no other defensive capabilities, however, so even with all of that health you should still build it in a secure location.*

Each wing has a different theme and houses technologies in line with that theme, allowing you to pick and choose the order in which you add them based on the strategy you're employing. A crucial part of any Abbasid Dynasty strategy is deciding which wings to prioritize in a given situation. The technologies available in each of them are not found anywhere else, so it's important to be familiar with everything each one offers, so you don't have to spend valuable seconds reading what each of them can do.

It's important to note that the technologies within each wing are still gated by Age requirements, so when you're deciding which wing to construct, the order in which its technologies become available to you is another consideration. As you progress through the Ages you'll also unlock technologies in the **House of Wisdom** itself; there are four in total that unlock, but the order is based purely on Age advancement, not which wings you construct. You may also notice that while there are four wings, you can still only advance three Ages; you can still build whichever wing is leftover in the Imperial Age to get access to the technology it houses, but you'll have to pay a lot of extra resources to do so.

The name of the wing gives you a general indication of what part of the game the technologies within it will benefit, and while they can be built in any order, by their nature, some of them are more beneficial than others at different points in the game. For example, when you're trying to grow your economy during the early stages of the game, all of the technologies in the **Economy Wing** are extremely beneficial, especially **Fresh Foodstuffs**, which is available in Age II and lets you produce Villagers at half the cost. Conversely, the **Trade Wing** is squarely focused on trade, so apart from niche strategies that involve heavy trading at the beginning of games, it's fairly safe to leave this to the later Ages, when trade becomes more important.

The Golden Age

The **Golden Age** system also centers on the **House of Wisdom**, but all it requires is the placement of the main building, not any of the wings. Through this system, you can unlock powerful economic and technological benefits, simply by employing some forethought with how you arrange your base. To progress through the **Golden Age** you need to construct buildings within the influence range of the **House of Wisdom**, and then once enough are placed, you'll advance a tier. The **House of Wisdom's** influence will extend one tile around any building placed within it, allowing you to expand the area covered to keep adding buildings.

TIER 1: 10 STRUCTURES

Villager Gathering Rate +10% for all Resources.

TIER 2: 30 STRUCTURES

Villager Gathering Rate +15% for all Resources.

Research Speeds +15%

TIER 3: 60 STRUCTURES

Villager Gathering Rate +20% for all Resources.

Research Speeds +20%

Production Speeds +20%

Planning your base arrangement so that as many buildings as possible lie within this influence range to contribute to the **Golden Age** is something you need to do from the start of every game. This means that the Abbasid Dynasty are at their best when they have one consolidated seat of power, rather than sprawling bases or multiple bases around the map. Later in games you'll have to spread out when nearby resources dry up, or aggressively place a forward camp near your opponent for faster military reinforcements, but making sure your main base is fully interconnected is still the number one priority.

*Buildings within the influence range of the House of Wisdom not only add to your **Golden Age** progress, but they'll also receive +5 fire armor, increasing their survivability considerably.*

Improved Berry Gathering

Similar to the Delhi Sultanate, the Villagers of the Abbasid Dynasty are capable of gathering Berries 25% faster than normal, making Berry gathering a great early source of Food. As the Abbasid Dynasty, you'll typically be playing fairly aggressively during the early stages of the game, so the safety of Berry gathering compared to hunting animals is not quite as important as it is with the more defensive orientated Delhi Sultanate—you'll likely be out scouting anyway, so you may as well hunt at the same time. Another similarity with the Delhi Sultanate is that the Abbasid Dynasty cannot gather Food from Boars, so if you see one, it's best not to engage.

Siege Infantry

The infantry of the Abbasid Dynasty have had similar advanced training to that of the Delhi Sultanate, but rather than focusing on defensive structures, the Abbasid Dynasty infantry has specialized in offensive siege units. From the earliest point they're available, Abbasid Dynasty infantry can build Siege Towers or Battering Rams while out in the field, and when you reach Age III, they'll also be able to produce deadly Springalds and mighty Mangonels.

The advantage of being able to construct these machines in the field without the need for any additional technologies cannot be overstated. With most civilizations, if you wanted to employ Battering Rams you would have to wait to Age II and learn **Siege Engineering** from a Blacksmith; with the Abbasid Dynasty, you can just build them straight away in Age I. Although it requires a lot of Wood, employing Battering Rams at such an early stage of the game can be devastating for your opponent, because there aren't many options to counter them.

Obviously, until Stone Walls come into play you won't have as much of a need for Siege Towers, but as soon as you see some, you can straight away build a Siege Tower to get your army on top of it. Later in the game when you get access to the heavy siege engines, they can often be the thing that gives you an advantage in battles. Without having to wait for the slow siege units, you can get your army into position much faster. When you do encounter an enemy army, you can gauge the composition of it and use some of your units to build the most appropriate siege unit for the job.

Combat Camels

One of the more unique aspects of the Abbasid Dynasty is their ability to use highly trained camels as part of their military. Both ranged and melee camels can be produced, and while their combat prowess is good, it's not their main strength: that would be their scent. Camels produce a natural musk that just so happens to be especially irritating to horses, and as such, if any of your camel units get near the horse cavalry of your opponent, all of those units will be affected by **Camel Unease**. While under that effect, all horse cavalry units deal 20% less damage, giving the Abbasid Dynasty an advantage against cavalry in general, and a huge advantage against cavalry-based civilizations such as the French or Mongols.

General Playstyle

When using the Abbasid Dynasty your playstyle will tend to differ from game to game, and will more often than not depend a lot on what your opponent is doing. The flexibility provided by the different wings of the **House of Wisdom**, coupled with cheap and powerful counter options, means you can play very reactionary, and employ whatever tactics are best at any given moment. The more game knowledge you accumulate about what each civilization is capable of, the more you'll be able to transition from reacting, to predicting based on the

The mighty War Elephants of the Delhi Sultanate are not as sensitive to the scent of camels, and thus even though they are considered cavalry units, they will not suffer the effects of ***Camel Unease****.*

civilization your opponent is playing. The one constant, however, is that the Abbasid Dynasty excels at early aggressive play, which makes quick and effective scouting one of the most essential things you can do.

Dark Age (Age I)

The first thing to keep in mind is that you should build the **House of Wisdom** well before you want to advance to the next Age, so that it's ready to go once you have the resources to build a wing. Building it before you start moving Villagers onto Gold is a generally safe approach. Make sure to place it next to either your starting Town Center or first Lumber Camp (and ideally next to both), so that you can start making progress in the **Golden Age** system.

The rest of your base should then be built outwards from that central position, with as many buildings as possible right next to each other. If you do need to build something outside of the area of influence, try and connect it later with Houses or other buildings so that every building contributes to the **Golden Age**. Try to take advantage of the increased Berry gathering rate with your Villagers to increase your early game Food income while your Scouts are out surveying the map and hunting animals. Once you have the resources, add your desired wing to the **House of Wisdom** to advance to the next Age as quickly as possible.

Dangerous Tactics

Due to the ability of Abbasid Dynasty Spearmen to construct Battering Rams in Age I, you can choose to take a hyper-aggressive approach during this Age. This is essentially an all-or-nothing strategy, because it will require a completely different Villager distribution and a lot of resources, and if you don't defeat your opponent with your first attack, there's a good chance you won't be able to recover. Focus most of your Villagers on Wood, with significantly less on Food, because you're going to need a lot of Wood for a Battering Ram. While you're saving up Wood, build a Barracks and start producing Spearmen while using your Scout to locate your opponent's base. After finding their base and building up a small group of Spearmen, march ALL of your units, including your Villagers, close to the opponent's base, and then have them construct one Battering Ram. When everything is ready, roll them into the base and start destroying the enemy's Landmark(s) with your rams and Villagers while your Spearmen deal with any defending units. If you do this fast enough you can catch your opponent off-guard and secure an early victory.

*The main part of the **House of Wisdom** building only costs 50 Wood and can be constructed by a single Villager in a reasonable time; the earlier your build it, the easier it will be to build your base around it, so there's no reason to wait!*

Age Advancement

Although you can build any wing you like, some are naturally better suited to the early stages of the game, and the Economic Wing is one of them. The Fresh Food Stuffs technology can have a dramatic effect on your economic growth during the next Age by reducing Villager production costs, and is a very strong option.

The Feudal Age is a prime time for the Abbasid Dynasty to start playing aggressively and that will nearly always involve producing Camel Archers. The Camel Support technology from the Military Wing can provide your army with some extra survivability by raising the armor of all infantry units near a camel by +1, increasing the chances of you coming out on top in battles.

Feudal Age (Age I)

Regardless of which wing you chose to reach this Age with, now is the time to start ramping up military production so that you can take advantage of the access to strong early game technologies and units. Spearmen should still be your primary infantry unit, but you should also build an Archery Range and produce one or two Camel Archers to support them, and then build a Blacksmith and research the first tier of the melee upgrades. The **House of Wisdom** will also gain the ability to research **Phalanx** during this Age. This technology will double the attack range of your Spearmen, upgrading their potency.

This aggressive approach works on water maps too, because the Abbasid Dynasty can construct Docks 50% cheaper than other civilizations, which means you can put the Wood you saved towards either more Docks or more Ships, in an attempt to conquer the waves.

The combination of upgraded Spearmen and Camel Archers is a very deadly one at this stage of the game, so if you can produce a good-sized army in a decent amount of time, it's well worth launching an attack. Remember that once you get close to your opponent's base you should have some of your Spearmen build Battering Rams to aid in your assault and provide protection from incoming ranged attacks.

Age Advancement

Between the Military Wing and the Economic Wing, whichever one you didn't build to reach the Feudal Age is a solid option for advancement to the Castle Age. The Military Wing gains access to Camel Rider Shields, which improves the defense of your camel units, and the Economic Wing gets Agriculture, which lets you improve your Villagers' gathering rate from Farms.

The Culture Wing is another strong option for this Age, because you'll have a lot of potential technologies to research during the Castle Age, and the -30% reduction in costs from learning Preservation of Knowledge at this wing can add up to significant savings.

Castle Age (Age III)

In this Age you'll gain access to some strong cavalry units in the form of Lancers and Camel Riders, which are the melee counterpart to your Camel Archers. The Camel Handling technology at the **House of Wisdom** can also be researched now, providing a +15% movement speed increase to all camel units. Camel Riders are always a decent addition to your army, but if your opponent is fielding any kind of cavalry, especially heavy melee cavalry, then they should be considered essential.

This is also the Age in which you should try to establish a forward base near your opponent. The Abbasid Dynasty have an easier time holding such bases in this age because you'll be able to have your infantry build Springalds and Mangonels, making it much harder for your opponent to counterattack. Trying to finish off your opponent in this Age should be of utmost importance, because if the battle continues on into the Imperial Age, the options available to other civilizations may start to outpace those of the Abbasid Dynasty, and things will get progressively more difficult.

Age Advancement

Building a fourth wing in the Imperial Age is a huge additional resource cost, so you need to choose carefully here, and then only build the final wing if you can easily afford it. If your opponent is fielding a lot of powerful single units such as War Elephants, then the Faith technology of the Culture Wing can be extremely beneficial, because it allows your Imam to convert single units without needing to hold a Relic.

If resources are proving to be an issue, then Improved Processing from the Economic Wing will allow your Villagers to drop off 8% more resources, or the Grand Bazar at the Trade Wing can enable your Traders to bring back a secondary resource on every trip. The bonuses from the Golden Age should be enough to offset the need for these resource technologies if you've been constructing your base efficiently, so keep that in mind when making your choice. The Boot Camp technology from the Military Wing will increase the health of all infantry by +15%, so if you've made it to this point without the Military Wing, then it should be a high priority to make the battles in the next Age a bit easier.

Imperial Age (Age IV)

In this Age you'll start to encounter a lot of powerful siege units that can decimate the Abbasid Dynasty's infantry-heavy armies. Thankfully, such things can be countered by the anti-siege weapon: the Culverin. If you've been using infantry to construct all of your siege units up to this point you'll need to build a Siege Workshop to produce Culverins. Building a University and researching **Chemistry** to give them some additional damage is a big additional investment, but it can be just the thing that helps this unit tip battles in your favor. If you've been building your base to take full advantage of the **Golden Age**, the increased gathering rates you gain from it can mean that you don't have to dedicate as many Villagers to resource gathering as normal. That will give you more population space for military units, allowing you to outproduce your opponent.

A large, fully upgraded infantry army can still hold its own in the Imperial Age, if it's supported by camel units and Culverins to counter your opponent's most powerful units.

Abbasid Dynasty Masteries

Born of the fertile crescent in the modern-day Middle East, the Abbasid Caliphate ruled over the Islamic world for hundreds of years. It oversaw a great period of flourishing and technological innovation known as the "Golden Age of Islam", bringing the medieval world racing towards the modern era.

- Profile Image [1]
- Text [2]
- Coat of Arms Pattern [3]
- Coat of Arms Sigil [4]
- Monument [5]

Commerce and Science	Accrue a sum total of 1,000 resources before the first wing of your House of Wisdom is complete	The resources can be from any source; Food, Wood, Stone or Gold and they add together. The Abbasid Dynasty should be able to maintain peak resource collection while building their Landmark.	1000XP	The Fertile Crescent [2] Windmill [1]
The Path Taken	Research the first technology available from a wing in your House of Wisdom, before reaching the Castle Age (III)	Each of the wings gives you one unique technology to choose from. These are important to your development and should be researched as soon as possible.	1000XP	The Battle of the Camel [2] Eastern Windmill [4]
Test of Strength I	Win a 1v1 Custom or Skirmish match against the Easy A.I.	Defeat a single Easy A.I. opponent in a Custom or Skirmish match. Go to the Single Player screen to create a Skirmish match.	1000XP	An Enduring Dynasty [2] Camel [1]
Support the Strong	Defeat 30 enemy units with Infantry who are receiving support from Camels	Research the Camel Support technology and then stand your infantry within radius of a camel to gain the benefit. Infantry include non-cavalry ranged units.	1000XP	The Round City of Baghdad [2] Abbasid Engineer [1]
Love of Knowledge	Research 30 technologies discounted by the Preservation of Knowledge	For a technology to count, it must be started after researching Preservation of Knowledge.	1000XP	From Alchemy to Chemistry [2] Camel & Rider [4]
Culture of Trade	Accrue 5000 Gold from your Traders after researching Spice Roads	Gold accrued only counts once you have researched Spice Roads.	1000XP	Mill Power [2] Abbasid Ship [1]
Test of Strength II	Win a 1v1 Custom or Skirmish match against the Intermediate A.I.	Defeat a single Intermediate A.I. opponent in a Custom or Skirmish match. Go to the Single Player screen to create a Skirmish match.	1000XP	Baghdad at its Height [2] Trader [5]
Expeditious Production	Produce 100 military units after achieving Tier 3 of the Golden Age	Tier 3 of the Golden Age increases production speed of your units. The production of military units only counts after achieving Tier 3.	1000XP	Medieval Metallurgy [2] Camel Rider [1]
Smell of Defeat	Defeat 30 enemy cavalry units with your Camel Riders	Camels are designed as anti-cavalry, use Camel Riders in this manner to defeat enemy cavalry.	1000XP	The Great Mosque of Samarra [2] Sun Frame [4]
Heart and Mind	Heal 1500 health on friendly units using your Medical Centers	After researching Medical Centers, bring injured units nearby to receive healing.	1000XP	Diplomacy by Elephant [2] Iman [1]
Test of Strength III	Win a 1v1 Custom or Skirmish match against the Hard A.I.	Defeat a single Hard A.I. opponent in a Custom or Skirmish match. Go to the Single Player screen to create a Skirmish match.	1000XP	The End of an Age [2] Ulayya Bint Al-Mahdi [1] Camel Rider [5]
bounty of the Earth	Increase the yield of 18 Berry Bushes and accrue 9000 Food	The Abbasid Dynasty can increase the Food available per Berry Bush by placing a Mill nearby.	1000XP	A Mathematical World [2] Abbasid Sailor [1] Minaret [4]
Resourceful in Warfare	construct 10 ranged siege units with your melee infantry	Abbasid melee infantry units can construct ranged siege units in the field.	1000XP	Glass and Optics [2] Rabia Al-Adawiyya [1]
No Higher Honor	Win a Wonder Victory after achieving Tier 3 of the Golden Age	Reaching Tier 3 of the Golden Age indicates a strong economy, culture and military structure is in place. This should make a Wonder victory achievable.	1000XP	Age of Automation [2] Abbas Ibn Al-Muttalib [1]
Test of Strength IV	Win a 1v1 Custom or Skirmish match against the Hardest A.I.	Defeat a single Hardest A.I. opponent in a Custom or Skirmish match. Go to the Single Player screen to create a Skirmish match.	1000XP	The Ceremonial Dynasty [2] Astrological Instrument [4] Ulayya Bint Al-Mahdi [5]

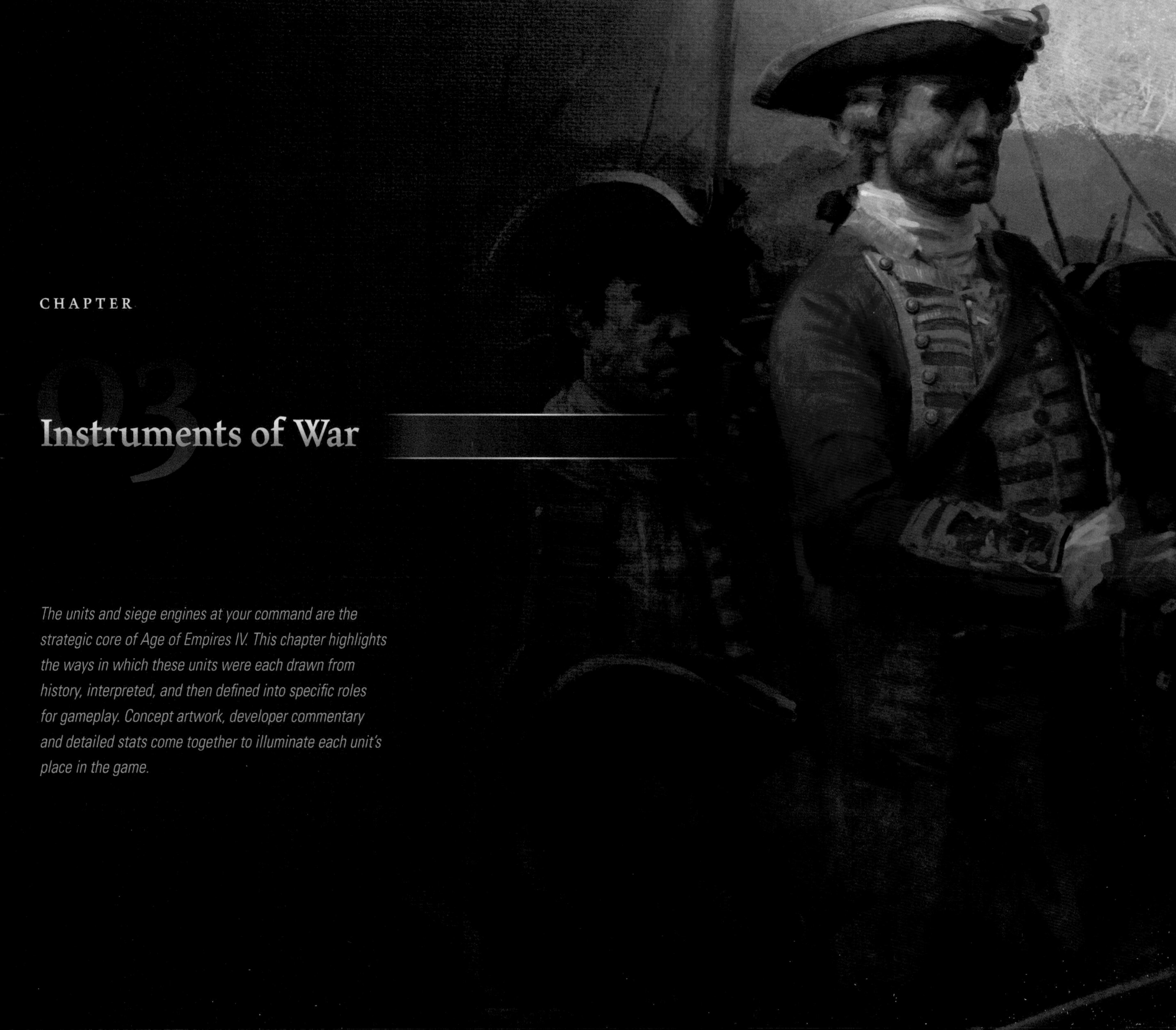

CHAPTER

03

Instruments of War

The units and siege engines at your command are the strategic core of Age of Empires IV. This chapter highlights the ways in which these units were each drawn from history, interpreted, and then defined into specific roles for gameplay. Concept artwork, developer commentary and detailed stats come together to illuminate each unit's place in the game.

About this Chapter

Throughout this chapter we present the stats and attack values for each unit in the game. To ensure that you understand what each of these values means, we'll provide short descriptions of each one here, linked to some example tables.

Unit Details

1 **Icon** This shows you the unit's in-game icon.

Age These small markers at the top of the icon tell you which Age the unit becomes available during.

Unique Icon Tells you if a unit is unique to the civilization named in the same entry.

Flags These show you which civilization has access to the first or main version of the unit. Sometimes the stat tables will show which civilizations have access to a particular unit type.

Weapon Shows which weapon type the unit uses.

Torch Shows whether the unit can use a torch against buildings/siege units.

2 **Primary Uses** This box gives you a top-level idea about the main functions of the unit.

Training Details and Unit Stats These stat tables show you the unit's basic production details.

3 **Building Required** Shows the main building that a unit is produced from. Sometimes a unit can be produced from multiple different buildings; those are handled on a case-by-case basis in Chapter 5.

4 **Time, Food, Wood, Gold, Population Capacity** These show you how long it takes to produce a unit, how much it costs, and its impact on your population total.

5 **Health** Shows how much health the unit has.

Melee/Ranged Armor Shows how much armor the unit has.

Movement Speed How many in-game tiles the unit can move across every second; the higher the number, the faster they are.

Attacks

6 These tables give you the details on any attacks the unit can make use of.

Damage Shows how much damage the attack deals. If an attack has multiple projectiles, then the second number will show how many projectiles are used, so 12x3 would be three projectiles in a single volley, each dealing 12 damage.

Counter Bonus Shows if the attack can inflict bonus damage against specific targets—if so, this value will tell you how much is added.

Bonus Against This tells you which target type you'll receive that amount of bonus damage against.

Attack Range Shows how far the attack can reach, measured across in-game tiles.

Attack Speed Shows how frequently the unit will initiate the attack. A 1-second attack speed means that an attack is started every second.

Abilities

7 Boxes like this one detail any manually activated abilities a unit may have.

Age Lets you know which Age you need to reach in a game before you gain access to the ability.

Cooldown This shows how long in seconds until the ability can be used again once activated.

Duration This shows how long in seconds the ability last once activated.

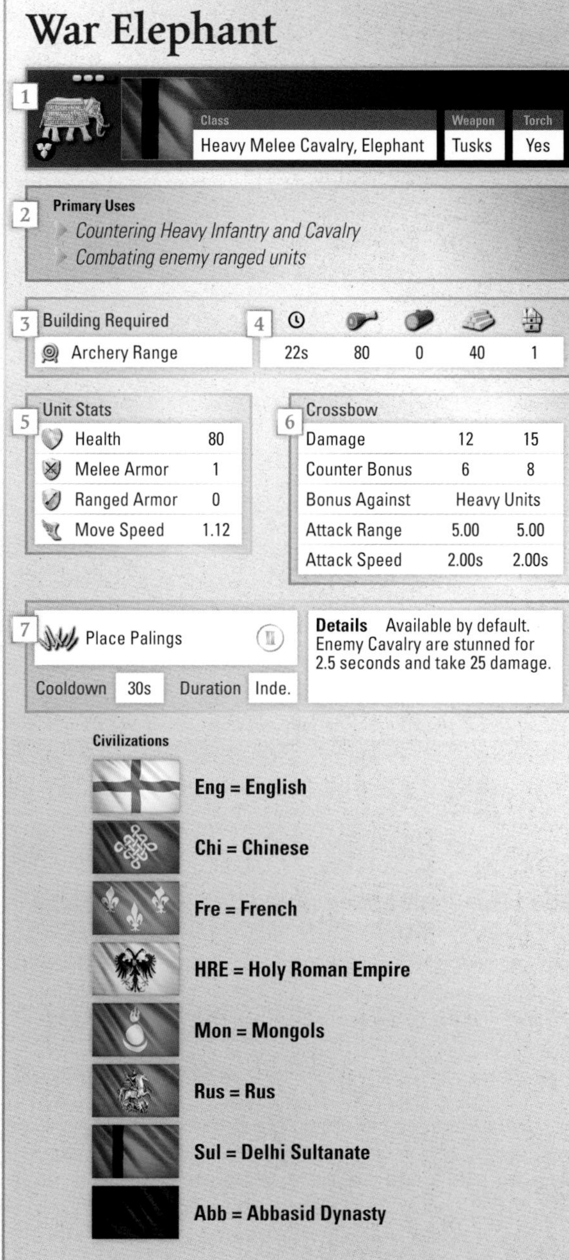

War Elephant

1

Class	Weapon	Torch
Heavy Melee Cavalry, Elephant	Tusks	Yes

2 **Primary Uses**
- *Countering Heavy Infantry and Cavalry*
- *Combating enemy ranged units*

3 Building Required	4 Time	Food	Wood	Gold	Population
Archery Range	22s	80	0	40	1

5 Unit Stats	
Health	80
Melee Armor	1
Ranged Armor	0
Move Speed	1.12

6 Crossbow		
Damage	12	15
Counter Bonus	6	8
Bonus Against	Heavy Units	
Attack Range	5.00	5.00
Attack Speed	2.00s	2.00s

7 Place Palings

Cooldown 30s Duration Inde.

Details Available by default. Enemy Cavalry are stunned for 2.5 seconds and take 25 damage.

Civilizations

Eng = English

Chi = Chinese

Fre = French

HRE = Holy Roman Empire

Mon = Mongols

Rus = Rus

Sul = Delhi Sultanate

Abb = Abbasid Dynasty

Imperial Official

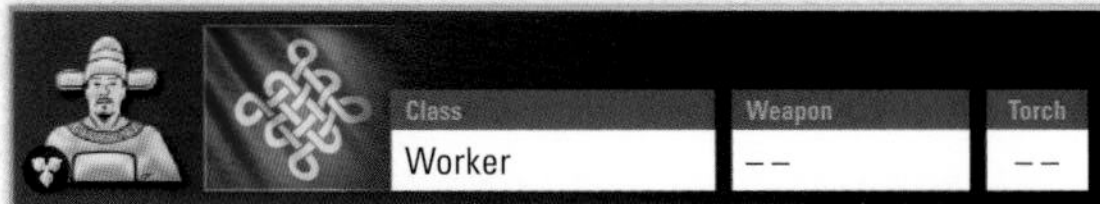

Class	Weapon	Torch
Worker	--	--

The Imperial Official plays a key part in the Chinese Taxation economic system, because it's the sole unit capable of collecting the Gold that is generated from the taxes applied to buildings every time a drop-off is made or unit produced. You can only have four Officials at a time (the current amount and total are displayed above your resources), and while you can train them from the start of a match, their hefty training price and the limited availability of buildings at that point, means it's often better to wait until the Feudal Age before training one.

Buildings within the influence range of the **Imperial Palace** generate taxes at double the normal rate, so try to plan your base layout to get the maximum benefit.

Abilities & Technology

Imperial Officials have a few upgrades that you can acquire through the **Imperial Palace** that significantly increase their efficiency. **Imperial Examinations** allows them to carry double the amount of resources, significantly cutting down on the amount of walking back-and-forth they need to do. Imperial Officials also start with the **Supervise** ability, which lets you manually assign one of them to oversee a building and increase its effectiveness. Supervising a production building leads to 200% faster production times from it, whereas a resource drop-off location will give you +20% additional resources for every deposit made. Like other Worker units, Imperial Officials also have access to the Seek Shelter ability so that they can automatically garrison the nearest available building if you need to protect them quickly.

Primary Uses

- *Collecting Taxes*
- *Supervising buildings to make them more efficient*

Training Details

Building Required	Time	Food	Wood	Gold	Population
Town Center	20s	150	0	0	1

Unit Stats	
Health	75
Melee Armor	0
Ranged Armor	0
Move Speed	1.12

Chinese Imperial Official

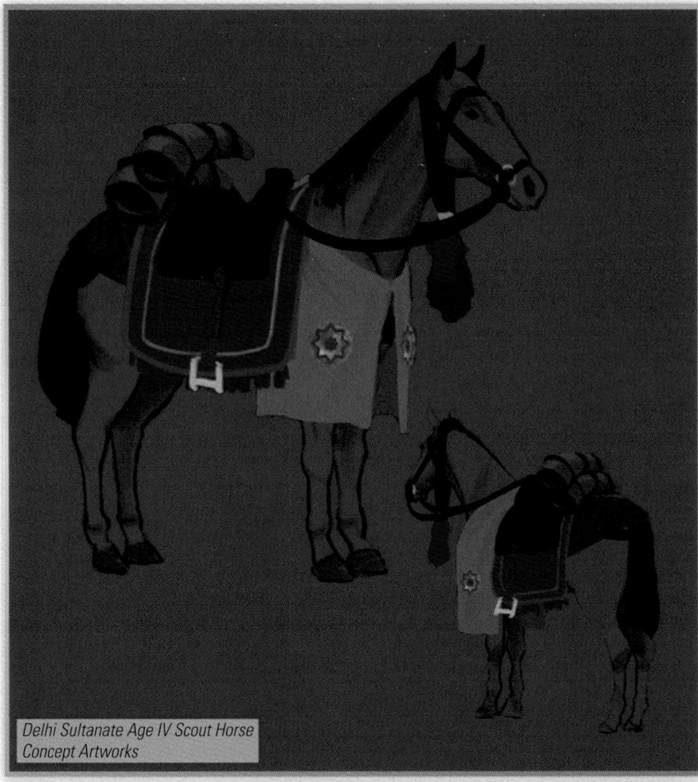

Delhi Sultanate Age IV Scout Horse Concept Artworks

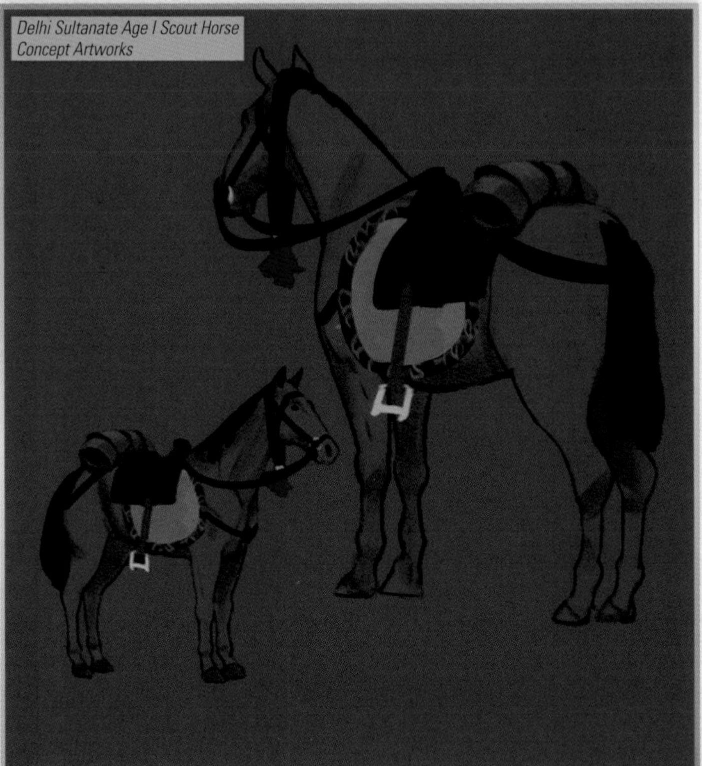

Delhi Sultanate Age I Scout Horse Concept Artworks

Scout

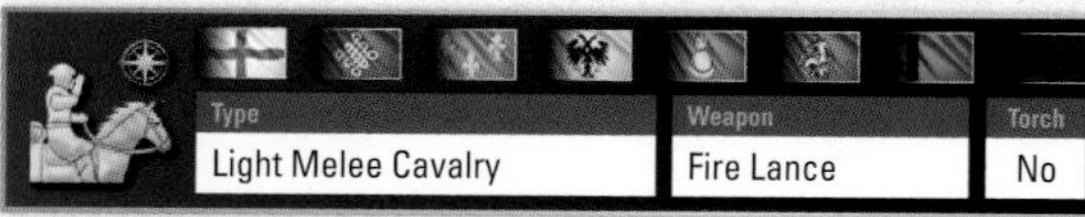

Type	Weapon	Torch
Light Melee Cavalry	Fire Lance	No

The Scout is a light and fast cavalry unit that has exceptional visual range, making it ideal for revealing unexplored parts of the map and spying on opponents. While they can attack, their low damage makes them little more than an annoyance to stronger units. Since they're always out exploring, they'll usually be the first to find wild animals, and they deal enough damage against these to make them excellent hunters. You'll start most games with at least one Scout, and you should try your best to keep it alive, because early in a match your resources and production queues are much better dedicated to Villagers.

English Scouts

Primary Uses

- *Scouting*
- *Sheep herding*
- *Hunting Animals*

Training Details

Building Required	Time	Food	Wood	Gold	Stone	Pop
Town Center*	20s	60	0	0	1	

*If the building is under the influence of an Ovoo, Mongols can pay an additional 60 Stone for x2 of the unit.

Unit Stats	
Health	110
Melee Armor	0
Ranged Armor	0
Move Speed	1.62
Fire Lance	
Damage	4
Counter Bonus	10
Bonus Against	Scouts
Attack Range	0.29
Attack Speed	3.75s
Bow	
Damage	3
Counter Bonus	--
Bonus Against	--
Attack Range	2.88
Attack Speed	0.62s

Delhi Sultanate Age III Scout Concept Artworks

Tactics & Usage

From the moment a game begins, your Scouts should never be idle. Between scouting the area for resources, searching out your opponent, or hunting wildlife, there's always something they can be doing. Once you reach Age II you can acquire the **Professional Scouts** upgrade from a Mill, allowing your Scouts to carry the corpses of any animals they kill on the back of their horse. While this requires a bit of micromanaging, being able to take advantage of the faster gathering rate from animals in the safety of your own base should not be overlooked. 3

As you prepare for battle it can also be beneficial to have one or two Scouts as part of your main army; their huge sight range will allow you to spot enemies sooner, making sure you're never caught off guard. Scouts are also the only units in the game that can see into Stealth Forests, which means that not only can they help reveal the area around a forest to make it easier for you to set up your own ambush, but they can also ensure that you're not walking into an enemy trap.

The Scout is the only unit in game that can herd sheep. Once a sheep has been picked up by a Scout, it follows the unit wherever it goes until it's dropped off at a building.

Rus are the exception to producing multiple Scouts early on because, thanks to their Hunting Cabins, they can train them without the need of a Town Center. The additional Gold from the Bounty system also makes having multiple Scouts very beneficial.

Trader

Type	Weapon	Torch
Worker, Cavalry	--	No

Traders are an extremely important unit for your economic growth, because they provide one of your few means of obtaining that most precious of resources: Gold. While exploring a map you'll often come across neutral trading posts, and if you tell one of your traders to travel to it, they'll return to the Market their assigned to with some Gold. While Trading Posts are the most common building you'll establish trade routes with, you can also establish a trade route with an allied Market. All civilizations can train Traders at the Market (French can also train the at the Chamber of Commerce, and Mongols through the Silver Tree Landmark), and while their initial training cost is quite high, you'll quickly recover that cost after just a couple of trades.

Holy Roman Empire Trader

Primary Uses

Trading to generate Gold

Training Details

Building Required	Time	Food	Wood	Gold	Population
Market	35s	0	75	75	1

Unit Stats	
Health	90
Melee Armor	0
Ranged Armor	0
Move Speed	1.00

Longer trade routes yield more Gold upon a Trader's return, but the roads can often be dangerous, and due to their slow movement speed and low health, Traders are extremely vulnerable and need to be well protected.

Tactics & Usage

While their cost can be recovered relatively quickly once you have an established trade route, that initial cost can still pose a risk early in games when you don't have a lot of Gold to spend or units to protect your Traders. You'll need to thoroughly scout the area and try to gauge if a route is safe enough to take the risk on producing some early game Traders. This can be somewhat easier in co-op team games, where you'll be able to share the scouting and protection costs between players.

As you progress later into the game and Gold Veins begin to run dry, Traders will become vital. Units that require Gold to train are usually superior to regular units, such as Spearmen and Archers. Thus, ensuring that you have a healthy supply of it will allow you to maintain a tactical advantage as the game progresses. Control over Markets and trade routes will often decide the outcome of a game at this stage in both 1v1 and team games.

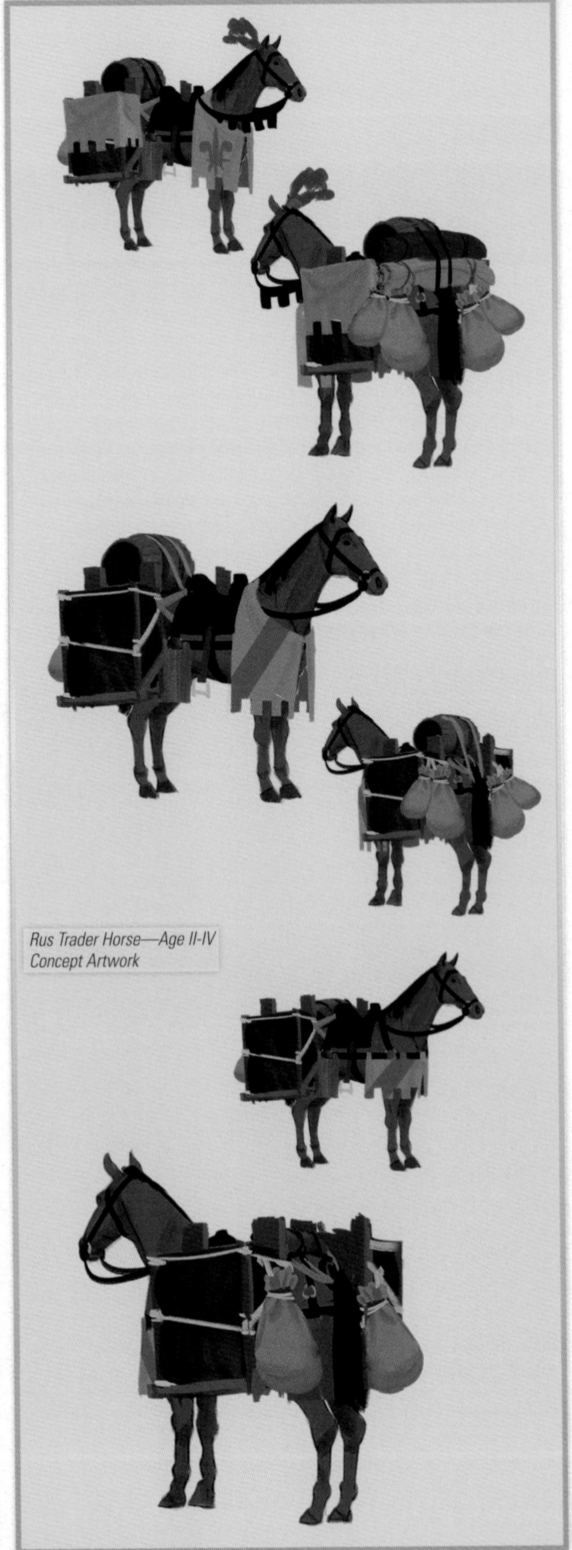

Rus Trader Horse—Age II-IV Concept Artwork

Villager

Type
Worker
Weapon
Knife and Bow
Torch
Yes

Villagers are the most important unit in the game, and the foundation from which everything else grows. They are almost solely responsible for constructing and repairing the buildings that form your bases, gathering the food that allows you to train your units, and mining the gold that lets you learn advanced technologies. For a healthy, booming economy, Villagers should make up at least half of your population. That amount may vary slightly depending on the unit types and strategy you employ: an army consisting mostly of Archers and Men-at-arms will need less economic resources than one composed entirely of War Elephants. That being said, the minimum 50/50 ratio is still a healthy goal to keep in mind as your economy grows, and will usually mean you have enough resources to accomplish your goals.

English Villagers

Primary Uses

- *Constructing Buildings*
- *Acquiring Resources*
- *Maintaining the Economy*

Training Details

Building Required	Time	Food	Wood	Gold	Stone/Pop
Town Center	20s	50	0	0	1

*If the building is under the influence of an Ovoo, Mongols can pay an additional 200 Stone for x2 of the unit.

Unit Stats		
Health		50
Melee Armor		0
Ranged Armor		0
Move Speed		1.12
Attacktype	**Knife**	**Bow***
Damage	6	5
Counter Bonus	--	--
Bonus Against	--	--
Attack Range	0.29	5.0
Attack Speed	3.75s	3.25s

*Only Eng use Bows to attack other military units, the other civilizations use weaker ones only to hunt.

Usage & Abilities

Villagers are only equipped with simple farm tools that deal minimal damage, which makes them easy pickings for opponents looking to cripple your economy—be sure to keep them safe at all costs! The **Textiles** technology from the Town Center in Age II can help with this—it provides Villagers with +25 health. Like almost all other units, Villagers can garrison inside buildings, either by moving them into one manually or by using the Seek Shelter ability. English Villagers can, however, put up a bit more of a fight, because they are armed with traditional weapons that enable them deal double the damage of other Villagers. While that won't make them an offensive unit, it does make them much better at hunting animals, and in a pinch, at defending themselves.

Generally, it's best to keep producing Villagers until you have over 100 upon nearing the population cap. Extra Town Centers will help to reach that number faster, though there may be some cases that require you to halt production. Upgrades that affect your economy are important to make early, since they'll allow you to collect more resources with fewer Villagers

Deciding on how and where best to deploy your Villagers is also something to constantly think about because it can change from moment-to-moment in a match. Villagers can collect Food faster from animals than picking berries for example, but animals are usually further away from your base so it can be a lot riskier. Similarly, as you cut down forests for Wood, you'll need to keep an eye on the tree line and replace your Lumber Camps whenever they're more than 3-4 tiles away from the trees to minimize the travel time for your Villagers. That same rule of placing drop-off buildings as close to resources as possible applies to other resources as well, but since those are mainly static you won't need to keep an eye on them as much.

Always keep an eye on the "Idle Villagers" button above your resources in the HUD as that lets you know if some of your Villagers are idle. Clicking it will take you straight to them so you can give them a new task.

Constructing buildings can be sped up by assigning more than one Villager to the job, but unless you're constructing a single important building it isn't always the best idea. If, for example, you're making five Stables, you'd be better off having one Villager work on each of them, since that would work out faster overall. If your base comes under attack, don't be afraid to pull your Villagers away from construction or resource gathering, because Villagers can also repair damaged buildings and Siege units; well timed repairs can give you enough time to bring in reinforcements to the area and fend of the attack before losing a key building. After a battle it's also important to check if any buildings are still on fire, or they will eventually burn down—your trusty Villagers are the only units that can put these fires out.

Male and Female French Villagers—Age III
Main Concept Artworks

Male and Female French Villagers—Age IV
Concept Artwork

Readable Character Designs

"The camera distance required for AOE4 was a significant yet familiar challenge for us. I think it's important to note that we approach readability from the player's perspective. An animator can craft the most amazing piece of animation, yet that animation may lose all clarity in context with gameplay. To achieve the best possible result for our players we work closely with several different departments. We especially work with artists to create character designs that work with our rig archetypes and iterate with them in gameplay until character silhouettes, colours and weapon sizes all feel just right."

– Brent Breedveld
Principal Animator, Animation Director, Relic

Villagers Throughout the Ages

"We started by looking at all aspects of a civilization during the time period which the game takes place in; namely 1000AD to 1600AD. We even looked a little bit outside of those years to see if there was anything we could draw on. We looked at the armor and weapon technology, what their architecture looked like, what life looked like for the average civilian and for the elites, which helped influence the costuming for the villager units throughout the Ages, such as the Castle or Imperial Age.

But all the questions such as how simple does an Age 1 or Age 2 French villager look compared to how they look in Age 3 and 4? What kind of clothing do they wear? These were important questions which required a chunk of time to research historical authenticity, as well as readability for the player. It was important to understand how powerful your own civilization was versus an enemy civilization by looking at them, and also having that feeling that gratification when you Age-Up and seeing all your units and buildings visually upgrade."

– Stuart Ng
Senior Concept Artist, Relic

Chinese Male and Female Villagers
Head/Hair 3D Sculpts

Abbasid Dynasty Male and Female Villagers—Age I-IV
Concept Artwork

3

Arbalétrier

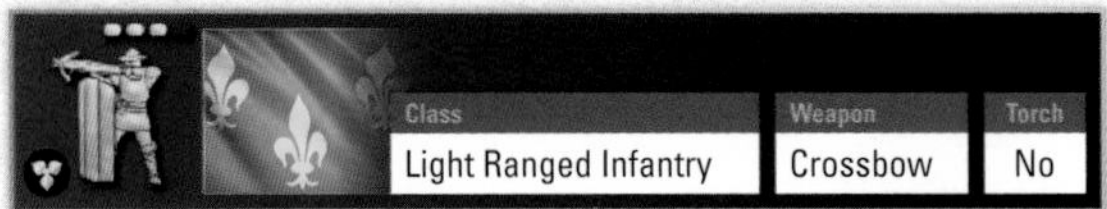

Class
Light Ranged Infantry
Weapon
Crossbow
Torch
No

The Arbalétrier is a unique version of the standard Crossbowman that only the French have access to, and it's available from Age III onwards. They come equipped with a few special abilities and have access to some additional technologies that give them an edge over the traditional Crossbowman, and make them much more viable in scenarios where Crossbowmen would have difficulty. Just like normal Crossbowmen, Arbalétriers have a damage bonus against Heavy units and can be used as a counter against them.

French Elite Arbalétrier

Special Abilities & Technologies

Arbalétriers have access to two unique technologies: **Gambesons** (Age III) and **Crossbow Stirrups** (Age IV). **Gambesons** is a very strong upgrade that increases melee armor by +5. If you're training a lot of Arbalétriers, it's worth acquiring this upgrade as soon as you can.

Crossbow Stirrups will increase your reload speed by 25%. This upgrade has a hefty price tag, but the effect is so strong that ideally you should purchase it right after the Elite upgrade, and even before any Blacksmith or University improvements.

Deploy Pavise

Upon activating this ability, your Arbalétriers will deploy a shield directly in front of them that grants an additional 5 ranged armor for 30 seconds, or until you move them away from the pavise, making the Arbalétrier a lot more durable against other non-Siege ranged units.

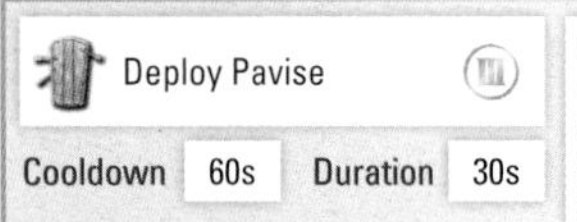

Details Gain an additional 5 Ranged Armor that remains active until the duration expires or the Arbalétrier moves away. Cannot be deployed while on a Stone Wall.

While the Pavise is a strong defensive tool, it's important to note that it cannot be deployed when standing atop a Stone Wall. Because of that, once enemy ranged units are close enough, you're better off moving the Arbalétrier back to ground level.

Tactics & Usage

Due to their special upgrades and abilities, Arbalétriers can easily outperform Crossbowmen—they can survive for longer in most engagements, and can fire faster to inflict more damage. Archers, for example, are considered a soft counter to Crossbowmen because they cost less and fire faster, but **Deploy Pavise** helps give Arbalétriers the upper hand over a similar-sized group of Archers, so you can engage with confidence. Like most ranged units, Arbalétriers are at their best when supported by melee units, but thanks to their unique abilities and strengths they can operate quite well on their own.

Primary Uses
- *Countering Heavy Infantry and Cavalry*
- *Combating enemy ranged units*

Training Details

Building Required	Time	Food	Wood	Gold	Population
Archery Range	22s	80	0	40	1

Upgrade Unlock Requirements			Time	Food	Wood	Gold
Elite Arbalétrier	Fre	IV	1m 30s	300	0	700

Unit Stats		
Health	80	95
Melee Armor	1	2
Ranged Armor	0	0
Move Speed	1.12	1.12
Crossbow		
Damage	12	15
Counter Bonus	6	8
Bonus Against	Heavy Units	
Attack Range	5.00	5.00
Attack Speed	2.00s	2.00s

Counters

If you face a mass of Arbalétriers, it's advised to counter them with either better, more expensive units, or a quick cheap counter. The former means heavy siege units like Mangonels or Cannons, while the latter refers to mostly Horsemen because they're considerably cheaper and quicker to make. If your units are caught off guard by a group of Arbalétriers and you can't flee or they are completely alone, try to close the distance as quickly as possible.

Archer

Type	Weapon	Torch
Light Ranged Infantry	Bow	No

Archers are a basic ranged infantry unit without any special or unique abilities, but that doesn't mean they should be underestimated. Their low cost, fast production speed, and relatively early availability means that you can quickly amass large numbers of them and use them to overwhelm unprepared opponents. The fact that their training costs only consist of Food and Wood also means that you can use any Gold you acquire on upgrades for these or other units, which can be especially important early in a game.

Holy Roman Empire Archers

Tactics & Usage

Archers are a key unit early in a game, when they can be used to harass enemy Villagers from a distance, or counter melee infantry. In Age II they shine as a raiding unit in groups that probe enemy bases, because they won't have to enter the range of Town Centers like melee or cavalry units would. They are, however, ineffective against buildings or fortifications, so you'll need to send in some melee or cavalry units once the Archers have cleared the way.

Archers are at their best in large groups, aiming to take out enemy units before they can get within melee range. When planning a large engagement, you should always have a contingent of melee or cavalry units with your Archers to act as a buffer between them and the enemy. Depending on which units you think you're going to face, the composition of that buffer should change. For example, if your opponent is anticipating that you're massing a large group of Archers, they'll likely be making cavalry units to try and counter them, which means you should bring a number of Spearmen with you so as not to be caught off guard. While a lot of the time it's Archers that need support, if you're using a lot of siege units, you should always have a group of Archers with them, because your opponent will likely try to counter the siege units with melee infantry, which the Archers excel at dispatching.

The speed and cheapness of Archers makes them one of the best units to stack in large numbers on top of your Stone Walls. From there they can take advantage of the extra range and rain arrows on your opponents en masse.

Counters

The natural counters to Archers are cavalry or siege units, as well as fortifications such as Towers and Keeps. To increase your chances of killing them, you'll want to try and catch them on their own or isolate them and close the distance quickly. Stealth Forests can help achieve this by allowing you to hide your units until the Archers are within range. Heavy Melee Infantry in comparable numbers can act as a soft counter to Light Ranged Infantry in that they can soak up more damage while closing the gap on the Archers; once they're within range, the Archers will be completely dominated.

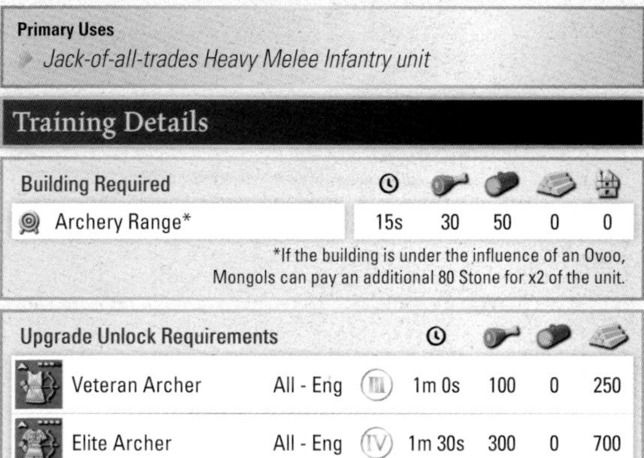

Primary Uses

- *Jack-of-all-trades Heavy Melee Infantry unit*

Training Details

Building Required	Time	Food	Wood	Gold	Stone
Archery Range*	15s	30	50	0	0

*If the building is under the influence of an Ovoo, Mongols can pay an additional 80 Stone for x2 of the unit.

Upgrade Unlock Requirements		Age	Time	Food	Wood	Gold
Veteran Archer	All - Eng	III	1m 0s	100	0	250
Elite Archer	All - Eng	IV	1m 30s	300	0	700

Unit Stats			
Health	70	80	95
Melee Armor	0	0	0
Ranged Armor	0	0	0
Move Speed	1.25	1.25	1.25
Bow			
Damage	5	7	8
Counter Bonus	5	7	8
Bonus Against	Light Melee Infantry		
Attack Range	5.00	5.00	5.00
Attack Speed	1.50s	1.50s	1.50s

In big enough groups, even heavy melee infantry like the Man-at-Arms will have a hard time dealing with Archers.

French Archer—Age III
Early Concept Artwork

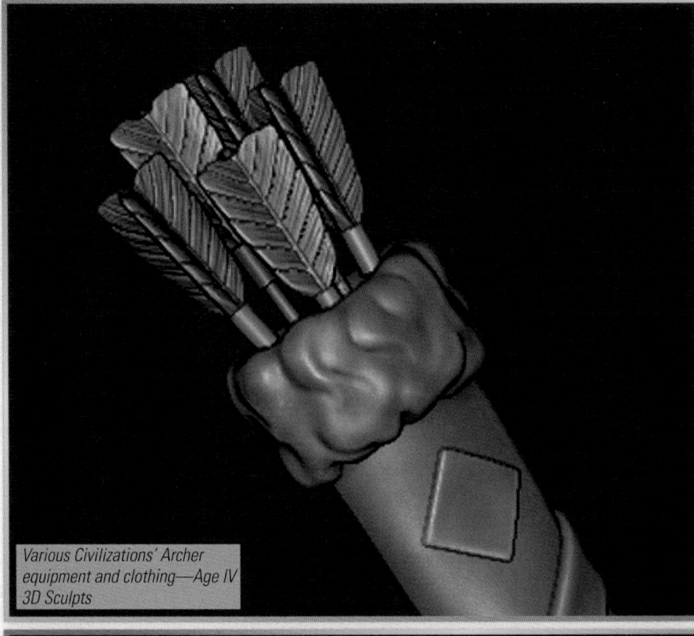

Various Civilizations' Archer equipment and clothing—Age IV 3D Sculpts

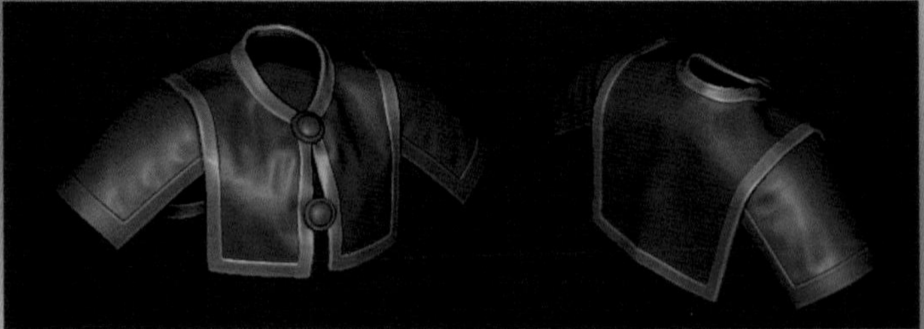

Ranged Unit Balance

"In a straight up, one-on-one fight, ranged units will generally lose to melee units. It's up to the ranged player to utilize additional facets like kiting, garrison, terrain bonuses, and walls to turn the tide in their favor.

Wall bonuses needed to be worth player's time to put their troops up there. However, the bonuses can't be too strong or they stall out the game and prevent. Part of the reason wall bonuses can be powerful is we've got counter units available like the ram to knock them down or the siege tower to deposit melee troops on the wall to kill pesky archers. 1 on 1 an archer loses to the man at arms, but there are a lot of opportunities for ranged players to flip the script and that dynamic gameplay makes it fun to play again and again!"

– Brent Breedveld
Principal Animator, Animation Director, Relic

Character Animation

"Motion capture was key in delivering the amount of character animation required for Age of Empires IV. Mocap provides a consistent look in the animation. This helps in that the movements can work well for all animation archetypes across all civilizations. The capture serves both gameplay and cinematic character animation in Age of Empires IV. A lot of research goes into planning the use of these weapons across the different civilizations. Much of this detail is directed on the day of the mocap shoot by the animation director. The animation director also brings a reference to display on a large screen in the motion capture space when specific direction is needed. This can be video or image reference to help the performers see clearly how something works. The Cranequin and Arbalest crossbow mechanisms come to mind. We had reference for those and built props so the actors could have tactile mechanisms to interact with. This helps us as a player feel that connection to the prop as well as the weight of the object and mechanism. "

– Brent Breedveld
Principal Animator, Animation Director, Relic

Abbasid Dynasty Archer—Age II-IV Concept Artworks

Longbowman

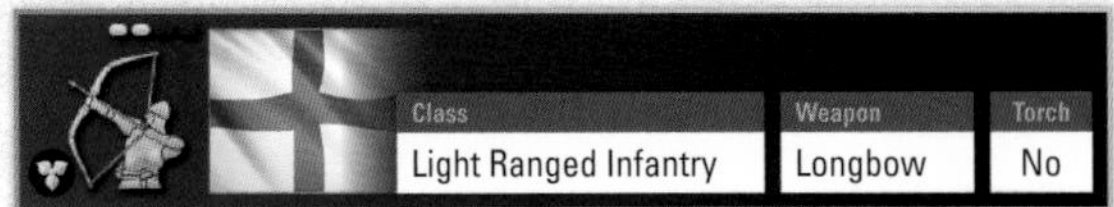

Class	Weapon	Torch
Light Ranged Infantry	Longbow	No

Unique to the English, the Longbowman replaces the standard Archer unit that other civilizations have access to. Their cost and health is similar to Archers, so they're quick and cheap to mass produce and maintain, but their increased attack power (+1), and range (+2 tiles) means they'll always come out on top against a similar number of Archers. Their only drawback in relation to the standard Archer is their slower movement speed (1 tile per second vs 1.25 for an Archer), but that difference is meaningless once the shooting begins.

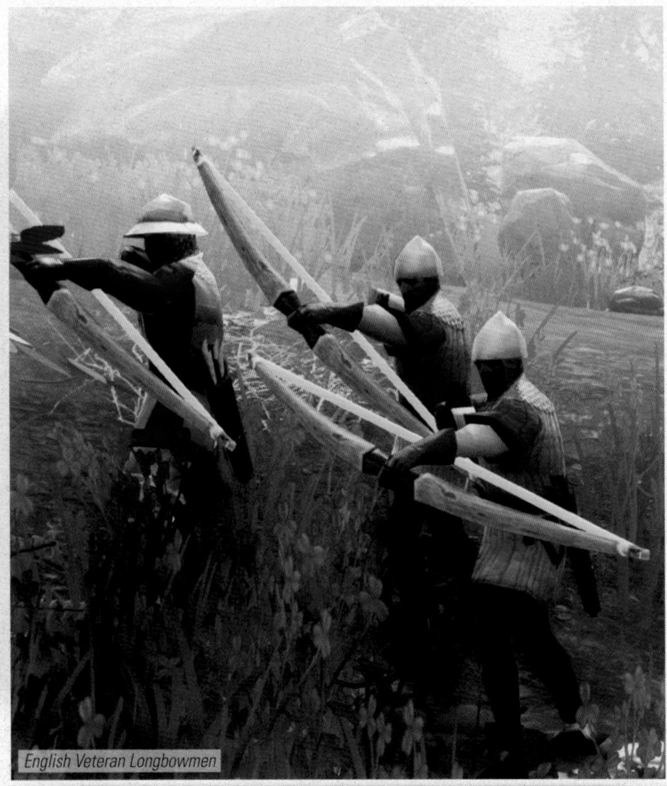

Primary Uses
- *Counter against Light Melee Infantry units*
- *Feudal Age Rush*

Training Details

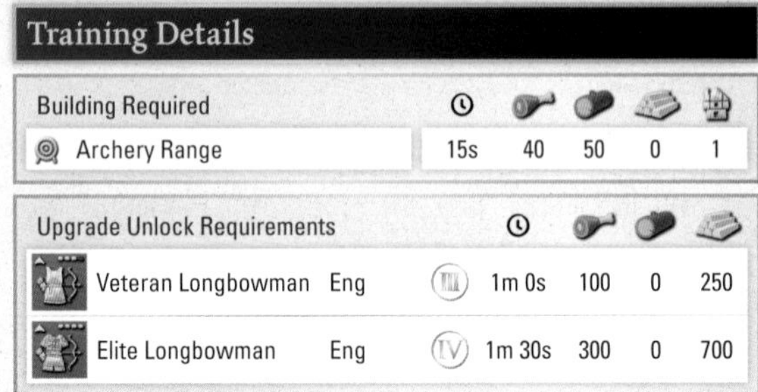

Building Required	Time	Food	Wood	Gold	Population
Archery Range	15s	40	50	0	1

Upgrade Unlock Requirements		Age	Time	Food	Wood	Gold
Veteran Longbowman	Eng	III	1m 0s	100	0	250
Elite Longbowman	Eng	IV	1m 30s	300	0	700

Unit Stats			
Health	70	80	95
Melee Armor	0	0	0
Ranged Armor	0	0	0
Move Speed	1.12	1.12	1.12
Longbow			
Damage	6	8	9
Counter Bonus	6	8	8
Bonus Against	Light Melee Infantry		
Attack Range	7.00	7.00	7.00
Attack Speed	1.50s	1.50s	1.50s

Longbowmen are very effective on elevated terrain. Due to the increased line of sight on top of hills and mountains, they can spot opposing units very quickly and make preparations ahead of time.

Special Abilities

 Place Palings

When activated, wood palings are placed in front of the unit and will remain there until the unit moves a few tiles away from them. Any cavalry that charge into those palings will be stunned and take a small amount of additional damage. This can buy significant time for reinforcements to arrive, and makes Longbowmen more valuable in stationary fights than normal Archers. The relatively short cooldown also means that you'll often have it ready to go in most engagements, so there's no need to save it for panic moments.

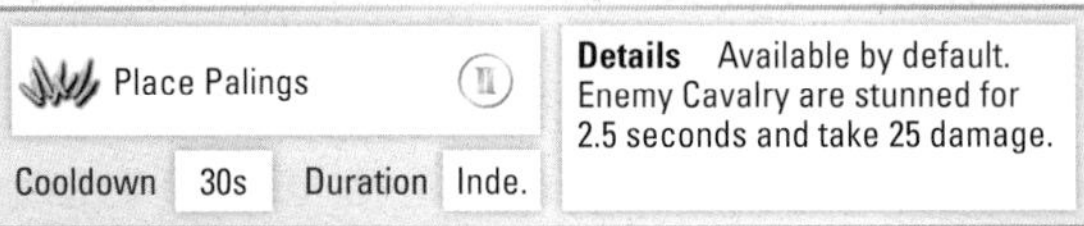

Place Palings (II)			
Cooldown	30s	Duration	Inde.

Details Available by default. Enemy Cavalry are stunned for 2.5 seconds and take 25 damage.

 Setup Camp

Upon activation, a campfire will be placed at the unit's feet, with a large circle around it that indicates its effective range. If you move outside of that range, the camp will disappear. This ability is very useful in stationary fighting, where the constant healing can help give you an extra bit of survivability. It also allows you to heal units between battles without a Monk. If you're expecting a fight, it's worth setting up a camp beforehand; it has the additional benefit of a field of vision increase, allowing units to engage enemies sooner.

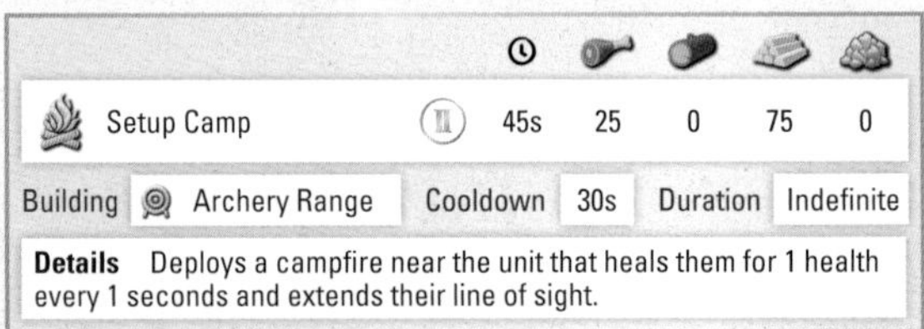

	Age	Time	Food	Wood	Gold	Stone
Setup Camp	II	45s	25	0	75	0

Building	Cooldown	Duration
Archery Range	30s	Indefinite

Details Deploys a campfire near the unit that heals them for 1 health every 1 seconds and extends their line of sight.

 Arrow Volley

This ability increases the Longbowmen's attack speed by 70%, allowing them to fire extremely quickly for its 15 second duration. It's best used in big fights against lots of units, or while retreating to help make hit-and-run tactics easier.

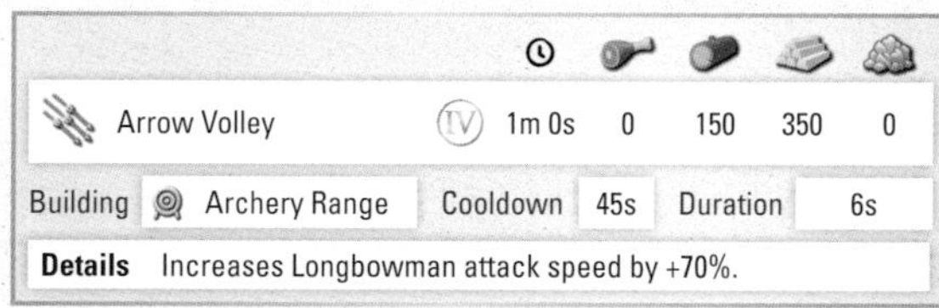

		⏱	Food	Wood	Gold	Stone
Arrow Volley	IV	1m 0s	0	150	350	0

Building	Archery Range	Cooldown	45s	Duration	6s
Details	Increases Longbowman attack speed by +70%.				

Tactics & Usage

Longbowmen are not very mobile; their power lies in stationary fighting, strengthened by their high range and special abilities. They're great for securing key locations such as hills and walls—a mass of Longbowmen atop a stone wall becomes a nearly impenetrable barrier for enemy forces. As with Archers, Longbowmen work best in large groups and enclosed spaces, where enemies are forced to walk through a rain of arrows and palings to try and reach you. Open areas, however, can be the bane of Longbowmen, since it gives your opponent much greater ability to flank and maneuver to avoid your arrows. It's usually best to accompany them with other units (ideally anti-cavalry and siege units) to mitigate their weakness against both cavalry and buildings, and help deal with any potential flanks.

The Council Hall, one of the English Feudal Age Landmarks, can also produce Longbowmen at the same cost as the Archery Range, but in half the production time. That, combined with their relative low cost, makes them an ideal rushing unit for attacks early in the game. Placing them close to your enemy's key resources early in the game will allow you to keep them from gaining a foothold there, hampering their economic growth. The Longbowmen's high range also allows them to harass the opponent at their base while staying out of range of their Town Center.

Close combat should also be avoided if possible, but the special abilities of Longbowmen do give them a better chance of victory in these situations compared to normal Archers.

Counters

To fight a group of Longbowmen, you have to attack their vulnerability: mobility. When their **Place Palings** is activated they are forced to stay at that spot, making them especially vulnerable to heavy siege units that can shoot them from afar. Once they've been forced to move, cavalry can easily catch up to them.

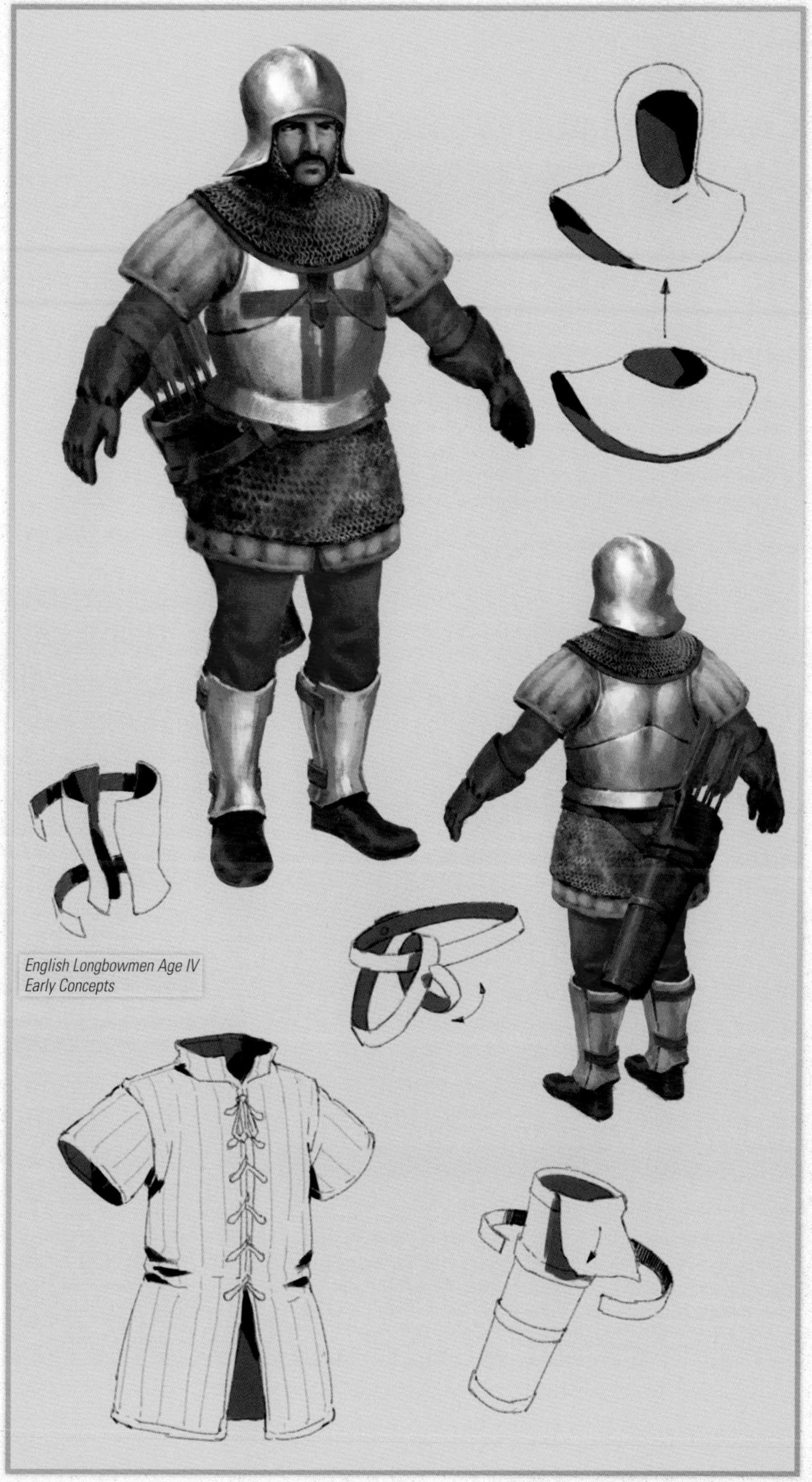

English Longbowmen Age IV Early Concepts

Crossbowman

Type	Weapon	Torch
Light Ranged Infantry	Crossbow	No

These ranged infantry units are armed with powerful crossbows that can pierce though the strongest plate armor, allowing them to shine against heavily armored units. While Archers can struggle to damage heavy units, Crossbowmen feel right at home against them. Their strength, however, does of course come at a cost. In this case it's their very slow reload times that hold them back, making them especially vulnerable at close range.

Rus Crossbowman

Tactics & Usage

Crossbowmen are instantly available after advancing to Age III, without the need for any upgrades. If you're starting to face heavily armored units such as Knights, it's possible to make a quick switch from producing Archers to Crossbowmen to counter them. Even more so than Archers, Crossbowmen should not be sent out on their own, because their long reload times and weak melee ability make them especially susceptible to Horseman charges.

As always, the units you pair them with will depend on what you think your opponent will use: if they're using cavalry to charge your Crossbowmen, put a wall of Spearmen in front of them; if they're peppering you with Archer shots, have some Horsemen charge them down. Generally, however, you should avoid having your Crossbowmen fight lightly armored units, especially Horsemen and Archers, because their strength of being able to deal damage to heavy units is completely wasted against light infantry. They're also pretty good in a defensive role atop walls, where they can deal a fair amount of damage and help stave off any enemy siege units.

Crossbowmen can reload while moving, so it's possible to temporarily keep enemy units somewhat at bay by using hit-and-run tactics and retreating away after every shot.

Counters

Although costly, Mangonels or Cannons are the perfect counter to Crossbowmen, since you can hit them from relative safety outside of their attack range. Even one or two of the siege units can be effective, especially if you pair them with some Horsemen or a large group of your own Archers, depending on what other units are accompanying the Crossbowmen. Crossbowmen are so ineffective at close range that your Horsemen will make short work of them if they can get close enough, and since Archers are so cheap to produce, you can overwhelm them with sheer numbers.

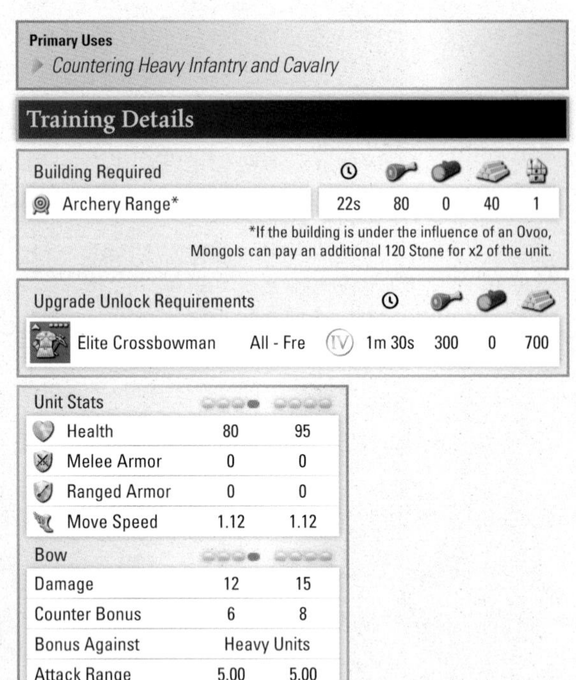

Primary Uses

Countering Heavy Infantry and Cavalry

Training Details

Building Required	Time	Food	Wood	Gold	Stone
Archery Range*	22s	80	0	40	1

*If the building is under the influence of an Ovoo, Mongols can pay an additional 120 Stone for x2 of the unit.

Upgrade Unlock Requirements		Age	Time	Food	Wood	Gold
Elite Crossbowman	All - Fre	IV	1m 30s	300	0	700

Unit Stats		
Health	80	95
Melee Armor	0	0
Ranged Armor	0	0
Move Speed	1.12	1.12
Bow		
Damage	12	15
Counter Bonus	6	8
Bonus Against	Heavy Units	
Attack Range	5.00	5.00
Attack Speed	2.00s	2.00s

Horsemen are a comparatively cheap tactical counter to Crossbowmen, especially in situations where you find yourself short on Gold.

Grenadier

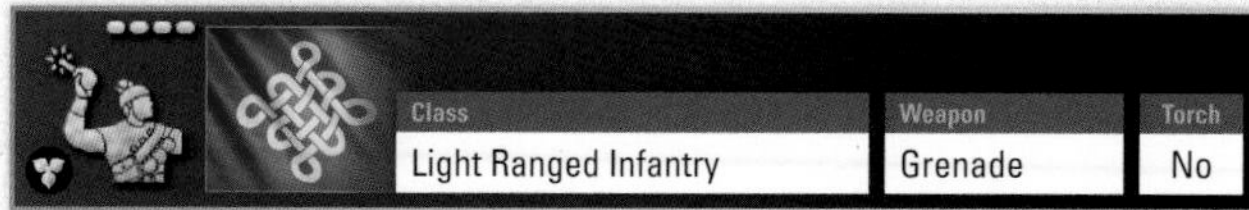

Class	Weapon	Torch
Light Ranged Infantry	Grenade	No

Grenadiers are a unique Chinese ranged infantry unit that come into play relatively late in the game at Age IV, once you have advanced to the Ming Dynasty. The best way to think of this unit is as "siege infantry," because instead of the arrows or bolts used by other ranged infantry, Grenadiers throw small explosive canisters that deal damage over a small area. This allows you to hit multiple units at once, if they're tightly grouped. For a late-game unit they also have a fairly low production time and cost, allowing large numbers of them to quickly bolster your army as soon as they become available.

Chinese Grenadiers

Primary Uses

- *Attacking large groups of enemy infantry*

Training Details

Building Required					
Archery Range	30s	120	60	60	1

Unit Stats	
Health	150
Melee Armor	0
Ranged Armor	0
Move Speed	1.12
Grenade	
Damage	15
Counter Bonus	--
Bonus Against	--
Attack Range	4.00
Attack Speed	1.50s
Grenade (Siege)	
Damage	30
Counter Bonus	--
Bonus Against	--
Attack Range	4.00
Attack Speed	1.50s

Tactics & Usage

If you want to make use of Grenadiers you'll need to plan ahead with your resources, because you'll need to progress through all of the Ages and build both Age IV Landmarks. Grenadiers are best suited to a support role rather than a primary unit within your army, where a small group of them can deal some additional area of effect damage and bolster your overall combat effectiveness. Keeping them in a supportive role also helps to offset their low health and slow movement speed, which if they were on their own, could easily be exploited by your opponent. Another way to offset those downsides and play to the strengths of Grenadiers is to use them in static defensive roles on top of walls or hills; such positions are often attacked by groups of enemies, and the additional range will help keep your Grenadiers safe.

Chinese Grenadier—Age IV Concept Artwork

A bunch of grenades thrown into a mass of enemy units will greatly enhance your chances of winning a fight.

Counters

Grenadiers are inherently weak against any sort of siege unit, so Mangonels and Cannons are very effective against them, and even Springalds can be used to snipe them one by one due to their slow movement speed. Other ranged infantry can be used to counter them, but if you go down this route, make sure to spread your units out by using the Spread Formation "C." The slow reload time of Grenadiers also means that cavalry are an excellent counter again them, because they'll take little damage during the initial charge and can easily overwhelm them once within melee range.

Handcannoneer

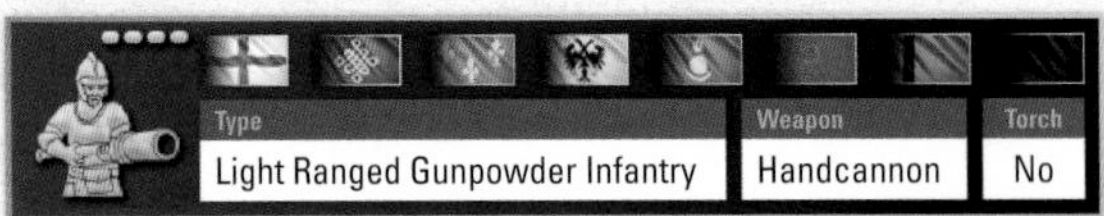

Type
Light Ranged Gunpowder Infantry
Weapon
Handcannon
Torch
No

Upon reaching Age IV, all civilizations except Rus (turn to P.161 to read about their specialized variant, the Streltsy) will be able to produce the powerful Handcannoneer. The role of this unit is somewhat similar to the Crossbowman in that it is a high damage, slow rate of fire infantry unit. The Handcannoneer packs an even bigger punch, however, albeit at the cost of some range.

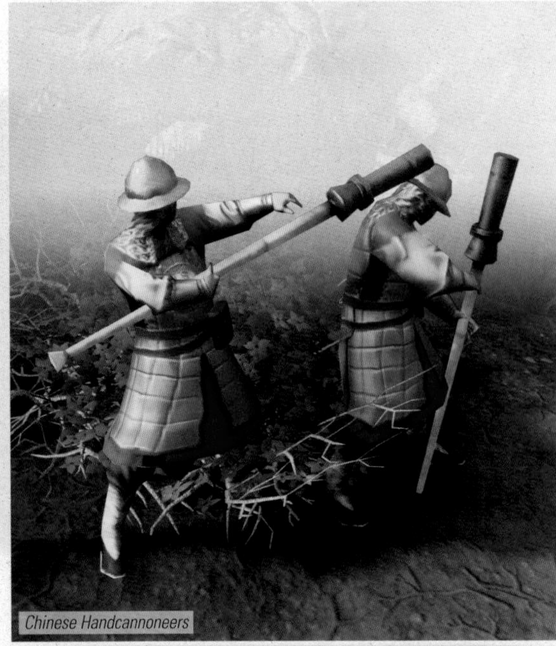
Chinese Handcannoneers

Tactics & Usage

The only thing that rivals the damage of the Handcannoneer is the cost it takes to produce them; if you're planning on working them into your army, you'll need plenty of readily available Gold. Time is also another factor to consider, with each Handcannoneer taking a full 35 seconds to produce. All of this means that Handcanoneers are not a unit that you can reactively decide to deploy at a moment's notice. Rather, it's one that requires some forethought as part of an overall strategy.

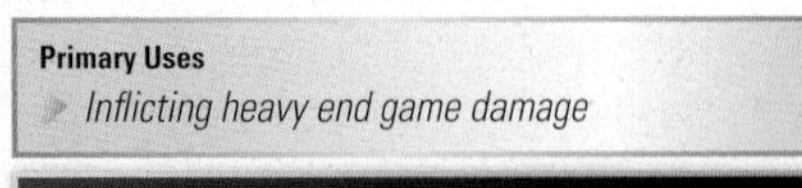

Training Details

Building Required					
Archery Range*	35s	120	0	120	1

*If the building is under the influence of an Ovoo, Mongols can pay an additional 240 Stone for x2 of the unit.

Unit Stats	
Health	150
Melee Armor	0
Ranged Armor	0
Move Speed	1.12
Handcannon	
Damage	42
Counter Bonus	--
Bonus Against	--
Attack Range	4.00
Attack Speed	2.00s

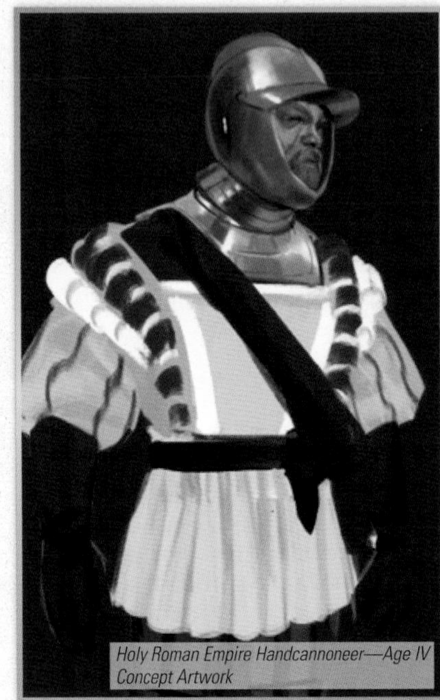
Holy Roman Empire Handcannoneer—Age IV Concept Artwork

Due to their high damage output, Handcannoneers do well against almost every unit. Because they have less range than most other ranged units, they do need to be accompanied by some support units to stand between them and the enemy units while they fire. Hancannoneers also deal minimal damage to buildings, so if you're using them as part of an army that's attacking a base, they're better suited to helping defend the area while your other units focus on destroying the buildings.

When placed on top of walls, Hancannoneers outperform other ranged infantry against enemy Battering Rams due to their high attack value, so they can be extremely useful when used in defensive roles.

Counters

Their low health, slow movement speed and weak melee attack means that Handcannoneers are vulnerable to heavy siege weapons and cavalry charges. While both of those options are effective on their own, combined they can be devastating. Have your Mangonels or Cannons fire at the Handcannoneers while your cavalry surround and charge them. Their lack of range can also be used to your advantage if you can exploit it with some upgraded Archers by keeping your distance and picking them off without getting close.

Landsknecht

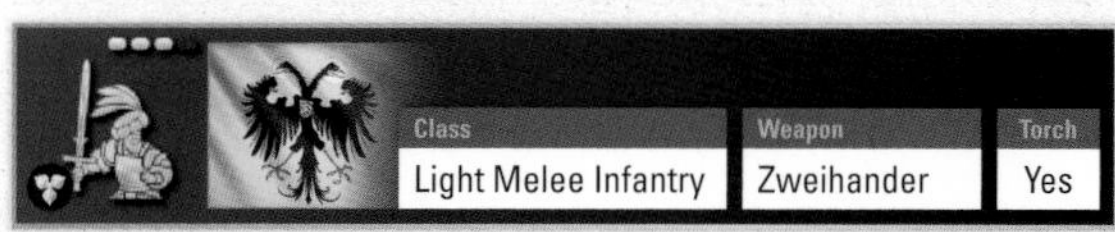

Class	Weapon	Torch
Light Melee Infantry	Zweihander	Yes

The Landsknecht is a mercenary unit that sells its services to the Holy Roman Empire, and the high Gold cost to produce the unit definitely reinforces that feeling. They carry a huge broadsword and use sweeping attacks to deal damage over a small area. The sheer weight of that sword, however, means that they sacrifice some armor in order to stay mobile, making them the epitome of a high risk, high reward unit.

Primary Uses

- *Attacking other groups of melee infantry*

Training Details

Building Required	Time	Food	Wood	Gold	Population
Barracks	22s	60	0	100	1

Upgrade Unlock Requirements			Time	Food	Wood	Gold
Elite Landsknecht	HRE	IV	1m 30s	300	0	700

Unit Stats		
Health	80	95
Melee Armor	0	0
Ranged Armor	0	0
Move Speed	1.25	1.25
Zweihander		
Damage	17	20
Counter Bonus	--	--
Bonus Against	--	--
Attack Range	0.29	0.29
Attack Speed	1.25s	1.25s
Charge Attack		
Damage	17	20
Counter Bonus	--	--
Bonus Against	--	--
Attack Range	0.54	0.54
Attack Speed	1.35s	1.35s

Holy Roman Empire Landsknechte

Tactics & Usage

The Landsknecht's main role is to deal heavy damage to clumped up units in messy fights—this is where lightly armored units will crumble under their attacks. Landsknechte deal damage within a frontal cone area rather than a straight line direct attack, so even though their attacks don't have any more range than other melee units, they cover a much larger total area, making them ideal for taking on groups of enemy infantry.

Because of the nature of Landsknechte attacks, towards the edge of the range they'll only be dealing 50% of their potential damage, so you'll want to get as close to the enemy as you can.

Because of their light armor, having them be the main unit in your army can be quite risky. Try to gauge the types of units your opponent is using to decide whether or not that risk will pay off. It's safest to pair them with other units, such as cavalry, because then if your opponent does lean into ranged infantry, your cavalry can absorb the initial hits while your Landsknechte move in behind them. If you're low on Food but have Gold, they can be used in most situations where you would use Men-at-Arms; just keep in mind that Landsknechte do not deal with incoming arrow fire as well, so pair them with other units accordingly.

Keeping them safe as they approach is especially important, because the initial charge attack of the Landsknecht is very powerful and covers a lot of range. This puts greater importance on making sure as many of them survive to get close to the enemy as possible, for maximum effect. The strength of that charge, and its area of effect attack, means they're also an excellent ambush unit from within Stealth Forests, since you can catch opponents unaware and not take as much damage while you close in. Using Landsknechte against any kind of heavy fortifications or siege units is not advised, because their low health means that they can picked apart quite easily. Make sure to position your Landsknechte away from such things, and only bring them in once they are either destroyed or distracted.

If you plan on producing Landsknechte as soon as you're able to, it's worth also building the **Burgrave Palace** Landmark. In this building you can create five Landsknechte (or other infantry units) in the time it would normally take you to produce one. This does require planning, since you have to commit the resources for all five at once, but it can be useful for both defensive and offensive purposes.

Counters

To counter a group of Landsknechte, you should avoid all types of melee units and go for any type of massed ranged unit (even Archers, as long as they can keep their distance) and heavy siege. A Landsknecht's low health means that sustained ranged attacks can pick them apart while they approach. If you see your opponent is using other units to defend them, try to focus on the Landsknechte first, because if they get within melee range, they're extremely deadly.

Man-at-Arms

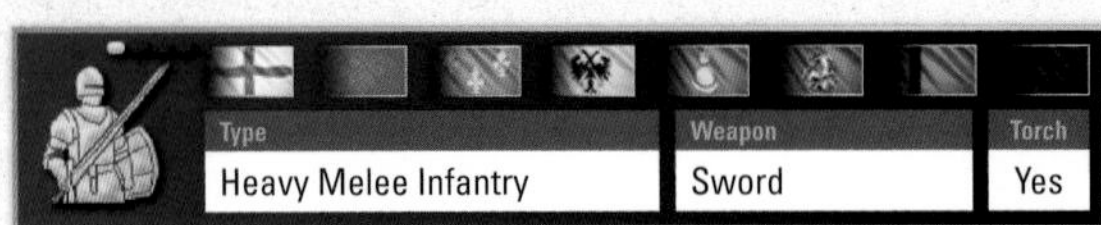

Type	Weapon	Torch
Heavy Melee Infantry	Sword	Yes

Palace Guard

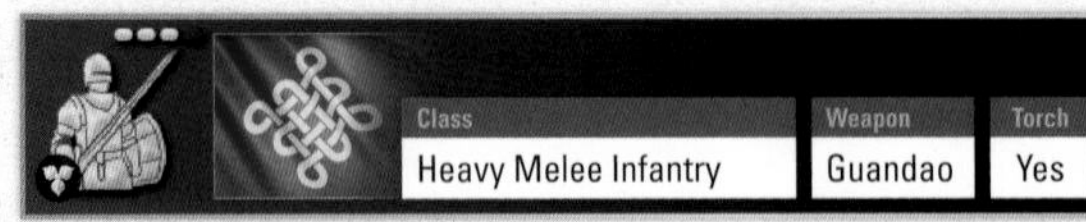

Class	Weapon	Torch
Heavy Melee Infantry	Guandao	Yes

The Man-at-Arms is a workhorse Heavy Melee Infantry unit that most civilizations get access to at Age III, but the English and HRE get access to them slightly earlier, and the Chinese get access to their own unique variant. As a sturdy all-rounder, the Man-at-Arms is equally at home fighting any kind of light unit, be it Archer, Spearman or even Horseman, and they're also a great unit for attacking buildings and siege units. Basically, regardless of what you're fighting, the chances are that Men-at-Arms will be able to lead the charge.

Primary Uses

- *Jack-of-all-trades Heavy Melee Infantry unit*

Training Details: Man-at-Arms

Building Required	Time	Food	Wood	Gold	Population
Barracks*	22s	100	0	20	1

*If the building is under the influence of an Ovoo, Mongols can pay an additional 120 Stone for x2 of the unit.

Upgrade Unlock Requirements		Age	Time	Food	Wood	Gold
Early Man-at-Arms	Eng	II	30s	25	0	75
Man-at-Arms	Eng/HRE	III	30s	50	0	125
Elite Man-at-Arms	All - Chi	IV	1m 30s	300	0	700

Unit Stats				
Health	100	120	155	180
Melee Armor	2	3	4	5
Ranged Armor	2	3	4	5
Move Speed	1.12	1.12	1.12	1.12
Sword				
Damage	8	10	12	14
Counter Bonus	--	--	--	--
Bonus Against	--	--	--	--
Attack Range	0.29	0.29	0.29	0.29
Attack Speed	1.25s	1.25s	1.25s	1.25s
Charge Attack				
Damage	8	10	12	14
Counter Bonus	--	--	--	--
Bonus Against	--	--	--	--
Attack Range	0.54	0.54	0.54	0.54
Attack Speed	1.25s	1.25s	1.25s	1.25s

Training Details: Palace Guard

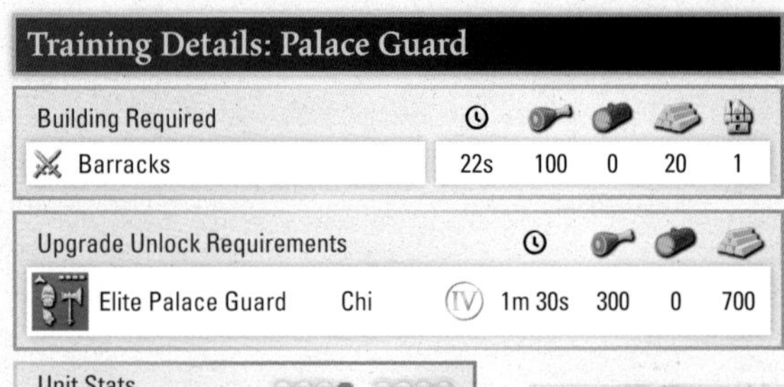

Building Required	Time	Food	Wood	Gold	Population
Barracks	22s	100	0	20	1

Upgrade Unlock Requirements		Age	Time	Food	Wood	Gold
Elite Palace Guard	Chi	IV	1m 30s	300	0	700

Unit Stats		
Health	125	145
Melee Armor	5	6
Ranged Armor	5	6
Move Speed	1.37	1.37
Guandao		
Damage	12	14
Counter Bonus	--	--
Bonus Against	--	--
Attack Range	0.29	0.29
Attack Speed	1.25s	1.25s
Charge Attack		
Damage	12	14
Counter Bonus	--	--
Bonus Against	--	--
Attack Range	0.54	0.54
Attack Speed	1.25s	1.25s

French Men-at-Arms

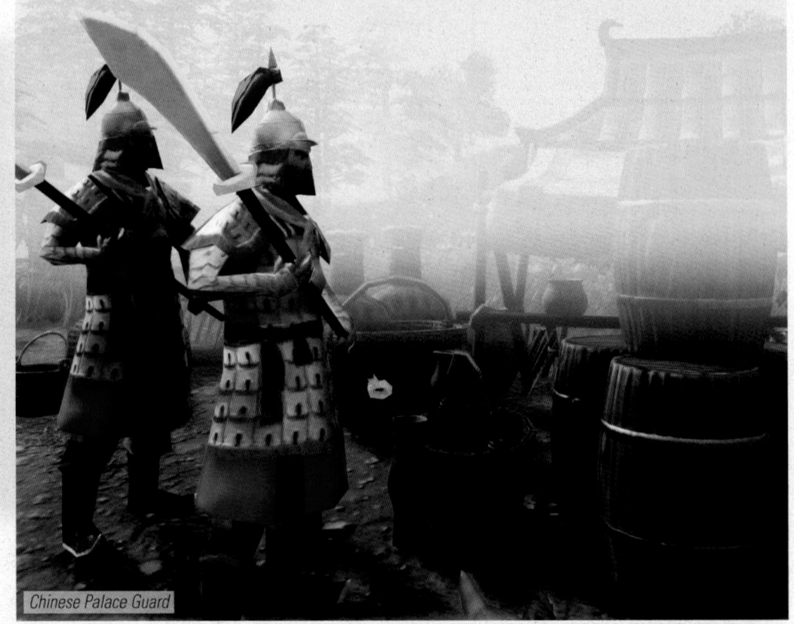

Chinese Palace Guard

Special Versions

Palace Guard (Chinese)

The Palace Guard is a version of the Man-at-Arms units that's exclusively available to the Chinese.They have more armor and are significantly faster than the standard Man-at-Arms, and benefit from a unique Chinese upgrade called **Battle Hardened** that provides them with more health.

Vanguard Man-at-Arms (English)

The English can produce Men-at-Arms from Age I in the form of the Vanguard Man-at-Arms, which they can then upgrade to Early Man-at-Arms in Age II. Producing them in Age I for the purpose of rushing is rarely worth it, because your Gold and Food income will likely be quite slow, and your opponent will probably be on their way to the next age by the time your Men-at-Arms arrive. That being said, if your opponent likes to venture outside the safety of their Town Center to look for animals, you might be able to catch them off guard and easily take out the hunting party.

Early Man-at-Arms (English, HRE)

Both the English and HRE gain access to the Early Man-at-Arms once they reach Age II, by which time your economy should be at the point where you can be quite aggressive with this unit. Since most hard-hitting units aren't accessible until at least Age III, Early Men-at-Arms are very hard to counter at this stage of the game, and as such they're ideal for extended Feudal Age play. Their relatively high armor for Age II and high attack means they can also try to take down defensive buildings and Landmarks if you gain the upper hand, which may lead to an early victory.

Men-at-Arms vastly outperform other light infantry units when it comes to withstanding and overcoming static defenses.

Due to their armour, Men-at-Arms are a good choice of unit to attack enemy Town Centers with.

Tactics & Usage

Generally, Men-at-Arms are designed to counter other light units that cost only Wood and Food, such as Archers, Spearmen and Horsemen. As such, they mostly come into play in Age III to repel a massed Feudal Age army, by taking advantage of their superior upgrades. Men-at-Arms are the perfect infantry to bolster your army in nearly every situation, and should only be avoided once a lot of units that can counter heavy infantry, such as Crossbowmen, Handcannoneers, or some siege units, come into play. Until then they can be a game changer that can be amassed and reinforced quickly, due to their low production time, and can be a key component of mid-game victories.

Early Men-at-Arms can be used to kill enemy villagers to slow their economy down early in games.

Rus Age II Man-at-Arms 3D Sculpt

Counters

Low numbers of Men-at-Arms can be countered by a group of Archers, but this is only effective if the Archers significantly outnumber the Men-at-Arms—other units become a better option if you're facing similarly matched numbers. Knights in somewhat equal numbers will overpower Men-at-Arms through sheer power, plus their much faster movement speed allows them to choose when to start the encounter. Any type of Mounted Archer is also extremely effective, because they can use their mobility to use hit-and-run tactics until the enemy infantry is defeated.

Outside of cavalry, the most effective counters are units designed to take down heavy infantry, such as Crossbowmen or Handcannoneers; unless those units are severely outnumbered, they will generally come out on top. Siege units, such as Mangonels, can be effective against a group of Men-at-Arms in sufficient numbers, but a lone Mangonel will still fall pretty quickly. Static defenses, such as Outposts, will also need some support from additional nearby units, so don't rely on them alone if you're trying to repel and incoming group of Men-at-Arms.

English Man-at-Arms Age IV Armor Concept Artworks

Using Color

"We researched what each civilization looked like, and most importantly, considered what sorts of building materials and types of cloth were available during these periods of time. We then tried to group colours into what made sense for each civilization; we tried to give each civilization its own colour identity. And atop it all, the team colours, UI, effects, and so forth had to work, so we layered the colour palettes for each civilization according to that sort of colour priority and structure."

– Stuart Ng
Senior Concept Artist, Relic

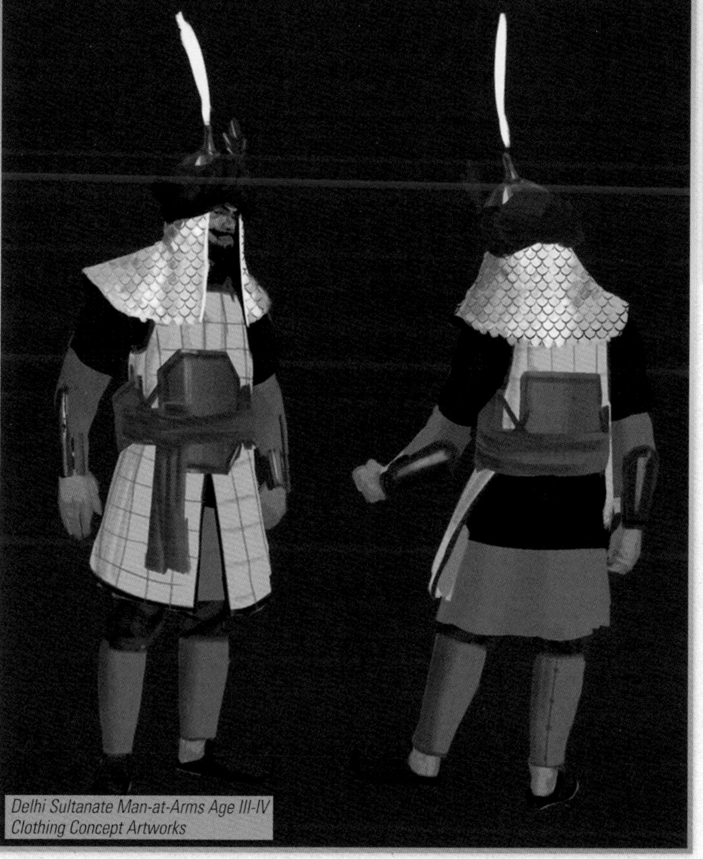

Delhi Sultanate Man-at-Arms Age III-IV
Clothing Concept Artworks

Abbasid Dynasty Man-at-Arms—Age ii-IV
Concept Artworks

The Use of Concept Art

"Concept art is the initial ideation in all game development, it's a quick way to 'realize' how far can one push the historical while balancing the readability and recognition. Even once objects are built in 3D there was still much work to be done to tweak and change. Concept is an aspiration, a shared idea in our minds realized for all to see, that's where we may remove the variances folks have in their own heads. The 2D concepts and even a 3D concept removes the assumptions quickly and then the real work of editing and all solving the same puzzle can begin.

Also concept helps with the 'compression' of a historical visual to make it more game friendly. It's simply faster in 2d and allows for a springboard for 3D to advance the iteration."

– Han Randhawa
Franchise Art Director, World's Edge

Monk

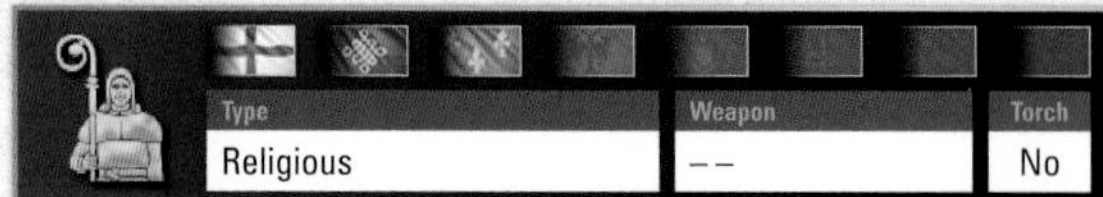

Type	Weapon	Torch
Religious	--	No

Imam

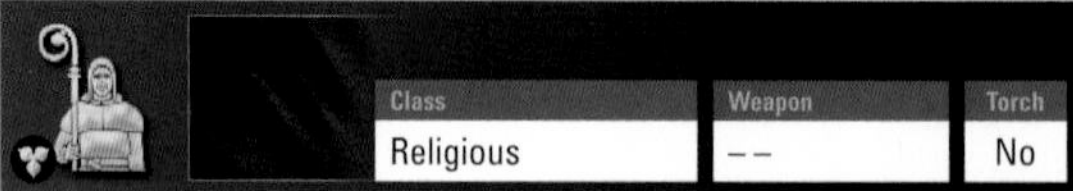

Class	Weapon	Torch
Religious	--	No

Shaman

Class	Weapon	Torch
Religious	--	No

Looking purely at their stats, you may think these units lack any kind of combat capability: low health, no armor, low speed and expensive production cost suggest that these units should be avoided, but nothing could be further from the truth. Monks, Imams, and Shamans are the ultimate support units and have one of the most important roles in the game. Although their names and the buildings they're produced from may differ, they're each functionally and statistically identical. Their abilities range from healing other units, to converting enemy units to your side, and if you're going for a Sacred Win Condition in Skirmish or Multiplayer, they're a necessity in order to win the game.

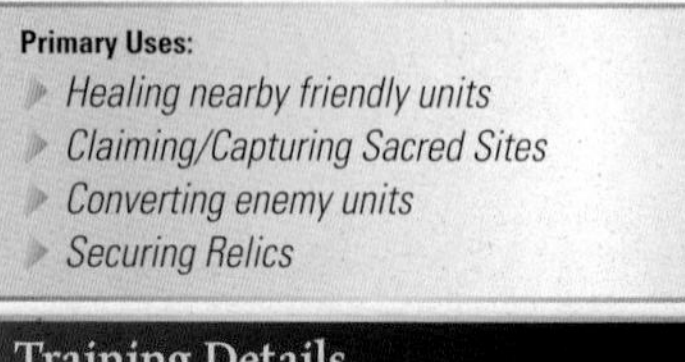

Primary Uses:

- *Healing nearby friendly units*
- *Claiming/Capturing Sacred Sites*
- *Converting enemy units*
- *Securing Relics*

Training Details

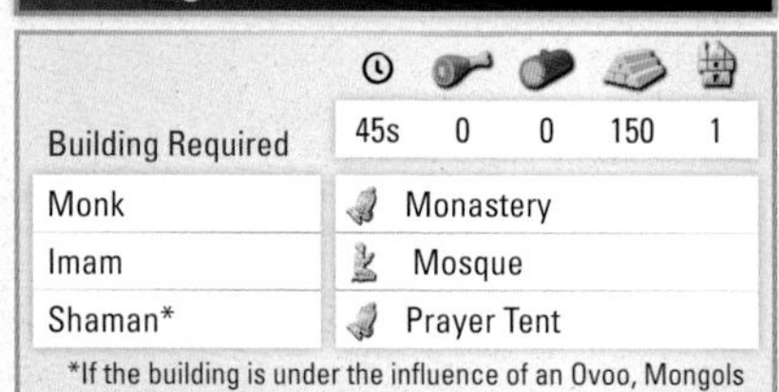

Building Required	Time	Food	Wood	Gold	Population
	45s	0	0	150	1
Monk	Monastery				
Imam	Mosque				
Shaman*	Prayer Tent				

*If the building is under the influence of an Ovoo, Mongols can pay an additional 150 Stone for x2 of the unit.

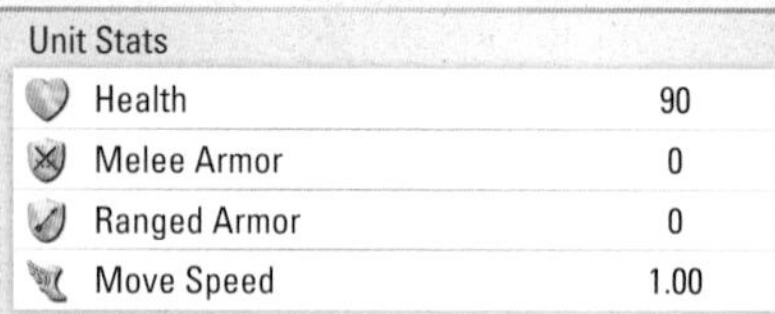

Unit Stats	
Health	90
Melee Armor	0
Ranged Armor	0
Move Speed	1.00

Usage & Abilities

Healing

These units have the power to heal any allied units close to them. This is especially useful with high Health units, such as Knights or elephants. Healing a Knight is worth almost as much as making a new one, and can tip the battle in your favor.

Relics

Relics are dispersed all over the map in random positions, though there are only ever a few in total. They enable your Monks, Imams or Shamans to act as an additional means of generating Gold by garrisoning it in a Monastery. This leads to gaining 100 Gold per minute, and each additional Relic you garrison will get you an extra 100 Gold per minute.

Conversion

These units also have the ability convert enemy units to your side. To do this you'll need to activate the ability while holding a Relic. A blue ring will appear around your character in a 5.5 tile radius, and any enemy unit within the radius will either get converted to your side

English Monks

Abbasid Dynasty Imams

Mongol Shaman

after a short time, or die if you have no population capacity available. When attempting to convert enemy units, keep in mind that you're unable to move for the duration of the ability, and are vulnerable units attacking you from outside of the conversion radius.

 Sacred Sites

Sacred Sites are also found randomly around the map, and once discovered, you can direct one of your Religious units in an attempt to capture it for your team by standing inside the area for a short period of time. Once a Sacred Site is in your possession it will generate 100 Gold per minute for as long as you hold it. The only way to lose possession is if the Religious unit of an opposing team stands in the area uncontested until it's captured for their side.

It takes about 6 seconds from the activation to the conversion of all enemy units inside the circle. The cooldown for this ability is two minutes.

Only Religious units can capture Sacred Sites, which means that with the exception of the Delhi Sultanates, who have access to a Scholar upgrade that lets them capture Sacred Sites before Age III, other civilizations have to wait until Age III before they can capture one. This holds true even for the HRE, whose Prelates still have to wait until Age III.

Counters

Since you don't have to worry about any offensive capabilities, the best units to end against Monks, Shamans and Imams are fast-moving light melee or ranged units that can close in quickly and finish them off before any potential reinforcements arrive. If there are already additional units forming a defensive perimeter, you may want to consider using a Springald. The Springald's main role is to snipe high value targets, and with a 10 tile range, it can do so from well outside the range of most other units.

Abbasid Dynasty Imam Age II Concept Artwork

Prelate

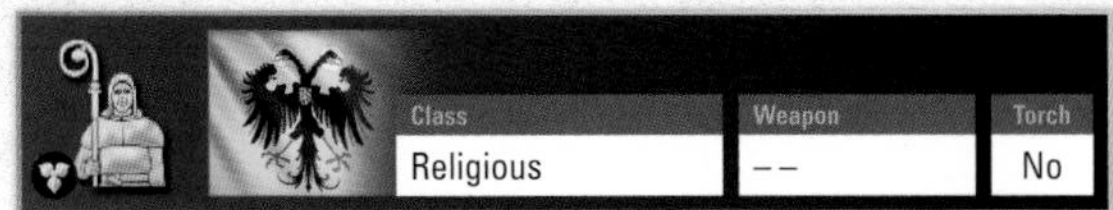

Class	Weapon	Torch
Religious	--	No

The Prelate is a unique Holy Roman Empire unit that also fulfills the role and duties of a Monk. For more information on Monks, please refer to P.154. Prelates can be produced straight away in Age I from your Town Center (or in Age III from a Monastery) for half the cost and time of other Religious units, but that's not their only claim to fame. Prelates are one of the most important units available to the Holy Roman Empire, because they can Inspire Villagers to gather resources at an accelerated rate, giving you a massive boost to the speed at which you can grow your economy.

Holy Roman Empire Prelate

Primary Uses

- *Boosting Villager gathering efficiency*
- *Healing nearby friendly units*
- *Converting enemy units*
- *Securing Relics*

Training Details

Building Required	Time	Food	Wood	Gold	Population
Town Center	20s	0	0	100	1

Unit Stats	
Health	90
Melee Armor	0
Ranged Armor	0
Move Speed	1.00

Abilities & Technology

Although you can produce Prelates from your Town Center during Age I, you'll have to wait until you can construct a Monastery in Age III to gain access to some of the unique technologies that they can take advantage of. **Benediction** makes inspired Villagers construct buildings 15% faster, while **Devoutness** makes them gather resources 10% faster. Finally, perhaps the biggest change comes from the **Holy Warriors** technology—it allows Prelates to Inspire military units, granting an additional +1 armor and +15% damage.

 Holy Inspiration

Through **Holy Inspiration**, the Prelate can boost the gathering rates of Villagers one at a time. Inspiring one Villager takes around three seconds, and since it has a duration of 30 seconds, one Prelate can effectively inspire a group of 10 Villagers if you want to maximize uptime. When you have the full 10 inspired, they will essentially be doing the work of 14 regular Villagers, so it's a significant boost to your resource intake. Depending on what strategy you're employing, you can then direct your more efficient Villagers to focus on the part of the economy that will benefit you the most. If you intend to produce a number of Prelates, you may want to send more Villagers than normal to mine Gold to cover their production cost, especially early in a game.

*While the boost from the **Holy Warriors** technology isn't huge, if you're facing off against an equally matched group of units, it's enough to give you the edge.*

Tactics & Usage

Producing at least one Prelate as early as possible in a game is highly recommended, especially since the cost can quickly be recovered by the inspired Villagers. Using Prelates early still requires a relatively balanced economy, and that can lead to a bit more micromanaging than you might be comfortable with. If you're using your inspired Villagers to mine Gold, for example, then use less than you usually would, saving a few to gather other resources with.

You can make this process a bit easier to manage by waiting until later in the game, when you're ready to build the Landmark to advance to Age II, because your economy will already be somewhat established by that point. Age II is when you'll be making significant advancements to your economy and military; by using this strategy you won't have to worry about every aspect of your economic growth, and can afford to have your inspired Villagers focus solely on the key resource for the strategy of your choice. For an even bigger boost, you might want to also consider building the **Aachen Chapel** Landmark between your resources and have your Prelate take up a garrisoned position inside it. This gives you a huge influence area around the building, saving you from inspiring a few Villagers at a time.

Regardless of how you've used them during the initial stages of the game, once you get into the later stages, Prelates are almost mandatory for the Holy Roman Empire. You'll need to put a lot of thought into where you position Prelates around the map, and always ensure they're close to a group of Villagers to keep up efficiently. But be careful: every dead Prelate will cost you greatly in economical output, and even every Villager that dies is more costly than normal because they're more efficient; always keep some military units or defensive buildings nearby to keep them as safe as possible.

Scholar

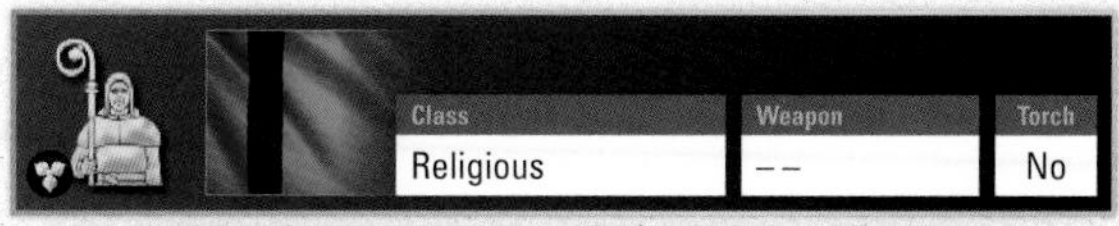

Scholars are the backbone that support all Delhi Sultanate technological advancement, and are and essential component of effective Delhi Sultanate play. You have access to both Scholars and the Mosque that produces them straight away in Age I, and for every Scholar (up to three) that you garrison inside the Mosque (or the Madrasa in Age IV), the speed at which research is completed is accelerated. Because the Delhi Sultanate have naturally longer research times, effectively using your Scholars is extremely important. Outside of that primary use, they also function and have the same abilities as the other Religious units in the game, for more information on which you can check P.154.

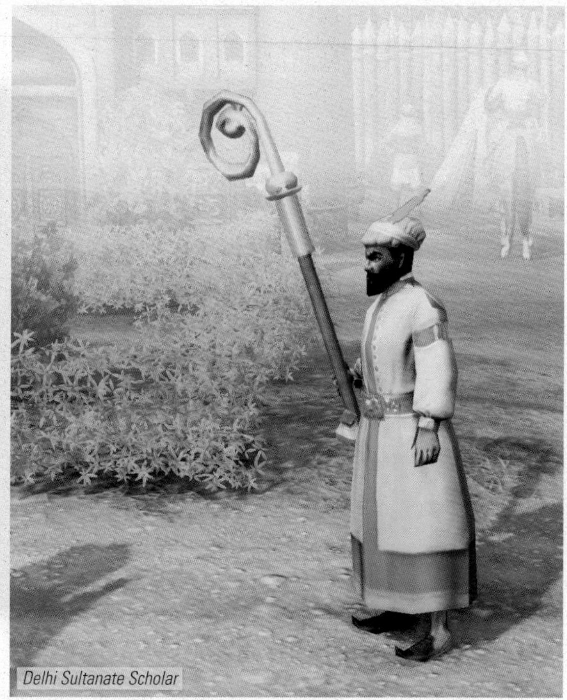

Delhi Sultanate Scholar

Primary Uses

- *Accelerating the rate at which research is completed*
- *Healing nearby friendly units*
- *Converting enemy units*
- *Securing Relics*

Training Details

Building Required					
Mosque	45s	0	0	150	1

Unit Stats	
Health	90
Melee Armor	0
Ranged Armor	0
Move Speed	1.00

Technology & Abilities

On top of their default ability to speed up technology research when garrisoned in a Mosque, Scholars also benefit from a number of unique upgrades that can further enhance their already impressive capabilities. Probably the most important of these is **Efficient Production**, which allows you to garrison Scholars inside buildings that produce military units, resulting in a +100% increase to production speed that can have a dramatic impact on how fast you can build your army.

Sanctity is especially useful during early stages of the game, because it allows Scholars to capture Sacred Sites before Age III, making them the only unit capable of doing so and giving them a huge advantage under certain win conditions. In addition, any sites that you do control will generate an extra +100% Gold, providing a boost to your early game economy.

The remaining upgrades are mainly geared towards improving your Scholars' ability to work in conjunction with your military units out in the field. **Zeal** will give any unit that's healed a +50% attack speed increase for three seconds, and **All-Seeing Eye** doubles the sight range of the Scholar, helping with general perception while moving with a group of military units. Finally, there's **Swiftness**, which increases the movement speed of your Scholars by +50%, allowing them to keep up with your faster units. With all these upgrades, Scholars outshine most other Religious units, and they're an indispensable support unit.

The utility of a Scholar is extremely beneficial for expensive military units such as the War Elephant, since they can not only keep health topped up, but also make them a lot deadlier when they're in combat.

Tactics & Usage

There are some important things to keep in mind if you want to get the most out of the Delhi Sultanate economy. Any technology that you've already started researching can still be sped up by new Scholars being garrisoned in the building, meaning that any research should be started immediately rather than waiting until you have more Scholars.

Not only does the speed increase count for the Mosque/Madrasa that the Scholars have garrisoned, it also extends to any other building in the surrounding influence range; if the influence range of two garrisoned Mosques/Madrasa overlaps, then that effect will stack for all buildings within the area covered by both Mosques/Madrasa. For more information on those buildings, turn to P.249/P.264. When it comes time to advance to Age II, you should strongly consider building the **Dome of Faith** if you intend to use a lot of Scholars, because it will enable you to produce them at half the cost.

Spearman

Type	Weapon	Torch
Light Melee Infantry	Spear	Yes

Spearmen are one of four military units that do not cost Gold, and are one of the cheapest units overall to produce. Their production time of 15 seconds means that Spearmen are extremely quick to train in large numbers, and because all civilizations except the English have access to Spearmen in Age I, they're a vital component to amassing a powerful early force. The Spearman should also be your first choice for battling enemy cavalry units due to their bonus damage against them. They can automatically use a Spearwall attack when cavalry units charge at them, and while it deals less damage than their normal attack, it has significantly more range, letting them get an early hit in before they start their regular attacks. All of that coupled with their ease of production and formidable attack speed means they'll nearly always come out on top in a direct engagement.

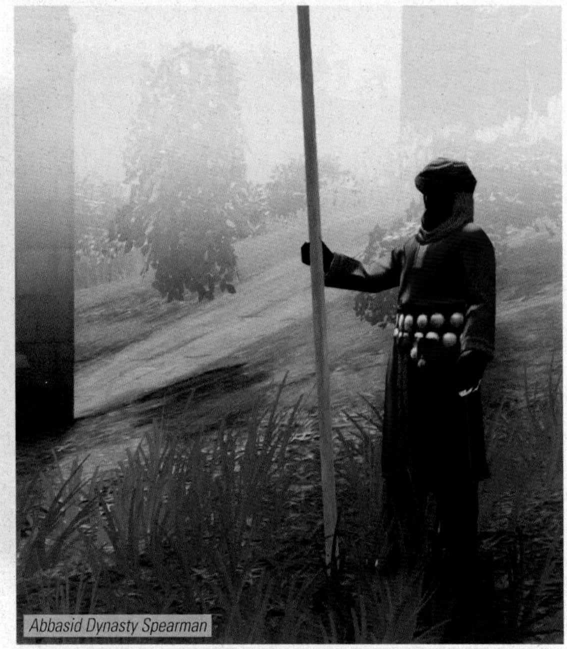

Abbasid Dynasty Spearman

Primary Uses

- *Counter against cavalry units*

Training Details

Building Required	Time	Food	Wood	Gold	Population
Barracks*	15s	60	20	0	1

*If the building is under the influence of an Ovoo, Mongols can pay an additional 80 Stone for x2 of the unit.

Upgrade Unlock Requirements		Age	Time	Food	Wood	Gold
Hardened Spearman	All - Eng	II	30s	25	0	75
Veteran Spearman	All	III	1m 0s	100	0	250
Elite Spearman	All	IV	1m 30s	300	0	700

Unit Stats				
Health	70	90	110	130
Melee Armor	0	0	0	0
Ranged Armor	0	0	0	0
Move Speed	1.25	1.25	1.25	1.25

Spear				
Damage	6	8	9	11
Counter Bonus	12	16	18	22
Bonus Against	Cavalry			
Attack Range	0.29	0.29	0.29	0.29
Attack Speed	1.75s	1.75s	1.75s	1.75s

Tactics & Usage

The places where the Spearman truly shine is in the early game and as guards for other units. Between the Dark Age and the Castle Age, the role of the Spearman can mostly be summed up as a cheap melee unit that can be mass produced and is good at taking down buildings. Gold tends to be a rare resource during this part of the game and should mainly be spent on upgrades or a small number of powerful units, and a mass of Spearmen in combination with Archers can do very well in this scenario.

As the game progresses and the more powerful units become commonplace, the Spearman's role tends to change from a primary attacking unit to one that is best used to protect other key units, such as siege and powerful ranged units from cavalry attacks. This is mainly due to the fact that as Gold becomes more readily available, the amount of potential units your opponent can produce that have the upper-hand against Spearmen significantly increases, and their effectiveness as the bulk of your army goes down accordingly. Of course, if your opponent is primarily using cavalry, Spearmen can still have a place, but if they're using heavy cavalry, you'll need to significantly outnumber the enemy units; the high health and charge strength of those units means that in an even fight they'll come out on top.

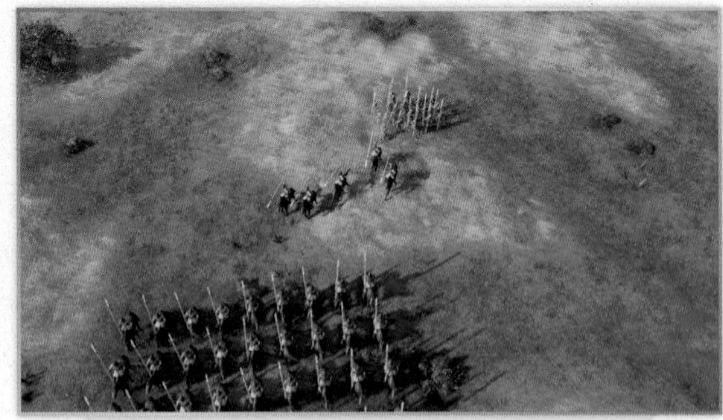

Spearmen's comparatively low movement speed does mean that cavalry units can sometimes escape unless forced to fight, and if you send them directly at enemy ranged infantry, they're likely to get picked off as they approach.

Counters

The cheapest and easiest counter to a large group of Spearmen is an equally large group of Archers. Archers can be produced just as fast and cheaply as Spearmen, so if you see your opponent amassing their Spearmen, make sure to do the same with some Archers. Once you have access to a steady Gold income, any of the heavy melee infantry units, or siege units such as Mangonels and the Nest of Bees, can decimate groups of Spearmen if they're not defended by other units.

Abbasid Dynasty Spearman—Age II-IV
Concept Artworks

Delhi Sultanate Spearman—Age IV
3d Sculpt

Rus Spearman—Age II
Concept Artwork

3

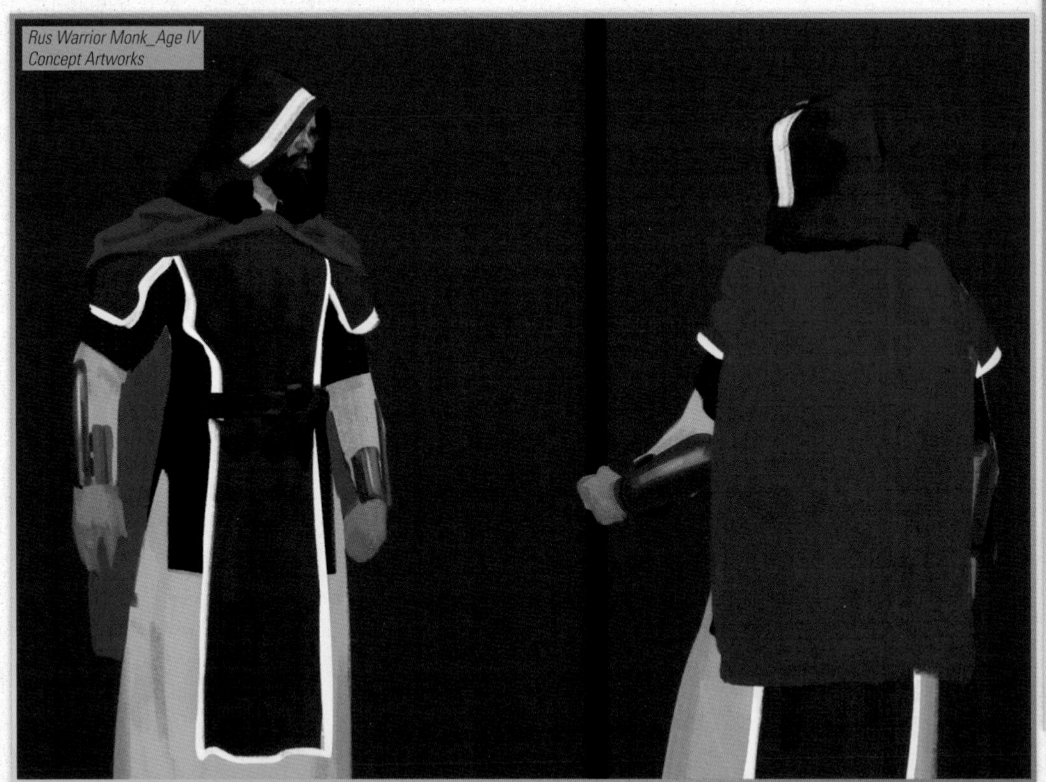

Rus Warrior Monk_Age IV
Concept Artworks

Rus Warrior Monk_Age IV
3D Sculpt

Rus Streltsy—Age I
Concept Artworks

Concepting Influences

"When concepting for Age of Empires IV, we looked at all three Age of Empires games prior, and also considered what the reaction and reception was from their respective audiences. We found that different players wanted different things in terms of aesthetics. Seasoned players favoured readability and clarity, whereas more casual players wanted an overall beautiful game primarily. We looked at Age of Empires II a lot, being Age of Empires fans ourselves. Although Age of Empires II was the game that defined what we remembered from the game's franchise, it was a 2D sprite-based game. While we tried to bring a lot of what was great about the original games' art into a modern 3D game, we did have to rely on art fundamentals such as color and value structure, saturation, contrast etc. when art directing the varyious aspects that make up the look of Age of Empires IV."

– Stuart Ng
Senior Concept Artist, Relic

Streltsy

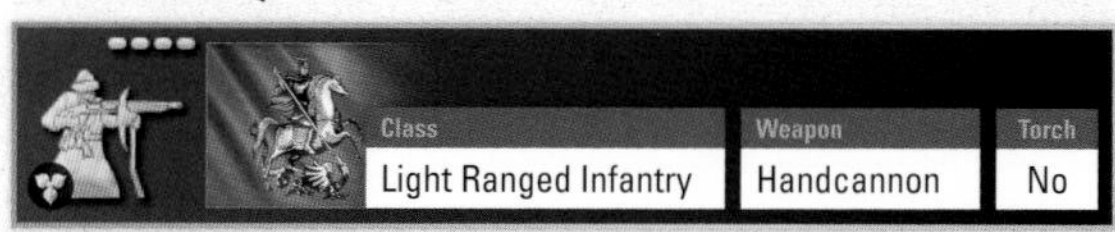

Class	Weapon	Torch
Light Ranged Infantry	Handcannon	No

Primary Uses

- *Inflicting heavy endgame damage*
- *Defending strategic locations*

Training Details

Building Required	Time	Food	Wood	Gold	Population
Archery Range	35s	90	0	90	1

Unit Stats	
Health	150
Melee Armor	0
Ranged Armor	0
Move Speed	1.12
Handcannon	
Damage	42
Counter Bonus	--
Bonus Against	--
Attack Range	4.00
Attack Speed	2.00s
Bardiche	
Damage	50
Counter Bonus	--
Bonus Against	--
Attack Range	0.29
Attack Speed	1.25s

The Streltsy is a unique version of the Handcannoneer that is only available to the Rus—for a more general overview of the that unit type, please turn to P.148. The stats of the two units are fairly comparable, but the Streltsy have much lower production costs, allowing you to field more of them. Where things really start to differ, however, is when you factor in some of the unique abilities that the Streltsy have; those are what make it stand above the normal Handcannoneer.

Special Abilities & Technologies

Double Time

Once researched at an Archery Range, this ability can be activated manually at any time. With **Double Time** activated, your Streltsy will gain +30% movement speed, and increase the speed at which they gain **Static Deployment** stacks by +50%, making it an incredibly powerful and versatile ability. Not only will it allow you to escape sticky situations, but it will allow you to move your Streltsy into key positions and build up their offensive capabilities quicker once there. Due to its low cost and great potential, it should be one of the earliest upgrades you consider for this unit.

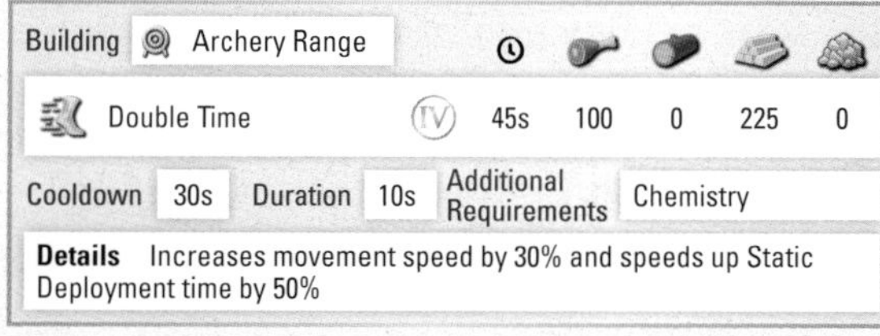

Building: Archery Range		Time	Food	Wood	Gold	Stone
Double Time	(TV)	45s	100	0	225	0

Cooldown: 30s | Duration: 10s | Additional Requirements: Chemistry

Details Increases movement speed by 30% and speeds up Static Deployment time by 50%

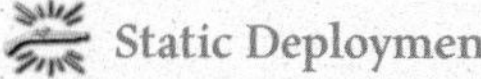

Static Deployment

Streltsy are excellent at stationary fighting and defense, and this passive ability is the primary reason for it. The Streltsy will start accruing **Static Deployment** stacks as soon as they stop moving, and for every five seconds they remain stationary they'll gain an additional +3 damage and +10% attack speed. This effect stacks up to a maximum of three times, for a total bonus of +9 damage and +30% attack speed, giving a huge boost to the Streltsy's damage output.

Tactics & Usage

Streltsy pack a tremendous amount of firepower for their production cost, especially if you can stand your ground with them to build up their stacks of Static Deployment. Because you want to avoid moving them when possible, Steltsy are best used to defend key positions around the map, or behind a large buffer of other units to give them time to build up stacks.

Rus Streltsy

Due to their high damage output, Streltsy do well against almost every other unit, and they even hold their own against melee units thanks to their heavy Bardiche attack. Ideally, they should still be paired with other units to act as a buffer, especially if your opponent is using a lot of cavalry.

Counters

If you want to counter a mass of Streltsy, heavy siege or big hordes of cavalry are a must. You'll need significantly more of them than you would against normal Handcannoneers, since Streltsy can inflict so much more damage. The best tactic is to surround them with cavalry units while Mangonels or Cannons fire at them from a distance. If you're running low on resources, fully upgraded Archers can also perform decently well in a pinch, as long as you can keep your distance.

Warrior Monk

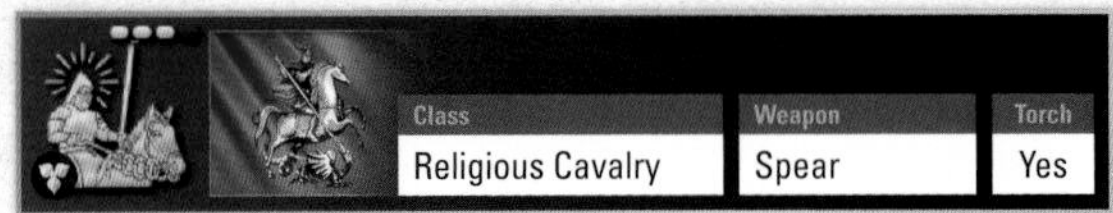

Class	Weapon	Torch
Religious Cavalry	Spear	Yes

The Rus Warrior Monk is a significantly stronger and more mobile version of the normal Monk, and its benefits easily outweigh the additional 40 Food and 50 Gold production cost. Not only can the Warrior Monk perform all of the functions that other Religious units can, it's also decent at attacking and can increase the attack of any surrounding allied units. No Rus army should ever be without one.

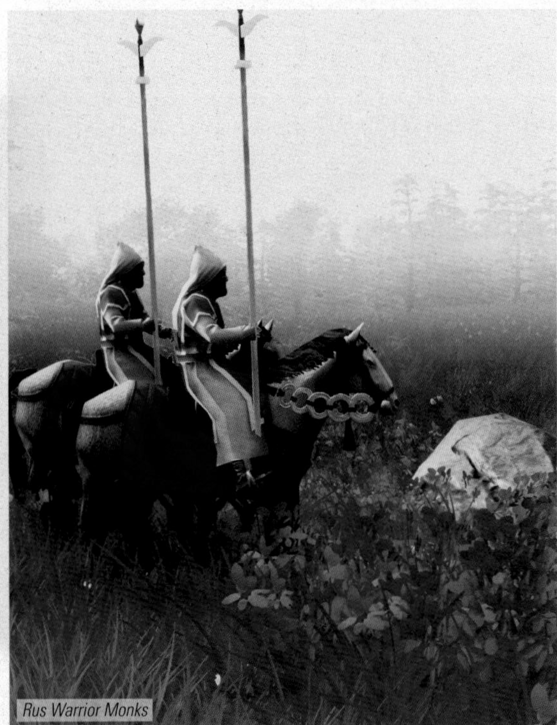

Rus Warrior Monks

Primary Uses

- *Boosting the combat effectiveness of friendly units*
- *Healing nearby friendly units*
- *Converting enemy units*
- *Securing Relics*

Training Details

Building Required	Time	Food	Wood	Gold	Population
Monastery	45s	40	0	200	1

Unit Stats	
Health	190
Melee Armor	0
Ranged Armor	0
Move Speed	1.62
Spear	
Damage	11
Counter Bonus	--
Bonus Against	--
Attack Range	0.29
Attack Speed	1.62s

Abilities & Technology

Blessing Duration is the first technology you have access to for improving your Warrior Monk. It's available through the normal Monastery, and grants an additional +10s to the duration of **Saint's Blessing**. If you want to use Warrior Monks to their fullest potential, however, you should also consider building the **Abbey of Trinity** to advance to Age III, because not only does it have all of the functionality of a Monastery, it also gives you access to an additional pair of very strong unique technology upgrades. The first of those is **Improved Blessing**, which makes the **Saint's Blessing** buff grant an additional +1 attack whenever it's active. **Saint's Reach**, meanwhile, extends the radius within which units will receive the buff by +3 tiles.

Saint's Blessing

Saint's Blessing is a passive ability that Warrior Monks have, and it's activated simply by striking any enemy unit. Once active, **Saint's Blessing** will increase the damage and armor of all nearby allied units by 20% for 10s, granting a massive boost to both survivability and offensive capabilities.

Tactics & Usage

Standard religious units have a few key downsides, including slow movement speed, low health, and no combat ability. The Warrior Monk has no such weaknesses, keeps all of their strengths, and has some additional strengths on top of that. Their decent health and attack, combined with their mobility,means they can hold their own in a fight while also providing healing to other units in addition to the power of conversion.

Warrior Monks are best used as part of a large army, so that as many units as possible can take advantage of the **Saint's Blessing** buff. To ensure that **Saint's Blessing** is activated as soon as possible in an encounter, keep the Warrior Monks towards the front of your army, leading the charge. As your army grows you'll want to have multiple Warrior Monks, spacing them out evenly between the units to maximize the **Saint's Blessing** coverage area.

In the late game stages when Gold is abundant, a large group of 10+ Warrior Monks will be a great benefit to your main army, and an intimidating sight to your foes.

Counters

The Warrior Monk has the same counters as the normal Monk, with two additions: Spearmen and Camel units. Because Warrior Monks are considered cavalry units, both Spearmen and Camel units are effective against them. Conversely, Archers are a lot less effective, to the point that Warrior Monks have an advantage, so avoid using them as a direct counter if possible.

Zhuge Nu

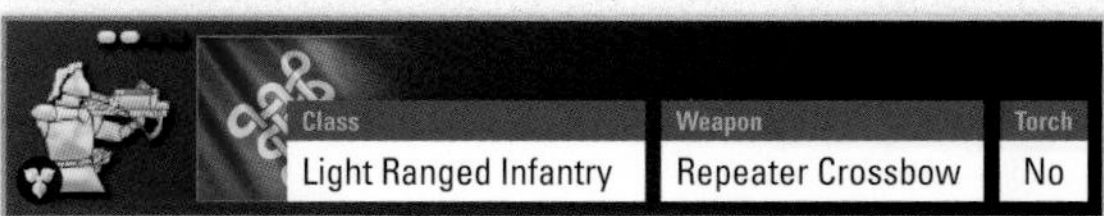

Class	Weapon	Torch
Light Ranged Infantry	Repeater Crossbow	No

The Zhuge Nu is the ultimate all-round ranged unit, and should be at the core of any Chinese army once you reach the Song dynasty and can produce it. You can think of them as early game Handcannoneers with higher range, and while they deal no bonus damage, the raw damage output of the three-round burst fired from their repeater crossbow is massive, and more than makes up for it.

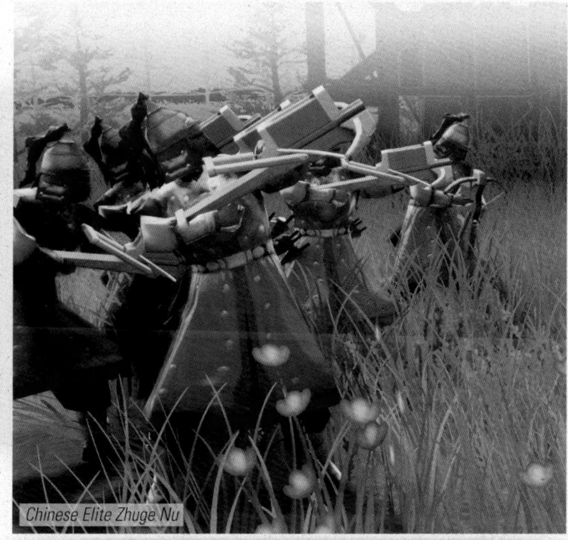

Chinese Elite Zhuge Nu

Tactics & Usage

The Zhuge Nu bring significant benefits, but they require a lot of planning and resources, especially given how late you gain access to them—you might have to sacrifice other advancements along the way. Zhuge Nu can only be produced after reaching the Song Dynasty, which means that you'll have to build both the **Imperial Academy** and **Barbican of the Sun**. That will require a big investment, and the Gold cost especially makes this difficult to achieve early on.

In the Song Dynasty you must reckon with the production cost of the Zhuge Nu, and that factors into how you should fold them into your army. If your army consists of normal ranged infantry, you should slowly replace them with Zhuge Nu as your resources allow. Zhuge Nu outperform Archers against armored units, and Crossbowmen against light units, making them the best overall choice for a ranged unit, so they should eventually make up the bulk of your ranged infantry.

There are no unique technologies that directly effect the Zhuge Nu, but they do benefit from all the normal ranged unit technologies. Although their strengths do offset some of the traditional weaknesses of ranged units, they are still relatively weak in melee range, and you should avoid being surrounded by large groups of cavalry unless you have a significant number of Spearmen to act as a defensive barrier. Spearmen, or any other cavalry unit, are ideal to pair with Zhuge Nu, and if you include some cavalry and siege units of your own, you've got the makings of a devastating force.

For all of their strengths, the one hurdle that Zhuge Nu have trouble overcoming are defensive structures, and they'll have a difficult time breaching them on their own. If you're attacking a base with a lot of these structures, make sure to bring some Torch carrying units or siege engines with you!

Counters

At first glance, Zhuge Nu seem very hard to counter, but they're hard to produce in large numbers early in the game due to their cost, so that's the best time to strike. In early- to mid-game, simply out-produce them with cheaper units and try to overwhelm them before too many take the field. Due to their relatively low health, they are weak against siege units and fortifications, so investing in some strong defensive can pay dividends in the long run.

Primary Uses

Inflicting heavy mid game damage

Training Details

Building Required	Time	Food	Wood	Gold	Population
Archery Range	22s	60	30	30	1

Upgrade Unlock Requirements		Age	Time	Food	Wood	Gold
Veteran Zhuge Nu	Chi	III	1m 0s	100	0	250
Elite Zhuge Nu	Chi	IV	1m 30s	300	0	700

Unit Stats			
Health	90	110	130
Melee Armor	0	0	0
Ranged Armor	0	0	0
Move Speed	1.12	1.12	1.12
Bow			
Damage	4x3	5x3	6x3
Counter Bonus	--	--	--
Bonus Against	--	--	--
Attack Range	4.50	4.50	4.50
Attack Speed	1.25s	1.25s	1.25s

The Zhuge Nu outperform the more standard Crossbowmen, but also need Wood to produce and are limited to the Song Dynasty.

3

Camel Rider

Class	Weapon	Torch
Light Melee Cavalry	Camel | Sword	Yes

Camel Archers are one of only four mounted ranged units in the game. All such units are ideal to employ against enemy melee infantry, but Camel units are also very useful for attacking or defending your own units from enemy cavalry, due to their innate Camel Unease ability. This added utility does make them a bit more expensive to produce than some of the other mounted ranged units, but the benefits and versatility they bring more than make up for the cost.

Primary Uses

- *Counter against Light Melee Infantry (Camel Archer)*
- *Counter against Light Ranged Infantry (Camel Rider)*
- *Soft counter against cavalry units*
- *Mitigating enemy cavalry attacks*

Training Details: Camel Rider

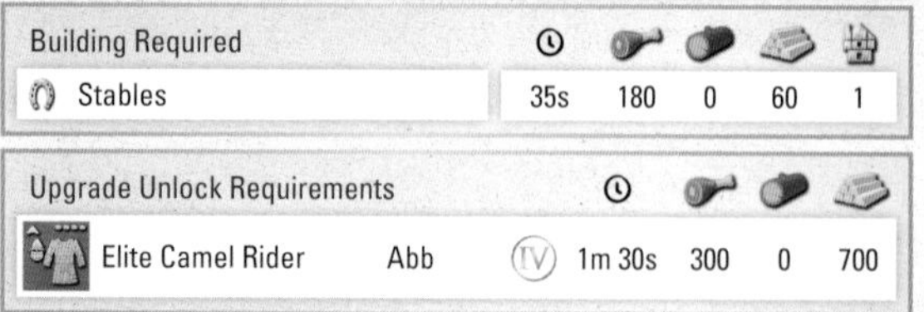

Building Required	Time	Food	Wood	Gold	Population
Stables	35s	180	0	60	1

Upgrade Unlock Requirements			Time	Food	Wood	Gold
Elite Camel Rider	Abb	IV	1m 30s	300	0	700

Unit Stats	Veteran	Elite
Health	270	320
Melee Armor	0	0
Ranged Armor	0	0
Move Speed	1.62	1.62
Sword		
Damage	9	10
Counter Bonus	18	20
Bonus Against	Cavalry	
Attack Range	0.42	0.42
Attack Speed	1.00s	1.00s

Camel Archer

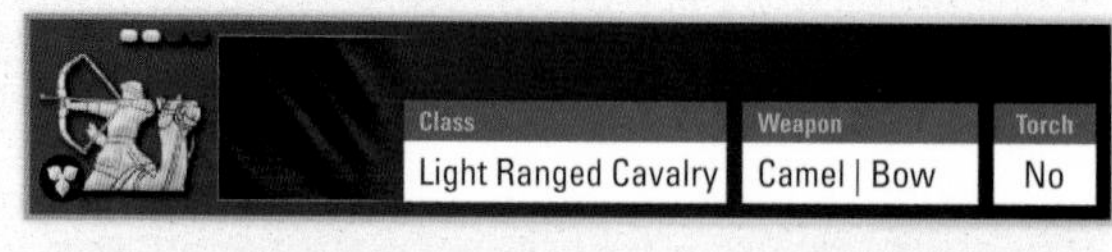

Class	Weapon	Torch
Light Ranged Cavalry	Camel | Bow	No

Training Details: Camel Archer

Building Required	Time	Food	Wood	Gold	Population
Archery Range	35s	180	60	0	1

Upgrade Unlock Requirements			Time	Food	Wood	Gold
Veteran Camel Archer	Abb	III	1m 0s	100	0	250
Elite Camel Archer	Abb	IV	1m 30s	300	0	700

Unit Stats	Hardened	Veteran	Elite
Health	175	210	250
Melee Armor	0	0	0
Ranged Armor	0	0	0
Move Speed	1.62	1.62	1.62
Bow			
Damage	10	12	14
Counter Bonus	20	24	28
Bonus Against	Light Melee Infantry		
Attack Range	3.75	3.75	3.75
Attack Speed	1.25s	1.25s	1.25s

Special Abilities

Camel Unease

All camel units have an innate passive ability called **Camel Unease** that causes allied units within close proximity of the camel take 20% less damage from enemy horse cavalry. This makes camels extremely useful in any fight where the opponent is using cavalry.

Camels also have access to a few unique technology upgrades through the **House of Wisdom's Military and Trade Wings**. From the **Military Wing** you can pick up **Camel Support**, which increases the armor of nearby infantry by +1 and is very useful if you intend on mainly using a couple of camels to support your main army. Camels are naturally somewhat slower than horse cavalry, so the **Camel Handling** upgrade

Abbasid Dynasty Camel Archer

Abbasid Dynasty Camel Rider

from the **Trade Wing** can help offset that difference by increasing the movement speed of all camel units by +15%. The final upgrade worth noting is also from the **Trade Wing**, and it's called **Camel Barding**. With it you can increase the armor of all camel units by +2 for a significant boost to their survivability, and is an upgrade we recommend prioritising over the general upgrades from the Blacksmith, if you intend on having a lot of camels in your army.

Small groups of Camel Archers can serve as excellent raiding parties, keeping the opponent on their toes.

Tactics & Usage

The most obvious use for camel units is to face off against horse cavalry, but that's not the only thing they can be used for. By virtue of being a cavalry unit, Camel Archers can perform well against most types of melee infantry, due to their mobility and ability to use hit-and-run style attacks—a playstyle that is enhanced by their additional counter bonus damage. Their quickness also makes them adept at performing quick, targeted attacks on Villagers or other key units at opportune moments.

Even in low numbers, camel units can be very effective early on to deter cavalry units your opponent might be probing your base with. Camel Archers can also form very effective small raiding parties with other units—such as ranged infantry or siege—that would otherwise be vulnerable to enemy cavalry counterattack. Just one camel mixed into a group can be a very effective tool that allows you to gain the upper hand in any fight that involves enemy cavalry units, or in the worst case scenario, draw enough attention to allow your other units to safely escape.

Camel Riders, on the other hand, perform similarly to Horsemen, in that they're great for countering enemy siege and light ranged infantry units, but they have the additional benefit of more health, allowing them to perform better against heavy melee infantry. Due to their relatively low attack, however, they don't quite fit into the same role as heavy melee cavalry, so that's still best filled by Lancers.

Later in the game, Camel Riders can serve as one of the main units in your army, especially if paired with some ranged infantry or siege units. This is because Camel Riders counter most of the units that your opponent might use to counter those additional unit types. While you can form the bulk of your army around Camel Archers, their relatively low damage output does mean that you'll want to pair them with some other powerful units at the front to absorb some of the incoming damage, especially given their high production cost.

This strategy does come with some risks, however. You'll usually only be able to amass a large number of Camel Archers in the later stages of the game (due to slow production times), and by that time your opponent has access to a lot of hard-hitting units that can out damage your camels. This is why, as the game goes on, Camel Archers tends to skew towards a supportive role.

While Camel Archers can work well in raiding groups, you should avoid using Camel Riders as pure raiders, because they're slower than other cavalry and more expensive than Horsemen, which are easier to replace and faster to produce.

Counters

At first glance, Camel Archers seem hard to deal with, because the traditional counter to ranged cavalry is heavy melee cavalry, a unit type that struggles against camel units unless you have a significant numbers advantage. Fortifications and heavy siege still work very well against them, however, due to their weak armor, and in the early- to mid-game you can overwhelm them with much cheaper and faster to produce infantry units. That tactic works especially well against Camel Riders, because large numbers of Spearmen are a very effective counter to them. Later in the game when you have more resources, however, you should include some high damage ranged units with your Spearmen to form an even deadlier counter group.

*If you're mainly going to use camel units in a supporting or supplementary role within your army, rather than a primary role, you should opt for the **Military Wing** on your **House of Wisdom** in Age II so that you can research **Camel Support** as soon as possible and pass the benefit on to your other troops.*

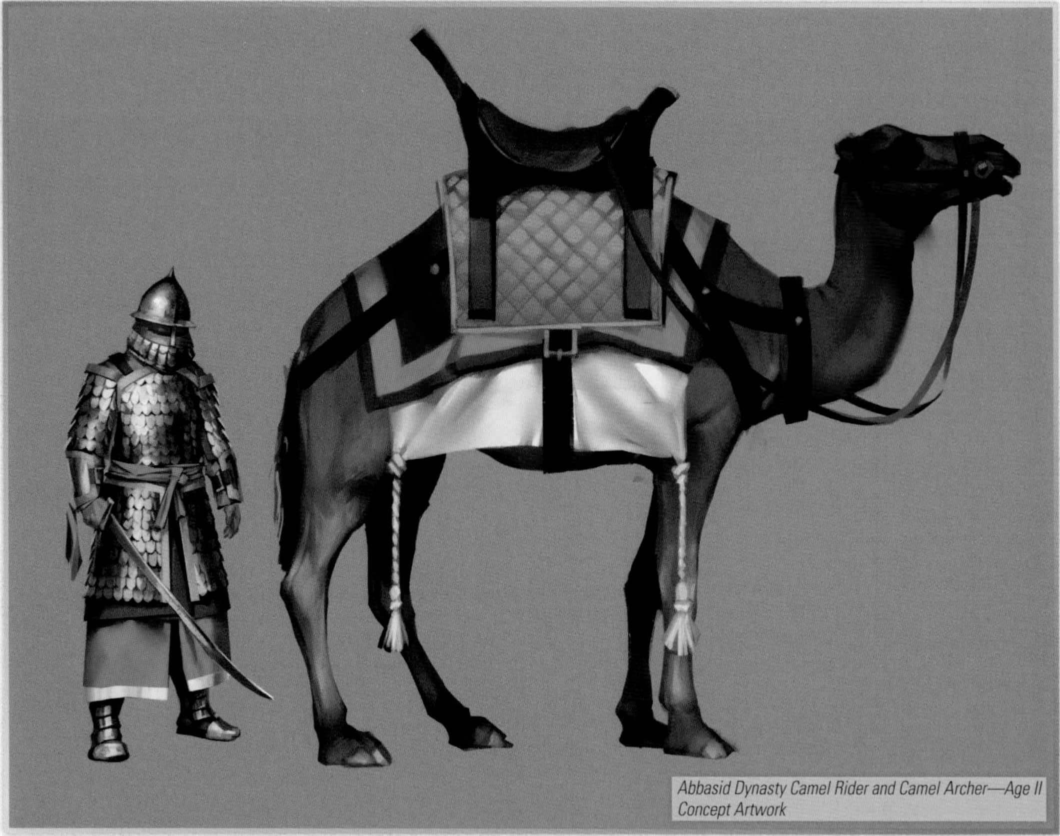

Abbasid Dynasty Camel Rider and Camel Archer—Age II Concept Artwork

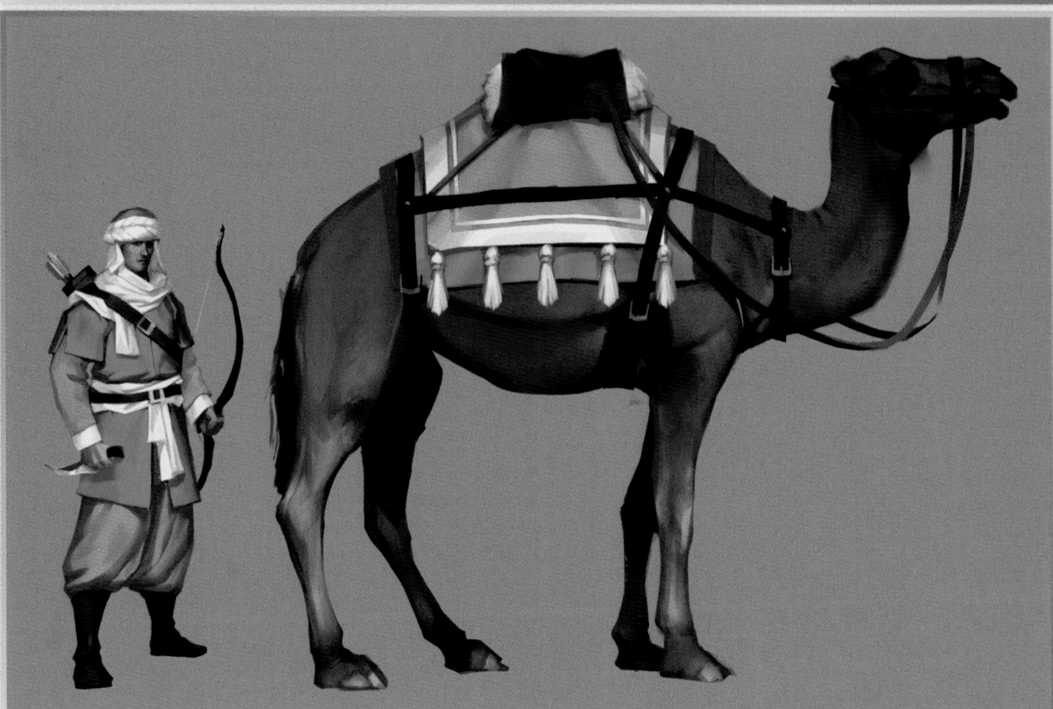

Accuracy in Animation

"In an accuracy vs. gameplay situation, gameplay must always be the winner. As an example from the very core design of the game, at one point in the project we had highly accurate horse movement and logic—they took time to get up to speed, had to decelerate, could only turn quickly at low speeds or when still, had to curve with momentum when turning and it wasn't great for gameplay, especially in a series that established itself on allowing a good degree of micro in terms of unit movement. Everyone that played it hated it... but wow did it ever look great.

While it's easy to close your eyes and picture fully accurate movement of vehicles, horses, and people, very rarely does that make a game compelling, especially in an RTS where players expect units to follow their orders to a near absolute degree. If this wasn't Age of Empires, maybe we could build a fully 'realistic' combat game that embraced all the rules of real-world physics and logic. I'm not surprised no one has really ever built that game though, because controlling it would be rather painful."

– Adam Isgreen
Franchise Creative Director, World's Edge

Creating the Horse Audio

"The sounds of horse footsteps, grunts, whinnies, and tack are layered together to create a foundation suggesting the speed and weight of these powerful units. Next, emotive human elements, like shouting and blood-curdling battle cries are mixed in to support the sense of urgency and intensity of the action on screen. Finally, all these layers of sounds are scaled to represent the number of cavalry units a player is controlling."

– Nick Bedell
Senior Sound Designer, Relic

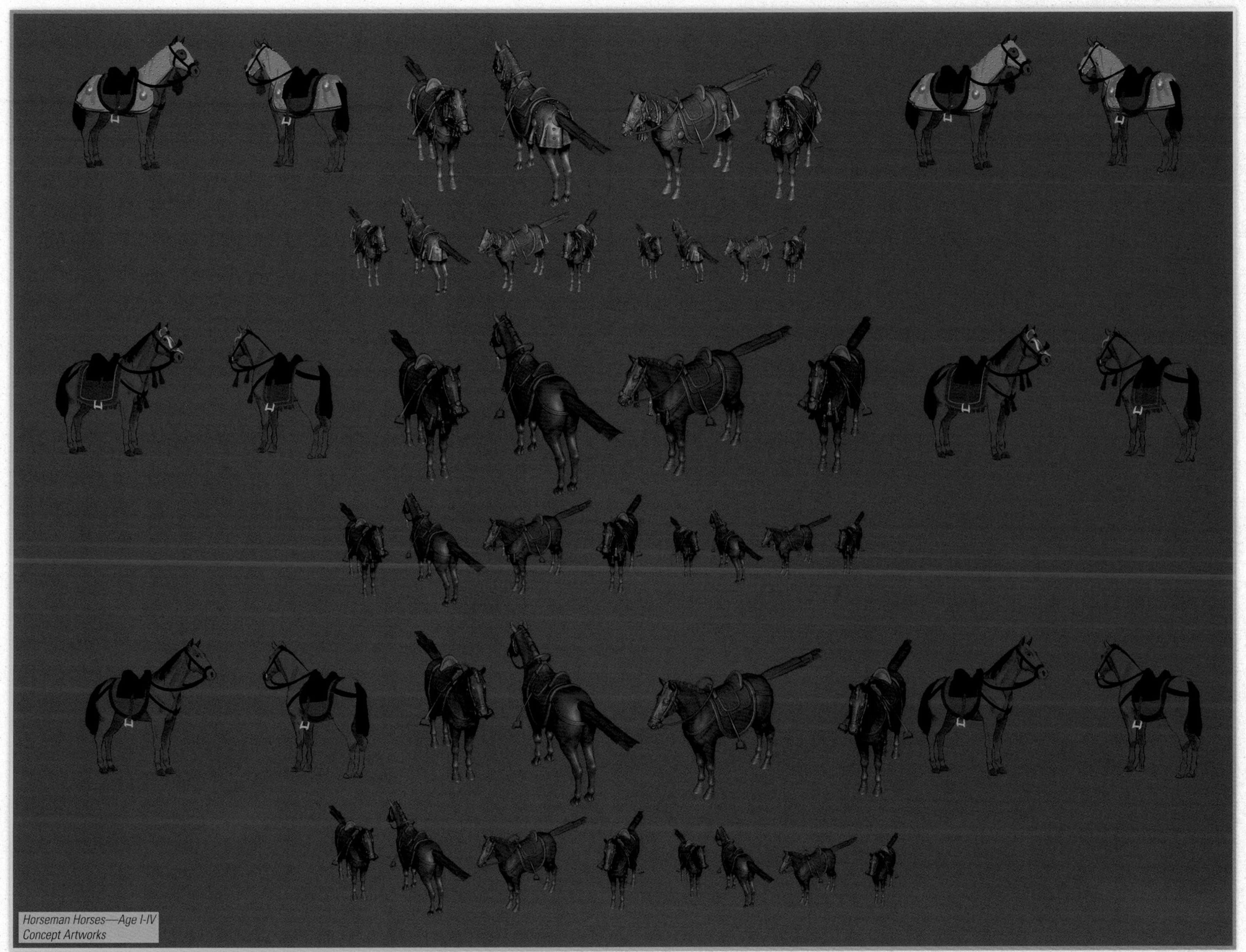

Horseman Horses—Age I-IV
Concept Artworks

3

Fire Lancer

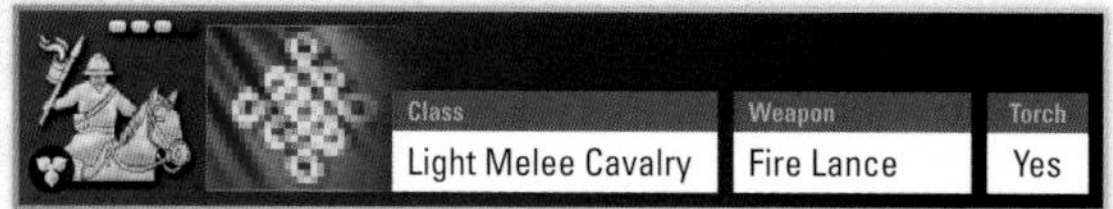

Class
Light Melee Cavalry
Weapon
Fire Lance
Torch
Yes

*The Fire Lancer is a unique Chinese mounted unit. You'll need to be in the Yuan Dynasty before you can produce it, meaning you'll need to build both the **Astronomical Clocktower** and the **Imperial Palace**. Because of their exceptionally powerful charge attack, coupled with the natural benefits that comes from being Light Melee Cavalry, they specialize in the role of a shock trooper in raiding parties against enemy siege units or buildings.*

Chinese Elite Fire Lancer

Tactics & Usage

Building an army that consists primarily of Fire Lancers is generally not a good idea, because compared to many other units they perform poorly in extended engagements. Their role is to get in and get out of fights quickly, taking out key buildings and units before your opponent knows what hit them. Their powerful charge attack is what makes this tactic so effective, because with a decently sized group, that one big initial hit is all you need. You can then retreat back to safety while you wait for the internal cooldown of the charge attack to reset, and then head back in and do it again.

In many ways you can think of them as better Horsemen that come at the cost of an additional small amount of Gold, because they do all of the same things, but with a couple of nice extra benefits. If you're in the Yuan Dynasty and feel you need Horsemen, produce Fire Lancers instead. Their already excellent raiding credentials are made even better when paired with the ability of the **Imperial Palace** to reveal the location of enemy Villagers for a short period of time, enabling you to launch targeted surgical strikes against your opponent.

Counters

Fire Lancers are countered by Heavy Melee Cavalry and all forms of Melee Infantry, with Heavy Melee Infantry performing especially well against them. To avoid being caught off guard by opposing Fire lancers, always protect your high value units with a group of Spearmen or similar units that can quickly contend with them.

If Fire Lancer raids become a threat as the game progresses, you might also want to station Spearmen alongside your Villagers to protect your economy, or invest in walls to deter them from just running straight into your base. Just make sure you also have some defensive units near the walls, so they don't just charge their way through them. It's for that reason that defensive buildings such as Towers or Outposts are not a good deterrent, because they tend to quickly fall to the charge of the Fire Lancers.

Primary Uses

- *Attacking enemy buildings and siege units*

Training Details

Building Required					
Stables	22s	80	20	20	1

Upgrade Unlock Requirements						
Elite Fire Lancer	Chi	IV	1m 30s	300	0	700

Unit Stats		
Health	135	160
Melee Armor	0	0
Ranged Armor	0	0
Move Speed	1.50	1.50
Fire Lance		
Damage	11	15
Counter Bonus	11	13
Bonus Against	Ranged Infantry	
Attack Range	0.29	0.29
Attack Speed	1.62s	1.62s
Lance Charge Attack		
Damage	21	25
Counter Bonus	--	--
Bonus Against	--	--
Attack Range	1.04	1.04
Attack Speed	1.40s	1.40s

Because of how quickly and effectively Fire Lancers can get behind enemy lines and destroy buildings, they're the perfect unit for raiding the opponent's base and decimating their economic capabilities.

Horse Archer

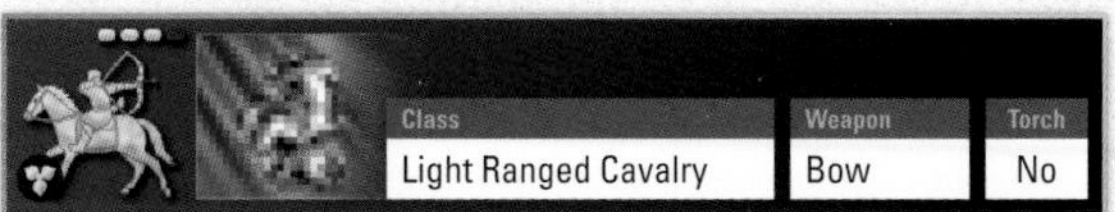

Class
Light Ranged Cavalry
Weapon
Bow
Torch
No

The unique Rus Horse Archer combines the ranged attacks from light ranged infantry with the speed and mobility of a cavalry unit, forming an excellent raiding or support unit that doesn't cost any Gold to train. Similar to the Camel Archers of the Abbasid Dynasty or the Mangudai of the Mongols, they excel at being able to engage and disengage from encounters very quickly, picking off enemy units on the periphery of engagements.

Rus Horse Archer

Tactics & Usage

Horse Archers are best suited to open terrain, where they can freely move around and get the biggest benefits from their quick movement speed. As part of your main army you can take advantage of that speed by moving them around within your ranks to always ensure that there are plenty of other units between them and whatever units your opponent is sending against your Horse Archers. Such forces will usually include melee infantry or cavalry, so keeping them at bay is a sure path to victory. If your economy is strong enough, Knights can be the ideal unit to have in front of your Horse Archers, because their mobility lets them work perfectly together. If you lack resources, however, Men-at-Arms or Spearmen can also fill that role.

The second area in which they shine is raiding—create small groups of five or so Horse Archers to act as raiding parties to weaken your opponent's economy by picking off Villagers one at a time. This approach is best employed during Age III, because by that stage of the game your economy should be producing enough Food to allow for multiple groups, and you'l have the ability to produce enough units to make up for any losses you suffer. This tactic does demand a lot of attention and unit control, but done well, it can pay off greatly and be devastating to your opponent.

Counters

The best counter to Horse Archers are heavily armored cavalry or heavy siege units, such as Mangonels and Cannons. Because Horse Archers are cavalry units, they also take considerable damage from anti-cavalry units, such as Spearmen. The problem with using infantry units such as those as a counter, however, is that they'll have trouble getting close enough. Horsemen can be a good middle ground here, because of their greater movement speed, and you can use them to help corner the Horse Archers so that your Spearmen can get close enough to attack. Both of those units are cheap enough to produce that small losses are acceptable. Defensive fortifications are also very effective against Horse Archers, so it's worth building some if you suspect that your opponent might send in raiding groups.

Primary Uses

- *Raiding enemy positions*
- *Ranged support unit*

Training Details

Building Required	Time	Food	Wood	Gold	Population
Stables	22s	80	40	0	1

Upgrade Unlock Requirements			Time	Food	Wood	Gold
Elite Horse Archer	Rus	IV	1m 30s	300	0	700

Unit Stats		
HP	135	135
Melee Armor	0	0
Ranged Armor	0	0
Move Speed	1.44	1.44
Bow		
Damage	12	14
Counter Bonus	--	--
Bonus Against	--	--
Attack Range	4.50	4.50
Attack Speed	2.00s	2.00s

The **Mounted Precision** upgrade that you can research from the Archery Range in Age IV is a cheap, but very powerful upgrade that gives your Horse Archers +2 range, making them even deadlier.

Horse Archers in combination with Horsemen make a mobile and effective raiding army, saving Gold for upgrades and ideal for the fast Food income of the Rus.

Horseman

Type	Weapon	Torch
Light Melee Cavalry	Spear	Yes

Horsemen are the standard and most readily available cavalry unit that all civilizations get access to during Age II. The Mongols can produce the Early Horseman during Age I, but their relatively high food cost means they're hard to mass produce at that point in the game. Horsemen form one part of the early game unit counter triangle alongside Archers and Spearmen—each of those unit types can effectively counter one of the others—learning where they fit into that is extremely important. Like other cavalry units, Horsemen also have access to a powerful charge attack that they use to initiate combat, so for one hit their potential damage increases significantly, making for a devastating opener when you have large groups of them.

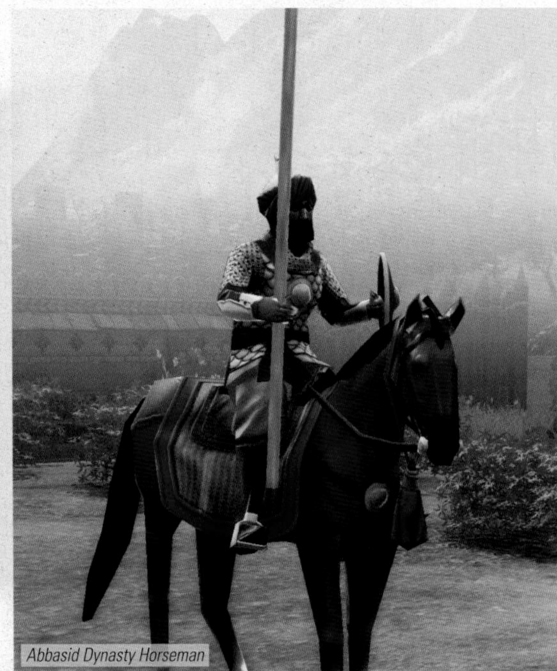

Abbasid Dynasty Horseman

Tactics & Usage

Horsemen shine the most during Age II as a counter to Archers or early in Age III as a means to counter siege units such as Mangonels and Springalds. Their speed lets them easily close in on those units, allowing you to make use of their strong charge attack and natural counter bonus to make quick work of them. That speed also makes them great for chasing down units that are attempting to disengage from a battle; if you see some units at the back of your opponent's army start to break off and retreat, don't hesitate to flank around with your Horsemen to cut them off.

In the later stages of the game, Horsemen tend to be outperformed by most of the stronger units that have become available, so their role tends to transition to raiding and distraction, rather than attacking. Sending a few of them all over the map, especially into parts of your opponent's territory that are not well defended, can be a great way of diverting attention, with the additional benefit of weakening their economy at the same time if your attacks are successful.

During the early stages of the game, Horsemen can be quite effective at hunting for enemy Villagers in exposed areas of the map.

Counters

Horsemen are countered by Heavy Melee Cavalry or all forms of melee infantry. Early in games it's important to have a groups of Spearmen around to protect your high value units or buildings, so that you're not caught off guard and can counter any early raiding groups of Horsemen. Spearmen can still fill that role well as you go deeper into the game, as long as other units are filling the ranks of your main army. You might also want to invest in some static defenses such as walls to help deter Horsemen from riding straight into your base, or key resource gathering hubs.

Primary Uses

- *Counter against ranged infantry*

Training Details

Building Required	Time	Food	Wood	Gold	Population
Stables*	22s	100	20	0	1

*If the building is under the influence of an Ovoo, Mongols can pay an additional 120 Stone for x2 of the unit.

Upgrade Unlock Requirements		Age	Time	Food	Wood	Gold
Horseman	Mon	II	30s	25	0	75
Veteran Horseman	All	III	1m 0s	100	0	250
Elite Horseman	All	IV	1m 30s	300	0	700

Unit Stats				
Health	125	155	190	225
Melee Armor	0	0	0	0
Ranged Armor	0	0	0	0
Move Speed	1.88	1.88	1.88	1.88

Spear				
Damage	7	9	11	13
Counter Bonus	7	9	11	13
Bonus Against	Ranged Infantry			
Attack Range	0.29	0.29	0.29	0.29
Attack Speed	1.62s	1.62s	1.62s	1.62s

Charge Attack				
Damage	7	9	11	13
Counter Bonus	7	9	11	13
Bonus Against	Ranged Infantry			
Attack Range	0.54	0.54	0.54	0.54
Attack Speed	1.62s	1.62s	1.62s	1.62s

Mangudai

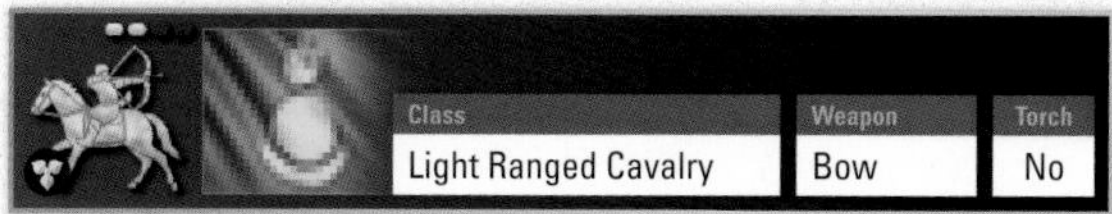

Class	Weapon	Torch
Light Ranged Cavalry	Bow	No

Mangudai are a special ranged mounted unit unique to the Mongols, and they're one of the core units involved in nearly all aspects of Mongol armies and tactics. They are perfectly suited to raiding trips into enemy territory, where they can decimate the economy and pick off slow or vulnerable targets. What makes them so perfect for these tasks is the fact that, unlike other ranged cavalry, they can shoot while moving, allowing you to target an enemy and deal constant damage to them while moving away and staying safe, instead of periodically stopping to fire.

Mongol Elite Mangudai

Tactics & Usage

The Mangudai's strengths—their mobility coupled with their ability to remain mobile while firing ranged attacks—make them the perfect raiding unit. In Age II, making large groups of them is a big investment, and it's also very easy for your opponent to counter and outnumber your Mangudai with

Mangudai's ability to shoot while moving makes them perfectly suited to ride-by raids on enemy Villager groups.

a cheaper Archer and Spearman army. This means you're better off using them in small raiding groups around the map to probe and attack enemy held territory, rather than committing to a predominantly Mangudai army.

By the time you hit Age III, however, you should be producing them in sufficient numbers to form the core of your army. Since they're a ranged unit, to get the most out of them you'll want to pair them with support units to act as a buffer between your units and your opponent's. Spearmen lend themselves very well to this task, since they only need Food and Wood for their production, leaving the Gold for more Mangudai.

The most powerful combination of units would be Lancers and Mangudai, but this is a very resource-heavy pairing that's difficult to avhieve before Age IV. This combination also requires a lot of micromanaging, but can be worth the payoff. Pairing Mangudai and Lancers can be made somewhat easier if you build the **Khagante Palace** to advance to Age IV. That building will produce a small army of either Mangudai, Lancers or Horsemen for free every 90s, allowing you to build up your main unit and support units at no cost.

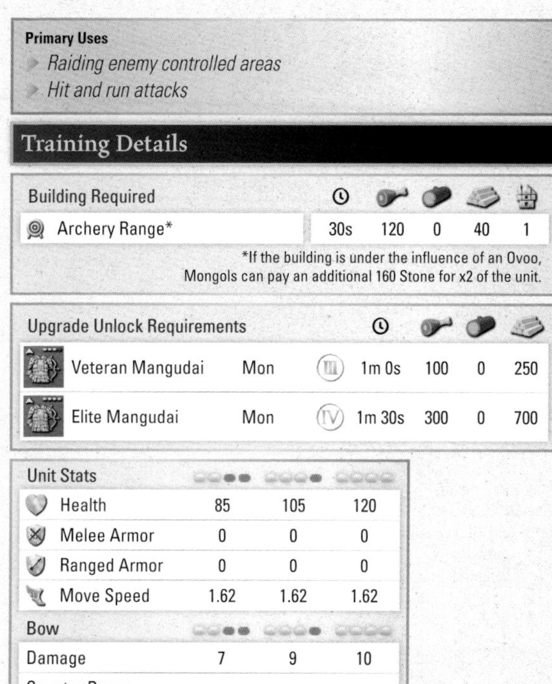

Primary Uses

- *Raiding enemy controlled areas*
- *Hit and run attacks*

Training Details

Building Required	Time	Food	Wood	Gold	Pop
Archery Range*	30s	120	0	40	1

*If the building is under the influence of an Ovoo, Mongols can pay an additional 160 Stone for x2 of the unit.

Upgrade Unlock Requirements		Age	Time	Food	Wood	Gold
Veteran Mangudai	Mon	III	1m 0s	100	0	250
Elite Mangudai	Mon	IV	1m 30s	300	0	700

Unit Stats			
Health	85	105	120
Melee Armor	0	0	0
Ranged Armor	0	0	0
Move Speed	1.62	1.62	1.62
Bow			
Damage	7	9	10
Counter Bonus	--	--	--
Bonus Against	--	--	--
Attack Range	4.50	4.50	4.50
Attack Speed	1.25s	1.25s	1.25s

Counters

As a cavalry unit, Mangudai are naturally weak to Spearmen, but it can be quite difficult for Spearmen to get close enough to attack without help from some cavalry of your own. Because they're a ranged unit however, Mangudai only deal minimal damage to buildings, which makes defensive buildings like Outposts, Towers and Keeps the best deterrents to Mangudai raiding parties. If you do need to counter them out in the field, your best option is Heavy Melee Cavalry, because they're fast enough to get close, and strong enough to finish them off. Heavy siege units, such as Mangonels or Cannons, can also be effective, especially if you can position them in such a way that makes it hard for the Mangudai to retreat to safety.

Khan

Class	Weapon	Torch
Light Ranged Cavalry	Bow	No

The Khan is a Mongol ranged cavalry unit that takes the place of the Scout that other civilizations start with by default. While it does share some functionality with Scouts (such as the extremely large vision radius), it has so much more to offer. You can have only one Khan active on the map at any given time, and it will automatically upgrade and gain new abilities as you progress through the Ages in a game. If your Khan dies, another one will emerge onto the battlefield from your Landmark Town Center after 120s have passed.

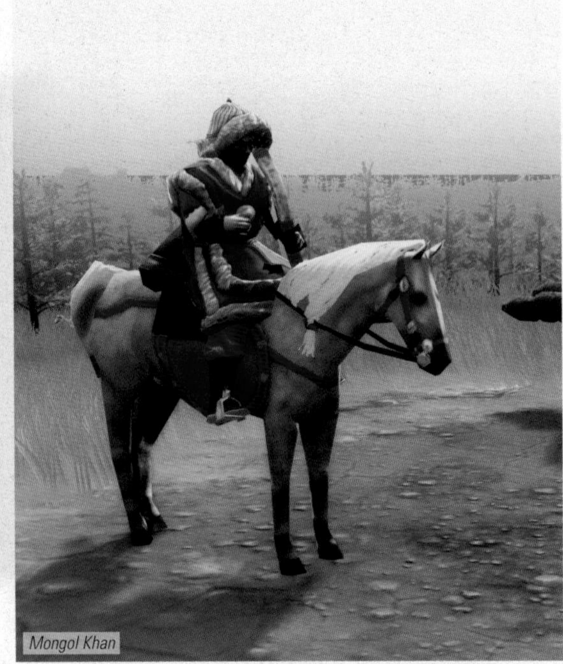

Mongol Khan

Primary Uses

- *Using abilities to support other units on the field*

Training Details

Building Required					
Automatically respawns from a Town Center upon death	0	0	0	0	1

Unit Stats				
Health	90	115	300	450
Melee Armor	0	0	1	2
Ranged Armor	0	0	1	2
Move Speed	1.62	1.62	1.62	1.62
Bow				
Damage	2	4	12	24
Counter Bonus	--	--	--	--
Bonus Against	--	--	--	--
Attack Range	5.00	6.00	7.00	7.00
Attack Speed	1.88s	1.88s	1.88s	1.88s

Special Abilities

The main thing that elevates Khans above Scouts is their special abilities; they can fire three different types of arrows that grant temporary bonuses, and they can release a trained falcon that grants you better vision for a period of time. Some of these abilities are available straight away, while others will unlock as you Age up when playing through a game, and learning when and where to use each one is a key part of effective Mongol military strategy, especially since only one signal arrow can be used at a time.

Due to its ranged attack, the Khan can go on the offensive right away and distract enemy Villagers. Just be aware that you;re missing out on potentially important scouting information by doing this.

Mousing over the signal arrow ability icons will show you their range, which can be useful when you first start using them so that you know your desired units will receive the buff.

 Scouting Falcon

Upon activation, a falcon will fly into the air directly above the Khan and begin circling the area, during which time you can freely move the Khan and any other units out of that area while maintaining the ability see what's happening there. This is extremely useful if you want to keep watch over a certain area without your enemy suspecting it, allowing you to spy on incoming armies or set up ambushes.

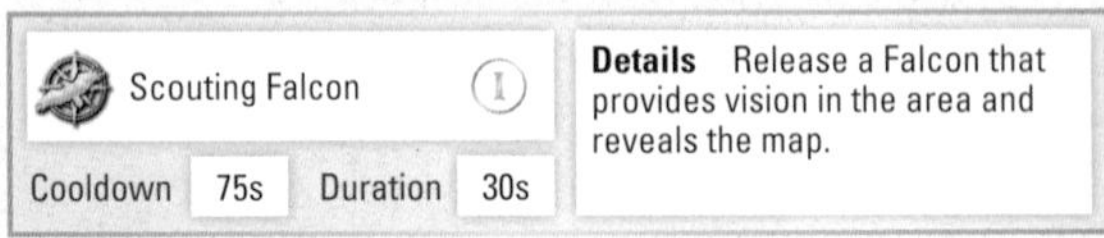

Scouting Falcon				**Details** Release a Falcon that provides vision in the area and reveals the map.
Cooldown	75s	Duration	30s	

 Maneuver Arrow

This ability helps with getting in and out of battles quickly, and pairs well with some of the other aspects of Mongol gameplay, Mangudai in particular. Getting into battles quicker can help immensely if you're trying to spring a trap in an area that's being scouted by the falcon, and the ability for Mangudai to shoot while moving is made even better by this arrow, because it's easier for them to stay ahead of the enemies they're attacking.

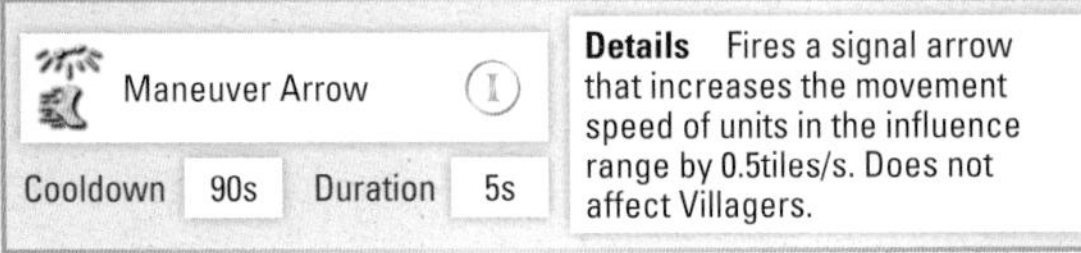

Maneuver Arrow				**Details** Fires a signal arrow that increases the movement speed of units in the influence range by 0.5tiles/s. Does not affect Villagers.
Cooldown	90s	Duration	5s	

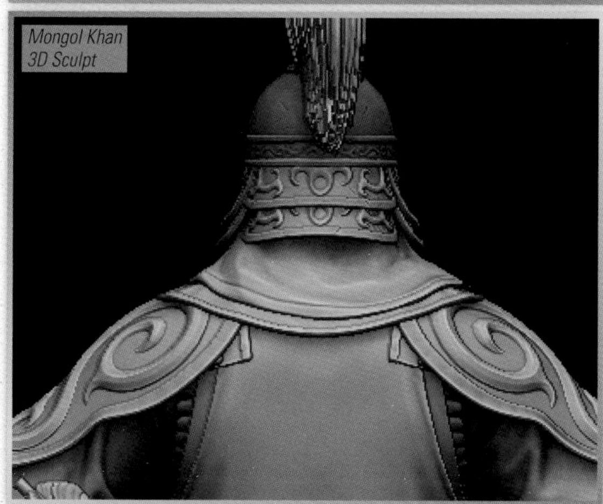

Mongol Khan 3D Sculpt

 Attack Speed Arrow

If you're using a large group of ranged units, you should always try to have a Khan amongst them and fire this arrow. Doing so will significantly increase the damage output of those ranged units, and give you a big advantage in the battle.

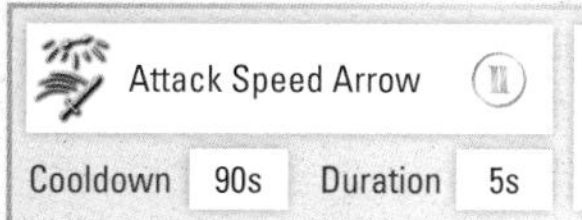

Attack Speed Arrow				**Details** Fires a signal arrow that increases the Reload Speed of ranged units in the influence range by 50%.
Cooldown	90s	Duration	5s	

Defense Arrow

This arrow is primarily for when things have taken a turn for the worse in a battle you're already committed to, and you need some extra survivability for all of your units. Its defense boost affects both ranged and melee units within the influence range. If you're mainly using hit-and-run style attacks with your Mangudai, then this ability won't benefit you a lot and either one of the others would be better.

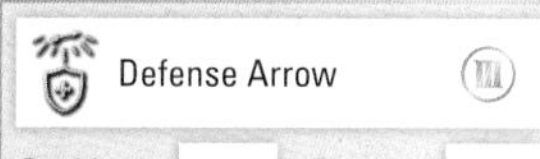

Defense Arrow				**Details** Fires a signal arrow that increases the armor of units in the influence range by 3.
Cooldown	90s	Duration	5s	

Tactics & Usage

The Khan is at its best when paired with mobile ranged units, especially groups of Mangudai. Since you start every game with a Khan, you should start making use of them immediately, which usually means taking on a typical Scout's responsibilities: revealing the map, and attacking any lone Villagers that you come across. You can even try to kill Sheep that follow the opponent's Scout and annoy Villagers from outside the enemy Town Center's range.

Once you have more military units or have produced an actual Scout, you should transition the Khan into a more supportive role. Your Khan should be placed within the bulk of your fighting force to ensure that as many units as possible can take advantage of the signal arrow buffs. Whenever you're defending an area or going on the offensive, make sure your Khan travels with you. The good thing is that, because a new Khan automatically takes the field if your current one falls in battle, you don't actually have to be overly protective with them. Just remember that their damage output is quite low, so you want to keep them away from the very front lines.

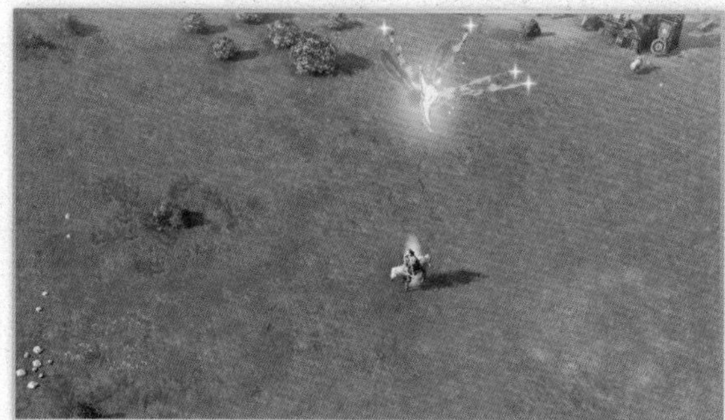

When firing one of the arrows available, an icon related to the enabled bonus can be seen.

The icon for your active Khan is always visible on the side of screen, so even if you don't have it selected, you can always see its health to know if it's in trouble. If your Khan dies, that icon also serves as a visual representation of the cooldown timer before another one takes the battlefield.

Counters

The Khan is weak against the same units that Mangudai are. This means Heavy Melee Cavalry are the best option to send against them, since they have the speed to actually catch them, and the damage to finish them off quickly. Because Khans are such a high value target, siege units such as Springalds and Culverins are also a good choice, since they have the ability to snipe the Khan in one or two shots even when it's surrounded by other units, significantly weakening the Mongol army in an instant.

Royal Knight

Class	Weapon	Torch
Heavy Melee Cavalry	Sword	Yes

Knights/Lancers are Heavy Melee Cavalry units that are available to all civilizations from Age III onwards with most civilizations, and although their names and weapons might be different, the role they fill in your army is the same. Any time you need a hard-hitting and mobile unit, Knights/ Lancers should be at the top of your list, because they're perfectly suited to gaining and maintaining control of the map, or for countering large amounts of siege or ranged units.

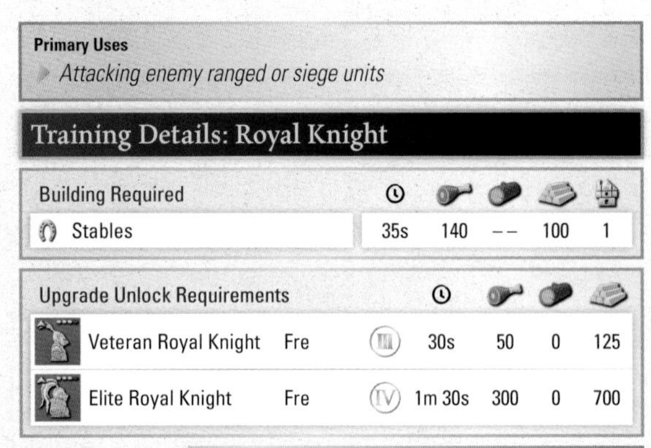

Primary Uses

- *Attacking enemy ranged or siege units*

Training Details: Royal Knight

Building Required	Time	Food	Wood	Gold	Population
Stables	35s	140	--	100	1

Upgrade Unlock Requirements		Age	Time	Food	Wood	Gold
Veteran Royal Knight	Fre	III	30s	50	0	125
Elite Royal Knight	Fre	IV	1m 30s	300	0	700

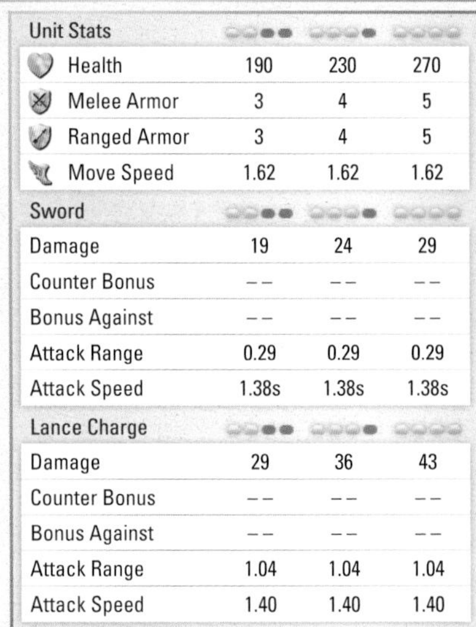

Unit Stats			
Health	190	230	270
Melee Armor	3	4	5
Ranged Armor	3	4	5
Move Speed	1.62	1.62	1.62
Sword			
Damage	19	24	29
Counter Bonus	--	--	--
Bonus Against	--	--	--
Attack Range	0.29	0.29	0.29
Attack Speed	1.38s	1.38s	1.38s
Lance Charge			
Damage	29	36	43
Counter Bonus	--	--	--
Bonus Against	--	--	--
Attack Range	1.04	1.04	1.04
Attack Speed	1.40	1.40	1.40

Knight/Lancer

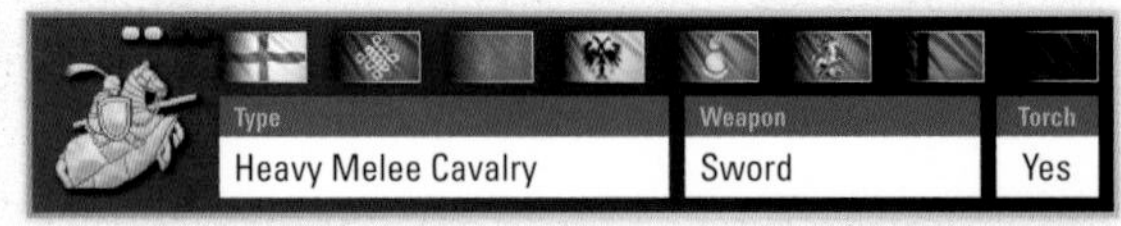

Type	Weapon	Torch
Heavy Melee Cavalry	Sword	Yes

Training Details: Knight/Lancer

Building Required	Time	Food	Wood	Gold	Population
Stables*	35s	140	0	100	1

*If the building is under the influence of an Ovoo, Mongols can pay an additional 240 Stone for x2 of the unit.

Upgrade Unlock Requirements		Age	Time	Food	Wood	Gold
Knight/Lancer	Rus	III	30s	50	0	125
Elite Knight/Lancer	All - Fre	IV	1m 30s	300	0	700

Unit Stats			
Health	190	230	270
Melee Armor	3	4	5
Ranged Armor	3	4	5
Move Speed	1.62	1.62	1.62
Sword			
Damage	19	24	29
Counter Bonus	--	--	--
Bonus Against	--	--	--
Attack Range	0.29	0.29	0.29
Attack Speed	1.38s	1.38s	1.38s
Lance Charge			
Damage	29	36	43
Counter Bonus	--	--	--
Bonus Against	--	--	--
Attack Range	1.04	1.04	1.04
Attack Speed	1.40	1.40	1.40

English Knight

Dehli Sultanate Elite Lancer

Special Abilities & Technologies

Knights/Lancers possess a powerful charge attack, during which they swap their normal weapons for a lance that improves both the range and damage of their initial attack when they enter combat. Once the charge attack is complete, they switch back to their normal weapon and commence their regular attack patterns.

Early Knight (Rus)

The Rus are able to produce Heavy Melee Cavalry in Age II, which gives them some useful options for countering enemy units that other civilizations do not have. The cost of 140 Food and 100 Gold does disincentivize massing a big army of Early Knights in Age II, but adding a few of them to your normal army composition will greatly impact your fighting power.

Age II is when a lot of Archers can often come into play, and if you manage to catch them on their own, they will stand no chance against your Early Knights.

Their effectiveness can be further improved thanks to some unique upgrades the Rus have. **Boyar's Fortitude** gives +20 health to all Rus cavalry, so if you produce a decent amount of Knights in Age II, you can give them all a big bump to health as soon as you hit Age III and can acquire this upgrade. Similarly, once Rus reach Age IV they have access to **Knight Sabers**, which increases the melee damage of their Knights by +4 and turns an already strong unit into a deadly one.

Royal Knight (French)

This special version of the Knight has only one key difference: for three seconds after their initial charge attack they gain bonus damage. Like Early Knights, they're available in Age II so are subject to the same resource constraints that make mass production difficult, but that extra damage can make the struggle worthwhile. Building the **School of Cavalry** as your Age II Landmark can help, since you can use it to produce your cavalry, and it will do so 20% faster than a normal Stable.

The French also have access to the **Chivalry** upgrade for their Royal Knights that lets them heal for +1 health every second. That upgrade can help to offset some of the risk in producing this unit, because you'll be able to heal up between fights and keep more of them alive. Then in Age III you can research **Cantled Saddles** to further increase the bonus damage after a charge attack by +10, giving you an even bigger advantage during the first moments of a fight.

Tactics & Usage

The primary use for Knights/Lancers is to counter ranged units and siege, especially from Age III onwards when your economy is strong enough to produce these units on a large scale. A few of them mixed in with other units, or a group of 10-15 on their own, can deal tremendous damage to your opponent's forces, and the earlier you can get them on the field the better.

Like other cavalry units, they can quickly engage and disengage from battles, giving you a nice tactical advantage against infantry because it allows you to choose when and where to fight. That mobility also makes them a great unit to establish a presence at key parts of the map quickly, or for quick raids into enemy controlled areas. Having a few of these units running around trying to catch your opponent off guard, or to keep them from expanding can pay off extremely well.

The high health of Knights/Lancers means they're very effective at shielding your own infantry from enemy ranged units, be they infantry or siege.

Late in the game, using a group of Knights/Lancers as your main fighting force can be a very effective strategy due to the speed at which they can catch opponents off guard by quickly surrounding or flanking their army. If, however, you're facing the Abbasid Dynasty, you should avoid investing heavily into Knights/Lancers, because they will be severely weakened against their unique camel units.

In general you'll want to pair your Knights/Lancers with units that counter their counter units. Archers are the obvious choice as an early cheap pairing, since they are the natural counters to Spearmen. Later in the game when resources become more abundant, Mangonels, Handcannoneers and mounted ranged units are the superior choice.

In siege situations, Knights/Lancers are best used to destroy approaching Battering Rams or Siege Towers.

Knights/Lancers perform well against standard Heavy Melee Infantry like Men-at-Arms, but you should avoid fighting their natural counters (such as Spearmen) directly, unless you significantly outnumber them.

Counters

Groups of Spearmen are the best counter option to Heavy Melee Cavalry early on. If you're facing a civilization that has access to Knights in Age II, you should build a sufficient number of Spearmen to deal with that threat. In later stages you might want to pair those Spearmen with Crossbowmen and Handcannoneers—just make sure that the Knights can't flank around the Spearmen and reach your ranged units.

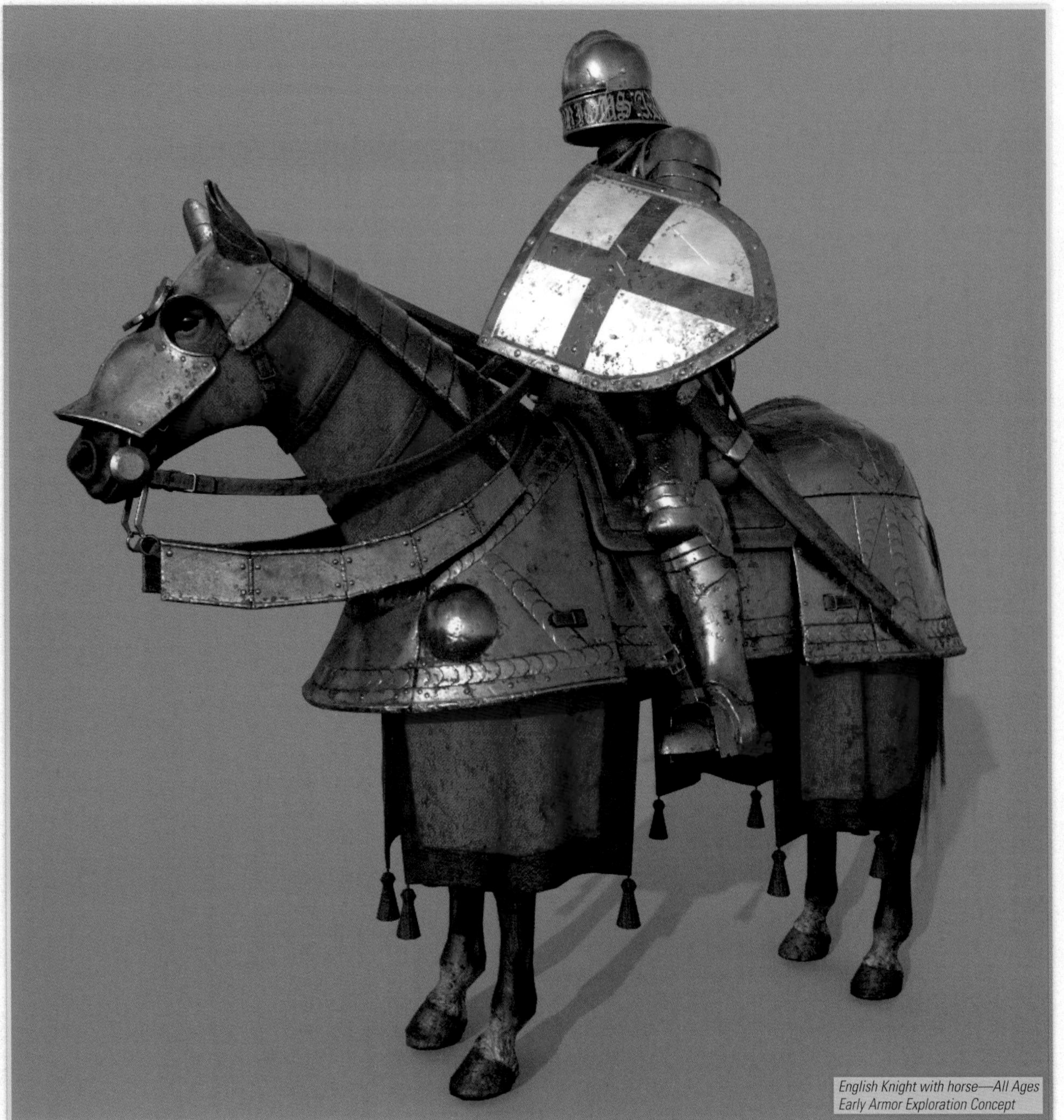

English Knight with horse—All Ages
Early Armor Exploration Concept

Horse Animation

"The units that presented the greatest challenge were the horses. We recognized early on that many units would be mounted on horses and each of those would carry different types of weapons and use them in interesting ways. Since this was an important part of the game, we decided to motion capture horses.

All of the base movement for horses and riders was captured from two riders who would swap out between seven different horses with markers over a three-day period. For the mounted character's carrying weapons, we motion captured performers on a completely different stage—each actor sitting on a prop horse with prop weapons. These animations were all combined later by animators, technical animators, and our engine. From there we simulated animation for the tail and baked it into the animation rather than taxing our game with real time physics. We were able to use all of this for our cinematics as well. The resulting quality of motion and detail of movement is something we're very proud of."

*– **Brent Breedveld***
Principal Animator,
Animation Director, Relic

English Knight's horse—Age I-IV
Horse Tack and Barding Exploration Concept

Tower War Elephant

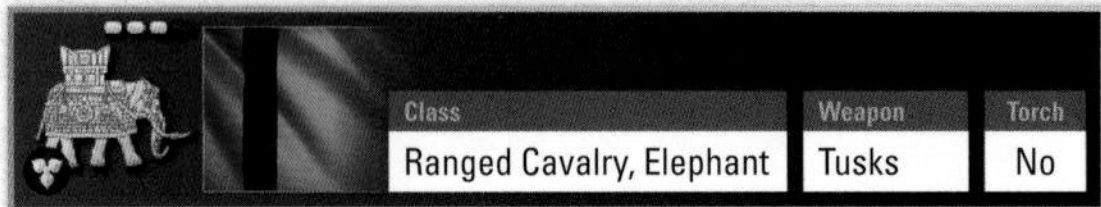

Class	Weapon	Torch
Ranged Cavalry, Elephant	Tusks	No

Tower War Elephants are one of the biggest and most imposing units in the game, and while they may lack some of the health and armor of their normal War Elephant cousins, they make up for it with additional versatility. Mounted on top of the elephant are a pair of highly trained Archers, allowing the Tower War Elephant to use both melee and ranged attacks simultaneously. Their impressive size, however, does have a significant impact on your economy, with each one counting as three population units towards your capacity.

Delhi Sultanate Tower War Elephant

Special Abilities & Technologies

Tower War Elephant can use both melee from its tusks and ranged attacks from the mounted Archers at the same time, making it rather special indeed. In Age IV you can further enhance those Archers by acquiring the **Siege Elephant** technology at the Archery Range. That upgrade turns the humble Archers into much stronger Crossbowmen, making the Tower War Elephant even better against armored targets. To give those Crossbowmen even more time to inflict that extra damage, you might want to consider getting the **Armored Beasts** upgrade from the Stable, because that gives all of your elephants +3 armor, allowing them to stay in fights for longer.

Primary Uses

- *Multipurpose cavalry unit*
- *Versatile siege unit*

Training Details

Building Required	Time	Food	Wood	Gold	Population
Archery Range	1m 0s	400	0	600	3

Unit Stats	
Health	960
Melee Armor	0
Ranged Armor	4
Move Speed	0.88

Attacktype	Bow	Tusks
Damage	15	30
Counter Bonus	40	--
Bonus Against	--	--
Attack Range	5.00	1.00
Attack Speed	1.25s	2.75s

Tusks (Siege)	
Damage	100
Counter Bonus	--
Bonus Against	Buildings/Siege
Attack Range	1.00
Attack Speed	5.75s

Tactics & Usage

Tower War Elephants are only really practical in Age IV, once your economy has a steady Gold income, and you have plenty of Farms. You can bolster your numbers with the **Palace of the Sultan's** ability to produce them for free, but you'll need a high population capacity to account for them all.

One of the primary counters to any cavalry unit are Spearmen, but thanks to the mounted Archers, Tower Elephants fare much better against them than normal cavalry.

The use of Tower War Elephants is somewhat similar to that of War Elephants, but there are a few areas where the addition of the mounted Archers are extremely beneficial. In addition to being able to attack Stone Walls, they can simultaneously shoot at infantry atop those walls to thin them out and allow your elephant to continue attacking. They can also act as an impressive support unit, mainly thanks to their ability to absorb a lot of damage while dishing out an impressive amount themselves. When used in conjunction with other strong melee units, or the even sturdier War Elephant, they can be hard for opponents to deal with.

Counters

To beat a Tower War Elephant you need to outnumber it significantly, either with a lot of strong ranged units, or an even greater number of melee units. Spearmen are still a good choice as a melee counter unit, because their ease of production means that you can make them in the numbers required. You're likely to lose a few trying to get close, but as long as enough get within range, they can get the job done thanks to their bonus damage.

Another option would be targeting the Tower War Elephant from a distance with a group of Springalds, but this is costly both in terms of resources and population. If you're confident in your micro unit control, Abassid Imams can also deal with them after researching the **Faith** technology, allowing them to convert these units without a Relic.

War Elephant

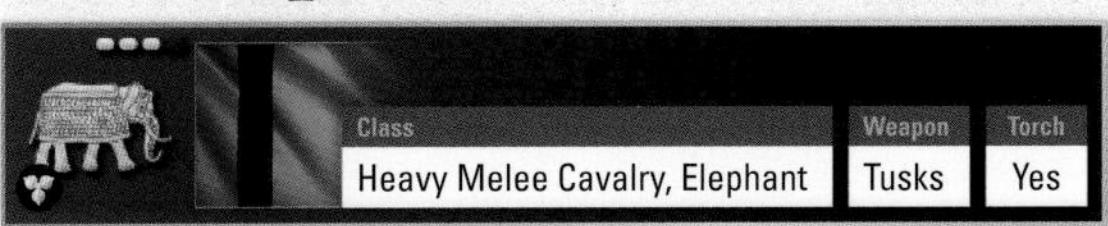

Class
Heavy Melee Cavalry, Elephant
Weapon
Tusks
Torch
Yes

Unlike the Tower War Elephant, normal War Elephants are entirely melee based, even down to the Spearman riding on their back. What they lack in attack diversity, however, they more than make up for with their raw ability to both absorb huge amounts of damage, and dish it out in turn. Just a few of these units acting together are capable of shredding armies and tearing buildings apart!

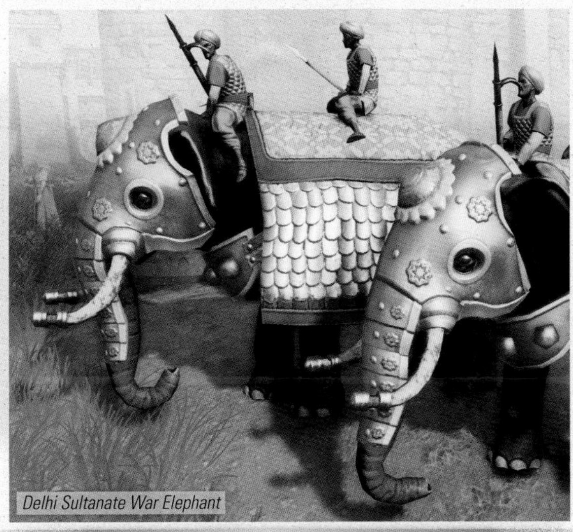
Delhi Sultanate War Elephant

Special Abilities & Technologies

As with the Tower War Elephants, it's important to take the mounted Spearman into consideration when you're working out how much damage this unit can deal. If you combine its tusks with the base attack of the Spearman, you'll be dealing 50 damage consistently, and if you go up against cavalry units, you also get the counter bonus damage from the Spearman, bringing you up to 90.

Along with the Tower War Elephant, these are one of the few melee units that can attack Stone Walls. While they lack the ability to directly attack any units standing atop the wall, their sheer amount of health means they can sustain their attack for much longer under fire. The **Armored Beasts** upgrade can help with that role, since it grants +3 armor to all elephants, and thus should be research immediately upon reaching Age IV.

Primary Uses

- *Destroying enemy buildings*
- *Destroying most enemy units*

Training Details

Building Required					
Stables	1m 0s	600	0	400	3

Unit Stats		
Health	1400	
Melee Armor	5	
Ranged Armor	2	
Move Speed	1.00	
Attacktype	Spear	Tusks
Damage	20	30*
Counter Bonus	40	--
Bonus Against	Cavalry	--
Attack Range	1.25	1.00
Attack Speed	1.75s	2.75s
Tusks (Siege)		
Damage	100	
Counter Bonus	--	
Bonus Against	Buildings/Siege	
Attack Range	1.00	
Attack Speed	5.75s	

*Switches to an 80 damage Charge attack for the initial attack

Tactics & Usage

War Elephants are best used either as a strong fighting unit within your overall military, or as a substitute to other siege units for destroying enemy buildings and fortifications. If you like to invest in heavy siege units once you reach Age III, then War Elephants are a great substitute that have the added benefit of not being vulnerable to melee units. Building a lot of them during Age III is cost prohibitive, but even a few are capable of dealing significant damage.

Once you get within range to charge your opponent's base, a heard of War Elephants is extremely difficult to take down without leaving a trail of destruction in their wake.

Because the most likely counter from your opponent at this stage of the game is Spearmen, you should try to pair your War Elephants with a lot of cheap Archers, as well as some Scholars to heal them. While the War Elephant is difficult for opponents to contend with, you should not get too complacent when using them. If you do run into trouble, it's nearly impossible to get out of it due to the elephant's slow movement, and with their high cost, you don't want to lose too many of these behemoths.

Counters

Although expensive, using Springalds to attack War Elephants from long range is very effective, and since the elephants move quite slowly it's difficult for them to escape or get close enough to destroy the Springald. The slow speed of the War Elephant is also what makes Spearmen a good option, because it's much easier for them to get close enough to launch an attack—just make sure you have a lot of them, because you'll take some casualties in the process. Putting a Religious unit with a Relic amongst those Spearmen is also not a bad idea, since they can act as a shield while you attempt to convert the elephant; just make sure to keep the Religious unit away from those tusks.

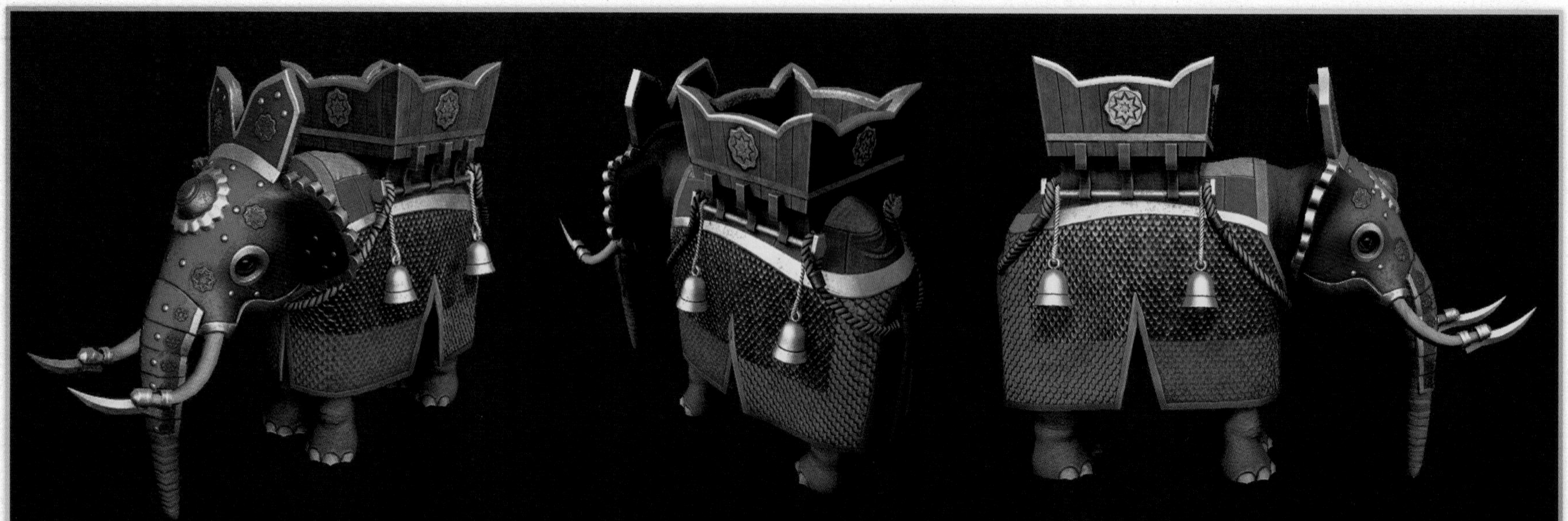

Delhi Sultnate Tower War Elephant—Age IV
Concept 3D Sculpt showing team color areas

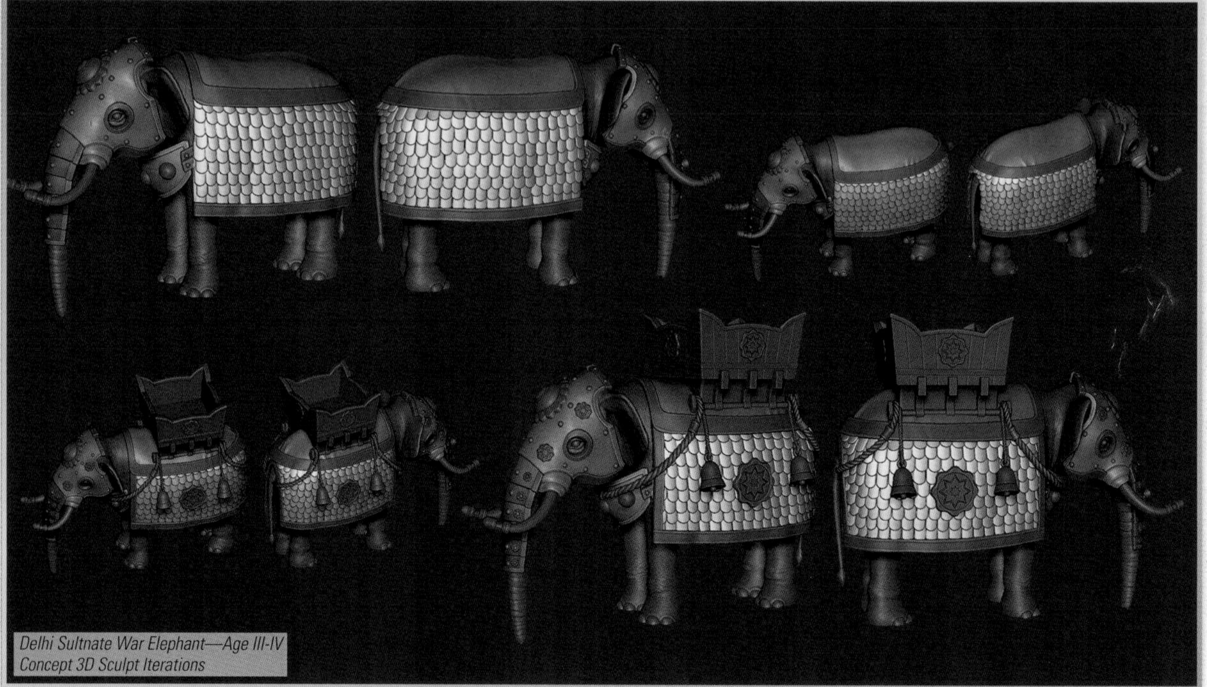

Delhi Sultnate War Elephant—Age III-IV
Concept 3D Sculpt Iterations

Elephant Balance

"One of my cherished memories from balance testing is witnessing a battle between 20 Knights and one War Elephant being healed by a pack of Scholars. The Knights were force attacking the elephant, so they were running circles around it while the Scholars did their best to heal. With so many Knights, the elephant health kept going down and down and down. Slowly though the elephant was whittling down the Knight count. The elephant's health bar got so low it looked completely empty. By this point it had landed the killing blow on enough Knights that the Scholars healing could keep up with the damage. They kept that poor elephant alive at 5 health while it killed the entire army of Knights!"

– **Eric Wrobel**
Senior Designer, Balance Lead, Relic

Delhi Sultnate Tower War Elephant—Age IV
3D Sculpts

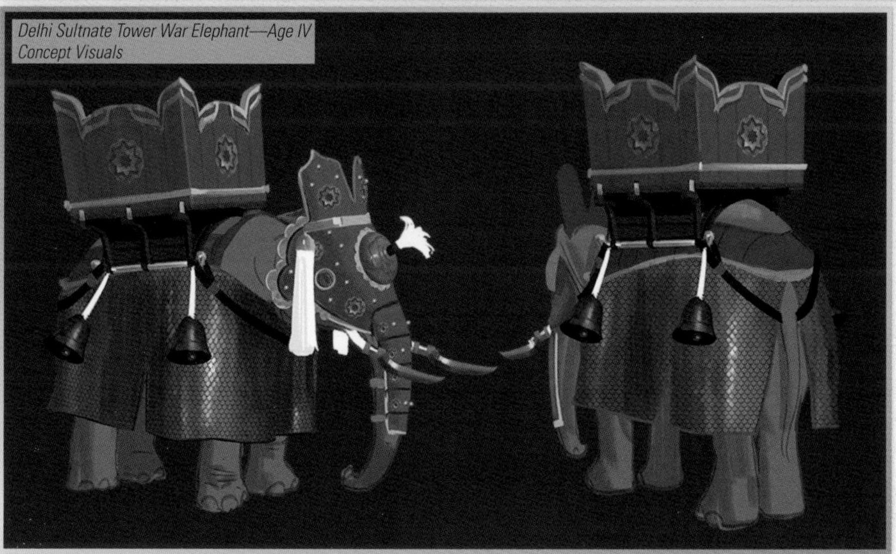

Delhi Sultnate Tower War Elephant—Age IV
Concept Visuals

Animating the Elephants

"Of all the things we worked on, I'm most proud of the way the Elephants turned out. Animators Anand Somasundaran and Yuri Lementy did such a great job with them—their keyframe animation is so strong. They had the added challenge of adding the rider animation from our motion capture. The elephants came together in the end and I had a lot of fun watching them work. I also like the villagers' animation. There are a lot of little details to those animations that, I think, bring a lot of life to the frame. There is personality there, yet the villagers still offer that AoE charm that players expect."

– Brent Breedveld
Principal Animator, Animation Director, Relic

Battering Ram

Type	Weapon
Siege	Ram (Siege)

*The Battering Ram is available to all civilizations, and is one of two siege units that infantry can construct in the field once you research the **Siege Engineers** upgrade, making it a very versatile unit. Their high health and ranged armor makes them perfectly suited to closing in on enemy buildings while under attack from ranged units, and once they get close, their rams can make short work of any building. That health and armor also comes into play with the other main function of the Battering Ram—as a troop transport. Up to 16 infantry units can safely fit under the protective covering of a Battering Ram, allowing you to get your squishy melee infantry close enough to enemy buildings to do some damage without falling to ranged attacks along the way.*

Battering Rams

Primary Uses

- *Protecting infantry units from incoming ranged attacks*
- *Destroying enemy buildings and fortifications*

Training Details

Building Required	Time	Food	Wood	Gold	Population
--	1m 20s	0	300	0	3

Unit Stats	
Health	900
Melee Armor	0
Ranged Armor	15
Move Speed	0.88
Ram (Siege)	
Damage	200
Counter Bonus	--
Bonus Against	--
Attack Range	0.29
Attack Speed	5.00s

Tactics & Usage

Heavily using Battering Rams in the Feudal Age takes a lot of commitment, and should only be done if you're going for a very specific style of high-risk, high-reward play, and are trying to end the game as quickly as possible. You're going to want to plan ahead, since you'll likely want to research **Siege Engineering**, and that takes a whole minute, which is time that can make or break a potential rush.

Battering Rams are a big investment, requiring 300 Wood, some upgrading time, and three population spaces, so you'll want to heavily lean towards gathering Wood with your Villagers to cover the costs. Once you have sufficient resources saved up, you'll want to move your infantry to a staging area, and only then build your Battering Rams, since that cuts down the risk of losing them along the way. Rams in this Age should primarily be used to take down defensive structures, such as Outposts and Walls, to clear a path for your other units, and to destroy Landmarks. If you can create an opening in your opponent's defenses, driving your Battering Rams straight for their Town Center or other Landmarks can lead to a devastating victory.

From the Castle Age onwards, you should be freely constructing Battering Rams with your infantry whenever the need arises. Their usage remains largely the same, but since your opponent's buildings are likely to be more spread out by this time, you'll often find yourself coming across buildings in exposed areas—the quickest way to destroy these could be to build some rams, depending on your group composition. Stone Walls also come into play at this stage of the game, and Battering Rams are a good, cheap option for bringing them down. As you move into Age IV, rams tend to make way for superior siege units, but by that point your economy should be strong enough that rams can be a quick, cheap, and disposable option while you use your more expensive units to take out priority targets.

Because they are available from the Feudal Age, Battering Rams are a good unit to use for early aggressive play into enemy territory, with the aim of destroying as many buildings as possible.

Counters

Countering Battering Rams is relatively simple: they're extremely resistant to ranged attacks, so using melee units is essential. Any melee unit will do, and while rams can't attack your units directly, you never know if there are infantry inside, so you should still attack them with sufficient numbers to cover that possibility.

Bombard

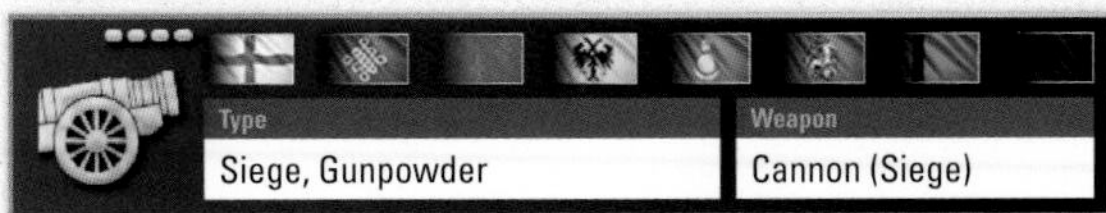

The Bombard is a powerful gunpowder siege available to most civilizations. Per shot, Bombard damage is similar to other siege units, but they sacrifice some range for much faster firing speed. If you get them close enough, very little can take out buildings faster.

Bombard

French Cannon

Cannon

Primary Uses

- *Direct attacks against buildings and fortifications*

Training Details

	Time	Food	Wood	Gold	Stone
All Variants	45s	0	400	600	3

Building Required	
Bombard*	Siege Workshop
Clocktower Bombard	Astronomical Clocktower
Cannon	Siege Workshop
Royal Cannon	College of Artillary

*If the building is under the influence of an Ovoo, Mongols can pay an additional 1000 Stone for x2 of the unit.

Unit Stats	Bombard	Clocktower B.	Cannon	Royal C.
Health	480	720	320	320
Melee Armor	0	0	0	0
Ranged Armor	12	12	12	12
Move Speed	0.88	0.88	0.88	0.88

Cannon (Siege)	Bombard	Clocktower B.	Cannon	Royal C.
Damage	170	170	200	220
Counter Bonus	340	340	400	440
Bonus Against	Buildings			
Attack Range	10.00	10.00	10.00	10.00
Attack Speed	5.25s	5.25s	5.25s	5.25s

Special Versions

Cannon/Royal Cannon (French)

The French get a unique version of the Bombard called the Cannon. Cannons deal more base damage and bonus damage than Bombards, and their lower health means they are a literal glass Cannon. As the French, if you build the **College of Artillery** to advance to Age IV, you'll also have access to the more powerful Royal Cannon. This version has most of the same stats as a normal Cannon, but its all-important damage stat is 20% higher, making it the superior version to produce if you have the choice.

Tactics & Usage

The best way to think of Bombards is as a more mobile Trebuchet with less range and faster attack speed. Unlike Trebuchets, however, Bombards/Cannons fire in a straight line, so they're unable to shoot over obstacles between them and their target. This changes their usage somewhat, making them better suited to breaching the outer defenses of your opponent's base rather than trying to target specific buildings inside it. Once inside a base, they're better at causing general destruction rather than targeted attacks.

If you're playing as the Chinese, all of the Bombards you produce will inflict 20% more damage by default thanks to the free Chemistry technology.

Counters

If you're looking to counter Bombards/Cannons with some siege units of your own, then Culverins should be your first choice. Not only do Culverins out-range bombards/Cannons, they also deal bonus damage against siege units, so they can make quick work of them in equal numbers. Melee infantry can also get the job done, but you should expect some casualties along the way—unless you manage to ambush them from a Stealth Forest.

Culverin

Royal Culverin

Primary Uses

- *Countering enemy siege units*
- *Sniping high value targets*

Although both a gunpowder unit and a siege unit like the Bombard, Culverins do not actually fill the same role because they're quite weak against buildings. Instead, Culverins are designed specifically to counter those siege engines that might be attacking your buildings or defending the enemy's base. With its long range it's perfectly suited to a sniping role.

Culverin

French Royal Culverin

Training Details

Both Variants	45s	0	400	600	3

Building Required	
Culverin	Siege Workshop
Royal Culverin	College of Artillery

Unit Stats	Culverin	Royal Culverin
Health	400	400
Melee Armor	0	0
Ranged Armor	12	12
Move Speed	0.62	0.62

Cannon (Ranged)	Culverin	Royal Culverin
Damage	85	102
Counter Bonus	200	204
Bonus Against	Siege	
Attack Range	12.00	12.00
Attack Speed	4.25s	4.25s

Special Versions

Royal Culverin (French)

Through the **College of Artillery**, the French can build their unique Royal version of the Culverin. It's identical to the normal version but deals 20% additional base and bonus damage, making it the better option to go with.

Tactics & Usage

Culverins are a more powerful gunpowder equivalent of a Springald, but instead of the ability to fire through enemy units, they deal large bonus damage to siege units. They also don't require any additional time to set themselves up before firing. Their range and bonus damage makes them very effective at countering Bombards and similar heavy siege units.

If your opponent is using siege units and they see you bringing Culverins to the fight, they're likely to try and destroy them as quickly as possible, so always keep some units nearby to defend your Culverins; they're very expensive to produce, so you'll want to keep them safe. Their high cost also means it's better to hold off building Culverins until you see your opponent starting to field siege units, because they're not very effective against large groups of infantry or buildings.

Counters

Culverins are primarily countered by large groups of melee and fast moving units that can close the distance quickly. Knights are ideal for this, since they cover both of the best options and are a powerful unit in their own right, but Horsemen can be quite on a budget. Similarly, Spearmen or Men-at-Arms can work well, but you'll need larger groups of them, and some are sure to be lost along the way.

Culverins are excellent at taking down single key enemy units, such as Monks or Khans. This is thanks to their combination of range and damage, which allows them to usually take out those units in a single shot.

Mangonel

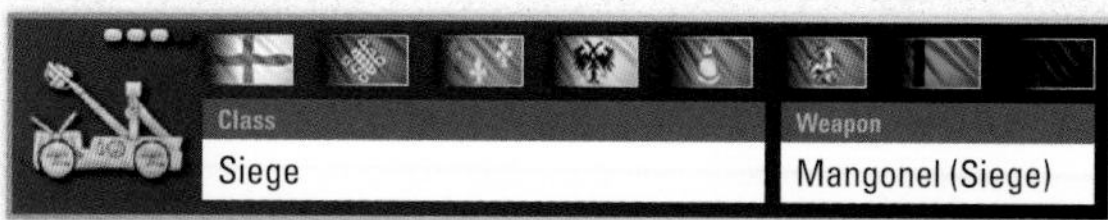

Mangonels are heavy siege units that require some set up time before they fire—and after firing, if you want to move them again. They fire volleys of three rocks over an area, and are primarily used to devastate groups of enemy infantry when you're either attacking or defending a position.

Mangonel

Special Abilities

In the single-player campaigns, Mangonels have the ability to toggle between their normal ammunition and incendiary ammunition, with the incendiary ammunition dealing more damage to buildings. While most units are only capable of attacking a single target, Mangonels can actually hit multiple targets within a roughly one tile radius of their projectile's impact point. The further away from that impact point, the less damage you'll deal. Up to around three quarters of a tile from the impact point you'll deal the full damage, and from there to a full tile away you'll deal 90% of the damage. You can still deal some damage just past the one tile mark, but it will only be 75%, and then it drops straight to zero one you reach the edge of the blast radius.

Tactics & Usage

Their high cost make the Mangonel a considerable investment when they first become available in the Castle Age, but as long as you never leave them unprotected, they can be put to devastating use. Pairing a Mangonel with both ranged and anti-cavalry units is usually a safe bet, because that will stop both of their main threats from getting close.

Used offensively, the Mangonel is best against large groups of infantry units—this is where you can get the maximum benefit out of their ability to deal damage over a large area. Ranged infantry are especially vulnerable to this form of attack, because the Mangonel can out-range most of them, and if they do close in, the Mangonel has a decent amount of ranged armor. If you see your opponent going for massive numbers of ranged units, a Siege Workshop and Mangonel is often the best response.

Additionally, they can support your other siege units during an assault on a fortified position by shooting infantry on top

*A Mangonel can also make use of a **Ground Attack** ability to target an area instead of specific units. This can be useful when timed correctly against incoming or retreating units to surprise your enemy; if you start firing just before they're within the normal attack range, you can get one early hit in before commencing normal attacks. You can also use this tactic to make it impossible for enemy units to enter a specific area.*

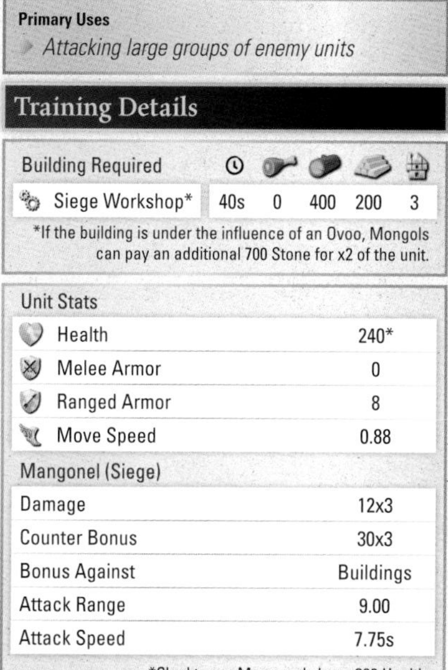

Primary Uses

Attacking large groups of enemy units

Training Details

Building Required	Time	Food	Wood	Gold	Pop
Siege Workshop*	40s	0	400	200	3

*If the building is under the influence of an Ovoo, Mongols can pay an additional 700 Stone for x2 of the unit.

Unit Stats	
Health	240*
Melee Armor	0
Ranged Armor	8
Move Speed	0.88
Mangonel (Siege)	
Damage	12x3
Counter Bonus	30x3
Bonus Against	Buildings
Attack Range	9.00
Attack Speed	7.75s

*Clocktower Mangonels have 360 Health

of Stone Walls—with the added bonus of dealing some extra damage to the walls themselves. If you're attempting this, however, be sure that you've taken down any Stone Wall Towers first, since they can easily destroy your Mangonel.

Defensively, the Mangonel is best used behind walls. They are able to shoot units approaching your walls without the danger of being caught off guard. If you have a Stone Wall with a Stone Wall Tower and some units on top, place a Mangonel behind it for an almost impenetrable defense—at least until Age IV siege units come into play.

Counters

Using other siege units to either out-damage or out-range Mangonels is often one of the best choices for dealing with them. Gunpowder siege units, such as Bombards or Culverins, can use their high damage output to win battles against them. Alternatively, in Age III, Springalds can be used, since they can attack from further away. If siege units aren't an option, then sturdy defenses such as Stone Wall Towers or Keeps work well, as can melee units if you close in quickly.

3

Clocktower Nest of Bees

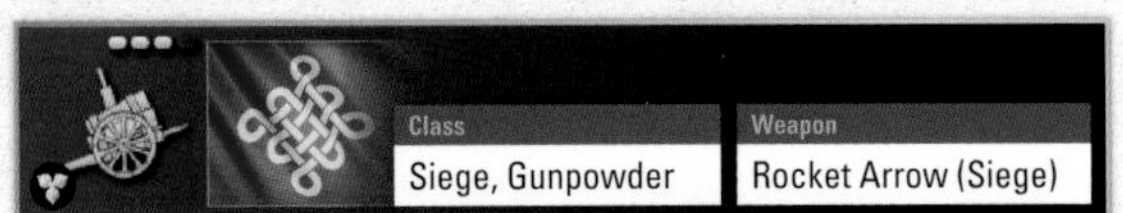

Nest of Bees

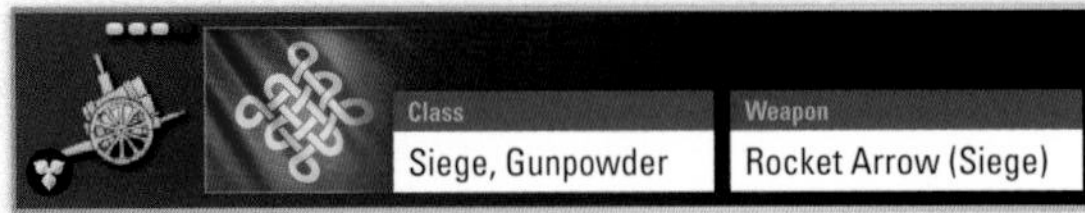

The Nest of Bees is testament to the superiority of Chinese gunpowder technology, and one of the most unique units in AoE IV. Upon firing, it launches a large volley of eight rockets, causing massive damage over a nearly one tile radius around the impact point. While that radius is smaller than that of a Mangonel, the Nest of Bees attack suffers no damage fall-off from the point of impact.

Chinese Clocktower Nest of Bees

Chinese Nest of Bees

Primary Uses

- *Attacking large groups of enemy units*

Training Details

	Time				
Both Variants	40s	0	300	300	3

Building Required	
Nest of Bees	Siege Workshop
Clocktower Nest of Bees	Astronomical Clocktower

Unit Stats	Nest of Bees	Clocktower Nest of Bees
Health	240	360
Melee Armor	0	0
Ranged Armor	8	8
Move Speed	0.62	0.62

Rocket Arrow	Nest of Bees	Clocktower Nest of Bees
Damage	6x8	6x8
Counter Bonus	--	--
Bonus Against	--	--
Attack Range	8.00	8.00
Attack Speed	5.50s	5.50s

*It's worth constructing the **Astronomical Clocktower** as your first Age III Landmark if you plan on producing a lot of Nest of Bees units, so that you can take advantage of the extra +50% health.*

Tactics & Usage

Nest of Bees are a reasonable investment, even early on in the Castle Age, due to their relatively modest cost compared to other siege units. They have the slowest movement speed of all units, however, so they're even more prone to counterattacks by enemy units, and protecting them should be an even higher priority than usual. As with most siege units, a mixture of cavalry and ranged units make for the best protective detail.

Their firing arc is high enough that they can be used as an effective infantry deterrent if you position them behind walls in your own base; such a stationary role helps to offset their slow movement speed. Similar to the Mangonel, however, Nest of Bees are at their best when firing into large groups of enemy units, especially since there's no fall-off to their damage past the point of impact, so you'll deal full damage to every unit you hit. They can also be used in a supportive role when you're attacking an opponent's base, due to how good they are at clearing out any units in the area. Just make sure that you bring your faster units in first, so that the Nest of Bees doesn't take a lot of damage as it slowly moves into place.

Counters

Depending on your playstyle, there are a few good options for dealing with Nest of Bees. If you're playing more defensively, Keeps or Stone Wall Towers with some upgrades can be an extremely effective means of keeping them away from your base without risking any of your units. Out in the field, however, your best options are melee cavalry units, since they can close in quickly and inflict a lot of damage to siege units. Other siege units, such as Culverins or Bombards, can also be quite effective, especially if you have them support your melee cavalry units from afar.

Royal Ribauldequin

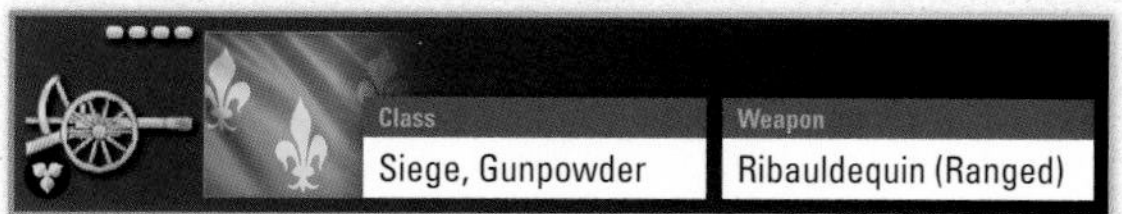

Ribauldequin

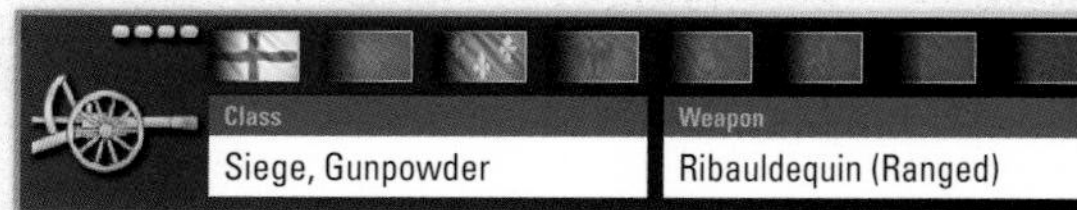

Ribauldequins are the ultimate anti-infantry gunpowder unit—you just have to get close enough to see the whites of the opposing unit's eyes to use them. Once they're within range, however, they can inflict a huge amount of damage over a large area very quickly, causing havoc among the enemy's ranks.

French Royal Ribauldequin

Ribauldequin

Primary Uses

- *Close range anti-infantry weapon*

Training Details

	Time	Food	Wood	Gold	Pop
Both Variants	45s	0	400	600	3

Building Required	
Ribauldequin	Siege Workshop
Royal Ribauldequin	College of Artillary

Unit Stats	Ribauldequin	Royal Ribauldequin
Health	480	480
Melee Armor	0	0
Ranged Armor	2	2
Move Speed	0.88	0.88

Ribauldequin (Ranged)	Ribauldequin	Royal Ribauldequin
Damage	42x12	50x12
Counter Bonus	--	--
Bonus Against	--	--
Attack Range	3.75	6.00
Attack Speed	6.25s	6.25s

Special Versions

Royal Ribauldequin (French)

The Royal Ribauldequin is another in the line of the enhanced royal versions of siege units that the French can build from the **College of Artillery**. The usage of this version is almost identical to the normal one, but the fact that it has nearly double the range means it's a lot safer, since you don't have to get quite so close to the enemy. It also deals more damage than the normal version, making it superior in every way.

Tactics & Usage

Everything about producing Ribauldequins carries a hefty Gold price tag; you're going to want to stockpile Gold during the initial stages of the game to ensure you produce them smoothly in Age IV. If Gold is not abundant, you're usually better off building Mangonels, since you can produce more of them for the same amount of Gold. They're essentially a gunpowder equivalent of a Mangonel in terms of their usage, but they sacrifice a lot of range for a significant bump to damage— a quintessential high-risk, high-reward unit. To mitigate that risk somewhat, always ensure there are some strong units in front of your Ribauldequin to act as a buffer, because at their high cost, you don't want to lose any of them.

Ribauldequin have a lot more health than Mangonels so can take a bit more of a beating, but due to their necessary proximity to enemy units, they're also a lot more likely to get into trouble.

Counters

Because of the amount of damage they can put out, taking on Ribauldequins head-on can be a risky proposition. Your best bet is to try to avoid getting into their firing range, and that means anti-siege units such as Culverins are by far the best option. Ribauldequin are also ineffective against buildings, so any strong defensive structures can be quite effective against them. If you have to use non-siege units to counter them, try to use the units that have the highest health possible, because they're going to need to absorb a lot of damage while they close in.

Siege Tower

Class	Weapon
Siege	--

Along with the Battering Ram, Siege Towers are one of only two siege units that can be built by your infantry units out in the field after researching the ***Siege Engineers*** *technology at the Blacksmith. A lot can change between first scouting an enemy base and the time your army gets there, and it is during such times that Siege Towers come into play. If you lack the means to destroy enemy Stone Walls, Siege Towers let you bypass them by transporting up to eight infantry units to the edge of the wall, and then deploying them to rush enemy units that have taken up defensive positions.*

Siege Tower

Tactics & Usage

Siege Towers have only one use: getting your infantry on top of Stone Walls. If your opponent has fully walled themselves in behind Stone Walls early in a game, these units will shine. To use them you'll need to garrison up to eight infantry units inside, and then right click on top of a wall to have the Siege Tower close in and release the units on top of it. Because you can only house eight units at a time, you'll usually want to send a few Siege Towers at once, so that you can storm the walls with a large force of units.

In the later stages of the game when there are heavier defenses available to your opponents, sending Siege Towers full of infantry will rarely be enough to infiltrate the enemy base on their own. If, however, you begin with your other siege units, and then use Siege Towers to deliver infantry to support them from the wall, you can force your opponent to fight on two fronts, making it easier for your units to create an opening.

The Abbasid Dynasty don't need to research ***Siege Engineering*** *before their infantry can build Siege Towers. This not only saves some resources, but also valuable time if your opponent is starting to place Stone Walls as soon as they're available.*

Counters

Because Siege Towers have no means of attacking, any units that deal melee damage can easily destroy them once they get close enough. The Springald bolts fired from Stone Wall Towers can be quite effective against Siege Towers, but in general, ranged attacks are quite ineffective against them due to their ranged armor.

Primary Uses

- *Transporting infantry units*
- *Deploying infantry units on top of enemy Stone Walls*

Training Details

Building Required	Time	Food	Wood	Gold	Population
--	45s	0	125	0	1

Unit Stats	
Health	480
Melee Armor	0
Ranged Armor	8
Move Speed	0.62s

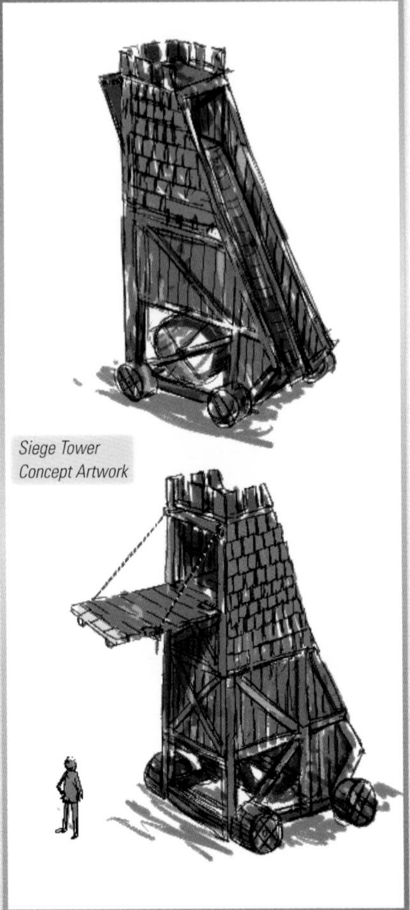

Siege Tower Concept Artwork

Springald

Clocktower Springald

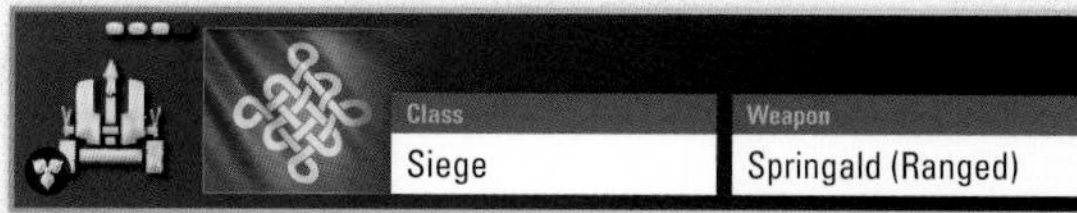

Primary Uses

- *Long range attacks on priority targets*

Training Details

	Time	Food	Wood	Gold	Stone	Population
Both Variants	30s	0	200	200	3	

Building Required	
Springald	Siege Workshop*
Clocktower Springald	College of Artillary

*If the building is under the influence of an Ovoo, Mongols can pay an additional 400 Stone for x2 of the unit.

Unit Stats	Springald	Clocktower Springald
Health	200	300
Melee Armor	0	0
Ranged Armor	8	8
Move Speed	1.00	1.00

Springald (Ranged)	Springald	Clocktower Springald
Damage	60	60
Counter Bonus	20	20
Bonus Against	Siege	Siege
Attack Range	10	10
Attack Speed	4.00s	4.00s

The Springald is a heavy siege unit that has to be deployed before it can start firing. They fire large bolts over great distances, and while those bolts deal very little damage to buildings, they're capable of inflicting massive amounts of damage to individual units. They can even pierce through other units to reach their intended target, although none of the units the bolt passes through will take any damage.

Springald

Chinese Clocktower Springalds

Tactics & Usage

The high damage per shot and relatively fast firing speed means that Springalds are mainly used for taking out high value targets, such as Monks or Mangonels, from a range at which most other units can't retaliate. It doesn't matter if that high value target happens to be standing behind a number of other units; the Springald's bolts can pass through multiple units and still inflict full damage once they hit their target. Additionally, although they only deal minimal damage to buildings, at the point of the game where defenses such as Stone Wall Towers become available, Springalds are a cheaper but less effective option than a Trebuchet.

Counters

Since Springalds have to deploy to fire, and they can only hit one unit at a time, large numbers of melee units that are spread out over a wide area, or ones such as cavalry that can move quickly, are most often the best forms of counter. Try to avoid closing in with any expensive or important units, because the Springald could easily pick them out of the pack, and instead stick with large numbers of cheaper units. Once your melee units do get close, the Springalds won't be able to put up much of a fight.

If your opponent's army is coming towards you in a giant wedge formation, at the back of which is a key support unit, it doesn't matter how many units are standing in front—a Springald bolt will always find a way through to its mark.

3

Counterweight Trebuchet

Counterweight Trebuchet

Trebuchets are extremely long-ranged siege units that specialize in attacking buildings or other stationary targets. It takes a long time for Trebuchets to deploy before they can commence firing, and even once they do, their projectile travel speed is among the slowest in the game, so hitting moving targets can be quite difficult. If used properly, however, you can rain down projectiles onto enemy buildings from so far away that they won't even know they're under attack until they've already been hit.

Special Versions

Traction Trebuchet (Mongols)

The Mongols have a unique version of the Trebuchet called a Traction Trebuchet. Their general usage is the same as a standard Counterweight Trebuchet, but they trade reduced damage and range for a much faster deploy time and attack speed, making them slightly better at hitting moving targets, especially infantry. Another thing that makes them good against infantry is the fact that the area of effect from the projectile impact is more than twice the size of the Counterweight Trebuchet, and the damage fall-off as you move away from the point of impact is also not as severe.

Clocktower Counterweight Trebuchet

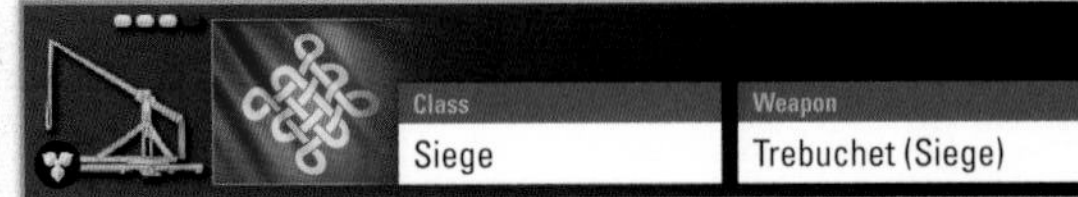

Chinese Clocktower Counterweight Trebuchet

Primary Uses

Long range building destruction

Training Details

	Time	Food	Wood	Gold	Stone/Pop
A Counterweight Trebuchet	40s	0	500	250	3
B Clocktower Counterweight Trebuchet	40s	0	500	250	3
C Traction Trebuchet	35s	0	400	150	3

Building Required	
A Counterweight Trebuchet	Siege Workshop
B Clocktower Counterweight Trebuchet	Astronomical Clocktower
C Traction Trebuchet	Siege Workshop*

*If the building is under the influence of an Ovoo, Mongols can pay an additional 650 Stone for x2 of the unit.

Unit Stats	A	B	C
Health	400	600	320
Melee Armor	0	0	0
Ranged Armor	8	8	8
Move Speed	0.62	0.62	0.88

Trebuchet (Siege)	A	B	C
Damage	150	150	100
Counter Bonus	300	300	200
Bonus Against		Buildings	
Attack Range	16.00	16.00	13.00
Attack Speed	12.50s	12.50s	9.50s

Traction Trebuchet

Mongol Traction Trebuchet

Pairing Traction Trebuchets with Mangonels gives you not only a fearsome grouping of anti-infantry siege units, but it allows you to stagger your units, making it harder for your opponent to destroy them if they get close.

Tactics & Usage

Trebuchets excel at taking down fortifications and buildings from outside any other unit's range. This makes them a great unit to force fights with—your opponent will need to leave their base if they want to stop your bombardments, or watch as their buildings crumble around them.

The small area of effect from the impact of a Counterweight Trebuchet, along with the slow travel speed of their projectiles, means they're not well suited to firing on infantry, but they can still be effective at dealing with other siege units. Because of their range, you can sometimes catch your opponent's siege engines as they start setting up to fire—this can mean that by the time they notice the incoming projectile, it'll be too late to move out of the way.

Since ships have to align themselves to fire, Trebuchets are a good long range defence measure vs naval units.

Their longer reload time between shots makes Trebuchets very vulnerable between attacks.

Counters

Trebuchets rely on their extreme range to keep them safe, so your best option is to close in on them as quickly as possible with melee units. Most of the time, you just need to make that first projectile miss, because once you're inside that range the slow speed at which Trebuchets transition back to their mobile state means it'll be too late to escape.

Fishing Boats

Fishing Boats are nautical units that are responsible for a lot of the same duties as the land-locked Villager. If you spot some birds circling above the water, you can send some Fishing Boats to that location to harvest the Fish beneath them, after which they'll drop them back off at the Dock. They can also repair other waterborne units, making them essential in drawn out naval battles.

Delhi Sultanate Fishing Boat

Tactics & Usage

The Fishing Boat can be used from very early on in the game to give a boost to your economy, especially if you're playing on a map with a lot of water. If you're going to build a Dock and Fishing Boats early, you'll want to put more Villagers on Wood than Food, because you'll need the extra Wood for all of the ships. Once you have them up and running, you can use the Fishing Boats to start bringing in more food.

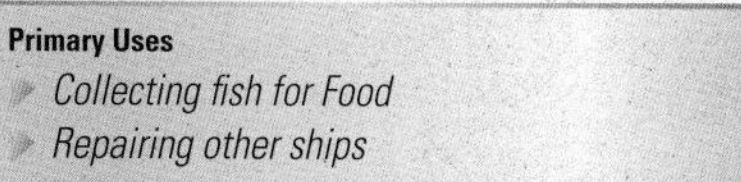

Primary Uses
Collecting fish for Food
Repairing other ships

Training Details (Age I)

Building Required					
Dock	25s	0	60	0	1

Unit Stats	
Health	125
Melee Armor	0
Ranged Armor	0
Move Speed	1.50

Delhi Sultanate Fishing Boats have an extra trick up their sleeve: the fisherman on board is actually a trained archer. As the only Age I ship capable of attacking, they're uniquely capable of harassing other Fishing Ships or Villagers trying to gather Shorline Fish at that time.

Try to prioritize Deep Water Fish over Shoreline Fish, because they're gathered significantly faster, and unless they're far away from your Dock, the extra travel time is usually worth it. Of course, the further away you get, the more likely you are to run into your opponent's naval vessels, and since the Fishing Boats of most civilizations do not have any weaponry, you need to make sure they don't get into too much trouble. Once you're ready to engage in some actual naval battles, you should always bring along a couple of Fishing Boats with your fleet, because they can repair damaged ships while out at sea, saving you from the need to sail them back to the dock to get repaired.

Transport Ship

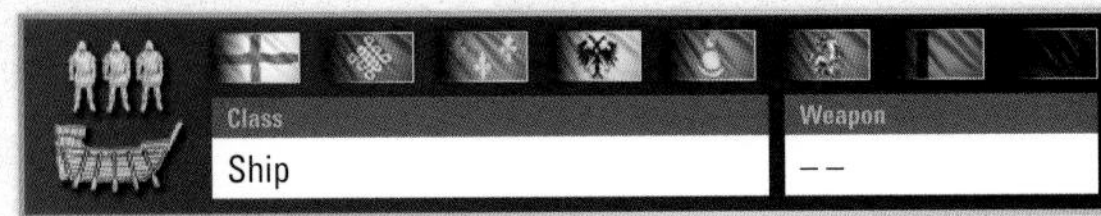

Class	Weapon
Ship	--

Transport Ships have the sole purpose of transporting your land units from one shore to another. Usually this will be for the purpose of bringing your army from your base across the water to your opponent's base, but they can also be useful for bringing Villagers to resources on small islands.

Chinese Transport Ship

Primary Uses

- *Transporting land-based units across bodies of water*

Training Details (Age I)

Building Required	Time	Food	Wood	Gold	Population
Dock	20s	0	100	0	2

Unit Stats	
Health	600
Melee Armor	0
Ranged Armor	0
Move Speed	1.50

You can garrison 16 units inside a Transport Ship, and even the huge War Elephants or Trebuchets only take up a single space, allowing you pack a lot of firepower into one Transport Ship.

Tactics & Usage

On maps with mostly water (e.g. Archipelago), Transport Ships can play an integral role in a strategy that combines both land and water units. If you're planning on most of your military units being ships, then it's worthwhile building a small contingent of land units and having some Transport Ships bring them to the enemy's shore to act as a diversionary force while your naval units launch your main attack. This tactic works best if you can land your Transport Ships undetected, so stick to the outskirts of the map, and try to land in a place that's unlikely to be visible to your opponent.

Alternatively, their cheap cost and early availability means that if you want to avoid naval battles, you can build up a large amount of land units and have Transport Ships get them into position for a quick, early land battle, potentially catching your opponent off guard. You can even use a Transport Ship to bring some Villagers and Scouts to your opponent's landmass and establish a secret base there.

On maps with rivers, Transport Ships can be used to transport units along the river to potentially catch your opponent off guard if they were expecting you to use the bridges and travel over land.

Counters

Learning to counter potential enemy Transport Ship landings is a big part of combat on maps with a lot of water, and there are some important things you should always keep in mind. If you don't want to get drawn into a land battle on your island, you should take preventative measures and be vigilant about minimizing your blind spots. First, place buildings like Houses along the shoreline and around your island to gain visibility, because if you spot a landing attempt right away, the element of surprise is gone. Outposts can also be used for this purpose, but they could have an impact on your ship production due to their Wood cost.

Having Scouts patrol along the shoreline is also an effective countermeasure, since their large vision radius lets them spot incoming Transport Ships. If any do manage to drop off their units, invest in land military of your own to repel them. If your opponent forfeited control of the water in favor of land units, then, there's a good chance you can come out ahead economically by taking control of the fishing spots.

Trade Ship

Class	Weapon
Worker, Ship	--

Trade Ships are the naval equivalent of the Trader unit and available to all civilizations from Age II onwards. They're used in much the same was as the Trader, albeit over water instead of land, and they also cost more to produce, both in terms resources and population capacity, since each ship counts as two towards your cap.

Abbasid Dynasty Trade Ship

On maps with rivers, you might be tempted to use Trade Ships to trade with allied docks. This, however, rarely works out better than normal trading over land, since it's a lot cheaper to produce land Traders, and they're a lot easier to protect.

Primary Uses

Trading to generate Gold

Training Details (Age I)

Building Required	Time	Food	Wood	Gold	Population
Dock	1m 0s	0	200	200	2

Unit Stats	
Health	300
Melee Armor	0
Ranged Armor	0
Move Speed	1.50

Tactics & Usage

Trader Ships in 1v1 Skirmishes can only be used effectively on maps with Coastal Trade Posts. If you select one and tell it to move to a Coastal Trade Post (or allied Docks in team games) it will pick up a delivery of Gold and Wood and bring it to your designated home market, which can be either a Dock or Market that you've built close enough to the coast.

Due to the nature of naval maps, Wood is often as valuable as Gold; there's not as much of it naturally available, and you need it for ship construction, so the first person to run out of Wood often looses. Naval trade routes also deliver Wood, however, so even if you run out of natural sources, a secure trade route will allow you to gain more. The longer the trade route, the more profitable each trip becomes.

Since they lack any offensive capabilities, Trade Ships are quite vulnerable to attack, especially later in games when the Gold they generate is even more valuable. The considerable costs of assigning naval units to protection duty are usually recouped after a few successful trades, however. You might want to build Keeps or Outposts on the islands where Coastal Trade Posts are located to gain some control over the area and help protect your trade route.

Trader Ships can be risky early in games due to their cost, but the sooner you establish your trade routes the better your long term gains will be. Control over Trade Posts and trade routes will often decide the outcome of the game at later stages, in both 1v1 and team games.

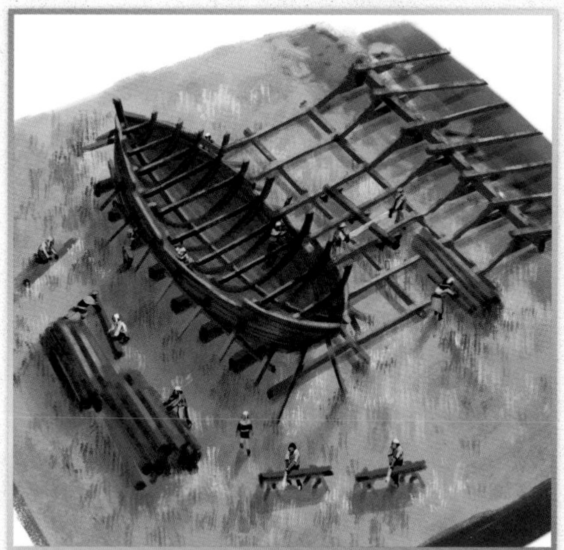

Concepts exploring ship contruction and naval combat.

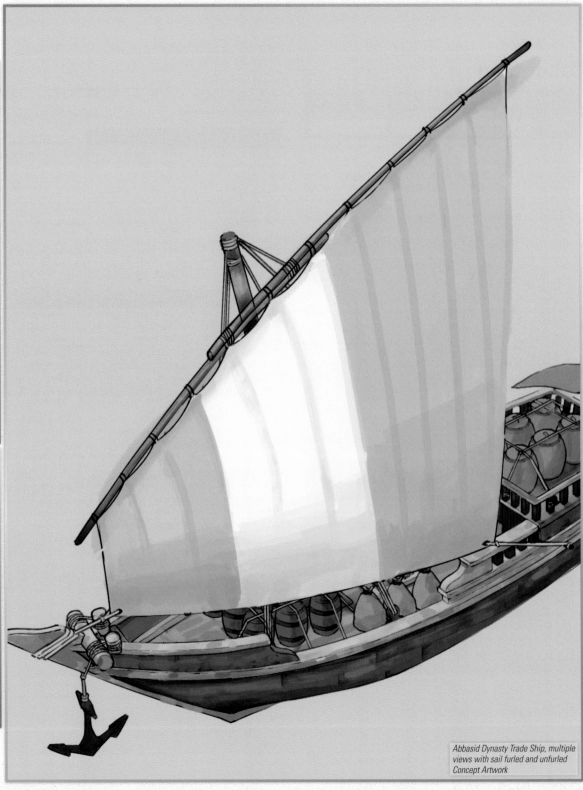

Abbasid Dynasty Trade Ship, multiple views with sail furled and unfurled
Concept Artwork

English Trade Ship, annotated Concept Artwork

Celebrating History

"We certainly [used the color palette to help create] a celebratory atmosphere in Age of Empires IV. Medieval history was chaotic, dark, and cruel, but there were many events and things about that part of human history which were important to how we've developed as a society. This was a period of time where gunpowder was playing a major role in transforming how battles were won and wars unfolded. How naval technology and navigation techniques helped to understand our world's geography and how that influenced trade and economy. And how the written word, philosophy and science of this time further laid the foundation for how our different cultures around the globe now rest upon. We wanted players to recognize this period of history with romanticism and imagination; and to do so with welcoming arms. We didn't want to push people away with 'doom and gloom'. Certainly, 'doom and gloom' is part of our history, but we didn't want it to be the overall tone of the game."

– Stuart Ng
Senior Concept Artist, Relic

Galleass

Class	Weapon
Ship	Bombard (Ranged)

The Galleass is only available to the French, and unlike all other gunpowder naval vessels, it has a bombard mounted on its bow, allowing to fire directly ahead, rather than being restricted to using broadside cannons.

French Galleass

Primary Uses
- *General purpose naval combat*

Training Details (Age III)

Building Required	Time	Food	Wood	Gold	Population
Dock	50s	0	360	300	6

Unit Stats	
Health	1200
Melee Armor	0
Ranged Armor	3
Move Speed	1.00
Bombard	
Damage	130
Counter Bonus	--
Bonus Against	--
Attack Range	8.00
Attack Speed	5.00s

Tactics & Usage

With higher production costs and the need for more population space than the other Age III ships, Galleass can be difficult to afford in any significant numbers early on in the Castle Age, but if you can build them, they can outshine nearly all other ships at that stage. Their long attack range makes them excellent for taking out buildings along the coastline, allowing you to get a head start on destroying fortifications, or even completely deny your opponent from establishing a foothold on key islands.

Galleass possess the same attack range as a Keep, so make sure to bring plenty of ships when you want to destroy one.

Their long range and forward-facing bombard also makes them a good choice to use against other ships, because they can easily out-range them, and you won't have to turn the ship to be able to fire, making it easier to stay within range if they try to escape. Their only real downside is their slow movement speed—other than that they're basically the ultimate all-round combat ship.

Counter

An effective counter against the Galleass is a superior number of Attack Ships. Due to their lower costs they are easier to mass produce, and if you build a lot of them you can significantly lower the enemy's numbers and hold control over the water. Warships also become a good option once you reach Age IV—paired with Attack Ships they make for a combination that can curtail the French Galleass force.

3

Demolition Ship

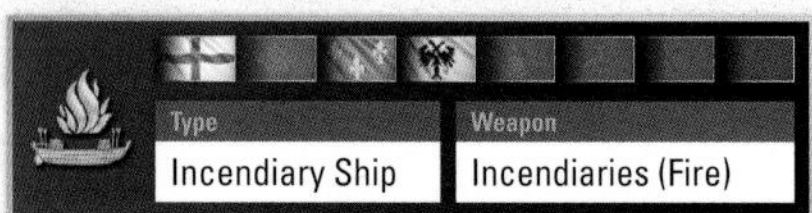

Explosive Dhow

Explosive Junk

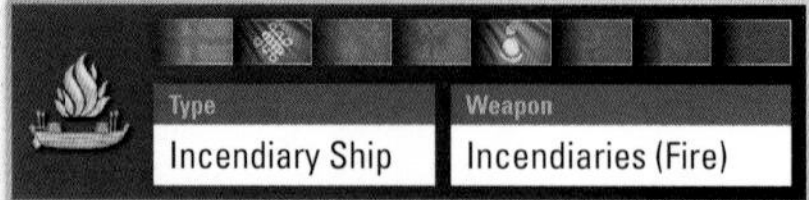

Lodya Demolition Ship

Incendiary Ships are mostly small, inconspicuous boats designed to slip into the enemy's fleet undetected, and then sacrifice themselves by detonating the massive amounts of explosives they have on board to damage or cripple as many vessels as possible.

English Demolition Ship

Delhi Sultanate Explosive Dhow

Explosive Junk

Lodya Demolition Ship

Primary Uses

- *Self-destructing to cause massive damage*

Training Details (Age III)

	Time	Food	Wood	Gold	Pop
All Variants	35s	0	160	80	2

Building Required	
All Variants	Dock

Unit Stats	Demolition	Dhow	Junk	Lodya
Health	200	250	200	250
Melee Armor	0	0	0	0
Ranged Armor	0	0	0	0
Move Speed	1.50	1.62	1.50	1.50

Incendiaries (Fire)	Demolition	Dhow	Junk	Lodya
Damage	300	500	300	300
Counter Bonus	200	200	200	200
Bonus Against	Warships			
Attack Range	2.00	1.00	2.00	2.00
Attack Speed	1.00s	1.00s	1.00s	1.00s

Tactics & Usage

Incendiary Ships are designed to deal a significant amount of damage to a dense group of opposing units by either triggering a manual detonation (default hotkey 'Q') or when they're destroyed. By hovering your mouse cursor over the detonate command you'll be able to see the radius around the vessel within which enemy units will be damaged—when first using these ships, it's worth making use of this to ensure that your intended targets are within range. Then after you've used it for a while and can gauge it by sight alone, using the hotkey will be much quicker and leave less chance for your opponent to escape.

Incendiary Ships can easily turn the tide of a close battle when used in tight spaces or sea straits when your opponent's ships are close together. Given their nature, however, an entire fleet comprised of them is not at all practical, so they're best used as a supporting unit, brought into a battle at an opportune time when your opponent is distracted by your other vessels.

Another less obvious use for Incendiary Ships—that can be equally devastating to your opponent—is to use them to target their shoreline economy. Shorline Fish are an essential part of the economy on water maps, and many opponents will use a lot of Villagers or Fishing Ships to gather them due to their high collection rate. These units are prime targets for a surprise assault by your Incendiary Ships, and if done correctly, you can take out entire groups of Villagers at once, and cause major damage to your opponent's economy.

The Explosive Dhow that the Delhi Sultanate and Abbasid Dynasty can build is the most dangerous Incendiary Ship; not only does it have a significantly stronger blast than the Incendiary Ships of other civilizations, it still costs the same amount so there's no additional risk in making them.

Even land units are not safe from the explosive force of Incendiary Ships. If you position them near shallow water or bridges that enemy units are likely to make use of, you can then move them in and detonate them when you see units starting to make their way across.

Counters

Against Incendiary Ships, you'll want to avoid them getting close to your units at all costs. Any kind of ranged naval unit or ranged fortifications can deal with Incendiary Ships well, if targeted carefully. Archer Ships are particularly suited for this role, since they can deal bonus damage against them.

Concept artwork exploring how ship-to-ship combat would need to work.

Naval Combat Balancing

"We really embraced asymmetry with Naval combat by giving each ship archetype unique stats even if they belong to the same class of ship. On land, this would be the equivalent of giving all Spearmen unique stats for example. We took this approach because there's far fewer boats available to each civ compared to land units, and so to broaden the Naval experience in AoE IV we made the civs play very differently from one another on water.

We still take a similar balancing approach, where each ship type fills a specific role, and we've created unique naval techs and bonuses for every civ which help to complement their ship roster too."

– Zak "ZeroEmpires" Robinson
Senior Designer, Balance, Relic

3

Lodya Fishing Boat

Lodya Transport Ship

Lodya Trade Ship

Lodya Attack Ship

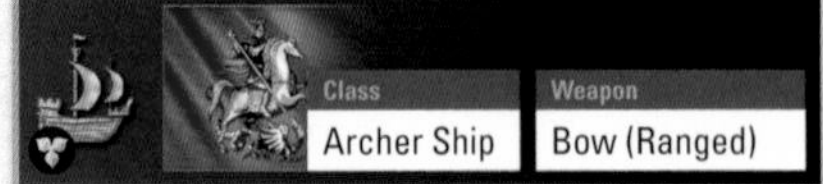

Rus Lodya Fishing Boat

Rus Lodya Transport Ship

Rus Lodya Trade Ship

Rus Lodya Attack Ship

Training Details (Age I and Age II)

Lodya Fishing Boat	25s	0	60	0	1
Lodya Transport Ship	20s	0	100	0	2
Lodya Trade Ship	1m 0s	0	200	100	2
Lodya Attack Ship	35s	0	120	60	2
Building Required					
All Variants	Dock				

Unit Stats	Fishing	Transport	Trade	Attack
Health	125	600	300	400
Melee Armor	0	0	0	0
Ranged Armor	0	0	0	3
Move Speed	1.50	1.50	1.50	1.62

Primary Attack	Fishing	Transport	Trade	Attack
Damage	--	--	--	8x5
Counter Bonus	--	--	--	--
Bonus Against	--	--	--	--
Attack Range	--	--	--	5.00
Attack Speed	--	--	--	2.25s

Lodya Role Switch

The Rus Lodya Ships have the unique ability to transform into any other Lodya Ship. This transformation ability is not free, however. If the ship you want to transform into has a higher production cost than the current ship, then you have to pay the difference. So the Lodya Fishing Boat has a production cost of 60 Wood, and if you want to transform it into a Lodya Demolition Ship, it will cost you 100 Wood and 80 Gold, to match the 160 Wood and 80 Gold production cost of the Demolition Ship. If your starting ship has a higher production cost than the one you want to transform into, then it still has a cost, but it's only 25 Wood. Time is also a consideration when transforming a ship; it takes a full 20 seconds to complete, so try and plan ahead when possible.

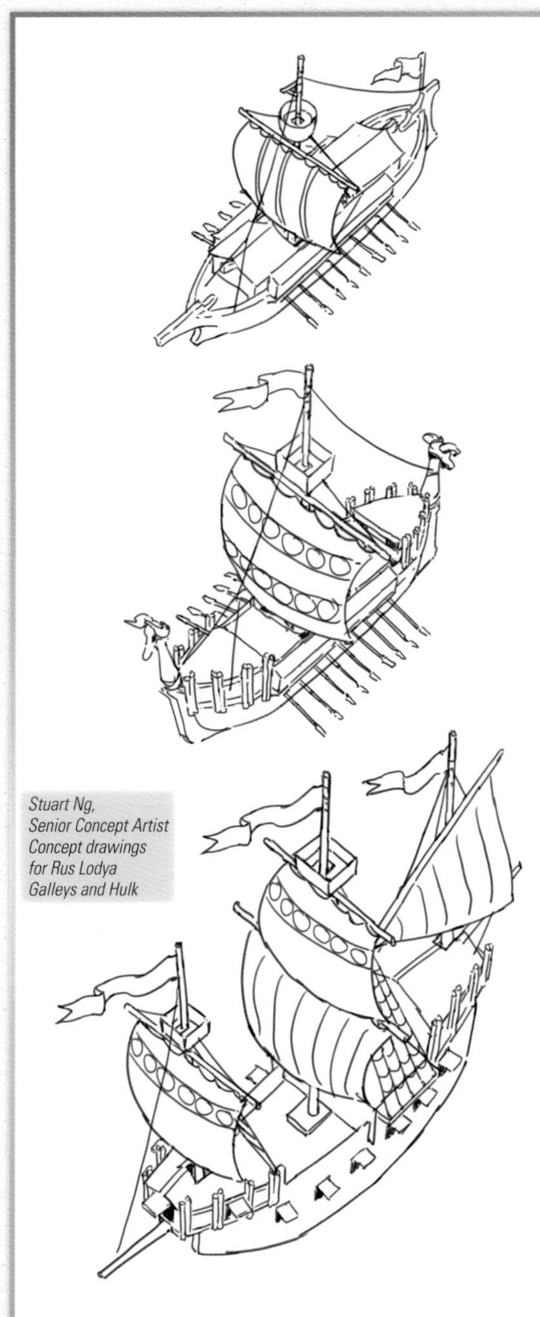

Stuart Ng,
Senior Concept Artist
Concept drawings
for Rus Lodya
Galleys and Hulk

*Given that Lodya Attack Ships are the only Rus military ship, it's important to upgrade them as much as possible, and the **Clinker Construction** and **Cedar Hulls** that both increase their health are among the most important.*

The Rus can convert their ships into other types at any time on the fly. There's still a resource cost, so you should only transform them when it's tactically advantageous.

Most of the Lodya Ships behave in the same way as their counterparts from other civilizations, but their ability to convert between ships opens up some unique tactical options. Lodya Fishing Ships, however, don't have to return to a Dock to drop off Food, making them extremely flexible, and very fitting to the Rus playstyle. It also allows for quick surprise assaults by converting your Worker ships into military ones to reinforce your army, very quickly giving you a larger fleet. If a naval battle goes well and you gain supremacy over the waters, you can then convert a number of your military vessels into Worker ships to give a quick boost to your economy. Because you already have all of the ships and are just changing their role, you don't need to worry about any additional burden on your population, which can free you up to produce more of other unit types.

Lodya Attack Ship Tactics & Usage

The Lodya Attack Ship is the only naval combat unit the Rus have access to, and as such, if you want to gain, maintain, or contest control of the water, you'll be using them for every stage of the game. Like the Dhow and Light Junk, Lodya Attack Ships can fire their five arrow volleys in any direction, but because they fire more arrows in every volley than both of those ships, they can see greater benefits from the Blacksmith's ranged attack upgrades. Those upgrades get applied to every projectile in a volley, so once you start stacking them up, the overall potency of each volley goes up significantly.

Because you won't gain access to the heavier-hitting ships when playing as the Rus, it's crucial that you take advantage of the omnidirectional firing of the Lodya Attack Ship to outmaneuver enemy ships and constantly try stay out of their firing lines. It's also faster than many of the other military ships, so it can get into and out of combat easier. Lodya Attack Ships will have a hard time keeping up in even numbers later in the game when those heavy-hitting ships and Attack Ships come into play; make use of their low cost and the convert ability to overwhelm your enemy early in the game and try to maintain control of the water.

Counters

Lodya Attack Ships can generally be countered by most of the anti-ship military vessels, such as Attack Ships, Warships or the Galleass. The main thing you need to be wary of is the role switch ability. If your fleet is closing in on a seemingly harmless group of Lodya Fishing Boats, do not get complacent and attack haphazardly because they could turn into military vessels at any time. In Age III you need to be even more vigilant, because that's when they gain the ability to convert into Lodya Demolition Ships, and you could be sailing into a trap. Keep your distance, and try to only attack Lodya Ships at the furthest reaches of your range and try to avoid being surrounded, even by seemingly harmless ships.

Baghlah

Hulk

War Junk

The Attack Ship class of units are your quintessential ship-killer naval vessels that are designed to both keep your own fleet safe from enemy vessels, and sail straight into enemy territory to decimate their ships. All attack ships are fitted with broadside ballista as their primary weapons, and as such you'll need to sail alongside the target once you're in range to get a shot on it, rather than heading straight towards it.

Variants

Baghlah (Abbasid Dynasty, Delhi Sultanate)

Baghlah are one of the lightest and fastest Attack Ships, but their size also means that they've been mounted with the smallest ballista so they deal less damage per shot than the other Attack Ships. To help offset the lower damage, the Baghlah has some Archers on deck that fires volleys of arrows alongside the ballista shots. Given the size of the vessel and its attacks, the Baghlah can be thought of as a hybrid between an Attack Ship and an Archer Ship.

Baghlahs perform much better against Incendiary Ships than the other Attack Ships because their arrow volleys do bonus damage against that ship type.

Hulk (English, French, Holy Roman Empire)

The European Hulk lives up to its name in that it has significantly more health an armor than the other Attack Ships, along with the longest attack range. If you love micro-controlling your vessels to keep them outside of the enemy's attack range while landing your own shots, then the Hulk is the ship you want—even if you make a mistake, they have the health reserves to give you time to recover. The French civilization also have the ability to build Hulks in Age II, and while their version is has slightly less attack range than other Hulks, the fact that it can be built a whole Age sooner allows the French to counter Archer Ships straight away.

War Junk (Chinese, Mongols)

Although the War Junk is the largest of the Attack Ships, it falls somewhere in the middle in terms of health and armor, but that size does come at the cost of some speed. The main benefit of the increased deck size is that it allows for an extremely large ballista to be installed, and while it does take a while to reload, per shot it packs the biggest punch of the group. To mitigate the slow rate of fire somewhat

Primary Uses
- *Ship-to-ship combat*

Training Details (Age III)

	Time	Food	Wood	Gold	Stone
Baghlah	45s	0	240	180	4
Hulk	45s	0	300	240	4
War Junk	45s	0	300	210	4
Building Required					
All Variants	Dock				

Unit Stats	Baghlah	Hulk	War Junk
Health	900	1000	900
Melee Armor	0	0	0
Ranged Armor	5	6	6
Move Speed	1.25	1.12	1.00
Ballista (Ranged)	**Baghlah**	**Hulk**	**War Junk**
Damage	50	100	120
Counter Bonus	--	--	--
Bonus Against	--	--	--
Attack Range	5.00	7.00*	6.50
Attack Speed	3.25s	3.95s	4.50s
Bow (Ranged)	**Baghlah**	**Hulk**	**War Junk**
Damage	10x5	--	--
Counter Bonus	5x5	--	--
Bonus Against	Incendiary Ships	--	--
Attack Range	5.00	--	--
Attack Speed	1.75s	--	--

*The French can build A Hulk in Age II, but their version only has a 6.00 attack range

you'll want to focus on one target with as many of your War Junks as possible—try to destroy the target in your opening volley rather than spreading your ships out between targets.

Tactics & Usage

Naval battles are almost inevitable on any water-based map, and since the main function of the Attack Ships is to destroy enemy vessels, they're all but an essential piece of the naval combat puzzle. By the time you reach Age III, the waters of the map are likely to be teeming with Archer Ships, because they're needed to both protect and destroy the Age I economy ships—this means lots of potential targets for your Attack Ships. You'll quickly be able to outperform an Archer Ship fleet if you can add even a few Attack Ships to your own upon reaching Age III. It's important to clear out the Archer Ships to get to your opponent's economy ships, so stockpile resources as you're getting ready to age up so that you can deploy some Attack Ships as soon as possible.

While Attack Ships do have an advantage over Archer Ships in general, it's important that you don't overextend with them. Because Archer Ships can fire from the front it's easy for them to shoot while following retreating units. Attack Ships are also slower than Archer Ships, and that means it's harder to escape if the Archer Ships get the upper hand.

Although they deal a decent amount of damage, Attack Ships still perform poorly against buildings, so it's best to keep them away from any coastal defenses unless you have a numbers advantage.

Counters

For most civilizations there are no real direct counters to Attack Ships until Age IV, when Warships come into play, but those are a cost prohibitive option. If you can catch Attack Ships off guard, Incendiary Ships during Age III can be quite effective due to the slow movement speed of the typical Attack Ship, and they're relatively cheap to produce. Land-based fortifications such as Keeps and Outposts can also be a good option to strike any that venture near the shore.

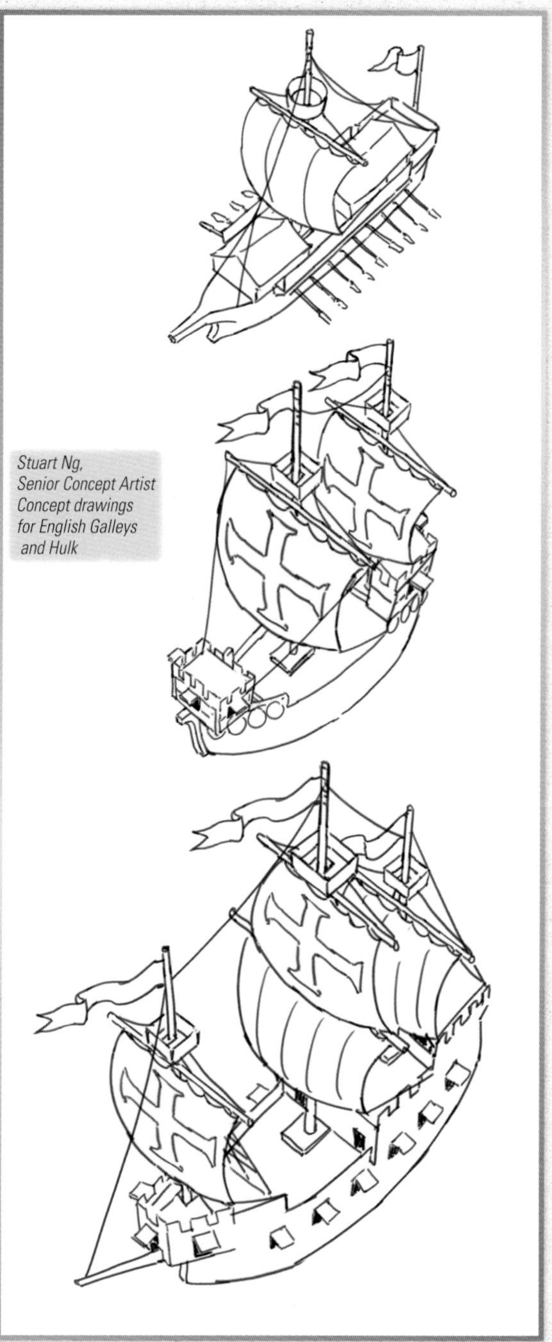

*Stuart Ng,
Senior Concept Artist
Concept drawings
for English Galleys
and Hulk*

Dhow

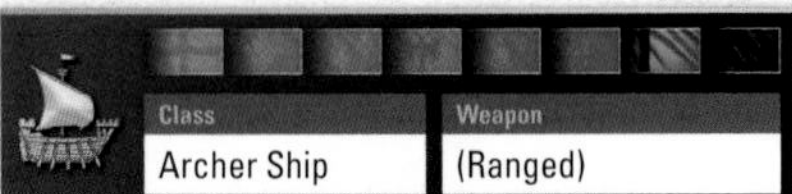

Galley

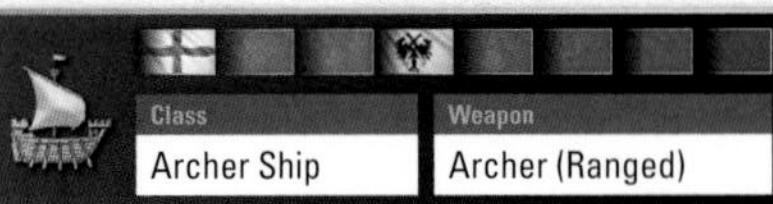

Junk

Light Junk

Archer Ships are the first offensively geared ship that most civilizations can build. If you want to gain control over the fishing industry on a map as soon as possible, Archer Ships will often play a key role in making that happen. These ships are lighter, faster, and more maneuverable than other combat ships, and are at their best when skirting the shoreline looking for targets, or sailing circles around the larger, slower vessels in your opponent's fleet.

Delhi Sultanate Dhow

Holy Roman Empire Galley

Chinese Junk

Mongol Light Junk

Primary Uses

- *Attacking enemy economy ships*
- *Close-range naval combat*

Training Details (Age II)

Dhow	40s	0	180	90	2
Galley	40s	0	180	180	4
Junk	35s	0	120	90	4
Light Junk	35s	0	120	90	2
Building Required					
All Variants	Dock				

Unit Stats	Dhow	Galley	Junk	Light Junk
Health	500	550	650	400
Melee Armor	0	0	0	0
Ranged Armor	4	5	2	3
Move Speed	1.88	1.50	1.62	1.75
Primary Attack	**Dhow**	**Galley**	**Junk**	**Light Junk**
Damage	8x4	10x6	8x4	10x3
Counter Bonus	5x4	5x6	5x4	5x3
Bonus Against		Incendiary Ships		
Attack Range	4.00	5.00	5.00	4.00
Attack Speed	2.00s	1.95s	1.95s	0.95s

Variants

Dhow (Abbasid Dynasty, Delhi Sultanate)

Dhows are the lightest and fastest of all the Archer Ships, and they also have one of the shortest attack range. Their four arrow volley pairs perfectly with their speed, because they can be fired from all sides of the vessel while it's turning, making it easier to hit targets while you're constantly sailing around them to stay out of harm's way. Their speed also means that it's almost impossible for other ships to escape from a battle with them, making Dhows one of the

When selecting the Archer Ship and holding the right mouse button, a range indicator shows the total attack range.

best ships for finishing off the opposition's vessels before they can retreat.

Galley (English, Holy Roman Empire)

Galleys fire a volley of six arrows from their bow, and can only hit units inside the highlighted cone in front of them. They're the slowest and most well-armored of the Archer Ships, which, when coupled with their narrow attack range, means that they're best used in straight-ahead assaults on other ships. As the most expensive Archer Ship, however, establishing early control of the waterways can be costly.

Junk (Chinese)

Like Galleys, Junks are in the heavier class of Archer Ship, and while they may lack some of the Galley's armor, Junks have significantly more health to compensate. Their cost is in line with other Archer ships, so you won't need to focus quite so heavily on Gold if you want to start producing them en mass early on. They also can only attack within a frontal cone, but the fact that the arrows they fire are slightly further apart than those of the Galley means it's easier to hit ships that are trying to out-maneuver them. Once you hit Age III, the **Extra Hammocks** upgrade adds additional crew to the ship, allowing for two additional arrows in each volley.

Light Junk (Mongols)

Light Junks are the Mongols' counterpart to the Dhow Archer Ship, and has the same ability to fire from all sides while moving and turning. This lightweight vessel is extremely nimble, and while not quite as fast as the Dhow, it's faster than the other Archer Ships so has no trouble closing in on targets. Once they're within range, their attacks pack more of a punch than the Dhow's, so they can finish off opponents faster. They are fast, powerful and relatively cheap to produce, so aim to produce a large fleet to compensate for their relative fragility.

Tactics & Usage

As the first available naval combat unit, Archer Ships can be used to gain territory control on maps where water is a key feature, whether it be the trade routes of the open seas, or key crossing points on rivers. They're almost essential on maps such as "Islands" or "Archipelago," where land-based resources are often within the attack range of naval units, and fishing spots are a big factor in your overall economy.

Because all naval units open fire automatically any time an enemy vessel is within attack range, keeping close to the target is extremely important to avoid having to manually tell your ships to attack as they move. That makes Archer Ships perfectly suited to hunting down and destroying the opposition's Fishing Boats and Trade Ships. Their speed lets them get into attack range quickly, to potentially get some attacks in before your opponent can react—and then they can easily pursue those ships once they start to flee, all while constantly firing.

Try to avoid fighting near the coast with your Archer Ships if you see defensive structures such as upgraded Outposts and Keeps along it. They have significantly more range than Archer Ships, and can easily catch you off guard while you're manoeuvring during a battle.

All Archer Ships have bonus damage against Incendiary Ships, so if you spot one within your opponents fleet, make full use of the Archer Ship speed to close in and destroy it before it can detonate.

Equally important to taking out your opponent's economy ships is protecting your own, and since Archer Ships are the first unit you can make that is capable of doing that, you should not neglect their importance in defensive play. Setting up blockades with Archer Ships to keep enemy vessels away from your precious fishing spots or trade routes can give you a significant economical advantage over your opponent. The earlier you gain control over these aspects of the map,the worse it will be for your opponent, and the extra resources you get can be used to build stronger ships as you age up to ensure that you keep control.

Counters

In Age II there is no naval counter to Archer Ships other than the Hulk that the French can build; all other civilizations have to also build Archer Ships if they want to contest water control. The only way to circumvent that would be to ignore water and force a land battle by transporting land units to your opponent's island, and fortifying your island with defensive buildings. Due to the placement of resources on water-dominant maps this can be a difficult strategy to employ, and you'll usually end up having to get into the water once land resources start to dry up. Once you reach Age III most civilizations gain access to Attack Ships, and since they are designed to be ship killers, thanks to their bonus damage against ships, they're by far the best units to use against any Archer Ships that your opponent has in the water.

Baochuan

Chinese Baochuan

Warships become available after reaching Age IV, and they are the largest and most powerful class of ships available. Each Warship comes equipped with a large number of broadside cannons that they can use to fire volleys of cannonballs over large distances, ideally at either enemy buildings or other Warships. All of that power does come at a cost, and in the case of Warships it's that each one counts as six towards your population capacity; if you want a large fleet of Warships, you'll need to make sacrifices in other areas.

Variants

Baochuan (Chi, Mon)

Following in the tradition of other east Asian naval vessels, the Baochuan is the biggest Warship, and this time it's also one of the most powerful ships in its class. Packing a whopping seven broadside cannons, Baochuans can inflict more than twice the damage per shot of a Carrack, and their huge amount of health allows them to absorb as much damage as they dish out. Their ability to take damage is just as important as their ability to deal it because their low rate

Carrack

English Carrack

Primary Uses

- *Destroying buildings and fortifications*

Training Details (Age IV)

Baochuan	1m 0s	0	480	480	6
Carrack	1m 0s	0	390	270	6
Xebec	1m 0s	0	480	300	6
Building Required					
All Variants	Dock				

Unit Stats	Baochuan	Carrack	Xebec
Health	2000	1400	1700
Melee Armor	0	0	0
Ranged Armor	6	5	5
Move Speed	0.75	0.88	1.25
Cannon (Ranged)	**Baochuan**	**Carrack**	**Xebec**
Damage	70x7	70x3	70x5
Counter Bonus	50x7	50x3	50x5
Bonus Against		Buildings	
Attack Range	9.00	8.00	9.00
Attack Speed	6.50s	4.50s	6.50s

Xebec

Delhi Sultanate Xebec

of fire does make them more susceptible to being out maneuvered by smaller, faster ships, and that health cushion allows you to take a few hits if you do mistime your shots.

Carrack (English, French, Holy Roman Empire)

Carracks are the cheapest Warship to build, with low damage per shot and health, which means they're best used in large numbers. They get roughly three shots to every two of a Baochuan, but they'll still come out behind in a battle of even numbers. If you're using Carrack against other Warships, always outnumber them or have support from other vessels and concentrate on one enemy ship at a time.

Xebec (Abbasid Dynasty, Delhi Sultanate)

With five broadside cannons at its disposal, the Xebec is in the middle of the pack in terms of per shot damage, but they retain the long attack range of the Baochuan, and its equally long reload time. Thankfully, they have best-in-class movement speed, far above a Baochuan, so if your micro unit control is good enough, you can dance in and out of a Baochuan's attack range during your shots. This speed also lets you get Xebec to their target much faster that most other military ships, potentially catching your opponent off guard.

Tactics & Usage

As with any premium Age IV unit, their costs are the main thing limiting production, especially their contribution towards your population capacity. If you've been building up a large naval fleet along with all of your land units, there's a good chance you could be getting near the population cap by the time you hit Age IV, so you might need to destroy some of your older, weaker units in order to make more room.

Warships excel at breaking down the defenses of fortified islands, without the need to invest a lot of resources into a landing party. They get a considerable bonus against buildings, so they can devastate entire coastlines as they sail by.

*If you invest in the **Chaser Cannons** research you can even out-range Keeps and Outposts.*

Warships are the most powerful of the naval combat units and as such will dominate late game water warfare. But be aware, they're also one of the slowest types of naval unit, which makes it hard to retreat once a battle stops going your way.

Counters

A superior number of Attack Ships can take down Warships, but you'll need a significant numbers advantage. Outside of that you'll have to rely on Warships yourself—without them it's unlikely that you'll be able to compete for control of the water, unless you outnumber your opponent significantly.

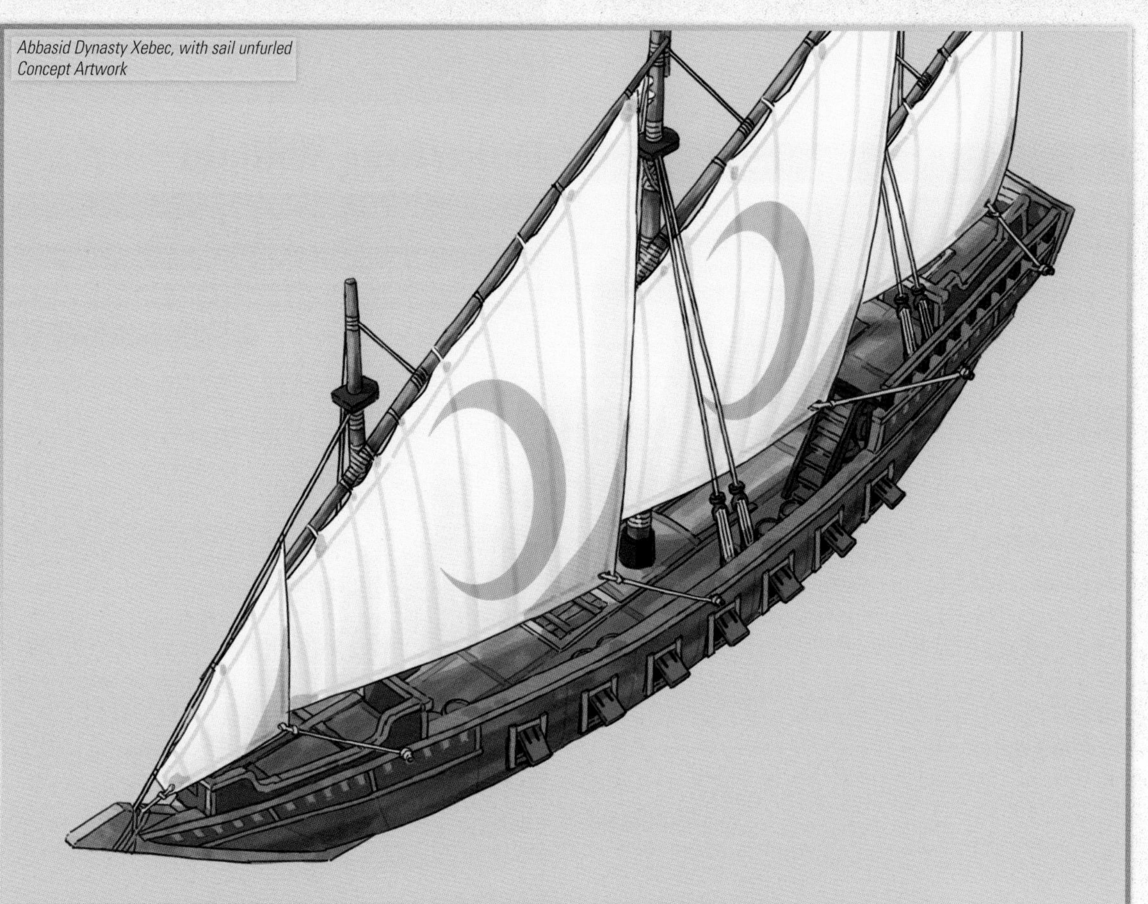

Abbasid Dynasty Xebec, with sail unfurled
Concept Artwork

Abbasid Dynasty Xebec, annotated with weapon and armor upgrade and sail furled
Concept Artwork

Overview

Hero units in AoE IV are key historical figures from the battles and time periods featured in the campaign scenarios, and as such they're only available to play during certain missions within that mode. They are generally very powerful units in their own right, but they also often have a number of unique passive and activatable abilities that enable them to support the other units in your army as well.

Engaging the opposing army with your Hero units first can draw a lot of potential damage and attention away from your main army, giving them the opportunity to move into a better position or get some uncontested attacks in. The main reason this is such as effective tactic is because, unlike normal units, any time a Hero unit falls in battle they can be revived by any of your other units and get straight back into the fight. Most Hero units also have the ability to heal themselves over time, so if you do want to keep them alive, any time they're at low health, simply withdraw them from combat and let them regenerate before you move them back in.

The activatable special abilities available to the Hero units should be used as often as possible in any situations where they would be useful because their cooldowns are usually low enough that you'll be able to use them in most encounters. By default they can be activated with one of the first 5 keys at the top of your keyboard (QWERTY) depending on the Hero and ability, and it's a good idea to memorize that key so you can activate the abilities quickly in the heat of battle if needed.

Duke/King William

Type	Campaign
Heavy Melee Cavalry, Leader	The Normans

Missions

1066: The Battle of Hastings   1069: North to York

Details

Unit Stats	
Health	450
Melee Armor	8
Ranged Armor	8
Move Speed	1.62
Lance	
Damage	45
Bonus	--
Attack Range	1.04
Attack Speed	1.40s
Sword	
Damage	30
Attack Range	0.29
Attack Speed	1.38s

- *Great in melee combat*
- *Weak against Spearmen and Crossbowmen*

Generating Enhancement

Fortitude Allows this unit to heal outside of battle at a rate of 2.5% of max health per second.

Manually Activated - Default: W

Attack Speed Increases ranged attack speed, and melee damage by 50% to all units within the radius for 15s with a 75s cooldown.

King Henry I

Type	Campaign
Heavy Melee Infantry, Leader	The Normans

Missions

1105: The Fall of Bayeux
1106: The Battle of Tinchebray
1119: The Battle of Brémule

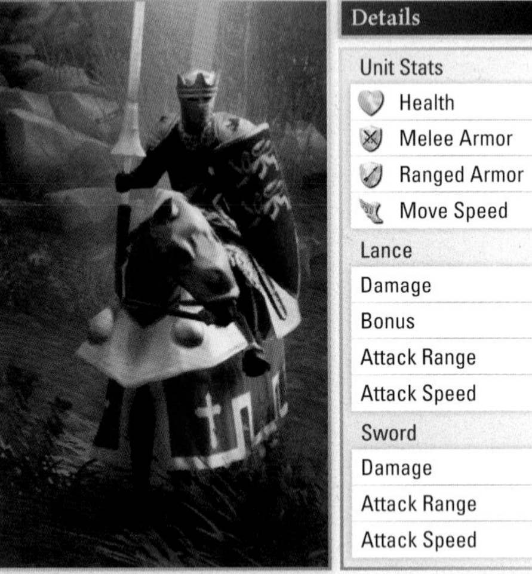

Details

Unit Stats	
Health	450
Melee Armor	6
Ranged Armor	6
Move Speed	1.62
Lance	
Damage	45
Bonus	--
Attack Range	1.04
Attack Speed	1.40s
Sword	
Damage	30
Attack Range	0.29
Attack Speed	1.38s

- *Great in melee combat*
- *Weak against Spearmen and Crossbowmen*
- *Nearby units gain increased spear and palings damage, armor and line of sight.*

Generating Enhancement

Fortitude Allows this unit to heal outside of battle at a rate of 2.5% of max health per second.

Manually Activated - Default: W

Armor Increases the melee armor of nearby units by +13 for 5s and +3 for a further 10s with a 75s cooldown.

Willikin of the Weald

Type	Campaign
Light Ranged Infantry, Leader	The Normans
Missions	
1216: The Siege of Dover	

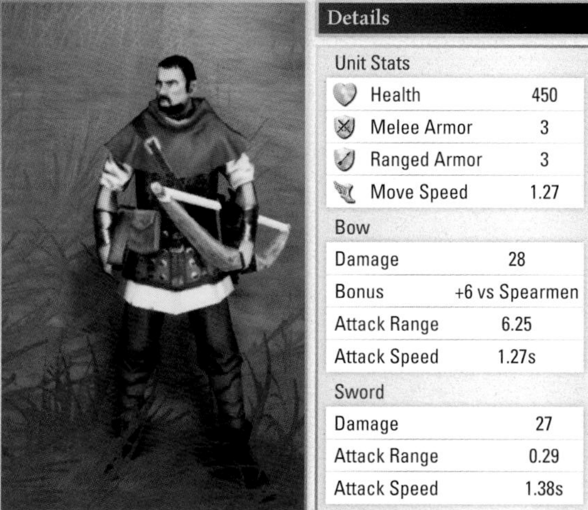

Details

Unit Stats	
Health	450
Melee Armor	3
Ranged Armor	3
Move Speed	1.27
Bow	
Damage	28
Bonus	+6 vs Spearmen
Attack Range	6.25
Attack Speed	1.27s
Sword	
Damage	27
Attack Range	0.29
Attack Speed	1.38s

- *Great in combination with Longbowmen for ranged fights*
- *Countered by cavalry*
- *Can see into Stealth Forests*

Generating Enhancement

Fortitude Allows this unit to heal outside of battle at a rate of 2.5% of max health per second.

Manually Activated - Default: Q, W, E, R

Place Palings When activated, wood palings are placed in front of the unit; charging cavalry will be stunned for 2.5 seconds and take 25 damage.

Arrow Volley Reduces Longbowmen's time between shots by 1s with a cooldown of 45s.

Movement Increases movement speed of nearby units for 15s with a cooldown of 45s.

Setup Camp Longbowmen nearby regenerate health and see further.

William Marshal

Type	Campaign
Heavy Melee Infantry, Leader	The Normans
Missions	
1217: Second Battle of Lincoln	

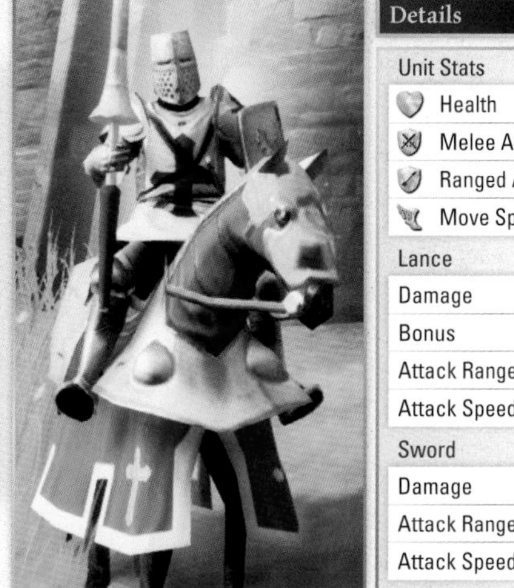

Details

Unit Stats	
Health	650
Melee Armor	9
Ranged Armor	9
Move Speed	1.62
Lance	
Damage	47
Bonus	--
Attack Range	1.04
Attack Speed	1.40s
Sword	
Damage	32
Attack Range	0.29
Attack Speed	1.38s

- *Great in melee combat*
- *Countered by Spearmen and Crossbowmen*

Generating Enhancement

Fortitude Allows this unit to heal outside of battle at a rate of 2.5% of max health per second.

Manually Activated - Default: W

Charge Increases attack and movement speed of nearby Knights for 15s.

Normans Campaign William the Conqueror 3D Sculpt

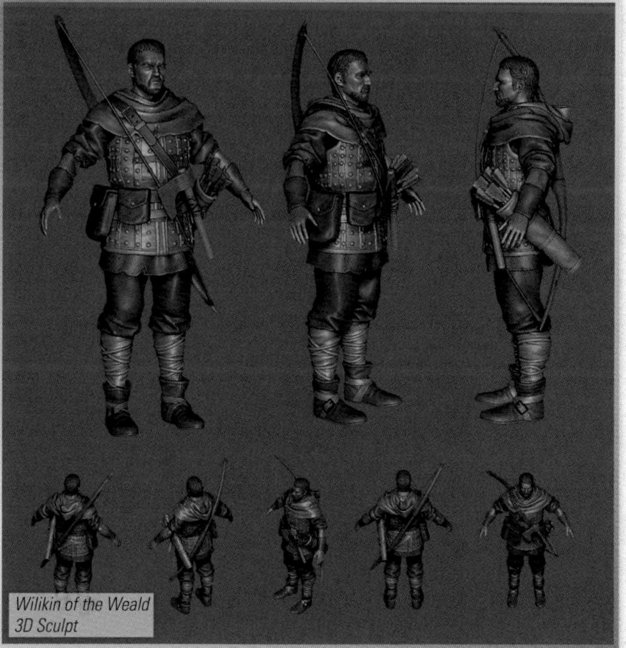

Wilikin of the Weald 3D Sculpt

Jean de Beaumanoir

Type	Campaign
Heavy Melee Infantry, Leader	The Hundred Years War

Missions
1351: The Combat of the Thirty

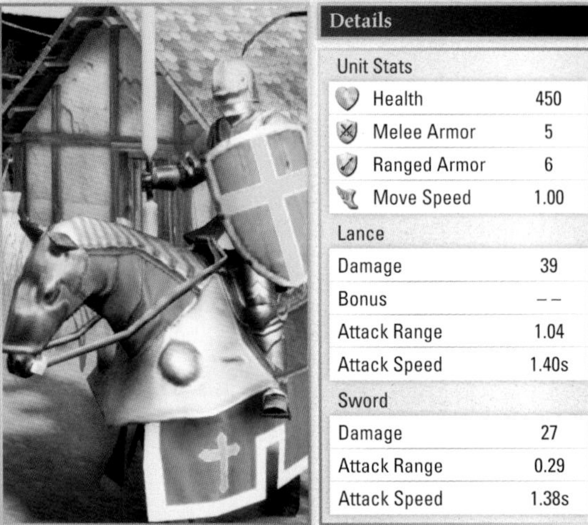

Details

Unit Stats	
Health	450
Melee Armor	5
Ranged Armor	6
Move Speed	1.00
Lance	
Damage	39
Bonus	– –
Attack Range	1.04
Attack Speed	1.40s
Sword	
Damage	27
Attack Range	0.29
Attack Speed	1.38s

- *Great in melee combat*
- *Weak against Spearmen and Crossbowmen*

Generating Enhancement

Fortitude Allows this unit to heal outside of battle at a rate of 2.5% of max health per second.

Manually Activated - Default: Q

Attack Speed Increases the ranged attack speed and melee damage of nearby units by 50% for 15s with a 45s cooldown.

Olivier Arrel

Type	Campaign
Heavy Melee Infantry	The Hundred Years War

Missions
1351: The Combat of the Thirty

Details

Unit Stats	
Health	200
Melee Armor	4
Ranged Armor	4
Move Speed	1.12
Ax	
Damage	15
Bonus	– –
Attack Range	0.29
Attack Speed	1.25s

- *Great in melee combat*
- *Weak against Spearmen and Crossbowmen*

Generating Enhancement

– –

Manually Activated - Default: E

Healing Restores the health of nearby units for 10s with a 45s cooldown.

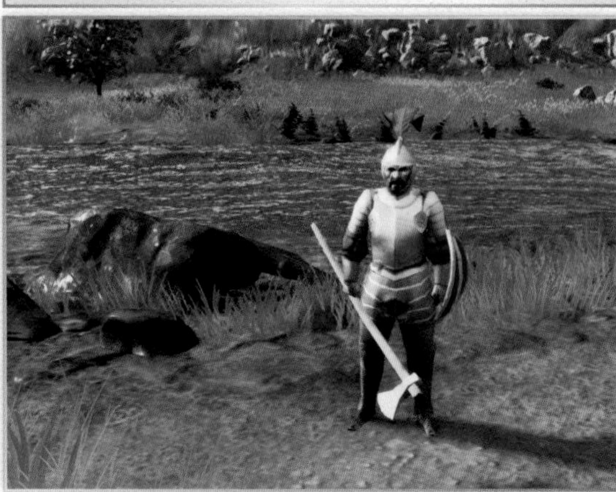

Guy de Rochefort

Type	Campaign
Heavy Melee Infantry	The Hundred Years War

Missions
1351: The Combat of the Thirty

Details

Unit Stats	
Health	200
Melee Armor	4
Ranged Armor	5
Move Speed	1.12
Mace	
Damage	13
Bonus	+3 vs Armored
Attack Range	0.29
Attack Speed	2.30s

- *Great in melee combat*
- *Weak against heavy cavalry and ranged units*

Generating Enhancement

– –

Manually Activated - Default: T

Sunder Decreases the melee armor of nearby enemies for 5s with a 45s cooldown.

Geoffroy du Bois

Type	Campaign
Heavy Melee Infantry, Leader	The Hundred Years War

Missions
1351: The Combat of the Thirty

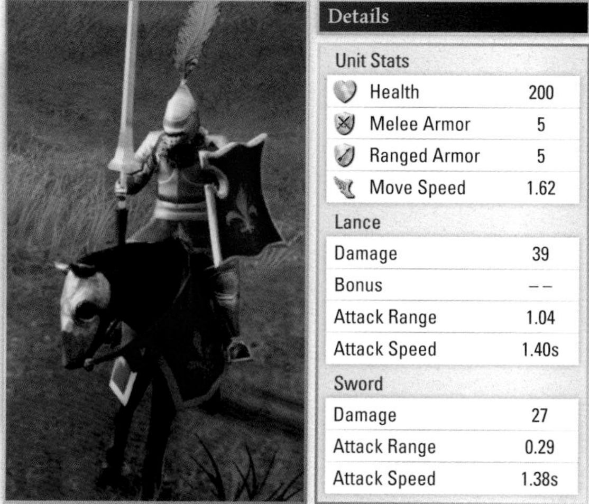

Details

Unit Stats	
Health	200
Melee Armor	5
Ranged Armor	5
Move Speed	1.62
Lance	
Damage	39
Bonus	--
Attack Range	1.04
Attack Speed	1.40s
Sword	
Damage	27
Attack Range	0.29
Attack Speed	1.38s

- *Great in melee combat*
- *Weak against Spearmen and Crossbowmen*

Generating Enhancement

--

Manually Activated - Default: R

Movement Increases movement speed of nearby units for 15s with a 45s cooldown.

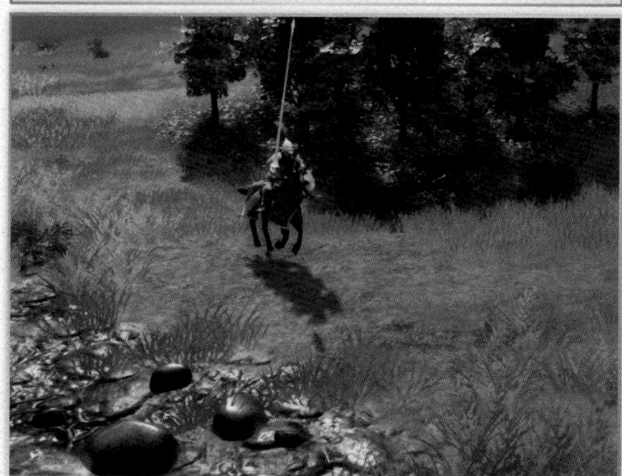

Yves Charruel

Type	Campaign
Heavy Melee Infantry	The Hundred Years War

Missions
1351: Combat of 30

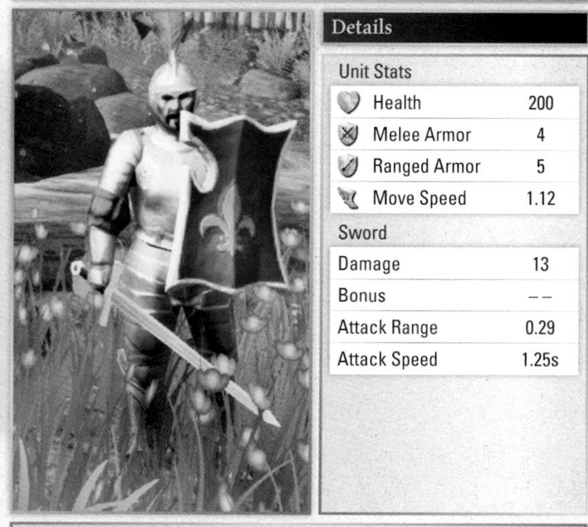

Details

Unit Stats	
Health	200
Melee Armor	4
Ranged Armor	5
Move Speed	1.12
Sword	
Damage	13
Bonus	--
Attack Range	0.29
Attack Speed	1.25s

- *Great in melee combat*
- *Weak against heavy cavalry and ranged units*

Generating Enhancement

--

Manually Activated - Default: W

Armor Increases melee armor of nearby units by +13 for 5 seconds and +3 for a further 10 seconds with a 45s cooldown.

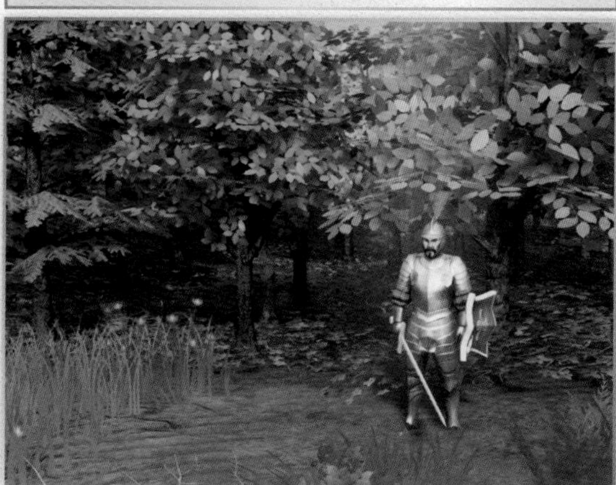

Civilizational Complexity

By creating the English and French in a way which feel more familiar to players coming from previous games in the franchise we hope that they can serve as a jumping-off point for newer players. The French have many passive economy bonuses which helps to reduce the macro overhead that a player has, allowing them to place more focus on their landmark choices and wielding their powerful Royal Knights. The English also have a very easy to learn influence system where they get extra benefit from placing farms around a mill. This helps to introduce players to the influence system mechanic in a way that feels natural.

Mastering these two civs gives players plenty of experience with unique game mechanics without throwing them in at the deep end. Once familiar and comfortable, progressing to civs with harder mechanics such as the Delhi Sultanate or the Mongols is the next step.

– Zak "ZeroEmpires" Robinson
Senior Designer, Balance, Relic

Jeanne d'Arc
3D Sculpt

Jeanne d'Arc

Type	Campaign
Heavy Melee Infantry	The Hundred Years War

Missions
1429: The Siege of Orléans   1429: The Battle of Patay

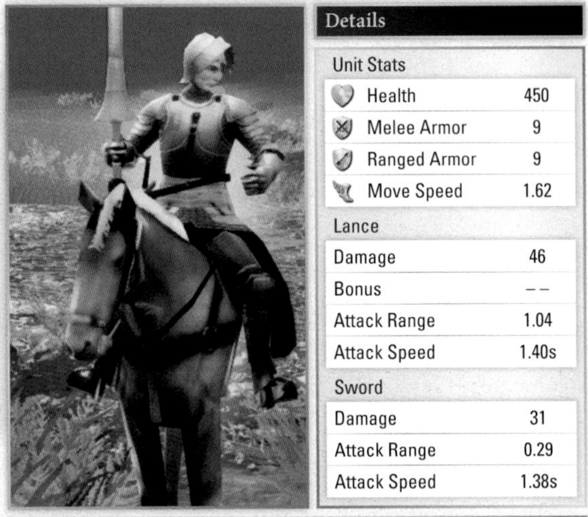

Details

Unit Stats	
Health	450
Melee Armor	9
Ranged Armor	9
Move Speed	1.62
Lance	
Damage	46
Bonus	– –
Attack Range	1.04
Attack Speed	1.40s
Sword	
Damage	31
Attack Range	0.29
Attack Speed	1.38s

- *Great in melee combat*
- *Weak against Spearmen and Crossbowmen*
- *Nearby units slowly regain health when out of combat.*

Generating Enhancement

Fortitude Allows this unit to heal outside of battle at a rate of 2.5% of max health per second.

Manually Activated - Default: W

Healing Restores health of nearby units for 10s with a 75s cooldown.

Jeanne d'Arc Tapestry
Hundred Years War Campaign Video Asset

Historical Objectivity

Throughout our research, writing, consultation, and editing we tried as far as possible to represent this history with objectivity. However, we also had to acknowledge that this is a video game and the player is placed on the side of one faction or another. In games, or films, or any other form of storytelling, it is common to celebrate the attributes and exploits of our protagonists and condemn or chastise the enemy. Finding a balance between cold objectivity and player-side celebration was something we were acutely aware of needing to hit just right.

We struggled especially with our French-side perspective on the Hundred Years War campaign. One of our historians pointed out that our slant on the war was decidedly pro-French – this was, after all, a war in which the French were dominated by crushing English victories for a very long time before gaining the upper hand. But, we felt that at some point the player point-of-view has to take precedence. A game that doesn't celebrate with the player does not feel like a satisfying experience. Objectivity is always important, but we do have to pat the player's faction on the back!

– Lauren Wood
Principal Designer, Narrative, Relic

General Subutai

Type	Campaign
Light Ranged Cavalry, Leader	The Mongol Empire

Missions: 1223: The Battle of the Kalka River 1241: The Battle of Mohi

Details

Unit Stats	
Health	450
Melee Armor	4
Ranged Armor	4
Move Speed	1.88
Bow	
Damage	14
Bonus	– –
Attack Range	7.50
Attack Speed	1.88s

- *Very mobile and great in ranged combat*
- *Weak against heavy cavalry and Spearmen*

Generating Enhancement

Master Tactician Increases sight range and decreases Signal Arrow ability cooldown times.

Fortitude Allows this unit to heal outside of battle at a rate of 2.5% of max health per second.

Manually Activated - Default: Q, W, E

Maneuver Arrow Increases movement speed of nearby units by 33% for 15 seconds with a 45s cooldown. Does not affect Villagers.

Attack Speed Arrow Increases reload speed of nearby ranged units by 50% for 15 seconds with a 45s cooldown.

Defense Arrow (The Battle of Mohi only) - Increases armor of nearby units by 3 for 15 seconds with a 45s cooldown.

Baidar

Type	Campaign
Light Ranged Cavalry, Leader	The Mongol Empire

Missions: 1241: The Battle of Liegnitz

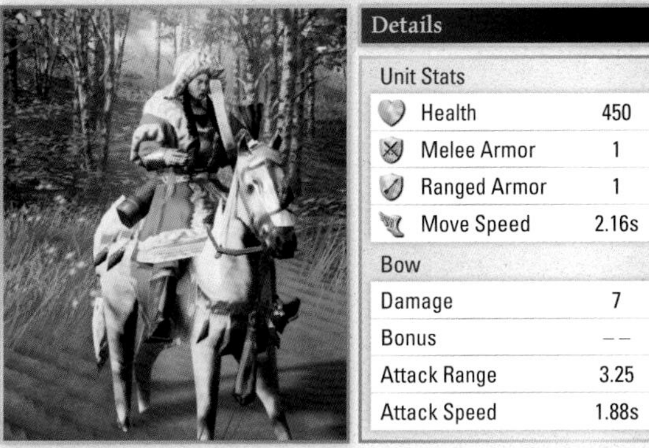

Details

Unit Stats	
Health	450
Melee Armor	1
Ranged Armor	1
Move Speed	2.16s
Bow	
Damage	7
Bonus	– –
Attack Range	3.25
Attack Speed	1.88s

- *Ideal support unit, weak in combat*
- *Weak against Spearmen, Crossbowmen and Heavy Melee Cavalry*

Generating Enhancement

Fortitude Allows this unit to heal outside of battle at a rate of 2.5% of max health per second.

Manually Activated - Default: Q, W, E

Maneuver Arrow Increases movement speed of nearby units by 0.5 tiles/s for 15s with a cooldown of 90s. Does not affect Villagers.

Attack Speed Arrow -Increases reload speed of nearby ranged units by 50% for 15s with a cooldown of 90s.

Defense Arrow Increases armor of nearby units by 3 for 15s with a cooldown of 90s.

Genghis Khan

Type	Campaign
Light Ranged Cavalry, Leader	The Mongol Empire

Missions: 1213: The Great Wall 1215: The Battle of Zhongdu

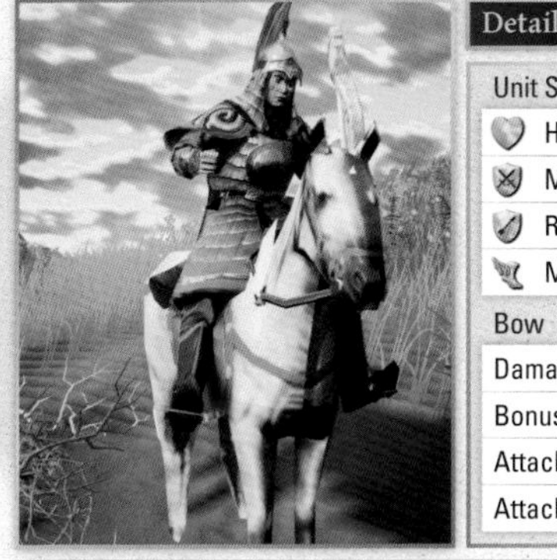

Details

Unit Stats	
Health	450
Melee Armor	0
Ranged Armor	0
Move Speed	1.88s
Bow	
Damage	8
Bonus	– –
Attack Range	7.50
Attack Speed	1.88s

- *Very mobile and ideal support unit*
- *Weak against heavy cavalry and Spearmen*

Generating Enhancement

Fortitude Allows this unit to heal outside of battle at a rate of 2.5% of max health per second.

Manually Activated - Default: Q, W, E

Charge Arrow Increases armor by 3 and speed of nearby units for 15s with a 75s cooldown.

Raiding Arrow Speeds up the rate at which buildings can be set ablaze, and increases the attack speed of nearby units by 50% for 15s with a cooldown of 75s

Defense Arrow Increases armor of nearby units by 3 for 15s with a cooldown of 75s.

Batu Khan 3D Sculpt

Mongke Khan

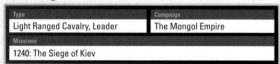

Type	Campaign
Light Ranged Cavalry, Leader	The Mongol Empire
Missions	
1240: The Siege of Kiev	

Details

Unit Stats	
Health	450
Melee Armor	4
Ranged Armor	4
Move Speed	1.88s
Bow	
Damage	14
Bonus	--
Attack Range	7.50
Attack Speed	1.88s

- *Very mobile and great in ranged combat*
- *Weak against heavy cavalry and Spearmen*

Generating Enhancement

Fortitude Allows this unit to heal outside of battle at a rate of 2.5% of max health per second.

Manually Activated - Default: Q, W, E, T

Maneuver Arrow Increases movement speed of nearby units by 0.5 tiles/sec for 15s with a cooldown of 90s.

Attack Speed Arrow Increases reload speed of nearby ranged units by 50% for 15s with a cooldown of 90s.

Defense Arrow Increases armor of nearby units by 3 for 15s with a cooldown of 90s.

Production Lets nearby buildings produce units and research technologies faster for 15 seconds with a cooldown of 75s.

Liu Zheng

Type	Campaign
Heavy Melee Infantry, Leader	The Mongol Empire
Missions	
1268: Blockade at Lumen Shan	1273: The Fall of Xiangyang

Details

Unit Stats	
Health	450
Melee Armor	7
Ranged Armor	7
Move Speed	1.62s
Lance	
Damage	47
Bonus	--
Attack Range	1.04
Attack Speed	1.40s
Sword	
Damage	32
Attack Range	0.29
Attack Speed	1.38s

- *Great in melee combat*
- *Weak against Spearmen and Crossbowmen*
- *Nearby defensive structures do more damage.*

Generating Enhancement

Fortitude Allows this unit to heal outside of battle at a rate of 2.5% of max health per second.

Manually Activated - Default: W

Construction Increases building and movement speed of nearby Villagers for 15s with a 75s cooldown.

Ismail

Type	Campaign
Heavy Melee Infantry, Leader	The Mongol Empire
Missions	
1273: The Fall of Xiangyang	

Details

Unit Stats	
Health	450
Melee Armor	7
Ranged Armor	7
Move Speed	1.20
Khanda	
Damage	17
Bonus	--
Attack Range	0.29
Attack Speed	1.25s

- *Great in melee combat*
- *Weak against Crossbowmen*
- *Can construct siege units in the field.*
- *Nearby siege units move and fire more quickly.*

Generating Enhancement

Fortitude Allows this unit to heal outside of battle at a rate of 2.5% of max health per second.

Manually Activated - Default: Q, R

Imperial Falcon Releases a Falcon that grants a massive amount of vision around Ismail for 120s with a 45s cooldown.

Grunt Work Constructs or repairs HuiHui Paos in the field.

Prince Dmitry

Type	Campaign
Heavy Melee Infantry, Leader	The Rise of Moscow

Missions: 1375: Tribute 1380: The Battle of Kulikovo 1382: Hold Against the Horde

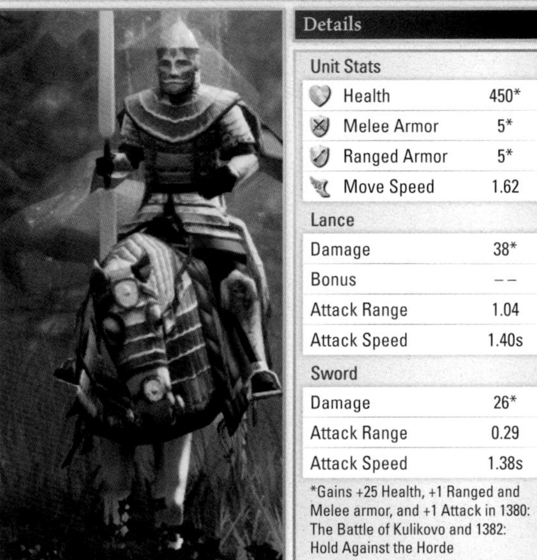

Details

Unit Stats	
Health	450*
Melee Armor	5*
Ranged Armor	5*
Move Speed	1.62
Lance	
Damage	38*
Bonus	– –
Attack Range	1.04
Attack Speed	1.40s
Sword	
Damage	26*
Attack Range	0.29
Attack Speed	1.38s

*Gains +25 Health, +1 Ranged and Melee armor, and +1 Attack in 1380: The Battle of Kulikovo and 1382: Hold Against the Horde

- *Great in melee combat*
- *Weak against Spearmen and Crossbowmen*
- *Nearby units regain health when out of combat*

Generating Enhancement

Fortitude Allows this unit to heal outside of battle at a rate of 2.5% of max health per second.

Manually Activated - Default: W

Healing Restores health of nearby units for 10s with a cooldown of 75s.

Ivan III

Type	Campaign
Heavy Melee Infantry, Leader	The Rise of Moscow

Missions:
1478: The Fall of the Novgorod Republic
1480: Great Stand on the Ugra River

Details

Unit Stats	
Health	450
Melee Armor	5
Ranged Armor	5
Move Speed	1.12
Sword	
Damage	15
Bonus	– –
Attack Range	0.29
Attack Speed	1.38s

- *Great in melee combat*
- *Weak against ranged units and heavy cavalry*

Generating Enhancement

Fortitude Allows this unit to heal outside of battle at a rate of 2.5% of max health per second.

Manually Activated - Default: W

Production Lets nearby buildings produce units and research technologies faster for 15s with a cooldown of 75s.

Ivan IV

Type	Campaign
Heavy Melee Infantry, Leader	The Rise of Moscow

Missions: 1552: The Siege of Kazan

Details

Unit Stats	
Health	475
Melee Armor	7
Ranged Armor	7
Move Speed	1.62
Lance	
Damage	47
Bonus	– –
Attack Range	1.04
Attack Speed	1.40s
Sword	
Damage	36
Attack Range	0.29
Attack Speed	1.38s

- *Great in melee combat*
- *Weak against Spearmen and Crossbowmen*

Generating Enhancement

Fortitude Allows this unit to heal outside of battle at a rate of 2.5% of max health per second.

Manually Activated - Default: W

Gunpowder Reload Speed Increases reload speed of nearby gunpowder units for 15s with a cooldown of 75s.

Prince Dimitri 3D Sculpt

CHAPTER

Building History

The buildings featured in Age of Empires IV are a collection of architectural wonders that provide a large part of each civilization's identity and majesty. From the humble mobile Ger to towering, nigh-impregnable walls, this chapter presents each of them in a way that highlights their design process and strategic uses.

About this Chapter

Throughout this chapter we present the stats and attack values for each building in the game (with the exception of Wonders, since they have no practical stats). To ensure that you understand what each of these values means, we'll provide short descriptions of each one here.

Building Details

1 **Icon** This shows you the building's in-game icon.

Unique Icon When this icon is present, the building is unique to the civilization shown.

Flags The flags shown here tell you which civilizations have access to the building.

Type Shows which category of building it is, which determines its function.

Age This tells you in which Age you can first construct the building.

2 **Building Stats** These stat tables show you the building's basic details.

Time, Food, Wood, Gold, Stone Shows you how long it takes to construct a building, and how much it costs.

3 **Health** Shows how much health the building has.

Armor Shows how much armor the building has.

Size Shows how many tiles the building occupies once built/placed.

4 **Influence/Aura** This lets you know if a building has either an influence range or generates an Aura. Auras have a circular radius around the building, whereas influence range adheres to the tile-based grid.

Influence/Aura Size Tells you how many tiles away from the building the area of influence or aura extends to.

Garrison Yes/No Lets you know if it's possible to garrison units inside the building.

Garrison Number If you can garrison units inside of a building, this number will tell you how many.

5 **Generating Enhancements** These are innate bonuses or abilities that some buildings generate around themselves. Examples include a damage buff to nearby units, or a unique means of repairing a building.

Attacks

6 These stats give you the details on any attacks the building can make use of.

Damage How much damage the attack deals. If an attack has multiple projectiles, then the second number will show how many projectiles are used, so 12x3 would be three projectiles in a single volley, each dealing 12 damage.

Counter Bonus If the attack can inflict bonus damage against specific targets, this value will tell you how much is added.

Bonus Against This tells you what target you'll receive that amount of bonus damage against.

Attack Range Shows how far the attack can reach, measured across in-game tiles.

Attack Speed Shows how frequently the building will initiate the attack. A 1-second attack speed means that an attack is started every second.

Units and Technologies

7 **Units Produced** This shows which units the building can produce, and the Age required to do so.

8 **Technology** This shows which Technologies the building can develop, as well which area of gameplay they affect and the Age in which they can be first acquired.

Farm

Type	Age
Food Source, Building	I

Compared to other Food sources, Farms are the second slowest means of acquiring Food; only faster than the standard gathering rate for Berries, and on par with Sheep. However, once most other sources of Food have run out, your Farms will still be producing, and as such they're an essential component for any long-lasting and prosperous empire. Farms can be constructed quickly and only a require a one-time investment of 75 Wood, after which you can assign a single Villager to tend and harvest the crops, which will regrow naturally overtime without any further investment required.

Building Stats

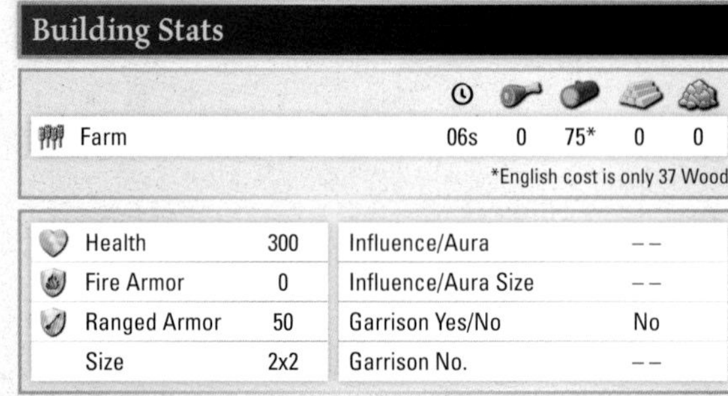

	Time	Food	Wood	Gold	Stone
Farm	06s	0	75*	0	0

*English cost is only 37 Wood

Health	300	Influence/Aura	--
Fire Armor	0	Influence/Aura Size	--
Ranged Armor	50	Garrison Yes/No	No
Size	2x2	Garrison No.	--

Make sure that all of your Farms are touching a collection site to ensure prosperous long-term Food production.

Usage

Because of their relatively high Wood cost during the initial phases of a game, it's best to start your Food gathering with the other sources of Food around your starting area. When the initial patches of Berries, Sheep and Deer in the vicinity of your Town Center start running dry, you'll have to make a choice between moving out onto parts of the map that are more exposed, or staying close to home and switching to Farms. Moving out for more huntable animals will be more lucrative than switching to Farms, but you'll risk losing Villagers—you'll need to weigh up the pros and cons of each approach when you reach that point in every game.

The Mongols do not build Farms, they instead rely on their Pastures to produce herdable Sheep for Food.

By the time those initial Food sources begin to run out, you should have acquired enough Wood for a smooth transition over to a farming based economy. It's important to make the switch to Farming a gradual one, while some of your Villagers are still hunting and gathering, because switching a large group of Villagers over to Farms at once might take more Wood than you have on hand at the time.

One of the golden rules for smooth economic growth is to minimize the walking time of Villagers. Following this premise, you should try to build Farms as close to collection sites as possible, meaning Town Centers and Mills. Because the area around those buildings is so important for minimizing that travel time, you should try to avoid blocking those areas with other structures, and reserve it for future Farms. Mills are a fairly cheap investment, so try to have all of your Farms around one and avoid stacking your Farms two or three deep away from a collection site.

English Farms with Mill—Age I

Strategic Considerations

Water Maps

As long as you have Fish at your disposal you should invest mostly into boats and not into Farms; you'll need the Wood for naval combat, and your income from Fish and other natural resources should be sufficient for the rest. Of course, if you lose access to these sources because your opponent has gained control of the water, you'll need to adapt and pivot to Farms quicker than you might have liked.

Chinese

The Chinese can build Granaries in the Yuan Dynasty, each of which improves the gathering rate of farmers in the aura area by 15%, and this effect stacks with each of the two additional Granaries you can build. Essentially, for the cost of 250 Wood you can build a superior Mill, which will benefit your Food economy greatly if you have a lot of Farms.

English

The English are the most formidable farming civilization in the game. They can build Farms 50% cheaper than other civilizations, and Farms built inside the influence area of their Mills have improved harvest rates starting at 15% in Age I, and increasing by 5% in each subsequent Age. At the Age I rate, Food gets collected almost as fast as Deer. Farming close to Mils should be prioritized with the English even more so than with other civilization, and no Farm should ever be outside of a Mill's influence range.

Ger

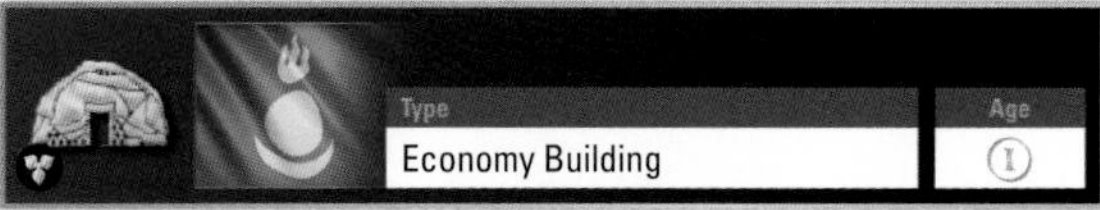

Type	Age
Economy Building	I

The Ger is a unique Mongol economic building, replacing the usual Lumber Camp, Mill and Mining Camp resource drop-off sites. Since it combines all of that functionality into one handy building, it's extremely versatile. Like all Mongol buildings, you can pack it up and move it, allowing you to always ensure it's placed for maximum efficiency. Although the cost is a bit higher than each of the normal drop-off buildings individually, if you place it strategically so that more than one resource can be dropped off there, it can actually work out cheaper.

Building Stats

	Time	Food	Wood	Gold	Stone
Ger	20s	0	100	0	0

Health	1000	Influence/Aura	--
Fire Armor	0	Influence/Aura Size	--
Ranged Armor	50	Garrison Yes/No	No
Size	2x2	Garrison No.	--

Usage

Gers are used in much the same way as every other resource drop-off site, the difference being that you never have to replace them as gathering areas dry up—you can simply pack them up and move to the next location! By making use of this ability, your Villagers will never have to travel far to drop off their goods and you'll never have to waste resources building more and more drop-off locations to keep up with the changing resource positions. As you progress into the later stages of the game, however, it's important to remember that when you pack up a building it counts as +1 towards your population capacity, so if you're already at maximum capacity, you might still need to build new ones rather than moving existing ones to avoid sacrificing military units.

Ger Technologies (P.45)

Technology	Type	Ovoo	Age
Forestry	Woodcutting		I
Forestry (Improved)	Woodcutting	✓	I
Survival Techniques	Hunting		I
Survival Techniques (Impr.)	Hunting	✓	I
Wheelbarrow	Villager		I
Wheelbarrow (Improved)	Villager	✓	I
Professional Scouts	Hunting		I
Professional Scouts (Impr.)	Hunting	✓	I
Horticulture	Food Gathering 1/3		I
Horticulture (Improved)	Food Gathering 1/3	✓	I
Fertilization	Food Gathering 2/3		I
Fertilization (Improved)	Food Gathering 2/3	✓	I
Precision Cross-Breeding	Food Gathering 3/3		I
Precision Cross-Breeding (Impr.)	Food Gathering 3/3	✓	I
Double Broadax	Wood Gathering 1/3		I
Double Broadax (Improved)	Wood Gathering 1/3	✓	I
Lumber Preservation	Wood Gathering 2/3		I
Lumber Preservation (Impr.)	Wood Gathering 2/3	✓	I
Crosscut Saw	Wood Gathering 3/3		I
Crosscut Saw (Improved)	Wood Gathering 3/3	✓	I
Specialized Pick	Mining 1/3		I
Specialized Pick (Improved)	Mining 1/3	✓	I
Acid Distillation	Mining 2/3		I
Acid Distillation (Improved)	Mining 2/3	✓	I
Cupellation	Mining 3/3		I
Cupellation (Improved)	Mining 3/3	✓	I
Husbandry	Pasture	✓	I
Husbandry (Improved)	Pasture	✓	I

Mongol Ger—Age I

Ovoo Influence

The technology that you can learn through the Ger is already capable of significantly increasing your resource gathering capabilities, but like most Mongol buildings, if you place one within the influence of an Ovoo you can take things a step further. All of the improved versions of the Gathering technologies can give you a noticeable bump to your economy, so depending on which resource is your priority, you should make it a point to acquire the improved technology for it.

Since Mongols are so heavily reliant on Sheep from Pastures for their long-term Food economy, make sure to build a Ger near an Ovoo to take advantage of the Improved economy technologies.

4

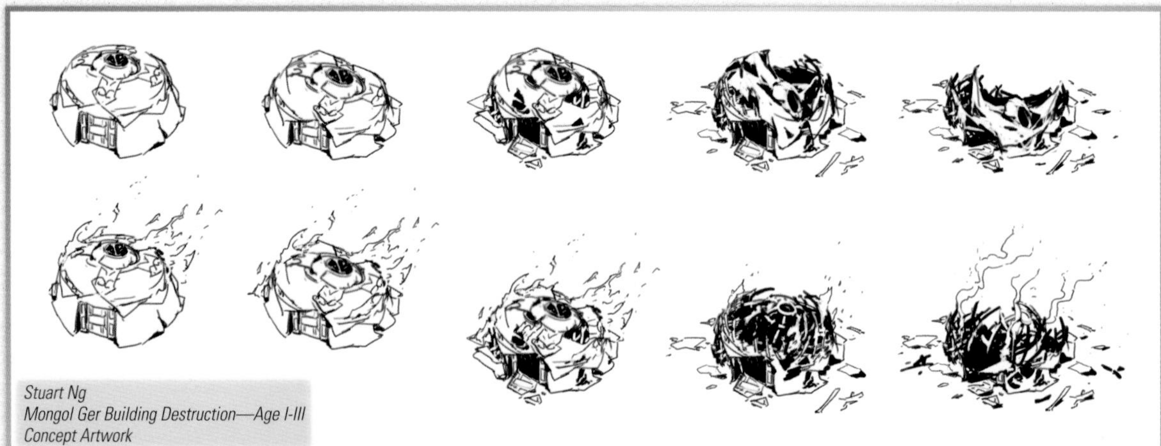

Stuart Ng
Mongol Ger Building Destruction—Age I-III
Concept Artwork

Mongol Housing Exploration—Age I-IV
Concept Sketches

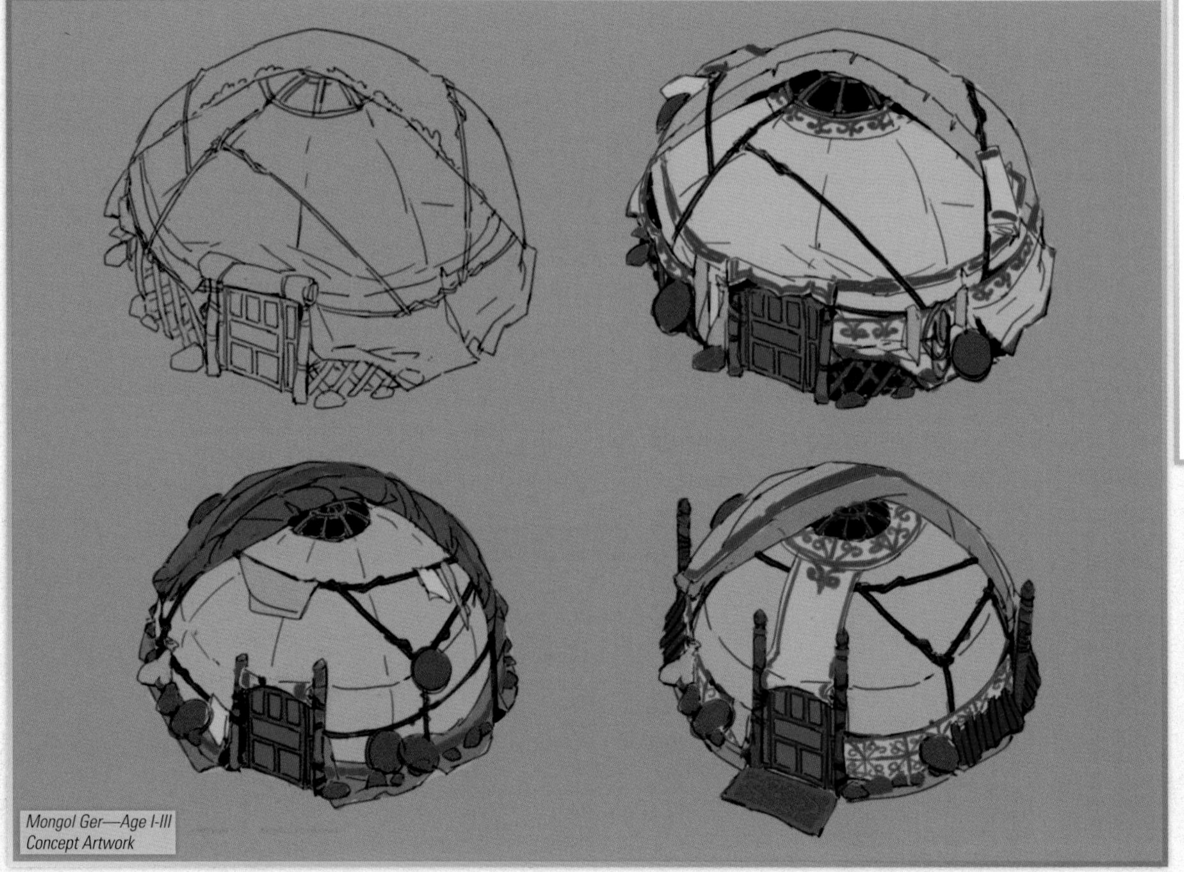

Mongol Ger—Age I-III
Concept Artwork

The Mongols' Expansion

"If I could have lived during one of the civilizations represented in the game, it'd be the Mongols. I'm fascinated by what the Mongol expansion across the Russia and Europe would have looked like. The thunderous sound of a 10,000+ Mangudai bearing down on enemy forces would be something to behold for sure."

– Christopher Rubyor
Design Director, World's Edge

Stuart Ng
Chinese Granery—Age II
Concept Artwork

Referencing Previous AoE Games

"All of the previous games in the franchise were reference points for AoE IV. We looked at each them and discussed their approaches to everything—from Aging up to resource types, collection approaches, buildings, tech, unit counts, and with the luxury of time being with us, the metas that developed for each game over the years and how we could represent those. We then thought about what was loved about those previous features and design conceits, and worked on merging and improving them as we constructed the core of Age IV. This was done hand-in-hand with our community, as we want to build a game for its fans and players."

– Adam Isgreen
Franchise Creative Director, World's Edge

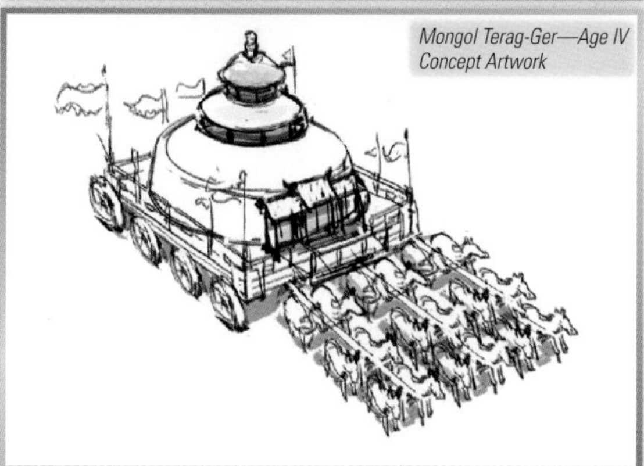
Mongol Terag-Ger—Age IV
Concept Artwork

Granary

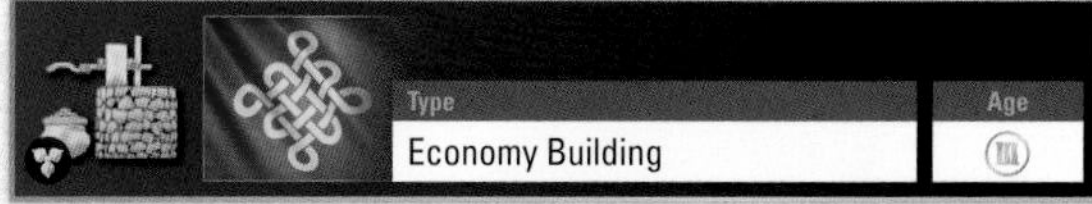

Type	Age
Economy Building	III

The Granary is essentially a superior version of a Mill that's available exclusively to the Chinese civilization in the Yuan Dynasty. At 250 Wood, it's significantly more expensive than a Mill, but since it comes with the bonus of increasing Villager gathering rate from nearby Farms by 15% the long-term benefits more than outweigh the initial cost, especially since you can only build three of them.

Building Stats

	Time	Food	Wood	Gold	Stone
Granary	35s	0	250	0	0

Health	1000	Influence/Aura	Aura
Fire Armor	0	Influence/Aura Size	7.5 Tiles
Ranged Armor	50	Garrison Yes/No	No
Size	4x4	Garrison No.	--

Usage

Generating Enhancement

Granary Improves the Farm gather rate of nearby Villagers by 15% (stacks with other Granaries).

Granaries are big buildings, and they need a lot of space to make full use of them. Each one is four times larger than a normal Mill, but its aura range extends far beyond that: one Granary can affect up to 56 Farms around it, with 28 being fully covered and another 28 partially. Furthermore, the gathering rate increase from a Granary can stack if the aura range of multiple Granaries overlap, so a Villager working a Farm within the aura range of all three Granaries can work even faster!

The area affected is indicated by the gold glowing circle you can see around the Granary before placing the structure, allowing you to precisely gauge their placement before committing to a build location. Be aware that farmers will only be affected by the enhancement if they're inside this area. So a Villager on a Farm at the edge of this circle will only gather faster if they're gathering from the part of the Farm that lies within the aura range. With three Granaries and a bit or planning it should possible to have most of your Farms affected by at least one Granary.

Chinese Granary—Age IV

Perfectly arranged Granaries and Farms are a work of beauty.

Mongol Ger—Age II-III
Concept Artwork

English Housing Exploration
Concept Sketches

Kevin Lam
Rus Houses—Age II
Concept Artwork

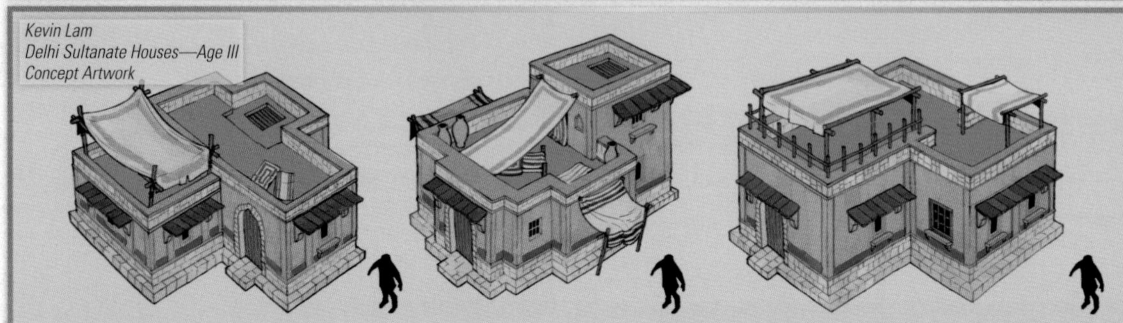
Kevin Lam
Delhi Sultanate Houses—Age III
Concept Artwork

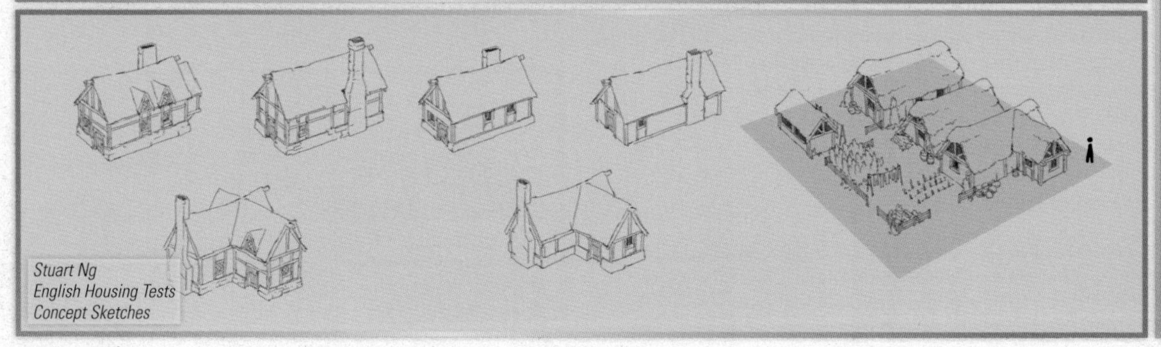
Stuart Ng
English Housing Tests
Concept Sketches

Kevin Lam
Abbasid Dynasty Housing Color Tests—Age III
Concept Artwork

House

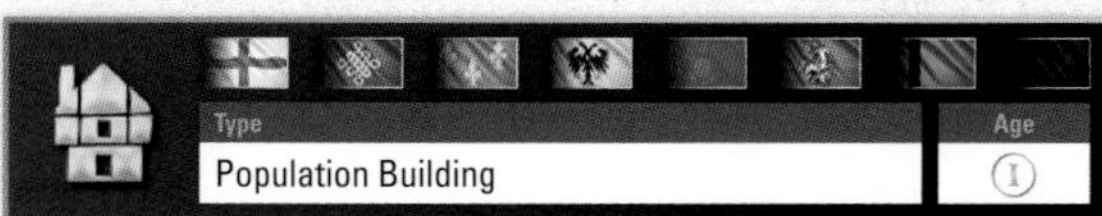

Houses will usually be one of the first buildings you'll want to construct at the start of every game, because for most civilizations, growing both your economy and military is impossible without somewhere for those units to live. The one exception to this is the Mongol civilization, since they start with the maximum population capacity by default. Each House you build will increase your maximum population space by 10, so you'll want to plan ahead and build them before you need them to ensure that you can keep producing units smoothly.

Building Stats

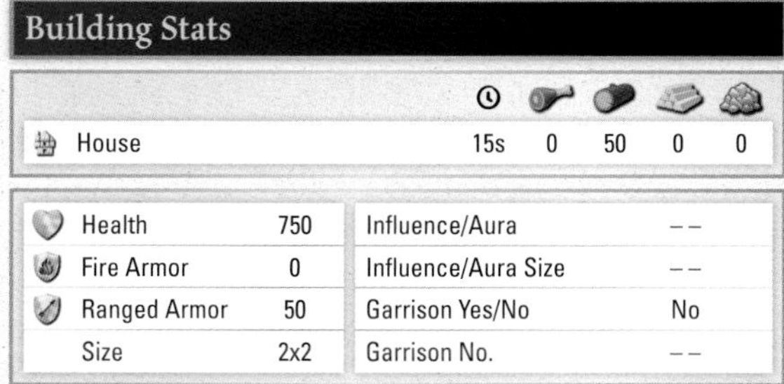

	Time	Food	Wood	Gold	Stone
House	15s	0	50	0	0

Health	750	Influence/Aura	--
Fire Armor	0	Influence/Aura Size	--
Ranged Armor	50	Garrison Yes/No	No
Size	2x2	Garrison No.	--

In the later stages of a game it's a good idea to build more houses than would be required for you to reach the 200 population limit. By doing that, if you lose some of them in a battle you have some overhead and can still rebuild your army without first having to increase your population capacity again.

English House—Age IV

Holy Roman Empire House—Age IV

Chinese House—Age IV

Rus House—Age IV

Abbasid Dynasty House—Age IV

Usage

You'll always start with six Villagers, a Scout and ten units of population space, and most of the time a lot of those units will get put to work immediately for hunting and gathering the nearby Sheep for Food. Sometimes, however, you'll need to send your Scout out to locate more Sheep straight away, leaving your Villagers with nothing to do. It's at these times you'll want to put those Villagers to work on building a House, because not only will it give you the population capacity increase you're going to need any way, but it will keep those Villagers busy until your Scout finds the Sheep.

It's important to check your population space periodically, because if you try to produce new units while you're at your current population capacity, those units will sit in the production queue until you build more Houses to increase the population capacity. This is called "being housed", and during the game, especially when following tight build orders, you should take every possible measure to ensure this doesn't happen to you, because the time lost can be the difference between winning and losing in close games.

However, it's not the best idea to just build a lot of Houses early in the game to prevent being housed, because that would require you to dedicate a lot of your Wood to them, and you'll need that for other things such as resource drop-off and military buildings. Ideally you want to always leave yourself a comfortable cushion between your current amount of units and your population capacity. At the start of the game when your total units increase quite slowly, you'll only need to build one or two Houses every now and then to stay ahead, but as you start producing more and more units, you'll need to dedicate more resources to Houses and build them a few at a time.

Houses can be placed anywhere in your base, but in general it's best to spread them around outside of your economy buildings rather than clumping them all together in a corner, just make sure to leave space around resources for either farming space or gathering sites. You do not want to block yourself off from your own resources. By placing them in this manner, any enemy units that approach your base are likely to attack them first rather than your precious Villagers, since they would be further inside the perimeter .

To avoid getting housed in the early phase of a game, it's good to let lumberjacks build houses from time to time.

Hunting Cabin

Hunting Cabins take on the role of Mills for the Rus, and they also play an integral part in the unique Bounty System—that of generating Gold. Similar to Town Centers and Stables, you can also produce Scouts from your Hunting Cabins, which can come in handy at times where you need one but don't want to clog up other production queues.

Usage

Generating Enhancement

Gold Generation Hunting Cabins generate Gold based on the number of nearby trees. Placing other Hunting Cabins nearby reduces this amount, however. Hunting Cabins generate Gold once every 30 seconds. During this period, all Hunting Cabins together can generate a maximum of 250 Gold.

First and foremost, Hunting Cabins are Mills and should be used as such for all of your resource drop-off needs. The more interesting part of these structures, however, is their role in the bounty system to generate Gold over time. Every time a Rus unit kills an animal they collect a bounty in the form of Gold, and as you kill more animals to collect more bounties you can reach higher tiers within the bounty system. The higher the Tier, the faster your Villagers are at collecting Food and the faster Gold is generated by your cabins.

The amount of Gold that's generated is determined by the number of trees within the aura range of the Hunting Cabin at the time it is placed. Gold is generated at a rate of 0.45 per tree within the radius, and the amount will not change if trees are cut down after the cabin is placed, but if you cut them down first and then place a cabin they will not count. In total, all cabins combined can generate 250 Gold per generation period, so once you hit that mark you shouldn't build any more unless they're needed as drop-off locations. The bounty system leads the Rus to favor hunting over berries and farming as a means of Food generation, which is risky at times, but if you can pull it off, it can pay dividends in the long run.

Rus Hunting Cabin—Age IV

Building Stats

	Time	Food	Wood	Gold	Stone
Hunting Cabin	40s	0	100	0	0

Health	750	Influence/Aura	Aura
Fire Armor	0	Influence/Aura Size	5 Tiles
Ranged Armor	50	Garrison Yes/No	No
Size	2x2	Garrison No.	– –

Hunting Cabin Technologies (P.45)

Technology	Type	Age
Survival Techniques	Hunting	I
Wheelbarrow	Villager	I
Professional Scouts	Hunting	I
Horticulture	Food Gathering 1/3	I
Fertilization	Food Gathering 2/3	I
Precision Cross-Breeding	Food Gathering 3/3	I

Rus Bounty System

Tier	Gold Req.	Gathering Boost	Gold Gen
1	100	+5% Villager Food Harvest Rate	27s
2	250	+10% Villager Food Harvest Rate	24s
3	500	+15% Villager Food Harvest Rate	18s

Unit Production

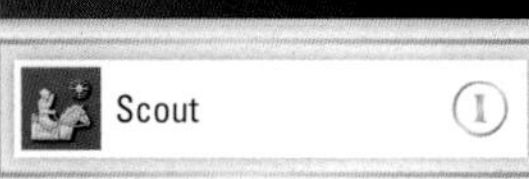

Lumber Camp Ideation
Concept Sketches

Stuart Ng
English Lumber Camp—All Ages
Concept Artwork

Lumber Camp

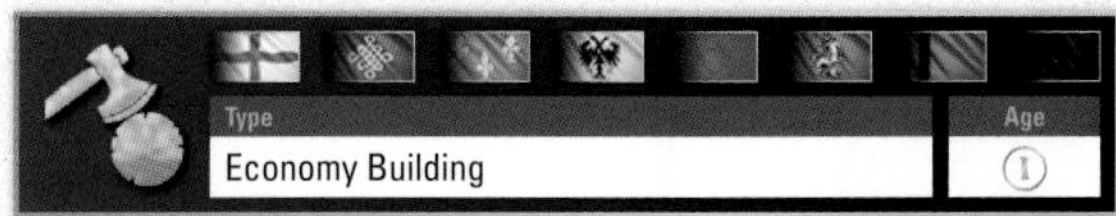

Lumber Camps are the standard Wood drop-off site, and they're available from Age I for all civilizations except the Mongols. Their low cost and early availability means that they should be used liberally whenever you gather Wood to cut down on the travel time of your Villagers as much as possible.

Usage

Lumber Camps will usually be one of the first drop-off buildings you construct, because Wood is arguably the most important resource. All of your production, drop-off sites and one of your main Food sources—Farms—need Wood to construct, so efficient collection of lumber is essential for the growth of your empire.

To improve efficiency, try to focus on one group of trees at a time, because Villagers will only collect from trees after they're cut down, which can take a while. If you find your lumberjacks spread out too much due to overcrowding around a group of trees, don't hesitate to make a second or even third Lumber Camp beside them to minimize walking time. Also, make sure to replace your Lumber Camps regularly: a good rule of thumb is to make a new one if it will fit comfortably between the old one and the forest.

Make sure not place new Lumber Camps on trees that have already been cut down or they will disappear, and then your poor Villagers will have to start cutting down fresh ones.

English Lumber Camp—Age I

Building Stats

	Time	Food	Wood	Gold	Stone
Lumber Camp	20s	0	50*	0	0

*French cost is only 25 Wood

Health	750	Influence/Aura	--
Fire Armor	0	Influence/Aura Size	--
Ranged Armor	50	Garrison Yes/No	No
Size	2x2	Garrison No.	--

Lumber Camp Technologies (P.45)

Forestry	Woodcutting	I	All
Double Broadax	Wood Gathering 1/3	II	All
Lumber Preservation	Wood Gathering 2/3	III	All
Crosscut Saw	Wood Gathering 3/3	IV	All

As stated earlier, Wood may be the most important resource in the game, so the upgrades that you can acquire from the Lumber Camp should also be high on your priority list. Collectively they can have a huge impact on the rate at which you can accumulate Wood—especially **Forestry** which, for a very low price, will allow your Villagers to chop down trees twice as fast.

Strategic Considerations

French

The French get a 50% discount on Mills, Lumber and Mining Camps, which means they can recoup the costs of those buildings in a minimal amount of time. This low price means you should be even more liberal with replacing your Lumber Camps, and split your Villagers across many Lumber Camps to ensure efficiency.

Holy Roman Empire

To further increase the rate at which you gather Wood as the Holy Roman Empire, always make sure that your Villagers gathering it are being inspired by a Prelate.

Historical Perspectives

"When I first started working on AoE IV I was excited because history provides us with a box that we can play in. Often in game development there is no defined box—the world is your oyster! This can of course be very exciting—but it can also make it harder to arrive at decisions you feel are 'right'. When you have a time period to turn into gameplay, that provides a pretty good place to start.

But history is messy, oftentimes told by the victorious. I've approached my job on AoE IV with the intent of delivering nuance and perspective on the history where possible, but in practice that's hard to do. History is told by the victor—this means you're not getting an encompassing perspective. Perhaps you're not even getting the truth—humans embellish, and sometimes we tell stories so many times that they change a little each telling.

To complicate matters further, history changes. Sources are invalidated or come into question because new information comes to light. For us, this meant leaning on historians for review. We cannot pretend to know as much as someone who has dedicated their life to this field does, and so we have to collaborate."

– Kristina Wiik
Senior Designer, Narrative, Relic

4

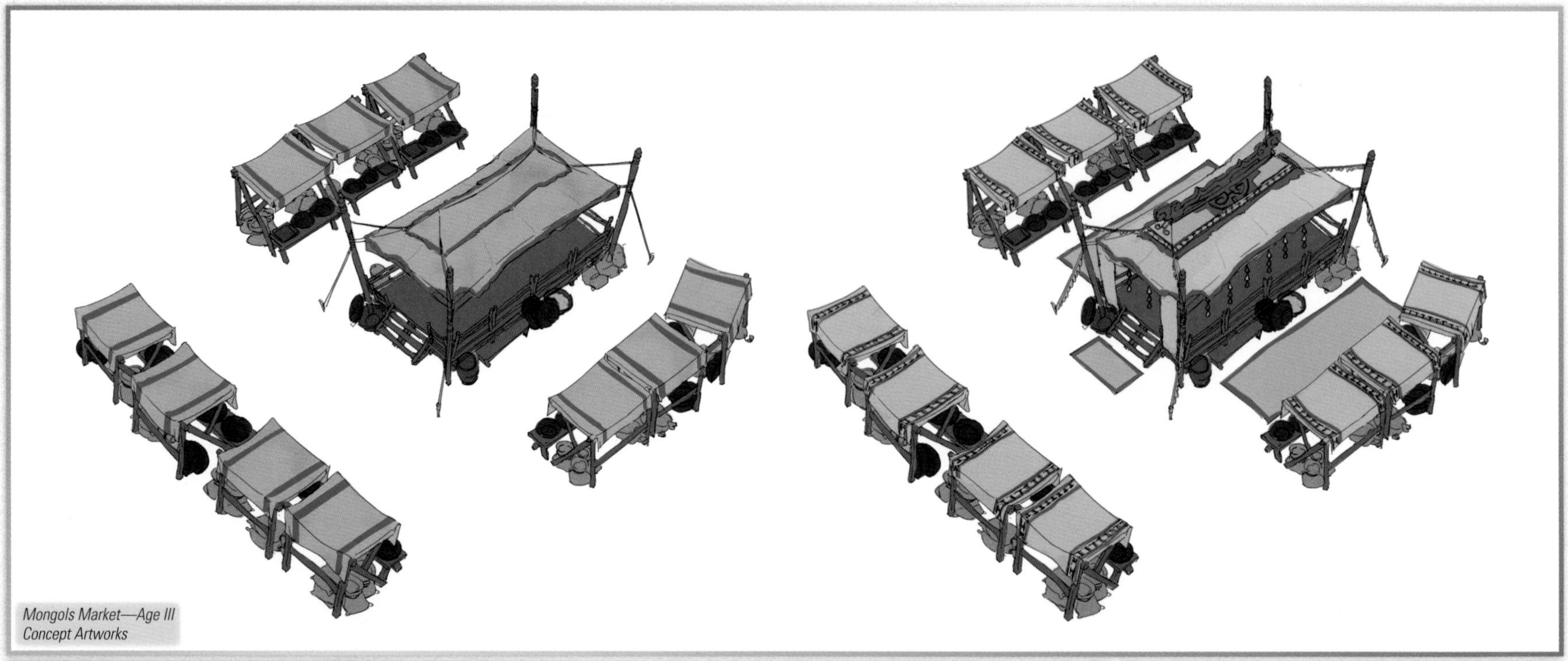

Mongols Market—Age III
Concept Artworks

Kevin Lam
Chinese Market—Age III-IV
oncept Artwork

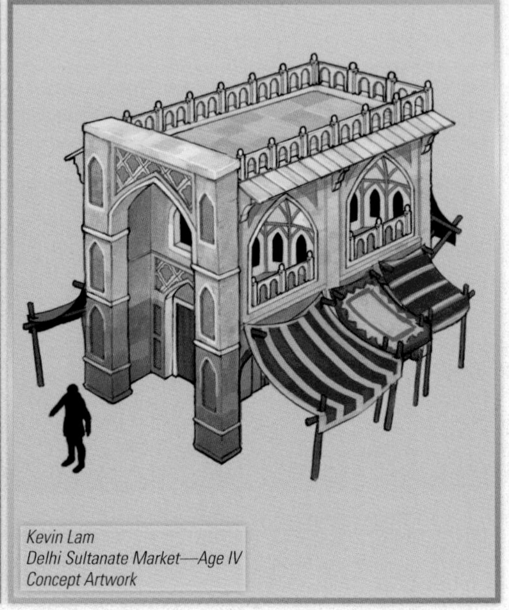

Kevin Lam
Delhi Sultanate Market—Age IV
Concept Artwork

Market

Type	Age
Economy Building, Trade Site	II

Markets are the hubs of economic trade in Age of Empires IV—through them you can buy and sell different resources to either bring in a lot of one that you're short of, or sell off one that you have in surplus. They also produce Traders, which can be used to establish trade routes for an additional, and often very important, source of Gold.

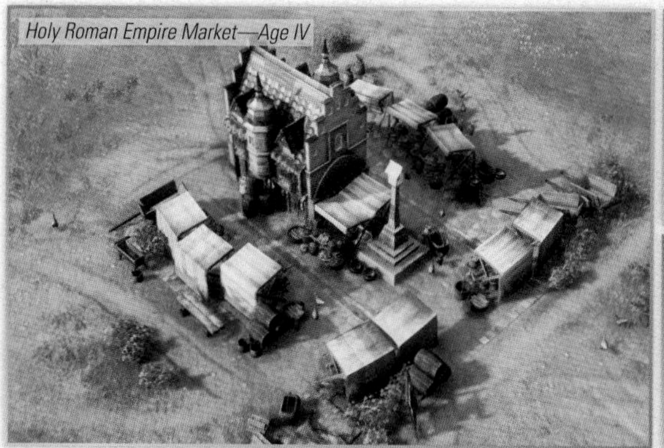

Holy Roman Empire Market—Age IV

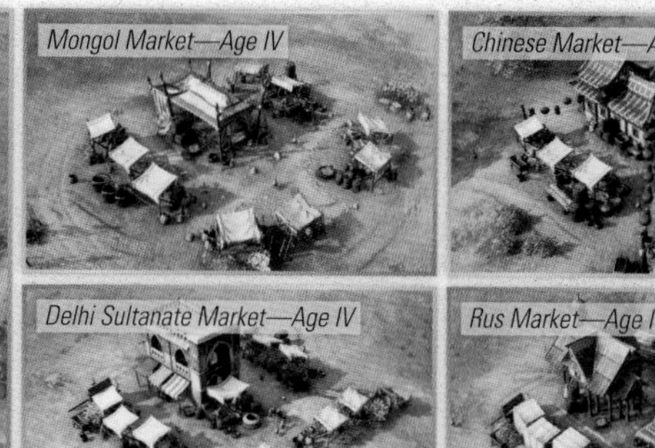

Mongol Market—Age IV

Chinese Market—Age IV

Delhi Sultanate Market—Age IV

Rus Market—Age IV

Building Stats

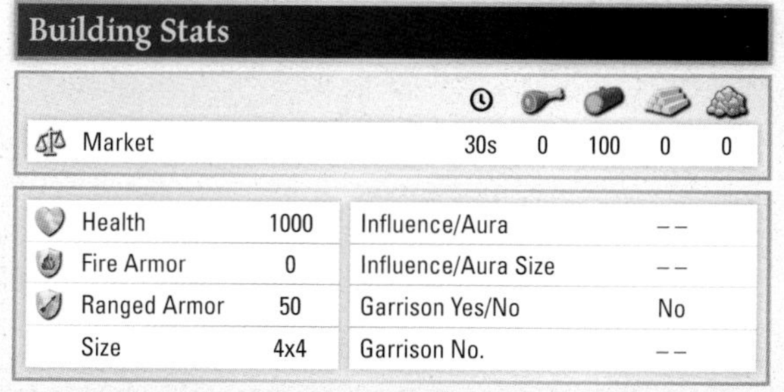

	Time	Food	Wood	Gold	Stone
Market	30s	0	100	0	0

Health	1000	Influence/Aura	--
Fire Armor	0	Influence/Aura Size	--
Ranged Armor	50	Garrison Yes/No	No
Size	4x4	Garrison No.	--

Usage

The buying and selling of resources is something that you should rarely plan for. In most games, however, it's either something that you will eventually need to do, or if things take a turn for the worse and you need something at a moment's notice, something you'll be happy you can do.

At the Market you can sell one type of resource that you have in stock but don't need urgently, or buy one that you can't wait for your Villagers to gather. This is a good option if you're trying to balance your economy to make up for a short-term deficit of one particular resource. Keep in mind though, that this is not a sustainable option and should only be used when necessary.

You'll always lose some resources when using the Market and each trade also has an impact on the exchange rate for that resource. If you trade Food for Gold for example, you'll get less Gold for the same amount of Food after every transaction. That process also effects trades going the other way; if you've traded a lot of Food for Gold, then the Market will have a lot of Food, so if you then wanted to trade Gold for Food, the price would be a lot lower than normal. This is why later in games you'll usually end up paying a lot for highly sought after resources such as Stone. Always try to balance your economy through assigning the right amount of Villagers to each resource to meet your goals, and only use the Market as a band-aid.

An early game Market can be especially important at times when you're being attacked and have to react quickly. Since you can't always predict which units your opponent will attack you with, you can end up in situations where you've gathered the wrong resources to build the units you need to counter what's attacking you. At these times it's also likely that your Villagers are either idle or have taken shelter to avoid being killed, so you can't divert them to the resource you need. In these situations, being able to buy and sell resources from the Market can be crucial to save you from defeat.

Besides trading one resource for another at the Market, they can also be used to produce Traders that you can send out to trade for Gold with other Markets or neutral Trade Posts. If there's still natural Gold on the map you'll generally want to use that for upgrades or military units, and you should only start to venture into Trader production once the availability of Gold on the map starts to fade. Trader production is quite a slow and expensive process, but when it comes time to use them, you'll want to set things up pretty quickly. The best way to achieve this is to build multiple Markets and have each of them produce Traders until you have the desired amount for your Gold income needs.

The amount of Gold that each Trader brings back to your base depends on the distance between the two Markets used for trading. Generally, the farther the distance, the more resources you gain, so if you place your Markets far apart, you'll gain a lot of resources. The downside of this is that it can be harder to keep the trade route safe.

Unit Production

Unit	Age	Civilizations
Trader	I	All

Market Technologies (P.45)

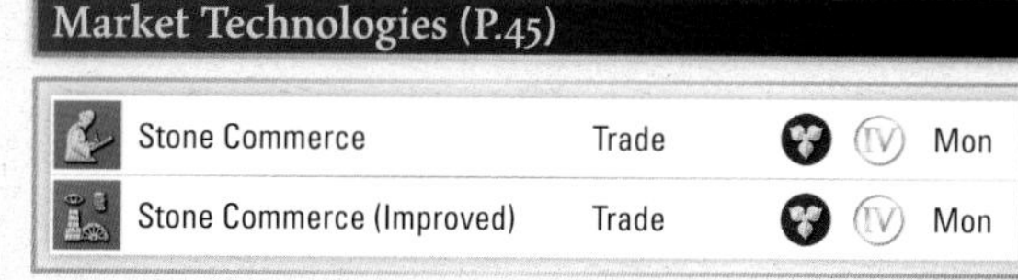

Technology	Type	Age	Civilization
Stone Commerce	Trade	IV	Mon
Stone Commerce (Improved)	Trade	IV	Mon

While most of your trades will be with either neutral or friendly locations, if your opponent placed a Market away from their base, and isn't monitoring or defending it, there's nothing stopping you taking advantage of that fact and sending your Traders to it for a long-range exchange.

4

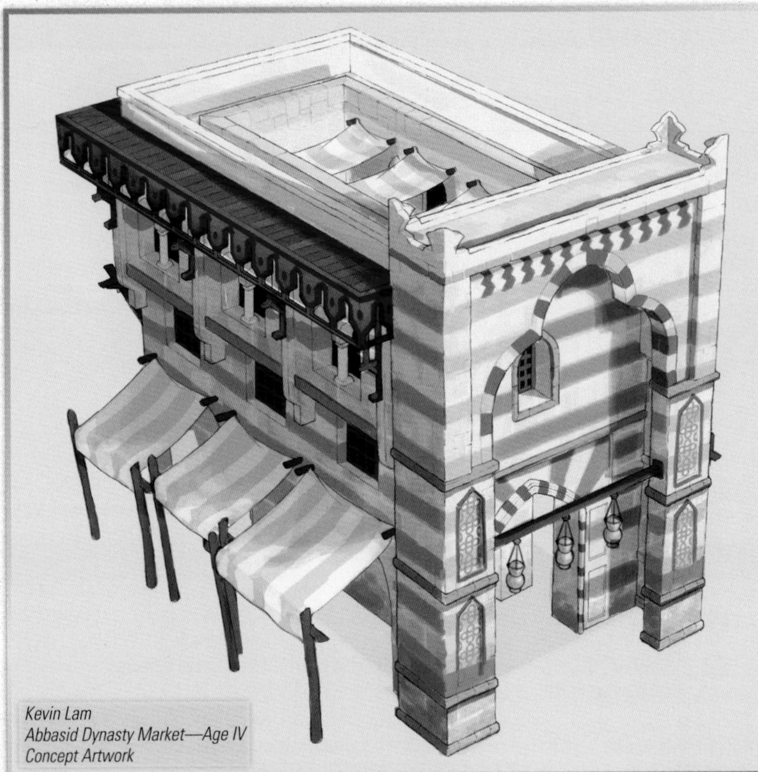

Kevin Lam
Abbasid Dynasty Market—Age IV
Concept Artwork

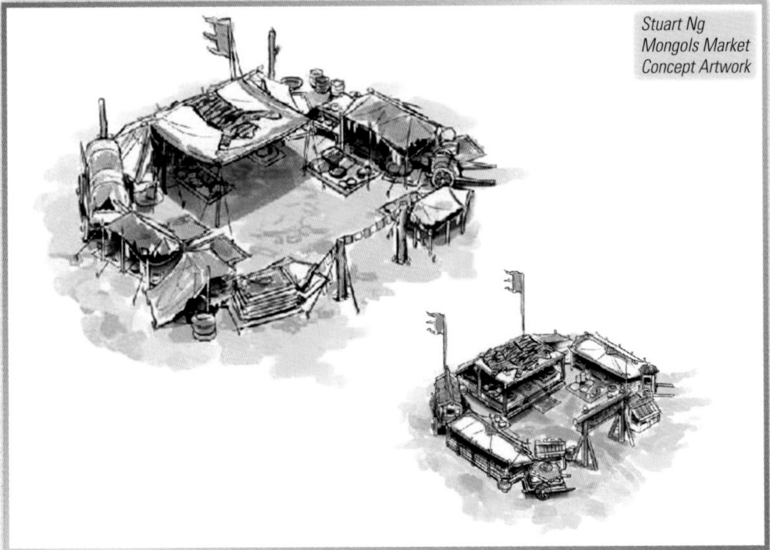

Stuart Ng
Mongols Market
Concept Artwork

Traders are a valuable yet vulnerable asset, and since they're slow and expensive to produce, you should try your best to keep them safe. In team games you can establish reasonably secure routes between yours and a teammate's Market on your team's side of the map, but you'll still want to keep an eye on it so that you can react quickly just in case your Traders do get attacked. To make sure your trade route is not only safe, but efficient you should ensure that there are no obstacles such as buildings in the way of your Traders, so that they can take the most direct route.

In highly contested games you may want to defend your trade route with walls or other fortifications.

In 1v1 games, trade routes can be risky, but they're often vital to winning games in the long-run. On most maps there's usually two neutral Trade Posts that can be used by either player; if you can gain control of both of them, you'll have a significant Gold advantage over your opponent, allowing you to produce more of the stronger endgame units than they can. Trade Posts are usually in open and exposed areas, so taking this approach is not without risk, but trying to keep control is worth the effort.

Strategic Considerations

Abbasid Dynasty

If you develop the **Trade Wing** for the **House of Wisdom** you'll gain access to three unique technologies that improve your trade rates, and the returns you get from each trade your Traders make.

French

For the French, neutral Trade Posts are revealed on the map by default upon starting a game. This not only lets you know exactly where you'll need to establish late-game trade routes, but it also gives you an indication of where you opponent's Town Center might be placed. Additionally, French Traders possess the unique ability to choose which resource they bring back, giving you a lot of late-game versatility. Trading Stone will be exceptionally useful, since it's the resource used for most defensive structures, and it tends to run out first.

Mongols

The Mongols can make use of their Silk Road ability to increase the amount of resources their Traders bring back from each trade, based on how many Traders you have. If you acquire the **Stone Commerce** technology from the Market, and have at least nine active Traders, they also bring back Stone as well as Gold with each trade.

Mill

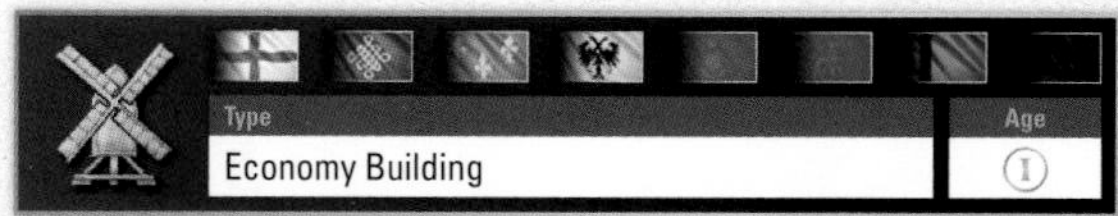

Type	Age
Economy Building	I

As with the other resources, having a drop-off location as close to the source as possible is key to an efficient income, and for Food, that drop-off location for most civilizations is the Mill. For a low cost, you can minimize the distance your Villagers have to carry their harvest, and gain access to a number of useful technologies to make them even more effective at that job.

Building Stats

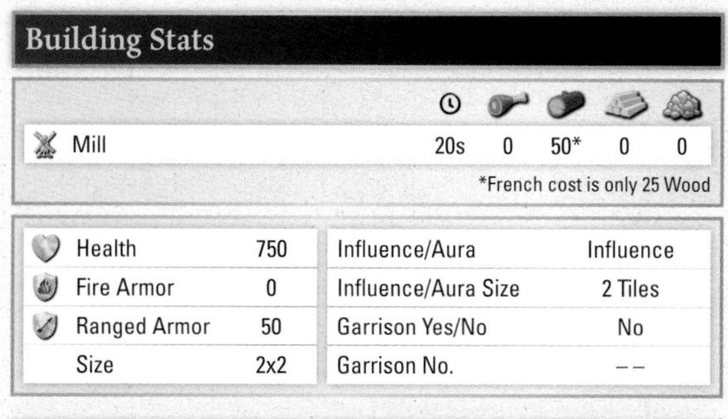

	Time	Food	Wood	Stone	Gold
Mill	20s	0	50*	0	0

*French cost is only 25 Wood

Health	750	Influence/Aura	Influence
Fire Armor	0	Influence/Aura Size	2 Tiles
Ranged Armor	50	Garrison Yes/No	No
Size	2x2	Garrison No.	--

Usage

Your first source of Food income in many games will be from the nearby Sheep around your Town Center; you should be looking to place your first Mill while you're still harvesting these, but only after you've placed your first Lumber Camp. The Berries close to your starting center or a near a group of Deer a little further out are both good options for where to place it, so go with whichever is the most convenient.

You don't want your entire early game Food income to be from Sheep only, so it's important to diversify early with either Deer or Berries to ensure your Food economy transitions smoothly through the Ages. You need about four Villagers on Sheep for continuous Villager production, but to reach the next Age you'll need to build up a surplus by adding more workers onto different Food sources.

Delhi Sultanate Mill—Age I

English Mill—Age I

Mill Technologies (P.45)

Technology	Affects	Age	Civilization
Survival Techniques	Hunting	I	All
Wheelbarrow	Villager	I	All
Professional Scouts	Hunting	II	All
Horticulture	Food Gathering 1/3	II	All
Fertilization	Food Gathering 2/3	III	All
Precision Cross-Breeding	Food Gathering 3/3	IV	All
Enclosures	Farm	IV	Eng

A decent setup would be about ten Villagers on Food, three or more on Wood and two on Gold. You want to add the Wood and Gold Villagers before you start building your Food surplus so that everything lines up nicely. These numbers can vary based on the civilization or specific strategy you're going for, but they're a good general reference point to keep in mind.

For the Mill placement, you always want to make sure that your Villagers spend as little time as possible walking, which means placing them directly adjacent to any Food source, or in the center of a group of Deer. By following this premise you can plan out your Farms in a way that avoids so-called "second row Farms", and in the long-run ensure that all Farms are in contact with a Mill.

If you have Villagers carrying non-Food resources, you don't have to worry about losing them if you task those Villagers with building a Mill, because all of those resources will still go into your bank once the building is complete.

Technology Overview

On water maps, a Mill may not be necessary for a long time if you have a thriving fishing economy. Everywhere else, however, you'll have to build them to ensure the prosperity of your empire if for no other reason that to gain access to the technology to improve your Food gathering rates that they house. On the following page we'll give you a quick overview of the technologies that become available in each Age and when you may want to acquire them.

4

Age I

Survival Techniques: This technology will greatly enhance your Villagers' hunting abilities, but although it's available straight away, you should only research it if you plan to stay in Age I for a long time, or do a lot of hunting early on.

Wheelbarrow: The **Wheelbarrow** upgrade is one of the most important early game economy upgrades, and it should be researched as soon as you can afford it. By increasing the carry capacity and movement speed of your Villagers, it will greatly improve all aspects of your economy by reducing Villager walking time, which is vital for a flourishing economy. If you're trying to push into the Feudal Age as fast as possible it's not worth delaying that for an economic upgrade such as this, but once you reach that Age, you should learn **Wheelbarrow** as soon as you can.

Age II-IV

Professional Scouts: This improves your Scouts by increasing their ranged damage against wild animals, along with the ability to carry a dead animal and drop it off at a desired spot. If you hunt a lot, and can handle the multitasking of killing animals and bringing their carcasses back to your base one by one, then this technology is worth investing in. It will also provide some additional safety for your Villagers, since they can stay within the confines of your base, and still take advantage of the faster gathering rates on hunted animals that your Scouts bring back for them.

Horticulture/Fertilization/Precision Cross Breeding: This series of upgrades is very useful and should not be ignored, but as you progress later into games, you may want to prioritize military upgrades over the higher tiers.

Strategic Considerations

Abbasid Dynasty/Delhi Sultanate

Both of these civilizations cannot gather Food from Boar, but they have improved gathering rates for Berries, and can double their yield if a Mill is nearby. By taking advantage of this you can make Berries about as efficient as Deer to gather, meaning you should always place your first Mill next to Berries, since you won't be missing out on anything.

Placing a Mill near Berry Bushes or Deer at the beginning of a game is vital to give a good start for your economy.

French

The French can build Mills at half the cost of other civilizations, so the choice between Berries or Deer as the location for your first Mill is very easy, since you can now do both for the same cost!

English

Generating Enhancement

 **Mill Influence** Farm harvest rate increased +15%/+20%/+25%/+30% by Age while within the influence of a Mill

The English have access to a unique late-game technology in the Mill called **Enclosures**, and with it, any Farm that is being worked on by a Villager will also generate Gold. Since your Farms will always be there, this technology gives you an excellent additional source of late-game Gold. Their inherent agricultural bonus also means that Farms within the influence of a Mill have faster harvest rates, and that bonus even increases as you progress through the Ages.

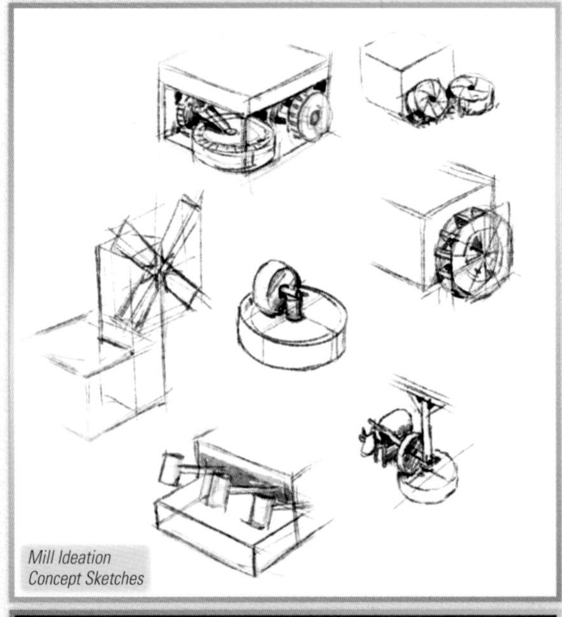

Mill Ideation Concept Sketches

History Consultants

"During development, we worked with a selection of historians and military history experts. They helped ensure that as much as possible of the game was faithful to history. They advised on everything from armour, building and weapons design, to the chronology of events, to cultural attitudes of past and present, to the untangling of myths from fact. You can see their influence in all parts of the game—in unit speech, in on-screen narrative, and most of all, in the documentary films."

– Lauren Wood
Principal Designer, Narrative, Relic

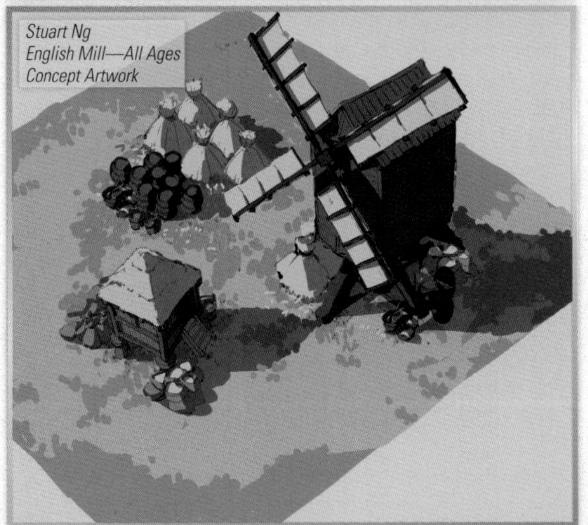

Stuart Ng English Mill—All Ages Concept Artwork

Mining Camp

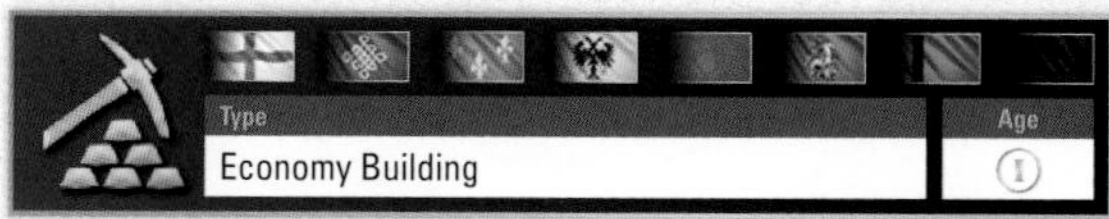

Mining Camps are the standard drop-off location for all of your hard-earned Gold and Stone. They also provide a cheap and convenient alternative to your Town Center, along with technology to make your Villagers better miners.

Building Stats

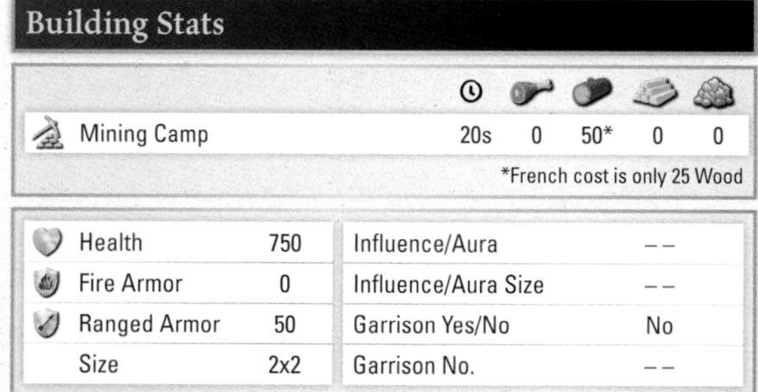

	Time	Food	Wood	Gold	Stone
Mining Camp	20s	0	50*	0	0

*French cost is only 25 Wood

Health	750	Influence/Aura	--
Fire Armor	0	Influence/Aura Size	--
Ranged Armor	50	Garrison Yes/No	No
Size	2x2	Garrison No.	--

Mining Camp Technologies (P.45)

Specialized Pick	Mining Technology 1/3	II	All
Acid Distillation	Mining Technology 2/3	III	All
Cupellation	Mining Technology 3/3	IV	All

Usage

Mining Camps should usually be the last of the three main drop-off sites that you build with most civilizations on a land-based map. Their initial use should be to aid you in gathering the Gold required to build a Landmark and advance to the Feudal Age, but if you plan on building more Town Centers at the start of Age II, you should also dedicate another Mining Camp and some Villagers to Stone.

Because of the nature of how Villagers work on and around Gold and Stone mines, the normal method of placing a single drop-off location on one side of the resource is not actually the most efficient way of working. If you take the route of placing a Mining Camp on one side of the mine, and you're mining with a lot of Villagers, the ones on the opposite side of the mine would have to walk around it to reach the camp. To make this more efficient, it's actually worth placing a second Mining Camp on the opposite side of the mine to your first one, so that no matter where the Villager is working they have the shortest possible travel time.

French Mining Camp—Age I

Technology Overview

Specialized Pick/Acid Distillation/Cupellation: Even though Gold is required for all economic and military upgrades, you should prioritize ones that benefit your Food and Wood gathering first, since that's what most of your Villagers will be dedicated to early on. Once you start wanting to produce units that require Gold, invest in this series of upgrades to speed up your income. Cupellation is generally les important than the first two upgrades, because by the time you reach Age IV a lot of mines tend to have run out and most of your Gold will come from other sources. That being said, if there's still plenty to mine at that time, and you can afford it, then it's well worth learning.

Strategic Considerations

French

Because you don't have to build as many Mining Camps as the other drop-off locations, and they tend to be built later—when you have access to more resources—the savings from the 50% discount are not as noticeable as with the other buildings. That being said, you will still save some resources over time, which is still a nice little bonus.

Holy Roman Empire

Given the importance of Gold, it's always worth having enough Prelates stationed at every Mining Camp to Inspire all of the Villagers working nearby; the faster you bring the Gold in, the faster you can spend it.

Rus

Due to their Bounty system, the Rus do not need access to a Mining Camp in order to get the Gold required to reach Age II—they can simply kill animals around the map with their Scouts to accumulate the Gold required. This means there's a bit less pressure on staking your first claim, but you should still try to establish some mines sooner rather than later.

While it is not always practical, it is possible to build a Mining Camp between a Gold and Stone deposit.

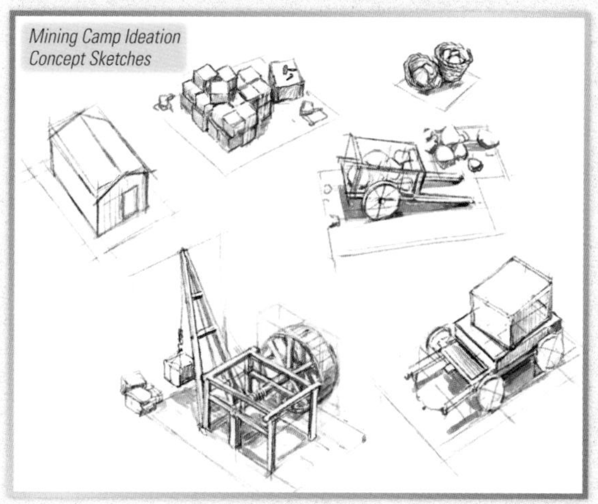

Mining Camp Ideation Concept Sketches

Ovoo

Type	Age
Economy Building	I

Ovoos are unique Mongol buildings that can only be built on top of a stone outcropping. You can only have one Ovoo built at a time; if you try to build a second one on another stone outcropping, the first one will be destroyed. The Ovoo is essentially the only way for Mongols to acquire Stone, because their Villagers cannot mine for it. It can also provide some unique bonuses to any other buildings within its influence range.

Building Stats

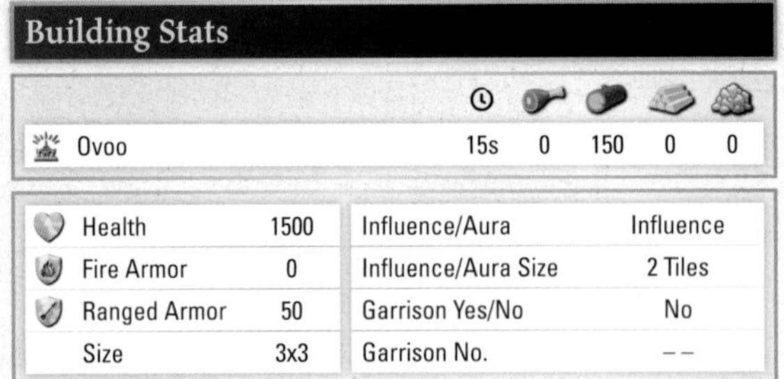

	Time	Food	Wood	Gold	Stone
Ovoo	15s	0	150	0	0

Health	1500	Influence/Aura	Influence
Fire Armor	0	Influence/Aura Size	2 Tiles
Ranged Armor	50	Garrison Yes/No	No
Size	3x3	Garrison No.	--

Usage

Not only do Mongols collect Stone differently to every other civilization, they also use it quite differently. Instead of sending Villagers to the Stone Outcropping, mining it, and then bringing it back to the drop-off building, Mongols construct an Ovoo directly on top of it. This is the only way for Mongols to get Stone for the majority of the game, because even if you have a Ger in the vicinity, Mongol Villagers will not mine a Stone Outcropping. Mongol Markets also do not trade in Stone, and it cannot be obtained through Tributes.

In the Imperial Age, Mongols do gain access to two other means of obtaining Stone, both of which are technologies that add Stone to resources that are acquired through raiding and trade routes. To compensate for this, Mongols do not require Stone for any of their buildings, and ones that traditional require Stone such as Town Centers have higher Wood costs instead. Stone for the Mongols is used exclusively for the additional benefits granted to buildings within the influence range of the Ovoo.

Mongol Ovoo—Age I

Ovoo Influence

The benefit granted to a building within the influence range of an Ovoo depends on the type of building it is. Military buildings can produce two of the same unit at once for the same cost in normal resources as a single unit, but with an additional Stone cost on top. The amount of Stone required is equal to the total amount of other resources the unit costs. So Spearmen usually cost 60 Food and 20 Wood for a single unit, but if your Barracks is within an Ovoo's influence range you can produce two Spearmen for 60 Food, 20 Wood, and 80 Stone. This can greatly speed up your production, but should be used wisely because Stone is hard to come by as Mongols. In the later stages of the game, however, it can be very useful in tight situations where you need a lot of reinforcements in a short amount of time.

With technology or economy buildings, the Ovoo's influence gives them access to improved versions of most of the normal technologies that you can learn through them. The principle for the cost stays the same if you go straight for the improved versions, but you can also choose to learn the normal version first, and then upgrade to the improved version later. In those situations, you only pay the additional Stone cost, not the other resources.

The Ger and Blacksmith stand out as key buildings that you should try and place near your Ovoo if only for the sheer amount of technology choices they give you. The improved versions of technologies such as **Biology** or **Elite Army Tactics** can make your military units significantly stronger, and the improved **Military Academy** will let you produce them even faster than normal. Outside of stat boosts, you can also gain a lot of new tactical opportunities with the improved **Siege Engineering** technology—it allows your infantry units to produce siege engines such as Mangonels and Trebuchets out in the field, instead of just the usual Battering Rams and Siege Towers.

Military buildings within the Influence of the Ovoo can train two units at the same time for an additional Stone cost.

If you're looking for more sources of Stone to keep up with learning all of the improved technologies, then you might want to consider building a Market near an Ovoo, since that will allow you to acquire the improved version of **Stone Commerce** which can increase your Stone income considerably. As you can see, trying to research all of the improved technologies available to the Mongols requires an extraordinarily large amount of Stone, but if you manage to get a lot of them, the Mongols can be a true late-game powerhouse.

Only a single tile of a building needs to be within the influence range of the Ovoo, so try to plan ahead to get the maximum amount of buildings around it.

Technology Overview

Age I

- Superior Mobility: This makes buildings pack and unpack 50% faster, which allows your base to be more mobile. While not necessary, due to the low cost it doesn't hurt to have this researched, especially if you're staying mobile with your buildings, or if you're forced to move by your opponent.

Age II

- Whistling Arrows: The Khan's signature abilities are their Signal Arrows, and through this upgrade you can extend both the duration and range of them. Later in games when your armies and the battles the wage are at their largest, this upgrade will prove very useful.

- Raid Bounty: Since raiding villages and razing buildings is a core part of Mongol gameplay, and this upgrade only makes that a much more lucrative venture, it should be considered a mandatory upgrade. In terms of Gold cost alone it will pay for itself after igniting only five buildings, and then it's all profit.

Age III

- Additional Torches: Increases the fire (torch) damage of all infantry and cavalry units by +3. This pairs well with the Mongol ability to gain resources from igniting buildings, so if you're using a lot of small groups around the map to set fire to buildings, then this upgrade will significantly speed you up. Because it's quite costly, however, you'll need to ignite a fair few buildings to recoup the costs. It can also come in handy it you tend to use infantry or cavalry units to land the finishing blows on your opponent's key buildings.

Age IV

- Stone Bounty: For the low cost of 100 Food and 225 Gold you'll get and additional 75 Stone for igniting buildings, on top of the other resources. This is a must get upgrade due to how valuable Stone is for improved technologies and production.

Ovoo Technologies (P.45)

Technology	Type	Age	Civ
Superior Mobility	Packing	I	Mon
Whistling Arrows	Khan	II	Mon
Whistling Arrows (Impr.)	Khan	II	Mon
Raid Bounty	Raiding	II	Mon
Raid Bounty (Improved)	Raiding	II	Mon
Additional Torches	Raiding	III	Mon
Additional Torches (Impr.)	Raiding	III	Mon
Stone Bounty	Raiding	IV	Mon
Stone Bounty (Improved)	Raiding	IV	Mon

Building Construction Method

"Since the construction animations were, as a mechanic, something that would be over quite quickly, it was most important that the readability was clear and that it looked cool. While the scaffolding and the construction process lends itself to depicting ancient construction methods, as a visual device, we needed it to indicate to a modern player what is going on. Sadly, we couldn't dive deeper into individual cultural methods (for example bamboo might have been used as scaffold in the east), as the asset count would go through the roof and challenge the game's performance."

– Han Randhawa
Franchise Art Director, World's Edge

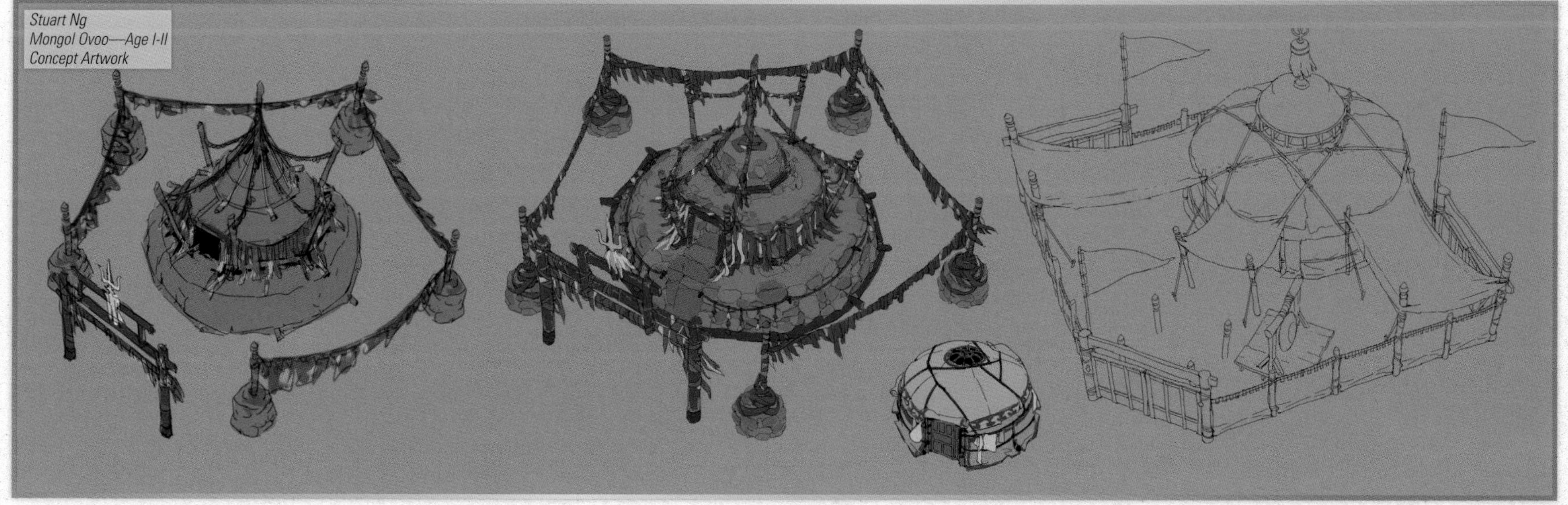

Stuart Ng
Mongol Ovoo—Age I-II
Concept Artwork

Pagoda

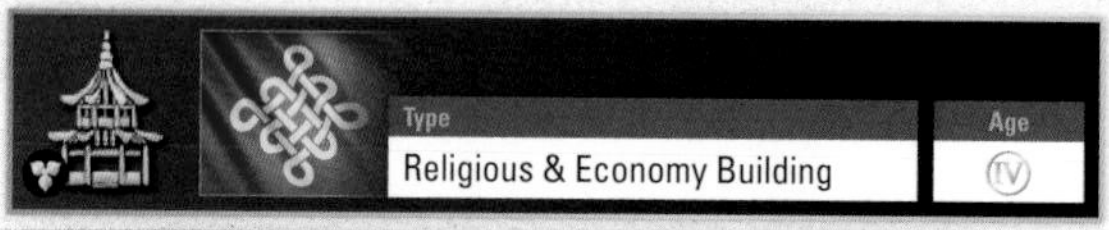

The Chinese Pagoda straddles the line between a religious and economy building, but on it's own it provides you with little tangible benefit. Once you have a religious unit garrison a Relic inside of one, however, it will begin automatically generating resources and turns into a nice supplemental source of income.

Building Stats

	Time	Food	Wood	Gold	Stone
Pagoda	40s	0	150	0	0

Health	2100	Influence/Aura	--
Fire Armor	0	Influence/Aura Size	--
Ranged Armor	50	Garrison Yes/No	No
Size	4x4	Garrison No.	--

Usage

Because they can only be built while in the Ming Dynasty during Age IV, Pagodas only come into play in the very late stages of a game. This means you might need to hold onto your Relics for some time until you get to put them to work inside one. A Pagoda with a Relic inside it will generate 50 of every resource every 30 seconds, and since it only costs 150 Wood to construct, in Wood alone it will pay for itself in 90 seconds. Because of that fact, as soon as you enter the Ming Dynasty you should immediately build a Pagoda for every Relic you have under your control to start the generation as early as possible. At this late stage in the game the Stone that you get from the Pagodas will be especially welcome, since it's usually the first resource that you'll run out of. Without a Relic inside, the only functionality a Pagoda has is that it will automatically generate taxes, at a rate of 10 Gold per Minute.

Chinese Pagoda—Age IV

You can only build a maximum of three Pagodas, so you should build one every time you gain control of a Relic until you reach the maximum amount.

To ensure the safety of your Pagodas, build them in a secure place, far from potential battle areas.

Stuart Ng
Chinese Pagoda—Age III
Concept Artwork

Building Silhouettes

"For iconic buildings, we looked at the major recognizable elements and tried to arrange them into a clear silhouette or layout. We want the player to recognize what the building is based on in reality, and be able to pick it out from the many, many other buildings of similar function and type. For example, mosques share a lot of the same geographical layout, so the initial goal was to make each one visually contrast one another. The same goes for castles in each of the different civilizations."

– Stuart Ng
Senior Concept Artist, Relic

Pasture

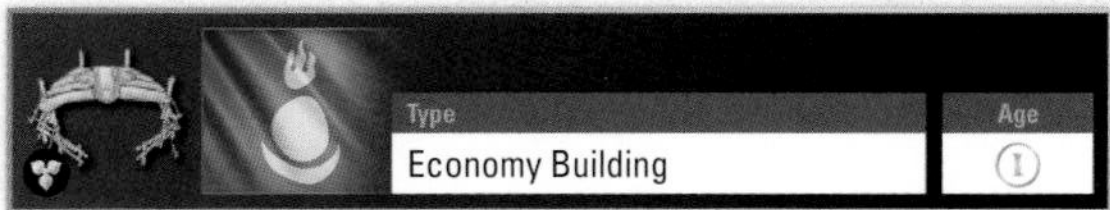

Type	Age
Economy Building	I

One of the main sources of early game Food for most civilizations comes from herding nearby sheep with Scouts and bringing them close to your base for your Villagers to hunt and gather from. Pastures streamline this process by automatically producing Sheep within the confines of a pen, saving you the need to go out and find them, and since Mongols cannot build Farms, this is their main source of safe and reliable Food income.

Building Stats

	Time	Food	Wood	Gold	Stone
Pasture	20s	0	150	0	0

Health	750	Influence/Aura	--
Fire Armor	0	Influence/Aura Size	--
Ranged Armor	50	Garrison Yes/No	No
Size	2x2	Garrison No.	--

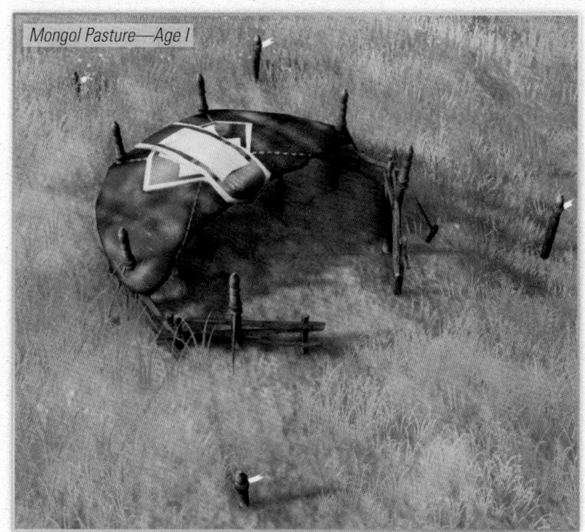
Mongol Pasture—Age I

Usage

Pastures are very similar to Farms, and as such you shouldn't invest in them too early when your Wood could be better spent elsewhere. Start building them once the nearby sources of Berries and other wildlife start to thin out to ensure a smooth transition from those sources.

Without any upgrades, five Villagers is the best amount to assign to one Pasture, because when they're done harvesting from one Sheep, the next one will be just about ready to appear. By the time you've unlocked all of the economy upgrades, along with **Wheelbarrow**, the number of Villagers required at each Pasture drops down to five since each of them is so efficient. The Improved versions of those technologies from Ovoo-influenced buildings will not change that number, they just make each trip with those Villagers even more efficient. There's also another benefit from building a Pasture near an Ovoo, and that's the fact that doing so will speed up the rate at which Sheep are generated. Under normal circumstances it takes 120s for each Sheep to spawn, but near an Ovoo that number is reduced to only 80s.

It's important to keep up with harvesting the Sheep at your Pastures, because you can only hold a total of 30 Sheep between all of your Pastures, after which they will stop producing new ones. This number only counts Sheep that are alive, so you can circumvent it a bit by killing off Sheep and harvesting them later. To be efficient, build a group of Pastures in a safe location around a drop-off site that your Villagers can bring the Food to. In the early part of a game you'll want to make that drop-off location your Town Center, since it's the safest and most effective arrangement.

Make sure to leave a one tile gap between the Pasture and your drop-off site so that your Villagers have room to work in.

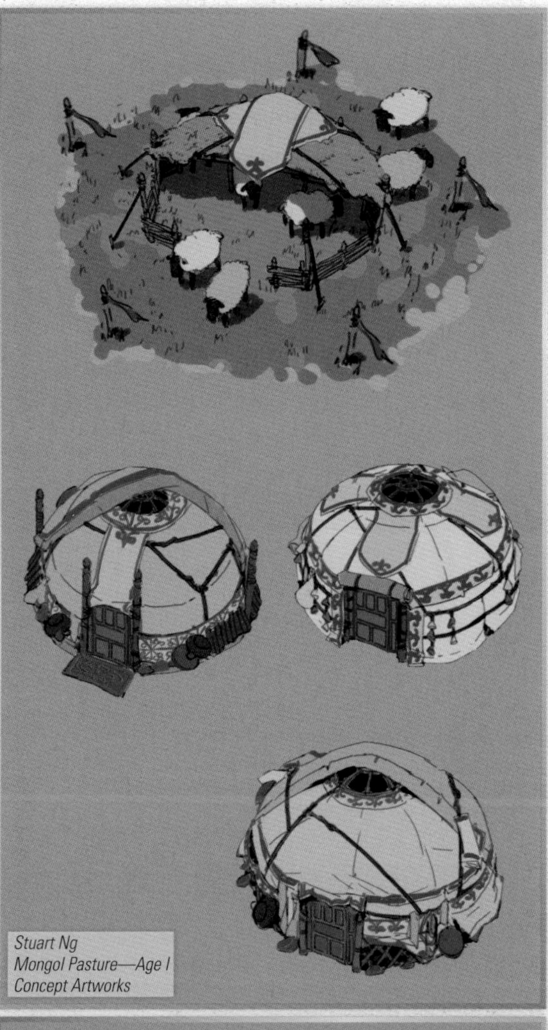
Stuart Ng
Mongol Pasture—Age I
Concept Artworks

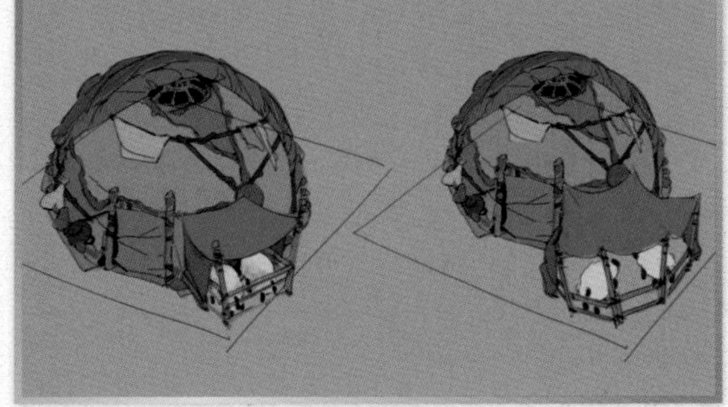

4

Town Center

Type	Age
Economy & Population Building, Landmark	II

Your Town Center is the first building you see and use in nearly every game, and since it produces arguably the most important unit in the game—Villagers—that makes it one of the most important buildings. Town Centers also act as drop-off locations for every type of resource, and your starting Town Center acts as a Landmark with some extra benefits that the ones you can build from Age II onwards do not have.

Building Stats

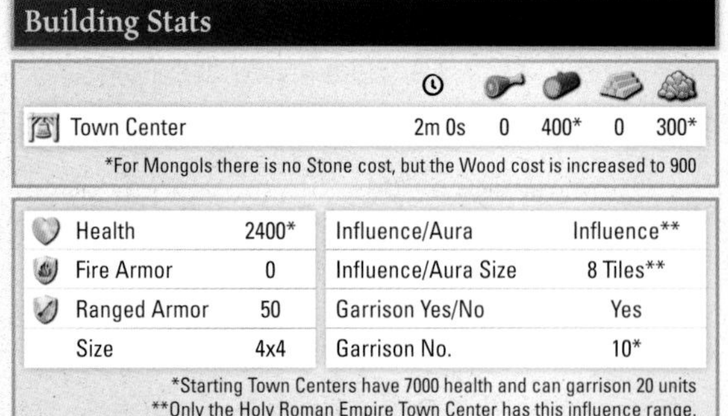

	Time	Food	Wood	Gold	Stone
Town Center	2m 0s	0	400*	0	300*

*For Mongols there is no Stone cost, but the Wood cost is increased to 900

Health	2400*	Influence/Aura	Influence**
Fire Armor	0	Influence/Aura Size	8 Tiles**
Ranged Armor	50	Garrison Yes/No	Yes
Size	4x4	Garrison No.	10*

*Starting Town Centers have 7000 health and can garrison 20 units
**Only the Holy Roman Empire Town Center has this influence range.

Usage

A helpful rule for players who are new to the game is to always be producing units from your Town Center, because that's the main way to keep your economy running and growing. Depending on your overall strategy or what units you're going for, you should be aiming for between 80-100 Villagers on average.

As you get more familiar with the game, there are some advanced strategies you can experiment with, where you go all in on military production after reaching a certain number of Villagers to get a short-term spike in military strength. Similarly, if your opponent has invested heavily into military units early on and starts attacking you, it might be best to halt Villager production and put all of your resources towards countering them.

Abbasid Dynasty—Age IV

Town Center Technologies (P.45)

Technology	Type	Age	Civilization
Textiles	Villager Technology	II	All

Attack Details

Arrowslits

Bow (Ranged)

Damage	8*
Counter Bonus	25
Bonus Against	Ships
Attack Range	8
Attack Speed	1.00s*

*Chinese Town Centers have defensive Handcannons that do 25 damage with an attack speed of 3.00

Unit Production

Unit	Age	Civilization
Imperial Official	I	Chi
Prelate	I	HRE
Scout	I	All
Villager	I	All

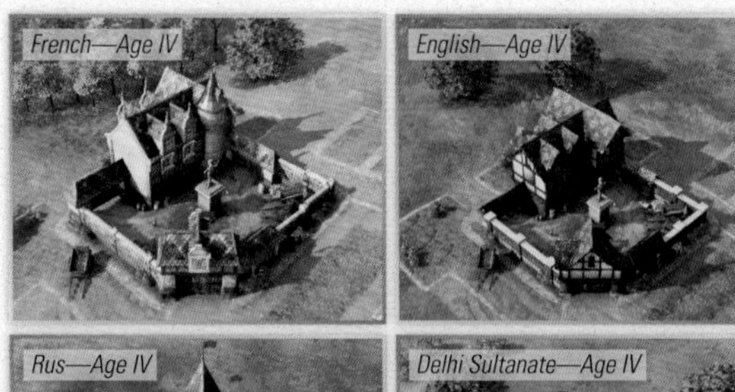

French—Age IV

English—Age IV

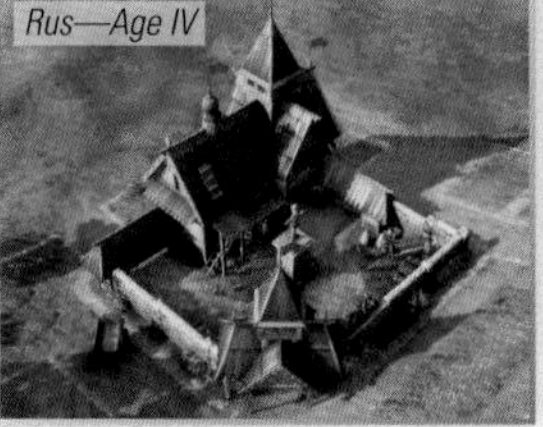

Rus—Age IV

Delhi Sultanate—Age IV

Building additional Town Centers once you're able to is also a good tactic to employ—they not only provide additional protection for your Villagers, but having more than one building producing Villagers allows you to reach your full economic potential faster. They're expensive to produce, however, so when you hit Age II you'll need to gauge the risks associated with when and how many you build. Sink too many resources into them and you might not have enough to defend your base if your opponent focused on military units, or if you want to attack, you might not be able to produce a big enough army.

In Age II you'll have to weigh your options: do you want to go with an economic focused strategy or a military focused one? Or maybe something in between? Your choice will depend on many factors, such as map type, civilization match-up, how much you know about your opponent's location and strength etc. For most matches, however, building more than two additional Town Centers for production will rarely be worthwhile.

Additional Town Centers can be used to try and establish control over deposits of Gold or Stone that are far from your main base or in exposed parts of the map during the later stages of a game.

Town Centers can also produce Scouts, but you should only produce additional ones when you have a plan for using them, because any Scout you produce and don't use is a wasted opportunity to produce another Villager. Some good uses for extra Scouts include hunting for Food, trying to lure your opponents into traps, or aggressively scouting the map to locate your opponent. Villagers that are produced early in games are worth more than ones in later ages, because if you have 10 of them, the next one will increase your economy by 10%, but if you have 100, that next one will only give you a 1% increase. Keep this in mind while deciding on when it might be worthwhile to produce another Scout.

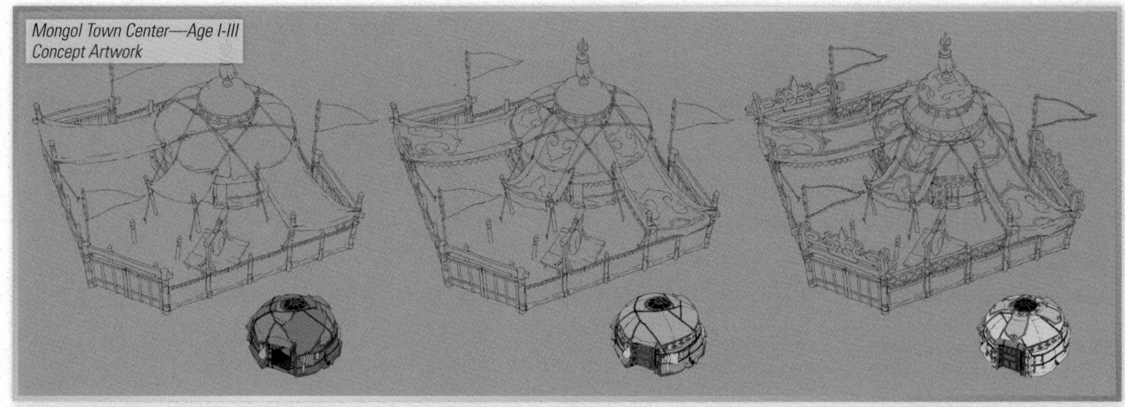

Mongol Town Center—Age I-III
Concept Artwork

Kevin Lam
Delhi Sultanate Town Center—Age I-IV
Concept Artwork

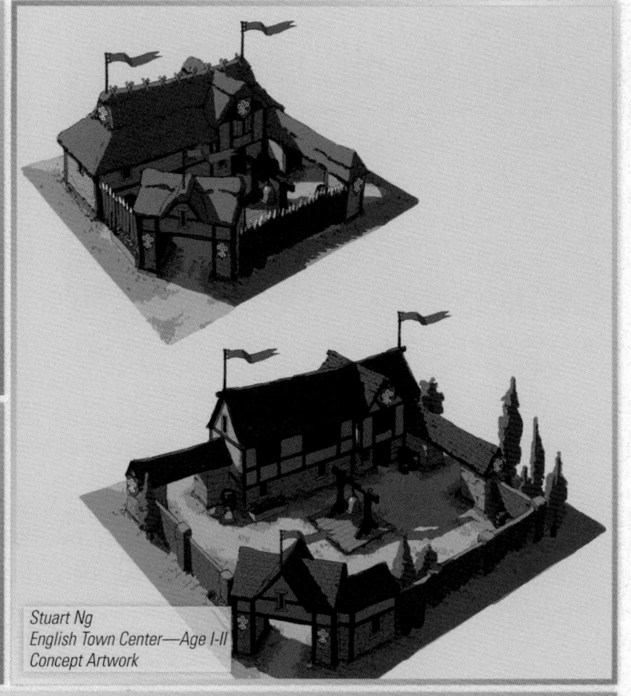

Stuart Ng
English Town Center—Age I-II
Concept Artwork

Kevin Lam
Chinese Town Center—Age I-IV
Concept Artwork

You should only stop production of Villagers for a Scout at your Town Center if you lose your initial Scout early in a game and have no other building that you can produce a Scout from.

Town Centers can also shelter up to 10 Villagers to protect them from enemy raids, and as long as they're garrisoned inside they'll fire arrows at the attackers. A fully garrisoned Town Center can deter small attacking forces, but if your opponent brings a large army or siege units, it won't hold out for long on its own. Your additional Town Centers should always be positioned with the purpose of serving as both a defensive structure, and a drop-off point for resources.

Starting Town Center

The Starting Town Center serves as your initial Landmark, and as such it's a little different from the ones you build later. Most of their stats are the same, but Starting Town Centers can fire a defensive arrow automatically without any units being garrisoned inside, and you can garrison up to 20 units inside instead of the usual 10. Both of those features combined means that its defensive capabilities are more than double that of a normal Town Center; each unit garrisoned inside Town Centers can fire an arrow that deals six damage, so at full capacity your Starting Town Center can dish out 128 damage per volley. Its status as a Landmark also means that in some game modes, if you haven't built another Landmark and your Starting Town Center gets destroyed, you'll lose the match.

Strategic Considerations

Chinese

Chinese Town Centers fire powerful Handcannons as their default attack rather than arrows, and can also produce the Imperial Official unit that's essential for collecting taxes from other buildings. For more information on that unit, please turn to P.134.

English

Generating Enhancement

 **Network of Castles** When enemies are nearby, this building sounds an alarm, causing nearby units to get a +25% increase to attack speed.

Due to their unique Network of Castles ability, English Town Centers are better at defending than those of other civilizations, because their attack speed is increased by 25% whenever an enemy is within its line of sight. Their Town Centers also fire twice as many arrows with each volley, making them even better at protecting your Villagers.

Holy Roman Empire

Generating Enhancement

 **Town Center Influence** Building gains the Emergency Repairs ability

Any buildings built within the huge 8 tile influence range around a Holy Roman Empire Town Center gain access to the **Emergency Repair** ability. This ability can be activated any time a building takes damage, and it repairs them by 150 health a second for 20 seconds. If your base is under siege, this ability can buy you a lot of time to bring in reinforcements, and potentially stop buildings from being destroyed. Holy Roman Empire Town Centers also allow you to produce their essential Prelate unit that boosts the productivity of your Villagers. Turn to P.156 to find out more about them.

Mongols

Unlike other civilizations, the Mongol Starting Town Center starts in its packed up form, which means you get to choose where to unpack it; try to select a location from which it can protect one of your resources, such as a forest or Gold Vein. Try not to stray too far from where you start with it, however, because that could hinder the protection of the other surrounding resources, and it also delays starting Villager production, slowing down your economic growth.

Stuart Ng
Mongol Town Center—Age I-IV
Concept Artwork

Village

You'll first need to reach the Song Dynasty before you can construct Villages, but the wait is more than worth it. The Village is essentially a superior version of the humble House, and three of them can take care of most of your population concerns. Keep in mind that if you lose one, you'll have to make up for the lost population space quickly, otherwise it'll be a long time until your next units will appear.

Building Stats

	Time	Food	Wood	Gold	Stone
Village	30s	0	100	0	0

Health	2000	Influence/Aura	– –
Fire Armor	0	Influence/Aura Size	– –
Ranged Armor	50	Garrison Yes/No	Yes
Size	4x4	Garrison No.	10

Usage

For a mere 100 Wood, Villages increase the maximum population space by 40 and are therefore very cost efficient. The same cost and build time would only get you two Houses, for only 20 population space. Because you can't build them until you reach the Song Dynasty though, there's a good chance that you would have had to build some Houses before reaching that point, and it's not worth demolishing them just to build Villages. You can also only build three Villages, but with your early-game Houses, you should rarely ever need that many.

Another ability of the Village is that you can garrison up to 10 units inside it, and that coupled with its high health means it has almost as much in common with a Town Center as a House. Because of these extra defensive capabilities, Villages are actually a very good building to provide some security to Villagers gathering resources, either within the confines of your empire, or at the borders of it.

Chinese Village—Age II

Even though it has some impressive defensive credentials, you don't want to place your Villages too offensively, because if one is destroyed, the loss of 40 population space could be devastating in a situation where you need to build units fast.

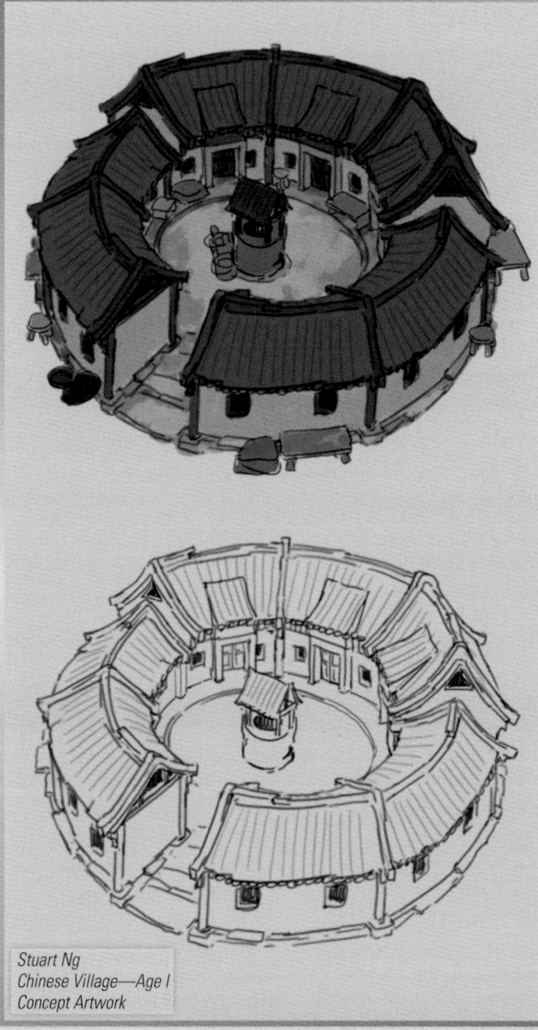

Stuart Ng
Chinese Village—Age I
Concept Artwork

Planning the Buildings

"For the buildings, the artistic imperative was that a shorthand art look needed to be created for ech one, a sort of compressed idea of the actual building, which was also true for past AoE environments. The surrounding details, from small fences to daily life accoutrements, helped embed the buildings into the terrain in a believable way. We had much more grandiose plans for animated Gaia, village life etc., but were eventually constrained by performance, and serving the gameplay always takes priority."

– Han Randhawa
Franchise Art Director, World's Edge

4

Archery Range

The Archery Range is one of the core military production buildings for every civilization, and through it you'll have access to a number of ranged units that specialize in attacking and countering other units, rather than buildings or siege engines.

Building Stats

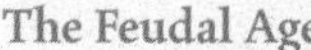

	Time	Food	Wood	Gold	Stone
Archery Range	30s	0	150	0	0

Health	1500	Influence/Aura	--
Fire Armor	0	Influence/Aura Size	--
Ranged Armor	50	Garrison Yes/No	No
Size	3x3	Garrison No.	--

Usage

Ranged units are best against slower moving units such as melee infantry or Villagers, but are weak against faster moving units such as cavalry. So although it's an important building, you should typically avoid having the Archery Range as your only military production building, since that would lead to an army that's easily countered by your opponent.

That logic also extends to your decisions about which units to produce from the Archery Range, because you won't want to always use every available type. Remember that your units also need upgrades, and as a match progresses you'll have to actively weigh the pros and cons between units and upgrades based on the situation at hand. Most importantly, if you realize your opponent has adapted to the army you're currently producing, don't cling to that type of production and instead move on to other units, otherwise you'll be facing an uphill struggle.

The Feudal Age

If you plan to go for ranged infantry as soon as you reach this age, you'll want to build two Archery Ranges at most, since that will allow you maintain a quick production of units for small armies that can harass your opponents. Since Archers are very vulnerable to any kind of cavalry, make sure to pair yours with an anti-cavalry unit. Even if you're choosing to take a more defensive approach that focuses mainly on economic development, it's risky to completely ignore military production buildings because you'll still want the option to produce units if the needed arises.

Castle Age Onwards

In the later stages of the game you're going to need a lot of Archery Ranges, because all ranged units are most effective when they're in large enough groups that they can kill enemy targets in a single volley. That means it's not only important to preserve your ranged units out in the field, but also to ramp up your production now that you should have enough economical support to sustain it.

Don't be afraid to build a lot of production buildings in order to quickly replace your army if it dies on the battlefield; resources in the bank won't win a battle. While most of your military production in the early game will be near your base, if your position allows it, establishing forward Archery Ranges closer to your opponent can give you a big advantage over them. Not only will it let you secure your position, but any units you produce there can reach your enemy's base faster, which is an excellent way to apply pressure.

In Age II, the easily produced Archers or Longbowmen serve as ideal counters to Spearmen.

In Age III you should start producing some anti-armor specialist units such as Crossbowmen to counter the heavier melee units that become available.

Archery Range Technologies (P.45)

Technology	Affects	Age	Civ
Setup Camp	Longbowman Ability Unlock	II	Eng
Arrow Volley	Longbowman Ability Unlock	IV	Eng
Gambesons	Arbalétrier	III	Fre
Crossbow Stirrups	Arbalétrier	IV	Fre
Siha Bow Limbs	Ranged Damage	III	Mon
Siha Bow Limbs (Impr.)	Ranged Damage	III	Mon
Mounted Precision	Horse Archer	IV	Rus
Double Time	Streltsy Ability Unlock	IV	Rus
Siege Elephant	Elephant	IV	Sul

Strategic Considerations

Abbasid Dynasty

From Age II onward the Abbasid Dynasty can produce Camel Archers. Though a costly unit, they're the ideal support unit for the other early melee and ranged infantry this civilization specializes in. If you've decided to incorporate them into your army, you should also consider developing the **Military Wing** of the **House of Wisdom** as your Age II Landmark to take advantage of complimentary technology it offers.

Chinese

In the Song Dynasty the Chinese are capable of fielding the iconic Zhuge Nu, which is a powerful ranged unit that does well against almost any other unit type. Their comparatively high cost and production time means that you'll need to build at least two or three Archery Ranges to produce a good-sized group.

Delhi Sultanate

The War Elephant isn't the only elephant unit the Delhi Sultanate have at their disposal. From the Castle Age onwards, they can also train the mighty Tower War Elephant, which carries two additional ranged units on its back that attack in conjunction with its massive trunk. Due to its high cost you'll only be able to afford to have a couple of Archer Ranges dedicated to producing it at a time, but if you can get a few of these rolling with other infantry and siege units to support them, you'll be hard to stop.

Unit Production

Unit	Age	Civ
Crossbowman	III	All - Fre
Elite Crossbowman	IV	All - Fre
Handcannoneer	IV	All - Rus
Archer	II	All - Eng
Veteran Archer	III	All - Eng
Elite Archer	IV	All - Eng
Longbowman	II	Eng
Veteran Longbowman	III	Eng
Elite Longbowman	IV	Eng
Zhuge Nu	II	Chi
Veteran Zhuge Nu	III	Chi
Elite Zhuge Nu	IV	Chi
Grenadier	IV	Chi
Arbalétrier	III	Fre
Elite Arbalétrier	IV	Fre
Mangudai	II	Mon
Veteran Mangudai	III	Mon
Elite Mangudai	IV	Mon
Streltsy	IV	Rus
Horse Archer	III	Rus
Elite Horse Archer	IV	Rus
Tower War Elephant	III	Sul
Camel Archer	II	Abb
Veteran Camel Archer	III	Abb
Elite Camel Archer	IV	Abb

English

With their iconic Longbowmen the English are able to strike fear into the hearts of enemy infantry and cavalry alike. The Longbowman is a staple of the English army throughout all ages. Early on, an Archery Range is not really necessary for the English, because they can build the **Council Hall** Landmark, which allows them to produce Longbowmen at twice the speed of an Archery Range.

Later in the game when you need to ramp up production even more or need access to other unit types, you should construct some Archery Ranges. Additionally, you can upgrade your Longbowmen through the Archery Range to gain additional special abilities that make your ranged infantry even more remarkable; if you invest a lot into Longbowmen, these upgrades should be considered mandatory.

Mongols

From Age II onwards the Mongols get access to the Mangudai, a very mobile and versatile mounted ranged unit that shoots while moving. Start production early from a single Archery Range while gradually improving your numbers and trying to minimize losses by poking at your opponent's army with hit-and-run attacks rather than direct engagements. Keep this up by continuously adding numbers and you can snowball the advantage you've established until you have an almost unbeatable mass of Mangudai.

An Archery Range for the Mongols is best paired with a Stable so that you can use melee cavalry to help get rid of siege units, and they can also act as a shield for your Mangudai without sacrificing any of your mobility. Be aware though, that this combination, although extremely potent, will be quite costly and your army will be hard to replace if you lose it. Mongols also have access to the **Siha Bow Limbs** upgrade that increases the ranged damage of your Mangudai and Khan units, and since it's cheaper than the next best option available in Age III, it should be a priority if you have a lot of Mangudai.

Rus

Similar to the Mongols, the Rus also get access to a mounted ranged unit in the form of the Horse Archer, but they have to wait until Age III for it. This unit can be used in much the same way as the Mangudai, with the exception that they do not shoot while moving. You'll want to have at least three or four Archery Ranges already built by the time you reach Age III if you want to switch to producing them in large amounts. Without that many Archery Ranges you won't be able to build them up in sufficient numbers to combat any decently sized army your opponent has waiting for you. Horse Archers get a huge power spike in Age IV with the **Mounted Precision** upgrade that gives them +2 range on their attacks, making large groups of them even scarier.

4

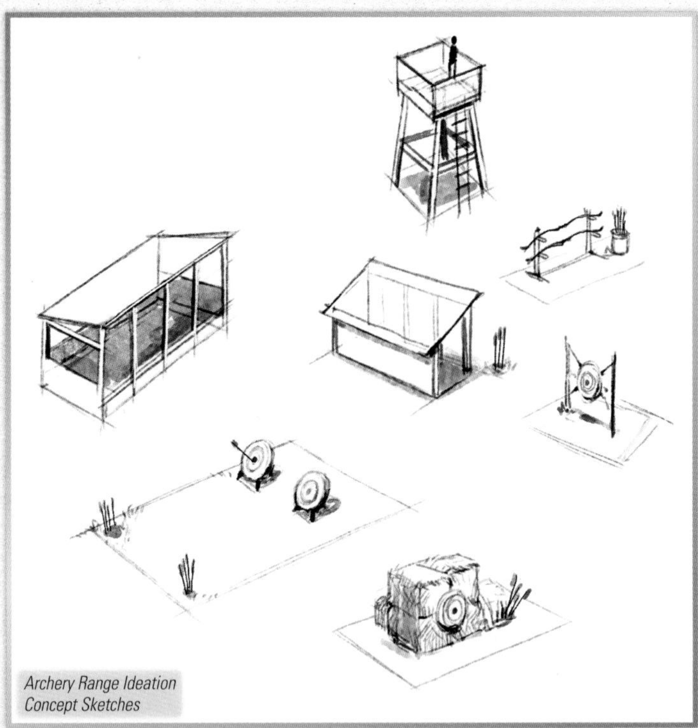

Archery Range Ideation
Concept Sketches

Mongols Archery Range—Age II-III
Concept Artwork

Visual Clarity

"We tried a lot of different scales and proportions and what we discovered was players needed the different aspects of buildings and units to indicate very clearly their respective function in a fairly short amount of time. Given that your camera view could be potentially darting around the map at varying frequencies, the buildings and units including the landscape, needed to be recognizable instantly, but also able to be scrutinized if you sat and gazed at them for a time. This was particularly challenging as different players had different ways of playing Age of Empires. Even something like determining how thick a wood beam would be, or the thickness of a spear, if you simply replicated how large they were in reality and expected it to be readable at a distance amongst a group of potentially hundreds or thousands of things happening on the screen; always assume you had to exaggerate it to a certain threshold."

– Staurt Ng
Senior Concept Artist, Relic

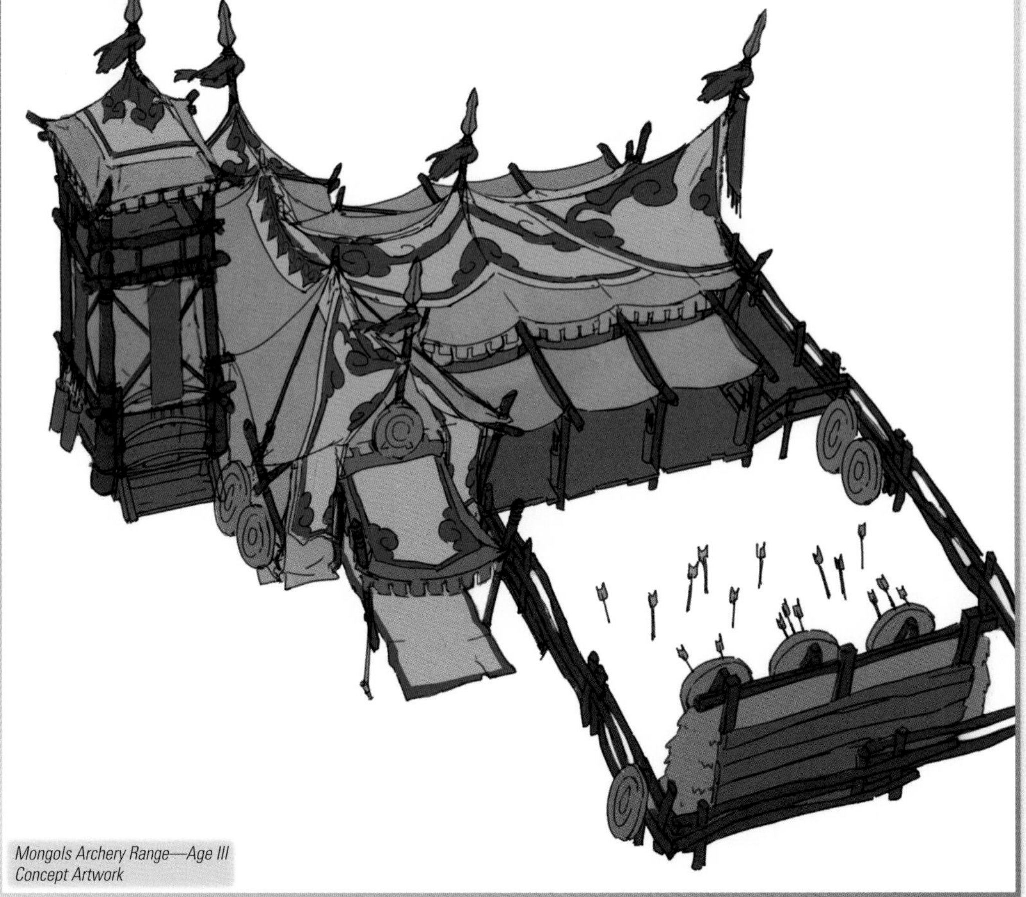

Mongols Archery Range—Age III
Concept Artwork

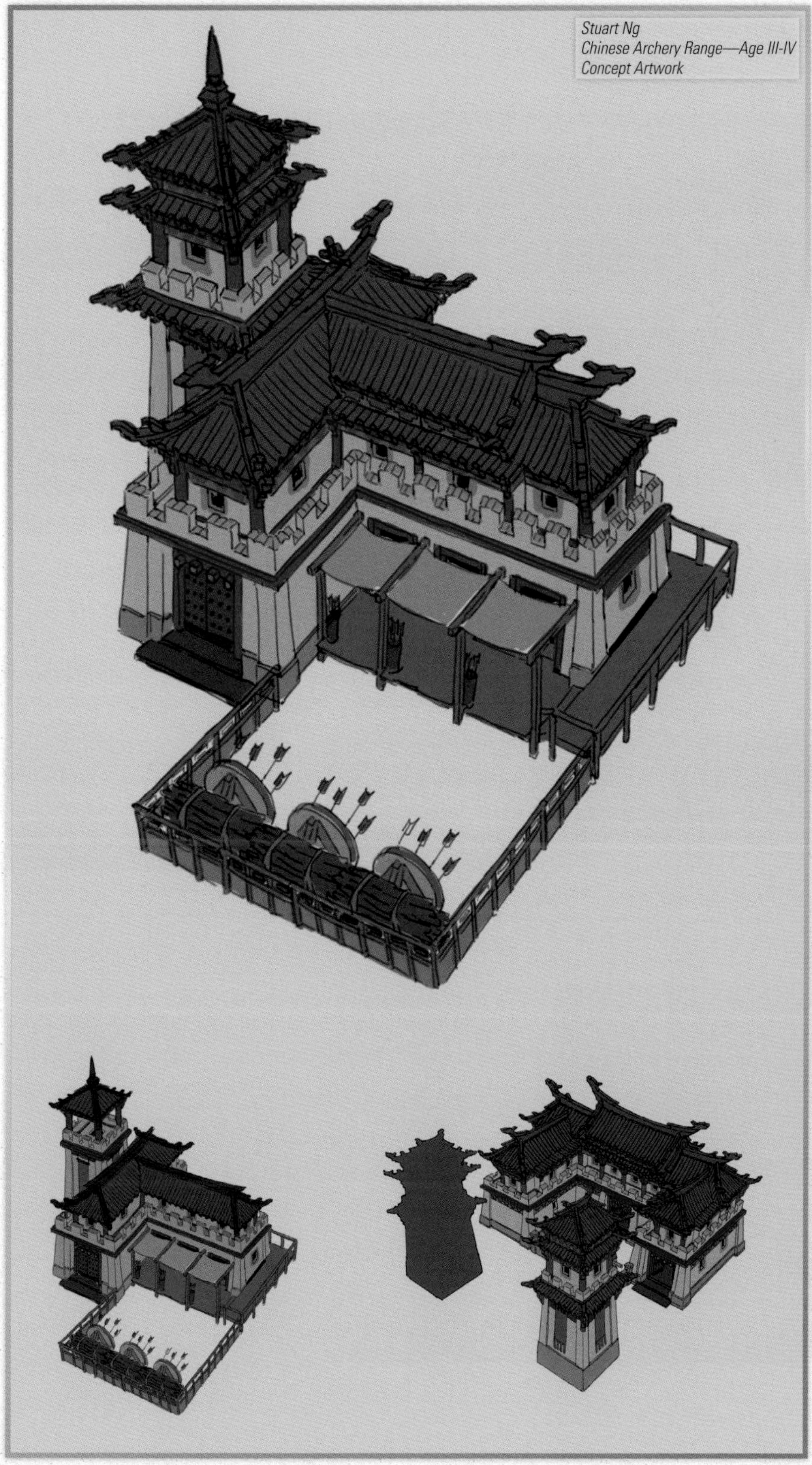

Stuart Ng
Chinese Archery Range—Age III-IV
Concept Artwork

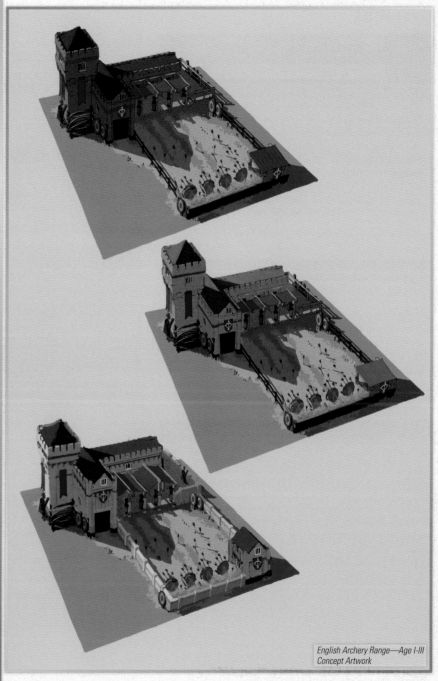

English Archery Range—Age I-III
Concept Artwork

4

Barracks

Along with the Archery Range, the Barracks forms the backbone of your military production. It's also the only military production building that every civilization has access to during the Dark Age, and as such, it's likely to be the one that you'll use for the longest amount of time. From your Barracks you're able to produce melee infantry ranging from light units during the earlier ages, all the way to heavy melee specialists later in the game.

Building Stats

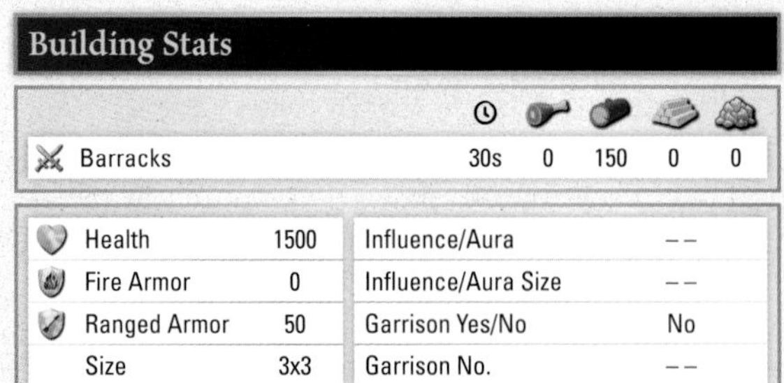

	Time	Food	Wood	Gold	Stone
Barracks	30s	0	150	0	0

Health	1500	Influence/Aura	--
Fire Armor	0	Influence/Aura Size	--
Ranged Armor	50	Garrison Yes/No	No
Size	3x3	Garrison No.	--

Although the Barracks are available from the start, you don't always have to build it straight away. Keep in mind that 150 Wood is a big investment early on and Spearmen alone are not very effective on the offensive.

If your opponent focuses on heavy cavalry play, Barracks are almost mandatory to produce the units required to efficiently counter their advances.

Usage

The Early Ages

Even though you have access to a Barracks from the start of a game, be careful not to over-invest in melee infantry because they can be easily countered by ranged units once you reach Age II. Try to produce them slowly, and save some resources so that you can produce your own ranged or melee cavalry units to pair with them and deal with any counters once those buildings become available.

The Late Ages

In the later stages of the game it's important that your resources are going out nearly as fast as they're coming in, which means you'll need to construct more production buildings based on your overall economic output and unit requirements. As a general rule, try to have as many buildings as you need for constant production, while not queuing more than 1-3 units at each building.

If you manage to secure a forward location on the map, make sure to claim it with more production buildings. This serves two purposes: first of all you can reinforce your army quicker, and second, if you get pushed back, your opponent has to tear down these forward buildings before advancing, giving you time to regroup and counterattack.

Strategic Considerations

Chinese

The Palace Guard that can be produced at Chinese Barracks is largely the same as the more common Man-at-Arms, but the **Battle Hardened** technology they gain access to in Age IV gives them a significant health boost and improves their survivability considerably.

English

The English are the only civilization that is capable of fielding the mighty Man-at-Arms unit as early as Age I. The so-called "Vanguard Man-at-Arms" is of course weaker than their later incarnations, but it's the best military unit available in the earliest stage of the game. Unlike other civilizations, however, they cannot produce Spearmen until Age II, which means that they have to rely on heavy melee infantry to fend off early attacks, and that comes at a considerably higher resource cost.

Additionally, the English Man-at-Arms benefit from a unique technology called **Armor Clad**, which becomes available in Age III and provides +2 melee and range armor, and so if you're using a lot of heavy melee infantry, you should prioritize this upgrade over the standard Blacksmith upgrades. This upgrade ensures that the English Man-at-Arms stays relevant in all stages of the game, making them an excellent addition to any army.

Holy Roman Empire

The Holy Roman Empire is the ultimate melee infantry civilization, and they're predestined to make heavy use of the Barracks. Similar to the English, the Holy Roman Empire gain access to Early Men-at-Arms in the Feudal Age, providing them with a sturdy defensive and offensive melee infantry unit.

It's in the Castle Age, however, where the Barracks of the Holy Roman Empire truly start to shine. They not only gain access to two unique and strong upgrades for their Men-at-Arms **(Heavy Maces** and **Two-Handed Weapons)**, but also to a unique light melee infantry unit: the Landsknecht. This unit specializes in taking down other infantry and groups of units by using their massive Zweihander to inflict damage across a small area in front of them, allowing them to hit multiple units at once. Furthermore, their Spearmen also get a unique upgrade, **Riveted Chain Mail**, which increases their melee armor by +3, and that extra durability lets them stand up to melee cavalry for longer so they can inflict more damage. It's the combination of all of these units and upgrades that make the other civilizations fear the Holy Roman Empire's infantry.

Abbasid Dynasty

The Barracks have a special role for the Abbasid Dynasty. Their early access to unique technologies for their Spearmen, combined with the ability to construct siege units right away in Age II, allows them to make extremely aggressive moves early on, making them a prime pick for players that like to play offensively as soon as the game begins.

Barracks Technologies (P.45)

Technology	Unit		Age	Civ
Armor Clad	Man-at-Arms	●	III	Eng
Battle Hardened	Palace Guard	●	IV	Chi
Heavy Maces	Man-at-Arms	●	III	HRE
Two-Handed Weapons	Man-at-Arms	●	III	HRE
Riveted Chain Mail	Spearman	●	IV	HRE

Unit Production

Unit		Age	Civ
Spearman		I	All - Eng
Hardened Spearman		II	All
Veteran Spearman		III	All
Elite Spearman		IV	All
Vanguard Man-at-Arms	●	I	Eng
Early Man-at-Arms		II	Eng/HRE
Man-at-Arms		III	All - Chi/HRE
Elite Man-at-Arms		IV	All - Chi/HRE
Palace Guard	●	III	Chi
Elite Palace Guard	●	IV	Chi
Landsknecht	●	III	HRE
Elite Landsknecht	●	IV	HRE

Stuart Ng
Chinese Barracks—Age IV
Concept Artwork

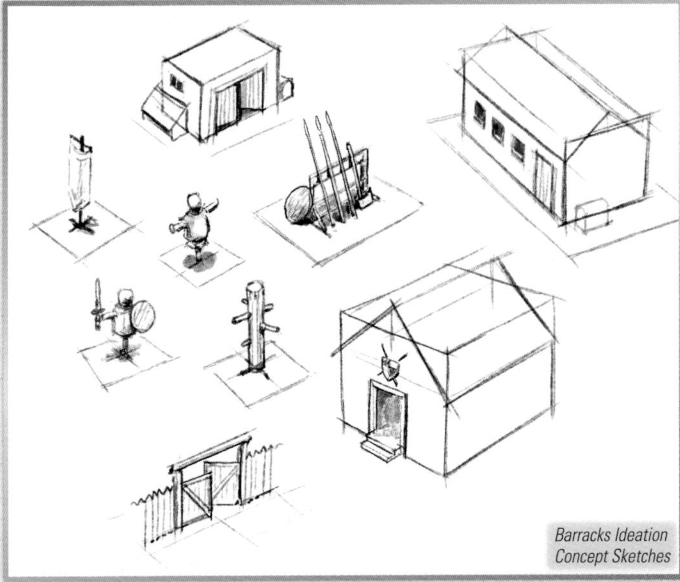
Barracks Ideation
Concept Sketches

Building Design

"We made sure that all buildings would have both busily detailed areas where player's eyes would be drawn, and negative spaces where their eyes could rest. Where we wanted the players' eyes to focus on the functionality and what not, is where we put the most contrasting or busy details. For areas such as walls, it made sense to have these as resting spaces. Walls and roofs take a good proportion of screen space in a fully built town, so we took advantage of these to story-tell using accents of colour to give the impression of a worn look."

– Staurt Ng
Senior Concept Artist, Relic

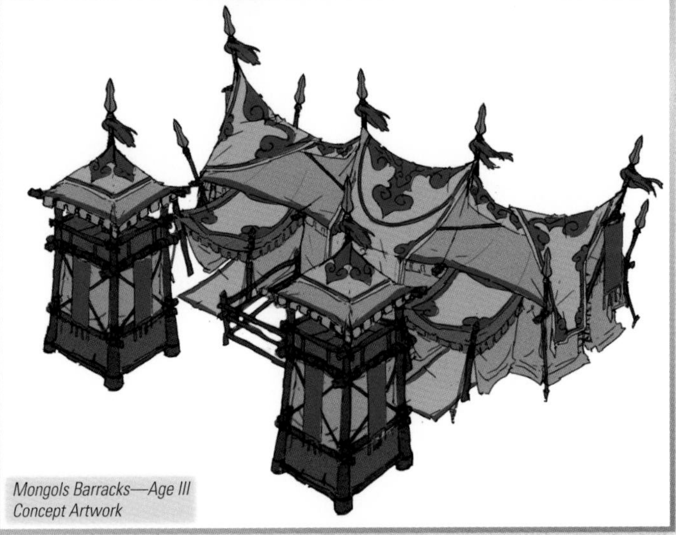
Mongols Barracks—Age III
Concept Artwork

Kevin Lam
Abbasid Barracks—Age IV
Concept Artwork

The Design Foundation

"Once we had concepted what the English would look like, that laid the foundation of some of the core buildings such as the barracks, archery range, stables, and siege workshop. We had ideas for the other buildings certainly, but as soon as we established the layout and shape language for those four core buildings, we began experimenting with how a French or Holy Roman Empire version of that same building type would look like. Our biggest reads were the look of the roof, windows, trims, and naturally the colour and value of the building. Playing with each of those aspects allowed us to come up with the different looks of each of the civilizations and establish a consistent way that players could look at each of the core buildings."

– Stuart Ng
Senior Concept Artist, Relic

Kevin Lam
Delhi Sultanate Barracks—Age I-IV
Concept Artwork

Stuart Ng
English Barracks—Age I-IV
Concept Artwork

Micro Versus Macro

"Macro in Age games is very tricky! You have to manage income for four different resources and keep production running smoothly by adding on new lumber mills, farms, and mining camps. When the enemy raids you, they can cause damage even if they don't kill any units! Forcing your lumber jacks to stop cutting wood could mean you no longer have the resources to keep your archery ranges producing. Where players spend their valuable attention resource between army micromanagement and economic development is a huge decision point!

Because the macro is complex we wanted the army management to be more forgiving. It doesn't make sense to have an entire army die in 3 seconds when so much time and attention is required to get the resources to build that army. So we have longer combat than pervious titles to allow for a more equal amount of player time spent between micro and macro."

– Eric Wrobel
Senior Designer, Balance Lead, Relic

Dock

Type	Age
Military & Economy Building, Trade Site	I

On any map where water is a dominant feature or bodies of water separate players, the Dock will play a pivotal role in all aspects of gameplay. Docks can create all manner of ships, both for combat and for economic purposes, so they have something to suit all playstyles and strategies. Because of their early availability, you can use them to work towards your goal right from the start of a match. Any ship that's within the aura range of a Dock also gets automatically repaired, so on maps with rivers or smaller bodies of water, your ships can easily return for a quick repair, saving you a lot of resources on new ships in the long run.

Building Stats

	Time	Food	Wood	Gold	Stone
Dock	30s	0	150*	0	0

*Abbasid Dynasty cost is only 75 Wood

Health	1500	Influence/Aura	Aura
Fire Armor	0	Influence/Aura Size	7.5 Tiles
Ranged Armor	50	Garrison Yes/No	Yes
Size	4x4	Garrison No.	3

Fishing Boats aren't the only things that can drop Food off at a Dock, any Villagers gathering Shoreline Fish can also take advantage of that service.

French—Age IV

Holy Roman Empire—Age IV

English—Age IV

Abbasid Dynasty—Age IV

Delhi Sultanate—Age IV

Strategic Considerations

Generating Enhancement

Automatically repairs nearby damaged naval units.

Open Water Maps (Warring Island, Archipelago)

You tend to start on your own island on water-based maps, and since you're usually separated from other players by an ocean, building a Dock as soon as you're able in Age I is almost mandatory. Your only other option is to play as if you were on a land-based map, and then build a Transport Ship to sail the army to your opponent's island. This is an extremely risky play, however, because if you don't manage to defeat your opponent with that initial attack, you'll be so far behind economically that it'll be very difficult to recover.

Building a Dock early lets you start taking advantage of the additional Food resources out in the water. As soon as you've established a Lumber Camp and have 150 Wood in the bank, tell your Sheep-gathering Villagers to build a Dock next to some Shoreline Fish. You should then begin collecting Food this way, because it's one of the fastest

Since naval units come with a huge cost, you don't need to invest into a lot of Docks early on. One or two Docks will be sufficient for quite a while, and only in the later stages of the game will you need to build more.

Another way to make use of Docks when your opponent has already seized control of the crossings is to build a Transport Ship and fill it with land military units and find a way to sneak them around your opponent's blockade in a flanking maneuver.

ways to accumulate Food in the game. Any new Villagers you produce should then be sent off to gather Wood so that you can start ship production in earnest. Food is harder to come by on land in these maps, which means you'll want to build lots of Fishing Boats.

River Maps (Danube River, Mongolian Heights, Confluence)

The fighting factions on river maps are separated by rivers that flow and carve their way through the land. Depending on the biome you get, the only way to cross the rivers will either be by bridge or ford; controlling these crossings, and thus the rivers flowing through the lands, is crucial for success, and that can primarily be achieved through your Dock. Incendiary Ships shine in the tight confines of rivers, because it's much harder for your opponent to escape their blast radius, and you can even use them against land units crossing over a ford carelessly. Once you have control of a crossing, make sure to block off the opponent's side of it with walls and other fortifications to make it even harder for them to reclaim it.

There are no Deep Sea Fish on these maps, only Shoreline Fish. This means your Dock will mostly be used as a military production building rather than a drop-off point. You can still collect the Shoreline Fish with your Villagers after building the Dock, and if you're lucky, there might also be a patch of Deer nearby that you could make use of. Keep in mind that the rivers on these maps can sometimes be quite far from your starting location, which makes early attempts at controlling them quite risky; you'll need to gauge the situation carefully in every match. Water may not be the main focal point on these maps, but it's an important component nonetheless.

Lake Maps (Ancient Spires, Black Forest, Boulder Bay, Nagari)

Lake Maps generally feature one or more lakes that players will either have to fight on or around. If you can control the bountiful Fish found in lake waters then you'll gain a significant economical and positional advantage over your opponent. Dominating these waters will not always ensure victory, because the lakes can still be circumvented and avoided

Black Forest is the exception among the lake maps, because the lake is always behind your base on that map, and you need only place a Dock to make Fishing Boats for the Fish, so there's no need for naval combat units.

Dock Technologies (P.45)

Technology	Affects		Age	Civilizations
Extended Lines	Fishing 1/2		II	All
Drift Nets	Fishing 2/2		III	All
Additional Sails	Naval		II	All - Abb
Navigator Lookout	Naval		III	All
Armored Hull	Naval		III	All - Chi/Mon
Extra Ballista	Attack Ship		III	All - Rus/Sul/Abb
Chaser Cannons	Warship		IV	All - Rus
Explosives	Demolition Ship		IV	All
Shipwrights	Naval		II	Eng
Extra Hammocks	Naval		III	Chi
Long Guns	Naval		III	Fre
Fire Stations	Naval		II	HRE
Piracy	Naval		II	Mon
Clinker Construction	Lodya Archer Ship 1/2		III	Rus
Cedar Hulls	Lodya Archer Ship 2/2		IV	Rus
Patchwork Repairs	Naval		II	Sul
Teak Masts	Naval		II	Abb

by land units. But if you ignore or neglect the lakes, you're essentially racing against the clock, because the person that controls them controls the resources they contain, and they could prove invaluable in later stages of the game. Having a mix of Fishing Boats and other ships to protect them, along with enough land forces, can be a hard balance to achieve on these maps, and depending on what your opponent is doing you might need to focus on one side more than the other. Finding the right balance will often be the key to victory on these maps.

Kevin Lam
English Dock—Age III-IV
Concept Artwork

Technology Overview

The Dock provides you with a suite of standard technologies that are available to most civilizations, but there are also some unique upgrades that play into the themes of individual civilizations. For example, the Holy Roman Empire get an upgrade that increases the repair rate of docks, emphasizing their defensive capabilities, and the Mongols have **Piracy**, which grants you resources for destroying enemy ships, mimicking their ability to plunder resources from igniting buildings.

Of the more universal upgrades—if you're on a map with a lot of Fish to gather—the ones related to fishing, such as **Extended Lines** and **Drift Nets**, are extremely important. In Age II you can gain access to **Additional Sails**; if you're engaging in a lot of naval battles this can be an equally important upgrade, since it allows you to better flee from battles, or chase down retreating enemy ships. That's more important on open water maps, because on lakes and ponds there's not as much space to run away.

In the Castle Age, the **Extra Ballista** upgrade is very important and should be one of your first purchases upon reaching that point. It adds another ballista emplacement to your ships that can shoot in every direction, increasing the damage output of your ships significantly. In Age IV, you gain the ability to research **Chaser Cannons**, which gives Warships +1 range, allowing them to out range Keeps. Although not from a Dock, you shouldn't neglect the **Chemistry** technology in this Age, because the extra damage can be a big boost for you gunpowder ships.

Unit Production

Unit	Age	Civilization
Fishing Boat	I	All - Rus
Transport Ship	I	All - Rus
Trade Ship	II	All - Rus
Galley	II	Eng/HRE
Hulk	III	Eng/Fre/HRE
Demolition Ship	III	Eng/Fre/HRE
Carrack	IV	Eng/Fre/HRE
Explosive Junk	III	Chi/Mon
Baochuan	IV	Chi/Mon
Dhow	II	Sul/Abb
Baghlah	III	Sul/Abb
Explosive Dhow	III	Sul/Abb
Xebec	IV	Sul/Abb
Junk	II	Chi
War Junk	III	Chi
Galleass	III	Fre
Light Junk	II	Mon
Lodya Fishing Boat	I	Rus
Lodya Transport Ship	I	Rus
Lodya Trade Ship	II	Rus
Lodya Attack Ship	II	Rus
Lodya Demolition Ship	III	Rus

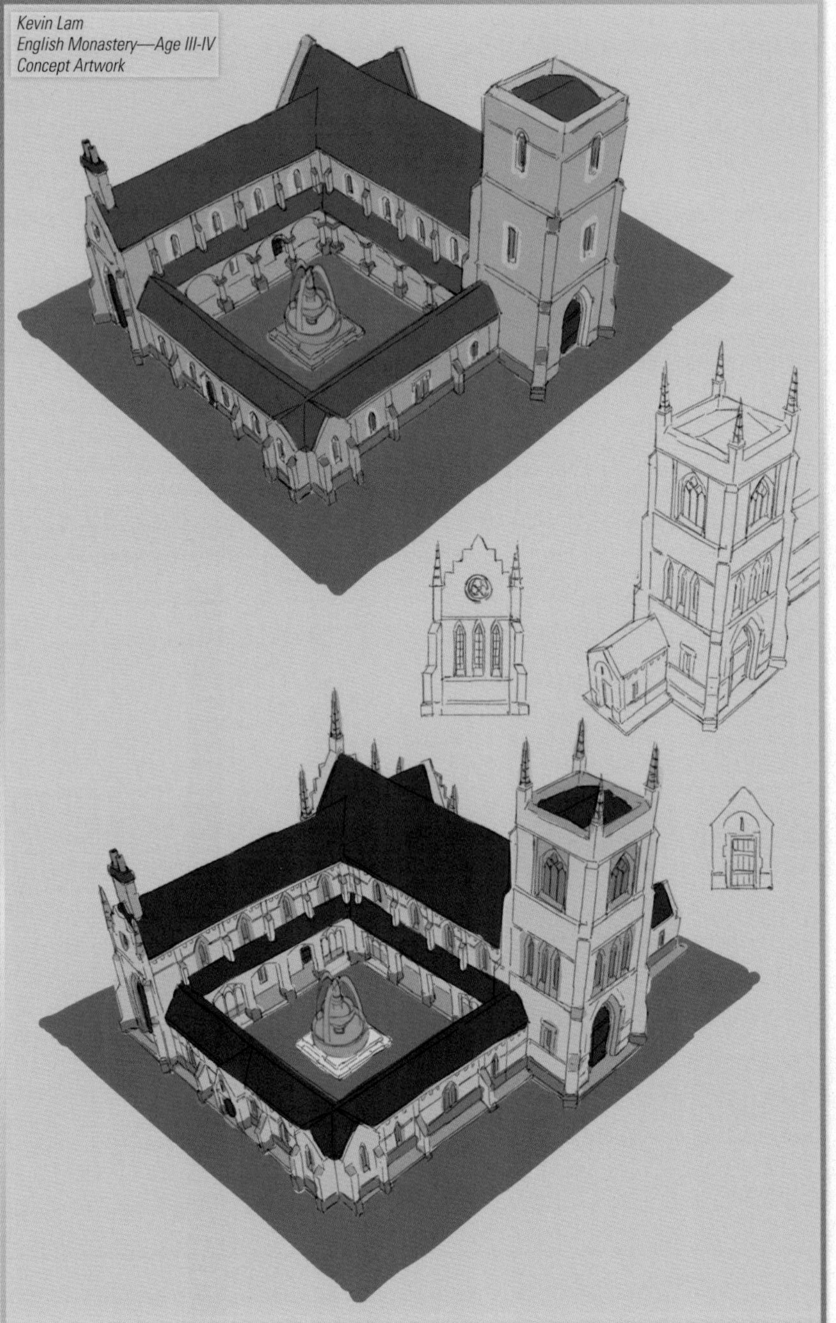
Kevin Lam
English Monastery—Age III-IV
Concept Artwork

Monastery

Type	Age
Religious Building	III

Prayer Tent

Type	Age
Religious Building	III

Religious buildings have two main purposes: producing religious units, and storing precious Relics to generate Gold over time. There's a lot of nuance within each civilization's individual religious buildings, but they'll always offer significant benefits to both your military and economy, regardless of your playstyle.

Building Stats: Monastery

	Time	Food	Wood	Gold	Stone
Monastery	25s	0	200	0	0

Health	2100	Influence/Aura	--
Fire Armor	0	Influence/Aura Size	--
Ranged Armor	50	Garrison Yes/No	No
Size	4x4	Garrison No.	--

Chinese Monastery—Age IV

Building Stats: Prayer Tent

	Time	Food	Wood	Gold	Stone
Prayer Tent	25s	0	200	0	0

Health	2100	Influence/Aura	--
Fire Armor	0	Influence/Aura Size	--
Ranged Armor	50	Garrison Yes/No	No
Size	4x4	Garrison No.	--

Mongols Prayer Tent—Age IV

Mosque

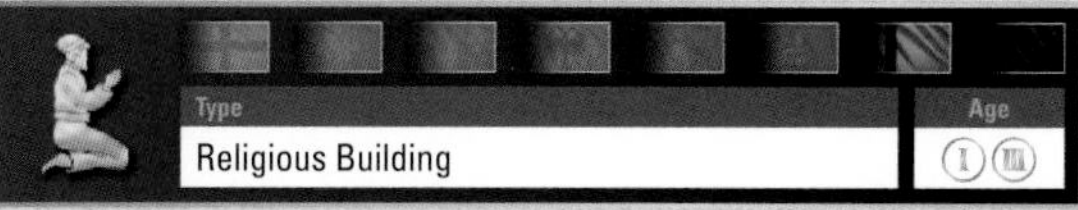

Type	Age
Religious Building	I III

Building Stats: Mosque (Delhi Sultanate)

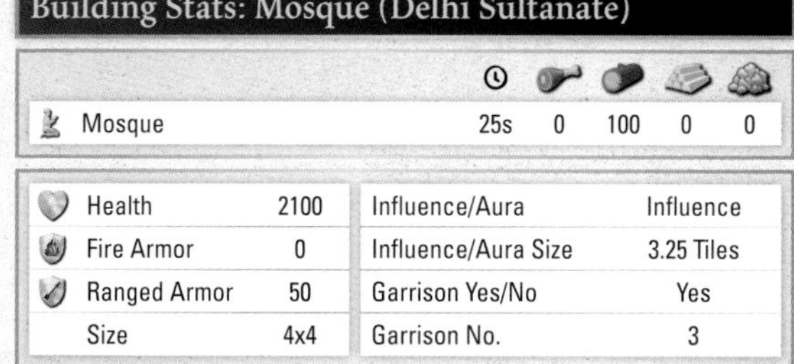

	Time	Food	Wood	Gold	Stone
Mosque	25s	0	100	0	0

Health	2100	Influence/Aura	Influence
Fire Armor	0	Influence/Aura Size	3.25 Tiles
Ranged Armor	50	Garrison Yes/No	Yes
Size	4x4	Garrison No.	3

Building Stats: Mosque (Abbasid Dynasty)

	Time	Food	Wood	Gold	Stone
Mosque	25s	0	200	0	0

Health	2100	Influence/Aura	--
Fire Armor	0	Influence/Aura Size	--
Ranged Armor	50	Garrison Yes/No	No
Size	4x4	Garrison No.	--

Delhi Sultanate Mosque—Age IV

Usage

Due to the amount of unique abilities that religious buildings and units offer, by the time you reach the Castle Age—which allows most civilizations to build them—building one should be strongly considered. Depending on the type of match and opponent you're playing against, your need for it may vary, but in game types where the Sacred win condition is active, they're all but essential. Under that win condition, all Sacred Sites must be captured by a religious unit and held for 10 minutes to win the game, and since they'll be highly contested areas, you may need to produce quite a few religious units.

Sacred Sites also generate a small amount of Gold over time, so even if that win condition isn't active, you should still try to capture them. Similar to Sacred Sites, Relics can also be used to generate Gold at a rate of 100 per minute each if you garrison one inside a religious building. In total you can store up to 20 Relics in one religious building, but you'll rarely find this many on the map. Even though their

4

late-game Gold generation is out-shined by other sources, such as Traders, Relics are still nice to have in long games since they can often give you just enough to get through a lull in your income.

Gold generation is not the only way that these buildings can aid your economy: they can also produce religious units that specialize in both healing your units, and converting enemy units to your side, both of which can save you a lot of resources. The religious unit—and subsequently the religious building—should be high on your priority list if you have high cost units with lots of health; it's better to heal those units while in or out of battle than to replace them every time.

Large groups of religious units will rarely be called for, so one or two religious buildings at most should be sufficient in most games.

If just a single tile of a Delhi Sultanate Mosque connects to another building, that building will benefit from the research time reduction.

Strategic Considerations

Delhi Sultanate

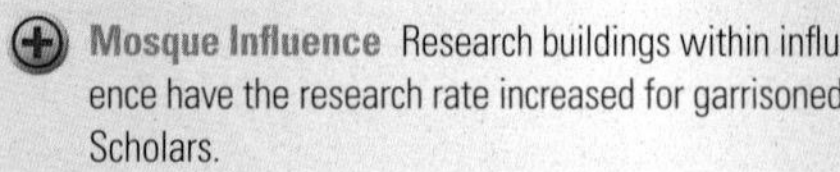

Generating Enhancement

Mosque Influence Research buildings within influence have the research rate increased for garrisoned Scholars.

The Delhi Sultanate's Mosque plays a key role in their development. It's a lot cheaper than the religious buildings of the other civilizations, and those savings extended even further, because the first one built also comes with a Scholar garrisoned inside, saving you the cost of training one. On those merits alone it should earn a spot among your mandatory builds during Age I.

Their Mosque also has a large influence range with many benefits that come from having buildings inside it, so when you place a Mosque, make sure as many drop-off, military and technology buildings as possible are within its boundaries. The Delhi Sultanate has no associated resource

Unit Production: Monastery

Unit	Age	Civilization
Monk	III	Eng/Fre/Chi
Prelate	III	HRE
Warrior Monk	III	Rus

Unit Production: Mosque

Unit	Age	Civilization
Scholar	I	Sul
Imam	III	Abb

Unit Production: Prayer Tent

Unit	Age	Civilization
Shaman	III	Mon

Monastery Technologies (P.45)

Technology	Type	Age	Civilization
Herbal Medicine	Healing	III	All - Mon/Sul/Abb
Piety	Religious	IV	All - Mon/Sul/Abb
Tithe Barns	Religious	IV	All - Mon/Sul/Abb
Benediction	Construction	III	HRE
Devoutness	Gathering	III	HRE
Inspired Warriors	Religious	III	HRE
Blessing Duration	Religious	III	Rus

Mosque Technologies (P.45)

Technology	Type	Age	Civilization
Herbal Medicine	Healing	III	Sul/Abb
Piety	Religious	IV	Sul/Abb
Tithe Barns	Religious	IV	Sul/Abb
All-Seeing Eye	Religious	I	Sul
Efficient Production	Religious	I	Sul
Sanctity	Religious	I	Sul
Swiftness	Religious	I	Sul

Prayer Tent Technologies (P.45)

Technology	Type	Age
Herbal Medicine	Healing	III
Herbal Medicine (Improved)	Healing	III
Piety	Religious	IV
Piety (Improved)	Religious	IV
Tithe Barns	Religious	IV
Tithe Barns (Improved)	Religious	IV
Monastic Shrines	Production	IV

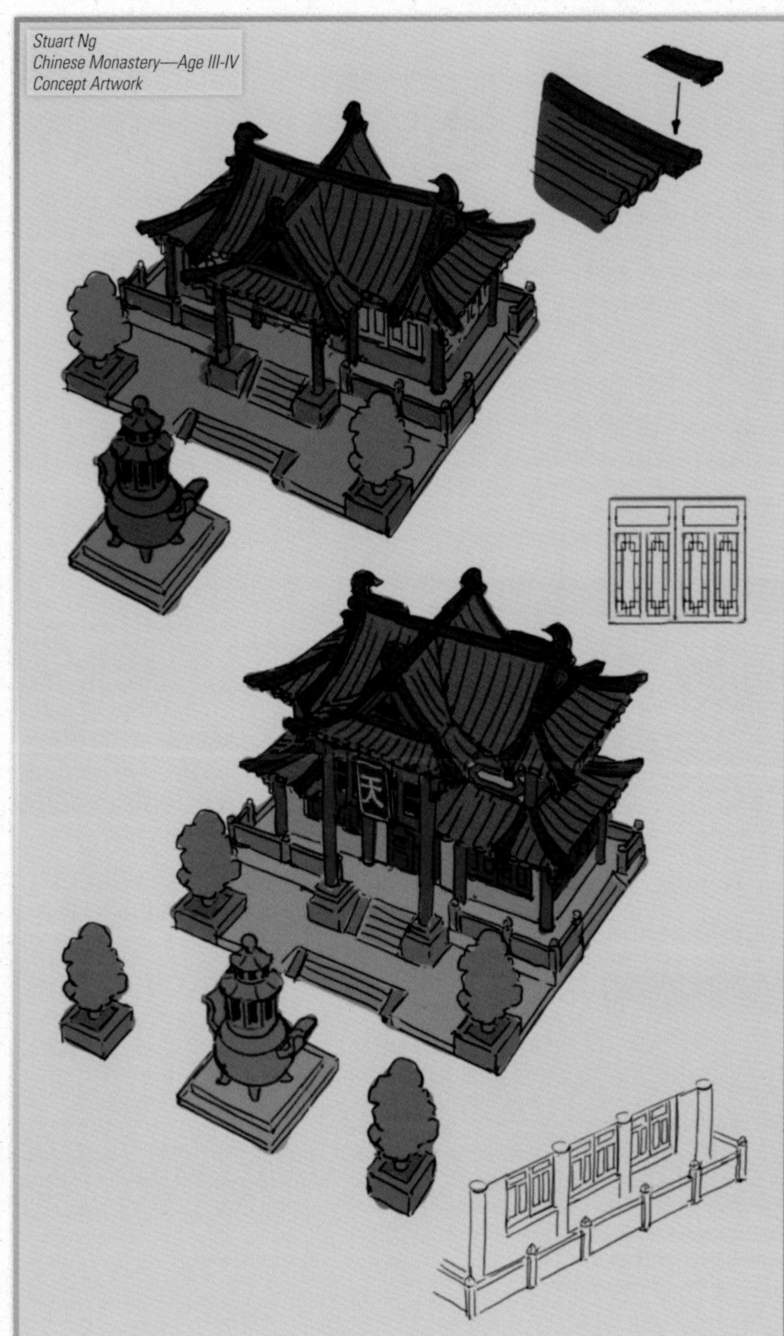
Stuart Ng
Chinese Monastery—Age III-IV
Concept Artwork

costs with acquiring any of their technology upgrades, but they complete at a significantly slower speed than other civilizations. Any Scholars garrisoned inside of a Mosque will reduce the research times at buildings within its influence range, and regardless of how far apart they are, all garrisoned Scholars count towards your global research time reduction. Each subsequent garrisoned Scholar leads to slightly less of a reduction than the previous one, but by the time you have nine garrisoned you'll be at time parity with other civilizations.

The research time for any upgrade started in buildings within the influence range of a Mosque will automatically speed up as you garrison more Scholars, so upgrades should be started immediately rather than waiting until you have more Scholars. At 150 Gold, however, Scholars are an expensive purchase early on. This means that your first additional Scholar should probably wait until after you reach the Feudal Age, because delaying the Age advancement for one Scholar is usually not worth it. Investing in more Scholars and more Mosques will be vital for the quick advancement of your empire once you begin aging up, so once you have the resources available, it's important to invest them into these buildings and units.

Holy Roman Empire

The Holy Roman Empire is in a unique position here compared to all the other civilizations, because they're able to produce their religious unit in Age I from a Town Center, taking away one of a religious building's roles. They also have the **Regnitz Cathedral** that can house up to three Relics each to generate Gold, another functionality that's usually reserved for a religious building. Therefore, an extra Monastery early in the Castle Age is only important if you want to make use of the special upgrades that you can access from it. The standout options are **Devoutness** for increasing the inspiring effect of the Prelate by another 10%, and **Inspired Warriors** to allow them to inspire military units.

Mongols

At first glance you might think that there's nothing special about the Mongol Prayer Tent compared to the religious buildings of other civilizations, but once you reach Age IV, you can access to a technology gives the Prayer Tent a lot of extra utility. **Monastic Shrines** basically allows Prayer Tents to act as mini Ovoos, in that any buildings within their influence range will have access to improved production and technologies, without having to be close to an Ovoo. The only thing it doesn't grant is the automatic Stone generation, but your Ovoo is locked in place at a Stone Outcropping, while you can freely move your Prayer Tent around like other Mongol buildings, so it's a fair trade-off.

Rus

Building a Monastery should be a high priority as soon as you reach the Castle Age when you're playing as the Rus, because they're the only civilization that are able to heavily invest in religious units for aggressive use. Warrior Monks have decent fighting ability and high mobility, two things that most other religious units are lacking. Their mobility means they can collect Relics and reach Sacred Sites long before other religious units, and also get to key engagements faster so they can heal, and even improve the combat effectiveness of your military units. To improve their supportive capabilities even further you should consider investing into the unique **Blessing Duration** upgrade that increases the duration of Saint's Blessing by 10 seconds.

Siege Workshop

If you have need of some heavy artillery to destroy your opponent's base or breach their defenses, there's a good chance that the tool for the job can be built at the Siege Workshop. Siege engines that specialize in taking out infantry can also be constructed here, so the Siege Workshop is a versatile and useful building to have in many situations, although depending on the strategy you're attempting to employ, it may not always be necessary.

Building Stats

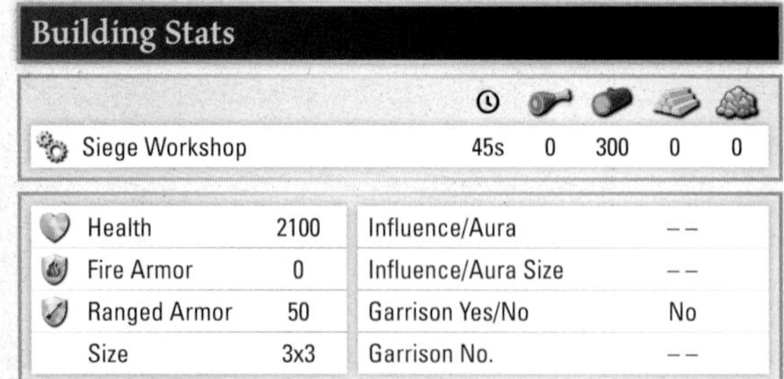

	Time	Food	Wood	Gold	Stone
Siege Workshop	45s	0	300	0	0

Health	2100	Influence/Aura	--
Fire Armor	0	Influence/Aura Size	--
Ranged Armor	50	Garrison Yes/No	No
Size	3x3	Garrison No.	--

Usage

You should consider building a Siege Workshop when it becomes available in Age III if you're planning on involving Springalds or Mangonels in your overall strategy. Springalds are best for taking out other siege engines or religious units, whereas Mangonels are better against large groups of infantry, so pay attention to the types of units your opponent is fielding and build the appropriate counter. If you're taking a more defensive approach, then you'll want to go with Mangonels since they can fire over your walls to help repel attacking armies.

Regardless of your approach during Age III, you should always make sure you build at least one Siege Workshop before you advance to the Imperial Age; the powerful gunpowder units you gain access to in that age can give you a massive power spike, especially if you get there before your opponent.

Siege Workshops should be built close to the locations they are needed so that if you see an opportunity to push your opponent back, your slow-moving siege engines can get there as soon as possible.

Late in games it's important to always have some siege engines in your army because there's nothing worse than winning a battle, but being unable to advance and breakthrough your opponent's defenses because you don't have any heavy siege engines with you.

Strategic Considerations

Chinese

As the Chinese civilization you'll have the unique bonus of getting **Chemistry** for free upon reaching the Imperial Age, giving all of the gunpowder units you produce an immediate boost in power producing.Additionally, the Chinese do not have access to Mangonels, so if you find yourself in need of an anti-infantry siege engine you should opt for the Nest of Bees instead, since it can accomplish similar things, albeit at a shorter range.

English

The English have the ability to research a special upgrade in the Imperial Age called **Shattering Projectiles**, which improves their Trebuchets by increasing the area of effect for every projectile. If you plan on only using your Trebuchets against buildings, then this upgrade should be a low priority. This upgrade is designed to make Trebuchets much more effective against large groups of infantry, effectively turning them into a longer range Mangonel, so if you're bringing Trebuchets with you to face other armies, then it's a worthwhile acquisition.

French

Gunpowder siege weapons are the French's forte, and not only do they get access to a more powerful version of a Bombard in the form of their Cannon, but they also get one of the most deadly anti-infantry weapons in the game: the Ribauldequin. If you want to use the French to their fullest potential, the **Chemistry** upgrade is arguably more important for them than most other civilizations.

You could instead opt to go the Landmark route and build the **College of Artillery** as your Age IV Landmark, giving you access to the Royal versions of gunpowder siege units. The downside to this approach is that you often want to produce siege units quickly and close to where they're needed, so you'll gain some damage, but lose some of that flexibility with the Landmark instead of a normal Siege Workshop. Because of the likely shift toward a lot of expensive siege engines in Age IV, make sure to save up plenty of Gold beforehand to ensure smooth production of them as the game continues.

Rus

While not directly related to the Siege Workshop, if you plan on using it to produce and use a lot of Siege Engines when playing as the Rus, you should consider building the **High Armory** as your Age IV Landmark. The upgrades available at this Landmark greatly improve any siege units fielded by the Rus, with **Siege Crew Training** allowing your Mangonels and Trebuchets to setup and teardown instantly, and **Fine Tuned Guns** increasing your Bombard attack speed. These upgrades make your siege weapons, and subsequently your whole army, much more mobile, allowing you to potentially raze buildings and be gone before your opponent can react.

Siege Workshop Technologies (P.45)

Technology	Unit	Age	Civilization
Greased Axels	Siege	III	All
Greased Axels (Improved)	Siege	IV	Mon
Roller Shutter Triggers	Springald	IV	All
Roller Shutter Triggers (Impr.)	Springald	IV	Mon
Adjustable Crossbars	Mangonel	IV	All - Chi
Adjustable Crossbars (Impr.)	Mangonel	IV	Mon
Siege Works	Siege	IV	All
Siege Works (Improved)	Siege	IV	Mon
Shattering Projectiles	Trebuchet	IV	Eng
Reload Drills	Bombard	IV	Chi
Reusable Barrels	Nest of Bees	IV	Chi
Pyrotechnics	Gunpowder	IV	Chi

Unit Production

Unit	Age	Civilization
Springald	III	All
Mangonel	III	All - Chi
Counterweight Trebuchet	III	All - Mon
Bombard	IV	All - Fre
Ribauldequin	IV	Eng/Fre
Culverin	IV	HRE/Abb
Cannon	IV	Fre
Nest of Bees	III	Chi
Traction Trebuchet	III	Mon

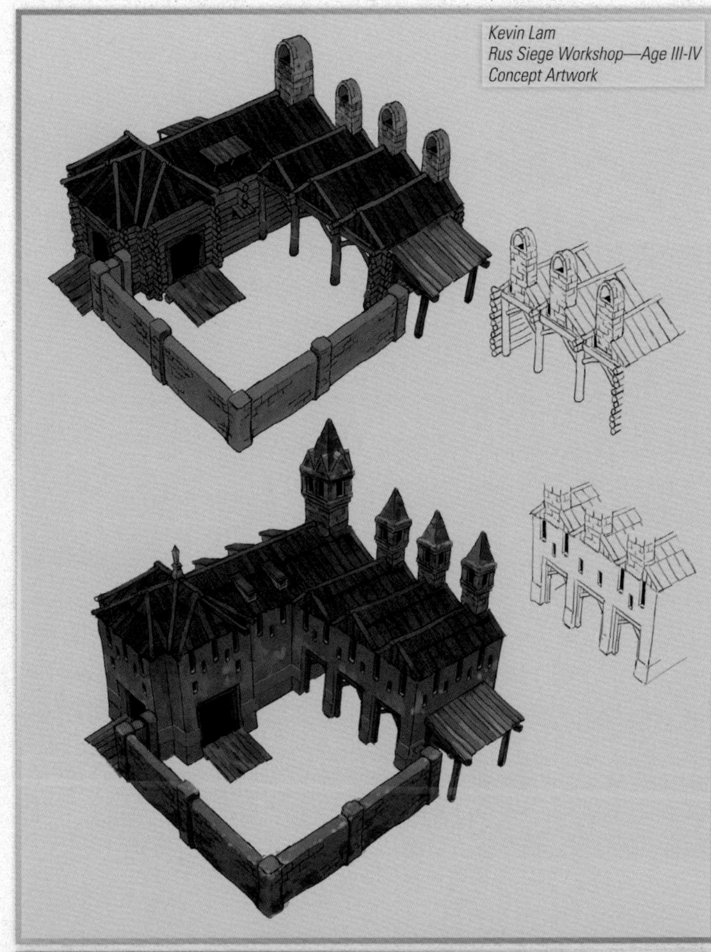

Kevin Lam
Rus Siege Workshop—Age III-IV
Concept Artwork

Balancing Siege Weapons

"The game's systems were built to be fun and accessible for a wide audience, but the overall balance is done with high level play in mind. For example, our siege weapons only deal splash damage to enemy troops. Making siege hit your own troops is a hardcore system that the elite players enjoy, but including it makes the game less accessible. After testing, we found that making siege weak against melee unit's torches added enough of a compelling positional dynamic to satisfy both player groups."

– Eric Wrobel
Senior Designer, Balance Lead, Relic

Stuart Ng
Chinese Siege Workshop—Age III-IV
Concept Artwork

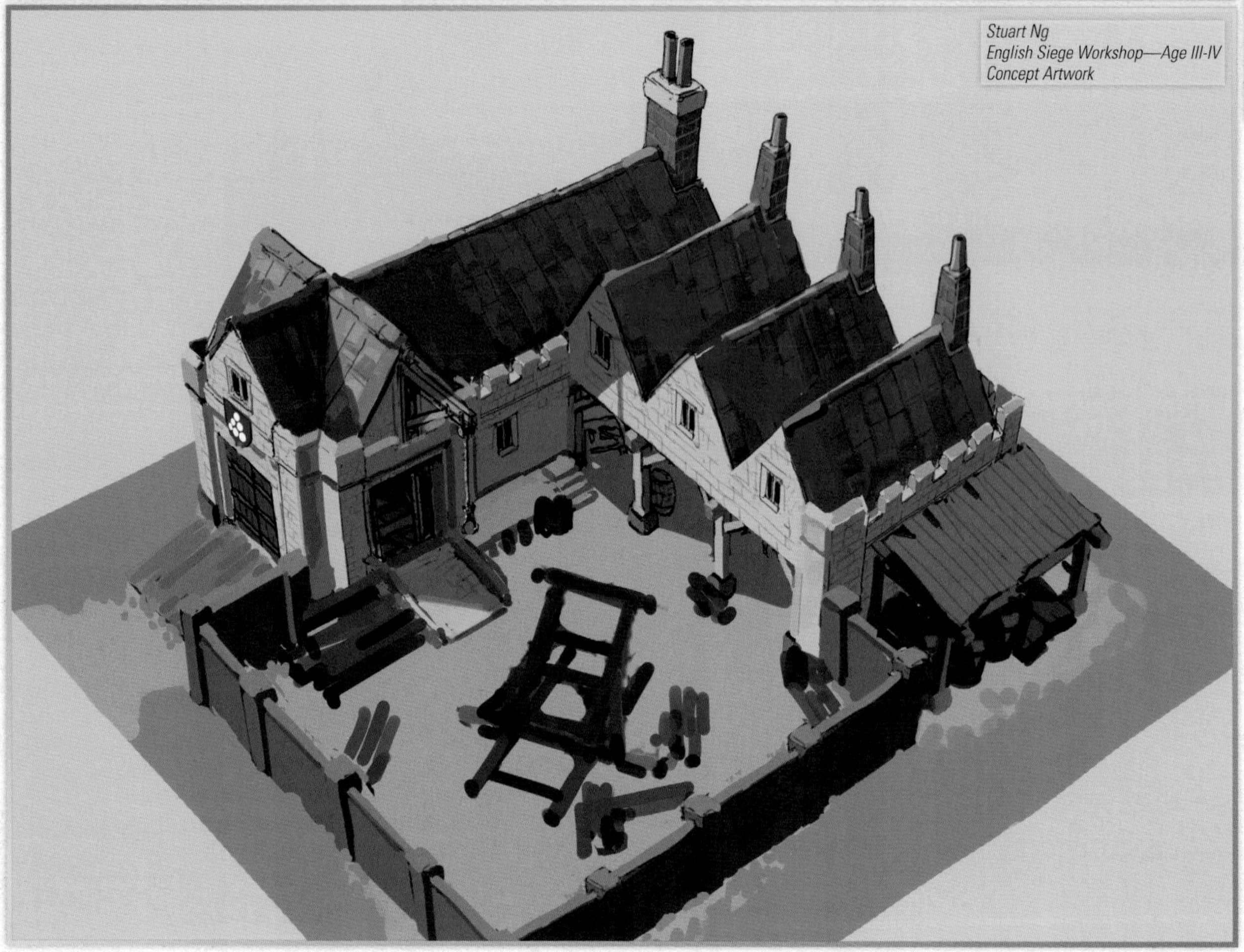

Stuart Ng
English Siege Workshop—Age III-IV
Concept Artwork

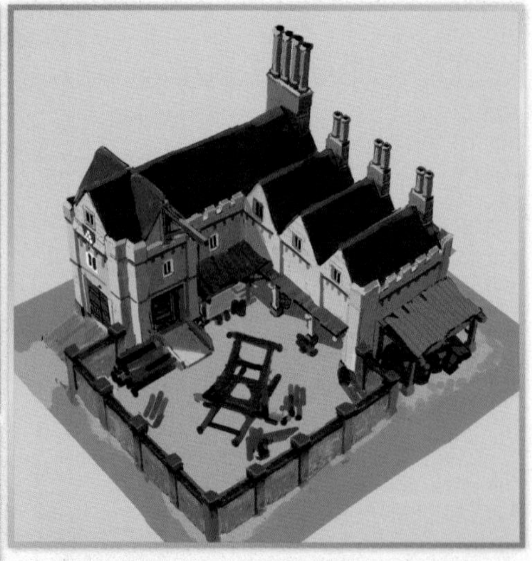

Ideas for Lighting

"Lighting was a major challenge. We have had fabulous ideas for time of day, changing weather, etc. but these kind of things all affect the surface and look of RTS units, readability, and recognition. It's imperative that the player can start committing to memory the shape-ology of the pieces. If we were to start shifting the light constantly, this changes what an element looks like slightly and we'd be in danger of breaking recognition muscle memory of key shapes. There are ways around that, but those always need more testing. One example we explored is the old hollywood western technique of "Day for Night,"—cameras couldn't pick up enough lighting during night shoots, so they shot during the day and added filters, which gave the image a wonderful quality that reminds me of classic storybook illustrators, like NC Wyeth, Howard Pyle and Dean Cornwell etc."

– Han Randhawa
Franchise Art Director, World's Edge

Stable

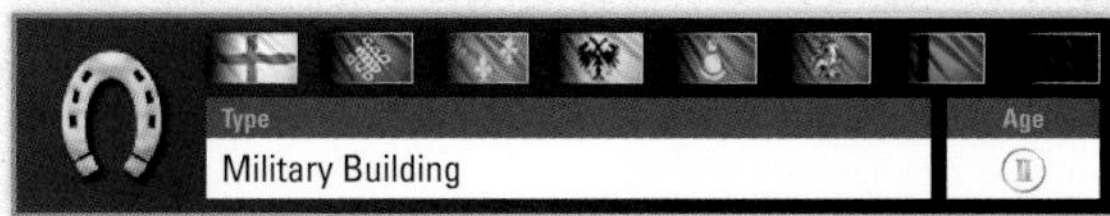

Stables are where you produce light and heavy melee cavalry, which you'll need for countering ranged infantry and destroying buildings; any ranged cavalry your civilization has access to is produced at their Archery Range. The speed of cavalry units opens up a world of tactical options from flanking to quick charges, so clever use of your Stables can often be a key component in victory.

Building Stats

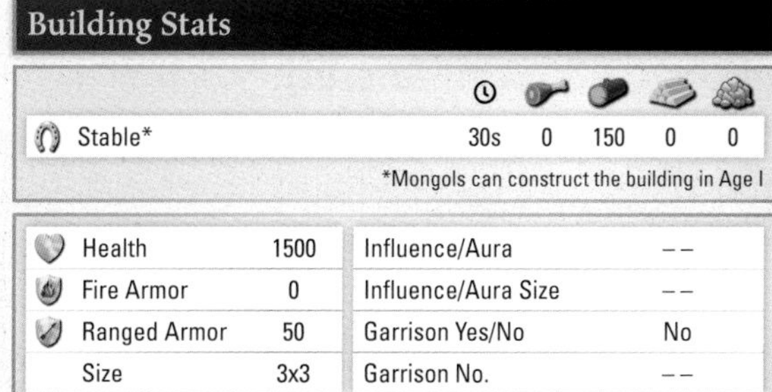

	Time	Food	Wood	Gold	Stone
Stable*	30s	0	150	0	0

*Mongols can construct the building in Age I

Health	1500	Influence/Aura	--
Fire Armor	0	Influence/Aura Size	--
Ranged Armor	50	Garrison Yes/No	No
Size	3x3	Garrison No.	--

Usage

In Age II, the main purpose of your Stable is to produce units that serve as counters to Archers as part of the Feudal Age Spearman/Archer/Horseman counter triangle. Furthermore, those units can act as fast-moving raiding units to harass enemy positions and Villagers. If you're facing down a mass of Archers, or enjoy a fast-paced playstyle, building a Stable should be a priority. This is especially true in scenarios where the distance between you and your opponent is very large, but you still want to rush them, which makes Horsemen the ideal early-game unit to use.

Heavy melee cavalry becomes available from Age III onwards for most civilizations, and then the role of cavalry extends to forming powerful groups of shock troopers, charging in and out of fights, and destroying enemy infantry and siege weapons as they go. If your opponent is using a lot of siege or ranged units, make sure to build enough Stables to produce plenty of cavalry units to counter them. On larger maps, cavalry tends to have a very prominent role since they can cover ground quickly, which will aid in maintaining map control. To make that job easier for them, however, you should build more Stables in forward positions to give them the quickest response time possible.

Due to their speed, cavalry can quickly charge ranged infantry to take them out before taking too much damage...

... that speed also gives you a lot of tactical flanking options to launch surprise attacks on your opponents while your main force distracts them.

Strategic Considerations

Chinese

If you progress to the Yuan Dynasty as the Chinese civilization, you'll be able to produce Fire Lancers from your Stables. These units serve as more powerful versions of the standard Horseman, and they specialize in razing buildings. If you haven't done so already by that point—and are considering doing some raiding along the outskirts of your opponent's position to weaken their perimeter—you should strongly consider building a Stable to gain access to this unit.

Delhi Sultanate

At a Delhi Sultanate Stable you'll gain access to the mighty War Elephant, which—for a significant price tag—can serve as a powerful meat shield for your other units, or as a siege weapon in its own right. Because of the War Elephant's siege capabilities, Stables can be considered a viable alternative to building a Siege Workshop once you reach Age III.

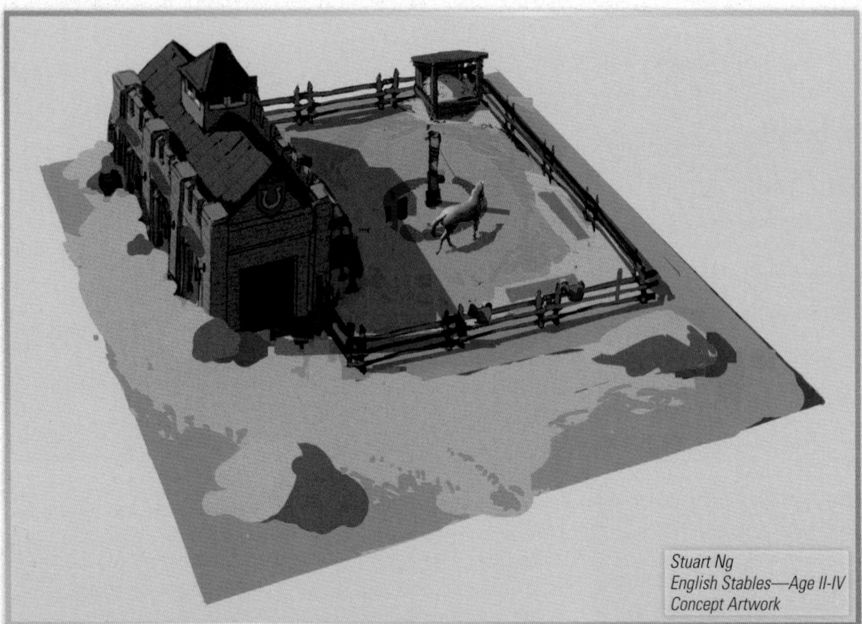

Stuart Ng
English Stables—Age II-IV
Concept Artwork

Unit Roles in Balancing

"With balance in AoE IV we really try to encourage combined arms; rarely is a single unit army combination the most effective.

A player making ranged units only will struggle to destroy buildings and so need to complement their army with either Melee Infantry, Cavalry, or Siege. They could research Siege Engineers from the Blacksmith and build a ram in the field or add a stable and train some supporting Horsemen which can torch buildings instead. Mangonels are a Longbow counter; they are designed to be "anti-mass" and deal large area-of-effect damage which can be especially damaging to lower health units. A player has a few options for countering Mangonels, though. From adding Springalds at the Siege Workshop which are especially good at countering other siege units, or training some mobile Horsemen which can flank the Siege units and torch them down quickly. "

– Zak "ZeroEmpires" Robinson
Senior Designer, Balance, Relic

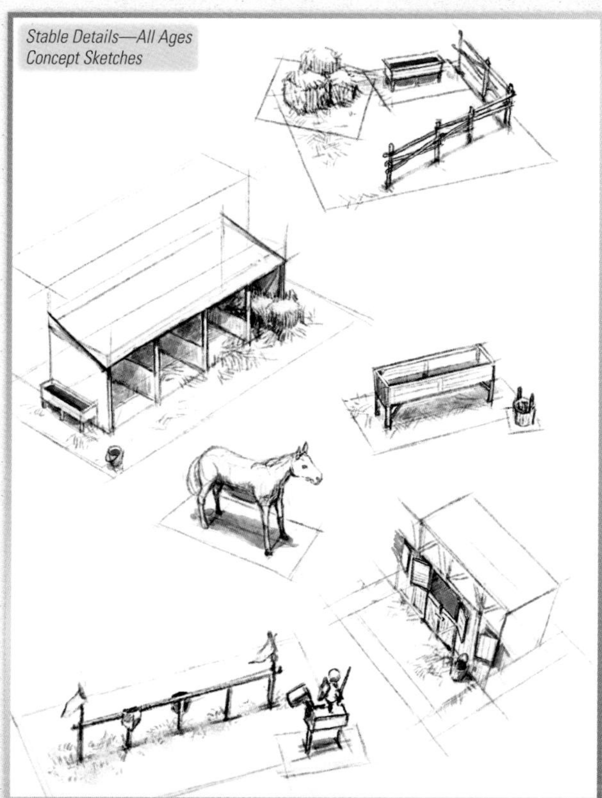
Stable Details—All Ages Concept Sketches

The Balancing Framework

"Asking whether building and unit costs and their effects on the economy came before their combat efficiency is like asking 'What came first the chicken or the egg?' We started by answering high level questions to provide a framework for the game and then modified things from there. How big should armies be in the feudal age? Do players have time to make strategic choices between the three archetypes: Rush, Tech, or Boom? How frequently do we want to see gunpowder units? Figuring out these high-level questions lead us to a starting point for determining numbers. But paper design only goes so far! It takes a huge amount of iteration to fit everything together and find the fun."

– Eric Wrobel
Senior Designer, Balance Lead, Relic

French

Along with gunpowder units, cavalry are one of the French civilization's strong points. They're one of three civilizations that are able to produce heavy melee cavalry from Age II, which can mix up the Feudal Age counter triangle significantly, giving the French cavalry a bigger punch early on.

Additionally, their special Royal Knights benefit from bonus damage for three seconds after their charge, as well as two unique technologies: **Chivalry** and **Cantled Saddles**. **Chivalry** gives Royal Knights the ability to regenerate health out of combat, so if you plan on producing a lot of them, this is an essential upgrade since it will save you a lot of resources over time. **Cantled Saddles** on the other hand increases the bonus damage after their initial charge, so if you're using them in large groups as shock troops, this upgrade will help to take out targets much quicker.

Mongols

Mongols are the only civilization that can build a Stable in Age I, giving them access to Early Horsemen, a unit that specializes in early game rushes. Early aggression should be seen as a risky move, however, that can either put you far ahead of your opponent, or set you back significantly if things go poorly. A very early rush with a few Horsemen (large groups will rarely be worth it) can be considered successful if you manage to force your opponent to produce Spearmen as a counter, and if you can idle their Villagers by destroying resource drop-off locations.

Rus

Like the French and Mongols, if you play as Rus you can produce heavy melee cavalry at their Stables in Age II, giving you the ability to create a unit your opponent might not be expecting or be able to counter. When you reach Age III you can increase the health of all your cavalry units with the **Boyar's Fortitude** technology, but given the cost of this upgrade, you should only consider it if you're heavily invested in the Castle Age or have Gold to spare. The **Knight Sabers** technology that you can acquire in Age IV should be considered an essential purchase and prioritized over any Blacksmith upgrades if you have a lot of Knights, because it increases their attack by +4.

Stable Technologies (P.45)

Technology	Affects	Age	Civ
Chivalry	Royal Knight	II	Fre
Cantled Saddles	Royal Knight	III	Fre
Boyar's Fortitude	Cavalry	III	Rus
Knight Sabers	Knight	IV	Rus
Armored Beasts	Elephant	IV	Sul

Unit Production

Unit	Age	Civ
Scout	II*	All
Early Horseman	I	Mon
Horseman	II	All
Veteran Horseman	III	All
Elite Horseman	IV	All
Early Knight	II	Rus
Knight	III	Eng/HRE/Rus
Elite Knight	IV	Eng/HRE/Rus
Lancer	III	Chi/Sul/Abb
Elite Lancer	IV	Chi/Sul/Abb
Fire Lancer	III	Chi
Elite Fire Lancer	IV	Chi
Royal Knight	II	Fre
Veteran Royal Knight	III	Fre
Elite Royal Knight	IV	Fre
War Elephant	III	Sul
Camel Rider	III	Abb
Elite Camel Rider	IV	Abb

*Mongols can produce this unit in Age I

Arsenal

*The English can build it in Age II during The Normans campaign.

The Arsenal is a Campaign mode only technology building that houses technologies for improving siege and ranged units, and it combines some of the functionality that's normally reserved for the Blacksmith and University/Madrasa in the Skirmish mode. In here you'll find a familiar suite of technologies, such as ranged attack and defense upgrades for infantry units, and the attack range and damage increases for your siege engines.

Building Stats

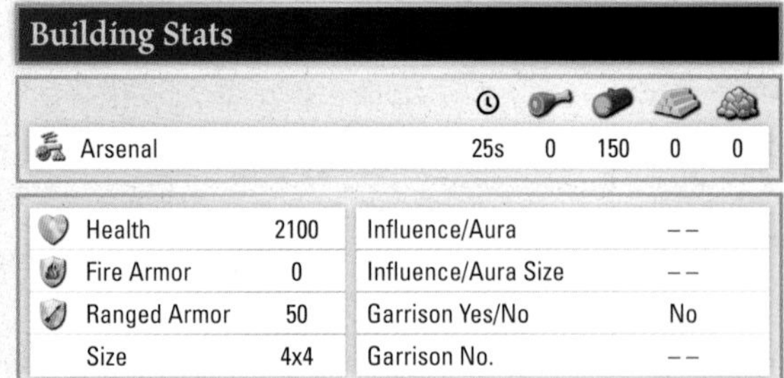

	Time	Food	Wood	Gold	Stone
Arsenal	25s	0	150	0	0

Health	2100	Influence/Aura	--
Fire Armor	0	Influence/Aura Size	--
Ranged Armor	50	Garrison Yes/No	No
Size	4x4	Garrison No.	--

Usage

The Arsenal can only be built from Age III onwards in most of the campaigns and since your Age is largely static in most missions, its availability will depend on which mission you're playing. If you can build one in the mission you're playing, however, you almost always should since the large variety of technologies available at the Arsenal means that it nearly always has something that you'll need. Due to the wide variety and amount of technologies, it can be very useful to build more than one Arsenal throughout the longer campaign missions, because having multiple upgrades researching simultaneously in different buildings will significantly speed things up.

Rus—Age IV

A lot of campaign missions require you to either assault an enemy position, or defend your own, and the siege engine upgrades available at an Arsenal will make accomplishing both of those objectives significantly easier.

To make use of both ranged and melee technologies during Campaigns, you have to build both Arsenal and Blacksmith.

English—Age IV

Exclusive Technologies

While most of the technologies found in the Arsenal are available from other buildings in Skirmish mode, it does have a few that are unique, and thus exclusive to the campaign scenarios.

Silk Bowstrings (Age III): Provides +2 range to Archers. This technology is a huge improvement for your Archers because it will allow them to start attacking enemy units from greater range, increasing the likelihood of killing them before they get close enough to attack. It should be high on your priority list if it's available and you're using a lot of ranged infantry.

Crannequins (Age IV): Improves the reload speed of Crossbowmen/Arbalétrier by 30%. One of the main weaknesses of these units is their long reload times, and since they're often used to take on dangerous targets, being able to reduce that time by such a significant amount can give you a big advantage in battle.

Corned Gunpowder (Age IV): This upgrade increases the damage of all ranged units by 20%, so it's a huge damage boost to a large number of different units: if this technology is available, it should always be learned.

Arsenal Technologies (P.45)

Technology	Effect		Age	Civilizations
Steeled Arrow	Ranged Damage 1/3	●	II	All
Steeled Arrow (Improved)	Ranged Damage 1/3		II	Mon
Balanced Projectiles	Ranged Damage 2/3	●	III	All
Balanced Projectiles (Impr.)	Ranged Damage 2/3		III	Mon
Platecutter Point	Ranged Damage 3/3	●	IV	All
Platecutter Point (Improved)	Ranged Damage 3/3		IV	Mon
Iron Undermesh	Ranged Armor 1/3	●	II	All
Iron Undermesh (Improved)	Ranged Armor 1/3		II	Mon
Wedge Rivets	Ranged Armor 2/3	●	III	All
Wedge Rivets (Improved)	Ranged Armor 2/3		III	Mon
Angled Surfaces	Ranged Armor 3/3	●	IV	All
Angled Surfaces (Improved)	Ranged Armor 3/3		IV	Mon
Incendiary Arrows	Ranged	●	III	
Greased Axles	Siege	●	III	All
Greased Axles (Improved)	Siege		III	Mon
Boiling Oil	Defensive	●	III	
Silk Bowstrings	Archer	●	III	All
Silk Bowstrings (Improved)	Archer		III	Mon
Adjustable Crossbars	Mangonel	●	IV	All
Adjustable Crossbars (Impr.)	Mangonel		IV	Mon
Crannequins	Crossbowman	●	IV	All
Crannequins (Improved)	Crossbowman		IV	Mon
Corned Gunpowder	Ranged	●	IV	Eng/Mon
Corned Gunpowder (Impr.)	Ranged		IV	Mon
Roller Shutter Triggers	Springald	●	IV	All
Roller Shutter Triggers (Impr.)	Springald		IV	Mon
Siege Works	Siege	●	IV	All
Siege Works (Improved)	Siege		IV	Mon
Setup Camp	Longbowman Ability Unlock	●	II	Eng
Chemistry	Gunpowder	●	IV	All

Kevin Lam
Delhi Sultanate Arsenal—Age III-IV
Concept Artwork

Stuart Ng
English Arsenal—Age IV
Concept Artwork

Blacksmith

The Blacksmith is home to numerous technologies that can significantly improve all civilizations' military units. Acquiring them is essential for long-term military success in every game mode. The main lines of technology can be separated in four categories: Melee Damage, Melee Armor, Ranged Damage and Ranged Armor, and in every Age you're able to research an improvement in any of these categories to increase either the damage or armor of your non-siege units.

Building Stats

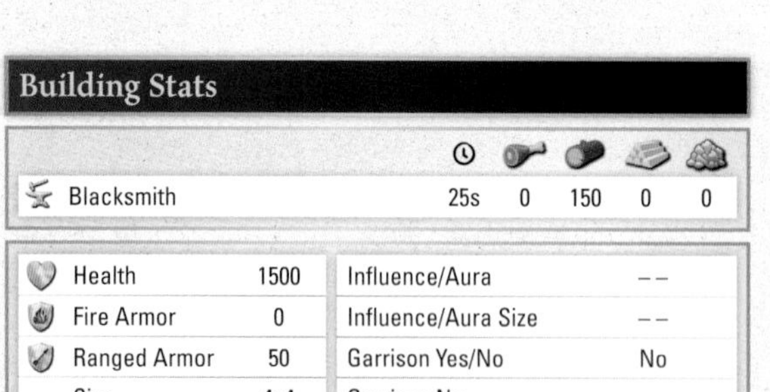

	Time	Food	Wood	Gold	Stone
Blacksmith	25s	0	150	0	0

Health	1500	Influence/Aura	--
Fire Armor	0	Influence/Aura Size	--
Ranged Armor	50	Garrison Yes/No	No
Size	4x4	Garrison No.	--

Usage

You should only consider not building a Blacksmith in Age II if you're taking a more defensive or economic approach in that Age, and combat is not part of your plan. If you're trying to overwhelm your opponent with a lot of military units early on, you might want to delay researching the upgrades at the Blacksmith in favor of more units. However, if the game draws on and your opponent has been acquiring those upgrades, they'll eventually be able to outclass your forces. As with many aspects of AoE IV, you'll need to pay close attention to the flow of the match and decide if you should go for military or economic upgrades first, or if you should place another production or research building.

Whichever path you take, you'll be sacrificing something, so if you choose to research the technologies at your Blacksmith, it's important to capitalize on the short term advantage you'll get in terms of military power. If your opponent is playing the long game with economic upgrades, it will only get harder to beat them as the game goes on. One thing you can do towards the later stages of games to improve your odds is to build multiple Blacksmiths so that you can acquire multiple upgrades at once to get bigger power spikes.

Make sure your Blacksmith is tucked away in a safe corner of your base where it would be difficult for your opponent to reach. You don't want key technology research to be delayed because your Blacksmith gets destroyed.

Technology Overview

Melee Damage

These upgrades will improve the melee damage output of your non-siege units by +1. If your current plan involves using a lot of melee units, then these upgrades should be high on your priority list, because they'll make your melee units perform better against all other units, regardless of type.

Melee Armor

These upgrades increase the melee armor of all non-siege units by +1, so if your opponent is using primarily melee units, you should learn this technology as soon as possible. This is especially true if you're using a lot of light infantry, because the lower the base armor of your units, the more useful this upgrade will be to you: for some units it could be a 100% increase, whereas units with already high armor might only get an extra 10%.

Ranged Damage

Ranged units should always prioritize dealing damage over everything else, because their goal is to defeat the enemy units before they can even get close. These upgrades make accomplishing that goal much easier, so they should be considered a mandatory acquisition whenever you're using a lot of non-siege ranged units.

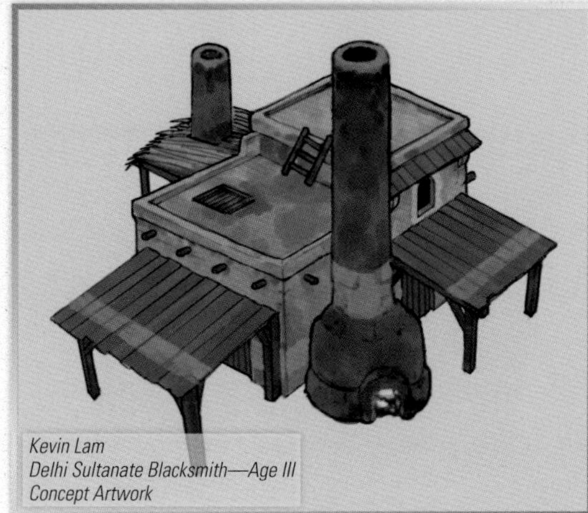

Kevin Lam
Delhi Sultanate Blacksmith—Age III
Concept Artwork

Ranged Armor

Of the damage and armor upgrades, these ones are generally lower on the priority scale, but if your opponent starts fielding large amounts of ranged units, then naturally you'll want to start learning them. You'll also want to make sure you have these upgrades when assaulting your opponent's base, because there will usually be a lot of defensive arrow fire, and you want your units to be able to withstand more hits.

Siege Engineering

This upgrade enables the infantry of most civilizations to build Battering Rams and Siege Towers out in the field, which makes it very useful to have when you're about to attack your opponent's base and see that they've set up a strong defensive perimeter. Because both it and the siege engines it unlocks are quite expensive, you'll probably only need to acquire it in Age II if you're playing very aggressively, otherwise it should be left until later in the game.

Military Academy

Being able to pump out your military units at a faster rate to add to and bolster your army is one of the best ways to increase your military strength, and that's what makes this upgrade useful at all stages of the game. When military production has to ramp up to either match or overwhelm your opponent, or when you need to replace dead military units as quickly as possible, you'll be glad you had this upgrade unlocked. It does, however, mean you'll burn through your resources faster so you need to keep an eye on them; that's much less frustrating than having the resources to fight back, but still losing because of slower production.

Strategic Considerations

Abbasid Dynasty

The Abbasid Dynasty can't research **Siege Engineering**, but that's because their infantry can already build Battering Rams and Siege Towers by default in Age I, which makes them perfectly suited for quick and early aggressive play.

Delhi Sultanate

In Age III the Delhi Sultanate gets access to the **Forced March** upgrade, which speeds up their infantry by 100% for ten seconds, with the caveat that they can't attack while the ability is active. Whether you're using hit-and-run attacks, or facing against an opponent that uses a lot of them, this can be a very useful technology for closing in or retreating quickly. Because all Delhi Sultanate technology is free but takes a long time to research, it can be very useful to build multiple Blacksmiths early in games, so you can start multiple technologies at the same time. Just make sure they're always within the influence range of your Mosques.

Holy Roman Empire

The Holy Roman Empire gets access to a very useful general purpose technology in the form of **Marching Drills** in Age II that increases the movement speed of all infantry by 10%. In the early parts of the game you should still prioritize armor and attack upgrades, but eventually this upgrade will be useful to have for chasing down Villagers and closing in on ranged units.

Mongols

The Mongols have more technologies available at the Blacksmith than any other civilization, because they have no Age IV technology building like the Madrasa or University. Some of the technologies from those buildings such as **Biology**, **Chemistry**, **Elite Army Tactics**, and **Incendiary Arrows** are instead learned at the Blacksmith. As with a lot of Mongol technology, if you place the Blacksmith within the influence range of an Ovoo you'll be able to research improved versions of many of them to get an even better effects.

Blacksmith Technologies (P.45)

Technology	Effect	Age	Civilization
Bloomery	Melee Damage 1/3	II	All
Decarbonization	Melee Damage 2/3	III	All
Damascus Steel	Melee Damage 3/3	IV	All
Steeled Arrow	Ranged Damage 1/3	II	All
Balanced Projectiles	Ranged Damage 2/3	III	All
Platecutter Point	Ranged Damage 3/3	IV	All
Fitted Leatherwork	Melee Armor 1/3	II	All
Insulated Helms	Melee Armor 2/3	III	All
Master Smiths	Melee Armor 3/3	IV	All
Iron Undermesh	Ranged Armor 1/3	II	All
Wedge Rivets	Ranged Armor 1/3	III	All
Angled Surfaces	Ranged Armor 1/3	IV	All
Siege Engineering	Siege Unit Unlock	II	All - Abb
Siege Engineering (Impr.)	Siege Unit Unlock	II	Mon
Military Academy	Production	III	All
Military Academy (Impr.)	Production	III	Mon
Incendiary Arrows	Ranged	IV	Mon
Biology	Cavalry	IV	Mon
Biology (Improved)	Cavalry	IV	Mon
Chemistry	Gunpowder	IV	Mon
Elite Army Tactics	Melee Infantry	IV	Mon
Elite Army Tactics (Impr.)	Melee Infantry	IV	Mon
Marching Drills	Infantry	II	HRE
Forced March	Infantry Ability Unlock	III	Sul

English Blacksmith Exploration
Concept Artworks

Delhi Sultanate Blacksmith—Age III
Concept Artwork

Chinese Blacksmith Exploration
Concept Artworks

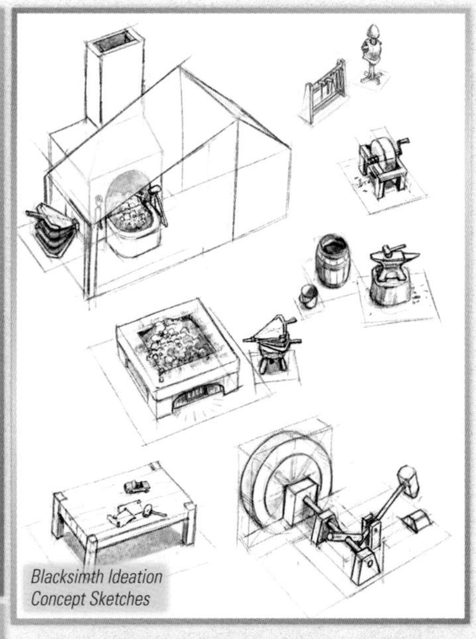

Blacksimth Ideation
Concept Sketches

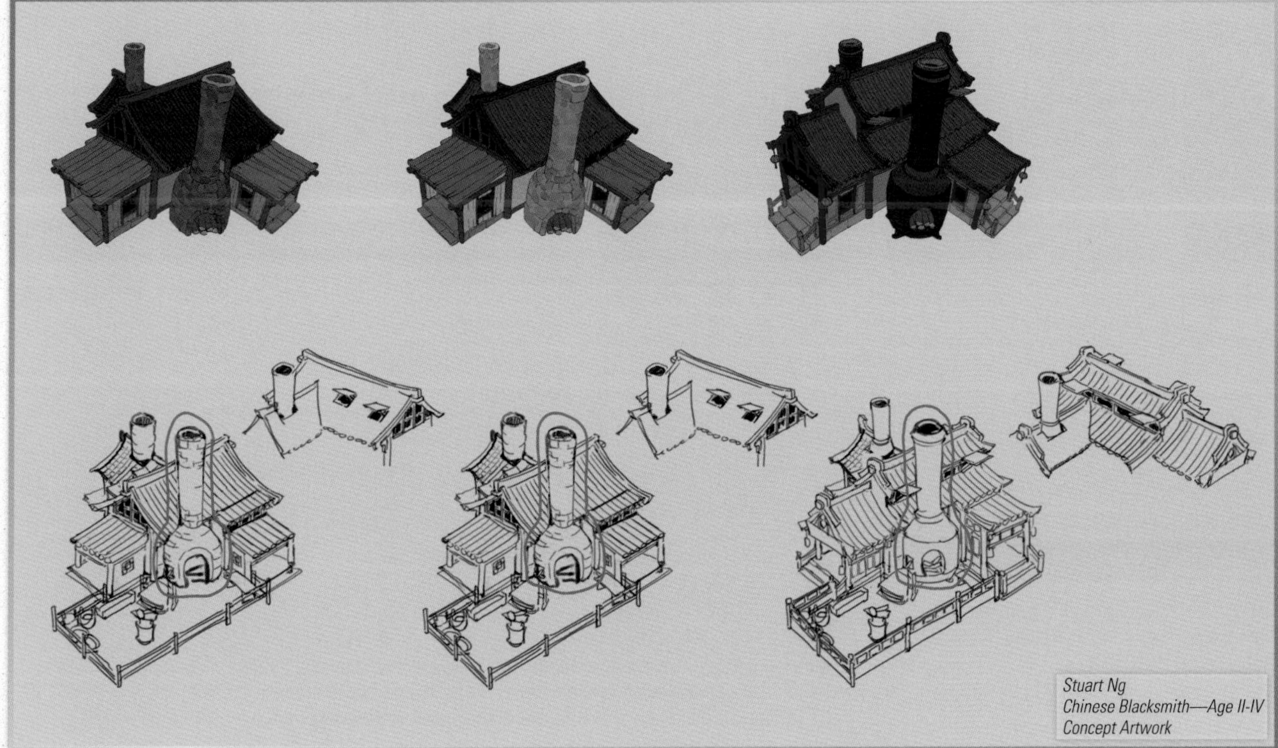

Stuart Ng
Chinese Blacksmith—Age II-IV
Concept Artwork

4

Artistic Influences

"As we began work, we looked at a variety of different art genres such as Orientalism, and Illuminated Manuscript art. We also looked at artists such as Craig Mullins and Graham Turner for inspiration. We tried to understand what made these genres and artists stand out for us, and what seemed to be universally accepted as key influences and definitions of what and who you think of when you think of medieval art. We constantly referred back to many of those artists and styles to understand their viewpoint of the middle ages; it was a good balance of grandeur, historical authenticity, and romanticism, which we felt Age of Empires IV should embody as much as possible."

– Stuart Ng
Senior Concept Artist, Relic

University

Madrasa

English University—Age IV Concept Artwork

While the Blacksmith is primarily focused on technology for your infantry, the University/Madrasa has technologies that can improve a number of different aspects of your economy and military. The technologies available in these buildings are both expensive and take a long time to research, so it's important to build your University/Madrasa as soon as you enter the Imperial Age to start working on them straight away.

English University—Age IV

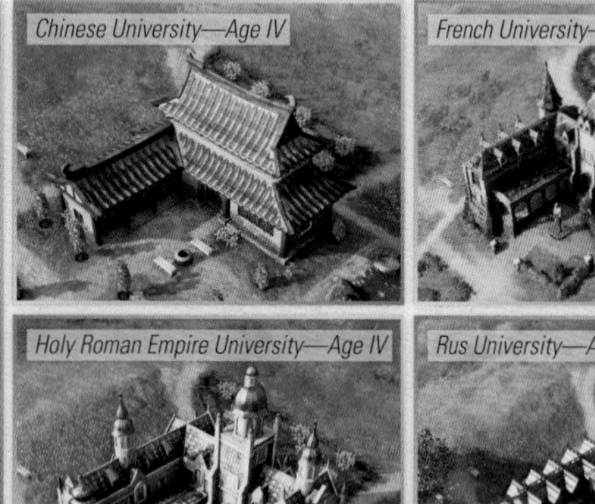
Chinese University—Age IV

French University—Age IV

Holy Roman Empire University—Age IV

Rus University—Age IV

Delhi Sultanate Madrasa —Age IV

Building Stats: University

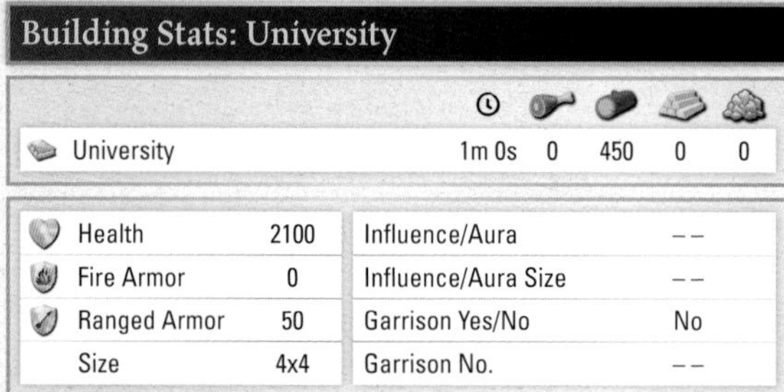

	Time	Food	Wood	Gold	Stone
University	1m 0s	0	450	0	0

Health	2100	Influence/Aura	--
Fire Armor	0	Influence/Aura Size	--
Ranged Armor	50	Garrison Yes/No	No
Size	4x4	Garrison No.	--

Building Stats: Madrasa (Delhi Sultanate)

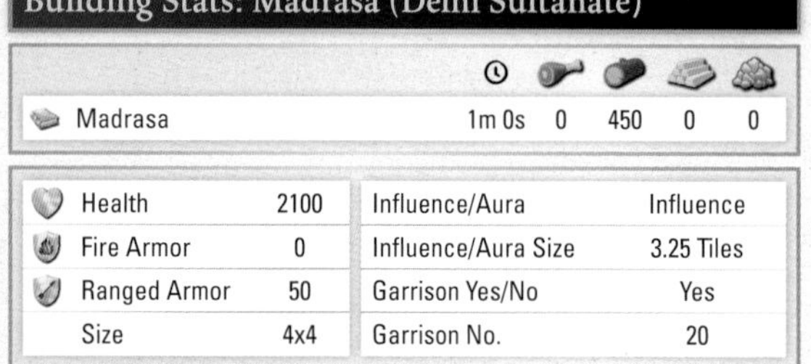

	Time	Food	Wood	Gold	Stone
Madrasa	1m 0s	0	450	0	0

Health	2100	Influence/Aura	Influence
Fire Armor	0	Influence/Aura Size	3.25 Tiles
Ranged Armor	50	Garrison Yes/No	Yes
Size	4x4	Garrison No.	20

Building Stats: Madrasa (Abbasid Dynasty)

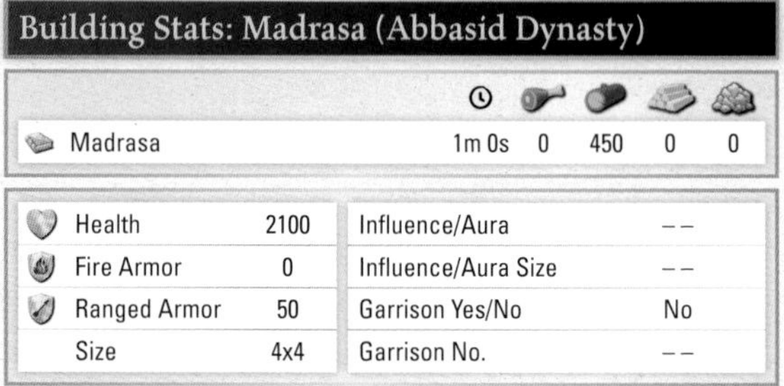

	Time	Food	Wood	Gold	Stone
Madrasa	1m 0s	0	450	0	0

Health	2100	Influence/Aura	--
Fire Armor	0	Influence/Aura Size	--
Ranged Armor	50	Garrison Yes/No	No
Size	4x4	Garrison No.	--

Technology Overview

Every technology available at the University/Madrasa can improve a specific part of your military or economy, so you'll need to prioritize them based on your needs at the time. For example, if you're focusing on cavalry, then **Biology** should be one of, if not the first upgrade you research, but if you're planning on using more gunpowder units, then you'll want to go with **Chemistry**.

Biology

If you're using a lot of cavalry, by the time you gain access to this technology you're likely to have a lot of expensive heavy cavalry units that would be costly to replace, and the 20% extra health they'll gain from this technology will significantly improve their survivability.

University Technologies (P.45)

Technology	Type		Age	Civilizations
Chemistry	Gunpowder Unit Unlock		IV	Eng/Fre/HRE/Rus
Geometry	Siege		IV	All - Mon/Sul/Abb
Biology	Cavalry		IV	Eng/Chi/HRE/Rus
Incendiary Arrows	Ranged		IV	All - Mon/Sul/Abb
Court Architects	Building		IV	All - Mon/Sul/Abb
Elite Army Tactics	Melee Infantry		IV	All - Mon/Sul/Abb
Ancient Techniques	Gathering	●	IV	Chi
Royal Bloodlines	Cavalry	●	IV	Fre

Madrasa Technologies (P.45)

Technology	Type	Age	Civilizations
Chemistry	Gunpowder	IV	Sul/Abb
Geometry	Siege	IV	Sul/Abb
Biology	Cavalry	IV	Sul/Abb
Incendiary Arrows	Ranged	IV	Sul/Abb
Court Architects	Building	IV	Sul/Abb
Elite Army Tactics	Melee Infantry	IV	Sul/Abb

As with other technology buildings, it can be worthwhile to build more than one University/Madrasa so that you can acquire all of the upgrades as soon as possible.

Chemistry

Gunpowder units are a big part of Age IV gameplay for a lot of civilizations, so unless you're playing as the Chinese who get this for free, researching this technology to increase the amount of damage they all do by +20% should be a high priority.

Court Architects

Defensive players that are using a lot of fortifications should strongly consider this technology, even though it is quite costly. The extra 30% health for all of your buildings will make it much harder for your opponent to break through your defenses, and allow you to survive in situations where you may not have otherwise.

Elite Army Tactics

Given the importance of melee infantry in taking out enemy ranged infantry, siege and buildings, being able to increase both their survivability and damage output with this technology can be a big boost to your military strength.

Geometry

This upgrade should be considered the counter point to **Court Architects** because the 30% increase to non-gunpowder siege engine damage is enough to offset the extra health granted by that technology if your opponent has researched it. If they haven't, then you'll be able to destroy their buildings that much faster.

Incendiary Arrows

This technology is one of the best upgrades for ranged infantry that you can learn, because it increases their damage by +20%. Given that by this point in a game you're likely to have a lot of ranged infantry units, the overall boost to the damage of your army can be quite significant. It should be pointed out, however, that while arrows will have a flame effect on them, this is purely visual and does not increase ranged damage against buildings or siege units.

Strategic Considerations

Chinese

For the cheap cost of 150 Wood and 350 Gold, the **Ancient Techniques** upgrade will increase the gathering rates of your Villagers by +5% for every Dynasty that you've achieved. If you've been progressing through even a couple of Dynasties, this technology can significantly improve your economy and should be acquired as soon as possible. Additionally, the Chinese get **Chemistry** for free, so if you're going to focus on gunpowder units you don't need to be in as much of a hurry to build a University as other civilizations.

French

As the French, you can learn the **Royal Bloodlines** technology, which is a superior version of the **Biology** technology that other civilizations have access to. Because cavalry are such a strong choice of unit when you're playing as the French, this technology is a must have acquisition.

Mongols

Having no access to either **Court Architects** or **Geometry** can make things very difficult for the Mongols during the later stages of the game when everything is fortified, so you'll need to make up for it in other areas. The rest of the University/Madrasa technologies are available at Mongol Blacksmiths, and it's important to try to research the improved versions of them to keep up with the other civilizations.

Delhi Sultanate

Generating Enhancement

 **Mosque Influence** Research buildings within influence have the research rate increased for garrisoned Scholars.

Like with their Mosques, you can garrison Scholars into a Madrasa and have them count towards your total garrisoned Scholars to increase research speeds. If you reach Age IV quickly and only have one Mosque, the extra research speed from the Scholars garrisoned here will be invaluable.

Keep

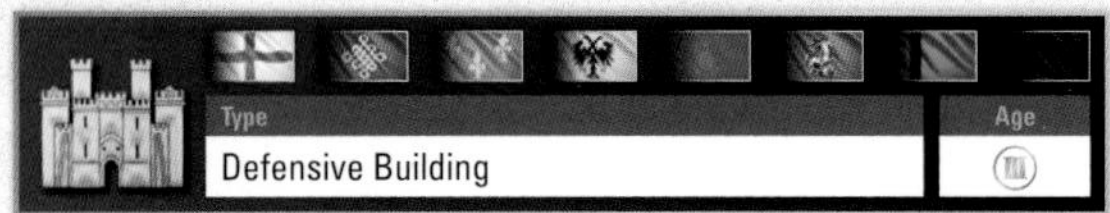

The Keep is a massive and powerful building, and it comes with a suitably massive price tag of 800 Stone. Its defensive capabilities, especially when garrisoned, are unrivaled by other buildings, and it's the ideal choice when trying to establish a froward defensive position for every civilization, except the Mongols, but they can simply move their base!

Building Stats

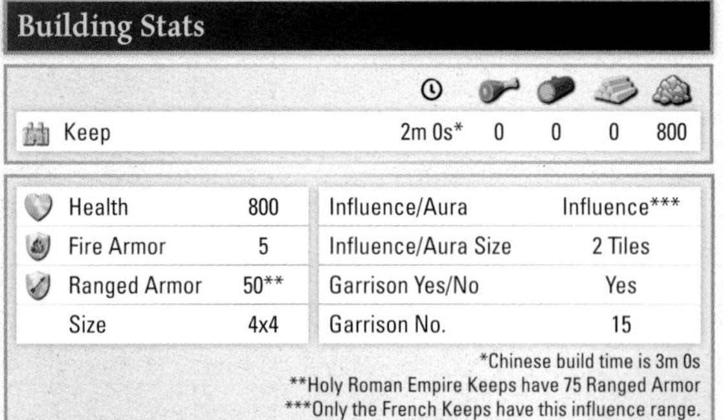

	Time	Food	Wood	Gold	Stone
Keep	2m 0s*	0	0	0	800

Health	800	Influence/Aura	Influence***
Fire Armor	5	Influence/Aura Size	2 Tiles
Ranged Armor	50**	Garrison Yes/No	Yes
Size	4x4	Garrison No.	15

*Chinese build time is 3m 0s
**Holy Roman Empire Keeps have 75 Ranged Armor
***Only the French Keeps have this influence range.

Usage

Keeps are primarily used to defend either your home base, or important places on the map such as neutral Trading Posts, Sacred Sites or huge Gold and Stone deposits. Due to their high cost, you'll need to choose your placement of them wisely, because you'll usually only be able to afford one or two of them at a time. Their already formidable defensive capabilities can be further improved with additional Springald and Cannon Emplacements that you can purchase for each individual Keep. The attacks from those emplacements are added to the normal attack of the Keep rather than replacing it, and you can also add the **Burning Oil** attack—which deals damage to units at the base of the Keep—making it ideal for fending off torch-bearing melee units or Battering Rams. Add in the ability to garrison up to 15 units inside for even more attacks, and you can start to see why Keeps can be such an intimidating challenge for your opponents.

Abbasid Dynasty Keep—Age IV

Chinese Keep—Age IV

French Keep—Age IV

Delhi Sultanate Keep—Age IV

English Keep—Age IV

While they are mainly used to defend a location, if you're feeling brave, Keeps can be placed near, or even inside your opponent's base, where it can bring the full force of all of its firepower to bear on them. This can be risky a play, because if you don't have enough forces in the area to support it, you're likely to suffer an expensive loss. But, if your gambit pays off, it will give you a dominating position in the game, which is very likely to lead to a victory.

If you're trying to defeat a Keep, you're going to need to either overwhelm it with sheer numbers of units in the Castle Age, or wait for the powerful siege engines available in Age IV that let you fire at it from a safe distance. When your opponent is attacking your Keep, it's worth deploying a couple of Villagers to repair it, especially if you're an Age below your opponent, since that can buy you valuable time to bring in reinforcements and strike back. Defending Keeps is worthwhile, but only up to a point, because it's not worth sacrificing your army to save a building; if you manage to build up a better army while your opponent exerts time and effort on your buildings. you may just come out ahead in the end.

Strategic Considerations

English

Generating Enhancement

Network of Castles When enemies are nearby, this building sounds an alarm, causing nearby units to get a +25% increase to attack speed.

Keeps are even useful on water maps because of their bonus damage against ships. When they're fully upgraded, only equally upgraded Warships are capable of taking them on, everything else has to steer clear.

Most Keeps fire a near continuous volley of arrows at any enemies that dare to get close enough, and for each unit garrisoned inside the Keep, and additional arrow dealing 10 damage is added.

Chinese Keeps fire slower, but significantly more powerful Handcannons by default instead of the usual arrows, but any units garrisoned inside still only add additional arrows to the attack, not more Handcannon shots.

The English Keep is special in that you're able to produce all military and siege units available to the English from it, making it not only useful for static defense, but also as a production tool. Their ability to produce siege engines is especially great, as you may not need to build a Siege Workshop if you're making effective use of your Keeps.

Since Keeps are usually placed towards the front of your base, the huge range at which the **Network of Castles** bonus extends around the Keep is even more useful for alerting you to encroaching enemy forces than it is with other buildings. You can also research the unique **Network of Citadels** technology to further increase the attack speed bonus from Network of Castles, making your Keeps even more powerful.

Depending on which upgrades have been researched for the Keeps, small details are added to the building, such as spots for Boiling Oil.

Keep Technologies (P.45)

Technology	Type	Age	Civilization
Springald Emplacement	Weapon Emplacement	III	All - Mon
Boiling Oil	Defensive	III	All - Mon
Cannon Emplacement	Weapon Emplacement	IV	All - Mon
Network of Citadels	Defensive	III	Eng
Extra Materials	Tower & Outpost	III	Chi
Enlistment Incentives	Influence	IV	Fre
Slate and Stone Construction	Building	III	HRE
Reinforced Defenses	Defensive	IV	HRE
Slow-Burning Defenses	Defensive	III	Sul
Village Fortresses	Keep	III	Sul

Chinese

If you're playing defensively as the Chinese, the **Extra Materials** technology that you can research at Keeps can help keep the health of your Stone Walls that are near Stone Wall Towers or Outposts topped up, since they'll automatically be repaired at a rate of 20 health per second. The main benefit of that is the fact that you'll no longer need to spend resources, or take precious Villagers away from other tasks to repair them.

French

Generating Enhancement

 **Keep Influence** Archery Ranges and Stables within influence have unit costs decreased by 25%

French Keeps have a unique area of influence around them, and if you build an Archery Range or Stable within it, the production cost of units from those buildings is reduced by 25%. Those savings can be further increased if you research the **Enlistment Incentives** technology, giving you an additional 10% off. When producing a lot of units, the 500 resources you spend on the technology will pay for itself very quickly.

Holy Roman Empire

Static defenses are a specialty of the Holy Roman Empire, and that's reflected in their unique Keep technologies. **Slate and Stone Construction** gives all of your buildings +5 fire armor, making them more resilient to Torch attacks, and **Reinforced Defences** gives your Walls, towers and gates +40% health, making them significantly more resilient to everything. Both of these upgrades should be acquired as soon as possible if you're playing defensively, but since it affects all buildings, **Slate and Stone Construction** should be researched first.

Delhi Sultanate

The Delhi Sultanate do eventually turn into a late-game powerhouse, but it can take a while to get there, so it's important to plan your defensive capabilities accordingly. **Slow Burning Defenses** grants all of your Walls, Keeps, and Outposts and additional +10 fire armor, and should be one of the first upgrades you research after building a Keep, because of the large durability boost it provides. During Age III you also get access to **Village Fortresses**, which makes all of your Keeps act like Town Centers, with all of the corresponding drop-off and unit production capabilities. That upgrade makes Keeps the perfect building for securing Gold Veins or other precious resources, because as well as offering protection, the Keep can now also serve as the drop-off point. The ability to produce Villagers from your Keep shouldn't be much of a factor at this stage of the game, but might come in handy if some of the ones you have nearby get killed and you need to replace them quickly.

Attack Details

Arrowslits
Bow (Ranged)

Damage	12x3
Counter Bonus	25
Bonus Against	Ships
Attack Range	8.00
Attack Speed	0.38s

Springald Emplacement
Springald (Ranged)*

Damage	60
Counter Bonus	50
Bonus Against	Ships
Attack Range	9.00
Attack Speed	6.25s

Cannon Emplacement
Cannon (Siege)*

Damage	85
Counter Bonus	85
Bonus Against	Ships
Attack Range	10.00
Attack Speed	7.00s

Handcannon Slits
Handcannon (Ranged)**

Damage	50x3
Counter Bonus	25
Bonus Against	Ships
Attack Range	8.00
Attack Speed	3.00s

Boiling Oil
Hot Oil (Siege)*

Damage	30
Counter Bonus	--
Bonus Against	--
Attack Range	2.00
Attack Speed	9.50s

*Requires the researching of their respective emplacements at the Keep.

**Only Chinese Keeps start with Handcannons instead of Arrows as their primary attack.

4

Kevin Lam
Delhi Sultanate Keep—Age III
Concept Artwork

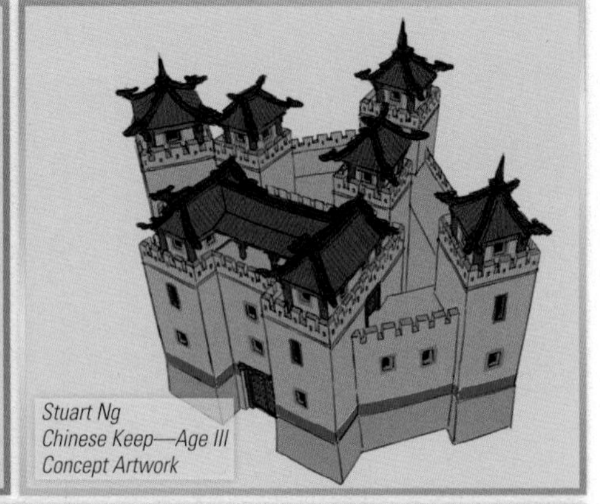

Stuart Ng
Chinese Keep—Age III
Concept Artwork

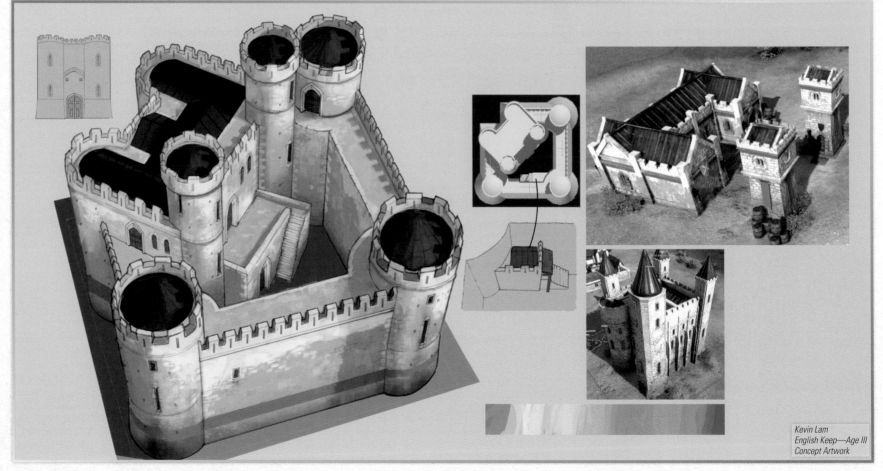

Kevin Lam
English Keep—Age III
Concept Artwork

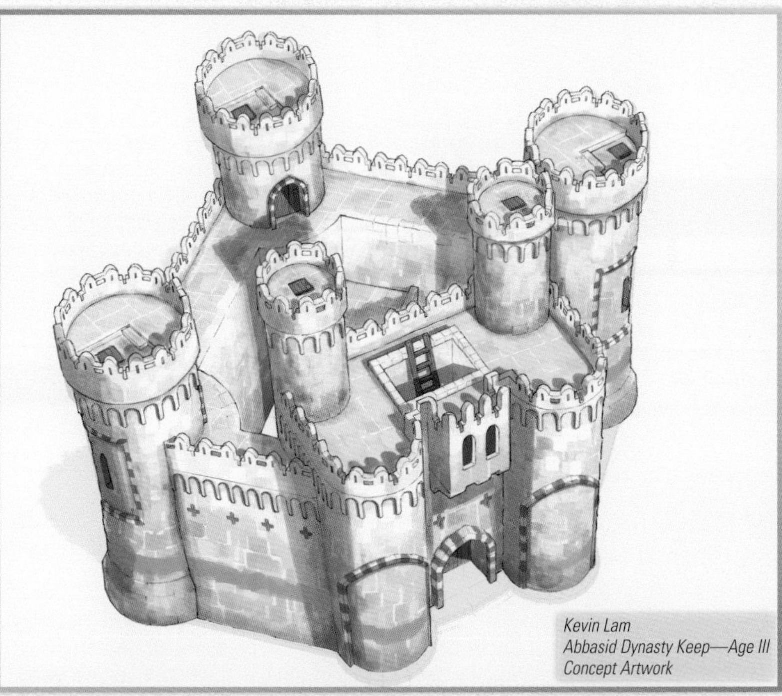

Kevin Lam
Abbasid Dynasty Keep—Age III
Concept Artwork

Stuart Ng
Mongols Outpost—Age I-III
Concept Artworks

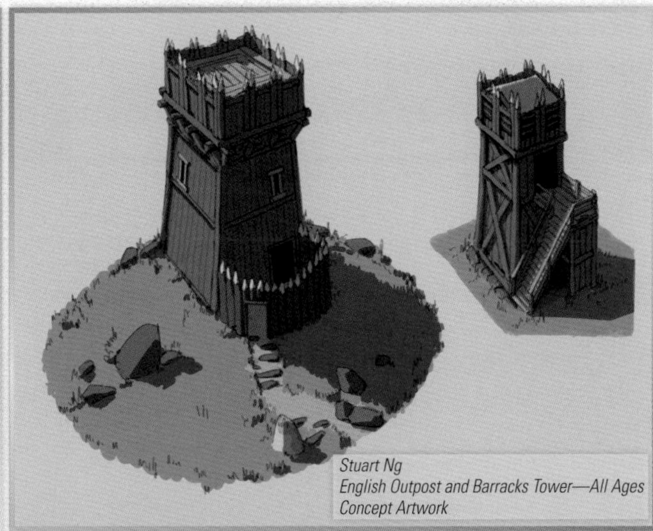

Stuart Ng
English Outpost and Barracks Tower—All Ages
Concept Artwork

Stuart Ng
Mongols Outpost—Age III
Concept Artwork

Researching Civilizations

"Each civilisation comes with its respective unique challenges. These challenges alter our approach to research and visualisation because many civilisations are far more historically heterogeneous than generally perceived. The Abbasid Dynasty civilisation, for example, was not only cosmopolitan due to its vast quilt of territories, but was led by different groups, at different physical locations at different times within the caliphate. So, the visual direction focused more on the regional architecture, costumes and armour of the prevailing caliph and the trick was finding visual consistencies across early Abbasid, Samanids, Buyid and Seljuq, Aghlabid, Fatimid, to the Mamluks so unit and building vernacular felt somewhat consistent with the rest of the civilisations.

Another example is with the Chinese civilisation. Architecture hadn't really fundamentally changed throughout the millennia, which meant the visual progression through the dynasties wasn't very compelling. So the emphasis was on regional architectural styles such as the rounded Hakka walled structures in Fujian to the decorative brick and stone motifs of the Hui Style architecture of the Huizhou prefecture of Anhui. Other civilisations were a challenge because either the reference is not easily searchable, or the material is not in our mother tongue. In cases when we simply had no data, we usually expanded our scope of research to include neighbouring cultures and their structures from classical and ancient periods to create something that feels historically believable."

– Zach Schläppi
Principal Artist, Art Director, Relic

Outpost

Wooden Fortress

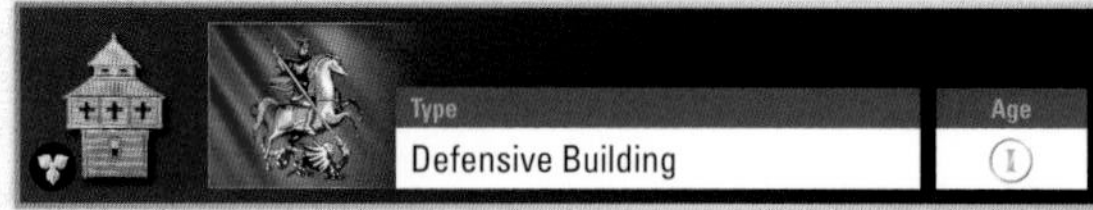

The Outpost is the first defensive structure that all civilizations other than the Rus can build, and they all have access to it in Age I. In its base form it provides a large vision radius to help you spot incoming enemies, and while it has no armaments of its own initially, you can garrison five units inside it to give it some firepower. With a bit of investment, however, additional weapon emplacements can be attached to increase its defensive capabilities.

Mongol Outpost—Age IV

Rus Wooden Fortress—Age IV

Building Stats: Outpost

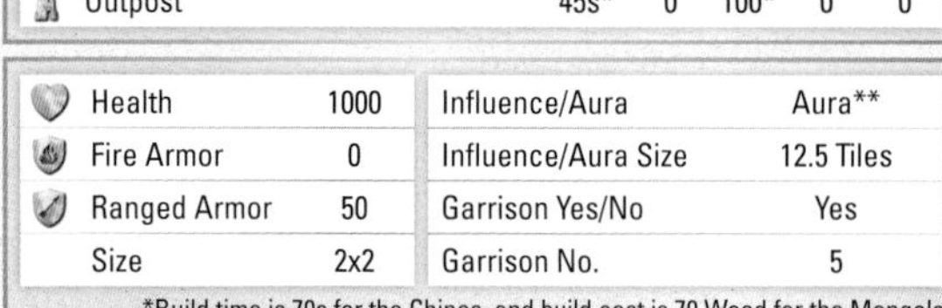

Outpost	45s*	0	100*	0	0

Health	1000	Influence/Aura	Aura**
Fire Armor	0	Influence/Aura Size	12.5 Tiles
Ranged Armor	50	Garrison Yes/No	Yes
Size	2x2	Garrison No.	5

*Build time is 70s for the Chines, and build cost is 70 Wood for the Mongols
**Only Mongol Outposts have this aura range.

Building Stats: Wooden Fortress

Wooden Fortress	50s	0	175	0	0

Health	2000	Influence/Aura	Influence
Fire Armor	0	Influence/Aura Size	3 Tiles
Ranged Armor	50	Garrison Yes/No	Yes
Size	2x2	Garrison No.	8

Usage

Outposts are primarily used to help defend key positions in your base—or around the map—during the initial stages of the game. The 100 Wood investment can be quite hefty depending on when early you build them, so you'll need to weigh your priorities. Sometimes you might be better off building Walls instead; if you want to play aggressively, you might be better off with no static defenses. Another upside to Outposts is that they can garrison units inside them, so if your base is getting attacked by a raiding party, they provide shelter spots for you in addition to your Town Center.

Outposts have access to a number of different weapon emplacements that become available from Age II onwards. They all cost some Stone to unlock, but the added firepower they provide makes an Outpost a much stronger defensive building. Only one emplacement can be fitted to an Outpost, so you need to decide carefully which one you want. The **Arrowslits Emplacement** is the weakest of the three, but you get access to it early so it's useful to help fend off small raiding parties. Later in the game you get access to the **Cannon Emplacement**, which is significantly more powerful and can help you against your opponent's siege engines and Warships. You'll need to try and gauge your opponent's tactics and unit selection, and then pick the appropriate countermeasure emplacement.

Strategic Considerations

English

Generating Enhancement

 **Network of Castles** When enemies are nearby, this building sounds an alarm, causing nearby units to get a +25% increase to attack speed.

English Outposts are a cheap way to extend your Network of Castles coverage, which can be especially important during the early stages of the game when there are fewer buildings capable of generating it.

Chinese

Instead of the usual **Arrowslits**, the Chinese get access to the more powerful **Handcannon Slits** emplacement in Age II, giving them a stronger Age II defensive option.

Mongols

Generating Enhancement

 **Yam** Cavalry and Traders near an Outpost get +15% speed for 20 seconds

The Outpost has a special place in Mongol gameplay; Traders or cavalry units within the Outpost's large area of effect (indicated by a big circle when the building is selected) will be affected by the **Yam** speed aura, which increases their movement speed by 15%. By placing Outposts along key routes—Trade routes or roads leading to your opponent's base—you can create highways for your units. The Yam speed aura is already useful when it's just affecting your Traders and cavalry, so if you already have Outposts setup to take advantage of it for them, learning the **Yam Network** upgrade here so all of your units can take advantage of it seems like an easy choice.

The Wooden Fortress is best built beside a forest and a Lumber Camp, where you'll be able to both protect your hard-working Villagers, and make use of the drop-off bonus.

Rus

Generating Enhancement

Wooden Fortress Influence Lumber Camps and Town Centers within influence return 20% more Wood

Unlike other civilizations, the Rus do not get the ability to build a standard Outpost. Instead, they can construct the Wooden Fortress, which has all the functionality of an Outpost, but with a few extra tricks to improve their utility, the most important of which is their ability to help increase your Wood income. Any Lumber Camp or Town Center built within the influence range of a Wooden Outpost will add an extra 20% to resources being dropped off there.

The Wooden Fortress can also have three more units garrisoned inside it, and unlike Outposts, you do not need to pick which weapon emplacement you want, because both of them can be fitted at the same time. When fully loaded, they're a significantly stronger defensive building than an Outpost.

If you do garrison your units inside of a Wooden Fortress a lot, then you should consider researching the **Castle Turret** technology, This upgrade increases the attack of their arrows by +2 giving them a big boost to power for a petty low cost of 75 Stone. Although it's difficult to collect Stone early in games on water maps, if you do manage to get enough, it can be worth spending some on the Castle Watch technology. The huge increase to the sight range of your Wooden Fortress can be invaluable on those maps for spotting incoming ships, and if that fortress also has weapon emplacements and is fully garrisoned, it also acts as an effective deterrent to those ships.

Outpost Technologies (P.45)

Technology	Type	Age	Availability
Arrowslits	Weapon Emplacement	II	All - Chi/Rus
Fortify Outpost	Defensive Emplacement	II	All - Mon/Rus
Springald Emplacement	Weapon Emplacement	III	All - Rus
Cannon Emplacement	Weapon Emplacement	IV	All - Rus
Handcannon Slits	Weapon Emplacement	II	Chi
Yam Network	Movement	III	Mon

Wooden Fortress Technologies (P.45)

Technology	Type	Age	Availability
Castle Turret	Weapon Emplacement	I	Rus
Castle Watch	Vision Emplacement	I	Rus
Arrowslits	Weapon Emplacement	II	Rus
Springald Emplacement	Weapon Emplacement	III	Rus

Balancing the Resources

"We spent a lot of time on resource balancing. In order to have a balanced match, we knew that resources needed to be placed in such a way as to not give one player or team a massive advantage over the other just due to unlucky resource spawns. Adding in randomness made this a huge challenge, but we developed a system that will dynamically calculate the areas of contention on a given map, based on where the player start positions were placed, and will place resources in those contention bands accordingly. For some maps, that could mean things like large gold deposits and boar spawning equidistant from players, and since our system takes actual unit pathfinding distance into account, this means maps that have the players navigating around mountains and other impasse can still have resources spawned in a balanced way. We built in special cases for islands and have separate tuning for resources that should appear close to players."

– Nick Taylor
Designer, Maps Lead, Relic

Attack Details: Wooden Fortress

Arrowslits
Bow (Ranged)

Damage	10
Counter Bonus	25
Bonus Against	Ships
Attack Range	8.00
Attack Speed	1.00s

Springald Emplacement
Springald (Ranged)

Damage	60
Counter Bonus	50
Bonus Against	Ships
Attack Range	9.00
Attack Speed	6.25s

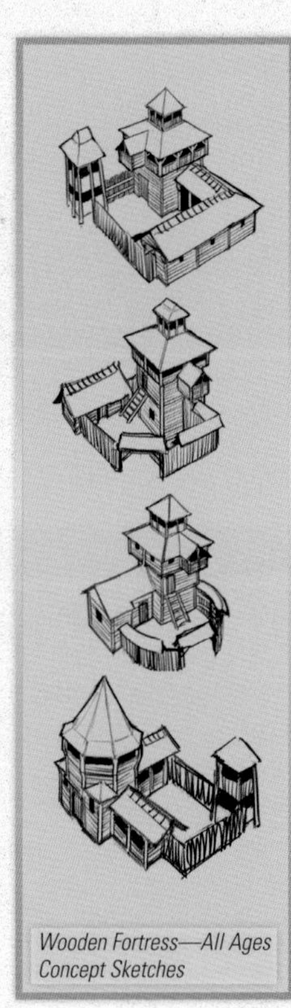

Wooden Fortress—All Ages Concept Sketches

Attack Details: Outpost

Arrowslits*
Bow (Ranged)*

Damage	10
Counter Bonus	25
Bonus Against	Ships
Attack Range	8.00
Attack Speed	1.00s

Handcannon Slits**
Handcannon (Ranged)*

Damage	25
Counter Bonus	25
Bonus Against	Ships
Attack Range	8.00
Attack Speed	3.00s

Springald Emplacement*
Springald (Ranged)*

Damage	60
Counter Bonus	50
Bonus Against	Ships
Attack Range	9.00
Attack Speed	6.25s

Cannon Emplacement*
Cannon (Siege)*

Damage	85
Counter Bonus	85
Bonus Against	Ships
Attack Range	10.00
Attack Speed	7.00s

*Only one additional emplacement can be fitted at a time.

**Only Chinese Outposts have access to the Handcannon Slits Emplacement.

4

Palisade Wall & Gate

Fortifide Palisade Wall & Gate

Palisade Walls and Gates are the first defensive structures available in the game and can be built from Age I onwards. They're used as cheap early game fortifications to block entry points into your base, and delay approaching enemies. While they're very strong against ranged infantry, they'll quickly crumble to melee infantry, cavalry or siege. Regardless of how quick they fall, they're always useful to act as an early warning system, letting you know that an opponent is trying to enter your base, and giving you time to move reinforcements to the area.

Palisade Wall & Gate—Age I

Rus Fortifide Palisade Wall & Gate—Age I

Building Stats: Palisade

	Time	Food	Wood	Gold	Stone
Palisade Wall	04s	0	15/5	0	0
Palisade Gate	10s	0	25	0	0

Health	1500	Influence/Aura	--
Fire Armor	0	Influence/Aura Size	--
Ranged Armor	50	Garrison Yes/No	No
Size	1x2	Garrison No.	--

Building Stats: Fortifide Palisade

	Time	Food	Wood	Gold	Stone
Fortifide Palisade Wall	03s	0	15/5	0	0
Fortified Palisade Gate	10s	0	25	0	0

Health	3000	Influence/Aura	--
Fire Armor	0	Influence/Aura Size	--
Ranged Armor	50	Garrison Yes/No	No
Size	1x2	Garrison No.	--

Construction

To build a wall out of palisades, click on your desired starting point, and then when you drag your cursor across the map, you'll see the outline of the wall and can move it to your desired end point. The initial section of wall costs 15 Wood, with each subsequent one only costing five, and even though you can build walls of any length, one section is considered anything up to two tiles—if you go over that you'll have to pay for the next section. While you're placing the wall you'll see the total cost of Wood for the whole thing in a small counter above it, allowing you check you have enough resources before committing to the build.

The initial 15 Wood cost has to be paid every time you start building a wall—even if you're finishing or branching off from a wall that you started earlier— so it's far cheaper to build one long straight section than multiple short ones. The reason for that is the start and end points of sections have additional palisades and serve as anchor points for the rest of the wall. If you're planning on adding a gate to your wall, it's important to remember that they can only be built over sections of wall that are at least two tiles in length, so plan your builds accordingly to avoid having to spend extra Wood on extensions.

Organic Cities

"In the early ideation stages of developing Age of Empires IV, we had tried a few different things to try to get players' cities and towns to look more organic. We also considered how towns were built around key structures in certain places, such as a defensible building like a motte and bailey or fort, or how a chapel might be positioned in relation to the civil housing. We had concepted many different visuals which would fill the spaces between buildings, so that your city/town would appear more lived in and believable beyond what you might expect from an RTS base. Some of this made it into the game, such as procedurally placed paths, gardens, roads, bushes, etc."

– Stuart Ng
Senior Concept Artist, Relic

Usage

Palisade Walls are mostly used for setting up defensive perimeters during the Dark and Feudal Ages, but even though they're weaker than Stone Walls, they do still have some uses later in the game. If you want to provide a light layer of defense to parts of your base that are not the focus of what's happening currently, then Palisade Walls can act as a cheap security system and prevent surprises.

If you're going to begin building Palisade Walls early in games, you'll want to put one more Villager on Wood gathering than you otherwise would. After putting your first four Villagers on Food (to sustain Villager production), and then the desired amount on Wood, the next Villager you produce should be the one to actually build the walls. You should start with areas that are easily closed off due to their proximity to geographical features on the map, with the focus being on the sides that are closest to your opponent's base.

If you need to cover a very large area with walls, then you may want to have two or more Villagers building them at once.

Keep in mind that every second your Villagers spend building walls instead of gathering resources will put your economy a second behind that of an opponent who isn't building walls. If you're building a lot of walls, the cost can easily exceed that of key early game military buildings like a Barracks. In return for those economic sacrifices you're essentially buying yourself the time it takes for your opponent to either navigate around, or tear down the wall, hopefully not before your army gets into position to counter them.

The main thing to be wary of when using walls is not to get lulled into a false sense of security, because while it's true there's less chances of being caught off guard, melee units especially can make short work of them; they can be a part of your defense, but they shouldn't be the only part.

Walls are more useful on some maps than others, depending on the geographical features and how open they are. It's especially hard to entirely wall off your base on open maps such as Dry Arabia or King of the Hill without spending all of your Wood on it. On these maps it's better to focus on sections, and just secure one side of your base with walls in an attempt to funnel your opponent's army around them to a point where your army is lying in wait. This way you're more secure, but most importantly, you'll save a lot of resources because of the much lower Wood investment.

Maps that are a lot more enclosed, such as Black Forest or Hill and Dale, are significantly more wall friendly, because there's usually only a few narrow approaches that your opponent can follow. Similarly, the narrow crossings or bridges on river maps are prime wall locations if you can get to them before your opponent. Even though you might consider building walls around your island when playing on an open water map, the Wood investment required to do so is almost certainly always better invested in naval units.

Mongols can't construct Palisade Walls or Palisade Gates due to their nomadic nature and focus on aggressive gameplay. The only structural defense they have is the Outpost, so you'll need to place them wisely.

Palisade Gate

Palisade Gates can only be built on top of a section of Palisade Wall that's at least two tiles long, and they're used to create a means for your troops to walk through a section of that wall that otherwise would be impassable. At 25 Wood they're easily affordable, and a must have in a fully walled base to maintain mobility. Gates can also be locked so even

Even if they're not the strongest, Palisades are available from Age 1 on and are quick and cheap to build.

your units can't walk through them, which can be useful when you're trying to position defensive units without exposing them to danger. Even if your units do walk through a gate and it opens, enemy units still won't be able to walk through it and enter your base; they have to destroy either the wall or the gate.

After selecting the Palisade Gate, but before confirming its placement, you'll be able to use the position of your mouse cursor to select which way the gate opens, indicated by the yellow marker above the gate. Make sure it opens outwards, or else enemies will be able to walk right into your base!

Rus Fortified Palisades

Because the Rus lack the ability to construct Stone defensive buildings, they'll instead shore up the normal palisade defenses to make them sturdier. The general usage of both the wall and gate are identical, the only difference is that these fortified versions have twice the amount of health. This extra defensive prowess comes at not additional cost either, so you get even more bang for your Wood.

Stone Wall, Tower & Gate

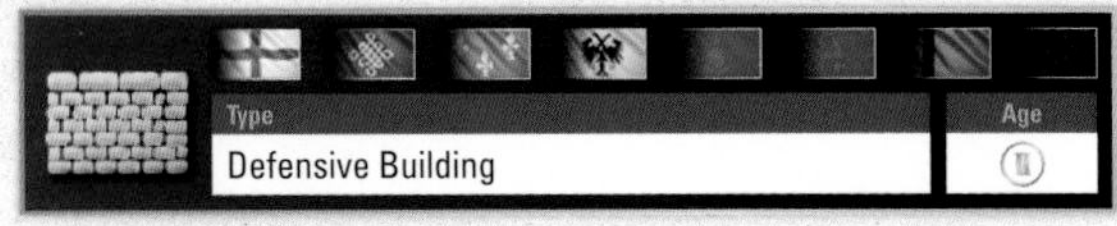

Type	Age
Defensive Building	II

Stone Walls are a significantly stronger defensive fortification compared to Palisade Walls, because not only do they have more health, but normal infantry and cavalry cannot damage them, only more powerful siege attacks and Battering Rams can. Not only are their defensive credentials impressive, but your infantry units can also take up positions atop them to gain a number of defensive and offensive bonuses. Keep in mind, however, that the cost of these walls is immense, so use them wisely, and only when you can afford to.

Building Stats

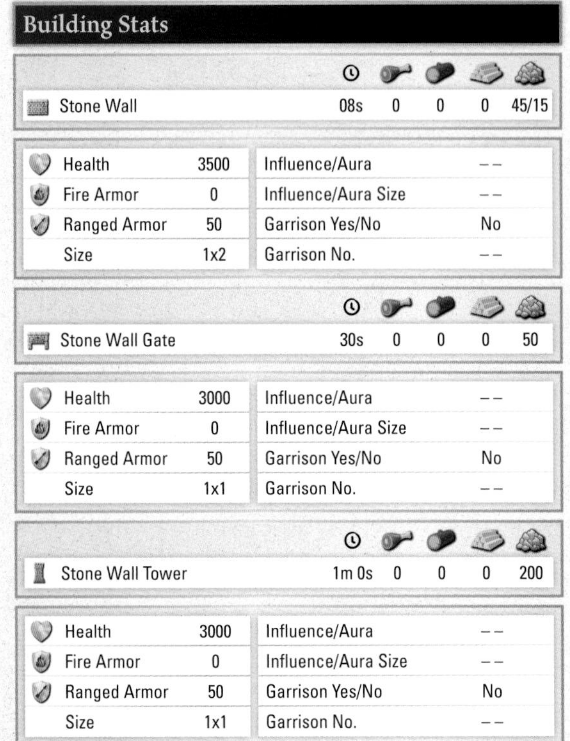

	Time	Food	Wood	Gold	Stone
Stone Wall	08s	0	0	0	45/15

Health	3500	Influence/Aura	--
Fire Armor	0	Influence/Aura Size	--
Ranged Armor	50	Garrison Yes/No	No
Size	1x2	Garrison No.	--

	Time	Food	Wood	Gold	Stone
Stone Wall Gate	30s	0	0	0	50

Health	3000	Influence/Aura	--
Fire Armor	0	Influence/Aura Size	--
Ranged Armor	50	Garrison Yes/No	No
Size	1x1	Garrison No.	--

	Time	Food	Wood	Gold	Stone
Stone Wall Tower	1m 0s	0	0	0	200

Health	3000	Influence/Aura	--
Fire Armor	0	Influence/Aura Size	--
Ranged Armor	50	Garrison Yes/No	No
Size	1x1	Garrison No.	--

Construction

Like Palisade Walls, the initial part of a Stone Wall costs three times the amount of a normal section, and since you're now dealing with the much scarcer Stone rather than Wood, you should be even more thoughtful about their placement. The initial section of a Stone Wall that you can build for 45 Stone takes up three tiles, but as you extend the wall, each section you pay for counts as two tiles. This is to ensure that the large drum towers that make the anchor points for Stone Walls are always clear of at least one normal section of wall, to allow for a gate or tower to be built in it if needed.

Usage

The defining feature that makes Stone Walls so special is the fact that you can position infantry on top of them along the battlements. Ranged infantry gain sight and attack range increases of +2 tiles, and any infantry unit on a Stone Wall gains a massive 66% damage reduction from enemy siege or ranged attacks.

To man these walls you'll first need to give your units a way to get on top of them, and Stone Wall Gates and Towers both have the requisite stairs you're in need of, giving them both some very useful additional functionality. Having ranged infantry on top of your wall, siege engines behind it, and some melee cavalry or infantry to go out and intercept the opposition's siege engines can be a near impenetrable defense until Age IV siege units come into play.

The one way an opponent can circumvent having to destroy your walls is by using Siege Wall Towers to deliver their infantry directly to the top of them, and this is another reason why it's always a good idea to have your own melee units nearby. For an efficient defense you should always repair damaged sections of Stone Walls, Towers or Gates with one of your Villagers; not only is this quicker, but it will save you a lot of Stone in the long run.

Holy Roman Empire Stone Wall, Tower & Gate—Age IV

English Stone Wall Towers have the additional benefit of generating the Network of Castles aura, which makes the Longbowmen defending from atop the nearby walls even deadlier.

Geographic features can save you some precious Stone when you're attempting to enclose your base in walls, just remember to complete that section of wall if what you're using is not a permanent part of the map.

Attack Details

Springald Emplacement	
Springald (Ranged)*	
Damage	60
Counter Bonus	50
Bonus Against	Ships
Attack Range	9.00
Attack Speed	6.25s

*Only one additional emplacement can fitted at a time.

Stone Wall Gate

A Stone Wall Gate can only be built on top of a clear section of Stone Wall, and it's used as both an access point for your units to pass through a walled off area, and as a means for them to get onto the ramparts atop the wall. Since they're a necessity if you're building Stone Walls, it's a good thing they're fairly affordable at only 50 Stone, because you're probably going to need to build a few of them along your wall to give yourself plenty of movement options. Like Palisade Gates, even if the portcullis is open, no enemies will be able to pass through it until the gate itself or surrounding section of walls is destroyed.

Stone Wall Tower

Stone Wall Towers are fairly expensive at 200 Stone, but they can be a highly effective defensive tool. Unlike Outposts, Stone Wall Towers come ready equipped with a Springald Emplacement so they're capable of fending off enemy units on their own without any further investment.

Care should be taken when you place Stone Wall Towers, because you can choose which side of the wall to place them on, and all of the weapons from the towers only fire forward. That fact can work in your favor when you're on the offensive, because if you can break through an undefended part of the wall and get behind them, they'll no longer be a threat. Also, unlike normal sections of Stone Walls, the Towers are susceptible to the torch attacks of melee units, and thus can be destroyed without the need for siege engines.

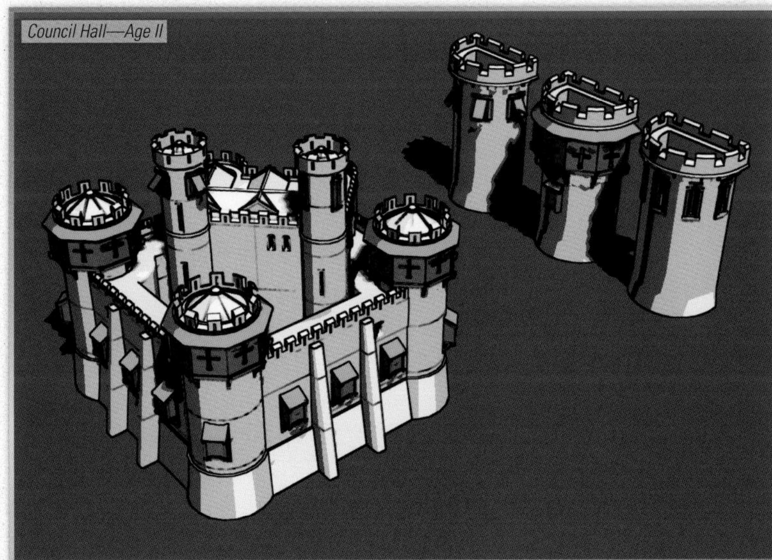
Council Hall—Age II

Council Hall

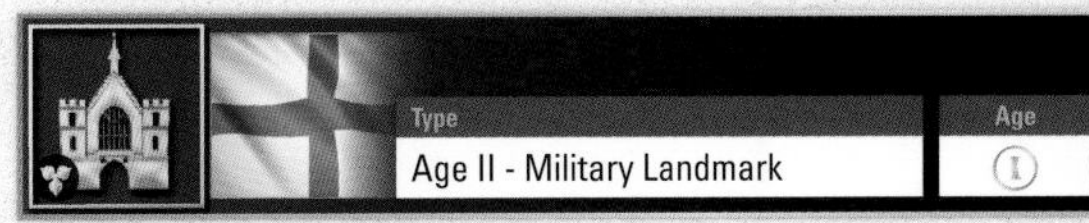

Type	Age
Age II - Military Landmark	I

Primary Uses

- *Advancing to Age II*
- *Producing Longbowmen quickly*

Building Stats

	Time	Food	Wood	Gold	Stone
Council Hall	3m 10s	400	0	200	0

Health	5000	Influence/Aura	--
Fire Armor	0	Influence/Aura Size	--
Ranged Armor	50	Garrison Yes/No	No
Size	4x4	Garrison No.	--

Council Hall—Age II

Prioritization and Usage

The **Council Hall** is the ideal Landmark to build for advancing to Age II if you plan on playing aggressively—or use a lot of Longbowmen—because this building's sole purpose is to produce one unit extremely quickly, and that unit is the iconic English Longbowman. It can produce them at twice the speed of a normal Archery Range, so if you're concentrating on Longbowmen, you can use the 300 Wood it would take to build the equivalent two Archery Ranges to build Barracks and Spearmen to pair with your Longbowmen instead. While this Landmark shines in early game rush attempts, it can still be useful if you're taking a more defensive approach and want to focus more on economic upgrades or additional Town Centers. The high production speed enables you to quickly produce units for repelling any early attacks by your opponent, and then you can put the bulk of your resources towards getting ahead economically. Due to their already excellent range, Longbowmen are also suited to defense duty from atop Stone Walls, making them invaluable for any defense-centric strategy.

Unit Production

Unit	Age
Longbowman	II
Veteran Longbowman	III
Elite Longbowman	IV

Council Hall Technologies (P.45)

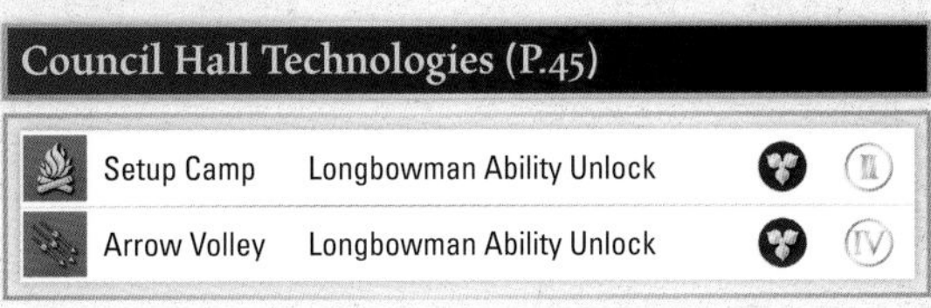

Technology	Effect	Age
Setup Camp	Longbowman Ability Unlock	II
Arrow Volley	Longbowman Ability Unlock	IV

Abbey of Kings

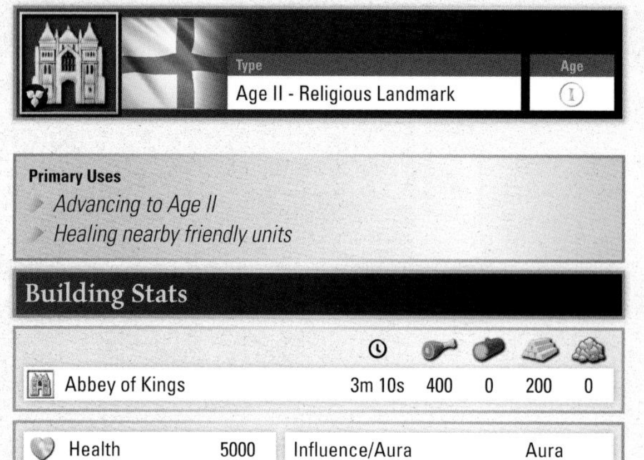

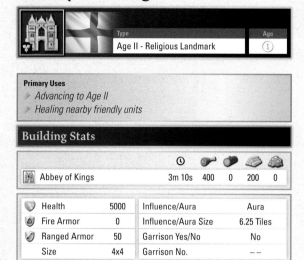

Type	Age
Age II - Religious Landmark	II

Primary Uses
- *Advancing to Age II*
- *Healing nearby friendly units*

Building Stats

	Time	Food	Wood	Gold	Stone
Abbey of Kings	3m 10s	400	0	200	0

Health	5000	Influence/Aura	Aura
Fire Armor	0	Influence/Aura Size	6.25 Tiles
Ranged Armor	50	Garrison Yes/No	No
Size	4x4	Garrison No.	--

Prioritization and Usage

Generating Enhancement

Abbey Healing Heals nearby friendly units by +4 every 1.5 seconds

Whereas the **Council Hall** has more immediate benefits when chosen as your Age II Landmark, the **Abbey of Kings** gets more useful the longer a game goes on and as you progress through the Ages. Once it's been built, any units within the aura range of the building will get healed for four health every 1.5 seconds, and that effect can benefit both your military and worker units. If you place the Abbey between your resources, you can use it to heal your Villagers during and after enemy raids.

Later in the game, when military production gets bigger, and units more costly, the benefits of the **Council Hall** taper off, but this is when the **Abbey of Kings** really starts to shine. Late game units are expensive, especially if you have a lot of them, so if you've built this Landmark you can simply bring them back to your base and heal them back up, saving you a lot of resources in the long run.

Abbey of Kings—Age II

King's Palace

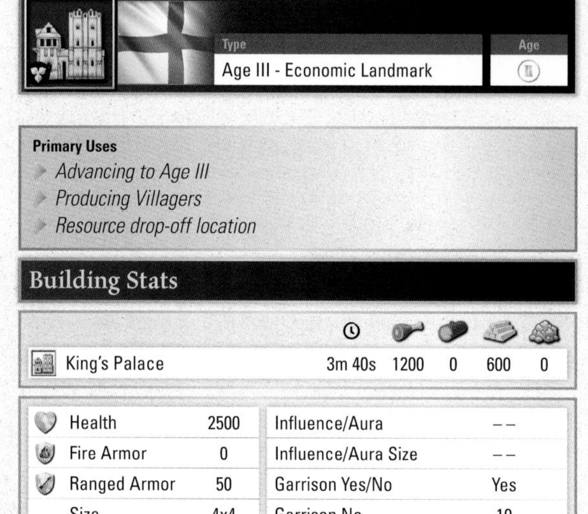

Type	Age
Age III - Economic Landmark	II

Primary Uses
- *Advancing to Age III*
- *Producing Villagers*
- *Resource drop-off location*

Building Stats

	Time	Food	Wood	Gold	Stone
King's Palace	3m 40s	1200	0	600	0

Health	2500	Influence/Aura	--
Fire Armor	0	Influence/Aura Size	--
Ranged Armor	50	Garrison Yes/No	Yes
Size	4x4	Garrison No.	10

Prioritization and Usage

Generating Enhancement

Network of Castles When enemies are nearby, this building sounds an alarm, causing nearby units to get a +25% increase to attack speed.

The **King's Palace** is essentially a Town Center with additional health, but it shares the functionality of an Age II Town Center, not your starting Town Center Landmark. That means it does not have any attacks by default, and you can only garrison 10 units inside, but it still increases your population capacity by 10. It's a good choice for an aggressive start to the game with lots of military, but in Age III you want to invest into economy by producing more Villagers. By going this route you can solidify any advantage gained early on, and save on the additional cost of another normal Town Center.

Ideally it should be placed in exposed areas of your initial base, or near areas with resources that you want to focus on, such as a forest or Gold Vein. If the Conquest win condition is active in the match, however, make sure not to build it too far from your initial base, because you'll want to be able to defend it quickly if needed. It's also quite possible that by the time you're ready to advance to Age III you've already built some other Town Centers, and if that's the case you'd be better off going with **The White Tower.**

King's Palace—Age III

Building Technologies (P.45)

Textiles	Villager Technology	II

Unit Production

Scout	III
Villager	III

Stuart Ng
Abbey of Kings—Age III
Concept Artwork

Stuart Ng
King's Palace—Age III
Concept Artwork

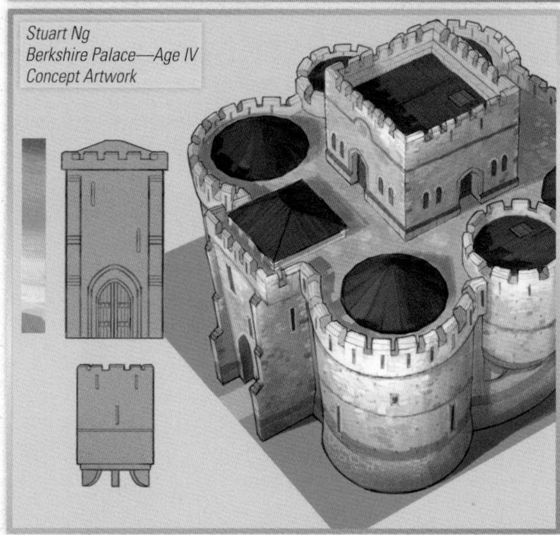

Stuart Ng
Berkshire Palace—Age IV
Concept Artwork

The White Tower

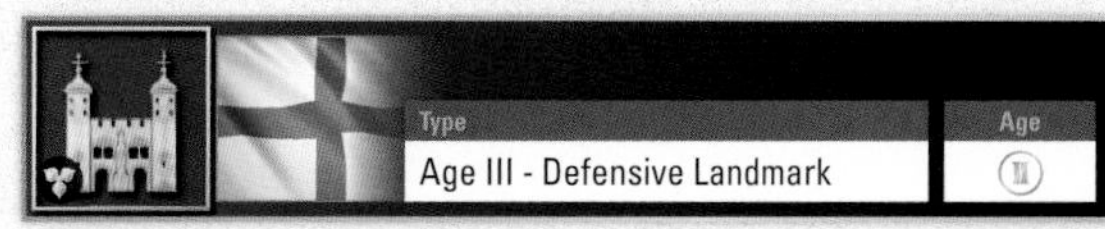

Type	Age
Age III - Defensive Landmark	III

Primary Uses

- *Advancing to Age III*
- *Fulfilling the role of a Keep, with all of the associated technologies, production, and offensive capabilities.*

Building Stats

	Time	Food	Wood	Gold	Stone
The White Tower	3m 40s	1200	0	600	0

Health	5000	Influence/Aura	– –
Fire Armor	5	Influence/Aura Size	– –
Ranged Armor	50	Garrison Yes/No	Yes
Size	4x4	Garrison No.	20

Building Technologies (P.45)

Springald Emplacement	Weapon Emplacement	IV
Boiling Oil	Defensive	IV
Network of Citadels	Defensive	IV
Cannon Emplacement	Weapon Emplacement	IV

The White Tower—Age III

Prioritization and Usage

Generating Enhancement

Network of Castles When enemies are nearby, this building sounds an alarm, causing nearby units to get a +25% increase to attack speed.

If you're about to enter Age III and are in need of a building to either defend an area, or to secure an advanced position, then **The White Tower** can help you accomplish both goals. The White Tower can do everything that an English Keep can do, including the ability to produce every type of military unit, so it's an extremely versatile building.

In a scenario where you have a superior army and map presence than your opponent, you can use **The White Tower** to aggressively place a Keep-like structure right on their doorstep. This is a very "all in" approach, but it's a much quicker option than advancing the Age first, and then placing a normal Keep in the same place. You do obviously risk losing the Landmark, but if you play it correctly, you'll save a lot of time and can keep up the pressure on your opponent, not to mention the 800 Stone saving it would have cost to build a Keep. Defensively, The White Tower is best if you're either being pushed back by your opponent, or if you've been investing into your economy during Age II and need some additional fortifications to help protect your investments.

Attack Details

Arrowslits
Bow (Ranged)

Damage	12x3
Counter Bonus	25
Bonus Against	Ships
Attack Range	8.00
Attack Speed	0.38s

Springald Emplacement
Springald (Ranged)*

Damage	60
Counter Bonus	50
Bonus Against	Ships
Attack Range	9.00
Attack Speed	6.25s

Cannon Emplacement
Cannon (Siege)*

Damage	85
Counter Bonus	85
Bonus Against	Ships
Attack Range	10.00
Attack Speed	7.00s

Boiling Oil
Hot Oil (Siege)*

Damage	30
Counter Bonus	– –
Bonus Against	– –
Attack Range	2.00
Attack Speed	9.50s

*Requires the researching of their respective emplacements at The White Tower.

4

Stuart Ng
The White Tower—Age II
Concept Artwork

XX Stuart Ng
Council Hall—Age III
Concept Artwork

The White Tower—Age II
Concept Artwork

Berkshire Palace

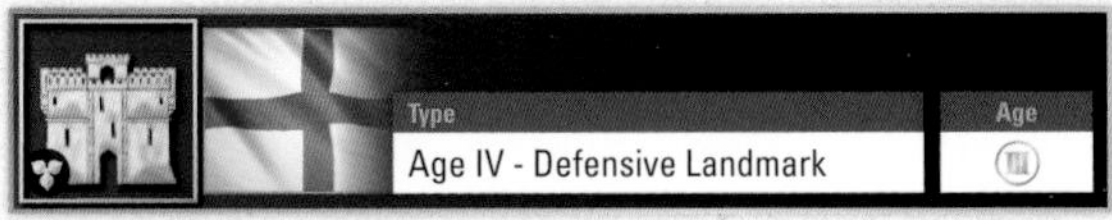

Type	Age
Age IV - Defensive Landmark	III

Primary Uses
- *Advancing to Age IV*
- *Defending Key Positions*
- *Producing any land military unit*

Building Stats

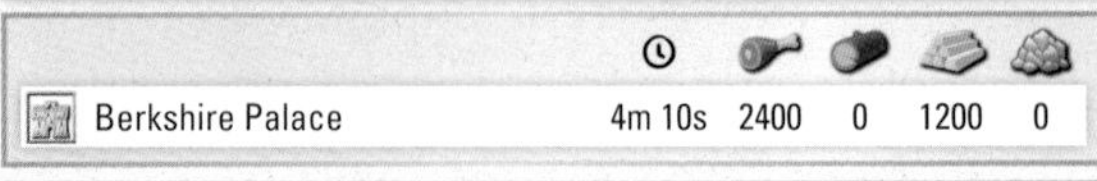

	Time	Food	Wood	Gold	Stone
Berkshire Palace	4m 10s	2400	0	1200	0

Health	5000	Influence/Aura	--
Fire Armor	5	Influence/Aura Size	--
Ranged Armor	50	Garrison Yes/No	Yes
Size	4x4	Garrison No.	20

Berkshire Palace—Age IV

Berkshire Palace Technologies (P.45)

Technology	Type	Age
Springald Emplacement	Weapon Emplacement	IV
Boiling Oil	Defensive	III
Network of Citadels	Defensive	IV
Cannon Emplacement	Weapon Emplacement	IV

Prioritization and Usage

Generating Enhancement

Network of Castles When enemies are nearby, this building sounds an alarm, causing nearby units to get a +25% increase to attack speed.

Similar to **The White Tower, Berkshire Palace** has all the functionality of a normal Keep, but also has 50% more attack range, and double the amount of default Arrowslits for twice the firepower. **Berkshire Palace** is a safe choice, because its capabilities are applicable to nearly any situation you might find yourself in. The extra attack range and damage make it one of the most formidable defensive structures in the game, even more so when fully garrisoned.

If you're using it to protect your Villagers in a key location, then a very sizable area will fall under its protective umbrella, and it's offensive strength allows it to tear through most raiding parties that don't include some heavy siege engines. Keeps are already one of the best fortifications on water maps, and **Berkshire Palace** shines here because the extra attack range makes it one of the few things that can outrange Warships, giving you a huge defensive edge against late game attacks.

Attack Details

Arrowslits

Bow (Ranged)

Damage	12x6
Counter Bonus	25
Bonus Against	Ships
Attack Range	12.00
Attack Speed	0.38s

Springald Emplacement

Springald (Ranged)*

Damage	60
Counter Bonus	50
Bonus Against	Ships
Attack Range	13.50
Attack Speed	6.25s

Cannon Emplacement

Cannon (Siege)*

Damage	85
Counter Bonus	85
Bonus Against	Ships
Attack Range	15.00
Attack Speed	7.00s

Boiling Oil

Hot Oil (Siege)*

Damage	30
Counter Bonus	--
Bonus Against	--
Attack Range	2.00
Attack Speed	9.50s

*Requires the researching of their respective emplacements at Berkshire Palace.

Wynguard Palace

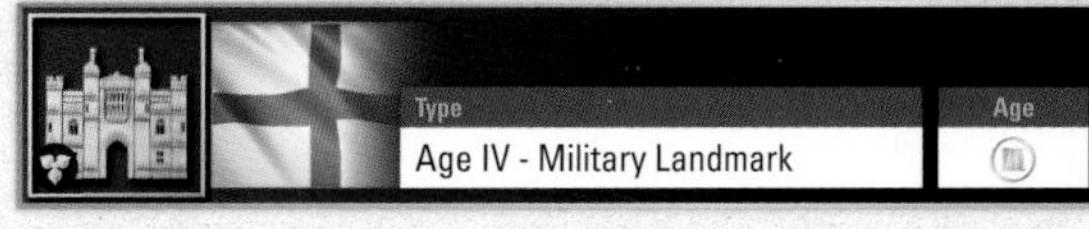

Primary Uses

- *Advancing to Age IV*
- *Producing the Wynguard Army*

Building Stats

	Time	Food	Wood	Gold	Stone
Wynguard Palace	4m 10s	2400	0	1200	0

Health	5000	Influence/Aura	--
Fire Armor	0	Influence/Aura Size	--
Ranged Armor	50	Garrison Yes/No	No
Size	4x4	Garrison No.	--

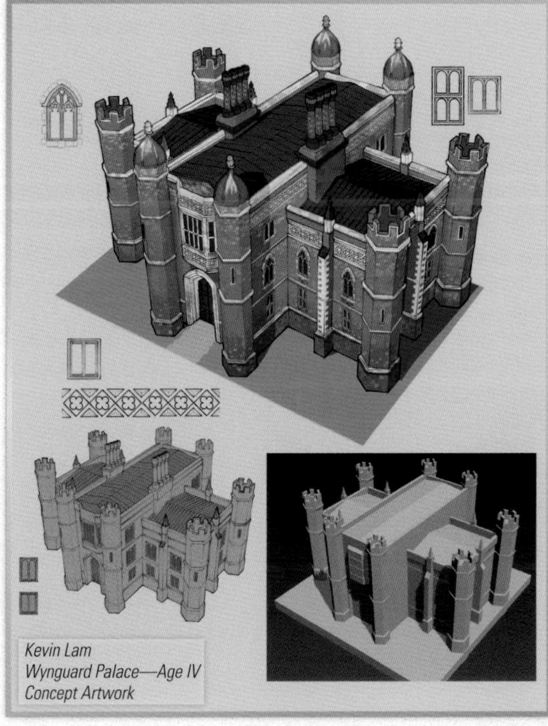

Kevin Lam
Wynguard Palace—Age IV
Concept Artwork

Wynguard Palace—Age IV

Prioritization and Usage

Wynguard Palace is a military Landmark with the sole purpose of producing the infamous Wynguard Army. This group of units consists of a Longbowman, Spearman, Man-at-Arms, Knight and a Trebuchet, and not only are they produced faster than producing them separately, but the total resource cost is also much lower. The cost is so much lower that a normal Trebuchet from a Siege Workshop alone is a lot more expensive. These units form a perfect group to protect the Trebuchet as long as you've been upgrading them while you've been Aging up, but if you're still using the base versions in Age IV, they might struggle against upgraded units. You'll mostly want to pick this Landmark over **Berkshire Palace** are if you're low on resources and need to produce a lot of units and siege engines with what you have available, in order to launch a counterattack against your opponent.

Wynguard Army Overview

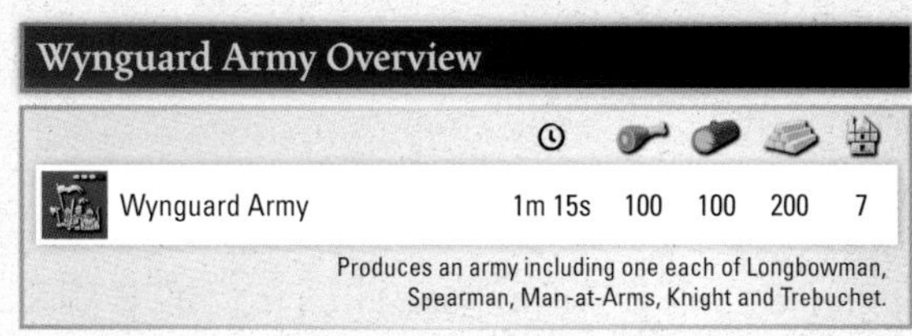

	Time	Food	Wood	Gold	
Wynguard Army	1m 15s	100	100	200	7

Produces an army including one each of Longbowman, Spearman, Man-at-Arms, Knight and Trebuchet.

Imperial Academy

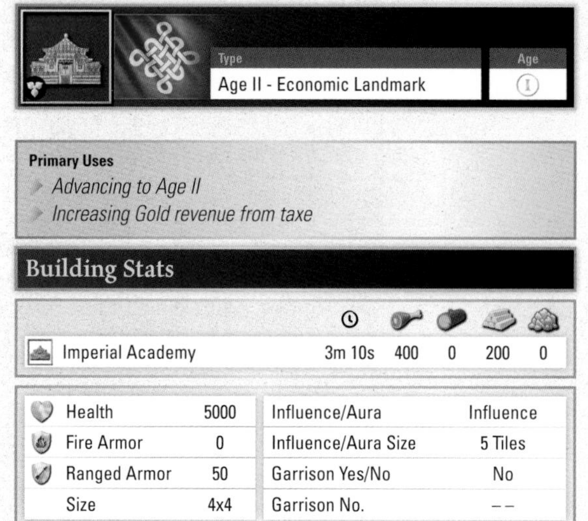

Type	Age
Age II - Economic Landmark	II

Primary Uses
- *Advancing to Age II*
- *Increasing Gold revenue from taxe*

Building Stats

	Time	Food	Wood	Gold	Stone
Imperial Academy	3m 10s	400	0	200	0

Health	5000	Influence/Aura	Influence
Fire Armor	0	Influence/Aura Size	5 Tiles
Ranged Armor	50	Garrison Yes/No	No
Size	4x4	Garrison No.	--

Prioritization and Usage

Generating Enhancement

Imperial Academy Influence Buildings within influence generate +100% Gold in taxes

This economic Landmark has the ability to double the rate at which buildings within its huge influence range generate Gold through the taxation system. Ideally you'll want to place this Landmark in a position where as many other buildings as possible are within its influence range to ensure you're getting the maximum benefits. The additional Tax Gold might not have much of an impact early in games, but as you progress and put more and more buildings within this influence range, the amount can really start to add up.

If you plan on building both of the Age II Landmarks so that you can advance to the Song Dynasty, it's usually better to build the **Barbican of the Sun** first for its defensive capabilities, and then build in the **Imperial Academy** afterwards. The only time when you might not want to build both of them is if you're investing all of your resources into technology and military units in an all-out early game rush. Even during that scenario you're usually better off building the **Barbican of the Sun**, because the benefits of being able to protect your economy are more immediate; only if you're confident in your abilities to keep your opponent away from your base and want the additional Gold should you build the Imperial Academy first.

Imperial Academy—Age II

Imperial Academy Technologies (P.45)

 Imperial Examinations | Imperial Official 

Barbican of the Sun

Type	Age
Age II - Defensive Landmark	II

Primary Uses
- *Advancing to Age II*
- *Defending key positions on the map*
- *Offers vision into Stealth Forests*

Building Stats

	Time	Food	Wood	Gold	Stone
Barbican of the Sun	3m 10s	400	0	200	0

Health	5000	Influence/Aura	--
Fire Armor	0	Influence/Aura Size	--
Ranged Armor	50	Garrison Yes/No	Yes
Size	4x4	Garrison No.	10

Prioritization and Usage

The **Barbican of the Sun** is similar to a Chinese Keep in that they share the same long-range defensive Handcannon attack. There are no further weapon emplacements or technologies that you can learn here, however. Building it is a relatively safe option if you're not sure about of your strategy yet, because it can provide benefits regardless of whether you're playing offensively or defensively.

You can't increase this building's attack capabilities, so if you notice your opponent's forces drawing near, make sure to garrison some units inside it to increase its firepower. If you're using the building to defend resource locations or production buildings, then you should always have some units nearby to fill that role. You don't even need to separate your infantry from your cavalry when attempting to garrison units, because this building can actually garrison cavalry units. The only scenario where you might not want this as your first Landmark as the Chinese is if you're sure your base or map position will be safe and secure for a long time, in which case you may want to opt for the **Imperial Academy** for some extra Gold income

Attack Details

Handcannon Slits	
Handcannon (Ranged)	
Damage	25
Counter Bonus	25
Bonus Against	Ships
Attack Range	8.00
Attack Speed	3.00

Barbican of the Sun—Age II

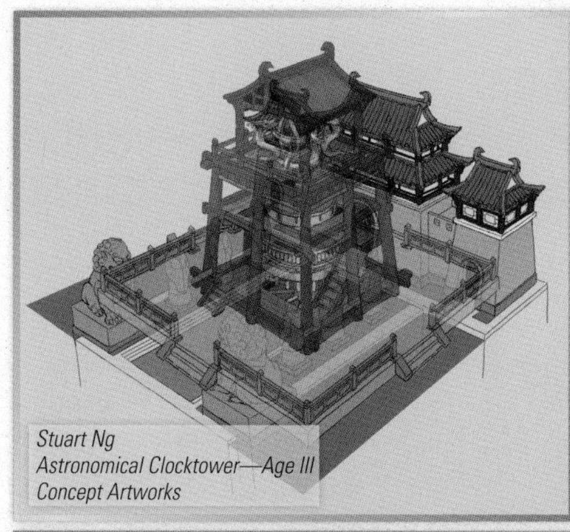

Stuart Ng
Astronomical Clocktower—Age III
Concept Artworks

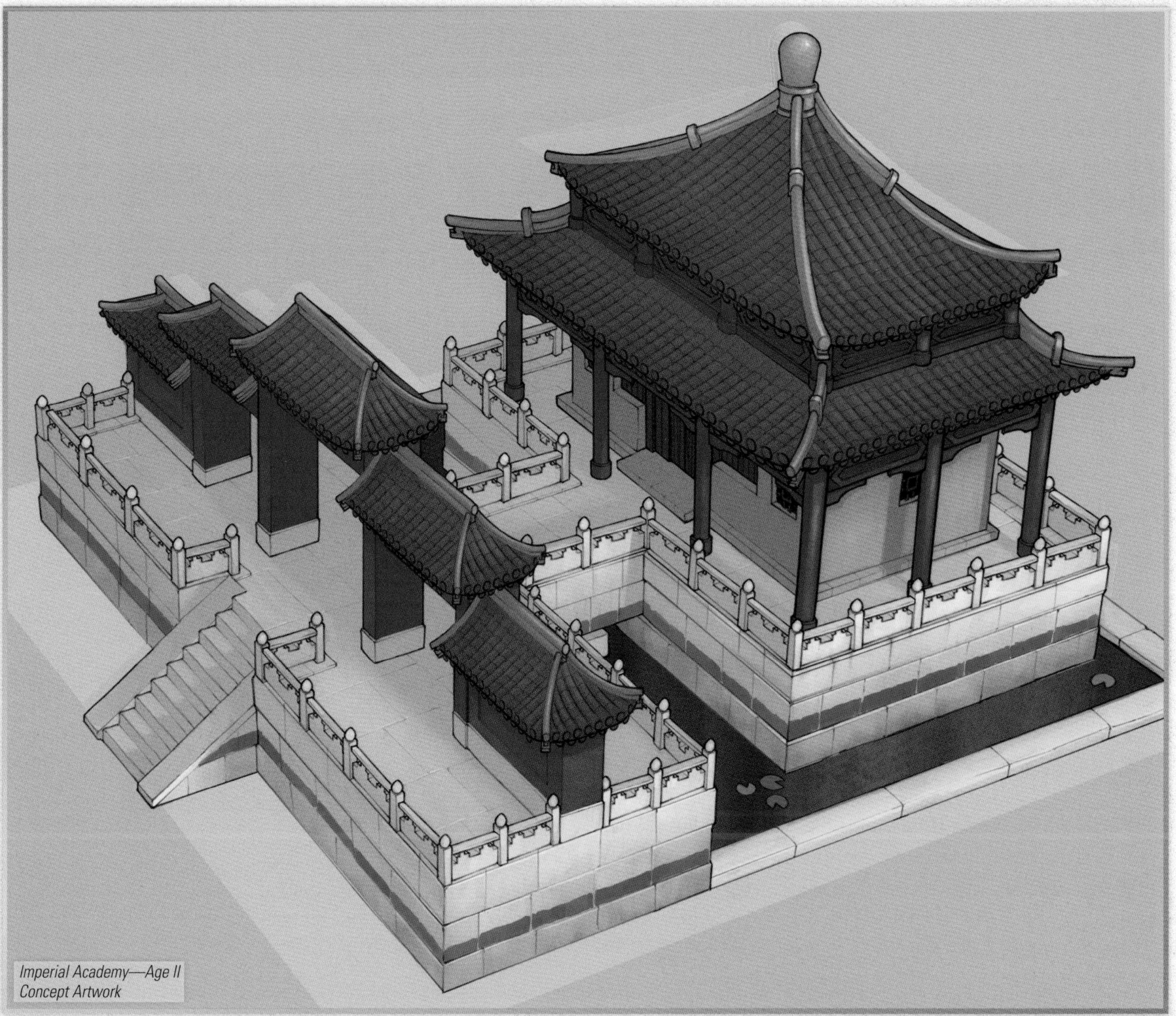

Imperial Academy—Age II
Concept Artwork

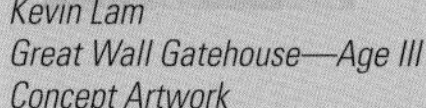

Kevin Lam
Great Wall Gatehouse—Age III
Concept Artwork

Kevin Lam
Barbican of the Sun—Age II
Concept Artwork

Astronomical Clocktower

Primary Uses
- *Advancing to Age III*
- *Producing siege engines with +50% health*

Building Stats

	Time	Food	Wood	Gold	Stone
Astronomical Clocktower	3m 40s	1200	0	600	0

Health	5000	Influence/Aura	--
Fire Armor	0	Influence/Aura Size	--
Ranged Armor	50	Garrison Yes/No	No
Size	4x4	Garrison No.	--

Astronomical Clocktower Technologies (P.45)

Technology	Affects	Unique	Age
Greased Axels	Siege		III
Roller Shutter Triggers	Springald		IV
Siege Works	Siege		IV
Reload Drills	Bombard	✓	IV
Reusable Barrels	Nest of Bees	✓	IV
Pyrotechnics	Gunpowder	✓	IV

The Astronomical Clocktower will instantly provide powerful defensive tools, such as the Nest of Bees.

Astronomical Clocktower—Age II

Unit Production

Unit	Unique	Age
Clocktower Springald	✓	III
Clocktower Nest of Bees	✓	III
Clocktower Counterweight Trebuchet	✓	IV
Clocktower Bombard	✓	IV

Prioritization and Usage

If you're planning on investing a lot into military units during Age III, or you've noticed your opponent using large groups of infantry, then the **Astronomical Clocktower** is the obvious choice of Landmark to pick for advancing to Age III. The siege engines you can produce here have the same offensive capabilities as those produced at a normal Siege Workshop, but these special Clocktower versions all have an extra 50% health, making them significantly more durable.

Being able to construct these siege engines as soon as you reach Age III can give you a bit of a time advantage over your opponent if they have yet to build a Siege Workshop, and the Nest of Bees in particular can be a great asset both offensively and defensively if produced straight away. The **Astronomical Clocktower** may not be the best initial choice of Landmark if your opponent is using a lot of cavalry, however; in those circumstances the **Imperial Palace** would be the better option. If you're going to try to reach the Yuan Dynasty then you'll need both of them anyway, so you'll need to judge the specific circumstances of the game and pick the best one at the time.

Stuart Ng
Astronomical Clocktower—Age III
Concept Artworks

Civilization Components

"We break apart the different components of a civ and balance the components against each other. Civilizations are made up of a four key pieces: Landmarks, unique units, unique technologies, and starting bonuses. This means we can make every civ achieve a powerful economy in unique ways such as hunting, raiding, or building religious units. However the net effect of these bonuses must end up being the same for each civ. The system works well with Age of Empires gameplay because civs have access to a shared pool of units. If one civ had more economy units, for example, then they'd have an advantage when making the shared units."

– Eric Wrobel
Senior Designer, Balance Lead, Relic

Stuart Ng
Imperial Palace—Age III
Concept Artwork

Landmark Naming

"Landmarks were afforded their own creative design, without having to share, which makes them a little easier I guess, with their own challenges for example taking a real-world building and "gamifying" it without losing some of the historical uniqueness. Landmarks really allowed the civ architecture and culture to shine through being as they are critical defining buildings for each Age. It's a celebration, a reward of reaching a mini milestone and progression; it feels great to get that landmark. Isn't that so appropriate, as in how history marches on and a remarkable unique structure can mark a milestone in the progress of a civilization? Historical buildings never fail to impress, elicit awe and grandeur. Humans are capable of creativity and ingenuity. Of course, there's always some less than immaculate history behind such buildings if one cares to dig deeper, never the less impressive as to what was possible."

– Han Randhawa
Franchise Art Director, World's Edge

Imperial Palace

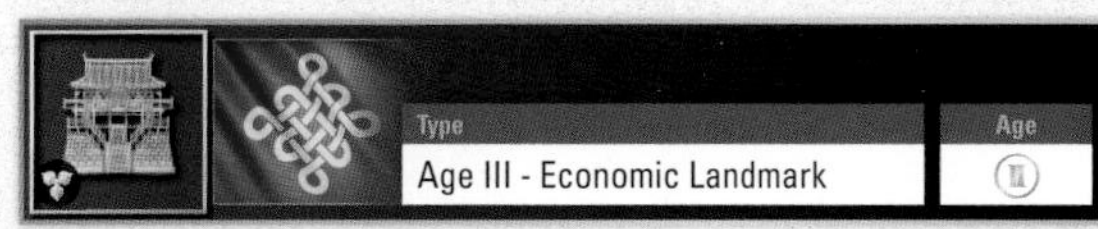

Primary Uses

- *Advancing to Age III*
- *Revealing the location of your opponent's Villagers*

Building Stats

Imperial Palace	3m 40s	1200	0	600	0

Health	5000	Influence/Aura	--
Fire Armor	0	Influence/Aura Size	--
Ranged Armor	50	Garrison Yes/No	No
Size	4x4	Garrison No.	--

With a little glimpse you can spot hidden Villagers and strategies of your opponent...

...to subsequently launch suprise attacks to take them down.

Imperial Palace—Age II

Prioritization and Usage

Manually Activated

Imperial Spies Clicking on this ability will reveal the location of all enemy Villagers on the map for 10 seconds, after which there's a 120s cooldown period before you can use it again.

The **Imperial Palace** has a number of useful offensive and defensive capabilities, but it's main functionality lends itself towards raiding and hit-and-run style gameplay—if that's the playstyle you're going for, then this should be your Age III Landmark. The first thing you'll notice when you place this building is that it has a huge sight radius, so it's perfectly suited to a forward position in your base where the extra sight range will give you advance warning of any incoming enemy troops. This extra time is especially useful if your opponent is using a lot of cavalry, since you'll need all the time you can get to move your troops into position to counter them.

On top of that you have the **Imperial Spies** ability, which is one of the best reconnaissance abilities in the game. Because it lets you see the area around the Villagers it reveals, it not only tells you their location, but also the location of any nearby buildings, allowing you to spot potential targets to put a dent in your opponent's economy. Being able to see the distribution of those Villagers can also give you information as to where best to send you raiding parties because you'll be able to identify both the largest groups, and least defended of them, so can plan your assaults accordingly.

4

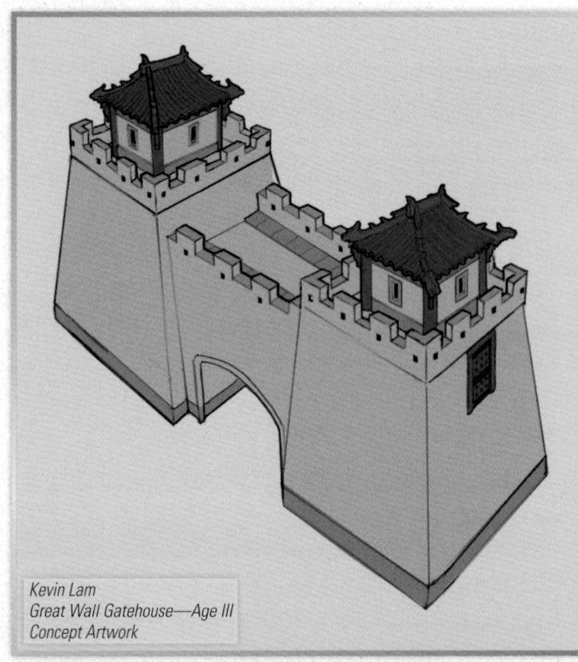

Kevin Lam
Great Wall Gatehouse—Age III
Concept Artwork

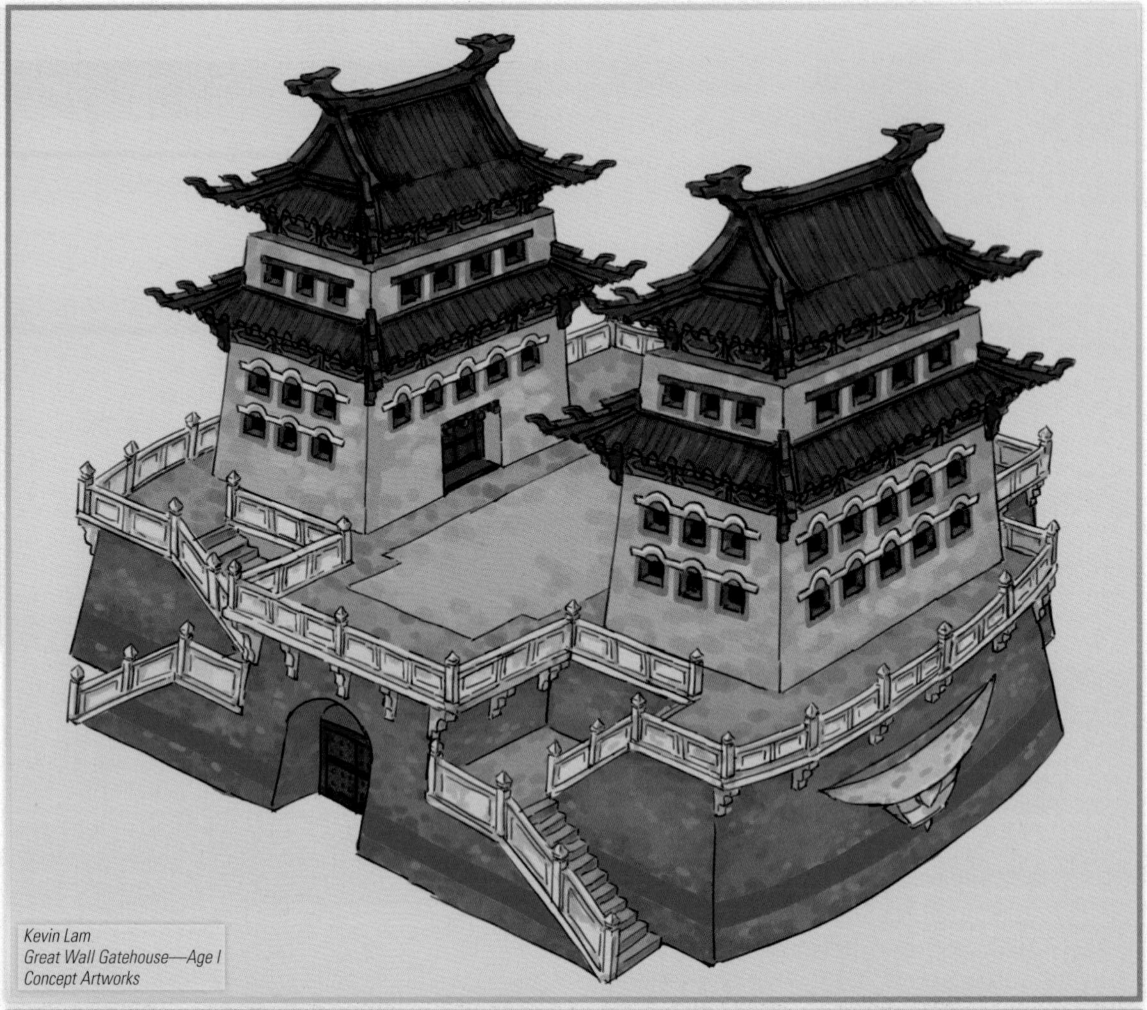

Landmark Naming

"Many historical landmarks are protected under each nations' laws and historical preservation efforts, so sometimes a culture may be OK with the depiction of a national landmark... but not if it was ever destroyed or damaged in the game. Being a game about combat and empire building, we had to err on the side of creating new or "in spirit" versions of famous landmarks, as we wanted to respect the wishes of each culture in how they wanted to be represented."

– Adam Isgreen
Franchise Creative Director, World's Edge

Kevin Lam
Great Wall Gatehouse—Age I
Concept Artworks

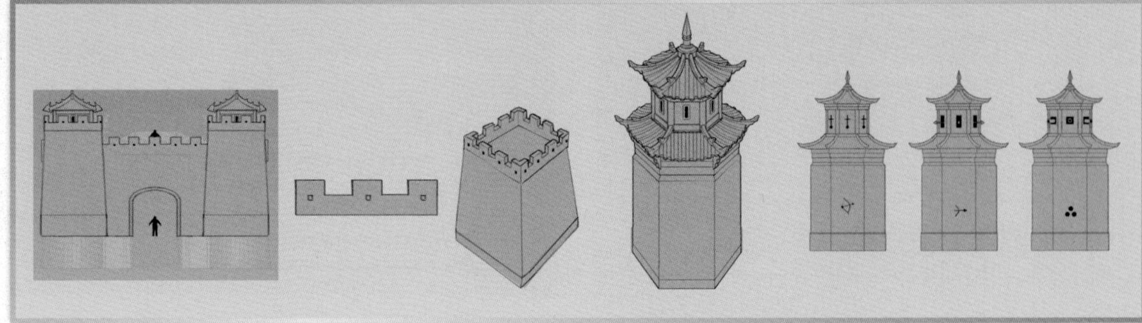

Great Wall Gatehouse

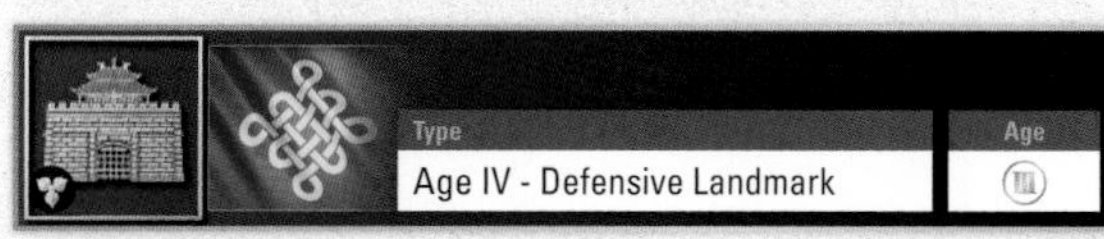

Type	Age
Age IV - Defensive Landmark	

Primary Uses

- *Advancing to Age IV*
- *Increasing the health of Stone Walls and Gates*
- *Increasing the damage done by units on top of nearby walls.*

Building Stats

	Time	Food	Wood	Gold	Stone
Great Wall Gatehouse	4m 10s	2400	0	1200	0

Health	10000	Influence/Aura	Aura
Fire Armor	0	Influence/Aura Size	7.5 Tile Radius
Ranged Armor	50	Garrison Yes/No	No
Size	2x3	Garrison No.	--

Prioritization and Usage

Generating Enhancement

Nearby troops on walls deal +50% damage

The **Great Wall Gatehouse** is the pinnacle of Chinese Stone construction, and its defensive prowess is sure to be an imposing sight to any would-be attackers. It can only be built on top of an existing section of Stone Wall that's at least five tiles in length, because like a normal gate, it requires a normal section of wall, or in this case, three of them. Once built, this excellent defensive asset will double the health of every Stone Wall or Gate that you have constructed, regardless of proximity to the Great Wall Gatehouse. The gatehouse itself also has an impressive 10000 health, making it incredibly hard for opponents to breach. Furthermore, any units on top of a wall within the gatehouses' aura will deal an additional 50% damage.

For obvious reasons, the **Great Wall Gatehouse** should only be built as your first Age IV Landmark in scenarios where

Great Wall Gatehouse—Age IV

you've already heavily walled the area around your base, or you're planning to build heavy fortifications in the near future. If you're playing a mobile, offensive style of gameplay then you may want to opt for the **Spirit Way** first, but if defense is your path, doubling the time it takes to break through your walls is hard to top.

4

Spirit Way

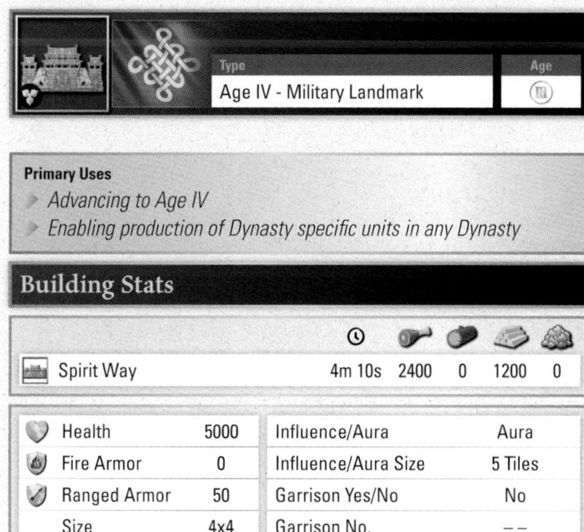

Type	Age
Age IV - Military Landmark	

Primary Uses

- *Advancing to Age IV*
- *Enabling production of Dynasty specific units in any Dynasty*

Building Stats

	Time	Food	Wood	Gold	Stone
Spirit Way	4m 10s	2400	0	1200	0

Health	5000	Influence/Aura	Aura
Fire Armor	0	Influence/Aura Size	5 Tiles
Ranged Armor	50	Garrison Yes/No	No
Size	4x4	Garrison No.	--

Prioritization and Usage

Generating Enhancement

All buildings can create previously achieved dynasty units. Buildings near this Landmark produce units at -30% cost.

Under normal circumstances, units such as the Zhuge Nu or Fire Lancer can only be produced in a specific Dynasty, and if you move out of that Dynasty you'll lose access to those units. If you chose the **Spirit Way** as your Age IV Landmark, however, it will unlock the ability to produce all units from any Dynasty that you've previously achieved at their respective production buildings. Additionally, if those buildings are within the aura range of the Spirit Way, you can produce Dynasty units from them at -30% of their normal cost. If you've been using a lot of Dynasty units while progressing through the Ages, then the Spirit Way is a good choice of Age IV Landmarks so that you can get access to them again. Even if you choose the **Great Wall Gatehouse** as

Spirit Way—Age IV

your Age IV Landmark, you should still build the Spirit Way afterwards, not only to advance to the Ming Dynasty, but also to give yourself more military flexibility.

School of Cavalry

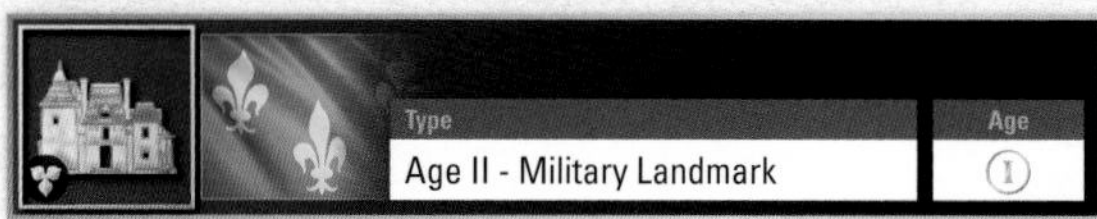

Type	Age
Age II - Military Landmark	I

Primary Uses
- *Advancing to Age II*
- *Producing cavalry units*
- *Increasing production speed of Stables by 20%*

Building Stats

	Time	Food	Wood	Gold	Stone
School of Cavalry	3m 10s	400	0	200	0

Health	5000	Influence/Aura	--
Fire Armor	0	Influence/Aura Size	--
Ranged Armor	50	Garrison Yes/No	No
Size	4x4	Garrison No.	--

Prioritization and Usage

The **School of Cavalry** acts in much the same way as a normal Stable in that it can produce all the French military cavalry units, but it also comes with the added bonus of increasing the production speed of all of your Stables, regardless of proximity by 20%. Since the School of Cavalry has no defensive capabilities of its own, you should build it close to your starting Town Center for some protection, just make sure to leave some space for potential Farms.

Cavalry are one of the most important unit types for the French, and that makes this building a very good choice of Landmark if you want to rush your opponent with cavalry units early in the game. If you want to play a more defensive or economic game, then this Landmark can still be useful because you'll be able to produce cavalry to defend your base at a faster rate. Given their reliance on cavalry in general, even if you don't have a use for it straight away, chances are you will eventually, especially during the later stages of the game where the increased production speed will be a huge boon to your military capabilities.

School of Cavalry Technologies (P.45)

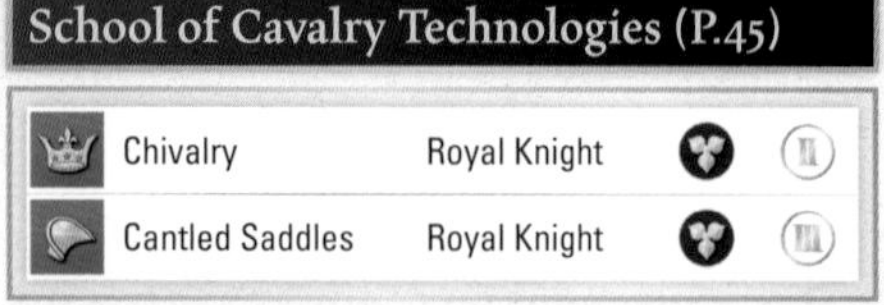

Technology	Unit	Age
Chivalry	Royal Knight	II
Cantled Saddles	Royal Knight	III

School of Cavalry—Age II

Unit Production

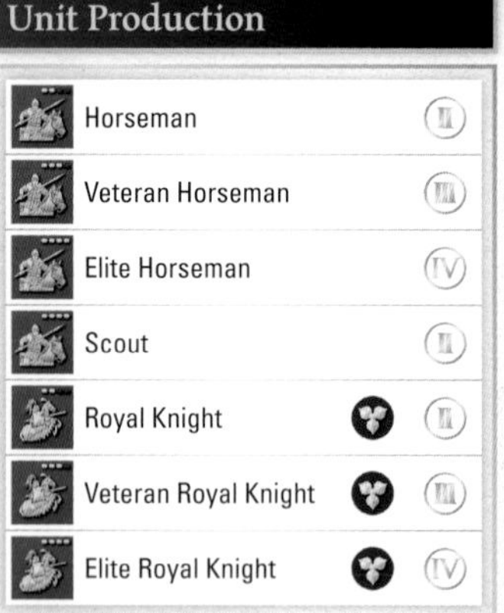

Unit	Age
Horseman	II
Veteran Horseman	III
Elite Horseman	IV
Scout	I
Royal Knight	II
Veteran Royal Knight	III
Elite Royal Knight	IV

Chamber of Commerce

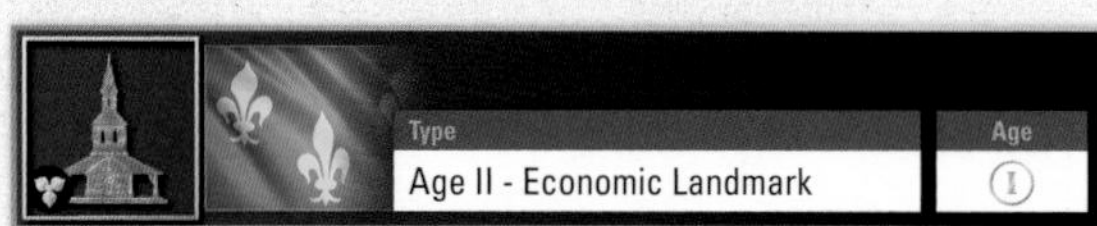

Type	Age
Age II - Economic Landmark	I

Primary Uses
- *Trading various resources for Gold*
- *Increasing the resources brought in by Traders and Trade Ships by 30%*

Building Stats

	Time	Food	Wood	Gold	Stone
Chamber of Commerce	3m 10s	400	0	200	0

Health	5000	Influence/Aura	--
Fire Armor	0	Influence/Aura Size	--
Ranged Armor	50	Garrison Yes/No	No
Size	4x4	Garrison No.	--

Prioritization and Usage

If you intend on focusing on economic growth rather than military during the early portion of the game, then the **Chamber of Commerce** could be a good investment to make. Because it acts the same as a Market, it provides you with a lot of economic flexibility from both selling/buying resources you're deficient in, and the ability to produce Traders for additional Gold income. Where it differs from and exceeds the capabilities of a normal Market is the fact that it also increases the amount of resources that Traders or Trade Ships return to a Market or Dock upon dropping off their goods by 30%. If you establish some long trade routes, the extra 30% can add a lot of extra value to every trip your trade units take. Outside of the choice to go for an economic approach, if you're either planning on not using a lot cavalry, or are facing an opponent that's using a civilization like the Abbasid Dynasty that are strong against cavalry, then the Chamber of Commerce is a good neutral choice to pick for reaching Age II.

Chamber of Commerce—Age II

Unit Production

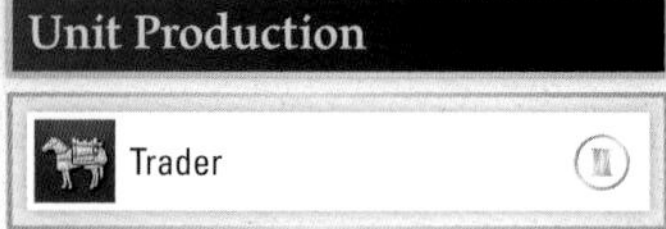

Unit	Age
Trader	II

Kevin Lam
Royal Institute—Age II
Concept Artwork

Kevin Lam
Guild Hall—Age III
Concept Artwork

Kevin Lam
Red Palace—Age III
Concept Artwork

Royal Institute

Primary Uses

- *Advancing to Age III*
- *Researching unique technologies*

Building Stats

	Time	Food	Wood	Gold	Stone
Royal Institute	3m 40s	1200	0	600	0

Health	5000	Influence/Aura	--
Fire Armor	0	Influence/Aura Size	--
Ranged Armor	50	Garrison Yes/No	No
Size	4x4	Garrison No.	--

Royal Institute—Age III

Royal Institute Technologies (P.45)

Technology	Affects
Enlistment Incentives	Influence
Royal Bloodlines	Cavalry
Crossbow Stirrups	Arbalétrier
Chivalry	Royal Knight
Cantled Saddles	Royal Knight
Gambesons	Arbalétrier

Prioritization and Usage

The **Royal Institute** takes all of the unique French technology upgrades that are normally found in other buildings and brings them all together under one convenient roof. Additionally, this building ignores the usual Age requirements for these technologies, giving you the opportunity to learn technologies such as **Royal Bloodlines** or **Crossbow Stirrups** in Age III instead of their normal place in Age IV. Having access to all of these upgrades at once, and at a -20% discounted rate can give you a huge boost to your overall military strength if you're using a lot of cavalry and Arbalétrier units. If you're not using those units, then the value proposition for this Landmark declines steeply, so make sure they're going to be a big part of your strategy before committing to it. If you're not sure, then the additional resources from the **Guild Hall** is a much safer bet because they can be used for any units or buildings.

Guild Hall

Type	Age
Age III - Economic Landmark	III

Primary Uses
- *Advancing to Age III*
- *Generating Resources*

Building Stats

	Time	Food	Wood	Gold	Stone
Guild Hall	3m 40s	1200	0	600	0

Health	5000	Influence/Aura	--
Fire Armor	0	Influence/Aura Size	--
Ranged Armor	50	Garrison Yes/No	No
Size	4x4	Garrison No.	--

Prioritization and Usage

The **Guild Hall** is an excellent general purpose Landmark that can aid you in every stage of the game, regardless of your playstyle. Once built, it will start automatically generating one of the four main resources: Food, Wood, Gold and Stone, and store it in a bank inside the building, after which, when you have the building selected, you can click the **Collect Resources** button to move them to your usable resources. At any time you can switch between which one of the four resources you want to generate, and any that have accumulated of the previous type will be moved to your usable resources when you change.

The building starts off generating 20 resources every 20 seconds. After a minute this rate will increase by +20, making it generate 40 per 20 second interval. The growth rate continues to increase at that pace while resources are stored until it's generating 200 resources every 20 seconds! After withdrawing the resource you'll start back at the base generation rate of 20. Ideally you'll want to leave the resources generating so that you're getting the top rate of 600 per minute, and only withdraw it when you need it to accomplish a specific part of your strategy. Choosing a **Guild Hall** as your Age III Landmark is a very safe choice, because in the long run you're either going to need more of whatever specific resource you're using for your strategy, or more of the rarer resources in general. Stone can be especially useful later in the game due to its scarcity, and with this building alone you can accumulate enough Stone for an additional Keep after a reasonable amount of time. Similarly on island maps where you need as much Wood as possible to keep up production of naval vessels, having an additional source of it that requires no additional effort will always be welcome.

Guild Hall—Age III

College of Artillery

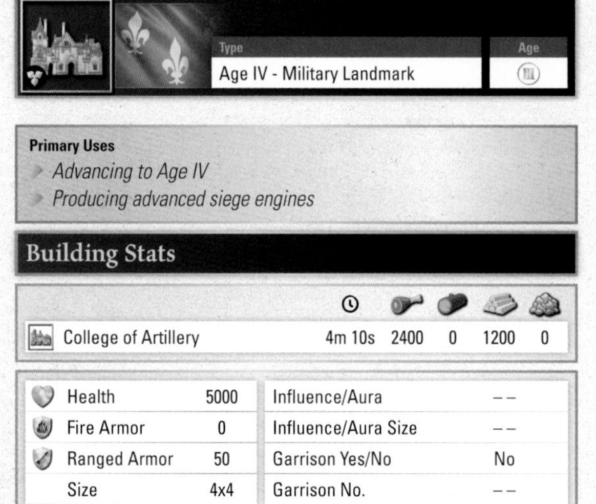

Type	Age
Age IV - Military Landmark	III

Primary Uses
- *Advancing to Age IV*
- *Producing advanced siege engines*

Building Stats

	Time	Food	Wood	Gold	Stone
College of Artillery	4m 10s	2400	0	1200	0

Health	5000	Influence/Aura	--
Fire Armor	0	Influence/Aura Size	--
Ranged Armor	50	Garrison Yes/No	No
Size	4x4	Garrison No.	--

Prioritization and Usage

The **College of Artillery** is where the French can produce the advanced "Royal" versions of the Cannon, Ribauldequin, and Culverin, and they're all substantially more powerful than the standard versions from a Siege Workshop. These unique gunpowder siege units can easily out damage the units in a similar class that other civilizations can field and some, like the Royal Culverin, have no normal version available at the French Siege Workshop. This unit adds a lot of tactical options to a French army, and is almost worth the price of the Landmark alone. If you're planning on making heavy use of siege engines either offensively or defensively during this stage of the game, then the **College of Artillery** should be your Age IV Landmark.

College of Artillery—Age IV

Unit Production

Unit	Age
Royal Cannon	IV
Royal Ribauldequin	IV
Royal Culverin	IV

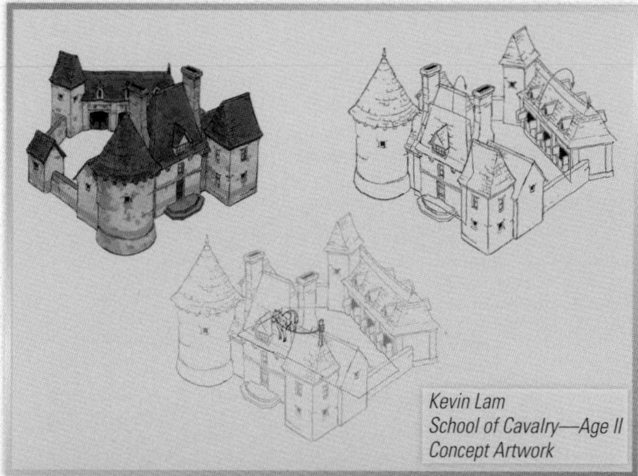

Kevin Lam
School of Cavalry—Age II
Concept Artwork

Landmark Design

"The landmarks each had their own challenges. There was a lot of research for each building, what did it look like during that time period, what sort of renovations occurred throughout the life of the building, what is the function of the landmark, and we considered all of that while also allowing it to visually contrast with the other landmarks within the civilization, and other civilizations as well. We tried to create visual distinction between all the landmarks. The design team provided us with a lot of information to start our work, but in some cases, we were allowed to explore and consider what sort of landmarks would best represent a civilization thematically.

– Stuart Ng
Senior Concept Artist, Relic

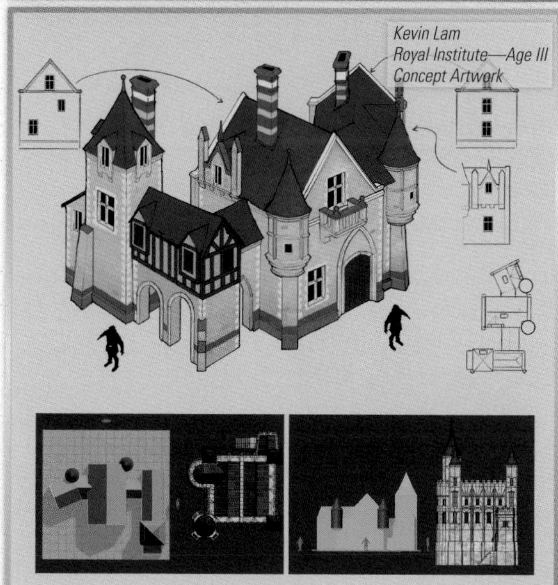

Kevin Lam
Royal Institute—Age III
Concept Artwork

Red Palace

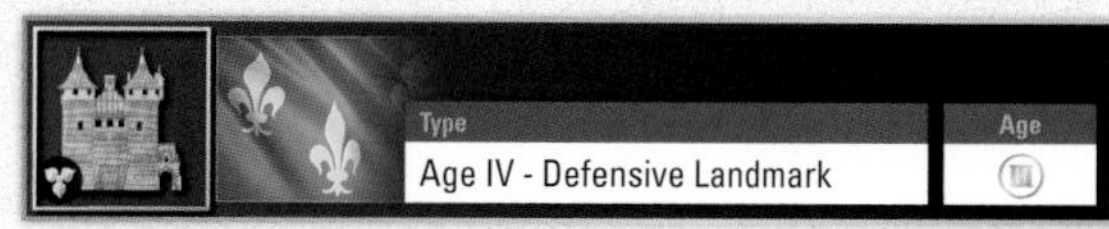

Type	Age
Age IV - Defensive Landmark	IV

Primary Uses

- *Advancing to Age IV*
- *Defending key positions*
- *Reducing unit cost at Archery Ranges and Stables*

Building Stats

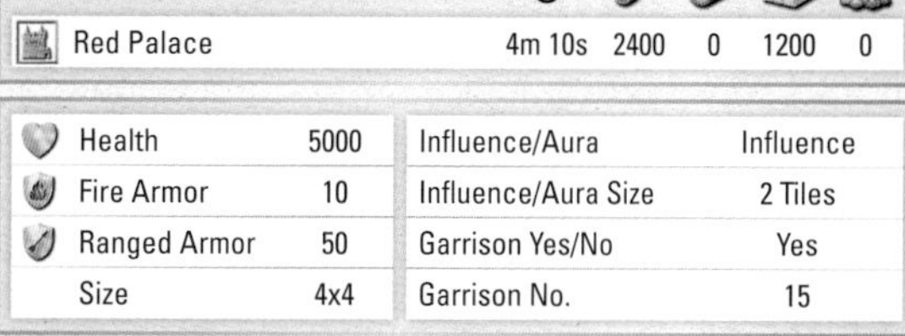

Red Palace	4m 10s	2400	0	1200	0

Health	5000	Influence/Aura	Influence
Fire Armor	10	Influence/Aura Size	2 Tiles
Ranged Armor	50	Garrison Yes/No	Yes
Size	4x4	Garrison No.	15

Red Palace Technologies (P.45)

Springald Emplacement	Weapon Emplacement	IV
Boiling Oil	Defensive	IV
Enlistment Incentives	Influence	IV
Cannon Emplacement	Weapon Emplacement	IV

Prioritization and Usage

Generating Enhancement

 **Keep Influence** Archery Ranges and Stables within influence have unit costs decreased by 20%

The **Red Palace** is the ultimate defensive French building, and can pack more firepower than many of their other buildings combined. At it's core the **Red Palace** acts in the same way as a Keep, but instead of firing standard arrows, it fires much stronger Arbalests, and when you garrison units inside it, instead of firing arrows, each one of them adds another Arbalest. Fully garrisoned, the Red Palace can fire off 18 rounds of 50 damage a volley, which is a huge amount, and can easily dismantle large infantry or cavalry groups with little or no assistance. You also still have the usual Keep armaments of a Springald and Cannon Emplacements that can be researched and equipped simultaneously for even more destructive power.

Any Archery Ranges or Stables placed within its influence range will have their production costs reduced by 20%, and if you research the **Enlistment Incentives** technology (also available at this building), you can reduce that by a further 10%. All of these things combined make the **Red Palace** the perfect Landmark to pick if you're looking to establish a forward base near your opponent, because the Red Palace can provide the production buildings, and the surrounding units with a lot of cover fire and safety.

Red Palace—Age IV

Attack Details

Arbalest Slits	
Arbalest Slits	
Damage	60x3
Counter Bonus	50
Bonus Against	Ships
Attack Range	10.00
Attack Speed	1.38s
Springald Emplacement	
Springald (Ranged)*	
Damage	60
Counter Bonus	50
Bonus Against	Ships
Attack Range	9.00
Attack Speed	6.25s
Cannon Emplacement	
Cannon (Siege)*	
Damage	85
Counter Bonus	85
Bonus Against	Ships
Attack Range	10.00
Attack Speed	7.00s
Boiling Oil	
Hot Oil (Siege)*	
Damage	30
Counter Bonus	--
Bonus Against	--
Attack Range	2.00
Attack Speed	9.50s

*Requires the researching of their respective emplacements at the Red Palace.

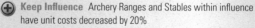

Meinwerk Palace

Type	Age
Age II - Military Landmark	I

Primary Uses
- *Advancing to Age II*
- *Researching technology at reduced costs*

Building Stats

	Time	Food	Wood	Gold	Stone
Meinwerk Palace	3m 10s	400	0	200	0

Health	5000	Influence/Aura	--
Fire Armor	0	Influence/Aura Size	--
Ranged Armor	50	Garrison Yes/No	No
Size	4x4	Garrison No.	--

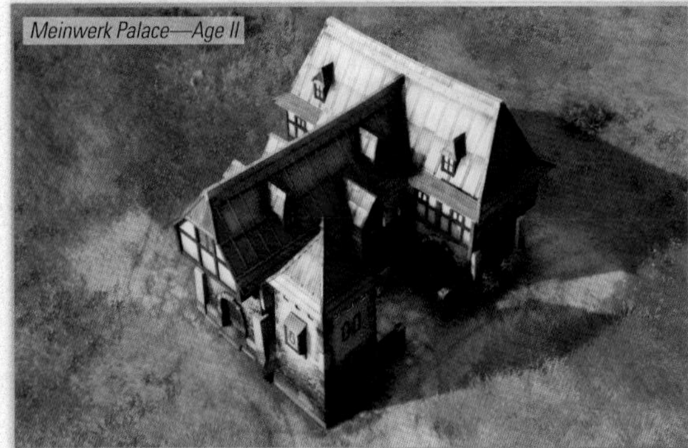

Meinwerk Palace—Age II

With the Meinwerk Palace you can upgrade your early infantry or other military units immediately upon entering the Feudal Age to on the offensive.

Prioritization and Usage

Meinwork Palace has all of the functionality of a Blacksmith and can research all of the technologies found within one, it can just research them 25% cheaper. By choosing this as your Age II Landmark you can forgo the need to build a Blacksmith after reaching that Age, allowing you to get a jump on your opponent in terms of technological advancement. If you have a lot of infantry units that can take advantage of these technologies, then the faster you can access them, the faster they can reap the benefits. This works well in conjunction with an aggressive playstyle where you've invested a lot into military early in the game in an effort to rush your opponent as early as possible, and if you have more advanced units when you do clash with your opponent, you're likely to come out on top.

Meinwerk Palace Technologies (P.45)

Technology	Effect	Age
Bloomery	Melee Damage 1/3	II
Decarbonization	Melee Damage 2/3	III
Damascus Steel	Melee Damage 3/3	IV
Steeled Arrow	Ranged Damage 1/3	II
Balanced Projectiles	Ranged Damage 2/3	III
Platecutter Point	Ranged Damage 3/3	IV
Fitted Leatherwork	Melee Armor 1/3	II
Insulated Helms	Melee Armor 2/3	III
Master Smiths	Melee Armor 3/3	IV
Iron Undermesh	Ranged Armor 1/3	II
Wedge Rivets	Ranged Armor 2/3	III
Angled Surfaces	Ranged Armor 3/3	IV
Siege Engineering	Siege Unit Unlock	II
Military Academy	Production	III
Marching Drills	Infantry	II

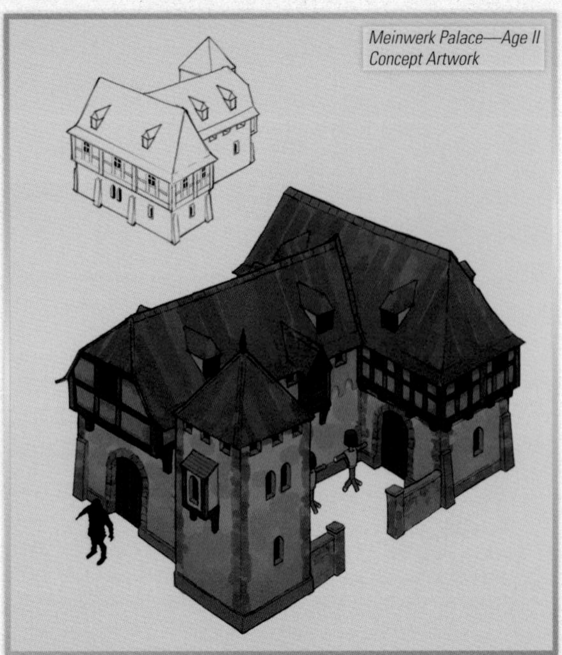

Meinwerk Palace—Age II Concept Artwork

Kevin Lam Aachen Chapel—Age II Concept Artwork

Kevin Lam Bulgrave Palace—Age III Concept Artwork

Aachen Chapel

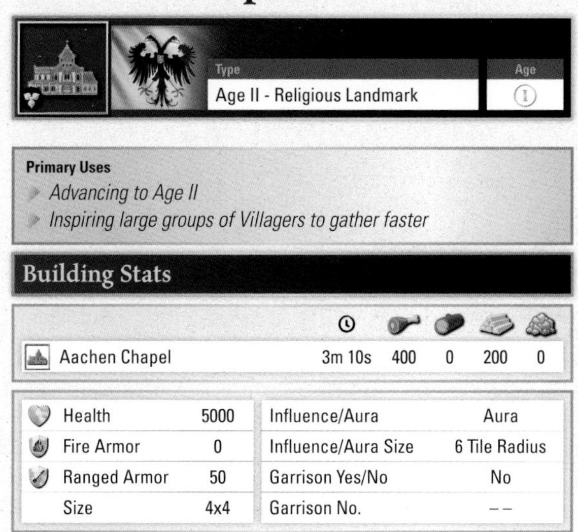

Type	Age
Age II - Religious Landmark	II

Primary Uses
- *Advancing to Age II*
- *Inspiring large groups of Villagers to gather faster*

Building Stats

	Time	Food	Wood	Gold	Stone
Aachen Chapel	3m 10s	400	0	200	0

Health	5000	Influence/Aura	Aura
Fire Armor	0	Influence/Aura Size	6 Tile Radius
Ranged Armor	50	Garrison Yes/No	No
Size	4x4	Garrison No.	--

Prioritization and Usage

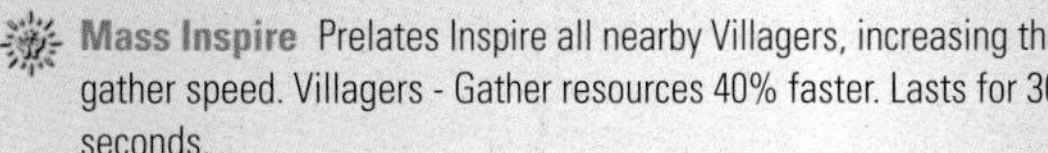

Generating Enhancement

Mass Inspire Prelates Inspire all nearby Villagers, increasing their gather speed. Villagers - Gather resources 40% faster. Lasts for 30 seconds.

Where the **Meinwerk Palace** can provide you with a significant boost to your military power, the **Aachen Chapel** can do the same for your economy with its ability to spread a Prelate's Inspiration over a large area. After garrisoning a Prelate inside the **Aachen Chapel**, any Villagers within the aura range will receive the Inspired buff for 30 seconds, and if they're still within range once the buff wares off, it will just reapply again immediately for near constant up time.

To make full use of this Landmark, try to build it in an area where a large number Villagers will either be working for a long time, or constantly moving through; in the middle of a group of Farms, or between a forest and drop-off point are ideal. You don't want to have to manually keep moving Villagers into the aura area to get the buff because that would waste a lot of time, and in those circumstances you'd be better off assigning another Prelate to the job. The boost to your economy from being able to have such a large group of Villagers gathering much faster should not be underestimated, and can quickly prove useful regardless of what type of strategy you're going for.

Aachen Chapel—Age II

Burgrave Palace

Type	Age
Age III - Military Landmark	III

Primary Uses
- *Advancing to Age III*
- *Producing groups of military units at once*

Building Stats

	Time	Food	Wood	Gold	Stone
Burgrave Palace	3m 40s	1200	0	600	0

Health	5000	Influence/Aura	--
Fire Armor	0	Influence/Aura Size	--
Ranged Armor	50	Garrison Yes/No	No
Size	4x4	Garrison No.	--

Burgrave Palace Technologies (P.45)

Technology	Unit	Age
Riveted Chain Mail	Spearman	II
Heavy Maces	Man-at-Arms	III
Two-Handed Weapons	Man-at-Arms	IV

Prioritization and Usage

Burgrave Palace is essentially five Barracks in one. From it you can train groups of five melee infantry at once, and while the total resource cost is the same as producing five individual units from one Barracks, the production time is equal to just one unit. Sustaining production from this building can be extremely resource intensive, but if you can keep up, then you won't need to build another Barracks until much later in the game where even more production may be needed.

Since it has such high production capabilities, it can give you a powerful melee infantry force in a very short amount of time, which can be used to quickly overwhelm your opponent. It can also be used defensively as an emergency tool to quickly produce a group of units that can fend off an attack on your base. Just keep in mind that both of these approaches require spending a lot of resources, so if your production is already stretched thin when it comes time to choose your Age III Landmark, you might not be able to get full use out of **Burgrave Palace**. Similarly, if you're intent on having your army mainly comprised of cavalry and ranged infantry, then the more general benefits of the **Regnitz Cathedral** might be a better fit.

Bulgrave Palace—Age III

Burgrave Palace Production

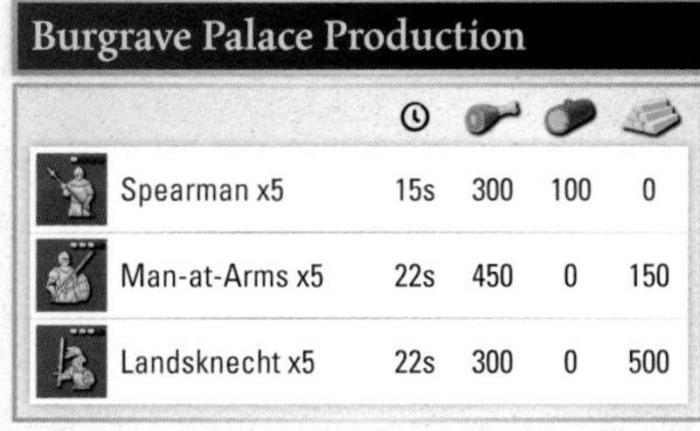

	Time	Food	Wood	Gold
Spearman x5	15s	300	100	0
Man-at-Arms x5	22s	450	0	150
Landsknecht x5	22s	300	0	500

4

Regnitz Cathedral

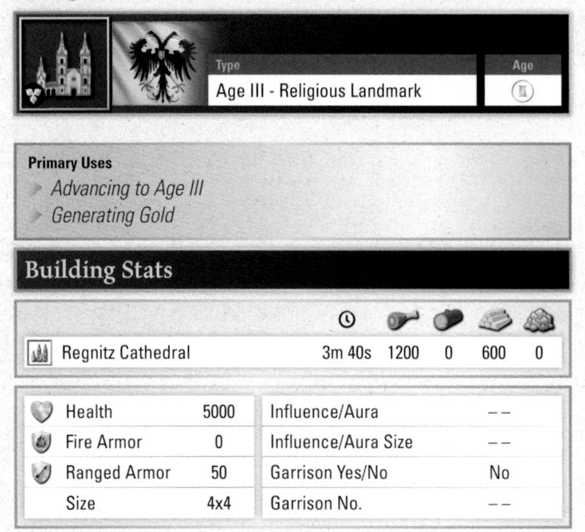

Type	Age
Age III - Religious Landmark	III

Primary Uses

- *Advancing to Age III*
- *Generating Gold*

Building Stats

	Time	Food	Wood	Gold	Stone
Regnitz Cathedral	3m 40s	1200	0	600	0

Health	5000	Influence/Aura	--
Fire Armor	0	Influence/Aura Size	--
Ranged Armor	50	Garrison Yes/No	No
Size	4x4	Garrison No.	--

Prioritization and Usage

Regnitz Cathedral has the ability to provide you with a substantial boost to your Age III Gold income if you can manage to take full advantage of it. You're able to place three Relics inside this Landmark, and once there, they'll generate +200% more Gold than at a normal building. Depending on how many Relics you have in your control when it's time to advance Ages, or how many you're confident you can acquire soon after, the benefits of this Landmark may vary for you.

If you're planning on building this Landmark, it's a good idea to produce a few Prelates earlier in the game so that you can have them ready to collect Relics as soon as you need them. The **Regnitz Cathedral** is more of a defensive, long-term investment for your economy, so if that's your playstyle then this is the Landmark you should go for over the military focused **Burgrave Palace**.

Regnitz Cathedral—Age III

Palace of Swabia

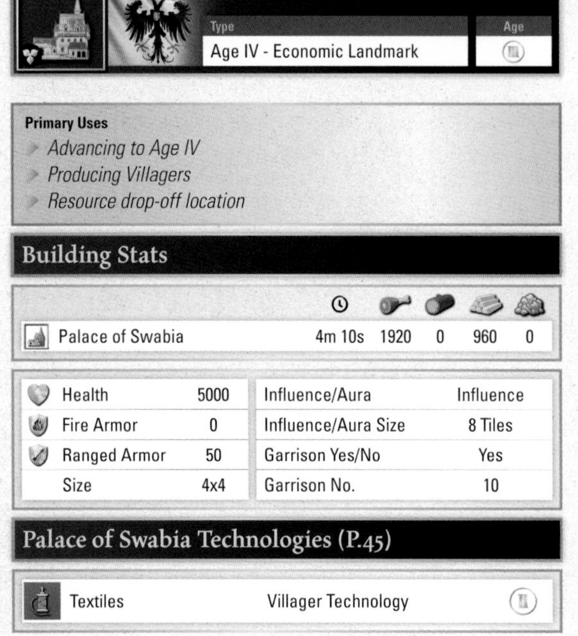

Type	Age
Age IV - Economic Landmark	III

Primary Uses

- *Advancing to Age IV*
- *Producing Villagers*
- *Resource drop-off location*

Building Stats

	Time	Food	Wood	Gold	Stone
Palace of Swabia	4m 10s	1920	0	960	0

Health	5000	Influence/Aura	Influence
Fire Armor	0	Influence/Aura Size	8 Tiles
Ranged Armor	50	Garrison Yes/No	Yes
Size	4x4	Garrison No.	10

Palace of Swabia Technologies (P.45)

Textiles	Villager Technology	II

Prioritization and Usage

You can take advantage of one of the main benefits of the **Palace of Swabia** before you even place it on the field, and that's the fact that it is 20% cheaper to build than other Age IV Landmarks. This discount allows you to advance to Age IV before your opponent, thus gaining access to the advanced units and technologies within it before them and giving you a significant advantage. To be able to research all of those technologies as quickly as possible you're going to need a sizable workforce, and that's where this Landmarks other signature ability comes into play. From here you can produce Villagers 75% faster than normal, and at 75% of the cost, allowing to give your economy a huge boost very quickly.

Since this Landmark has all of the functionality of a Holy Roman Empire Town Center it can also serve as the drop-off location for those resources, so you'll want to place it close to whichever one you desire so that you don't have to spend time constructing an additional drop-off building. If, however, you've already invested a lot into your economy and have multiple Town Centers producing Villagers before you're ready to advance to Age IV, then it would be worth saving up a bit more and investing in **Elzbach Palace** instead since that will provide more benefits.

Palace of Swabia—Age IV

Villager Production Details

	Time	Food	Wood	Gold
Villager	05s	12	0	0

Unit Production

Villager	IV
Scout	IV
Prelate	IV

Kevin Lam
Regnitz Cathedral—Age III
Concept Artwork

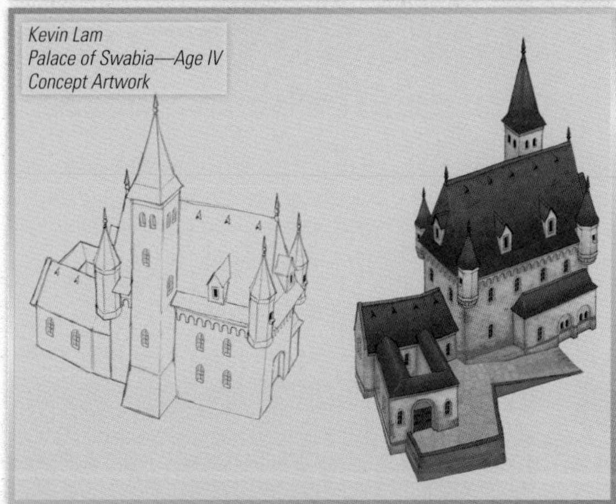

Kevin Lam
Palace of Swabia—Age IV
Concept Artwork

Stuart Ng
Elzbach Palace—Age IV
Concept Artwork

Elzbach Palace

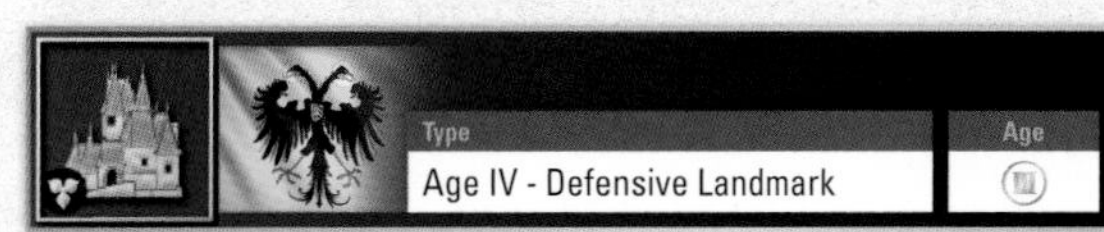

Primary Uses

- *Advancing to Age IV*
- *Defending key positions*
- *Increasing the survivability of surrounding buildings*

Building Stats

	Time	Food	Wood	Gold	Stone
Elzbach Palace	4m 10s	2400	0	1200	0

Health	7500	Influence/Aura	Influence
Fire Armor	5	Influence/Aura Size	8 Tiles
Ranged Armor	50	Garrison Yes/No	Yes
Size	4x4	Garrison No.	20

Elzback Palace—Age IV

Elzbach Palace Technologies (P.45)

Technology	Type	Age
Springald Emplacement	Weapon Emplacement	IV
Boiling Oil	Defensive Technology	IV
Cannon Emplacement	Weapon Emplacement	IV
Slate and Stone Construction	Building Technology	IV
Reinforced Defenses	Defensive Technology	IV

Prioritization and Usage

Generating Enhancement

Elzbach Palace Influence Elzbach Palace Influence Buildings take 33% less damage.

While many of the Landmarks based off Keeps further enhance their offensive capabilities, in fitting with the defensive theme of the Holy Roman Empire, **Elzbach Palace** is decidedly defense focused. The Landmark itself has 50% more health than a traditional Keep, and any building within the huge influence range takes 33% less damage from all sources. Along with the usual weapon emplacements, you can also research the unique **Slate and Stone Construction** and **Reinforced Defenses** technologies, both of which also add to the durability and survivability of your buildings and fortifications.

If you're planning on taking a defense approach in a match, or just really want to make an area and group of buildings as secure as possible, choosing this as your Age IV Landmark is a pretty straightforward choice since it can accentuate and amplify all aspects of that gameplay style. Like other Keeps, you can use it aggressively by placing it near your opponent's base, but rather than holding the area through force, with this Landmark you should aim to establish a blockade of walls and buildings within the influence range to deny your opponent access to resources.

Attack Details

Arrowslits*

Bow (Ranged)

Damage	12x3
Counter Bonus	25
Bonus Against	Ships
Attack Range	8.00
Attack Speed	0.38s

Springald Emplacement

Springald (Ranged)*

Damage	60
Counter Bonus	50
Bonus Against	Ships
Attack Range	9.00
Attack Speed	6.25s

Cannon Emplacement

Cannon (Siege)*

Damage	85
Counter Bonus	85
Bonus Against	Ships
Attack Range	10.00
Attack Speed	7.00s

Boiling Oil

Hot Oil (Siege)*

Damage	30
Counter Bonus	– –
Bonus Against	– –
Attack Range	2.00
Attack Speed	9.50s

*Requires the researching of their respective emplacements at Elzbach Palace.

4

Deer Stones

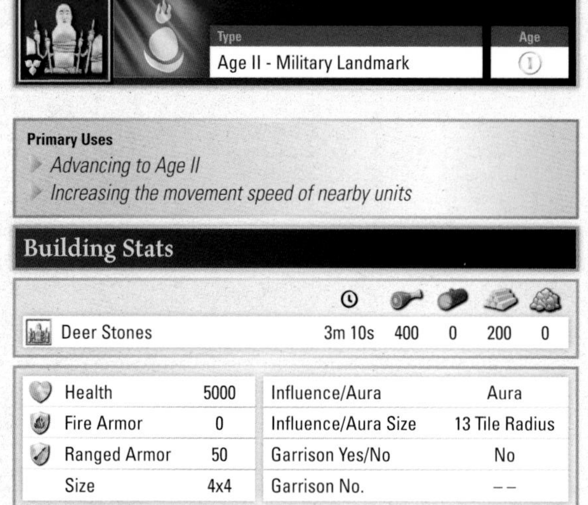

Type	Age
Age II - Military Landmark	I

Primary Uses
- *Advancing to Age II*
- *Increasing the movement speed of nearby units*

Building Stats

	Time	Food	Wood	Gold	Stone
Deer Stones	3m 10s	400	0	200	0

Health	5000	Influence/Aura	Aura
Fire Armor	0	Influence/Aura Size	13 Tile Radius
Ranged Armor	50	Garrison Yes/No	No
Size	4x4	Garrison No.	--

Prioritization and Usage

Generating Enhancement

Yam Cavalry and Traders near an Outpost get +15% speed for 20 seconds.

When unpacked, the **Deer Stones** Landmark has a large aura radius, within which any unit will automatically and continuously receive the **Yam** speed aura that increases their movement speed by +15%. Once a unit moves out of the aura, the buff will remain active for 20 seconds before dropping off. The large area that this buff can be applied over means you can affect a lot of units, both military and economic. If you unpack the Landmark near an area where you're gathering a lot of resources, then all of the Villagers working there can reap the benefits and drastically cut down on their walking time.

Place it near military production buildings, and any units produced will acquire the buff automatically when they appear and can move to your rally point marker or combat area at much greater speed. This is all made possible because the **Yam Network** technology (normally an Age III technology) is unlocked immediately for free as soon a the Landmark is constructed. That upgrade makes it so that any unit near one of your Outposts also receives the **Yam** speed aura. Because of the flexibility and number of uses this is an excellent all-round pick for an Age II Landmark that can fit any playstyle.

Deer Stones—Age II

The Silver Tree

Type	Age
Age II - Economic Landmark	I

Primary Uses
- *Advancing to Age I*
- *Trading and selling resources for Gold*

Building Stats

	Time	Food	Wood	Gold	Stone
The Silver Tree	3m 10s	400	0	200	0

Health	5000	Influence/Aura	--
Fire Armor	0	Influence/Aura Size	--
Ranged Armor	50	Garrison Yes/No	No
Size	4x4	Garrison No.	--

The Silver Tree Technologies (P.45)

Stone Commerce	Trade	II
Stone Commerce (Improved)	Trade	IV

Prioritization and Usage

Establishing lucrative trade routes with large numbers of Traders is a cornerstone of Mongol gameplay, and if you're leaning into those elements, then **The Silver Tree** is the ideal Age II Landmark to choose. It has all of the functionality of a normal Market, but it can produce Traders at half the cost, and in half the time, which can make it significantly quicker and cheaper to start trading once you reach Age II, especially since you won't need to build an additional Market. All it takes is one roundtrip to a neutral Trade Post on most maps for a Trader produced at this Landmark to offset their production cost and start earning profit.

Given all of the benefits that come from establishing and securing trade routes for the Mongols, **The Silver Tree** is ideal for players that are focusing more on economic growth than military. The only times you might not want to go for this Landmark is if you're playing on a map where water is the dominant feature and you can't really establish any form of land trade.

The Silver Tree—Age II

Unit Production

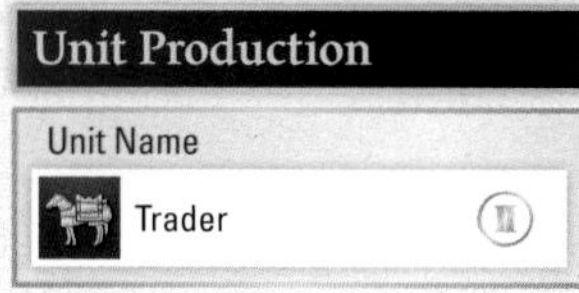

Unit Name	
Trader	II

Stuart Ng
Kulrutai—Age III
Concept Artwork

Stuart Ng
Kulrutai—Age III
Concept Artwork

Concepting the Silver Tree

"I very much enjoyed concepting the Mongol Karakorum Silver Tree. It was inspired by a real-world monument, and because there is no surviving version of it today, we had to research text records, accounts, or illustrations which interpreted what it could have looked like. We had joked that it was the Mongol "Party Tree", which it pretty much was. The Mongols would return from battle, then sit by this monument which had 3 silvery dragons intertwined spouting alcohol from its mouths. Beneath it were workers that had to continually refill the fountain with drink, and an angel would sit atop the entire monument."

– Stuart Ng
Senior Concept Artist, Relic

Kurultai

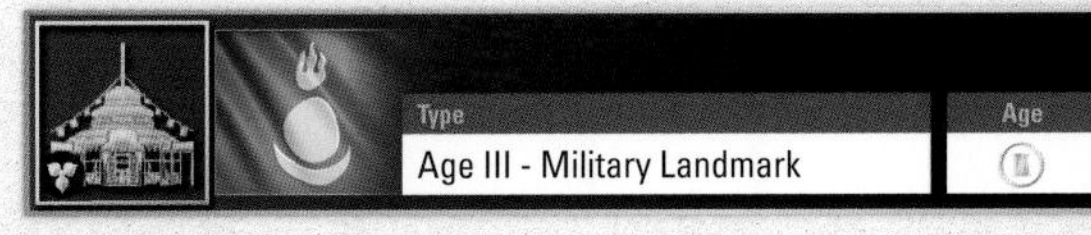

Type	Age
Age III - Military Landmark	III

Primary Uses

- *Advancing to Age III*
- *Healing and increasing the damage of nearby units*

Building Stats

	Time	Food	Wood	Gold	Stone
Kurultai	3m 40s	1200	0	600	0

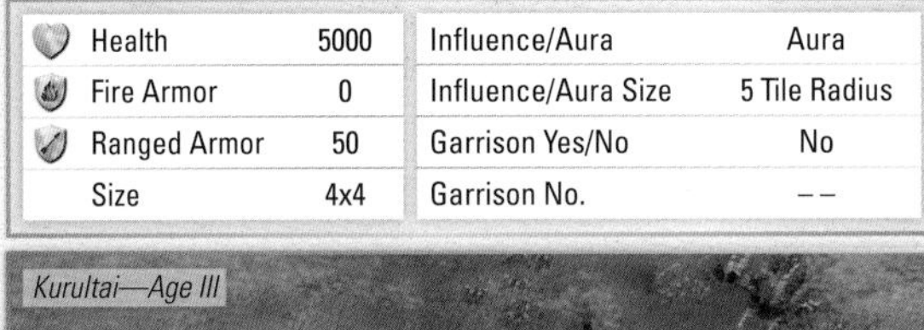

Health	5000	Influence/Aura	Aura
Fire Armor	0	Influence/Aura Size	5 Tile Radius
Ranged Armor	50	Garrison Yes/No	No
Size	4x4	Garrison No.	– –

Kurultai—Age III

Prioritization and Usage

How much benefit you get out of the **Kurultai** depends entirely on where and how you're using the Khan unit. The **Kurultai** has an average sized aura, and if the Khan is within it, any damaged unit will immediately start healing, and all units receive a huge +25% damage bonus for 30 seconds.

Because all of the abilities of the **Kurultai** are so linked to the proximity of the Khan, if you're mainly using the Khan as a raiding unit with groups of your military, far from any defensible position, then you may see more benefit from the **Steppe Redoubt** as your Age III Landmark. The **Kurultai** is thus best used in your base area as a defense tool in conjunction with the Khan to aid you against enemy assaults in games where there's a lot of back-and-forth attacks. If your Villagers keep getting attacked by small raiding parties, then you can position the **Kurultai** and your Khan nearby so that those Villagers can walk through the aura area and get healed up.

If you're playing in a game where the Conquest win condition is not enabled, then you can use the **Kurultai** in an aggressive manner where you place it near highly contested areas within quick reach of your raiding parties. This tactic is best used in combination with cavalry units since they can cover ground much faster, allowing you to put the **Kurultai** in a slightly safer place, while still giving your army time to make use of the damage bonus.

Steppe Redoubt

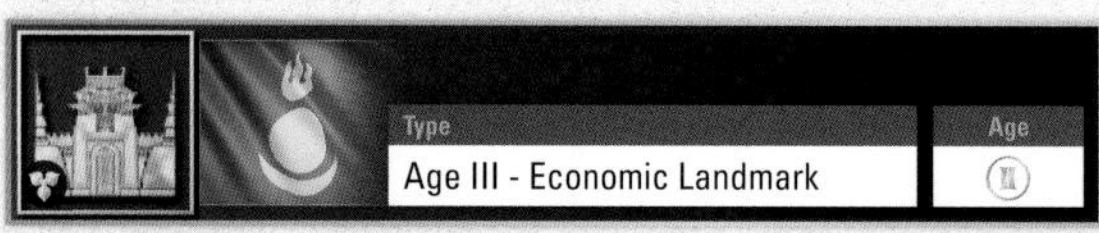

Primary Uses

- *Advancing to Age III*
- *Resource drop-off locationResearching technology*

Building Stats

	Time	Food	Wood	Gold	Stone
Steppe Redoubt	3m 40s	1200	0	600	0

Health	5000	Influence/Aura	--
Fire Armor	0	Influence/Aura Size	--
Ranged Armor	50	Garrison Yes/No	No
Size	4x4	Garrison No.	--

Stuart Ng
Steppe Redoubt—Age III
Concept Artwork

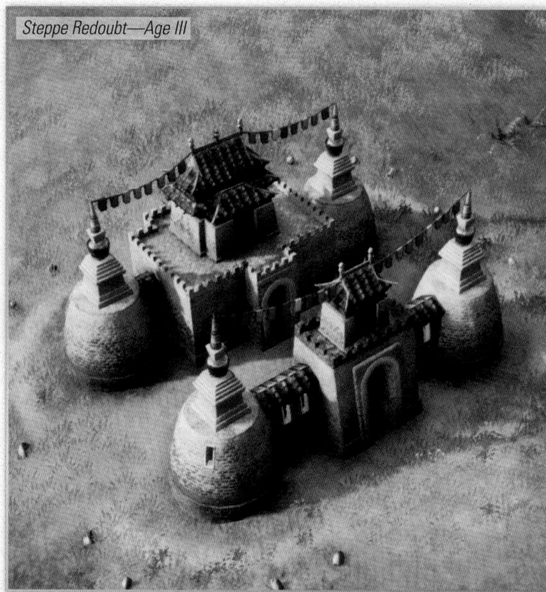

Steppe Redoubt—Age III

Prioritization and Usage

The **Steppe Redoubt** is a more economic focused Landmark than the **Kurultai**, so if the strategy you're employing is focused on economic strength, then this would be a good choice of Age III Landmark. It has all of the properties and abilities of a normal Ger, but comes with the significantly higher health of a Landmark so it's a bit safer to place further from your base. One of the main benefits of this Landmark over a normal Ger, however, is the fact that any Gold your Villagers drop off here is increased by 50%, so even though it can be used near any resource, you should ideally place it near a Gold Vein.

Like all Mongol buildings, it can also be packed up and moved, so once a Gold Vein is depleted, simply move it to another one. Due to the amount of technologies that the Mongols have the ability to research at a Ger, having this as your Landmark can also speed up their acquisition since it gives you another place to research things without having to construct another Ger.

Steppe Redoubt Technologies (P.45)

Technology	Type	Age
Forestry	Woodcutting	I
Forestry (Improved)	Woodcutting	I
Survival Techniques	Hunting	I
Survival Techniques (Impr.)	Hunting	I
Wheelbarrow	Villager	I
Wheelbarrow (Improved)	Villager	I
Professional Scouts	Hunting	II
Professional Scouts (Impr.)	Hunting	II
Horticulture	Food Gathering 1/3	II
Horticulture (Improved)	Food Gathering 1/3	II
Fertilization	Food Gathering 2/3	III
Fertilization (Improved)	Food Gathering 2/3	III
Precision Cross-Breeding	Food Gathering 3/3	IV
Precision Cross-Breeding (Improved)	Food Gathering 3/3	IV
Double Broadax	Wood Gathering 1/3	II
Double Broadax (Impr.)	Wood Gathering 1/3	II
Lumber Preservation	Wood Gathering 2/3	III
Lumber Preservation (Impr.)	Wood Gathering 2/3	III
Crosscut Saw	Wood Gathering 3/3	IV
Crosscut Saw (Improved)	Wood Gathering 3/3	IV
Specialized Pick	Mining 1/3	II
Specialized Pick (Impr.)	Mining 1/3	II
Acid Distillation	Mining 2/3	III
Acid Distillation (Improved)	Mining 2/3	III
Cupellation	Mining 3/3	IV
Cupellation (Improved)	Mining 3/3	IV

The White Stupa

Primary Uses

- *Advancing to Age IV*
- *Generating Stone over time*
- *Granting access to improved technology and production*

Building Stats

	Time	Food	Wood	Gold	Stone
The White Stuppa	4m 10s	2400	0	1200	0

Health	5000	Influence/Aura	Influence
Fire Armor	0	Influence/Aura Size	2 Tiles
Ranged Armor	50	Garrison Yes/No	No
Size	4x4	Garrison No.	--

The White Stupa—Age IV

Prioritization and Usage

By the time in games that you're normally looking to advance to Age IV, one of the most precious resources, Stone, is usually starting to become quite scarce, and since the Mongols rely on it a lot for their improved technology and production, any sources of it are a welcome sight. That's where the **White Stuppa** comes into play. It has all of the functionality of an Ovoo, but does not have to be built on a Stone Outcropping, and when unpacked, it automatically generates 240 Stone per minute. That amount of Stone alone is enough to produce a lot of units through improved production, or if you save up for a few minutes, you can afford most improved technologies.

In terms of placement, you'll want to get maximum benefit out of the improved functionality it enables in any buildings built within its influence range, so either build it near them, or move them within range afterwards. Because you'll generally need Stone regardless of your playstyle, and all of the other Ovoo benefits it comes with, it's hard to go wrong with picking the **White Stuppa** as your Age IV Landmark.

Stuart Ng
The White Stupa—Age IV
Concept Artwork

The Mongols' Flexibility

"Mongol moving buildings gives the civilization a ton of flexibility and helps them to save some wood too. Given that they are unable to build walls, having the ability to relocate can help to cover that weakness, while also making the Mongols a truly nomadic civ in AoE IV. Some of the Mongol Landmarks (which can also be moved!) encourage the player to put them in more exposed positions, such as the Kurultai which could be used aggressively, or the Silver Tree which you might place away from your base to set up an early trade route. Because Landmarks are also conquest victory conditions it can be a double-edged sword to place them in dangerous locations, and if you're caught with a packed landmark it becomes an easy target for enemy forces!"

- Zak "ZeroEmpires" Robinson
Senior Designer, Balance, Relic

4

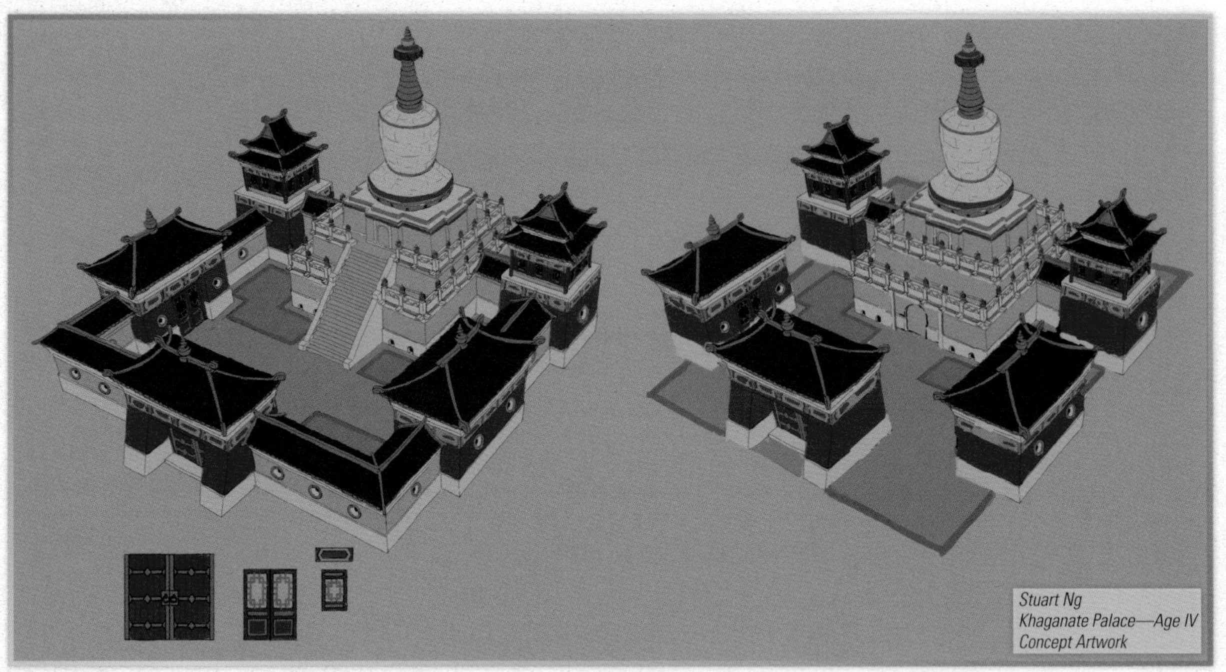

Stuart Ng
Khaganate Palace—Age IV
Concept Artwork

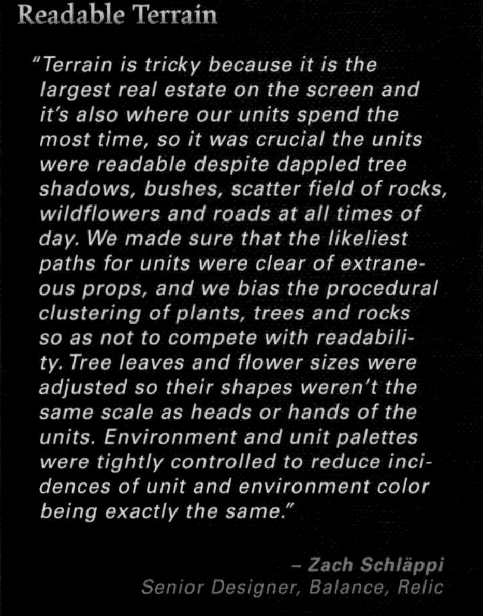

Readable Terrain

"Terrain is tricky because it is the largest real estate on the screen and it's also where our units spend the most time, so it was crucial the units were readable despite dappled tree shadows, bushes, scatter field of rocks, wildflowers and roads at all times of day. We made sure that the likeliest paths for units were clear of extraneous props, and we bias the procedural clustering of plants, trees and rocks so as not to compete with readability. Tree leaves and flower sizes were adjusted so their shapes weren't the same scale as heads or hands of the units. Environment and unit palettes were tightly controlled to reduce incidences of unit and environment color being exactly the same."

- Zach Schläppi
Senior Designer, Balance, Relic

Khaganate Palace

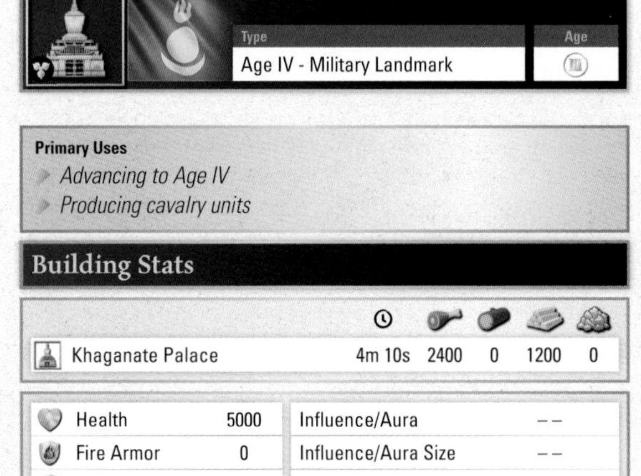

Type	Age
Age IV - Military Landmark	

Primary Uses
- *Advancing to Age IV*
- *Producing cavalry units*

Building Stats

	Time	Food	Wood	Gold	Stone
Khaganate Palace	4m 10s	2400	0	1200	0

Health	5000	Influence/Aura	--
Fire Armor	0	Influence/Aura Size	--
Ranged Armor	50	Garrison Yes/No	No
Size	4x4	Garrison No.	--

Prioritization and Usage

There's an element of risk associated with picking the **Khaganate Palace** as your Age IV Landmark due to the unpredictable nature of its ability, but if you can work with or plan around it, it can give you a nice boost to your military strength. Once built, the **Khaganate Palace** will spawn a small army of cavalry units every 90s, and that army can consist of either Horsemen, Mangudai, or Lancers. You have no control over which unit type will spawn, everything is left in the hands of fate. If you're struggling with producing enough military units to contest your opponent, then this Landmark can help with that because the units it produces do not cost any resources, and they'll continue to spawn even if you've completely run out of all resources.

The downside to this, however, is that there's also the possibility that your population space might be clogged up with units that you're not using. To try and negate that situation happening, you should build the core of your army out of the three unit types this Landmark produces if you decide to pick it, otherwise the more predictable technology advantage provided by **The White Stupa** might be more suitable for you.

Khaganate Palace—Age IV

Army Spawn Details

	Amount	Spawn Time
Horsemen	8	90s
Mangudai	6	90s
Lancers	4	90s

Kevin Lam
Kremlin—Age II
Concept Artwork

Researching the Buildings

"We actually researched a lot of how buildings were constructed during these centuries, and for each civilization. We tried to understand how the support frames actually worked, which helped define the look of each civilization, and when that type of architecture was used in which century. Even though you might not see the much of the interiors of buildings compared to the exterior, we felt it was important to understand how it was built inside. Some of the support framework would be seen on the exteriors of the building. We did take some creative license in simplifying some of the architecture for the sake of readability from a great distance, and considering how many and how much there would be on screen at any given time."

– Stuart Ng
Senior Concept Artist, Relic

Kremlin

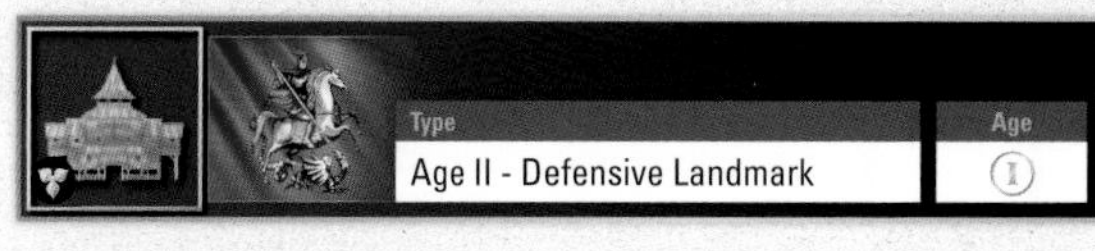

Type	Age
Age II - Defensive Landmark	II

Primary Uses

- *Advancing to Age II*
- *Defensive fortification*

Building Stats

	Time	Food	Wood	Gold	Stone
Kremlin	3m 10s	400	0	200	0

Health	5000	Influence/Aura	Influence
Fire Armor	0	Influence/Aura Size	4 Tiles
Ranged Armor	50	Garrison Yes/No	Yes
Size	4x4	Garrison No.	8

Kremlin—Age II

Kremlin Technologies (P.45)

Springald Emplacement	Weapon Emplacement	III

Prioritization and Usage

Generating Enhancement

Wooden Fortress Influence Lumber Camps and Town Centers within influence return 20% more Wood.

The **Kremlin** is a very safe choice to go with for Age II Landmark because it's a stronger version of the already strong Wooden Fortress. Not only does it have significantly more health, but it also comes with the **Arrowslits, Castle Turret,** and **Castle Watch** technologies unlocked by default, giving it a much greater defensive presence than a Wood Fortress. Also like a Wooden Fortress it comes with Wooden Fortress Influence, so placing this Landmark near one of your Lumber Camps will not only make that area very secure for Age II, but you'll also get more Wood in the process. If you expect aggressive play by your opponent, or are in great need of Wood either because you're on a water map or for a strategy you're trying to use, then the **Kremlin** is definitely the Landmark to choose.

Attack Details

Arrowslits

Bow (Ranged)

Damage	12
Counter Bonus	25
Bonus Against	Ships
Attack Range	8.00
Attack Speed	1.00

Springald Emplacement

Springald (Ranged)*

Damage	60
Counter Bonus	50
Bonus Against	Ships
Attack Range	9.00
Attack Speed	6.25s

*Requires researching of the emplacement at the Kremlin.

4

The Golden Gate

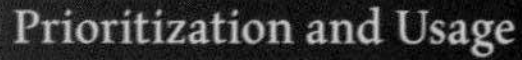

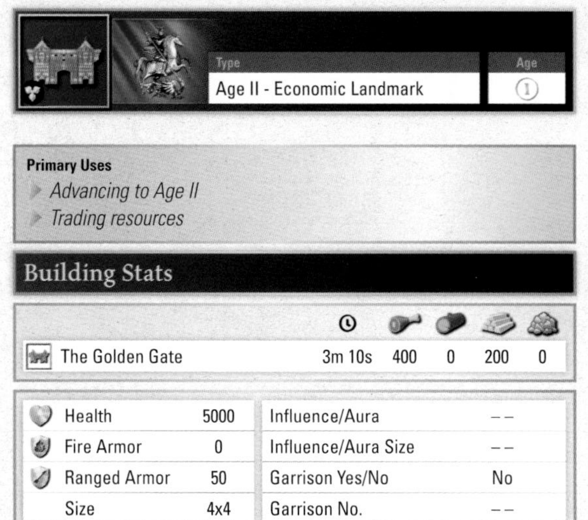

Type	Age
Age II - Economic Landmark	II

Primary Uses
- *Advancing to Age II*
- *Trading resources*

Building Stats

	Time	Food	Wood	Gold	Stone
The Golden Gate	3m 10s	400	0	200	0

Health	5000	Influence/Aura	--
Fire Armor	0	Influence/Aura Size	--
Ranged Armor	50	Garrison Yes/No	No
Size	4x4	Garrison No.	--

Prioritization and Usage

Passive Ability

Supply Generation Generates supplies every 60s that can used to ensure a favorable trade.

As an Age II Landmark, **The Golden Gate** should be considered a long term investment rather than one that you see immediate benefit from. It has most of the functionality of a normal Market in that you can buy and sell various resources for Gold, but it lacks the ability to produce Traders, so you'll still need to build a normal Market for them if you're looking to establish a traditional trade route. Normal trading is not **The Golden Gate's** forte, however, because it has the ability to automatically generate a cache of supplies every minute, and they can be used to ensure that when you complete a trade (either buying or selling), you gain an extra 50 resources.

So if the exchange rates are neutral, you could buy 150 Food for 100 Gold, or sell 100 Wood for 150 Gold for example. These supplies accumulate over time, so it's possible to save them up and use them when needed, which can give you a massive influx of a particular resource in a time of dire need. Because of the fact that it's best to save up the supplies for either a big push on your opponent to finish them off, or in an effort to make a defensive stand towards the end of the game, this Landmark should be built when you plan to play a slower, longer game.

The Golden Gate—Age II

High Trade House

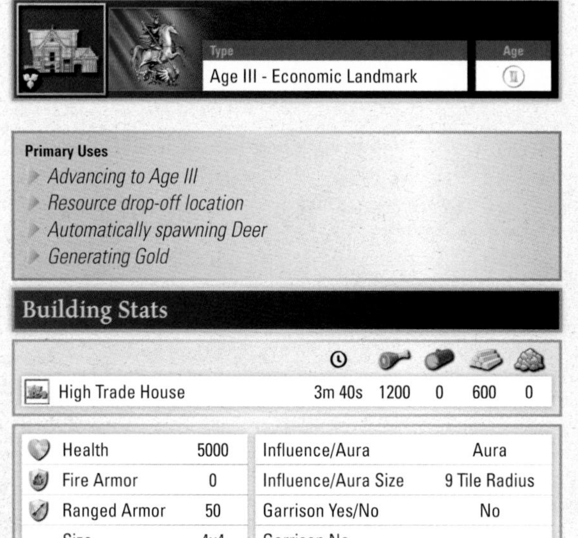

Type	Age
Age III - Economic Landmark	III

Primary Uses
- *Advancing to Age III*
- *Resource drop-off location*
- *Automatically spawning Deer*
- *Generating Gold*

Building Stats

	Time	Food	Wood	Gold	Stone
High Trade House	3m 40s	1200	0	600	0

Health	5000	Influence/Aura	Aura
Fire Armor	0	Influence/Aura Size	9 Tile Radius
Ranged Armor	50	Garrison Yes/No	No
Size	4x4	Garrison No.	--

Prioritization and Usage

Like a Hunting Cabin, the **High Trade House** Landmark automatically generates Gold over time based on how many trees are nearby, but the amount it generates is 200% higher than that of the Hunting Cabin, which means it has the potential to be a lot more lucrative. To take full advantage of the Gold generation you should place this Landmark away from other Hunting Cabins, and close to as many trees as possible.

Once it's placed, you can then send your Villagers in to start the deforestation without affecting the amount of Gold generated, but unlike a a normal Hunting Cabin, you should also send some additional Villagers because this Landmark has another trick up its sleeve. Every 60 seconds a Deer will spawn close to the **High Trade House**, so it's worth having a group of Villagers to kill and gather the Food from them. This constant and consistent source of additional Food can provide a nice boost to your overall Food income which, coupled with the Gold generation, make this an excellent Age III Landmark if you're focusing on your economy.

High Trade House—Age III

Kevin Lam
High Trade House—Age III
Concept Artwork

Civilizational Balance Process

"Starting at the paper design level, we try to balance like for like systems against each other. For example, each Landmark at each Age should provide the player with an approximately equal raw value. Each civilization has various economic bonuses which we total together and try to normalize across all eight of them. By breaking each system down and modelling them across each of the civs, we build a solid foundation.

This approach requires many assumptions to be made, however, and so from this basis we playtest, playtest, and playtest to flag any nuances that a paper design cannot capture when it comes to all these interacting systems.

From there we iterate, measure, and iterate again—the more we play, the more accurate our assumptions and models can become on paper, and the more accurately we can judge the strength of each comparable system."

– Zak "ZeroEmpires" Robinson
Senior Designer, Balance, Relic

Abbey of the Trinity

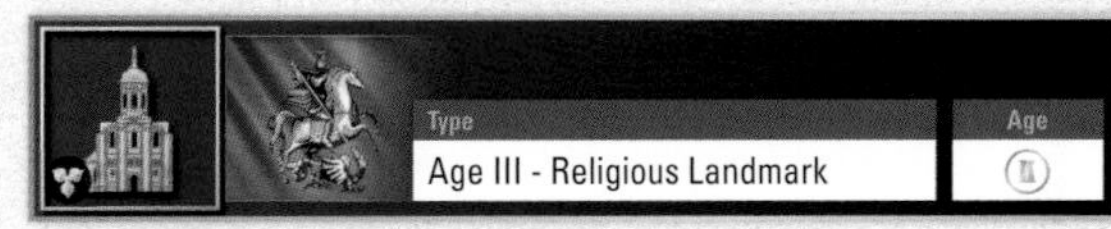

Type	Age
Age III - Religious Landmark	III

Primary Uses

- *Advancing to Age III*
- *Housing religious Relics*
- *Researching unique religious technologies*

Building Stats

	Time	Food	Wood	Gold	Stone
Abbey of the Trinity	3m 40s	1200	0	600	0

Health	5000	Influence/Aura	--
Fire Armor	0	Influence/Aura Size	--
Ranged Armor	50	Garrison Yes/No	No
Size	4x4	Garrison No.	--

Abbey of the Trinity—Age III

Prioritization and Usage

If you plan on making heavy use of the Warrior Monk unit, then the **Abbey of the Trinity** should be considered an essential choice for your Age III Landmark. Not only can it produce Warrior Monks at half the cost of a normal Monastery, but it also grants you access to a pair of unique technologies that further increase the **Saint's Blessing** buff. **Improved Blessing** grants an extra +1 damage to the buff, and **Saint's Reach** increases the range of it by 3 tiles, allowing it to affect a great many more of your units. The ability to produce Warrior Monks for half the cost will make it much easier for you to collect Relics and gain control of Sacred Sites early in Age III, which can help you greatly with Gold generation at a time when gold Veins are starting to dry up. If your goal is to expand your control of the map, and thus the game, having Warrior Monks as part of your armies, giving them all of the additional benefits that you can add to **Saint's Blessing** from this building will make it much easier to achieve.

Abbey of the Trinity Technologies (P.45)

Technology	Type	Unique	Age
Improved Blessing	Religious	✓	III
Saint's Reach	Religious	✓	III
Blessing Duration	Religious	✓	III
Herbal Medicine	Hunting		III
Piety	Religious		IV
Tithe Barns	Religious		IV

Unit Production

Unit	Age
Warrior Monk	III

4

Spasskaya Tower

Type	Age
Age IV - Defensive Landmark	IV

Primary Uses
- *Advancing to Age IV*
- *Defending key positions*

Building Stats

	Time	Food	Wood	Gold	Stone
Spasskaya Tower	4m 10s	2400	0	1200	0

Health	8000	Influence/Aura	--
Fire Armor	5	Influence/Aura Size	--
Ranged Armor	50	Garrison Yes/No	Yes
Size	4x4	Garrison No.	20

Prioritization and Usage

Spasskaya Tower doesn't feature any unique abilities, but unlike other Landmarks based on Keeps, this one comes fully-formed with all of its weapon emplacements already unlocked, making it an extremely strong defensive building as soon as it's placed. It also features a lot more health than a traditional Keep so it can fare a bit better when used offensively away from your base. Where it shines, however is as a defensive powerhouse, protecting either exposed parts of your base or highly contested areas such as Sacred Sites and Trade Posts. If you're under a lot of pressure from your opponent and need some extra defensive firepower, or have no need of the technologies available at the High Armory, then **Spasskaya Tower** is a good all-round choice for an Age IV Landmark.

Attack Details

Arrowslits	
Bow (Ranged)	
Damage	12x3
Counter Bonus	25
Bonus Against	Ships
Attack Range	8.00
Attack Speed	0.38s
Springald Emplacement	
Springald (Ranged)	
Damage	60
Counter Bonus	50
Bonus Against	Ships
Attack Range	9.00
Attack Speed	6.25s
Cannon Emplacement	
Cannon (Siege)	
Damage	85
Counter Bonus	85
Bonus Against	Ships
Attack Range	10.00
Attack Speed	7.00s

Spasskaya Tower—Age IV

Spasskaya Tower Technologies (P.45)

Boiling Oil	Defensive	IV

High Armory

Type	Age
Age IV - Military Landmark	IV

Primary Uses
- *Advancing to Age IV*
- *Researching unique siege engine technologies*

Building Stats

	Time	Food	Wood	Gold	Stone
High Armory	4m 10s	2400	0	1200	0

Health	5000	Influence/Aura	Aura
Fire Armor	0	Influence/Aura Size	7 Tile Radius
Ranged Armor	50	Garrison Yes/No	No
Size	4x4	Garrison No.	--

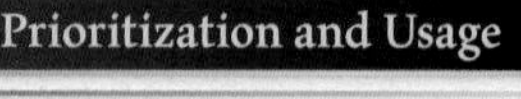

Prioritization and Usage

Generating Enhancement

High Armory Production Bonus The cost of siege engines in nearby Siege Workshops is decreased by 20%

The sole purpose of the **High Armory** is to make your siege engines hit harder, further, and faster, and since siege engines are relevant in the late stages of almost every game, these increases be very important. As an added bonus, if you place this Landmark near a Siege Workshop, their production costs will be reduced by 20%, allowing you to field more siege engines than your opponent.

If you're planning on obtaining this Landmark, try to have a couple of Siege Workshops built and ready to go before you're ready to advance to Age IV, and then you can place this Landmark right next to them and start mass producing. The technologies available at this Landmark all affect different siege engines, so you should prioritise them based on which units or defenses your opponent has. The only time you might not want to build the **High Armory** is if you're playing in a team game and your allies are focusing on siege, so at those times you the **Spasskaya Tower** might be a better option.

High Armory—Age IV

Spasskaya Tower Technologies (P.45)

Wandering Town	Ram	IV
Siege Training Crew	Mangonel & Trebuchet	IV
Fine Tuned Guns	Bombard	IV
Banded Arms	Springald	IV

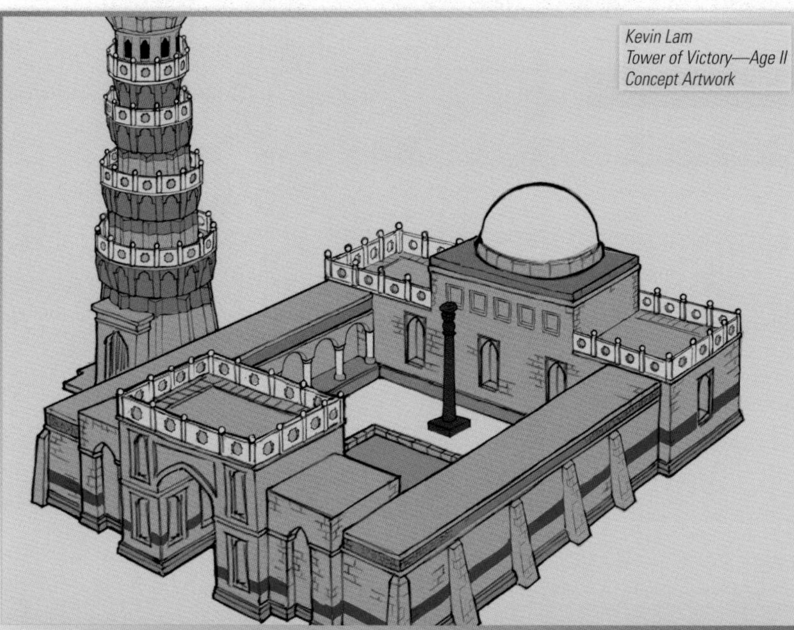

Kevin Lam
Tower of Victory—Age II
Concept Artwork

Making the Buildings Recognizable

"The challenge with buildings was the orbiting camera. The buildings must be quickly recognisable from any angle which led us to prioritize rooftops, towers and building footprints, followed by skirts (landscaping around the structure) and walls.

As with the characters, the first important step is categorizing the buildings and attributing certain architectural characteristics, shape language and material to each of those categories based on function: Industrial, residential, institutional/religious, military and landmarks. Since we had to prioritize, we used a simple system in which we ask: What will the player see first, most often, and will it produce units/vehicles or not? This generally drove the priorities of which buildings should be benchmarked, given extra or less layer of detail, or would get the roof treatment. For example, residential buildings, like houses, would be one of the first structures to be built and seen because they govern population capacity and would be the most numerous; they received most detail, diversity, and because the player will not interact with them and doesn't need to notice them but anyone else watching the game will see them repeatedly. Military buildings such as barracks, archery range, stables and siege works are critical to the player need to be actively seen and is often used by the player for unit production and upgrades. Which is why all military unit producing structures have the more eye-catching shinier metal roofs."

– Zach Schläppi
Principal Artist, Art Director, Relic

Tower of Victory

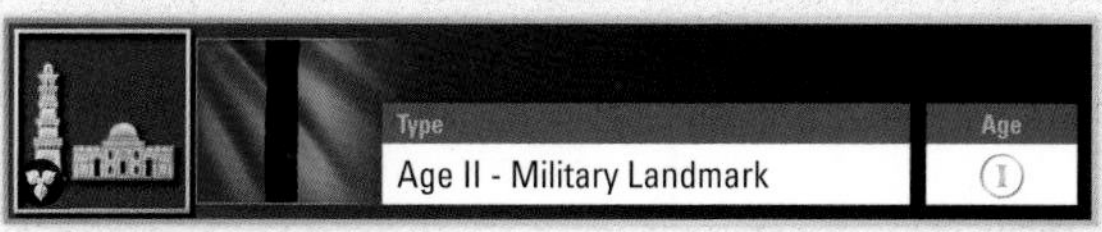

Type	Age
Age II - Military Landmark	(I)

Primary Uses

- *Advancing to Age II*
- *Enhancing infantry units*

Building Stats

Tower of Victory	3m 10s	400	0	200	0

Health	5000	Influence/Aura	Aura
Fire Armor	0	Influence/Aura Size	5 Tile Radius
Ranged Armor	50	Garrison Yes/No	No
Size	4x4	Garrison No.	--

Generating Enhancement

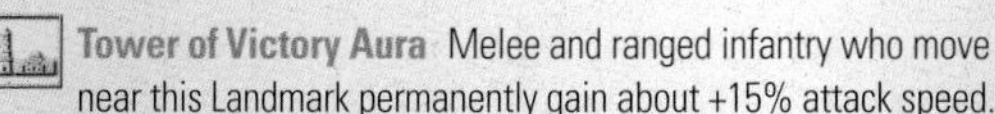

Tower of Victory Aura Melee and ranged infantry who move near this Landmark permanently gain about +15% attack speed.

Tower of Victory—Age II

Prioritization and Usage

The Delhi Sultanate tend to start slow and get stronger as the game goes on, therefore their gameplay tends to be somewhat passive in earlier stages. This Landmark can help you overcome some of those early game hurdles by giving a boost in power to all of your infantry units. Any infantry unit that passes through the aura range of this Landmark will have their attack speed permanently increased by 15%. This increase is obviously good for all infantry, but it's especially useful for the slow-firing late game heavy-hitters like Crossbowmen and Handcannoneers.

Because your units only need to pass through the aura once to receive the buff, you should ideally place this Landmark in a position between your production buildings and the rally point where your army is gathering. By doing that you'll ensure that as many units as possible walk through the area and get the buff on the way to their destination. If you intend on making use of a lot of military infantry units rather than the religious benefits provided by the **Dome of the Faith**, then this should be your choice of Landmark to reach Age II.

Dome of the Faith

Type	Age
Age II - Religious Landmark	II

Primary Uses

- *Advancing to Age II*
- *Producing Scholars at reduced cost*

Building Stats

	Time	Food	Wood	Gold	Stone
Dome of the Faith	3m 10s	400	0	200	0

Health	5000	Influence/Aura	--
Fire Armor	0	Influence/Aura Size	--
Ranged Armor	50	Garrison Yes/No	No
Size	4x4	Garrison No.	--

Prioritization and Usage

Scholars are vital for the long-term economic and military growth of the Delhi Sultanate, because the speed at which they can research technology is determined by the amount of Scholars garrisoned inside Mosques. Producing enough Scholars to be able to research things quickly regardless of your playstyle requires a lot of Gold, so the fact that the **Dome of the Faith** can produce them for half the cost makes it an excellent pick for your Age II Landmark. As soon as it's built, it should be used to produce Scholars constantly, and you should only stop if you're in desperate need of Gold elsewhere, or you have enough Scholars to research things at a pace you're happy with.

Unit Production

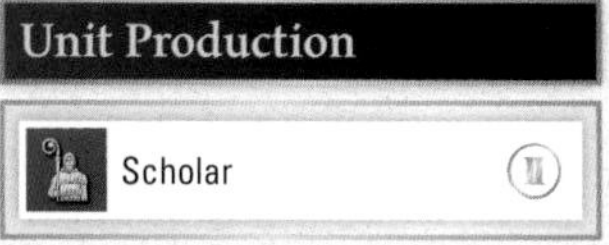

Unit	Age
Scholar	II

Dome of the Faith—Age II

Compound of the Defender

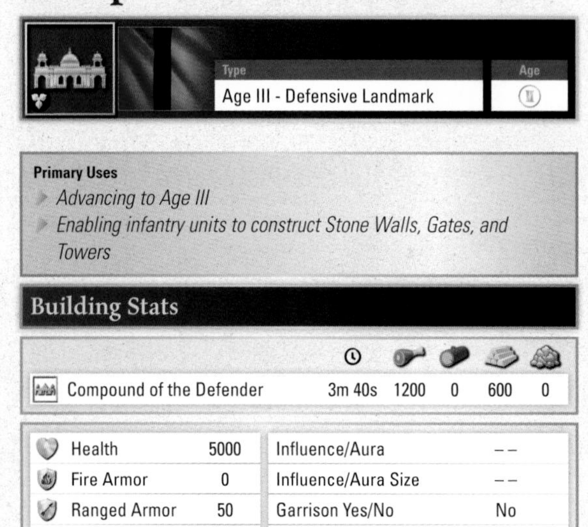

Type	Age
Age III - Defensive Landmark	III

Primary Uses

- *Advancing to Age III*
- *Enabling infantry units to construct Stone Walls, Gates, and Towers*

Building Stats

	Time	Food	Wood	Gold	Stone
Compound of the Defender	3m 40s	1200	0	600	0

Health	5000	Influence/Aura	--
Fire Armor	0	Influence/Aura Size	--
Ranged Armor	50	Garrison Yes/No	No
Size	4x4	Garrison No.	--

Prioritization and Usage

As its name implies, the **Compound of the Defender** Landmark has a distinctly defense orientated focus, so if you're taking a defensive approach during a match, this would be the choice of Landmark to reach Age III. Once built, it enhances the intrinsic ability of Delhi Sultanate infantry to construct Palisade Walls and Gates by adding their Stone equivalents to the list of things they can build in the field. As an additional benefit, the Stone cost of all buildings, fortifications or emplacements is reduced by 25% once this Landmark is placed.

If you're planning on fortifying your base with Stone defensive structures, then it's worth waiting until you've placed this Landmark because, not only will you be able to construct them at a much lower cost, but you can also use your military infantry to do the work, rather than taking Villagers off resource gathering duty for it. While defense is their primary purpose, with a bit of creativity, Stone Walls constructed by your infantry can also be used to surprise your opponent just as you're about to engage them; a few quickly constructed walls can funnel your opponent's units into chokepoints that your elephants can take advantage of, and this tactic can be especially useful if your opponent doesn't have any units capable of destroying the walls, because then you can set up entire blockades.

Compound of the Defender—Age III

House of Learning

Primary Uses

Advancing to Age III

Building Stats

House of Learning	3m 40s	1200	0	600	0

Health	5000	Influence/Aura	--
Fire Armor	0	Influence/Aura Size	--
Ranged Armor	50	Garrison Yes/No	No
Size	4x4	Garrison No.	--

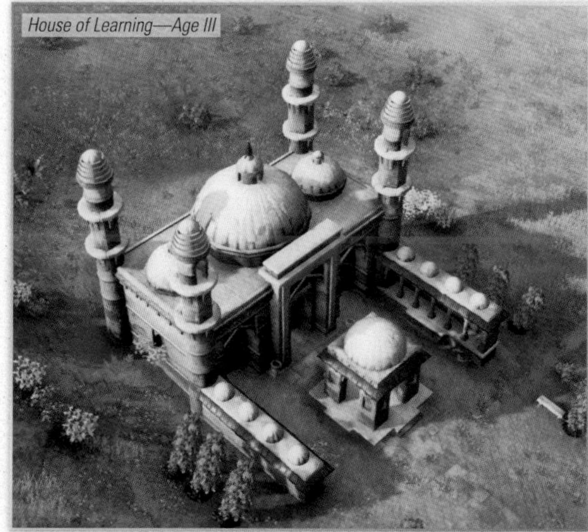

House of Learning—Age III

House of Learning Technologies (P.45)

Reinforced Foundations	Population	IV
Tranquil Venue	Mosque	IV
Lookout Towers	Outpost	IV
Honed Blades	Man-at-Arms & Knight	IV
Hearty Rations	Villager	IV

Prioritization and Usage

If you went with the **Dome of the Faith** as your Age II Landmark, then the **House of Learning** is a good follow-up as your Age III Landmark, because you can take advantage of all of those Scholars to research the unique technologies available here. In total there are five technologies that you can research at this Landmark each affecting various aspects of your economy or military units and none of them are available anywhere else.

To cut down on the amount of Houses you need to build, or if you're struggling with population capacity, then the **Reinforced Foundations** technology can give you a quick boost by adding +5 capacity to all of your Houses and Town Centers. **Tranquil Venue** turns your Mosque into a place of healing, and you can get **Lookout Towers** to increase the sight range of your Outposts, which can be useful if your opponent is raiding you a lot. If you're looking a good all-round boost to your economy, then increasing the carrying capacity of your Villagers with the **Hearty Rations** technology will be a good acquisition. Finally, if Men-at-Arms or Knights are part of your army, then you should strongly consider learning **Honed Blades**, because it increases their attack power by +3.

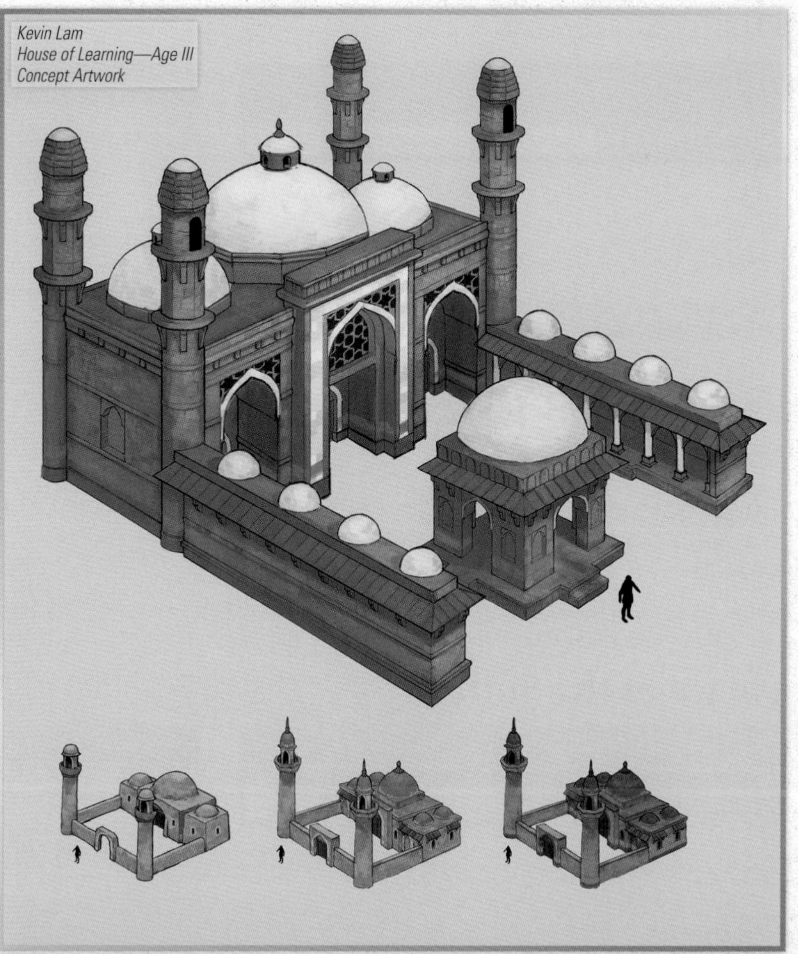

Kevin Lam
House of Learning—Age III
Concept Artwork

Designing for Player Skill Levels

"From a balance perspective, we place a lot of importance on balancing around the top level of play and have skilled, dedicated, play-testers to assist with putting the game through its paces. We are going to be supporting multiplayer ladders so we must ensure that the game balance works for players who are looking to win by any means possible.

It's also at the top of our minds to consider how changes impact players at all skill levels as we aim to create a game that is easy to pick up but difficult to master."

– Zak "ZeroEmpires" Robinson
Senior Designer, Balance, Relic

Hisar Academy

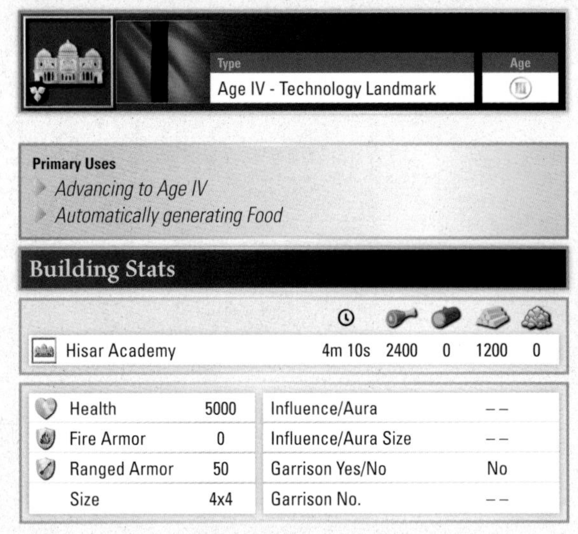

Type	Age
Age IV - Technology Landmark	IV

Primary Uses
- *Advancing to Age IV*
- *Automatically generating Food*

Building Stats

	Time	Food	Wood	Gold	Stone
Hisar Academy	4m 10s	2400	0	1200	0

Health	5000	Influence/Aura	--
Fire Armor	0	Influence/Aura Size	--
Ranged Armor	50	Garrison Yes/No	No
Size	4x4	Garrison No.	--

Prioritization and Usage

The **Hisar Academy** will automatically start generating Food as soon as it's placed, the amount of which is based on how many different technologies you've researched. Each learned technology will generate one Food every five seconds, so the more things you've unlocked, the larger amount you'll receive. Everything from unit upgrades, to weapon emplacements count towards this number, so it doesn't matter if you've been focusing on military or economic upgrades, this Landmark can still be useful to you. It's usefulness only grows the longer the game goes on, because if you have a lot of technology researched, the Food it generates can allow you to have less Villagers gathering Food, meaning more of your population capacity can be used for military units instead.

Hisar Academy—Age IV

Palace of the Sultan

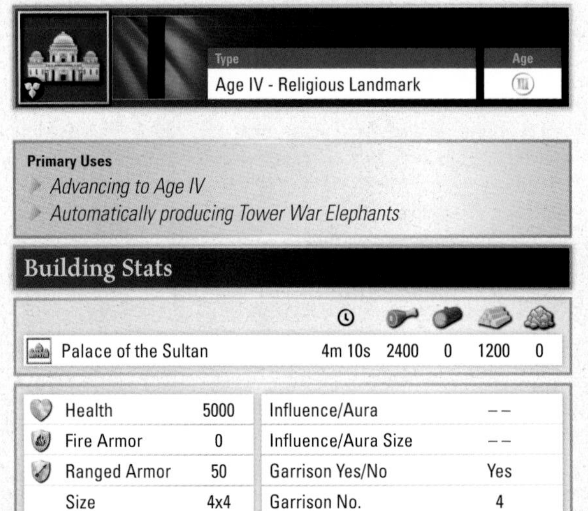

Type	Age
Age IV - Religious Landmark	IV

Primary Uses
- *Advancing to Age IV*
- *Automatically producing Tower War Elephants*

Building Stats

	Time	Food	Wood	Gold	Stone
Palace of the Sultan	4m 10s	2400	0	1200	0

Health	5000	Influence/Aura	--
Fire Armor	0	Influence/Aura Size	--
Ranged Armor	50	Garrison Yes/No	Yes
Size	4x4	Garrison No.	4

Prioritization and Usage

As soon as it's placed, the **Palace of the Sultan** will start automatically producing powerful Tower War Elephants at no cost, but at a relatively slow pace. You can, however, garrison up to four Scholars inside the Landmark, each of which will reduce the production time, and at its fastest, you'll be getting one Tower War Elephant every 1m 40s. Even at its fastest it's still slower than producing them from an Archery Range, but the fact that you don't have to spend the huge cost of 400 Food and 600 Gold for each one more than makes up for that.

Because of their immense strength and versatility, Tower War Elephants are useful regardless of your current strategy, and the savings you make from producing them for free at this Landmark will rarely be matched by the Food generated at the Hisar Academy. The main thing you need to be wary of with this Landmark is your population capacity, because constantly producing Tower War Elephants can soon fill it up, so if you're getting close to capacity, remember that you can stop production at any time.

Palace of the Sultan—Age IV

Kevin Lam
House of Wisdom Ideation
Concept Sketches

House of Wisdom

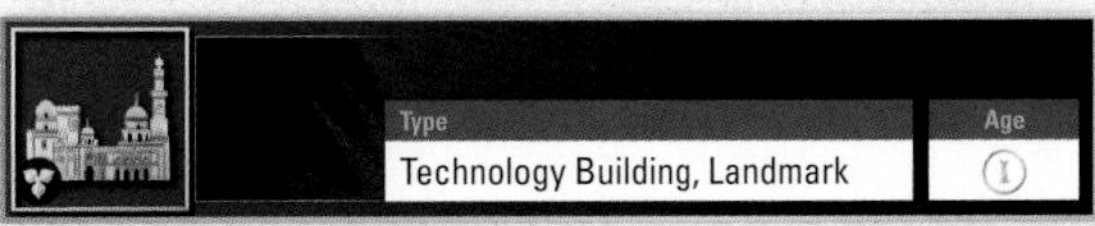

Type	Age
Technology Building, Landmark	I

Primary Uses
- *Advancing through the Ages by adding additional Wings*
- *Enabling progress towards the Golden Age*
- *Granting access to unique technologies*

Building Stats

	Time	Food	Wood	Gold	Stone
House of Wisdom	30s	0	50	0	0
Age II Wing	2m 0s	400	0	200	0
Age III Wing	2m 0s	1200	0	600	0
Age IV Wings	2m 0s	2400	0	1200	0

Health	2000*	Influence/Aura	Influence
Fire Armor	5	Influence/Aura Size	2 Tiles
Ranged Armor	50	Garrison Yes/No	No
Size	5x5	Garrison No.	--

*Building gains an extra 5000 health with each additional wing added.

House of Wisdom—All Wings

House of Wisdom Overview

Generating Enhancement

 **House of Wisdom Influence** Buildings within influence gain +5 Fire Armor. Structures built within **House of Wisdom** influence area help progress to the Golden Age.

The **House of Wisdom** is the only Landmark available to the Abbasid Dynasty, and as such it both stands out and works quite differently to the Landmarks of other civilizations. The main **House of Wisdom** building is very quick to construct, and only requires only a paltry 50 Wood, and while it's still considered a Landmark, building it won't actually advance the Age of your civilization. What it does do, however, is give you access to the unique Golden Age system, which provides you with a number of beneficial effects based on how many buildings are within the influence of the **House of Wisdom**. For that reason alone it's worth constructing as soon as you have the resources so that you can start receiving the Gold Age benefits.

To actually advance the Age you'll need to construct one of the different wings that you can add onto the main **House of Wisdom** Building. Each wing is themed after a different aspect the game, and comes with a number of different technologies that play into that theme. Each wing you add will advance another Age, and since you can pick from any of them every time, you have total freedom over the order in which they're acquired and can prioritize them as you see fit. It's important to note, however, that the technologies from each wing as still gated by Age requirements, so you won't get access to them all at once and should plan for which technology is most useful to you in the Age that you're actually advancing to.

When you want to advance, first select the **House of Wisdom**, and then choose the wing you want. Unlike other Landmarks, each wing is fairly quick to construct, so if you're gathering resources quickly, you should be able to advance the Age before opponents playing other civilizations. Also unlike other Landmarks, the construction of wings does not require Villagers, allowing you to keep them on resource gathering rather than tasking them with construction.

Eventually all wings can be built, so you don't have to worry about not gaining access to any of the unique technologies found within them.

Along with your starting Town Center, the **House of Wisdom** will be your only Landmark as the Abbasid Dynasty, and when first constructed, it only has a lowly 2000 health and is quite vulnerable because it has no built-in defensive capabilities. Try to build it in a safe location that is guarded by other defensive structures, but still with enough room around it to get maximum benefit out of the Golden Age mechanic. Thankfully, technology is not the only benefit that comes from construction additional wings on the **House of Wisdom**, they also significantly add to its durability. For each wing you construct, the main building gains an additional 5000 health, so by the time you have all wings built, it will have a massive 22000 health and take a significant amount of effort by your opponent to destroy.

The Golden Age

The Golden Age mechanic is another feature unique to the Abbasid Dynasty that you gain access to up constructing the main **House of Wisdom** building. There are three tiers in total that you can progress towards, each one offering an increasing number of benefits to your overall economy and production capabilities. For a building to count towards the Golden Age it needs to be built within the influence range of the **House of Wisdom**, and while it's impossible to fit 60 buildings within the default influence range, the influence range of the **House of Wisdom** itself is rather special. If just a single tile of a building is within the influence range of the **House of Wisdom**, its influence will extend out to include that building, and an additional tile around it. This is the main reason why you should build the **House of Wisdom** as soon as possible, so that you can have it at the heart of your base, and place all other buildings adjacent to it and each other, spreading outwards.

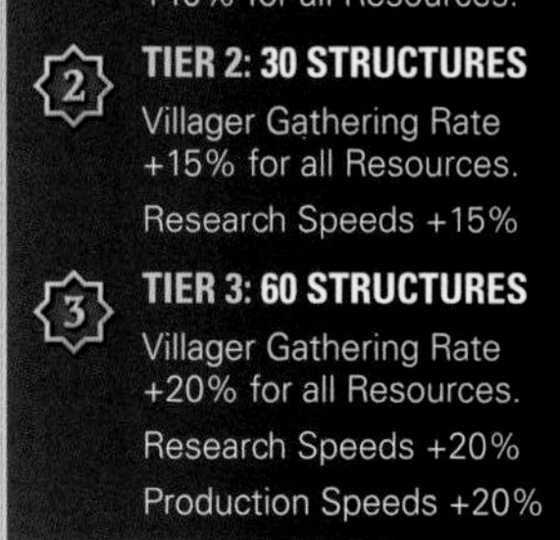

1
TIER 1: 10 STRUCTURES
Villager Gathering Rate +10% for all Resources.
2
TIER 2: 30 STRUCTURES
Villager Gathering Rate +15% for all Resources.
Research Speeds +15%
3
TIER 3: 60 STRUCTURES
Villager Gathering Rate +20% for all Resources.
Research Speeds +20%
Production Speeds +20%

Fortifications such as Palisade or Stone Walls and Gates, Stone Wall Towers, and also Farms will not contribute progress towards the Gold Age, but all other buildings are compatible.

It can take a lot of planning and forward thinking to ensure that buildings are still placed in an optimal position while progressing towards the Gold Age, but with a bit of practice, it can soon become second nature.

Because of the fact that the House of Wisdom is the only additional Landmark next to your starting Town Center, you have to make sure it is well protected through all the Ages.

House of Wisdom Technology Overview

Because none of the wings offer any offensive, defensive or unit production abilities, the main determining factor you have to take into account when deciding the order to build them is the technologies they offer. To better enable you to make that choice, we'll go over those various technologies here, along with the ones that unlock at the House of Wisdom itself as you Age up.

Unlike choosing the wings, you cannot choose the order in which these technologies become available, you simply have to build additional wings to advance the Age and they will unlock in sequence.

Phalanx (II)
Increases the attack range of Spearmen by 100%, and should be considered a high priority acquisition if you're using a lot of Spearmen during Age II. It can also be useful later on for increasing the attack range of the Spearmen riding on the back of of the War Elephant.

Camel Handling (III)
Increase Camel Movement Speed by +15%. Camels are naturally slower than some of the horse cavalry units, so this technology can literally help them close the gap if you're encountering an opponent that has good cavalry movement skills.

Camel Barding (IV)
Add +2 armor to all camel units. This is a solid defensive upgrade for your camel units that works well in conjunction with some of the other camel related technologies available at the **Military Wing**.

Composite Bows (IV)
Reduce the reload time of Archers by -25%. Like other Age IV technologies, this one is quite expensive, but it should be a mandatory acquisition if you have a lot of Archers in your army because it gives them a huge boost to their overall damage output.

Culture Wing Technology Overview

The **Culture Wing** focuses on technologies improving overall development and religious unit and building functionality. If you're going to be researching a lot of technology in general as you play, then the Culture Wing should be a frontrunner for the first wing you construct, because the earlier you gain access to the **Preservation of Knowledge** technology, the more you'll save in the long-run.

House of Wisdom—Culture Wing

'Preservation of Knowledge (II)

Reduces the cost of all technology by 30%. This is a very solid technology to research early in the game because it will allow you to save resources on any subsequent technology that you research. It can be especially important if you plan on staying in Age II for a long period of time due to the amount of technology available to research in that Age.

Medical Centers (III)

Keeps heal nearby units for +2 health every 1 second. This technology is useful regardless of whether you're using Keeps offensively or defensively, because it allows you to heal your more powerful and expensive units wherever they are, and it's definitely a good choice for an Age III upgrade.

Faith (IV)

Gives your Imams the special ability to convert a single unit of your choice, rather than all units within an area of effect, and they can do so without needing to hold a Relic. This can technology can be especially useful against very powerful units that you want to take out of action as quickly as possible, such as the Delhi Sultanate's own War Elephants. It's a very micro intensive playstyle, and can be hard to execute in the large scale battles that take place during the later stages of the game, but can be a very nasty surprise for your opponent when performed successfully.

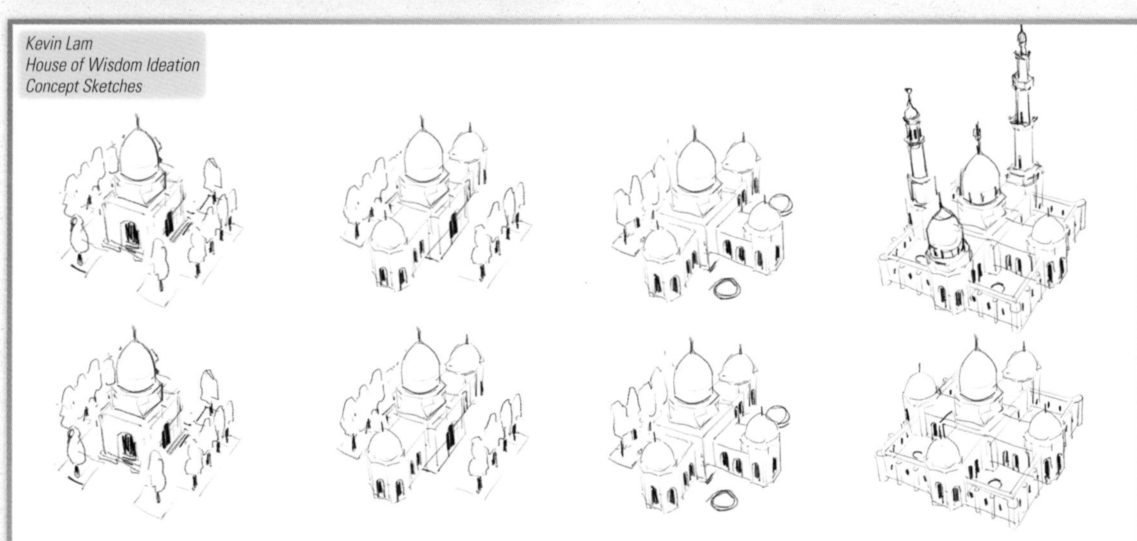

Kevin Lam
House of Wisdom Ideation
Concept Sketches

Economic Wing Technology Overview

As the name suggests, this wing focuses on improvements of your economy, and is a good all-round choice regardless of the Age because economy is the backbone of your empire, and the ability to improve it is always welcome

House of Wisdom—Economic Wing

Fresh Foodstuffs (II)

Reduces cost of Villagers by 50%. This upgrade can greatly improve your economy, and will come in especially handy if you decide to build additional Town Centers early in Age II. Because Villagers indirectly affect nearly any strategy regardless of which resource it focuses on, the benefits of this technology can be far reaching, and the only time it's not useful is if you're employing extremely aggressive all or nothing strategies that does not require Villager production.

Agriculture (III)

Improves the Villager gathering rate of Farms by 15%. This is also a technology you eventually want to research if it looks like it's going to be a longer game, because most Food income will be from Farms during the later stages.

Improved Processing (IV)

Villagers drop off +8% more resources. This will make your Villagers more efficient gatherers, meaning you'll need less of them and can use the additional population space for more

Military Wing

The **Military Wing** provides technology that benefits Camel and infantry units, so if there's a lot of fighting going on in the game you're playing, these upgrades can give you the edge that just might lead to victory.

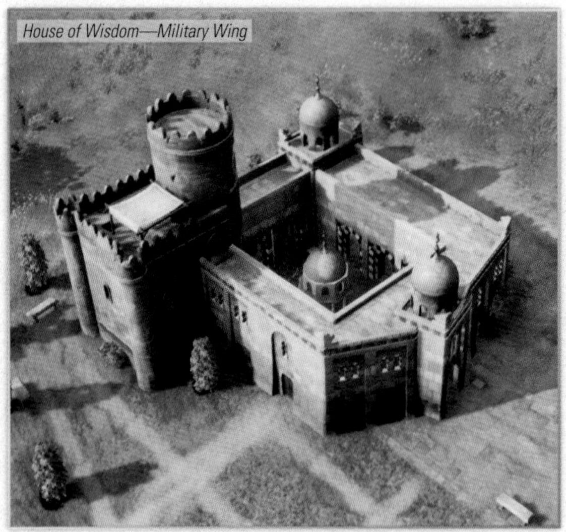
House of Wisdom—Military Wing

Camel Support (II)

This technology gives Camel units the ability to increase the armor of nearby infantry units by +1. While this is a useful upgrade that emphasis the support role of your Camel units, it should only be a priority if you intend to focus heavily on lots of Camels and infantry during the early stages of the game. In general, however, some of the technologies available at other wings during Age II are more useful overall.

Camel Rider Shields (III)

Camel Riders gain +3 melee armor through this technology. Since you gain access to Camel Riders in this Age, this can be an excellent upgrade to acquire for them and makes a good case for picking the **Military Wing** for your Age III ascension.

Boot Camp (IV)

This technology increases the health of your infantry by a substantial 15% and is one you'll want to eventually acquire, unless you're going for a pure cavalry and siege engine army.

Trade Wing

Trade is the key to wining longer games, but since it's not as relevant early in the game, the **Trade Wing** should be your go to wing for either Age III or Age IV depending on how the individual game is playing out. The only time you wont want to eventually build this wing is if you know the game will end before Gold Veins and other resources start to run dry and Trade moves to the forefront.

House of Wisdom—Trade Wing

Spice Roads (II)

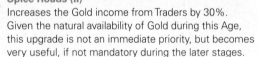

Increases the Gold income from Traders by 30%. Given the natural availability of Gold during this Age, this upgrade is not an immediate priority, but becomes very useful, if not mandatory during the later stages.

Armored Caravans (III)

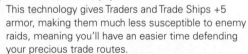

This technology gives Traders and Trade Ships +5 armor, making them much less susceptible to enemy raids, meaning you'll have an easier time defending your precious trade routes.

Grand Bazaar (IV)

The **Grand Bazaar** technology makes your Traders return not only Gold, but also 25% of their Gold amount as a secondary resource of your choice, which can be toggled at your Markets. Given how valuable, useful, and scarce Stone is at this point in games, this upgrade can make acquiring it a lot less troublesome and should be acquired as soon as possible if you've already established trade routes.

Kevin Lam
Great Palace of Flensburg
Concept Artwork

Kevin Lam
Great Palace of Agra
Concept Artwork

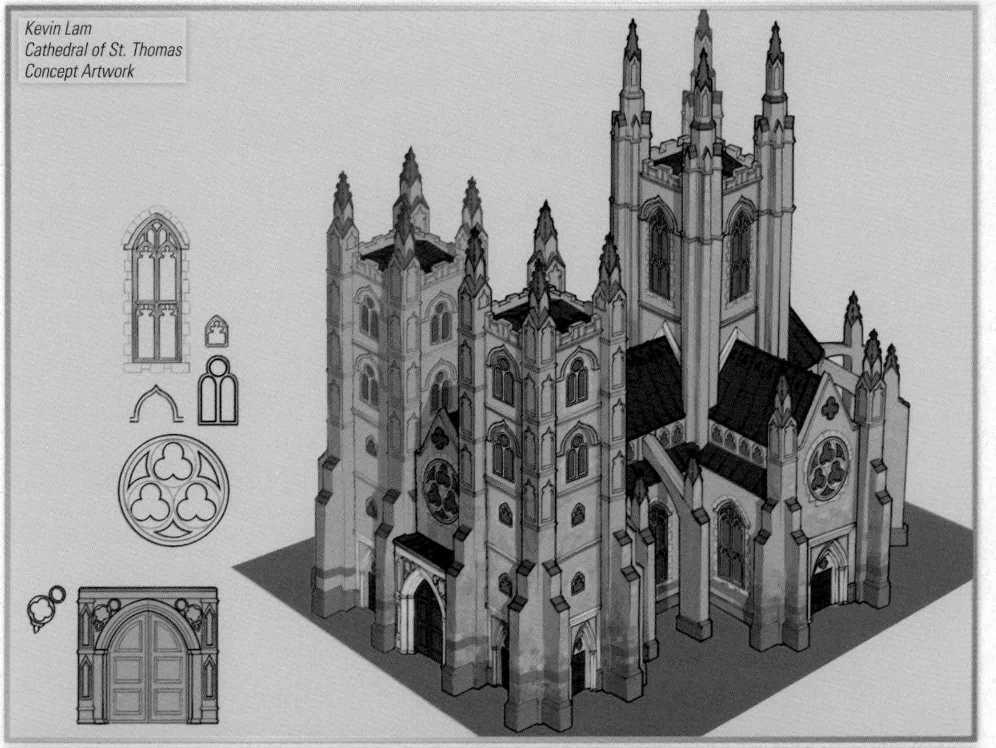

Kevin Lam
Cathedral of St. Thomas
Concept Artwork

Designing Shared Buildings

"When designing the shared buildings, we started with the "easiest" civ—the English. We broke down the assets into categories: residential, commercial, industrial, military and institutional. To ensure we had consistent historical references I created architectural one-sheets containing a series of reference photos, and corresponding outline sketches to reference callouts to show examples of doors, windows, roof lines and other iconic shapes for each category of building for each Age.

I focused on visual themes that can be threaded from the first Age to the fourth. For example, although the French had both round and angular architectural knaves, I chose the round profile for the French architecture to contrast with the more angular Holy Roman Empire, and because it tied quite nicely with the rounded ends of the early 9th century French thatch homes of the Romanesque religious architecture hundreds of years later, traced to the rounded turret towers in the later 15th and 16th Century castles. Historians may take issue with this style of visual distillation of a millennium of architectural evolution into a couple of buildings, but it's needed to help players quickly distinguish the buildings. For consistent readability, all generic unit-producing buildings always share the same basic footprint—this was done for both gameplay and production reasons."

– Zach Schläppi
Principal Artist, Art Director, Relic

Wonders Overview

Primary Uses

- *Achieving victory when the Wonder win condition is active*

Wonders are some of the most iconic buildings belonging to each civilization, and they come with a cost that's as impressive as their features. Most civilizations have to pay 3000 of every resource, but since the Mongols cannot mine Stone, they have to pay 4000 Food, Wood and Gold instead, and then on top of the cost, they take 15 minutes by default to construct.

Wonders are only relevant in games where the Wonder victory condition is active, although they can be used to show off your economic might and intimidate your opponent if you have the resources to spare. With that victory condition active your opponent(s) will be informed as soon as you start constructing a Wonder; when construction has finished, they'll have a further 10 minutes to destroy it or you'll automatically win the game.

A Wonder victory is feasible if you are in a situation in a 1v1 or team game where no player is able to make progress for a long time and you're essentially in a stalemate. By building it you force your opponents to make a move or they'll lose the game, just make sure you've built up sufficient resources and defensive fortifications to be able to defend it and secure victory.

Even though they're massive buildings, they have no offensive or defensive capabilities, and due to their low health and armor, they can be destroyed relatively quickly and need to be well defended. If you lose your Wonder, your Investments will very often be for naught, and you may end up losing the game. if you no longer have resources to invest into units and defenses. Only decide to build a Wonder if you're in a relatively secure position that can be easily defended.

Furthermore, when you're ready to start construction, make sure you assign as many Villagers as you can spare. Because your opponent gets alerted as soon as you start building a Wonder, they have the opportunity to counter build one, and if it gets finished before yours, you end up at a disadvantage and could potentially lose the game. It's also important to note, that if you decide to stop construction before the Wonder is finished, you'll still get all of your resources back, just like with any other building.

Building Stats

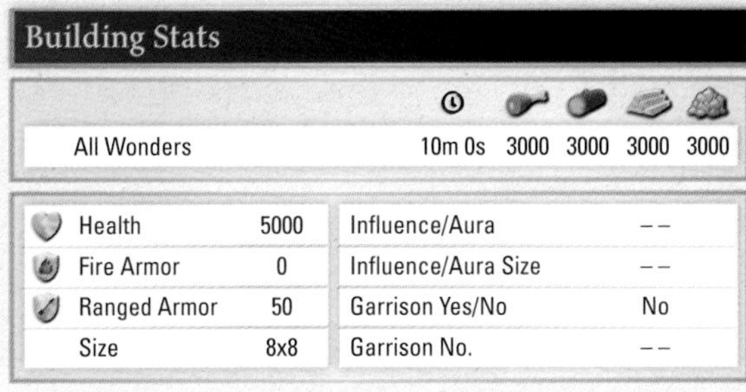

	Time	Food	Wood	Gold	Stone
All Wonders	10m 0s	3000	3000	3000	3000

Health	5000	Influence/Aura	--
Fire Armor	0	Influence/Aura Size	--
Ranged Armor	50	Garrison Yes/No	No
Size	8x8	Garrison No.	--

Kevin Lam
Cathedral of the Tsar
Concept Artwork

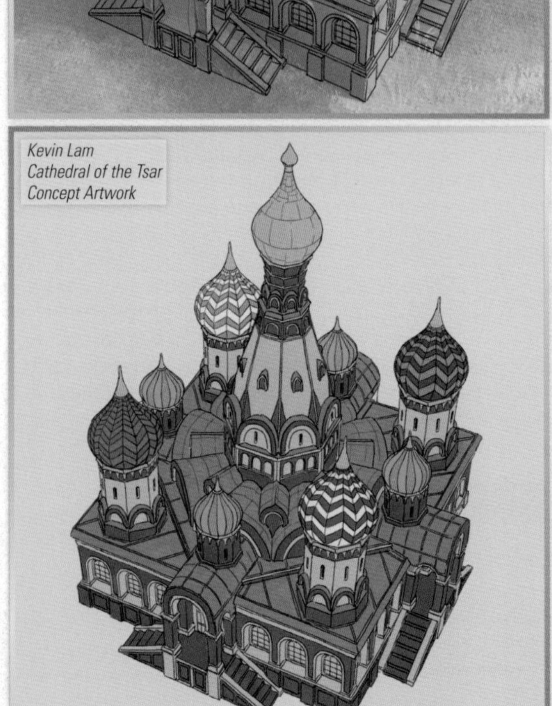

Kevin Lam
Cathedral of the Tsar
Concept Artwork

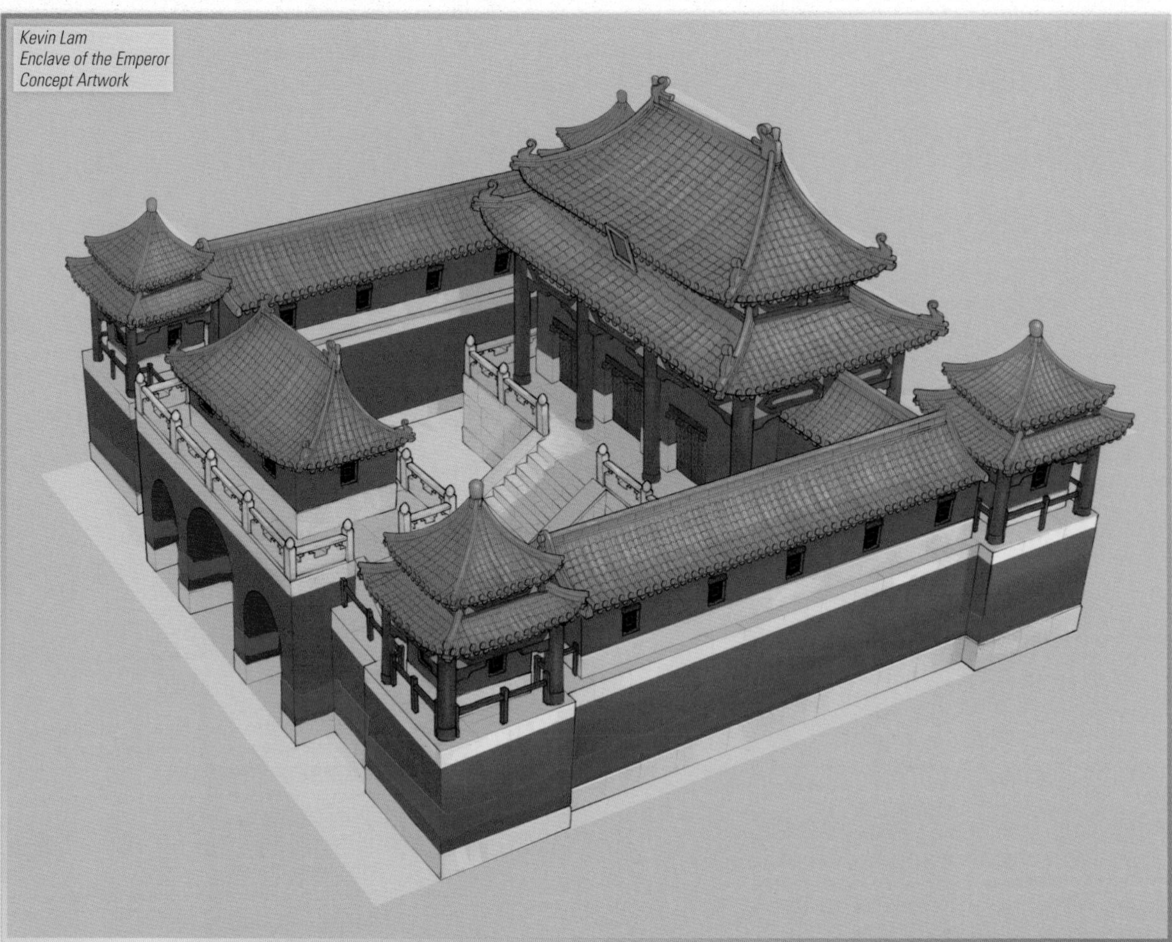

Kevin Lam
Enclave of the Emperor
Concept Artwork

Adding Emotion to Design

"I wanted the player to feel more connected emotionally to what was going on the ground without cross-purposing gameplay. That meant introducing more emotion, such as leveraging the medieval trope of "doom and gloom" to make the unexplored areas more menacing, rock shapes more jagged, trees imperfect and contrast that with the "celebratory view of history". But due to the delicate nature of RTS, we used color, shape and detail in a more controlled, intentional fashion to make the quality of the art feel more depthful and rich. We wanted civilizations worth defending, with more individual cultural weight and character. We want the act of creating a settlement as enjoyable and meaningful as capturing sacred sites or winning battles."

– Zach Schläppi
Principal Artist, Art Director, Relic

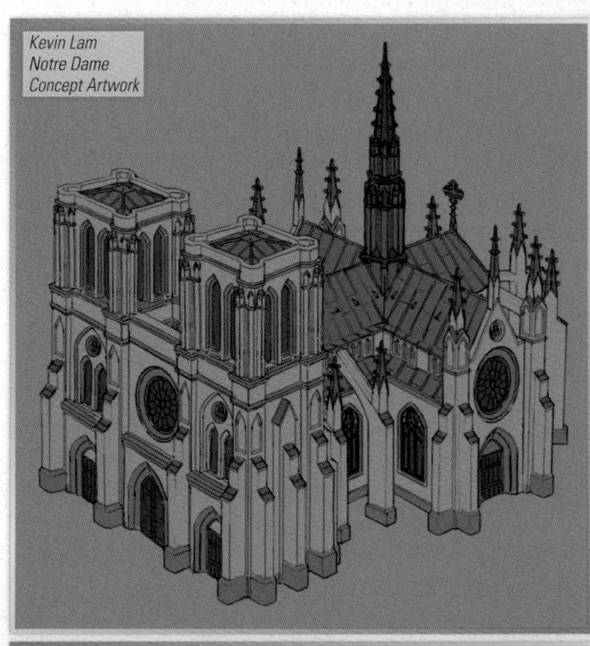
Kevin Lam
Notre Dame
Concept Artwork

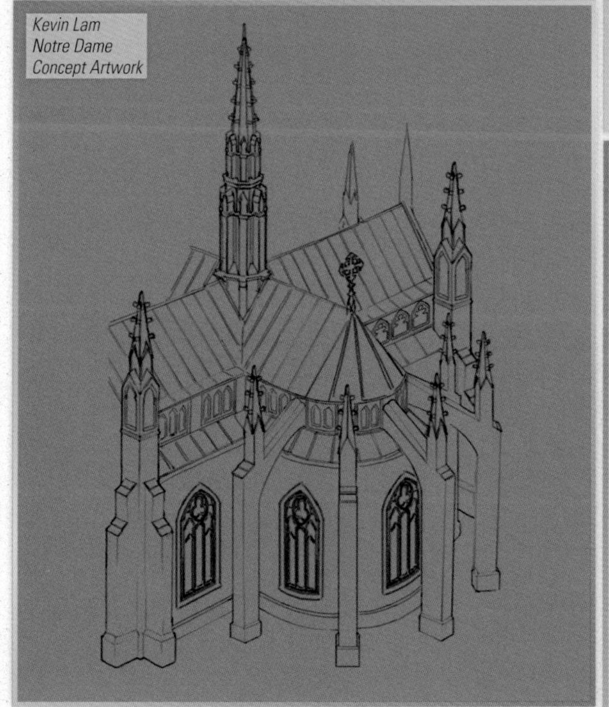
Kevin Lam
Notre Dame
Concept Artwork

Stuart Ng
Prayer Hall of Uqba
Concept Artwork

Stuart Ng
Monument of the Great Khan
Concept Artwork

CHAPTER

A Walk Through History

Beginning with the explosive Battle of Hastings in 1066, the Age of Empires IV campaigns follow 500 years of medieval history. Chart the formation of England's modern nation after the Norman conquest, follow France's struggles through the epic Hundred Years War, witness the rapid expansion of the great Mongol Empire and the rise of Moscow from village to superpower. This chapter will walk you through each mission in turn and ensure you get as much from the journey as possible.

About this Chapter

This chapter is comprised of separate walkthroughs for each of the game's four single-player campaigns. For each one, guidance is provided for completing each of the main objectives, and the text is linked to overview maps that show important strategic positions. Occasionally, artwork or commentary from team members at Relic and World's Edge will appear when there's something relevant to show or provide context for.

Illuminated Histories

Many of the missions feature "Illuminated History" text boxes that we've included as a bonus for readers who might appreciate an extra bit of history. These texts were written for the game during production by Bonnie Jean Mah, Lauren Wood, and Kristina Wiik, members of Relic's writing team. They would have been made into short, narrated interlude movies, but were ultimately never used in the final version and ended up on the cutting room floor. They were intended to provide some additional context by detailing some other historical events that took place at the same points in time as the missions, and we've placed them at the points they would have appeared in the game.

Icon Legend

Each overview map has its important objective locations marked, along with **Position Points** that are bolded in the text to make finding specific positions easier. Sometimes, when there are a few of the same object closely grouped together, a number next to the icon will show how many are in the area.

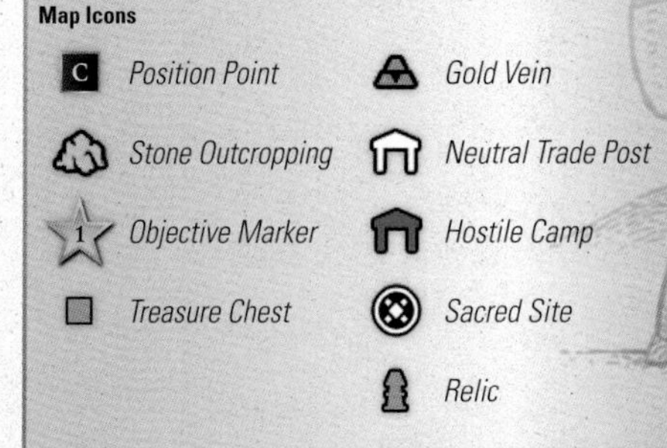

Stuart Ng, Relic *An annotated paintover of York City, and a wooden keep concept used as inspiration and reference for the York Keep, created while designing the second mission of the Normans campaign.*

Normans

1066

Conquest

The Battle of Hastings

In 1066, William of Normandy set out to wrest the Kingdom of England from his Anglo-Saxon rival. Only one man could be king.

William of Normandy began his conquest of England. But to end the Anglo-Saxon rule, he would first have to kill their king.

Rewards

- Building a Castle
- Nova Stella, Novus Rex!
- The Norman Conquest

Objective 1

Attack Harold's Saxon Army

You begin this mission at the base of Senlac Hill with an army of ranged and melee infantry. Your first goal is to break the foundation of the Anglo-Saxon army, but although there are a lot of allied units, you can initially only control a small group led by Duke William. The others serve as reinforcements that will join you as needed, so don't worry too much if you lose some units in your initial charge. To start your attack, select all of your units, then click the **Attack Move** command and left click near your opponents to move up and engage them. Remember to use Duke William's special **Attack Speed** ability as often as possible, because it will drastically improve the performance of your army.

One of your other units can always revive your leader unit if they die, so you don't have to worry too much about them going down in battle.

Objective 2

Feign a Retreat

After realizing the futility of further attacks on the shield wall, a change in tactics is required. Select your entire army and move them back down the hill as quickly as possible to minimise losses, and sensing weakness, the opposing army will break ranks and follow you.

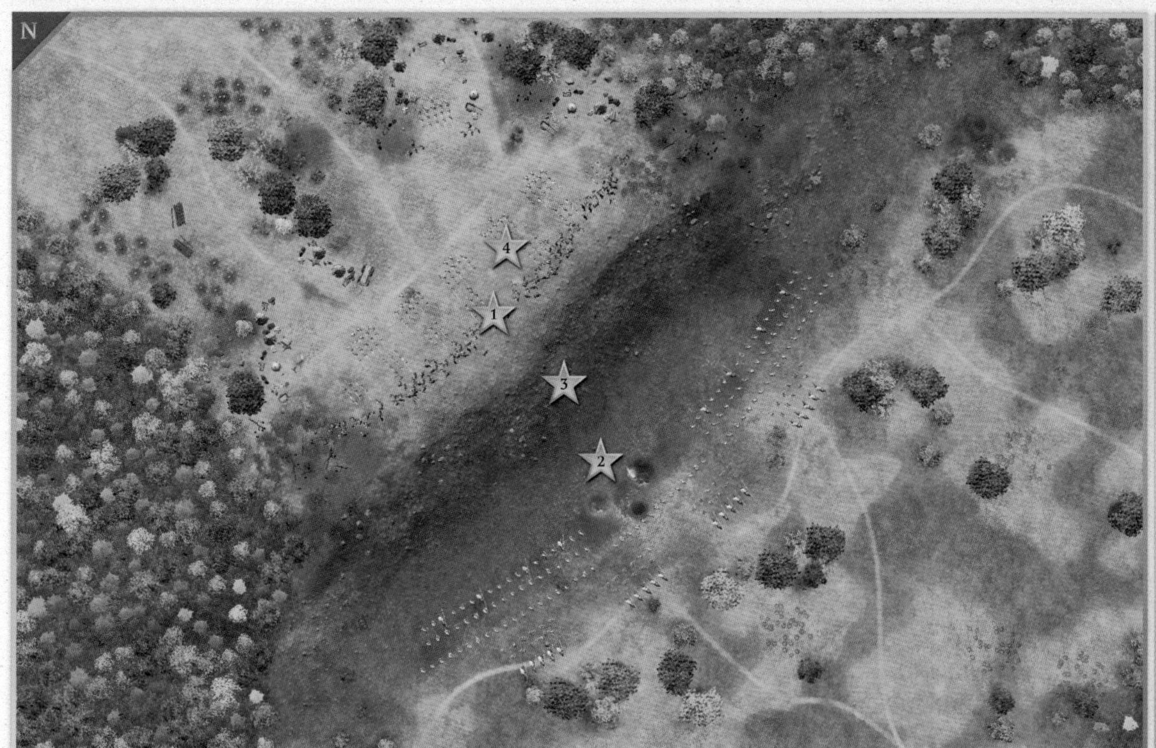

Historical Battles

"In terms of the moment-to-moment re-enactment of a battle, the closest [Age of Empires IV campaign mission] to history is probably the Battle of Hastings in the Norman Conquest campaign. For example, we show the Saxon tactic of the "shield wall" and William the Conqueror's feigned retreat. The battle is paced out in a close facsimile of the actual events of the battle, ending with the death of King Harold.

The Battle of the Kalka River in the Mongol Horde campaign also attempts to recreate the shrewd manoeuvring of General Subutai in trapping his enemy in an ambush.

There are many other examples throughout all the campaigns where real historical strategies are played out. Where we have embellished a little to produce well-rounded missions, we have always stuck closely to the types of events and strategies that would have been utilised at the time."

– Lauren Wood
Principal Designer, Narrative, Relic

Make sure not to push too far up the hill because you could end up surrounded by the enemy forces; stick to the crest of the hill and let them come to you.

Objective 3

Attack Harold's Saxon Army

Re-engage Harold's army now that they're exposed, and try to keep your army as grouped up as possible to ensure that the maximum number of units get the benefit of Duke William's **Attack Speed** ability. Keep up the pressure until the enemy units that broke rank are defeated, at which point they will send in groups of Spearmen. Thankfully, allied Archers were waiting in the wings for just such an eventuality. Quickly select and group up all of your new Archers and have them attack the approaching Spearmen, and then fold them into your main army and keep attacking the enemy units on the hill.

You'll see a progress bar under the objective on your screen, and that represents the amount of enemy reinforcements that you've defeated; fill the bar and you'll complete the objective. From this point on, small groups of reinforcements consisting of Archers and Men-at-Arms will become controllable near the line of allied units, so keep checking and add them to your main army as they become available. After defeating all of the enemy Spearmen, the next threat comes from their Archers, so to counter them you'll gain a large number of cavalry units; group them up and charge them up the hill to engage the Archers ahead of your other units.

Objective 4

Slay King Harold

Now that you've broken through all of their defensive ranks, King Harold's army is in disarray, which means now is the time to strike him down. Try to ignore the other enemy units at this time, and focus on clearing a path to King Harold and defeating him to win the battle.

The Bayeux Tapestry: 1077

Surviving wars, neglect and the march of time, the Bayeux Tapestry tells the story of the Norman invasion of England in 1066. Revered as an artistic masterpiece and historic record, the tapestry was created as a work of propaganda. For this is a chronicle told by the conquerors. When the Normans invaded, William the Conqueror killed King Harold, took the crown and claimed the country. The tapestry presents their side of the story. Its artwork depicts the actions of the Anglo-Saxon earl, Harold, who swore on holy relics to be loyal to William when he eventually inherited the English crown. But when the old king died, Harold broke his sacred oath and claimed the throne for himself. The invasion was divine retribution. This message would have come through loud and clear to the conquered people of England. And nine hundred years later, we can follow William's story, beat by beat, just as the Anglo-Saxons did. Through the Bayeux Tapestry, the Normans are still reaching through time to tell their version of history.

– Illuminated History

Conquest

North to York

Rewards

- Domesday Book
- North to York
- The Crossbow

England was under Norman rule, but not all were content with the Conqueror King.

King William's army faced an uncertain march to York, fraught with resistance from those opposed to Norman rule.

Objective 1

Capture Middlethorpe

Your initial army is vastly superior to the rebels in Middlethorpe. Victory is certain, but you can minimize your losses by attacking with all your army at once, and then once the battle begins, select your cavalry and flank around to attack the enemy archers from behind. After defeating all of the rebels you'll need to build up your economy so that you have the resources to fuel your advance on York.

*Remember to use King William's **Attack Speed** ability as often as possible in fights to give your army a significant advantage.*

In capturing Middlethorpe you also received five Villagers, and the first thing you should do is have them build a Lumber Camp at **Position A** and start gathering Wood there. Have your Town Center produce four more Villagers, and then when the first one is ready, have it build two Houses near the other ones in the village to complete that part of the objective. Once the houses are complete, have each of your four new Villagers build a Farm near the Town Center to start gathering Food and finish the final part of the objective.

Objective 2

Capture Fulford

With the newly arrived reinforcements there should be no problem taking Fulford. On the way there you'll encounter a group of archers at **Position B**, which you should engage with your cavalry first. Once you arrive, attack with your whole army, again bringing your cavalry round to engage the archers as a priority. Try to focus on the rebel units only and leave the buildings alone, because as with Middlethorpe, Fulford will come under your control when the area is clear.

With a second village under your control, you can now build up your military strength even more thanks to the nearby Gold Veins. You'll need 400 Food and 200 Gold to build the required Landmark, so have the Fulford Town Center produce two Villagers, and then send them along with the five that are standing nearby to work on the Gold Vein at **Position C**.

If you have an abundance of Food and Wood, you can sell some of it at the Market in Fulford to speed up the acquisition of Gold required to build your Age II Landmark.

Once you have the resources, build the **Council Hall** Landmark at the entrance of Fulford with the Villagers that were mining Gold, and then have them build a Stable nearby before going back to gathering Gold. A band of Danish raiders will launch an attack on Fulford as soon as construction of the Landmark is complete, and another group of reinforcements for you will also arrive at the same time, so use your combined army ready to repel the raiders.

You'll now get an optional objective to stop the Danish raids by either destroying their camp at **Position D**, or paying them a Tribute of 800 Gold. If you opt to pay them, all you need to do is click the Players & Tribute button in the top right of the HUD and click on the Gold to offer payment. Provided you haven't lost too many units thus far, you should have an army of around 80 units, and that's sufficiently strong for a smooth victory over the Dane camp, but if you need additional units, produce Longbowmen from the **Council Hall** and Horsemen from the Stables. If you chose to destroy the camp you'll also be able to pick up two Treasure Chests inside it for some additional Gold. It doesn't matter which option you go with, but picking one is important to stop the raids, otherwise building up and attacking York will be much more difficult.

Objective 3

Reclaim York

Now is the time to build up and upgrade your army for the final assault on York, so to facilitate that, build two Barracks and a Blacksmith in Fulford. Groups of raiders will start coming from York to attack your base at this time, so while you're preparing, position your army towards the front of Fulford to repel them. You should also produce some more Villagers at Middlethorpe and have them build and work on Farms to increase your Food acquisition rate to allow for constant military unit production.

Recommended Army	
Spearmen	30
Men-at-Arms	30
Archer	45
Horsemen	20

Recommended Upgrades			
Barracks	Hardened Spearmen	Early Man-at-Arms	
Blacksmith	Bloomery	Fitted Leatherwork	Siege Engineering

There are two paths into York: the direct route at **Position E**, and the scenic route at **Position F**. There are less defenses along the scenic route, but with the army you've amassed you should have no trouble taking the direct approach. When you're ready, march your army towards **Position E**, taking out any enemy units along the way, and then when you reach the bridge, have some of your units build two Battering Rams. Send the rams over the bridge to start destroying the first gate and draw some enemy fire, and then have your main army follow behind them to speed up the process.

After breaching the first gate and entering the city you'll get the objective to destroy York Keep at **Position G**. Continue moving towards it with your rams leading the charge, destroying the gates blocking your way as you come to them. When the Keep is in sight, send everything to attack it because the mission will complete as soon as it's destroyed, regardless of how many enemy units are left.

The Keep in York is heavily guarded, so make sure to have some rams ready.

Henry I of England: r. 1100 - 1135

In 1090, trembling on the battlements of Rouen castle, a traitor begged for mercy. Henry, son of William the Conqueror, had no second thoughts before delivering his sentence. Ignoring the traitor's pleas, Henry pushed him to his death as an example to all. Ten years later, Henry became king of England and continued to make quick examples of thieves and betrayers. He ordered blindings, mutilations and hangings without trial. And to ensure none escaped justice, he employed a network of spies to sniff out his enemies. Henry was also fond of life's indulgences. He held gut-busting banquets in halls adorned with elaborate riches. He amused himself with a collection of exotic animals and with a long procession of mistresses.

Henry was also an astute king—highly educated and a skillful negotiator. In the interests of order, he introduced a justice system, an exchequer and a Charter of Liberties, which ensured fair treatment of his subjects. Despite his quick brutality and lavish excesses, Henry was one of the most successful monarchs of his era. He would rule over a loyal and peaceful England for the duration of his 35-year reign.

– Illuminated History

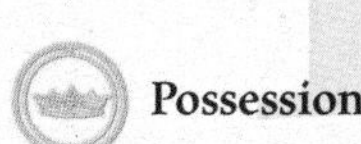

1105

Possession

The Fall of Bayeux

Rewards

Mail Making

Possession

In Normandy, William the Conqueror's sons ignited a bitter feud over control of their empire.

King Henry I descended on Bayeux with the full force of his army, intent on taking what he believed was his.

Objective 1

Destroy Bayeux

You'll get attacked by a small group of enemy units as soon as this mission begins, so ready your army for them and use King Henry I's **Armor** ability to reduce the amount of damage you take. A group of reinforcements will then join you and you'll need to put them into groups to allow for quick and easy control.

It's best to put your units on control groups 1-4 first, since that makes it easy to select a group and use their abilities. A good setup would be: 1 - Spearmen, 2 - Longbowmen, 3 - Cavalry, 4 - Leader. When your units are nicely grouped, move them down the hill towards **Position A**, taking out the patrolling enemy groups along the way. When Bayeux's Stone Walls come into view, the sheer scope of your undertaking becomes clear, and a much bigger and stronger army is called for.

Try to be consistent with your unit grouping by always assigning the same units types to the same number, doing this builds up muscle memory that will speed up your unit selection in the long run.

A nearby forest village at **Position B** has the resources you need to build up a suitable force to take Bayeux, so start heading in that direction, making sure to stay away from the walls around Bayeux so that the archers and defensive towers along them don't pick off your units. There are more roaming enemy cavalry patrols along the way too, so make good use of your Longbowmen's **Place Palings** ability against them. When you reach the village, defeat the units defending it to claim it as your own.

To break through the walls of Bayeux you're going to need to construct Battering Rams, which means you'll need to build up your economic and military capabilities first. You get a total of 16 villagers, of which eight are automatically assigned and the others are idle, so start by having the idle ones build a Blacksmith, and then have four of them build Farms around the mill.

The remaining four should build a Mining Camp near the Gold Vein and start working on gathering Gold. Enemy attacks are infrequent at this time, so there's no need to rush your preparations. Have your Town Center start producing Villagers so that you can grow your economy quickly, while building an Arsenal, two Barracks and two Archery Ranges to strengthen your army.

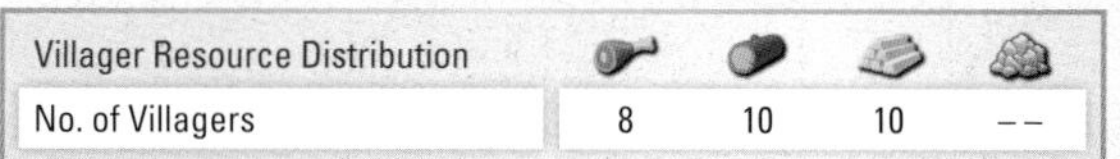

Villager Resource Distribution	Food	Wood	Gold	Stone
No. of Villagers	8	10	10	--

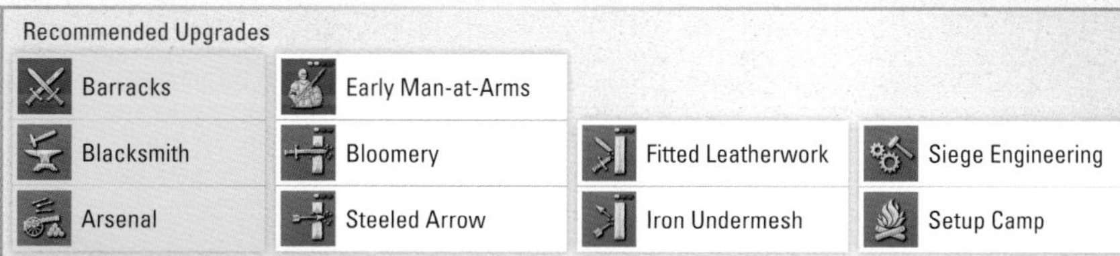

Recommended Upgrades			
Barracks	Early Man-at-Arms		
Blacksmith	Bloomery	Fitted Leatherwork	Siege Engineering
Arsenal	Steeled Arrow	Iron Undermesh	Setup Camp

*The **Setup Camp** ability you can research for your Longbowmen at the Arsenal greatly increases their survivability, and is an essential acquisition.*

Produce Men-at-Arms from your Barracks until you have around 25 of them, switching to Spearmen once your Gold starts to run out, and have your Archery Ranges produce Longbowmen. As soon as Siege Engineering has been researched, have your infantry construct five Battering Rams, and then continue producing Spearmen and Longbowmen until you hit the 200 population capacity, building Houses as needed.

Once your army is ready, it's time to march on Bayeux. Rather than attacking the gates head on where most of the defenses are located, send your Battering Rams to the wall at **Position C** near the enemy Monastery and destroy the Stone Walls and Towers there. While your rams are working on the wall, move your Longbowmen within range and Setup Camp with them while they rain arrows on the enemy units atop the walls. After breaching the walls and moving your army inside Bayeux you'll no longer have to worry about attacks from the Stone Wall Towers. To claim Bayeux you need to not only defeat all of the units defending it, but also destroy a large number of its buildings; keep your army together advancing street-by-street clearing units, and your Battering Rams behind them destroying buildings until Bayeux is yours.

The Battle of Tinchebray

The brother-versus-brother fight for Normandy would be decided on this day.

King Henry I's bid for Normandy hinged on capturing his brother. But the castle at Tinchebray protected Duke Robert. Henry would take any measure necessary to lure him out.

Rewards

 The Battle of Tinchebray

The Taking of Caen

Objective 1

Raze Villages to Draw out Robert's Army

You have limited resources and units in this mission, and what you do have is not strong enough to break through the walls that Robert Curthose is hiding behind, so you need to try and lure him out by burning the buildings of the surrounding villages. Start by marching your army to Martigny at **Position A** and attack the enemy units defending it. When they're all defeated, go about destroying all of the buildings.

*The forces at Martigny are no match for your army, but to minimize your losses, remember to use King Henry I's **Armor** ability to increase the defense of units near him.*

After completely razing Martigny you'll get the ability to call in reinforcements, albeit ones that cost Gold to hire; you have no means of mining Gold, which means you'll need to rely on Treasure Chests. There are six in total around Martigny, giving you 600 Gold to spend on reinforcements, and you should spend it on one group of Knights, and one group of Infantry. Once you've obtained and grouped up your new units, take your army towards another Treasure Chest at **Position B**, making sure to grab the other two chests near the fork in the road on the way.

On the way there, Robert will call in some reinforcements of his own and they'll enter the map from the road near the chest you're going towards. You need to defeat these reinforcements before they can join up with Robert, so once they're within range of your army, attack them with everything you have. After defeating them, turn your sights on Frênes at **Position C** and give it the same fate as Martigny.

Objective 2

Defeat Duke Robert and his Army

Enraged by the destruction you've caused, Robert's army will storm out of the castle and begin marching towards your units. If you picked up every Treasure Chest along the way, you should have 800 Gold after burning Frênes to the ground; spend it on another group of Knights, and three groups of Infantry. These reinforcements arrive in the same location as the previous ones, so you'll need to be quick with combining your forces before Robert's army reaches you. Bring your army at Frênes down to the reinforcements at Martigny, because that is where you should make your stand. Defeat Robert and his army and the battle is won.

If you engage Robert's forces as they approach Martigny you can fight them downhill, which is easier to control than an uphill battle.

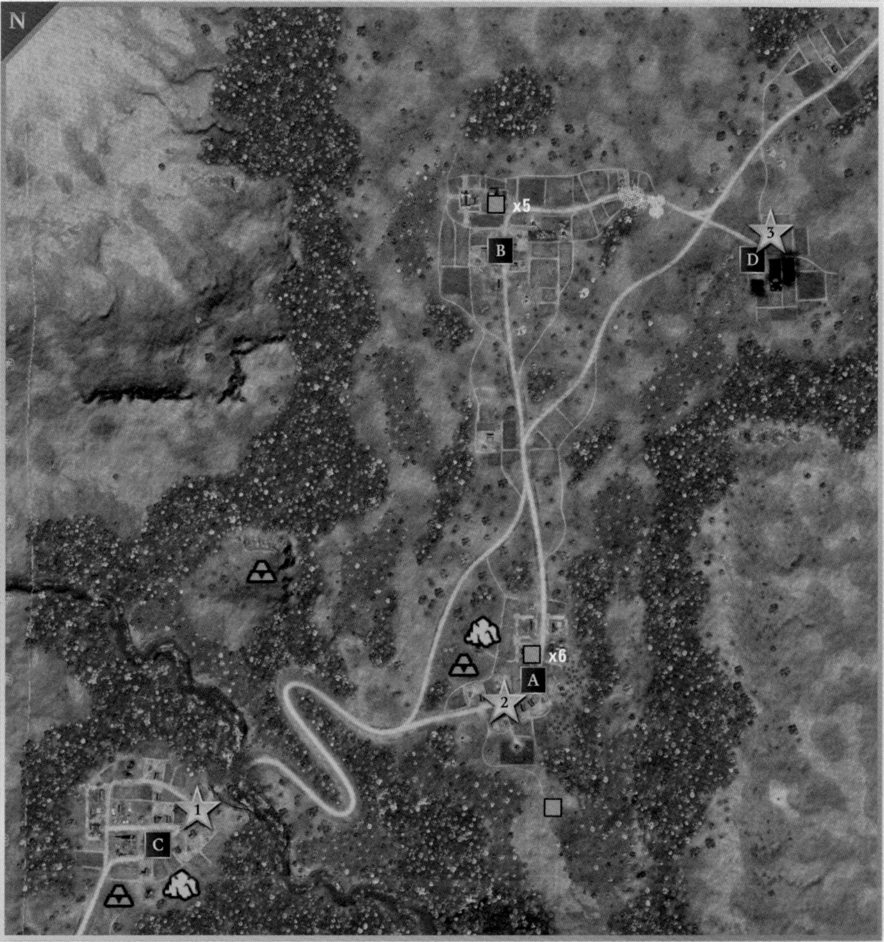

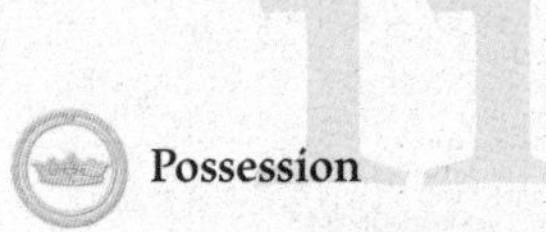

The Battle of Brémule

Rewards

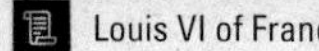

- Falconry & Hawking
- Louis VI of France
- The Battle of Brémule

Two heavyweight kings fought face-to-face to decide the fate of Normandy.

A chance encounter in the farmlands of Normandy saw King Henry I face open battle against France's illustrious King Louis VI.

Objective 1

Hold off the French

King Louis and the large army he commands will begin attacking the outlying villages of Grainville **(Position A)** and Cressenville **(Position B)** as soon as the mission starts, and it will be impossible for you to hold them. To minimize your losses, move every unit from both of those villages back to the more fortified town of Fleury **(Position C)** where the bulk of your forces are.

As your retreating units make their way to Fleury, focus on building up your economy until King Henry arrives, with the goal of building a Landmark to advance to the Castle Age as quickly as possible. To set up your economy in the most efficient way, ensure your Town Center has at least one Villager in its production queue at all times. Prioritise tasking your first six Villagers to gather Food from Sheep, followed by Villagers to Stone and Gold, placing new Mining Camps closer to each of of those resources for added efficiency. The next Villagers should go on Wood, and any after that should build additional Farms around your Town Center.

Villager Resource Distribution					
No. of Villagers	Start	12	6	5	3
	Goal	30	20	10	5

Warning: *When King Louis' army takes control of the outlying villages you'll lose population capacity; build additional Houses inside Fleury to ensure you can maintain smooth production of units.*

A few minutes into the mission an army will attack the main entrance to Fleury. In preparation for this attack, build an additional Outpost near the existing three, and consider upgrading them to Fortified Outposts once you have the resources to do so. When the enemy attack commences, make sure that your cavalry avoids the enemy Spearmen by flanking around them, allowing them to attack the Archers at the rear. King Henry and his reinforcements will arrive a short while after the enemy attack begins, and with these units you'll be able to safely defend Fleury.

Each Outpost can have three units garrisoned inside it, with each one adding an extra arrow to each attack volley. Before you get attacked, make sure to garrison some of your Longbowmen inside to maximise your defensive capabilities.

Objective 2

Capture Grainville and Cressenville

The French army is still way too strong for you to take head on, so for now, continue building up your economic and military strength. Small batches of the French army will attack you every few minutes, but they should be easy to fend off with your current army. If you have a quick look at King Louis' army at **Position D**, you'll notice that it is predominantly cavalry, with Spearmen and Archers as support, so you should focus your military and upgrades towards countering that. Keep producing Villagers and have them build an Arsenal, and an additional Barracks and Archery Range before moving to resource gathering, and then start researching upgrades.

*The **King's Palace** is a good choice for Age III Landmark because it will speed up your Villager production without the need to build an additional Town Center, giving you a big boost to your economy.*

Keep producing Spearmen and Longbowmen while researching your upgrades, and then once they're done and you reach 200/200 population capacity, it's time to start retaking the land that was taken. Push out to Grainville at **Position A** using the **Attack Move** command so that you deal with the small groups of enemies along the road, and then send the full might of your upgraded army directly into the village to easily defeat the enemy forces there. Once the village is yours you can use it as a forward base because it already has some military production buildings, and you now have control over another Gold Vein, so once the one in Fleury runs out, send those Villagers here. It's also worth constructing a Monastery in Grainville so that you can produce a Monk to heal your units, and take some time to pick up the Treasure Chests left behind by the French.

Soon after defeating the army at Grainville a larger detachment of King Louis' army will counter attack, but they should easily be repelled by your forces. As soon as that is done, and you've produced any reinforcements needed, march for Cressenville at **Position B** and recapture that village as well. Similar to Grainville, after capturing Cressenville you'll have to fend off a French counter-attack, and then it's finally time to face the main army.

Objective 3

Defeat King Louis' Army

Only one fight now stands between you and victory, and with your full army and the right tactics, defeating the French forces at **Position D** should be a forgone conclusion. It's worth noting, however, that if you are defeated, King Louis' army will remain in place, and you should have more than enough resources to rebuild.

As usual, you'll need a lot of units to defeat King Louis' Army.

Approach the French army cautiously and try to bait the French cavalry into charging by moving your Spearmen slowly forwards; when they charge, retreat your Spearmen back behind your Longbowmen, and have the Longbowmen deploy their Palings to stun the cavalry. While they're stunned, bring your Spearmen back up to engage them, as your cavalry flank around behind to engage the French Archers. If it all goes to plan, you should beat King Louis' forces and reign victorious.

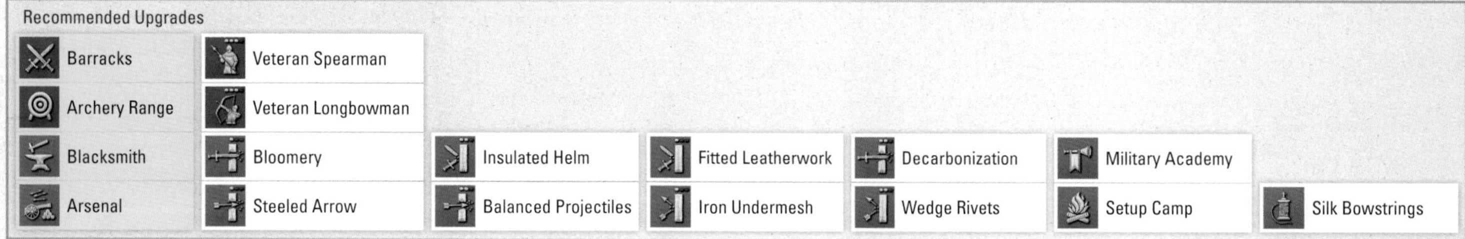

Recommended Upgrades

Barracks	Veteran Spearman					
Archery Range	Veteran Longbowman					
Blacksmith	Bloomery	Insulated Helm	Fitted Leatherwork	Decarbonization	Military Academy	
Arsenal	Steeled Arrow	Balanced Projectiles	Iron Undermesh	Wedge Rivets	Setup Camp	Silk Bowstrings

1141

The Anarchy

First Battle of Lincoln

Rewards

- The Anarchy
- The Empress's Flight
- The Trebuchet

The Empress Matilda made her move for the English throne, fueling the fire of the civil war.

The castle at Lincoln was under siege. Inside, forces loyal to The Empress Matilda awaited relief from her half-brother, Robert of Gloucester. To break the siege, Robert would have to capture the king.

Objective 1

Set up an Ambush

Stealth Forests are the perfect places to setup an ambush, so move your units into the one directly ahead of you. The large vision range of your Scouts will easily let you spot any approaching enemies, while you remain hidden from their sight. You should also use the **Stand Ground** command on your units to ensure they don't break ranks prematurely.

Objective 2

Eliminate Enemy Reinforcements

Three columns of enemy reinforcements will start moving through the area as soon as your units have taken up their ambush position, and you need to stop them from joining the siege. The first column of reinforcements travels along the road in front of you starting from **Position A**, so simply wait for them to walk past, and then spring your ambush. When attacking, you can minimize your losses by surrounding the enemy Longbowmen to force as many as possible into melee combat, in which they will deal a lot less damage.

Keep at least one of your Scouts out of direct combat to ensure they stay alive; their huge sight radius will prove extremely useful for timing your ambushes.

The second column starts from **Position B**, so quickly move your units to **Position C**, because the Stealth Forest there provides a better ambush site. After defeating them, the final column of reinforcements will start from **Position D**, so head back to **Position C** again and spring your ambush from there. You'll receive a fresh batch of your own reinforcements at **Position B** as soon as the final enemy column has been defeated, so group up with them and march on the next objective.

Objective 3

Destroy the Enemy Market Town

Only two small enemy groups defend the market town, so your new army should have no problems defeating them, after which you can safely destroy all of the buildings. Another large group of reinforcements, comprised mainly of Knights, will join your cause after you destroy the market, so group up with them to increase the strength of your army.

Objective 4

Rendezvous with the Welsh Allies

A group of allied Welsh units will now enter the area and start making their way towards Lincoln, but enemy units are waiting along their route and will soon ambush them. Quickly start moving your army towards your allies, but when you get close, your units will also get ambushed. To ensure the safety of your allies, engage the enemies that are attacking your units with your infantry, and then have your cavalry flank around to help the Welsh units. After defeating all of the ambushers, follow the Welsh units towards Lincoln.

Objective 5

Gain Entry to Lincoln

Breaking your way through the blockade outside of Lincoln can be difficult, but if you apply what you've learned so far, you can make things much easier for yourself. Rather than a head-on attack, enter the Stealth Forest at **Position E** and flank around the blockade with your entire army. Once you're behind them, send your cavalry to attack the enemy ranged infantry and siege engines while your infantry clashes with the enemy Spearmen. After defeating the blockade, you're finally free to enter Lincoln.

Because your Longbowmen will likely end up in close-range combat in this fight, make sure to use their Setup Camp ability to offset some of the damage they'll take.

Objective 6

Defeat the Besieging Forces

In Lincoln you gain military buildings, Villagers and a Town Center with which to start building up your military and economic strength to repel and defeat the forces besieging the town from **Positions F**, **G**, and **H**. There are three idle Villagers next to your Town Center, so have them go to **Position I** and join the other Villagers gathering Wood, and then start your Town Center producing more Villagers to gather Gold from the vein near your Wood gatherers.

You won't really need any additional cavalry for this part of the mission, but Longbowmen to man the walls and Men-at-Arms to attack are very useful. You have a **Council Hall** in Lincoln, so any Longbowmen you want should be produced from there because of the reduced production time. Because the attacking forces are so heavily comprised of infantry, Mangonels can be extremely effective, so a lot of your Gold should go towards producing them and you should be selective with your technology upgrades.

***Warning:** Be careful with taking out all of the enemy camps too quickly. You'll want to have a good amount of units left after clearing them because King Stephen's main force will attack afterwards. Discovering his army at **Position J** will also trigger his attack, so stay close to Lincoln and give yourself time to build up your forces.*

The eastern camp at **Position F** poses the biggest threat because that's where Lincoln's defenses are the weakest, so if you made it through the blockade with at least 80 units, you should attack there and clear the camp as soon as possible. If a lot of your units are low on health, send them to the **Abbey of Kings** inside Lincoln to get healed up first. Take out the camp at **Position G** next after bringing in reinforcements to get you back to 80 units. Before clearing the final camp at **Position H** however, build up a significantly stronger army that includes around 100 infantry units, and four Mangonels. Now when you attack that camp you'll already have a sufficiently strong army for what comes next.

Objective 7

Capture King Stephen

King Stephen will attack with his main force from **Position J** as soon as the final camp is destroyed, so retreat back to just outside of Lincoln's walls and make your stand under the cover of the defenses there. Have your Mangonels focus on attacking groups of infantry, while any cavalry you have left or melee infantry need to destroy the enemy Mangonels as soon as possible before they can decimate your army. If you find yourself outnumbered, do not fret. King Stephen will not call in reinforcements, so you can stay by the safety of the Lincoln Keep while you regroup. He will regenerate health over time, but he'll fall easily if you rebuild and launch a second full assault.

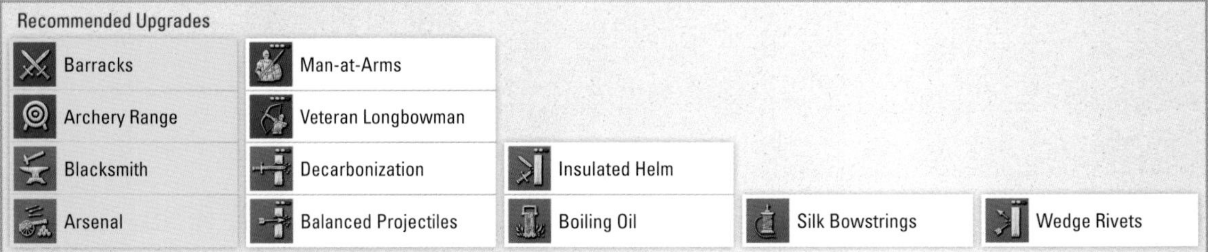

Recommended Upgrades

Barracks	Man-at-Arms			
Archery Range	Veteran Longbowman			
Blacksmith	Decarbonization	Insulated Helm		
Arsenal	Balanced Projectiles	Boiling Oil	Silk Bowstrings	Wedge Rivets

Matilda: The Empress Who Fought to be Queen: 1102 - 1167

In the English civil war known as the Anarchy, Matilda fought against her cousin, Stephen, for the right to rule. The daughter of King Henry I, Matilda was uniquely prepared to lead a kingdom. Her father had married her off to the Holy Roman Emperor when she was just 12 years old. As Empress and Queen of the Romans, Matilda grew up learning how to command. In the years when the Emperor was at war, she governed the realm in his stead. But after the emperor's sudden death, King Henry married Matilda off again, this time to Geoffrey of Anjou. In 1135, the king died. He'd named Matilda as his heir, and she expected to become queen. But the barons betrayed their oaths of loyalty and crowned her cousin. Matilda went to war to regain her crown. After almost twenty years of bloodshed, however, it was not to be. She negotiated a peace with Stephen that ensured her son would inherit the kingdom. Her descendants were kings of the powerful Angevin Empire, ruling over lands in both England and France. The Empress never became queen. But in her own way, Matilda achieved victory.

– Illuminated History

The Anarchy 1153

The Siege of Wallingford

Rewards

- The Angevin Empire
- The Siege of Wallingford

The future rule of the empire was at stake. Kings would be made... and unmade.

Matilda and Stephen's battle for the crown would all come down to Wallingford. If Matilda's army could hold the castle, she could restore her claim to the throne.

Objective 1

Defend Wallingford

You start this mission with limited units and defenses that you must use to defend the town of Wallingford for ten minutes, until your reinforcements can arrive. Attacks on Wallingford will start almost immediately, so you'll need to contend with them while simultaneously building up your economy and military to help with the defense.

Your main army should be used as a mobile force that gets sent to any point of the wall that's being attacked, so when they're not being used, keep them in a central location to make that easier. It can be beneficial to go outside of your walls sometimes to finish off enemy groups, but you should always bring your units back inside and allow your fortifications and Longbowmen on the walls to do the brunt of the work. The three gates at **Positions A**, **B**, and **C** are where most of the enemy attacks are focused, so the bulk of your static defenses should be centered around those locations.

Keeping your walls and gates intact is also key to the defense of the town, so it's worth keeping a couple of Villagers nearby to perform emergency repairs when needed.

One of the biggest things that can help you defend the town is Mangonels to quickly take out groups of enemy units, so after fending off the first attack, have the two idle Villagers near your Town Center build a Siege Workshop. Start producing Villagers from both the Town Center and the **King's Palace** Landmark so speed things up, and send the first ones to work on the Gold Vein at **Position A**.

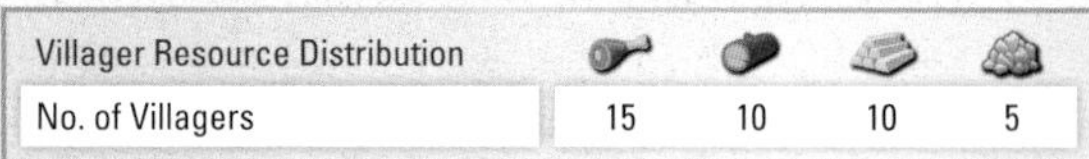

Villager Resource Distribution				
No. of Villagers	15	10	10	5

You also have access to a **Council Hall** Landmark, so start producing Longbowmen from there to take advantage of the reduced production time, and position them on top of the walls near the gates. When you have enough Stone and Gold, start building Stone Wall Towers next to each of gates you're defending, and then produce Mangonels and place one behind the walls near the gates to quickly take out enemy infantry. After producing the Mangonels, put your remaining Gold towards upgrades. The Stone and Gold deposits in Wallingford won't last long, so when they run out, evenly distribute the Villagers from them to Wood and Food, with Farms being your Food source. Because Gold is scarce, for the bulk of your army you should stick to producing units that only require Food and Wood such as Longbowmen and Spearmen.

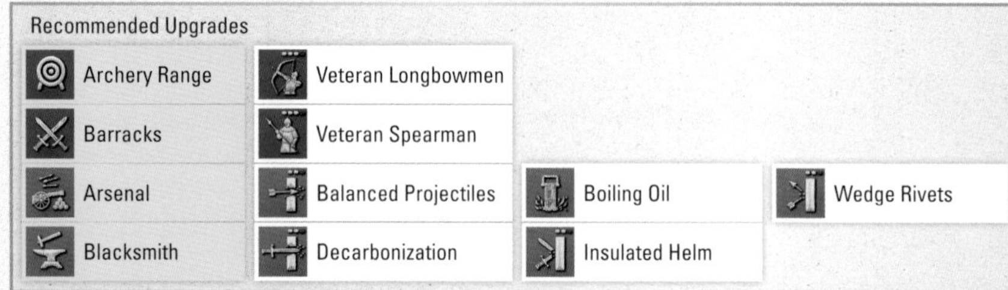

Recommended Upgrades			
Archery Range	Veteran Longbowmen		
Barracks	Veteran Spearman		
Arsenal	Balanced Projectiles	Boiling Oil	Wedge Rivets
Blacksmith	Decarbonization	Insulated Helm	

Objective 2

Destroy the English Outposts

After ten minutes your reinforcements will arrive at **Position E**, but the attacks will keep coming until you destroy the enemy outposts at **Positions F-I**, so you'll now have to manage battles on two fronts at once. While you build up your main force and use it to defend Wallingford, use the reinforcements to attack the outposts, starting with the one closest to them at **Position F**. If you need additional Gold for upgrades, remember that you can sell off some of your other more sustainable resources at the Market until you have enough.

Your attacking army should easily be strong enough to clear that first outpost and push on to the next one at **Position G** without needing additional units, but after those first two, send some reinforcements to bolster their numbers. Continue destroying the remaining outposts with your attacking army, reinforcing it as needed while you continuously produce military units back in Wallingford to both defend and ensure a constant supply of units to your attacking army.

Because you'll no longer need to contend with attacks coming from the direction of the destroyed camps, you can focus your defenses on the remaining sides of Wallingford.

Objective 3

Defeat the Final Wave

As soon as the final outpost is destroyed, quickly bring your army back towards Wallingford because the enemy will launch one final desperate attack in an attempt to sack the town. Rather than meeting the incoming attackers out in the open, wait for them to get close to your walls so that you can take advantage of your static defenses, and then consolidate all of your units and make one last defensive stand. This final wave contains a lot of infantry and cavalry, so make sure your Mangonels are in a good position to bombard them, while your infantry forms a blockade in front of them. As long as you were constantly producing units this whole time, you should have no trouble fending off this last attack and securing the safety of Wallingford.

Making Age of Empires IV Unique

"One of the key things [in making Age of Empires IV unique] is how we diversify and celebrate the civilizations represented: their languages and how they developed; music and how it was influenced by everything from religion to instrumental technology and access; how neighbouring cultures impacted theirs; the inventions and scenarios that drove their intellectual development and technological leaps. We present this in-game and in supplemental content to create a better picture of each civilization. I've never seen us celebrate cultures to the depth that we do in Age of Empires IV, and I'm very proud of what Relic Entertainment and all our partners have created.

Speaking specifically to gameplay, we walk a fine line between satisfying the players that already love Age from its previous iterations and modernizing and finding new ways to shift players' mental planning around warfare and empire growth. Siege and wall combat is a good example of an area we felt we could lean into that's specifically unique to Age IV, as players love building vast empires. How could we better represent the defense of those massive empires?"

– Adam Isgreen
Franchise Creative Director, World's Edge

1216

Rebellion

The Siege of Dover

Rewards

- Rebellion
- The Key to England

King John's poor stewardship of England sparked an invasion to overthrow his fragile rule.

King John had angered the English barons. In full revolt, they invited the French to invade and take advantage of his weakness. One key fortification stood in their way: the castle at Dover!

Objective 1

Hold off the French Siege

Dover is under siege as soon as the mission starts, and you'll find yourself having to fend off four waves of French attackers, with a diminishing period of time between each one to prepare. The first wave should be easily handled by the Longbowmen on your Stone Walls, but to make it easier on them, research the upgrade to **Veteran Longbowmen** at the Archery Range straight away. After fending off that first wave, you'll have 10:00 minutes to prepare for the next.

Start producing additional Longbowmen from the **Council Hall** Landmark now and set the rally point on top of the wall near one of the gates so that they get into position straight away. If you see any siege engines among the attacking French units, make sure to attack them with the group of Horsemen you start with before they can inflict too much damage on your walls.

While your units are holding the line, use the time to make additional preparations. Start by having your Town Center and **King's Palace** Landmark produce Villagers until you have five more that you can send to help gather Stone, and another five to build and work at Farms for Food. You'll also want some additional static fortifications, so produce a few extra Villagers and have them construct Stone Wall Towers near the gates along the wall.

The French have their siege units at the ready as soon as the mission starts.

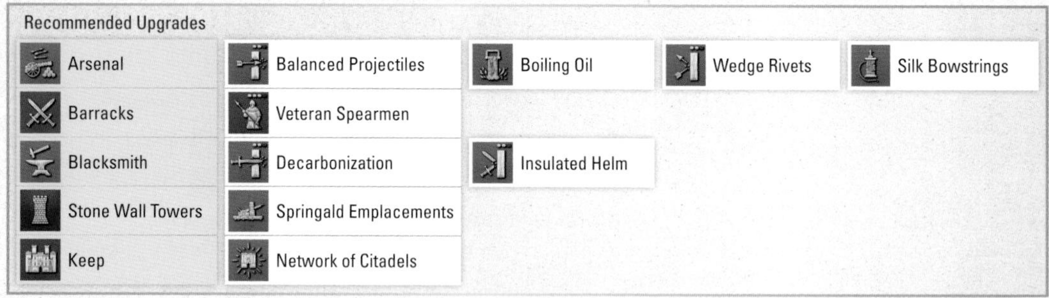

Recommended Upgrades				
Arsenal	Balanced Projectiles	Boiling Oil	Wedge Rivets	Silk Bowstrings
Barracks	Veteran Spearmen			
Blacksmith	Decarbonization	Insulated Helm		
Stone Wall Towers	Springald Emplacements			
Keep	Network of Citadels			

After fending off the first wave, Willikin of the Weald will arrive at an outlying town at **Position A** with the aim of disrupting the French forces attacking the castle by recruiting local Longbowmen to the cause. You have 10 minutes now to prepare for the next wave, and Gold will make that much easier. The town where Willikin starts will come under your control when he arrives, so have the Market there build five Traders while Willikin makes his way to another town at **Position B**. Along with a few more Longbowmen to recruit, you'll also find a neutral Trade Post here, so establish a trade route to it with the Traders you're producing to start earning Gold.

French siege weapons will start making their way towards the castle from **Position C** at this time, and with a few more recruits, Willikin just might be able to stop them. Thankfully, more recruits await in the small towns at **Positions D** and **E**, so have Willikin visit both of them so they join up. While that's going on, keep producing units at your main base, including some Spearmen to backup your Longbowmen, and use your new Gold to start doing some research.

The French siege reinforcements drive straight past the Stealth Forest at **Position F**, so once you have all of the recruits, position them and Willikin there, and put them on **Stand Ground**. This group of units should be sufficiently strong to defeat the small siege weapon convoys, but to ensure victory, make sure to use their **Arrow Volley** ability for some extra damage. If any of the French units do slip past you they'll join the next attack wave, so anything you do here will only help your main force.

Mood concept for the English civilization's landscape.

Willikin has to do a lot of running between towns to find the recruits, so to speed up that process, make use of his ***Movement Speed*** *ability to cover ground in less time.*

If you need additional Wood for more Longbowmen and Spearmen at this point, build a Town Center near **Position A** and produce some more Villagers there to gather it. Now that you have some Gold income it's also worth building a Siege Workshop at your main base to produce some Mangonels, because they'll help considerably with your defense. The second wave of French attackers should be hitting you about now, but if you've been preparing sufficiently, you should be able to fend them off easily and will now have 8:00 minutes to prepare for the next wave.

More allies will want to join the fight now, so have Willikin and your ambushers quickly move to the small camp at **Position G** to recruit them because more French reinforcements will start trying to join the next wave, and you'll need to get into a new position to stop them. These siege weapons travel along the road from **Position H**, which is too far from an Stealth Forest to attack from, so you'll need to be a bit more proactive. Hide them in the Stealth Forest at **Position I**, and then go out and attack each group as they pass you by. If you're slow in getting here and some have already moved past this point, you can attack them further up the road as they round the corner.

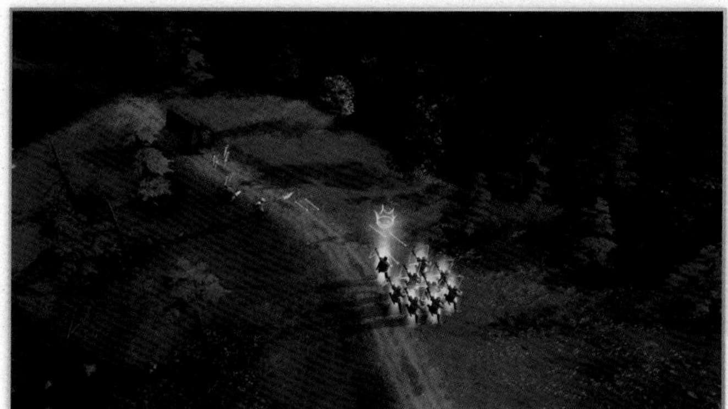

Some of the French siege reinforcements can be sneaky and veer off the road, so always keep an eye on their progress, and if needed, send Willikin and his troops out to attack them.

Aim to have about five or six Stone Wall Towers at the two gates the French attack by the time the third enemy wave reaches you, and upgrade as many of them as possible with **Springald Emplacements**. If you need more Stone for construction, remember that you can buy some for Gold at the Market in the town at **Position A**. You should also be able to reach the population capacity by this point, so then it's just a waiting game for the next attack.

Before the final wave hits you'll have another 8:00 minutes to repair and rebuild your main base, and you can also intercept more French reinforcements with Willikin. They travel along the road from **Position C** again this time, so quickly move his group back down to **Position F** so you can ambush them as they pass. Your ambush group might be running pretty low at this point, but if you've been upgrading and building up your main defending force sufficiently, you should be able to easily fend off the final attack even if you don't stop any of the siege engines. Once the final attacking wave is defeated, the mission is complete.

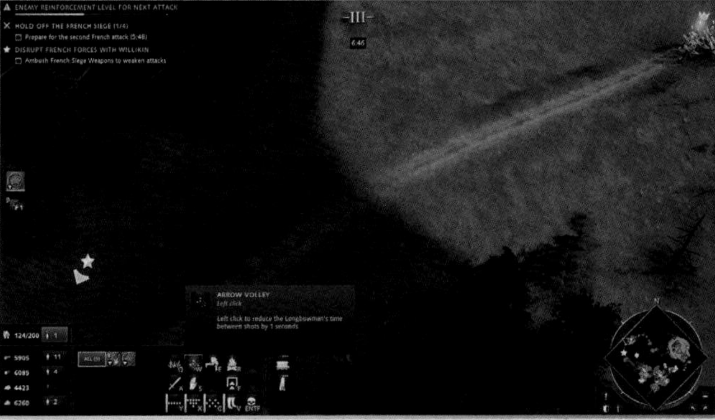

The ***Arrow Volley*** *ability allows the Longbowmen to have a higher firing rate , making them very effective against large enemy groups.*

 Rebellion 1215

The Siege of Rochester

King John clung to the throne, but the cost would be a bloody battle against his own people.

Rewards

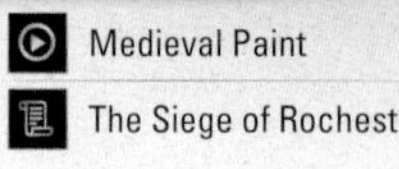

Medieval Paint

The Siege of Rochester

The castle at Rochester had fallen to rebel control. King John had to lay siege against his own barons.

Objective 1

Capture Chatham

The army at Chatham is no match yours, so march in there and take the village by force. Leave your Scout behind during this first engagement; it will be useful for the rest of the mission and you don't want to lose it in the first battle.

Objective 2

Destroy Rochester Keep

Capturing Chatham was an easy task, but keeping it won't be. Groups of enemies will constantly attack you while you're trying to build up your forces to mount an attack on Rochester, so you're going to have to multitask building your economy while defending your base. Your Villagers are especially vulnerable to these early attacks, so focus on defending them at all costs. Most of the attacks come from either the forest at **Position A**, or the road at **Position B**, so split your army and have them guard those locations.

Villager Resource Distribution					
No. of Villagers	Start	8	6	2	4
	Goal	20	10	15	4

Assign your starting Villagers to the resources shown in the table, and make sure to build Lumber and Mining Camps near the gathering points to speed things up, with Food coming from additional Farms built around your Mill. Start producing more Villagers at your Town Center and have them go to the Gold Vein just up the road from your base. While this is happening, use your Scout to explore the surrounding forests to locate Sheep to bring back to your base for even faster Food gathering.

Magna Carta

England's Magna Carta was created as a peace treaty to end a bitter civil war between rebel barons and their king. The rebels had captured London, forcing King John to negotiate peace terms that would limit his power and hold him to the same laws that governed his people. But the peace failed. And by the time war ended in 1217, John's son, King Henry III was in power. Henry reissued the charter to help heal the country. And from that day on, Magna Carta—the Great Charter—bound monarchs to the same laws as their subjects. It established that the people are protected by the due process of law, including a fair trial by their peers. And it led the way to creating a Parliament that operates independently of the crown. Magna Carta has influenced founding and human rights charters throughout history, including the United States' Constitution and Bill of Rights. Only four copies of the original treaty from 1215 survive. But the power of its words still affects countless lives across the globe today.

– Illuminated History

You get some Monk units when you take Chatham, so have one of them capture the Sacred Site in town to start generating some additional Gold, and then capture the one just outside of town as well.

As soon as you have 500 Wood and 400 Stone, build a second Town Center near the Gold Vein at **Position C** to provide some extra protection for your workers there and start the expansion of your base. To help with defense, build a Siege Workshop next and produce a couple of Mangonels from it, and then when you have enough Stone, wall off the enemy approach route at **Position A** by building a wall from the coast to behind the forest there. Build a gate and a couple of Stone Wall Towers along that wall, and then after stationing a few Longbowmen on top of it, it should be secure enough for you to move the rest of your units to **Position B** to help defend that area.

The enemies attack with a lot of Battering Rams to try and destroy your buildings, which means that you'll want your initial military units to be melee ones, and with that in mind, build two Barracks on the forest side of your second Town Center to produce Spearmen. Keep saving resources as much as possible, and then when you have 1600 Food and 1200 Gold, build the **Berkshire Palace** Landmark near the road at **Position B**. Not only will that Landmark advantage you to Age IV, but it will also provide a significant amount of defense and produces units right where you need them.

Build two more Archery Ranges near the Barracks you previously built, and between all of those and the Berkshire Palace you should now have enough military production, and your infantry should consist mainly of Men-at-Arms and Longbowmen. Now it's also time to start focusing on upgrades by building a Blacksmith and Arsenal; if you start running out of Gold, build some more Stone Walls around the Gold Vein at **Position D** to defend it and have your Villagers gather from there.

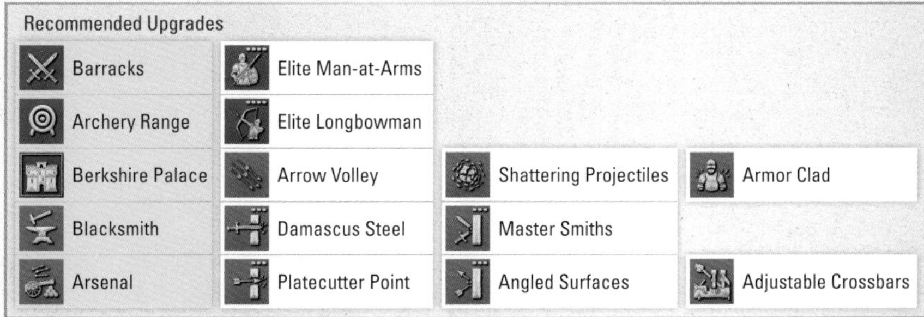

Recommended Upgrades

Barracks	Elite Man-at-Arms		
Archery Range	Elite Longbowman		
Berkshire Palace	Arrow Volley	Shattering Projectiles	Armor Clad
Blacksmith	Damascus Steel	Master Smiths	
Arsenal	Platecutter Point	Angled Surfaces	Adjustable Crossbars

Once you have enough units produced that you can afford to spare around 80 of them and still have enough to defend your base, it's worth taking some time to complete a couple of optional objectives that will significantly weaken Rochester's defense. Rochester is sending groups of Traders to a Market along the river, and you can cut off that trade route by blockading the road at **Position E**. Defeat six Traders with your army and there won't be enough food for everyone, leading to a large number of rebels deserting and leaving the castle.

Your Monks can also pick up the Relics that are scattered around the map and bring them back to your Monastery to generate additional Gold.

With the supply lines broken, bring your army back to base to heal and rebuild, and then turn your sights towards **Position F** where there are a number of Mills you can destroy to further cripple Rochester's food supply. Around this time, however, the attacks on your base will start including Mangonels, so it's important to keep a close eye on your minimap to spot them as they approach or else they can decimate your infantry. When your army is ready again, take it to **Position F** and destroy all four Mills and the defending armies, making sure to stay away from the walls of Rochester. Even more rebels will flee the castle now, making your final assault that much easier.

Many units still remain inside the castle walls, however, so even though you've made things easier, you shouldn't get complacent. It's also important to remember that your goal is to destroy the Keep, so nothing else matters. The easiest route to the camp is through the walls at **Position G** because that area has the weakest defenses. Trebuchets are the key to cracking Rochester's defenses, so make sure your army has at least four of them, and then rally them all near **Position G** and begin your assault.

Take out the Stone Walls with your Trebuchets, and have your infantry fend off any enemy units that try to stop you. Make sure not to advance inside the castle area too quickly; go slow, and thin out the units inside gradually to avoid getting overwhelmed. Reinforce your army as needed, and then advance past the first wall into the city itself and start clearing that area, but do not actually destroy the inner walls that surround the Keep. Your Trebuchets can reach the Keep from outside of those walls, and making a hole in the walls will make protecting them a lot harder. Done correctly, you should never have to fight the large army in the interior part of the castle, and your Trebuchets can safely bombard the Keep until you're victorious.

William Marshal: Knight of Legend

At the Battle of Lincoln in 1217, legendary knight William Marshal rode into battle at the head of a desperate army. He was 70 years old. But charging headlong into a bad-odds fight was nothing new. As a young knight with few resources, William fought on the tournament circuit, competing in brutal mock battles that had very few rules. His audacious exploits—such as grabbing his enemy's bridle and dragging horse and rider back to camp to hold for ransom—won him fortune and fame. But real war soon put those tournament skills to the test.

William fought in Normandy and in Jerusalem, and when he returned from the Holy Land he became a commander in King Henry II's service. He defended the kingdom for Henry II and his descendants: Richard, John, and the boy king Henry III. In 1217, William Marshal was regent to the young king during the baron's rebellion. He bet the future of the kingdom on a daring plan to attack the rebel-held city of Lincoln. Once again, he charged directly at his enemy - and again, his audacity won the day. William Marshal ended the war, secured peace for England and ensured that the kingdom he had served so faithfully would endure.

– Illuminated History

Second Battle of Lincoln

Rewards

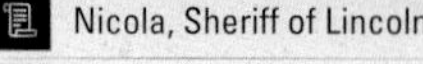

- Nicola, Sheriff of Lincolnshire
- The Norman Legacy
- The Second Battle of Lincoln

The succession of a child king left England vulnerable to revolt. Its protection fell to an aging knight and a female sheriff.

Rebel barons and their French allies besieged the castle at Lincoln. The king's knight, William Marshal, was tasked with retaking the city by force.

Objective 1

Defend Lincoln Castle until William Marshal Arrives

The castle is under siege as soon as the mission starts, so you'll need to act quickly and decisively to fend off the attackers and keep your walls intact. William Marshal and his reinforcements will arrive in six minutes, but until then you're on your own. You can't build any economy buildings at this stage, but you can build military buildings, produce military units, and repair buildings.

Start by using your idle Villagers to build a Siege Workshop and have it produce two Mangonels to quickly deal with enemy infantry, and then start producing Longbowmen from your Archery Range and have them man your walls. You're going to need resources to build up your economy soon, so try not to spend more than is needed. You have a small group of Men-at-Arms by default, so use them to go outside of your gates and deal with enemy Battering Rams, just make sure to bring them back inside quickly. If any of your walls and towers do take damage, send your Villagers in to repair them straight away, and then just keep defending until William Marshal arrives.

Your Longbowmen can run all the way along your Stone Walls, so move them around to where they're needed most.

Objective 2

Destroy Rebel Military Buildings

When William Marshal arrives he'll bring with him an army of Knights and ride through the town of Stowe, bringing it under your control. Before you try and do anything at the town, however, you need to put an end to the attacks on Lincoln, so group up William's army and march it straight through your gates, picking up your group of Men-at-Arms along the way. Take them into the rebel stronghold outside and start systematically destroying the enemy's military production buildings, starting at **Position A**, and working down to **B** and **C**.

A small group of enemy units will attack the other side of your castle at **Position D** while you're dealing with the military buildings, so position your Longbowmen along the walls to that side so they're ready. Destroying the nearby buildings will take care of the immediate threat, but enemy forts around the outskirts of town will still launch attacks at you every few minutes, so you need to stay vigilant.

Objective 3

Defeat the French Army

Your current military strength is not sufficient to destroy those forts, so now is the time to start building up. Start producing Villagers from the Town Center in Stowe at **Position E**, and while that's happening, send your army to the small French camp at **Position F** and defeat the group of enemy units there to give you access to the resource deposits. Use the Villagers you produced at Stowe to build a second Town Center at this location, and then have it too start producing Villagers. Farms are your best source of Food at the moment, so build more around the Mill in Stowe, and then build a second Mill nearby and surround it too with Farms.

Villager Resource Distribution				
No. of Villagers	16	15	20	5

As soon as you have the resources, advance to Age IV by building **Berkshire Palace** at **Position G** outside of your castle walls to provide some additional defense and give you access to some powerful upgrades. When that construction

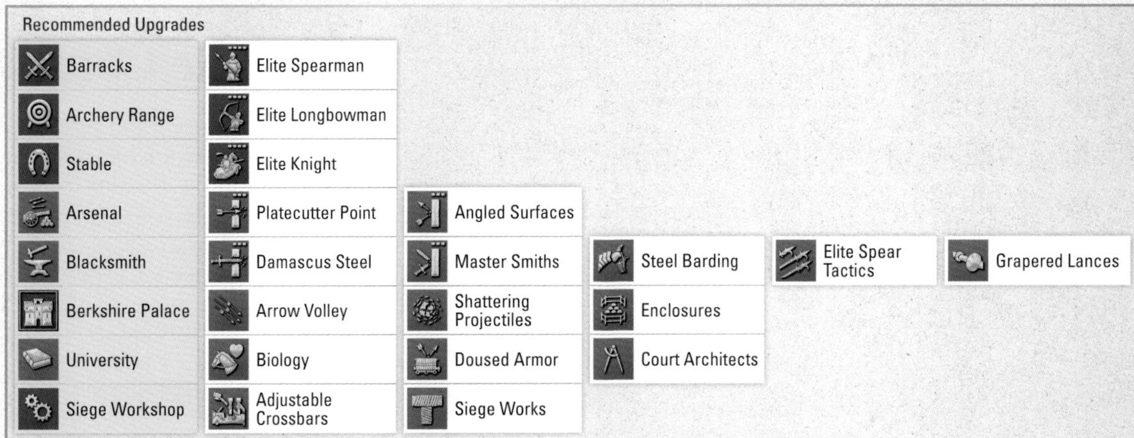

Recommended Upgrades

Barracks	Elite Spearman				
Archery Range	Elite Longbowman				
Stable	Elite Knight				
Arsenal	Platecutter Point	Angled Surfaces			
Blacksmith	Damascus Steel	Master Smiths	Steel Barding	Elite Spear Tactics	Grapered Lances
Berkshire Palace	Arrow Volley	Shattering Projectiles	Enclosures		
University	Biology	Doused Armor	Court Architects		
Siege Workshop	Adjustable Crossbars	Siege Works			

has finished, have those Villagers build a Blacksmith, Arsenal and University in Stowe so that you can start making some upgrades.

The French army consists mostly of Men-At-Arms, siege, Arbalétriers and Knights, and ths is well countered by a mix of light units such as Spearmen and Longbowmen, in conjunction with your own Knights and some Mangonels. The technologies you research should go towards benefiting those units while you have your military buildings start producing them, and to speed that process up, you should build two more Barracks, Archery Ranges, and two Stables in and around Lincoln.

Remember that you can produce units from the Berkshire Palace and the Keep inside Lincoln as well, so you can use them in place of some of the military production buildings.

Once you have an army of around 100 units made up of Spearmen, Longbowmen, Knights, Mangonels and a couple of Trebuchets, and you can leave some units behind for defense, it's time to mount your attack. The southern fort at **Position H** is both the closest and the weakest, so march your army there first. The fort has numerous Outposts and Mangonels inside, so it's important not to rush in there; take a slow approach and let your Trebuchets bombard the Outposts from safety, and use the rest of your army to fend off any enemy units that come out to attack you.

After destroying all of the buildings in the southern camp, take your army across the bridge towards the northern camp at **Position I** and form a blockade there while you bring in the rest of the units that you left behind in defense. The northern camp is uphill, which means the enemy will see you coming and you're likely to take more damage than usual. The enemy also has Springalds outside of the camp, and because of sight lines, they can start firing before your Trebuchets, which means you have to be bold and approach quickly with your army to destroy them.

While most of your units are dealing with the Springalds, have your Trebuchets start attacking the Outposts. When the Springalds are down, move your army inside the camp and have them take out the Mangonels, while your own Mangonels fire on the enemy infantry and cavalry to minimise your losses. Now it should be a simple matter of finishing off the last few units and destroying all of the buildings to firmly cement your victory in this battle.

Hundred Years War

Chivalry 1351

The Combat of the Thirty

England's king waged war for his claim to France. In the midst of violent raids and devastating battles, one tournament of champions would uphold the values of chivalry.

The French captain, Jean de Beaumanoir, would enlist thirty great fighters to defend France's claim to Brittany. On the opposing side, England's fiercest champions represented their king. The two sides would clash in an arena of chivalric combat.

Rewards

- A Tournament of War
- Chevauchée
- Chivalry

Objective 1

Recruit Champions to Combat the English

Your first objective is to recruit two champions to your cause. There are four that you can recruit, and it's worth getting them all to gain more options during the final battles. Each champion will have a small objective for you to complete before they'll join you, and if you fail it, you'll lose the chance to recruit them. The first champion you can recruit is located north of the town you start in, right at the first objective marker. When you get close to that position, a group of Villagers will be attacked by a pack of Wolves; if you want to recruit Olivier Arrel, you'll need to save them. Once you gain control over him, group him with the rest of your units and move towards the nearby houses and kill the Wolves there to secure his help.

The location of the other three champions will then be revealed on your map—head towards Geoffrey du Bois and his cavalry at **Position A**. As you get near his position you'll notice that a group of Longbowmen are attacking an Outpost, and you'll need to ensure the safety of that Outpost if Geoffrey du Bois is to join your army. Only use Jean and your cavalry units for this part of the fight, and have Jean lead the other units to draw their fire and minimise your losses. Once that initial group has been defeated you'll need to defend the Outpost from small incoming waves of enemies for 90 seconds; now is the time to bring in your other units and Olivier Arrel so that you can use his healing ability.

For your third champion, head towards **Position B**, where Guy de Rochefort awaits you. When you get close, a group of cavalry and infantry will attack; try to minimize your losses here by making frequent use of the special abilities your champions posses. The fourth and final champion, Yves Charruel, lies directly along your path on the bridge at **Position C**. You'll need to win a duel against him to recruit him, and Jean alone is more than up to the task.

Objective 2

Arrive at the Halfway Oak

To complete this objective, simply follow the road through the wooden gate here and enter the staging area.

The Black Death: 1347-1351

In the 1340s, France was under attack by the English in the Hundred Years War. As the countryside reeled under English raids, rumors reached France of an unstoppable wave of death sweeping across Asia. Was it a sign of the apocalypse? Divine punishment for humanity's sins? The people would soon see for themselves. For in 1347, the Black Death arrived in France. Spread by fleas and lice, the plague could not be outrun, and none were immune. Victims' skin erupted in pus-filled buboes. They developed acute fever, then began vomiting blood. Death soon followed.

France and England put war on hold as disease gripped each nation. The Black Death sped across France, gutting crowded cities and decimating the peasant population. With no one to work the fields, crops failed. Famine swept the land. The plague finally waned in 1351, but not before killing a quarter of France's entire population. And as one threat eased, another returned: the English invaded, and war resumed with a vengeance. France's suffering would continue....

– Illuminated History

Objective 3

Select Champions to Combat the Englisch

The English battle group in this area (in orange) will look different every time you play this mission, and you'll need to chose champions that can counter the group that you see. The general rules are:

- Men-at-Arms vs Spearmen
- Spearmen vs Cavalry
- Cavalry vs Archers
- Men-at-Arms vs Men-at-Arms

Against a combination of Spearmen and Heavy Infantry, choose Guy de Rochefort (Infantry) and Yves Charruel (Armor).

Objective 4

Round 1 of 2 - Defeat the English Soldiers

Enter the combat arena to begin the first stage of the battle, and if you've picked the right combination of champions, and use the abilities of your heroes to your advantage, you should have no trouble emerging victorious.

Objective 5

Reinforce Units and Research Technology

Now you get the chance to acquire some upgrades for your units at the Blacksmith near the gate leading to the combat area. The best ones to get are **Fitted Leatherwork** and **Insulated Helm**—once they've been learned, return to the combat arena.

Objective 6

Round 2 of 2 - Defeat the English Soldiers

Engage in the next round of combat in the same manner as you did in the first, and once all of the English soldiers have been defeated, the mission is complete.

Chivalry

1360

The Siege of Paris

Rewards

- Edward, the Black Prince
- Plate Armor
- The Siege of Paris

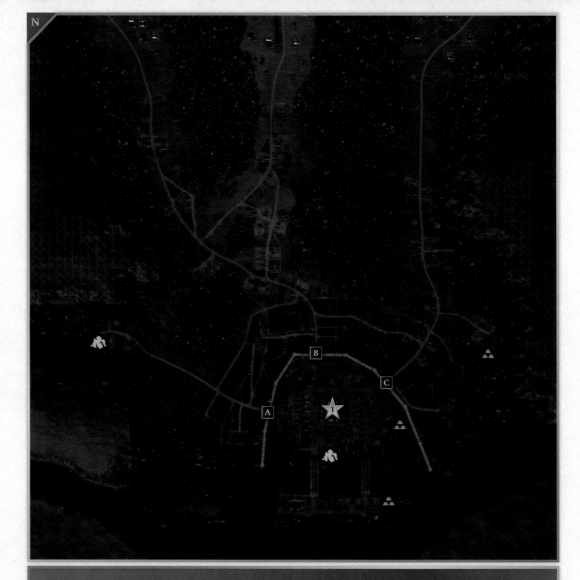

The fearsome Black Prince of England had set northern France ablaze. Poised for the final blow, his army closed in on the capital.

The English were coming for Paris. As Parisians took shelter behind the capital's walls, the French army prepared to defend the city. Only their determination and a few feet of stone stood between victory and defeat.

Objective 1

Defend Paris

You won't be able to defend the rural areas outside of Paris, so start by evacuating the 18 Villagers from the nearby areas and send them to your Town Center to drop their resources. Redistribute them the following way, and produce more Villagers until you can reach the goal amounts for each resource type.

Villager Resource Distribution					
No. of Villagers	Start	7	4	10	3
	Goal	10	12	13	5

Produce Arbalétriers at your Guild Hall; they are cheaper, and produce faster there than at an Archery Range.

Black Monday: 1360

In the Hundred Years War, England's King Edward III used fire and destruction to terrorize the people of France. On Easter Monday in 1360, he was planning an attack on the cathedral city of Chartres. Night fell and the temperature dropped. The wind gained strength until it became a storm of epic proportions. Enormous hail stones plummeted to earth, striking down men and horses in the darkness. For Edward, this horrific storm seemed to be divine wrath for his invasion. He knelt in prayer at the height of the tempest and vowed to make peace with the French. When the skies cleared, Edward was surrounded by the dead. A thousand English soldiers fell that night, along with six thousand horses. To Edward, the message was clear. His war must end. Three weeks later, he signed the Treaty of Brétigny. Edward's conquest was over. The terror of Black Monday had led to a fragile peace between England and France.

– Illuminated History

The enemy attack will begin in six minutes from this point, and the mission will fail if they make it into the heart of Paris and destroy the majority of the buildings, so now is the time to bolster your defenses. Start by building a Siege Workshop and commence Mangonel production as soon as you can afford them, and then add at least one Stone Wall Tower near each of the gates along your wall, adding more as you can afford them. To help deal with any enemies that get close to those towers, you should also research the **Boiling Oil** upgrade at the Arsenal. Along with the structural defenses, it's worth acquiring some upgrades for your units. For additional units, start producing Arbalétriers and Men-at-Arms, and then when you run out of Gold, switch to Archers and Spearmen.

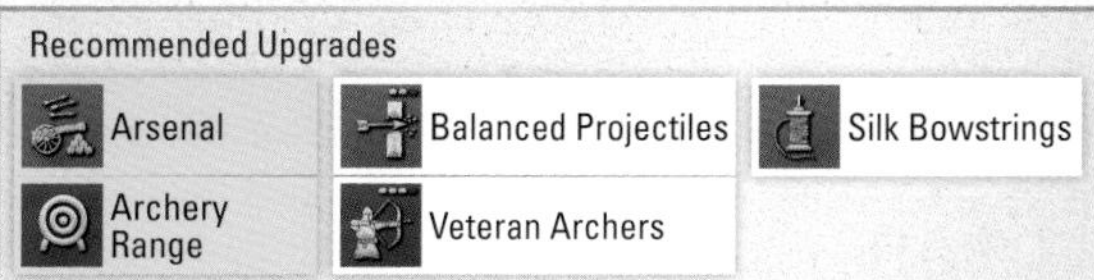
Recommended Upgrades

Arsenal	Balanced Projectiles	Silk Bowstrings
Archery Range	Veteran Archers	

Once your Gold Veins and Stone Outcroppings run dry, redistribute your Villagers to Food and Wood equally, and if you need more Gold, sell some of your Food or Wood at the Market. The enemy attack will start as soon as the timer runs out, and their forces will primarily attack near the gates at **Positions A**, **B**, and **C**, so focus your defenses there. You'll need to repel 10 waves of attacking enemies in total. Here are some additional tips to help you accomplish that goal:

Mining the Stone inside Paris to build Stone Wall Towers greatly increases your chances of defeating the English.

Tips for defending against the siege:

- *Have Mangonels stationed behind your walls; they're effective at taking out enemy units and siege engines.*
- *Ranged units on top of walls have higher range and take less damage, so use them in great numbers.*
- *Stone Wall Towers are useful for additional defense, especially with the Arrow Slits and Boiling Oil upgrades.*
- *Always have a mobile group of preferably cavalry units that can quickly move outside the castle momentarily to destroy enemy siege engines when they're unguarded.*
- *Have melee infantry ready to defend the bottom of your walls.*
- *Place one Villager at every gate ready to repair damaged walls/ buildings.*
- *Always move your units where they're needed.*

From wave 5 of the assault onwards, the enemy will bring Trebuchets to bear against your walls, and they're significantly more troublesome than anything you've faced thus far. To counter them you'll need to send groups of infantry and cavalry out from behind your defenses, so speed is of the essence. It can be worth using a few of your units to draw away some of the enemy units defending the Trebuchet, so that your main attacking group has a clear path to their target. This tactic can be quite effective if used to draw the enemy into the range of your defensive towers and Archers. As soon as all 10 waves have been repelled, the mission is complete.

Mangonels become one of the main threats once you reach wave 7, but you can target them with your Stone Wall Towers to minimize the need to send out your units.

Campaign Writing

"Writing a campaign mission is a multi-step process that usually begins with me rough-drafting some voice over for all the objective beats in the mission. I'll sit with the mission designer and we'll make sure that the intent of my writing matches with what they are planning for the mission. At that point, I can refine my writing and once that is at a level that I'm happy with, I will pass it to my peers and seniors for review.

Once I get the notes back on my writing, I will action these notes and do a full pass on the voice over script again. At this point it's in a good spot and ready for final review. Now is usually the time I'll play the mission a few times, get a good feel of the cadence and look for any opportunity to inject more history into the mission.

Take Combat of the 30—the opening mission for the Hundred Years War: this was a strange battle that needed context for the uninitiated to understand. As such, I was able to inject some flavour with the intent of providing the player with context on the knights of the era."

– Kristina Wiik
Senior Designer, Narrative, Relic

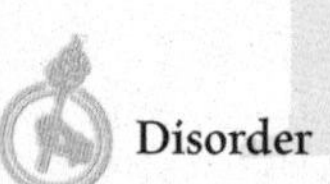

France in Chaos

Rewards

- Disorder
- Les Routiers
- The Warhorse

A storm of disorder threatened France's survival. The king's authority would have to be enforced...over invaders and peasants alike.

Taking the throne in 1364, the Dauphin became King Charles V of France. Facing threats from peasants, mercenaries and invaders, the first test of his power would be to bring control to a realm in disorder.

Objective 1

Stem the Peasant Rebellion

A large portion of your camp is engulfed in flames when you begin this mission, so begin by assigning Villagers to repair the burning buildings. You initial main goal is to capture two nearby villages (at **Positions A** and **B**), but your more immediate concern should be the threat posed by a band of English routiers at **Position C**.

Start by upgrading to **Hardened Spearmen** at your Barracks, and while that's researching, put your Town Center to work on producing Villagers and distribute them evenly between Food and Wood. There are Sheep near the outskirts of your camp, so it's worth taking a Scout outside to round them up and bring them in to get a jump start on Food gathering.

While your Scout is outside, it's worth having them go around and pick up some of the Treasure Chests that are dotted around the nearby forests.

The English routiers attack mainly with Horsemen, which is why it's good to upgrade your Spearmen, but the only ways you can put a stop to their attacks is to either destroy their camp, or pay them 800 Gold intribute. Both of those options are out of your grasp at the moment, because there are no Gold Veins nearby, and their camp is too strong for your current military. Instead, your best option is to build a second Barracks and produce more Spearmen to fend off their attacks and defend your camp. Building a Blacksmith to research the **Fitted Leatherwork** technology is also worth doing.

If you decide to pay off the English routiers, you can click the "Players & Tribute" button in the top right-hand corner of your screen to open the Tribute menu. Then simply click on the Gold icon to add increments of 100 Gold until you reach the desired amount, just note that they won't stop attacking until they receive the full amount.

With your defenses now set up, turn your attention to retaking Jouy from the rebels at **Position A**. At Jouy you'll face basic infantry, so bring your Archers and your Royal Knights if they're still alive. To minimise casualties, use hit-and-run attacks so that the enemy forces never get close to your Archers; the slow movement of the militia makes this relatively easy. Once Jouy is captured, you'll gain another Town Center, along with more Villagers working at Farms. Have both Town Centers produce Villagers until you have around 50 in total, then build another Barracks and Archery Range in Jouy and have them start producing units.

Your sights should now be firmly set on Croisy at **Position B**, which you can take in much the same way you did Jouy. This one is more important, however, because it has a precious Gold Vein. Once the village is yours, up your Villager count to 60, and put at least 15 of them on Gold. Rebuilding the Mining Camp closer to the Gold can help speed up this process.

***Warning:** Leave a few units (10-15) behind at Jouy to defend against enemy militia counter-attacks that will start arriving from the north after you retake the village.*

Now that the two smaller villages are yours, it's time to turn your attention towards Cocherel at **Position D**. Thanks to your new Gold supply, now is a good time to deal with the routiers by paying their one-time Tribute; you won't have to pay them again, so your defensive force can join your main army for the assault of Cocherel. You should also make some additional upgrades before commencing your attack.

Recommended Upgrades		
Lumber Camp	Forestry	Double Broadax
Mill	Wheelbarrow	Horticulture

Build two more Archery Ranges and Barracks in Croisy and have them produce Archers and Spearmen until you have around 60 units. Once ready, head towards **Position D,** have your infantry build a pair of Battering Rams before you get too close, and send one to attack each of the Outposts guarding the gate. If enemy units emerge, send your units to defend your rams, then advance on the gate once it's clear. When you're inside, concentrate on enemy units rather than buildings, since you'll gain control of everything once the units are routed.

Objective 2

Defeat Charles of Navarre's Army at Their Campsite

***Warning:** You must protect the Monastery in Cocherel, because you'll lose if it gets destroyed. The enemy often attacks with small groups of Knights, so keep some Spearmen nearby to counter them.*

You automatically advance to Age III after capturing Cocherel, so it's time to make some upgrades. Mangonels will help with the assault, so build a Siege Workshop to produce them.

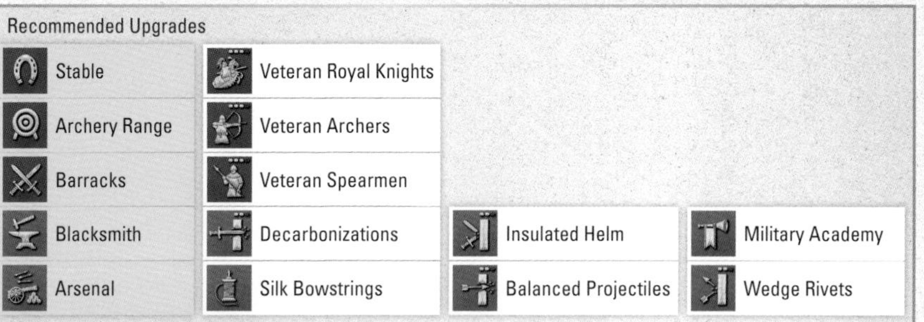

Recommended Upgrades			
Stable	Veteran Royal Knights		
Archery Range	Veteran Archers		
Barracks	Veteran Spearmen		
Blacksmith	Decarbonizations	Insulated Helm	Military Academy
Arsenal	Silk Bowstrings	Balanced Projectiles	Wedge Rivets

You get two Monks when you capture Cocherel, so after they heal your units, send them to capture the nearby Sacred Sites. Make sure to send some additional troops with them, because there are usually small groups of enemies defending them.

Send a Scout near the location of the enemy campsite to uncover the area. There are two ways to the top of the hill: one path **(Position E)**, is defended by Archers, and the other **(Position F),** has patrolling melee infantry. It's best to attack from both sides at once, so you'll need to split your army in two while leaving a decent sized group behind to defend the Monastery. The first should be made up of around 20 Royal Knights and 3 Mangonels, while the second has roughly 40 Spearmen, 40 Arbalétriers/Archers, and 2 Mangonels.

Have your Royal Knight brigade wait close to **Position E** while your infantry take the scenic route to **Position F**; launch your assault once both groups are ready. At **Position F**, have your Mangonels shoot the Archers and the Royal Knights defend them; 3 Mangonels can kill a group of Archers in a single volley, and once they've been defeated, have your cavalry flank the patrolling enemy infantry. At **Position E**, again, use your Mangonels to fire on the enemy units, and keep your own cavalry in front to defend them. Once the army is defeated, the mission is complete.

The Battle of Agincourt: 1415

October 25, 1415. Two armies faced off across a muddy field near the small French town of Agincourt. The French knew that victory would be theirs. They vastly outnumbered King Henry V's English army, an exhausted force weakened by hunger and disease. In one stroke, France could end the war and drive the English invaders from their land. As the fight began, the French cavalry charged through deep mud towards the enemy line. Then, they heard a terrible noise from above and iron-tipped arrows rained from the sky. The longbowmen shot one thousand arrows a second into the French ranks. Knights fell and sank into the mud. Pain-maddened warhorses trampled the fallen. And after they ran out of arrows, English archers used knives and hammers to slaughter the immobilized knights. Soon enough, King Henry had won the day by a staggering margin. Historians estimate that six to ten thousand French died, while only a few hundred Englishmen fell. At the Battle of Agincourt, France suffered one of its worst defeats in the Hundred Years War. And the English turned the miraculous story of Henry V's victory into legend.

– Illuminated History

A Grand Scale

"Age of Empires IV covers the rise and fall of entire dynasties and empires, rather than following the span of an individual's life. This approach sets each character's impact within the broader context of how their civilisation faired before and after their rule. This way, we bring the richness of medieval history to our players in a form that connects those events through the continuum of time to today."

– Lauren Wood
Principal Designer, Narrative, Relic

Disorder

1370

The Battle of Pontvallain

Discord and rivalry had divided the English army. Now was France's moment to strike.

In-fighting had split the English army into rival factions. As these scattered groups raided their way towards Pontvallain, the French army prepared to stamp them out.

Rewards

- Arrow Making
- Bertrand du Guesclin
- The Battle of Pontvallain

Objective 1

The Pontvallain Town Center Must Survive

To build an army powerful enough to defend the Pontvallain Town Center in the time allotted, you're going to need to build up your economy very quickly, while spending as little as possible on your military. With that in mind, you should aim to have at least 45 Villagers and 15 Traders active when there are around five minutes left on the countdown.

Trade is extremely important in this mission because it's your primary source of Gold, so the first thing you should do is send your two Traders to the Market in Pontvallain, while constantly producing them from the **Chamber of Commerce** Landmark at **Position A**. Two round trips is all it takes to bring in enough Gold to offset the cost of a Trader, so it won't be long before you're turning a profit. Any villagers that you produce should initially be put to work gathering Wood.

At **Position B** there's a small English camp that has a Gold Vein nearby and some Treasure Chests, making for a target too rich to pass up. Your starting army should be sufficient to clear the camp, but if you want to be safe, bring along a few additional Spearmen. Once the camp is yours, send at least eight Villagers up there to mine the Gold, while at the same time moving six of the Villagers at your base onto Food by killing the nearby Deer.

> ***Warning: Raiding Parties***
> *These raiding parties are the most difficult thing to deal with early on, because you'll have to balance developing your economy and repelling them at the same time. A few minutes into the mission you'll get an announcement that a raiding party is incoming, after which it takes them a little while to begin their attack on the outlying Farms. Before that happens, make sure to build a second Barracks in Pontvallain and have it research **Hardened Spearmen**, and then produce around 15 of them. That should be enough to deal with the first raiding party, and some allied units will lend some additional support for the second one. By the time the third group—consisting of Knights—arrives, they shouldn't pose much of a threat to your more developed army.*

After mostly focusing on your economy, once you reach the five minute mark, it's time to start working on your military units. At this point it's not worth investing more into Traders, because it takes 50 seconds to produce one, and a round trip takes around 3 minutes,

To make your Food gathering more efficient, build a Mill near the Deer you're harvesting.

which means you're better off investing whatever Gold you have into military. Next, build the **Royal Institute** Landmark in Pontvallain, along with four Stables, four Archery Ranges, a Blacksmith, and an Arsenal around it so that they can all benefit from the reduced production and research costs its influence range provides.

*It can be a tight fit getting all of your production and technology buildings around the **Royal Institute**, but the savings more than make up for the effort.*

The main English army consists of Longbowmen and Men-at-Arms. To counter them you should produce Royal Knights (great against ranged infantry and still good against Men-at-Arms), Arbalétriers to deal a lot of damage to the Men-at-Arms, and some additional Mangonels as backup. You'll want at least 20 Royal Knights and 30 Arbalétriers. While those units are being produced, build a Blacksmith and Arsenal and research the following technologies.

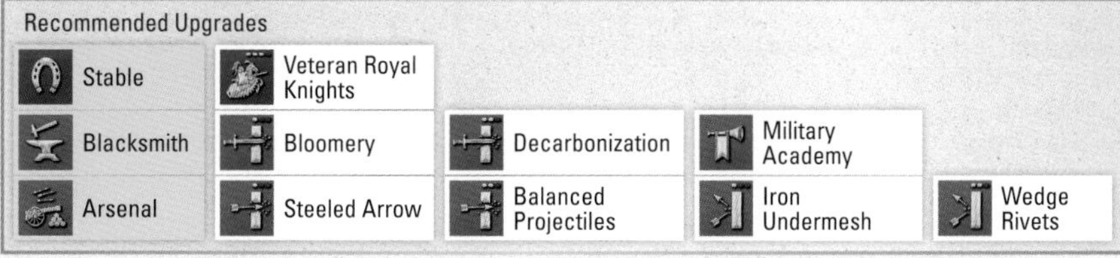

Recommended Upgrades

Building				
Stable	Veteran Royal Knights			
Blacksmith	Bloomery	Decarbonization	Military Academy	
Arsenal	Steeled Arrow	Balanced Projectiles	Iron Undermesh	Wedge Rivets

When the timer expires, the English army will make their move and launch their attacks along the three main routes into Pontvallain at **Positions C**, **D**, and **E**. As long as you've built up your forces to the recommended numbers, even a head on fight with all of them should be manageable, but intercepting them one at a time ensures they won't get close to your Town Center. Just make sure you return to Pontvallain again before the other groups arrive.

Spearmen are the natural counter unit to mounted units. Mass groups of them can take out even the strongest knights.

Desperation

The Siege of Orléans

The fate of a nation and the rise of a king rested on the shoulders of one fearless young woman: Jeanne d'Arc.

Jeanne d'Arc led the French army to the besieged city of Orléans. She found the walls surrounded and the people desperate. Firm in her faith, she would rally the French to fight back, and put her claim to divine calling beyond doubt.

Rewards

- Campaign Life
- Defiance
- Desperation

Objective 1

Defend Orléans

You'll be under siege from all sides as soon as the mission starts. Before you can even think about mounting an assault on the Keep at Les Tourelles, you'll need to set up a solid defensive foundation. To accomplish that, you're going to need resources, so start by producing more Villagers until you have at least 10 on both Gold and Stone. The enemy will attack the gates at **Positions A**, **B**, **C**, and **D**, but **Position A** tends to be attacked the most, so concentrate the bulk of your units there initially.

*A short while into the mission a friendly supply convoy makes its way along the road at **Position E** to drop off some resources. A group of English units will attempt to ambush the convoy near this position, so if you want the resources, you'll need to clear the road. A group of Knights along with Jeanne d'Arc are ideal for this job, but you should only go for it if you're confident in your defenses. More supply convoys will attempt the trip periodically for the rest of the mission, so if one doesn't make it through, you'll have more chances.*

Historical Accuracy

"History is never fully set in stone. Although our understanding is solid for many events, there are always room for further interpretation and deeper understanding. History is not just about the facts of what happened but is also about what those events meant to the people at the time and the generations that followed them – that is then always subject to reinterpretation and further study.

We tried to always speak to the truth of the people we were representing, taking the way they saw the world seriously. To cite just one example, there's been endless conjecture about the "truth" of Jeanne d'Arc. There's little doubt she existed and did amazing things, but did she speak to angels? Was she suffering from some form of hallucinations? Instead of indulging in those modern conjectures, we turned to understanding how she was seen at the time and took her beliefs seriously. What matters is that she believed she was operating on a holy mission and that informed her actions and the actions of those around her."

– ***Philippe Boulle***
Lead Narrative Designer, Relic

To solidify your defense, build two Stone Wall Towers at each gate, with a Mangonel behind them, and then a group of at least 10 ranged infantry on top of the wall near the gate. Another group of melee infantry should wait in the vicinity as well, acting as a last line of defense against Battering Rams. Keep your starting cavalry as a rapid response force that can quickly move between gates—it'll be your main attacking force to destroy Battering Rams and other siege engines. Make sure to replenish their numbers if you start losing some.

Recommended Upgrades

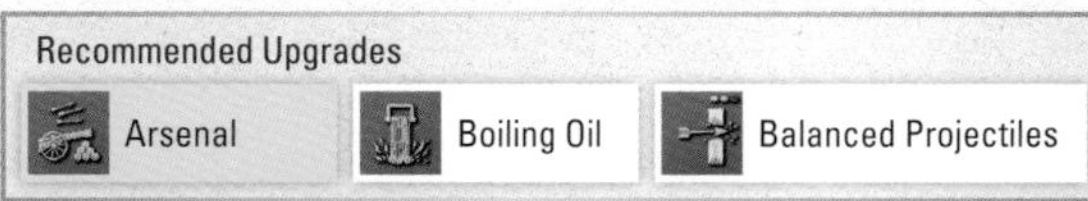

> ***Warning:*** *Stay within close proximity to your base while you set up your defenses, because you don't want to draw in the surrounding armies until you're ready.*

The assaults on your base will continue until the enemy camps surrounding you are destroyed, so once your defenses have been set up, it's time to switch to offense. There are four camps in total—one each at **Positions F**, **G**, **H**, and **I**—but before you attack them, you should first clear the enemy groups surrounding Orléans. To accomplish that, take a single fast unit and move close enough to get their attention, and then retreat back to draw them into range of your defenses; they don't have any siege units, so your Towers and ranged infantry will make short work of them.

*Make sure to use Jeanne's **Healing** ability. Units affected by it will appear with a golden shine and regenerate part of their lost health.*

Now you should build up the army you're going to use to attack the camps, comprising it of Men-at-Arms and Arbalétriers, with a few Mangonels and some Royal Knights to attack the enemy siege engines; aim for around 60 units plus your siege engines to comfortably take on a camp. Start with the one at **Position F**, and then work your way around clockwise, taking out the rest of them as you come to them.

Your army that was defending the gate at **Position A** can join your attacking army once the first two camps have been destroyed, and the same goes for your forces at gates **B** and **C** once the third camp is gone. Now it should be safe to concentrate all of your defensive forces at **Position D** while your army moves around to destroy the final camp, which will also mean that the supply convoy will no longer get attacked and can deliver the resources to you unimpeded.

Objective 2

Destroy the Keep at Les Tourelles

If you followed our recommendations, the majority of your forces should be near the camp at **Position I** at this time, which means that the nearby bridge should be the route you take towards Les Tourelles. It doesn't really matter which approach you take; this one just happens to be the closest. Build up your army until you hit the 200 population capacity, making sure you have a good mix of infantry, cavalry and siege engines, with at least three Battering Rams.

While you're producing units, cross the bridge with a good-sized force and take out the camp on the other side to use that as your staging area, and then once everything is ready, take your army down the road towards Les Tourelles. After clearing out the surrounding units, use your Battering Rams on the Stone Wall Gate, defending them with your other units. As soon as the gate is destroyed, quickly move your cavalry units inside and use them to destroy the enemy Mangonels, while simultaneously sending your Battering Rams to attack the Keep. The rest of your army is purely there to support and defend your Battering Rams; the English have no Villagers, so you'll be victorious as soon as the Keep catches fire, because they have no means of repairing it.

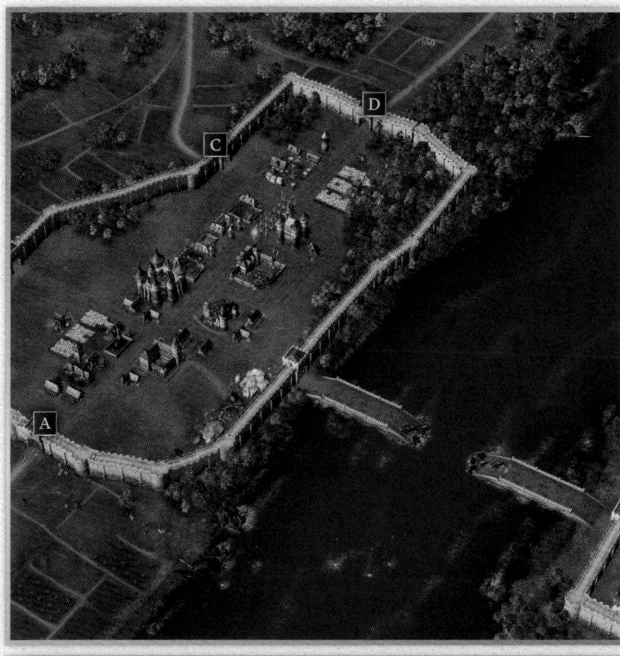

Narrative Objectivity

"Throughout our research, writing, consultation, and editing we tried as far as possible to represent this history with objectivity. However, we also had to acknowledge that this is a video game and the player is placed on the side of one faction or another. In games, or films, or any other form of storytelling, it is common to celebrate the attributes and exploits of our protagonists and condemn or chastise the enemy. Finding a balance between cold objectivity and player-side celebration was something we were acutely aware of needing to hit just right.

We struggled especially with our French-side perspective on the Hundred Years War campaign. One of our historians pointed out that our slant on the war was decidedly pro-French—this was, after all, a war in which the French were dominated by crushing English victories for a very long time before gaining the upper hand. But, we felt that at some point the player point-of-view has to take precedence. A game that doesn't celebrate with the player does not feel like a satisfying experience. Objectivity is always important, but we do have to pat the player's faction on the back!"

– Lauren Wood
Principal Designer, Narrative Lead, Relic

Blancing the Old with the New

"We thought about [balancing old and new elements] very carefully! Everything was debated and weighed as we discussed how much of the previous games should be in this one. What I really enjoyed was there were times that someone at World's Edge (like me, who often tends to do things like this to spark thought) would suggest a radical departure from an existing Age tenet, only to be countered by Relic in making sure that we upheld it instead. This worked both ways as we developed the game's feature set."

– Adam Isgreen
Principal Designer, Narrative, World's Edge

The Battle of Patay

Rewards

- Medieval Surgery
- The Battle of Patay
- The Cathedral of Kings

Jeanne d'Arc's perseverance had paid off. With the English in retreat, she could deliver the fatal blow.

Chased from the Loire Valley by Jeanne d'Arc's relentless pursuit, the remnants of England's forces fled for the safety of the north. At Patay, the French army could make sure they never made it.

Objective 1

Defeat the English on the the Road to Patay

This is primarily a combat mission with few opportunities to resupply, so try to minimize your losses and grab the Treasure Chests dotted around the map. Follow the path from the start and you'll be met by a few Longbowmen that have set up a defensive blockade behind some palings. You can face the Longbowmen head on, but if you take the side road at **Position A**, you can flank around their palings and take less damage.

Now that the road is clear you'll have the option to call in reinforcements, but to do so you'll need to spend precious Gold; you start with 3000 Gold, but you can acquire another 400 by picking up the nearby Treasure Chest. The next stop along the road is the small village of St. Sigmund at **Position B**, and there are a large number of English Spearmen there, so you'll want to pick reinforcements that can counter them. A good selection would be: 3x Archers (1200 Gold), 2x Infantry (1200 Gold), and 1x Royal Knights (1000 Gold).

Approach the village with your infantry leading the way, with the archers just behind them and your cavalry at the rear; make sure your cavalry do not charge into the Spearmen first or you'll suffer a number of unnecessary losses. After liberating the village you can safely pick up all the Treasure Chests to acquire another 2000 Gold, and this time you should invest that into 2x Royal Knights.

The Road to Patay is blocked by a Longbowmen with Palings. Assault them from behind by taking the side road.

Objective 2

Defeat the English Blockade

There's another English blockade further along the road, and just like the first one, they've set up defensive palings, but this time they have some additional firepower in the form of Mangonels. These siege engines can make quick work of your infantry, so cavalry should be the vanguard of your forces this time. Flank around the palings by taking the trail through the Stealth Forest at **Position C** and ignore the Archers in there for now, because your main focus needs to be the Mangonels. Once the Mangonels have been destroyed, move the rest of your army in and finish off the remaining English units. Jeanne d'Arc will arrive after the battle, and you should use her **Healing** ability to restore the health of your troops. You can also find another pair of Treasure Chests here, but don't acquire any more reinforcements just yet.

Objective 3

Eliminate the remaining English regiments

You now need to defeat the three remaining regiments of English forces. To do so smoothly, it's worth completing the optional objective to take control of Patay. To that end, it's best to head straight to **Position D** where the eastern regiment is stationed, and then go straight along the road to Patay. That group of enemies consists mainly of Horsemen and Longbowmen, so you shouldn't have any problems defeating them with the cavalry you've already built up.

While your military units are fighting, make sure to send your Scouts off to pick up the remaining Treasure Chests. If you are careful with your movement you can get around the central and western regiments without taking any damage, especially if you make use of the Stealth Forest in the middle of the map.

Upon reaching Patay you'll automatically take control, netting you some resources and Villagers to command. You don't need to establish a diverse economy at this point, so take all of your new Villagers and put them to work mining Gold so that you can just call in more reinforcements. When you have around 4400 Gold, invest it into 4x Infantry, and 2x Royal Knights, and once they arrive, start heading towards the central regiment at **Position F**. This group has a lot of Spearmen, so bring your infantry in first, and then flank around with your cavalry and destroy the two Springalds from behind.

Reinforcements are hired by the tribute menu on the top right of the UI.

To make room for your reinforcements, make sure to build a few Houses around Patay until you reach the 200 population capacity.

The final regiment to the west is the toughest group, consisting of 40 Men-at-Arms, 30 Longbowmen and 2 Mangonels. Depending on their position at the time you'll want to either head straight down the road, or flank around through the Stealth Forest. Your goal should be to attack the Mangonels with your cavalry before anything else, while the remainder of your units move in behind them to finish things off.

5

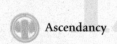

Retake Normandy

Normandy would see an explosive end to the struggle for its long-contested realm.

The advent of gunpowder weapons had ushered in a new era of warfare. While England's army still relied on the longbow, the French had a unique opportunity to overpower them.

Rewards

- Ascendancy
-  Compagnies d'ordonnance
- Medieval Guns

Objective 1

Capture the University

Before you can retake Normandy, you must first capture the University in the English-occupied town directly ahead of your starting position. Your army is more than up to the task, so an aggressive push into the town is the best approach. Try to avoid destroying any buildings, because they'll all become yours once the defending English have been finished off.

Objective 2

Research Chemistry

To research **Chemistry** you'll need to reach Age IV, and since you already have enough resources, you can do that by simply building the **Red Palace** and placing it near the gate at **Position A** to help with defense. The English will periodically send enemy groups to attack you, so it's a good idea to build up your resources and fortify your defenses. Start by placing a Lumber Camp near where your Villagers are chopping down trees, and then produce more Villagers until you have 10 on Wood and 15 on Gold. You should also produce some additional military units to maintain the safety of your base. Because your Outposts are your first line of defense, it's worth spending some of your Stone to fortify each of them. Once you have the resources available, start researching **Chemistry** at the University.

There are a lot of Sacred Sites on this map, and since Gold is so important, it's worth building a Monastery to produce Monks to capture them—over time you'll more than make up the Gold.

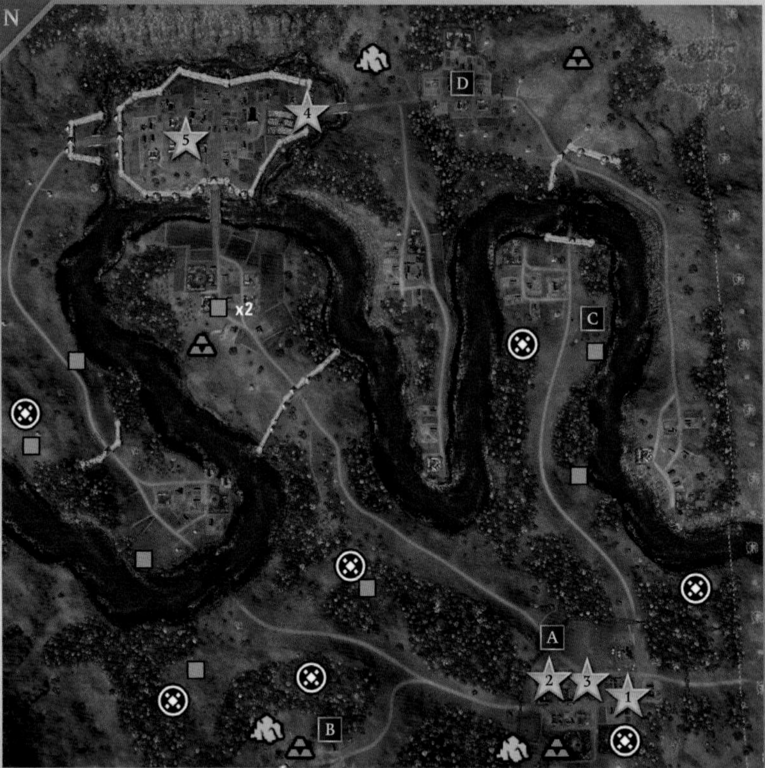

Villager Resource Distribution				
No. of Villagers	16	10	15	10

*Since the **Chemistry** research takes a long time to be finished, you should use the time to build up your army.*

Objective 3

Build Cannons

Begin production of the Cannons with the resources you have, and while they're building you should work on the optional objectives you were given; victory can be achieved without them, but completing the Mine and Trade Route objectives should be done to ensure success.

Rouen Mine is located at **Position B**, and it only has a small contingent of enemy units defending it. Take about half of your military units to the mine and clear the area, and if the mines within the walls of your base are starting to look depleted, move all of the Villagers working them to this new mining operation. Now is a good time to start researching some upgrades. Those upgrades will take a lot of time and Gold, so you might want to consider selling some Food at the **Chamber of Commerce** if you have an overabundance of it. While the technologies are being researched, build three more Barracks, and three more Archery Ranges to start mass-producing your military units. A mix of Men-at-Arms and Arbalétriers/Handcannoneers plus your Cannons and some additional siege units is ideal. Once you've started everything going, it's worth establishing a Trade Route to help with your Gold income.

Take a mixed group of around 40-50 upgraded units towards the neutral Trade Post at **Position C** and use them to clear out the defending units along the way. When the area is secure, build two more Markets back at your base and start producing Traders from them, sending them off to the neutral Trade Post as they become available. For a decent level of gold income, aim for around 10 Traders. It's also worth constructing some additional military production buildings near the neutral Trade Post, because this will be your staging area for the final assault.

Objective 4

Breach Rouen's walls

Keep producing military units until you've maxed out your population capacity, and if you have the Stone for it, consider researching the **Royal Artillery** upgrade at the Bureau Brother's Workshop so that you can add some Royal siege units to your army. Once all of your units are ready, move them all over to the staging area at **Position C**.

Before you can begin your assault on Rouen, you'll need to first get past a blockade, and clear out an enemy camp at **Position D**. Your Cannons are the key to breaching the Stone Walls, so keep them safely behind your main army. With that in mind, lead your army across the river and destroy the Stone Walls and Towers on the other side, and then advance on the camp, using your Cannons to safely destroy the Outposts. The camp itself is only lightly defended, so your army should have no trouble clearing the area once inside. Resupply your army by brining new units if needed, and then when you're ready, push on to Rouen and put your Cannons to work destroying its walls.

Recommended Upgrades

Barracks	Elite Man-at-Arms			
Archery Range	Elite Arbalétrier			
Arsenal	Platecutter Point	Crannequins	Siege Works	Angled Surfaces
University	Geometry	Corned Gunpowder	Superior Transport Construction	

Remember, as the French you can manually choose which resource your Traders return with, so if you're running low on Stone, don't hesitate to switch over to that instead of Gold.

Gunpowder units are more powerful than conventional units and can deal bonus damage against stone structures.

Objective 5

Destroy Rouen's Landmarks

Make sure to destroy the Stone Wall Towers around the gate so that your army can engage the defending forces without taking additional damage. Most of the enemy units shouldn't pose a threat, but the Mangonels can still inflict a lot of damage. Culverins are perfect for destroying Mangonels if you have them, otherwise your Cannons will suffice. Keep sending in reinforcements as needed while your siege engines work on destroying the Landmarks, and once all three have been destroyed, victory will be yours.

The Battle of Formigny

The Hundred Years War had raged through invasions, uprisings and devastation. France now stood on the threshold of victory.

In the last gasps of the Hundred Years War, England clung to its territories in the north of France, sending a vast army to defend them. At Formigny, it would meet the force of France's momentum head-on.

Rewards

- Castillon: End of the War
- Illuminated Manuscript
- The Battle of Formigny
- War's End

Objective 1

Defend Carentan to the Last Man

Hopelessly outnumbered, all your forces can do is fight and die with honor, while trying to take as many of the enemy with you as possible.

Objective 2

Drive the English from Normandy

After the defeat at Carentan you now find yourself in control of a huge French army, with the sole purpose of finally driving the English out of these lands. Number one on your list is an English army belonging to Thomas Kyriell, but first you'll have to find them. A small detachment of English soldiers have set up camp in a village called Bricquebec—at **Position A** not far up

While you're in Bricquebec, make sure to grab the Treasure Chest for some extra Gold.

The Bureau Brothers: 1453

In 1453, France's King Charles VII ordered his new artillery division to take the English-held city of Castillon. Charles had broken with the military tradition of appointing a commander from the aristocracy. Instead, he trusted this division to two self-taught artillery experts: Jean and Gaspard Bureau. Aided by revolutionary developments in gunpowder and gun manufacturing, the brothers destroyed English resistance in Northern France. At Castillon, Jean Bureau's division built a 300-gun artillery camp, placing the guns on makeshift walls to face the city. This gun placement allowed for interlocking cannon fire—a tactic to cover all angles of attack. When the English army arrived, they charged the French artillery camp from behind. But Jean Bureau quickly turned the cannons away from the walls of the city... and aimed into the ranks of the soldiers. Each round from the massive guns blasted through six men at a time. Amid the carnage, the remaining English soon fled, and France took the city. Castillon marked the last major battle of the Hundred Years War. King Charles' gamble on the Bureau Brothers—on their education and experience, rather than birthright—had paid off in victory for France.

– Illuminated History

the road from where you start—so head there first. You'll encounter a few scattered patrols along the way, but neither them nor the camp can hold up to your overwhelming forces.

Your next destination should be a nearby friendly village called Valognes at **Position B**, but on the way there it will come under attack by a group of English soldiers. Quickly move in and defeat them to save the village. As thanks, the locals give you access to their technology buildings and Market, so sell off 300 Food, and then start researching some upgrades.

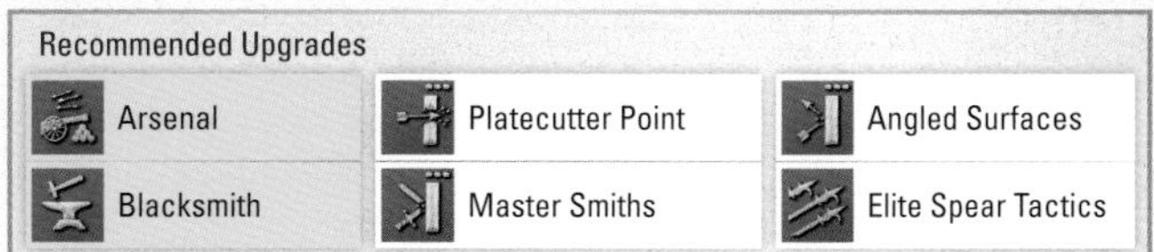

Recommended Upgrades		
Arsenal	Platecutter Point	Angled Surfaces
Blacksmith	Master Smiths	Elite Spear Tactics

Go back down towards Bricquebec now, and then head to **Position C**, where you'll find a friendly Monastery and some Monks that will join your team and heal your units. When all of your units are fully healed, set your sights towards your next target at **Position D**: the English camp, Saint-Sauveur. As with the previous camp, this one is no match for your army, so simply drive straight into the camp and lay it to waste.

After clearing Saint-Sauveur, pick up the Treasure Chest there, and then head to ***Position E*** *to find another one. If you now sell all of your Food at the Market in Valognes, you should have enough Gold to research the* ***Steel Barding*** *and* ***Grapered Lances*** *upgrades at the Blacksmith.*

You should be as strong as you're going to get now, which means it's time for the final showdown with Thomas Kyriell's army, located on the other side of the river near **Position F**. Just in front of the river crossing there is a small group of enemy units and a pair of Outposts—destroy those first, and then take some time to heal up again. You'll also now receive six Cannons as reinforcements.

The only way forward now is through the opposing army in a head-on clash, but you can still be smart about how you approach it. There are three crossings near each other at the river, and the army on the other side spans all three of them; to avoid being surrounded, it's important that you try to funnel the enemy down one of the outside crossings. Use your Cannons to fire on the English from a safe distance, and position your army in front of the Cannons to defend them, but try to avoid crossing to the other side of the river.

Always keep your artillery and siege units protected. Since they don't inflict any friendly fire damage, you can be assured that they won't kill your own units.

After a few rounds of Cannon fire, the English will launch their attack on you, so be ready to defend and keep your Cannons firing on them to take out as many units as possible. As the tide of the battle turns, the English will retreat—use the reprieve to heal up, and then slowly cross the river. The English will now reform their ranks at **Position G**—once again it's a very wide formation so you should move your troops along the treeline to the west so that you only attack a small portion of it at once. As before, try to use your Cannons to lure them out of position and pick off small groups at a time.

During this part of the fight, a formidable contingent of Breton Elite Royal Knights will join you at **Position H**—quickly select them all and use them to perform a flanking attack on the rear of the English army. When your two groups combine, victory is finally within your grasp. The last vestiges of the English army are now holed up in the nearby town of Formigny; one final push is all that's needed.

Use your Cannons to blow a hole in the Stone Walls at **Position I**. Doing so provides you with a good angle to fire on the Outposts inside Formigny, to clear the way for your infantry and cavalry to enter the town. The few remaining enemy units inside the town pose no significant threat to your army, and after defeating them all, victory is yours.

Mongol Empire

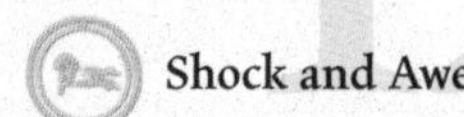

1223

Shock and Awe

The Battle of the Kalka River

In 1223, the Mongol army made a thunderous arrival in the west. They would test their tactics and flex their might against an unsuspecting new enemy: the Rus.

The great Mongol tactician, General Subutai, lured the Rus army to a battle site he had carefully chosen: the banks of the Kalka River.

Rewards

- Drums & Signal Arrows
- Shock and Awe

Objective 1

Prepare your Army to Ambush the Rus

This first mission focuses on combat only, and will get you familiar with the units and fighting style of the Mongol army. You start with one Khan (General Subutai), 36 Mangudai, 68 Lancers, and 36 Horsemen. Begin your preparations by moving all of your Horsemen to **Position A**, and 30 of your Lancers to **Position B**. The remainder of your forces should hide in the Stealth Forest at **Position C**.

Objective 2

Destroy the Rus Army

Once you've moved your units into both of the flanking positions, it's time to lure the Rus into your trap. Take one or more of your Mangudai—horse archers that fire their bows while moving—and ride it near the Rus army to get their attention, and then retreat back towards **Position C**. Your army is vastly outnumbered (the Rus field around 400 units comprised of Hardened Spearmen and Veteran Archers), so in a head-on clash, you would lose. This means you'll need to take a more strategic approach.

*The Khan's **Signal Arrows** provide extremely powerful buffs for a short period of time, and you should make use of them any time they're available to give your army a huge power boost.*

When the Rus army nears the ford they will mostly stand their ground, with only a few groups moving across, but you should not call in your Lancers just yet. Approach the Rus Spearmen with your Mangudai and Khan, and make use of the Khan's **Movement Arrow**

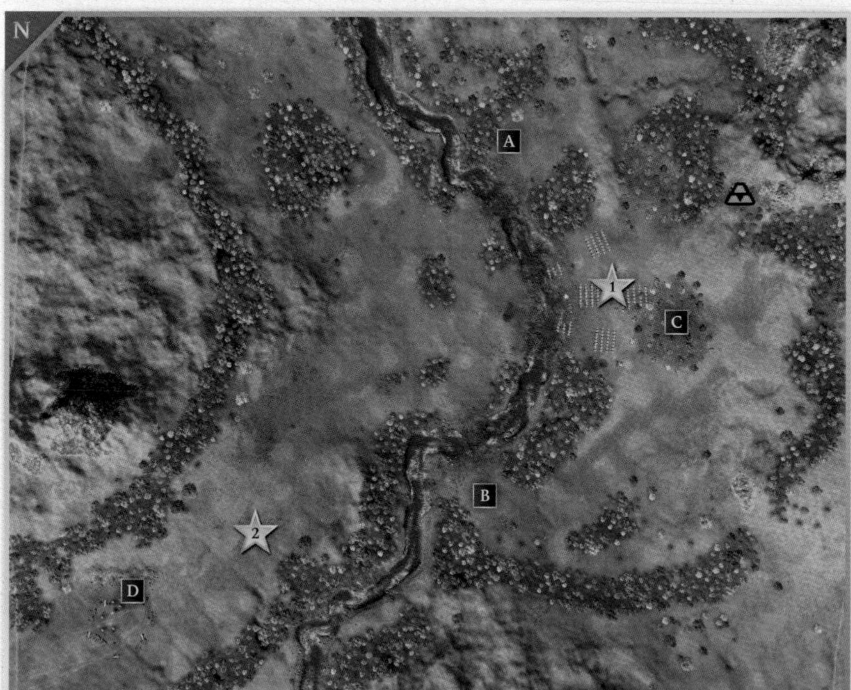

The Secret History of the Mongols: 1228

In a gold-plated box in Mongolia rests one of history's most precious relics: a document known as "The Secret History of the Mongols". Written soon after Genghis Khan's death, it tells the story of humanity's most formidable conqueror, and the world that made him. We learn that he was born under an omen of greatness—clutching a large blood clot in his fist. We see how the murder of his father and a destitute childhood hardened his survival skills. And how the shattering of a blood oath led to a tribal war that affirmed his place as khan. The Secret History also tells of the Mongol way of life, it lays out Genghis Khan's new laws and celebrates his great conquests. Thanks to the detailed accounts in the Secret History, we can hear the words of Genghis Khan and feel the impact of the Mongol empire echoing through history.

– Illuminated History

ability for hit-and-run attacks. Maintain your distance, and keep picking off Spearmen until there are only a few groups left, and then bring in your cavalry from both flanks and have them focus on the archers; if you attack with everything at once, the Rus army should stand no chance at this point.

The last remnants of the Rus army will flee back to their enclosure at **Position D**, where some additional forces are stationed, and you'll need to advance on that position to finish them off. If you have at least 50 units left, a simple straight-ahead charge with all of your units will suffice, otherwise you should use hit-and-run attacks with your Khan and Mangudai to weaken them again before moving in for the final blow.

Choosing the Time Periods

"We explored everything from prehistoric to modern, and as we dove deeper into each of them, what kept resonating with the period we chose is that civilization-specific approaches to combat still were prevalent; they lived and breathed and changed as the cultures matured, grew into new territories, and interacted with others. The further forwards we go in time, the more that combat and technology homogenises across the planet, to the point that in modern times, most weapons are built by a handful of superpowers and nations, regardless of who wields them. As we're a series that celebrates history and cultures, we didn't feel as if we were going to be able to celebrate them as well in settings like that."

– Adam Isgreen
Franchise Creative Director, World's Edge

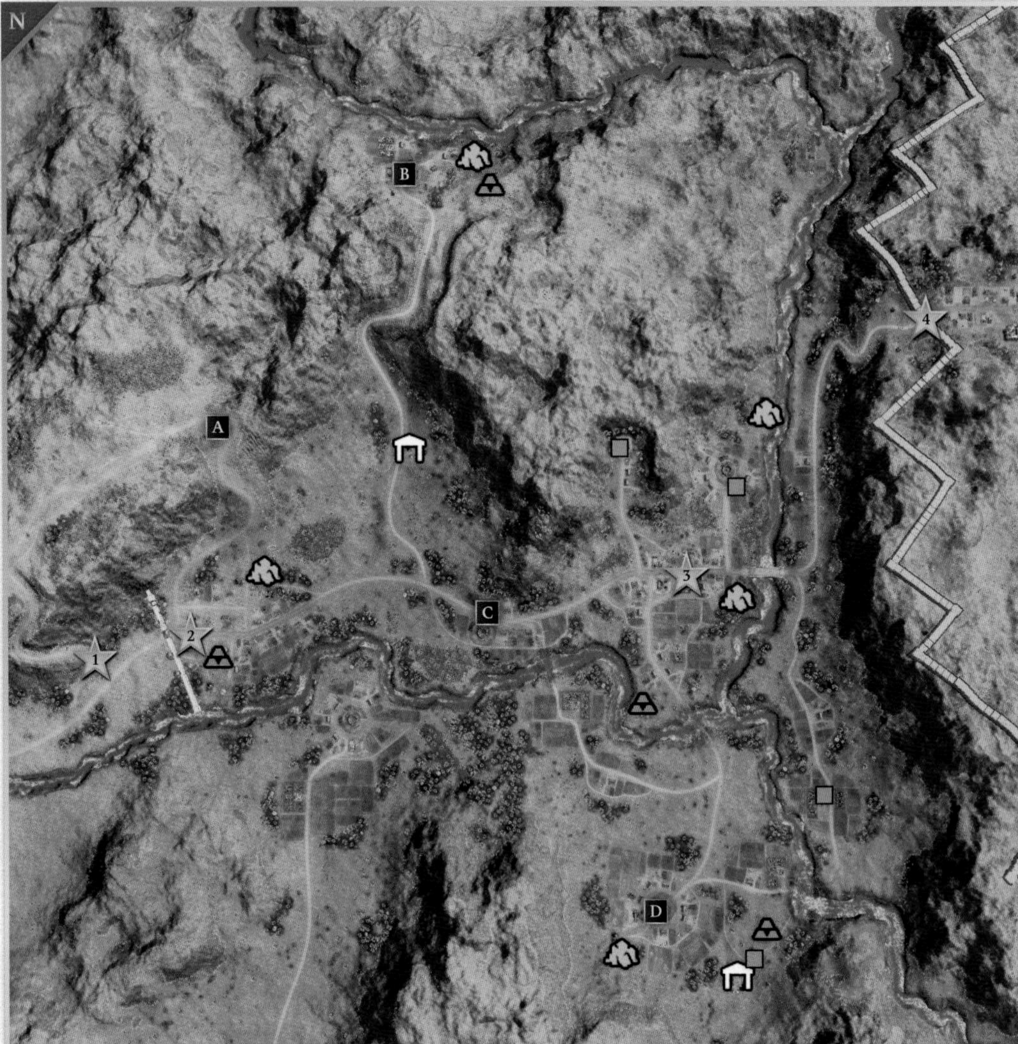

The Covenant: 1203

The Mongol clan leader, Temujin, fled for his life across the steppe. He had dared to rise above the station of his bloodline and was being hunted by his high-born enemies. Exhausted and starving, Temujin and his men hid at a remote, mud-choked lake. The end was surely near. But as darkness turned to day, a foreign merchant appeared. Temujin had no goods to trade. But rather than leave them to die, the merchant offered food and horses. And in return, Temujin agreed to be his guide. The mercy of this stranger affirmed Temujin's core belief: that actions outweighed birthright. He vowed to honor the good deeds of this stranger. And to unify the tribes under one nation where great deeds by ANY Mongol would be rewarded. Raising a mud-filled fist to the sky, Temujin led his men in an oath of brotherhood. Merit over bloodline. They sealed the covenant by drinking the lake's muddy waters. Temujin would go on to become Genghis Khan, the legendary leader of the Mongol people. And he would build his great empire with a meritocracy at its heart.

– Illuminated History

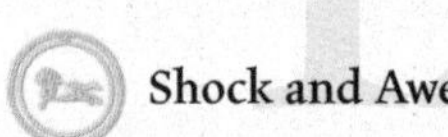

The Great Wall

Rewards

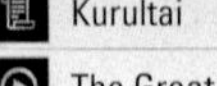

- Kurultai
- The Great Wall
- The Mongol Horse

Ten years before the Mongols' first assault on Europe, Genghis Khan descended on his most ambitious target yet: The Great Wall of China.

Genghis Khan's bid to expand his empire had brought him to the Great Wall of China. But in his path to the wall stood the mighty Jin fortress of Zhangjiakou.

Objective 1

Plan your Attack

You'll need to survey the area before your main forces can advance, so move your two Scouts along the mountain path and follow the trail. There are a couple of small enemy patrol groups in this area, but you can avoid them by traveling through the Stealth Forest near the edge of the mountain. Continue until you reach **Position A**, at which time the plan will come to light, and the main Mongol forces will arrive.

Objective 2

Destroy the Keep at Zhangjikou

Lead your army along the same mountain path used by your Scouts until you meet back up with them. At the bottom of the path is a large contingent of Chinese Archers and Spearmen; you have enough units to deal with them, but you should make use of the Khan's **Charge Arrow** ability to minimize your losses. Try to stay away from the Keep while battling the units and destroying the surrounding buildings, and only attack it when the area is clear.

Objective 3

Destroy Yanqing

Before you bring in the Mongol caravan, make sure to clear the Chinese Archers from atop the walls or they'll easily pick off your Villagers. Once it's safe, bring the caravan in and unpack the buildings in the following way:

- **Town Center:** Close to where the Keep was so it's near to the Gold and Wood.
- **Pastures:** Next to the Town Center

The optional objective to collect 2000 resources by burning buildings can be acheived naturally by simply destroying the buildings in Zhangjikou. It teaches that, as the Mongols, you should always raze buildings for resources—remember this whenever playing as them.

- **Barracks:** Near the Stone Outcropping to make a barrier against incoming attacks.
- **Ger:** Near the forest outside of the wall to better protect your Villagers.

You should have enough resources to immediately advance to Age II, so use all of the Villagers that came with the caravan to construct the **Silver Tree** Landmark near the Ger you just unpacked. The functionality of this building will be extremely beneficial as the mission proceeds. Start producing Villagers and send them to work at the nearby Gold Vein, and after the **Silver Tree** is constructed, build three more Pastures near your Town Center. Pastures are the Mongols' primary source of Food, so assign six of your Villagers to work on the them, and then put four on Wood at the forest near the Ger.

Around this time you should get a warning about raids from outlying villages in the area, so make sure your military units are positioned towards the outskirts of your base to stop incursions. This mission can be very difficult if you don't destroy those villages—and gain the extra resources from the buildings—but you should make some preparations first.

Your Gold Vein will be depleted quickly, so you'll soon need another source of Gold. Thankfully, there's a neutral Trade Post, and because you have the **Silver Tree**, you can produce Traders and establish a trade route with it. You'll need a relatively strong army to secure the trade route, so start by building a Blacksmith, and then aim for the following Villager distribution and technology acquisitions. When the Gold Vein is depleted, move those Villagers onto Food as well.

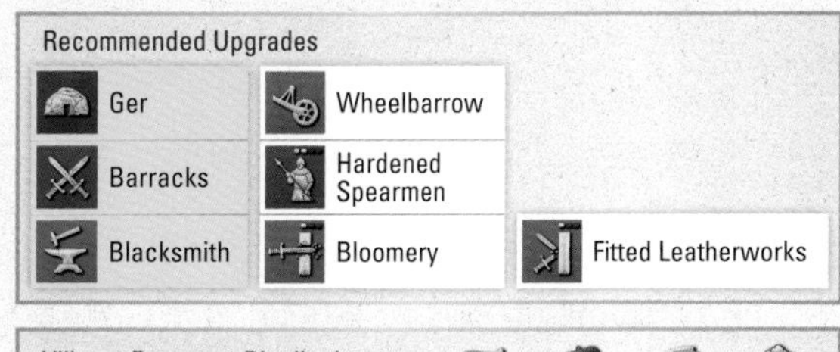

Recommended Upgrades		
Ger	Wheelbarrow	
Barracks	Hardened Spearmen	
Blacksmith	Bloomery	Fitted Leatherworks

Villager Resource Distribution	Food	Wood	Gold	Stone
No. of Villagers	20	10	8	--

Your army should consist mostly of Mangudai and Spearmen. To produce them quickly, build two more Barracks and three Stables and have them make as many as you can afford. When you have around 30 Spearmen and 30 Mangudai, it's time to group them with your Khan and move out while your buildings keep producing more units.

Move your army towards **Position B** (making sure to defeat any enemy units you encounter along the way), and you'll find a neutral Trade Post—remember its location. Upon reaching **Position B**, defeat all of the enemy units and make sure to destroy all nine of the buildings in the village. Next, move your army back down to the Trade Post and bring in some fresh units from your base to reinforce them and make sure the path between the Trade Post and your **Silver Tree** Landmark is clear of enemies.

Start producing Traders at the **Silver Tree** and have them begin trading with the Trade Post as they become available. Produce a total of nine Traders so that you can take advantage of one of the unique Mongol traits of bringing back additional resources from trades based on the number of active Traders along a route. Once the trade route is secure, turn your sights towards **Position C** where the next village is located, and bring an army of around 60 units to attack it. After destroying that village, pack up all of your military production buildings and move them there so that you have access to faster reinforcements.

Access to your base is essentially cut off now, so bring the remainder of your military units along too. Leaving behind a contingent of units for defense again, take the remainder of your army across the nearby ford and head for the southern village at **Position D**, laying waste to any units and buildings that you come across along the way. All of the foundations have been laid by this point, so simply keep producing Spearmen and Mangudai until you hit the 200 population capacity, and then send your army to destroy Yanqing village and anyone defending it.

When you move out to attack the sources of the raids, leave behind your ranged infantry and melee cavalry to defend your base.

Objective 4

Breach the Great Wall

As a precaution, advance your military buildings again and station them in Yanqing. Now you're going to need something that can break through the Great Wall, and that requires some siege engines. Battering Rams are your best option, and building four of them also happens to be an optional objective; research **Siege Engineering** at your Blacksmith, and then have your infantry construct four Battering Rams.

March your army and rams towards the Stone Wall Gate that's blocking your path, and while your infantry and cavalry deal with the defending units, send two Battering Rams to each of the Outposts. When the defenses are down, focus everything on the gate. After it's destroyed, send your Battering Rams straight for the Keep while the rest of your army defends them. You'll be declared victorious as soon as the Keep is burning.

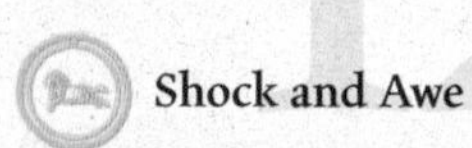

Shock and Awe

The Battle of Zhongdu

Rewards

- Making the Mongol Bow
- Spirit Banner
- The Battle of Zhongdu

The quest for world domination brought Genghis Khan to the walls of China's prosperous capital: Zhongdu.

Zhongdu was a shining beacon of trade, healing and technology. To take the great city for himself, Genghis Khan would employ a slow but reliable strategy: starvation.

Objective 1

Accumulate Wealth to Gather Followers

As is the Mongol way, the wealth you need is acquired by pillaging villages and burning the buildings. To start earning, simply head along the road to the buildings at **Position A**, destroy them, and then continue to **Position B** and do the same there. Upon reaching the prerequisite Gold amount, followers in the form of some additional military infantry, a handful of Villagers, and a Town Center, Pasture, and Ger buildings will join you. Gold is an important resource at the moment, so set up camp near the Gold Vein at **Position A**, and have your current Villagers start gathering Food from the nearby Berries or Sheep at the Pasture.

*The optional objective to acquire 500 more Gold is a repeating one, and every time you hit the milestone you'll get more reinforcements. To complete the first one quickly, send your starting army from **Position B** along the mountainside path to **Position C**—destroy all the buildings in your path and you'll reach 500.*

Objective 2

Starve Zhongdu by Eliminating Suppliers

Warning: *Time is of the essence here. As more Traders deliver their resources to the city you'll see a progress bar fill, indicating their current level of military supplies. Each time that bar fills, a group of enemy units will be dispatched to attack either your base or your army, depending on where it is, so stopping the supplies will make your life much easier.*

Before you can make a move on any of the Traders and Markets, you'll want to bolster your economy a bit more. Keep producing Villagers until you have around 20 of them, and when you have enough resources, have four of them construct the Age II Landmark **The Silver Tree** before switching to the Gold Vein, and all of the rest should build four more Pastures and focus on Food. You'll get more Villagers and buildings as reinforcements, so there's no need to produce more than is necessary.

There are two ways to complete this objective: Either eliminate the Traders en route to their destination, or destroy the Markets they originate from. Both have their pros and cons, but trying to focus on four different Traders and their escort units at the same time requires a lot of micromanaging of your units and reinforcements, so it's easier to take a two-pronged approach at destroying the Markets. Before you begin, however, make sure to build a Blacksmith and complete the following upgrades.

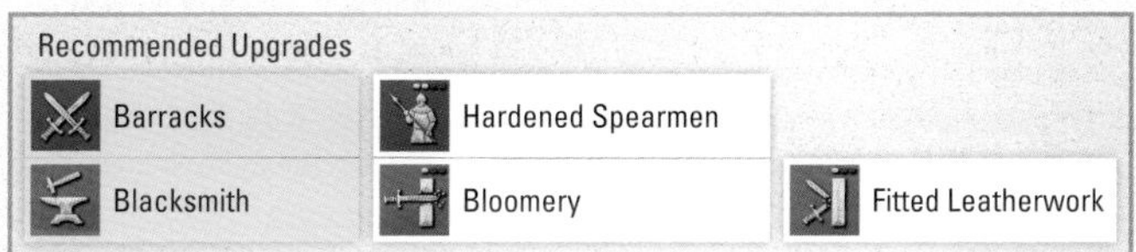

Recommended Upgrades		
Barracks	Hardened Spearmen	
Blacksmith	Bloomery	Fitted Leatherwork

Between your starting army and the initial reinforcement groups, you should have at least 60 military units, so if you haven't received a Stable yet from the reinforcements, build one now and have it start producing Mangudai while your Barracks focuses on Spearmen. When you have around 20 additional units that you can leave at your base for defense, move your main army across the river towards the Market at **Position D**, destroying any buildings along the way to speed up the reinforcements. There will be a small group of enemy units defending the Market, but nothing your army can't handle, especially if you're making use of the Khan's **Signal Arrows**.

The progress bar among the objectives keeps track of your razings.

While your army is taking care of that first Market, build another Barracks and Stable to speed up your unit production, and once you have another group of 60+ units (still keeping 20 or so behind for defense), move them in the opposite direction and have them destroy the Market at **Position E**. Send reinforcements to either army if needed, and when your northern army is finished at their first target, have them work around to the next one at **Position F**, and your southern army can do the same to **Position G**.

Make sure to use the "Attack Move" command when moving either of these armies so that they attack any buildings or Traders they encounter along the way.

Objective 3

Sack Zhongdou

Once all of the Markets have been destroyed, it's finally time to make your assault on the main city itself, and then set fire to three Landmarks once you're inside. To get past the Stone Wall defenses you're going to need some siege engines, so have your Blacksmith research **Siege Engineering**. The best place to begin your assault is **Position H**, because there's a nice open area to stage your assault from, and there's no Keep behind the walls on this side.

Build up your forces until you have around 40 Mangudai, 40 Early Lancers, and 40 Spearmen, and then have them move to **Position H** and build six Battering Rams. Use three rams to attack each of the Stone Wall Towers opposite the Gate in this area while your army protects them, and then have everything focus on the Gate. Because you destroyed all of their supply routes, the army inside is severely depleted, so once you breach the walls, your army should face little resistance, and while they deal with the units, have your rams work on the Landmarks until you're victorious.

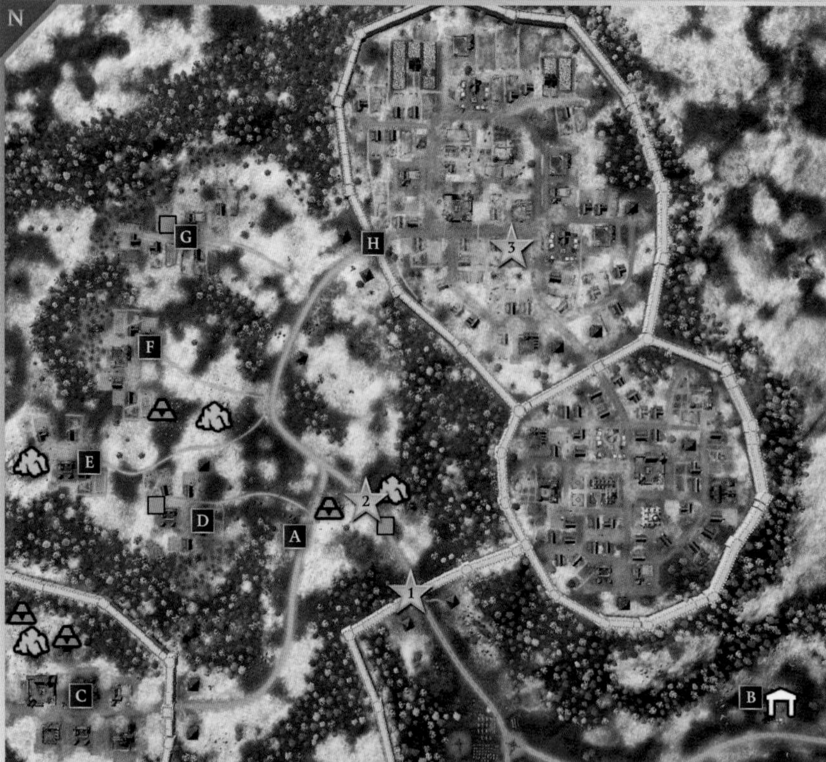

1240

 Conquest

The Siege of Kiev

One by one, the Rus princedoms had fallen to the invaders from the east. Only Kiev remained standing on the threshold of the west.

Angered by Kiev's defiance, Mongke Khan knew he must make an example of the proud city. Europe would hear of Kiev's mistake—paid for in blood and ash.

Rewards

- The People of the Felt Walls
- The Yam
- Western Conquest

Objective 1

Destroy the Gate to Kiev

Before you can begin an assault on the gate itself, you'll need to deal with its defenses. Start by having one of your Trebuchets attack each of the Wooden Fortresses, and then use your army to deal with the units that were garrisoned inside. Turn your Trebuchets on the gate next—once it's destroyed, move your army through the hole cautiously because more enemy units await on the other side.

Objective 2

Unpack the Mongol Camp at a Safe Location

The area on the other side of the gate you just destroyed has all of the resources you need to set up your initial camp, but there are enemy soldiers defending the area so move your army in first to clear the way. Move all of your buildings except the **Deer Stones** to this new area; have the **Deer Stones** unpack outside of the wall to save space since you don't need it close by. Make sure to keep your Trebuchets well back from any action too, because you want to make sure they survive.

Unpack your Town Center on the patch of snow just past the wall, your Ger near the Gold Vein and Berries, and then your two production buildings around the Stone Outcropping. As part of the camp convoy you also got 12 Villagers, so put six of them on Gold and the remaining ones on Berries and have your Town Center start producing more to put on Wood.

*Keep your army near **Position A**; Rus Traders frequently travel along this road and you can kill them and plunder their resources. Enemy raids can also come from that side, so you're covering both bases.*

Objective 3

Destroy the City of Kiev

There are three parts of the city you need to destroy, but before you can make a move on any of them, you're going to need to build up your economic and military strength. Start by building an Ovoo on the Stone Outcropping near your Town Center, and make sure the Barracks and Stables you have are within its influence range. Build another Barracks and an Archery Range also near the Ovoo, and then build five Pastures to secure a sustainable Food supply.

Villager Resource Distribution				
No. of Villagers	15	10	10	--

> **Warning:** *Don't push out from your small base too early. You'll trigger raids and attacks from different directions that can be difficult to contend with.*

Your resources should be coming in smoothly by this point, so once you have 1200 Food and 600 Gold, build the **Kurultai** Landmark in the middle of your base to advance to Age III. The healing and damage bonus from this Landmark can help you deal with any potential enemy raids. Now that you have sustainable Food income, you should establish the same for Gold, so build a Market and create a trade route with the neutral Trade Post at **Position B**. Keep producing traders until you have around nine for a decent income and bonuses from the Silk Road trait.

Turn your attention towards your military now—begin producing Spearmen and Archers with the double production ability at those buildings because of their proximity to the Ovoo. You can also use your Khan's **Production** special ability to drastically increase the production speed. Next, build a Blacksmith and Arsenal outside of the nearby wall to make space and start making some upgrades.

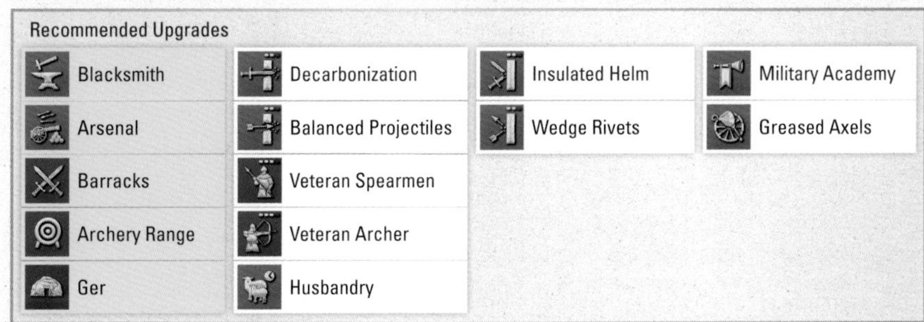

Recommended Upgrades			
Blacksmith	Decarbonization	Insulated Helm	Military Academy
Arsenal	Balanced Projectiles	Wedge Rivets	Greased Axels
Barracks	Veteran Spearmen		
Archery Range	Veteran Archer		
Ger	Husbandry		

You face a lot of enemy groups in this mission, so it's also worth building a Siege Workshop now and have it produce two Mangonels. As soon as you have enough military units to form an army of around 30 Spearmen and 30 Archers with your siege units and Khan—while still leaving behind a defensive group—it's time to move on your first target: the trade district at **Position C**.

Start approaching that position, using your Mangonels and infantry to take out the enemy groups along the way, and then use your Trebuchets to destroy the Wooden Fortresses and entrance gate. After breaching the area, move in with your infantry leading the way and your Mangonels behind to take out the remaining forces and destroy the buildings.

After securing the trade district you can move some of your Villagers there and build another Ger near the Gold Vein.

Take some time to build your military back up at this point. If you're having trouble dealing with enemy raids, you might want to consider moving some of your base to the trade district since it's a much more secure area. Before beginning your assault on the main city, you should clear out the surrounding areas to put an end to the raids on your base. Max out your population capacity with military units, including at least three Mangonels, and then start working your way around the map from **Position D** to **Position G**, taking out the enemy camps one at a time. If you lose units during a battle, produce some more and bring them in as reinforcements.

When the surrounding area is clear, build up your forces once more before tackling the main city because the interior is heavily defended. Use your Trebuchets again to destroy the defensive structures and gate leading into the main city, and your Mangonels to hit the enemy units atop the walls. Now you can move in with your main army, while sending in reinforcements as needed—keep destroying buildings until nothing is left standing in either part of the city to complete the mission.

Conquest

1241

The Battle of Liegnitz

Disciplined and relentless, the Mongols struck at Europe's eastern front with their most reliable strategy: divide and conquer.

Led by Genghis Khan's grandson, Baidar, the Mongols made the first of their dual attacks on central Europe. The Polish army scrambled to face them, arriving at the field in scattered groups.

Rewards

- Nomad Music
- The Battle of Liegnitz
- Warriors on Campaign

Objective 1

Destroy the Polish Army

There's no economy management in this mission, so your only concerns are producing and upgrading your military units. A 20:00 minute timer will start ticking down as soon as the mission starts, and when it reaches zero, a large Bohemian army will arrive to reinforce the existing Polish troops; while that won't end the mission, it will make completing it significantly harder, so speed is of the essence.

The key to success in this mission lies in the incredibly powerful Nest of Bees units that you get at the start; use them wisely, and don't waste them.

In order to produce more units, you're going to need resources, and just as the optional objective indicates, the best way to acquire them is to raid the nearby settlements. Leave your Nest of Bees units behind for now, and with your Khan and cavalry, head to **Position A** and destroy all of the buildings along the way. Once that side has been razed, return to your base, and then do the same thing on the other side towards **Position B**. Make sure to use the Khan's **Maneuver Arrow** ability to speed up your movement and make this process faster, and don't forget to burn the Farms as well. After clearing both sides you should have at least 5000 of each resource, so it's time to make some upgrades.

Historical Considerations

"In the Battle of Liegnitz there's a siege weapon called Nest of Bees. This is unique to the Chinese civ, but we know from history that the Mongols came across gunpowder weapons during the conquest of the Jin Dynasty, prior to their campaigns in Europe. There are sources that state the Mongols brought the gunpowder weapons from China into Europe, and while this isn't entirely set in stone, it makes for great gameplay. We also know the Mongols were incredible early adopters of new technology, and so it's reasonable to assume that when they came across gunpowder weapons in China, they would bring this with them if possible.

We are able to justify the use of the Nest of Bees here because we know the Mongols integrated Chinese experts into their armies and benefited greatly by borrowing from other cultures—in the Blockade at Lumen Shan we get to play with a Chinese leader who fought for the Mongols in their campaigns to conquer the Song Dynasty. In short, we have to weigh the probability of the historical accounts and also look at the overall picture—is it likely that this happened or not? In the above example we were able to lean on the fact that we know the Mongols were very open to borrowing from other cultures. Additionally, we believe the inclusion of the unique unit presents a fun premise and challenge for the player, that also serves to illuminate the history surrounding the Mongols."

– Kristina Wiik
Senior Designer, Narrative, Relic

Recommended Upgrades			
Blacksmith	Decarbonization	Insulated Helm	Military Academy
Arsenal	Balanced Projectiles	Wedge Rivets	

Use your remaining Gold to produce Mangudai and Lancers at a 2:1 ratio, and if you have Stone, use that at the Stables close to your Ovoo to produce two at a time and speed you up. When most of those units are ready, bring your entire army—including the Nest of Bees units—towards **Position C** and engage the first group of Polish soldiers. Keep producing units with any resources you have left, and use them to reinforce your main army as needed. Use your cavalry to counter the enemy's cavalry, and have your Nest of Bees focus on their infantry. If you need more Gold to continue producing Lancers and Mangudai, sell some Wood at your Market.

Send your Scouts ahead to lure smaller groups of enemy soldiers towards your main army so that you always fight on favorable terms. Just be mindful of charge attacks from enemy cavalry.

Because you only need to worry about defeating the groups of Polish soldiers, you can ignore the small camps at **Positions D** and **E** if you have enough time left. If, however, it's looking like the Bohemians will arrive before you finish, then it's worth burning them down with your army for the additional resources, because you'll want to produce as many units as possible. One of the groups of enemy soldiers are comprised entirely of cavalry and they patrol around the area—always keep an eye open for them, because you don't want to fight them at the same time as another group. If you spot them and the area is clear, take them out so they don't surprise you later.

The enemy group at **Position F** should be your next target, and this group is led by Landsknechte and Spearmen, a potentially deadly combination for your cavalry. Use hit-and-run tactics to weaken and lure them into range of your Nest of Bees so that they can deal the bulk of the damage, just make sure to keep them safe. The **Defensive Arrow** ability with your Khan can also help in this fight. The final group is at **Position G**, so after bringing in some reinforcements, move your army to engage them—if you kill them all in the allotted time, the mission will be complete. In the unfortunate event that you run out of time and have to contend with the Bohemian army, retreat back to your base and wait for them to come to you while producing as many units as possible. It will be a hard fight to win, but it's not impossible.

The Battle of Mohi

Rewards

- General Subutai
- The Battle of Mohi
- The Multibow Crossbow

Duped by the Mongols' provocative raids, the Hungarians chased down these new invaders... exactly as Batu Khan intended.

Luring the Hungarian army to a carefully chosen battle site, Batu Khan and General Subutai prepared their warriors for another tactical fight.

Objective 1

Destroy the Hungarian Army

At the start of this mission you have control over a small scouting party, while Batu Khan's much larger allied force waits behind you. In order to gather intelligence for them you need to advance over the bridge ahead with your small group of units and scout the area. A number of enemy units lie in wait on the other side, so as soon as you're attacked, quickly retreat back to your allies so that they can kill your attackers.

Batu Khan is now determined to launch a full-scale attack, and you're given 13 minutes to prepare your own army and perform a flanking maneuver with them. As with the previous mission, time is of the essence. A mobile camp that includes some buildings and Villagers will arrive to facilitate your preparations, so start unpacking your Town Center at **Position A** between the Stone Outcropping and Gold Vein. Unpack the Ger in the middle of the nearby Berries, and the military buildings next to the Stone Outcropping. You also get a **Kurultai—** put that towards the front of your base so that your military units get the most benefit out of it.

For a large amount of your allotted time you should focus on improving your economy, so that when it comes time to produce units, you have plenty of available resources and can produce them quickly. To that end, start by building an Ovoo on the Stone Outcropping, and then build five Pastures around your Town Center while you research **Husbandry** at the Ger. Finally, build a Blacksmith and and Arsenal to make some much needed upgrades, and then you can finally put your starting Villagers to work gathering resources.

Villager Resource Distribution					
No. of Villagers	Start	5	5	--	--
	Goal	15	5	10	--

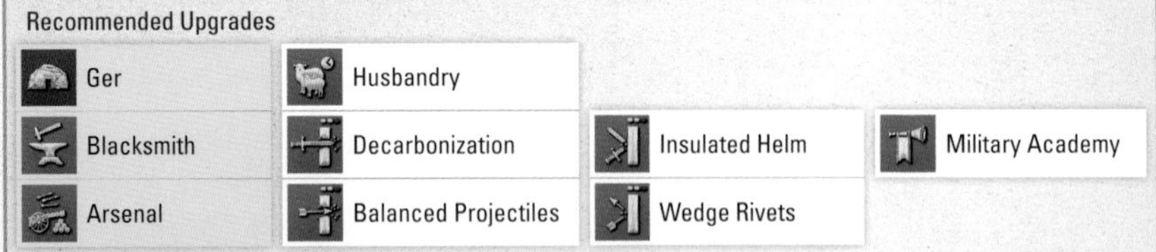

Recommended Upgrades			
Ger	Husbandry		
Blacksmith	Decarbonization	Insulated Helm	Military Academy
Arsenal	Balanced Projectiles	Wedge Rivets	

Once the Berries start to run out, switch your Food gathering Villagers to Sheep at Pastures to ensure continuous Food income.

When you have enough resources, build two more Barracks and Stables around the Ovoo, and with roughly five minutes left, start producing Spearmen and Mangudai, taking advantage of improved production as much as possible. While those units are being produced, send a Villager to **Position B**, where you'll find a broken bridge that you can repair, giving you access to the other side of the river.

Xanadu: 1256 - 1430

Returning from his famed travels in China, the Venetian merchant Marco Polo described the wonders he had seen. Perhaps the most enduring vision was that of Kublai Khan's decadent summer capital, Xanadu (or Shangdu). Polo wrote, "Within the bounds of this royal park there are rich and beautiful meadows... watered by many rivulets... where a variety of animals are pastured. In the centre there is a beautiful grove of trees, where the Khan has built a royal pavilion, ornately carved and gilded." Polo goes on to describe Kublai Khan's vast hunting grounds, his herd of sacred white horses, and his elaborate banquets, attended by dignitaries from all over the empire. Xanadu was the great crossroads of the Mongol Empire, where cultures converged, and where old met new. After the site was abandoned in 1430, Xanadu became a place of legend and romance, inspiring dramatic works from cultures across the world. In his well-known poem, "Kubla Khan", Samuel Taylor Coleridge sums up the mystique surrounding Xanadu and its hold over the great Khan: "Weave a circle round him thrice, And close your eyes with holy dread. For he on honey-dew hath fed, And drunk the milk of Paradise."

– Illuminated History

Split your army into two halves at the one minute mark, and then send one half to **Position C**, and the other to **Position D** so that they're ready to initiate the flank as soon as Batu Khan makes his move. Keep producing units so that you have reinforcements ready if you need them, but if you time your attack along with Batu Khan's, you should have no trouble defeating the Hungarian forces.

After the coordinated attack you'll no longer be under any time constraints, and once you've killed enough of the Hungarian ambushers, any that remain will start fleeing until they regroup at one of two supporting groups of units at **Positions E** and **F**. Take some time now to build a Siege Workshop, have it produce three Mangonels, and then move those along with any other reinforcements across the bridge to join your main army.

You don't need to kill all of the remaining enemy units, only enough to drive them back to their camp at **Position G**, which usually equates to fully clearing one of the support groups. The road towards **Position E** has more room to maneuver, making it the easier side to take. Once all of your units are in place, charge the enemies head-on, making sure to use your Mangonels because the enemy units tend to group up a lot. When it comes time to attack the camp, send your Spearmen against the enemy cavalry and Outposts with support from your ranged units and Mangonels. The mission will end once you've killed the majority of the enemies in the camp.

Shangdu: 1258

Kublai Khan's decadent summer capital, Shangdu, was more than just an idyllic retreat... It was a crossroads where cultures converged... and collided. Kublai wanted Shangdu to represent both the old country of Mongolia and his new dynasty in China. Shangdu's careful design incorporated important aspects of both cultures. His portable Cane Palace was constructed of Chinese bamboo, but resembled the circular design of a Mongol ger. Vast hunting grounds—which paid homage to the ways of Kublai's ancestors—sat beside crops farmed in the Chinese method. Despite his efforts to appease both peoples, violence erupted between religious groups in Northern China. Kublai knew that such instability could threaten the empire itself. And so, in 1258, he convened a debate between the two groups at Shangdu. Which religion should the empire officially adopt? Each side presented its case. And for Kublai, the answer was clear. Buddhism won out. It would afford him greater power over more people as their "Universal Emperor". Today, Buddhism is widely practiced throughout the world, thanks, in part, to Kublai's choice eight hundred years ago... at his cultural crossroads in Shangdu.

– Illuminated History

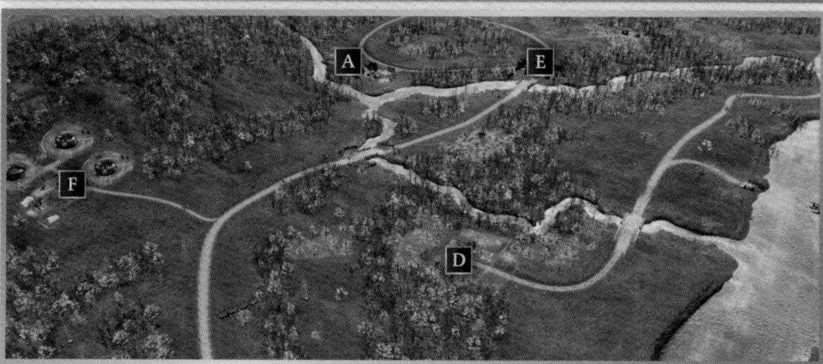

1267

Domination

The Song Fortress

Rewards

- Domination
- Queens of the Empire

Kublai Khan set his sights on the throne of China. But in his way stood an impregnable fortress and its unyielding garrison.

Eager in his quest to become Emperor of China, Kublai Khan sent his army to seize the richest cities of the Song Dynasty. Sitting on either side of the Han river, the twin fortresses of Xiangyang and Fancheng braced for a direct assault.

Objective 1

Seize Fancheng

There are no time constraints to worry about here, so it's worth taking a scenic route to the objective marker to collect some resources that will be useful later in the mission. Start by heading up to the village at **Position A** and setting it ablaze for the resources, and then go down towards **Position B**, ignoring the nearby blockade for now. Neutral villagers are busy cutting down a forest, creating an opening that you can move though to reach another village to burn down at **Position C**.

After burning down the first village, cut back through the forest to snag a hidden Treasure Chest. There are many of these scattered throughout the mission, and because they're always worth going for, the route we planned out takes you close to all of them.

Cross the river now so that you can pillage the village at **Position D**. While moving there, make sure to stay away from the river bank near the city, because the defensive towers on that side can hit your units from there. You can cut through the nearby forest to reach the large enemy camp that's stopping you reaching the objective marker, but there's more resources to be had first. Circle back down to **Position E** and break through the small blockade there, and then continue along the road towards the next blockade and use the small ford beside it to flank around and attack it from behind. You get resources for burning down the small tents here, so it's worth taking the time to do it.

There's another small village that you can plunder for resources at **Position F**, and then it's time to head towards the camp. There are some small blockades along the main road, but if you go to **Position G** you'll find an opening in the forest that lets you flank behind them.

A battalion of reinforcements will arrive on the other side of the camp once you get close, so have them plunder the spoils from the village at **Position H**, and then perform a coordinated pincer attack on the Song Camp with both of your armies. After burning the camp to the ground, head towards **Position I** and you'll get an optional objective to bring your units to a nearby temple; neutral Monks will heal them there, so make sure you capitalize on their services. Continue to the objective marker now and meet up with the allied forces there.

Objective 2

Protect the Allied Trebuchets from Song Soldiers

Allied Trebuchets will move to the river bank and begin bombarding the city, but the enemy troops are not just going to sit there and take it. Three waves of enemies will attempt to destroy the Trebuchets, and they all come from a nearby bridge at **Position J**; move your army there to intercept them all before they get close to the Trebuchets. After fending off the attackers, your allied forces will come under heavy gunfire and retreat, at which time you'll receive a mobile camp.

Objective 3

Besiege Fancheng and Xiangyang

Your mobile camp will try to split up and go to different parts of the map, but you should group them up and take them all down near **Position C**. For this part of the mission you have to move units to defend three bridgeheads; your existing army has the western one covered, and **Position C** gives you quick access to the other two. You also want to keep all of your buildings together, because one of them is the **White Stuppa** Landmark which acts like an Ovoo and you'll want to place as many of your production buildings around it as possible.

If you did all of the plundering and treasure grabbing so far, you should have over 10,000 of each resource—with the exception of Stone, which won't be far behind—and that's more than enough to make your army. Focus on producing strong cavalry units like Lancers and Mangudai, or if you go for infantry, Men-at-Arms and Crossbowmen, and research the improved technologies at the Blacksmith. Keep going until you hit the population capacity, and then split your units evenly and send them to the other two bridgeheads. If you need more Gold, set up the Market that came with the mobile camp and establish a trade route with the neutral Trade Post back at **Position A**.

Objective 4

Hold the Bridgeheads Against the Counter Attack Waves

If you've made all of the upgrades from the Blacksmith, your forces should have no difficulty fending off the attacking waves. Just make sure not to step onto the bridge where the towers can shoot you—let the enemy units come to you. The **Stand Ground** command will help ensure your units stay in place. Keep producing units at your base so that you can send reinforcements if needed, and after three waves, you'll complete the mission.

Blockade at Lumen Shan

The Song's unwavering defense of their fortress forced the Mongols to switch strategies—from assault to starvation.

Kublai Khan enlisted the expertise of the Chinese defector, General Liu Zheng. The Mongols would employ his insights to undermine the strength of the twin cities.

Rewards

- Blockade at Lumen Shan
- Mongol Heavy Cavalry
- The Silk Road

Objective 1

Take Control of Lumen

Before marching on the Song base, take some time to explore the nearby forests with your army; there are a number of small patrolling enemy groups, and some Treasure Chests to pick up, and taking care of those things now will make things easier in the long run. When you're ready, bring the full might of your army to bear on the Song base and burn it to the ground. The local villagers are so happy to have been liberated that they'll give you control over the town of Lumen, which means for this mission you'll primarily be using Chinese buildings and technology.

Objective 2

Blockade the Road North

It's important not to complete this objective too quickly, because when all of the roads have been blocked off, you'll trigger the next phase of the mission, so take some time to build up your resources and defenses before then. Start by building a Lumber Camp with the two Villagers that are already gathering Wood, while the Town Center starts producing extra Villagers to gather other resources in the distribution shown in the table.

Small groups of enemy units will periodically attack you from south of Lumen during this phase of the mission, but your starting army is more than capable of fending them off if you position them on that side of the town.

Villager Resource Distribution				
No. of Villagers	10	5	15	8

Around this time you'll receive an optional objective to take over a town called Bohekou at **Position A**. Not only is that an excellent staging area for the blockade you need to deploy on that side of the map, but there's also a Blacksmith there, making for one less building to construct. Send half of your military over to Bohekou to secure the area, and split the remaining half on either side of Lumen. Now that you have a free Blacksmith, you only need to construct an Arsenal and University to start working on some upgrades.

Recommended Upgrades			
Blacksmith	Damascus Steel	Master Smiths	
Arsenal	Platecutter Point	Angled Surfaces	
University	Biology	Court Architects	Corned Gunpowder

There's already a Barracks and Archery Range in Bohekou, so all you need to add is a Siege Workshop on that side to cover your military production. At Lumen you'll need to construct all three buildings, ideally towards the southern side of the towns. When all of your production buildings are in place, upgrade to **Elite Spearmen** and **Elite Archers**, and then start producing a group of five Villagers to begin work on the blockade.

Where you place your blockade is key to the success of this mission, because they'll have to be strong enough to stand up to eight waves of enemy attacks, and if 20 enemy units make it past your blockade, it's an automatic fail. **Position B** is the perfect location for your first one because it's a natural choke point, and placing it this far down essentially cuts off half of the map from the enemy. It will also give you a safe path from which to establish a trade route from Lumen to the neutral coastal Trade Port at **Position C** if you need additional Gold.

Take all of your military units at Lumen and your group of Villagers, and move them to **Position B**, taking out any enemy units along the way. Once there, build a Stone Wall from the treeline to the riverbank, with enough room to build a gate in the middle and a Stone Wall Tower on either side. Upgrade one tower with a Springald and the other with a Cannon.

While that construction is going on, have your military buildings in Lumen produce a group of 10 Grenadiers, a few Archers, and two Nest of Bees, and then move them down to your blockade to join your other units. Put the ranged infantry up on the wall with the Nest of Bees behind it, and keep those Villagers behind the wall, but nearby in case they're needed for repairs during the next phase. Repeat this process at **Position D** just south of Bohekou (the area here is wider, so you can build additional Stone Walls Towers for extra security), and then prepare yourself for the next phase once both blockades are complete.

The extra range from being atop a wall makes your Grenadiers even more effective for defending the blockade.

Objective 3

Hold the Blockade

When the enemy waves begin attacking your blockades, wait for them to get close so that your ranged infantry and tower defenses can do a lot of the work, and then use your cavalry to quickly attack high priority targets such as siege engines. Send reinforcements down as needed, or alternatively, build Monasteries nearby and have Monks heal your units between battles. Attack waves will alternate sides, and because you've staggered the distance of the blockades from their starting points, you'll have plenty of time to manage each wave before switching to the other. Once all eight waves have been defeated, the mission is complete.

Domination

The Fall of Xiangyang

Rewards

- Legacy of the Mongols
- Mongol Capitals
- The Fall of Xiangyang

The mighty stone walls of Xiangyang met the immense power of the Great Trebuchet in the final stand of the Song fortress.

Kublai Khan's siege engineer, Ismail, brought with him a devastating new trebuchet. With this mighty weapon, he could strike at the fortress with a force like no other.

Objective 1

Prepare your Siege Engines

At the start of this mission you'll get an optional objective to help defend allied villages at **Positions A** and **B** to maintain the trade income they provide you with. These villages will get attacked by groups of elite cavalry units roughly every 30 seconds, and they'll become overwhelmed very quickly without your help. The extra resources from them are very important, so the first thing you should do is group up all of your military units and send half to each of the allied camps to join with their forces.

Be careful when moving around this area. The impact craters along the riverbank serve as a stark warning as to the destructive power of the Chinese defensive cannons if you get too close to them.

Next, go to the **Silver Tree** at **Position C** and start producing Traders until you have seven more, and then establish a trade route with the Market at one of the allied towns you're defending. While the Traders are being produced, go to your Town Center and start producing Villagers; have them first build two more Pastures, and then keep putting them on Food and Wood until you have 15 on each resource before starting to research some upgrades.

To make sure that the two allied trading villages remain safe, send a couple of Villagers to build two additional Barracks at each of them, and have them keep producing Spearmen to counter the enemy cavalry. When you reach 1000 Stone you can finally make use of Ismail's unique ability to construct a Huihui Pao, so have him build one of these trebuchets just outside of your main base; with their huge attack range they can hit a target from well outside the range of the Chinese defensive towers.

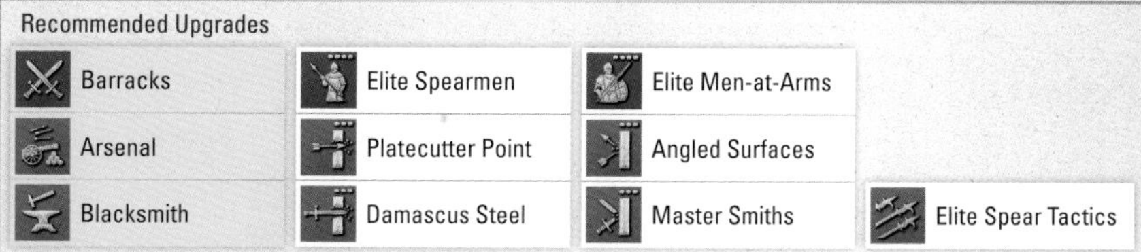

Recommended Upgrades

Barracks	Elite Spearmen	Elite Men-at-Arms	
Arsenal	Platecutter Point	Angled Surfaces	
Blacksmith	Damascus Steel	Master Smiths	Elite Spear Tactics

Objective 2

Assault Fancheng

Now that you have a Huihui Pao you can begin your assault on Fancheng, but in order for your forces to be able to enter the city safely, you'll first need to take down the defensive towers that line its walls. If you have enough Stone, it's worth taking the time now to build additional Huihui Pao to speed up the bombardment process. The city itself is cut off from the surrounding area, which means you'll need to repair a bridge so that your army can cross the river.

The nearest one is at **Position D**, so have Ismail use his **Imperial Falcon** ability to scout the area and reveal targets for your Huihui Pao to destroy. Once your bombardment begins, the Chinese Archers atop the walls will start moving into the area to try and defend it, so after destroying the towers, have your Huihui Pao bombard them as well to help clear the path for your army. When it's safe to do so, bring in some of your Villagers to repair the bridge at **Position D**. Build two more Barracks around the Ovoo in your base and have them start producing Men-at-Arms until you have around 15 of them; as soon as the bridge is complete, march the group of Men-at-Arms into the city.

Entering the city with a force of this size will be sufficient to complete the "Assault Fancheng" objective, which has the extremely beneficial effect of stopping the raids on the allied trade villages. You're now free to regroup your forces near the bridgehead, and take some time to prepare for your final assault.

Objective 3

Sack Fancheng

You should have large reserves of Gold by this stage in the mission thanks to the constant trading, which means you can afford to produce an expensive army. Start replacing all of your cheap infantry with Elite Men-at-Arms and Handcannoneers, and build some Mangonels at a Siege Workshop. To be able to produce and get the most out of this army you should also research the **Chemistry, Corned Gunpowder, Adjustable Crossbars,** and **Siege Works** technologies at the Arsenal.

If you're really patient, you can actually destroy nearly every building and unit in Fancheng from afar with your Huihui Pao—this is commonly known as "death by a thousand bombardments".

While you upgrade and produce units, bombard the cities from afar with your Huihui Pao to make the upcoming fight much easier. Move your army across the bridge into Fancheng when it's ready, and start destroying the buildings and defeating the enemy units. While you're in this area, try to stay away from the bridge leading down to Xiangyang, because the Keep on the other side has immense range and will make quick work of your units if you're not prepared. Thankfully, your Huihui Pao can take care of all of the buildings on that side of the city from a safe distance. To complete the sacking of this city you need to defeat all of the units and destroy the **Barbican of the Sun** Landmark.

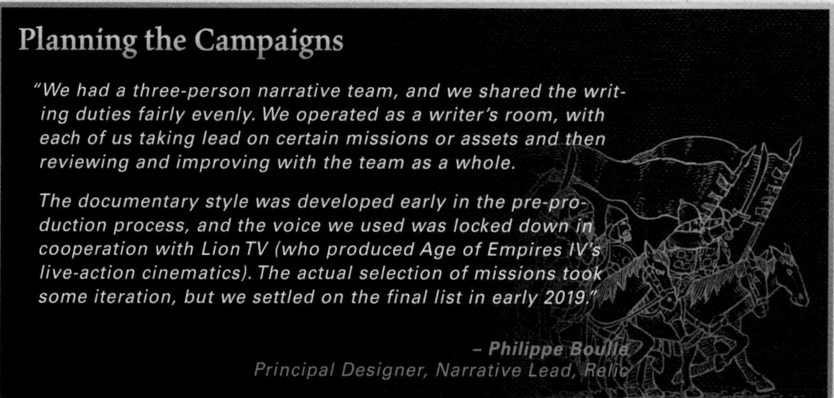

Planning the Campaigns

"We had a three-person narrative team, and we shared the writing duties fairly evenly. We operated as a writer's room, with each of us taking lead on certain missions or assets and then reviewing and improving with the team as a whole.

The documentary style was developed early in the pre-production process, and the voice we used was locked down in cooperation with Lion TV (who produced Age of Empires IV's live-action cinematics). The actual selection of missions took some iteration, but we settled on the final list in early 2019."

– Philippe Boulle
Principal Designer, Narrative Lead, Relic

Objective 4

Sack Xiangyang

The bridge leading to Xiangyang was destroyed to prevent you from crossing it, and a deadly Chinese Keep will fire on any of your units that move in to repair it. Thankfully, your Huihui Pao have a slight range advantage over the Keep, and a single bombardment from three of them is enough to destroy the fearsome building. Be careful when moving your Huihui Pao into range, however, because if you get even a tiny bit too close the Keep will open fire and it can destroy your siege engines in a single barrage.

Bring in some Villagers to repair the bridge after destroying the Keep, and move your Huihui Pao up slightly to start bombarding the Stone Wall Towers and defending units on the other side. After softening up their defenses, move across the bridge with your main army once it's repaired. There's a seemingly endless amount of enemy units on the other side of the bridge, so make sure to use your Mangonel to full effect on the large groups. Keep up the pressure by constantly bringing in reinforcements, and try to get your Huihui Pao into position near where the Keep once stood. From there, if you have Ismail nearby you can reveal the location of the **Imperial Palace** with his **Imperial Falcon** ability, and then your Huihui Pao can bombard it; as soon as the palace is burning, your victory will be complete.

Rise of Moscow

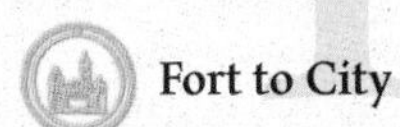

1238

Fort to City

Rebuilding Moscow

Rewards

- Daniel of Moscow
- Fort to City
- Horse Archers

In just a few short years, the once-proud Rus principalities were razed and annexed by the Mongol invaders of the Golden Horde. But one small town would rise from the ashes: Moscow.

Mongol raiders left the town of Moscow burned to the ground. But the resilient Muscovites were determined to rebuild their home—this time, stronger than before.

Objective 1

Protect Moscow

You start this mission with your base under siege by Mongol cavalry, and your first priority is to put out the fires before everything burns to the ground. The cavalry are too focused on burning buildings to attack your units, so you can safely move your Villagers around and repair buildings as you come to them, while the few Spearmen at your disposal can thin out some of the enemies. Don't produce any additional Villagers just yet, however, because any produced now won't count towards the next objective.

Objective 2

Rebuild Moscow

Moscow is safe for now, so it's time to start rebuilding; there's no time restrictions in this phase, so you're free to explore at your own pace. Task five of your Villagers with building a Lumber Camp and a Wooden Fortress near the forest at **Position A**, and the remaining Villagers should work the Farms near the Hunting Cabin at **Position B**.

The setting after you defeat the Mongols feels like a variation on the opening of a skirmish game.

Moscow and the Mongols: 1238

In 1238, a terrifying force tore through the lands of the Rus: the Mongols had invaded. Genghis Khan's grandson, Batu, burned his way across the Rus principalities. From the capital at Vladimir, to the gleaming jewel of Kiev, to the humble outpost of Moscow, the Rus lands became part of the Mongol empire. Batu Khan named the region "The Golden Horde," and established its capital at Sarai. He demanded staggering payments of tribute from all of the Rus principalities under threat of further violence.

Even as the Rus endured increasing hardship to appease their Mongol overlords, life was made worse by bitter conflicts between their own princes. The men pursued age-old feuds over who would hold the title of Grand Prince of Vladimir—and rule over all the Rus. But as more than a century passed under Mongol domination, the princes realized that to throw off the Mongol yoke, they had to set aside their rivalries. Only a united Rus would be strong enough to rebel against the Golden Horde. And at the forefront of that looming battle for independence stood Moscow.

– Illuminated History

There's no need to actually produce any new Villagers yourself; if you find one of the Hunting Cabins scattered around the map, the Villagers near it will join your side. The fastest way to accomplish this is to produce Scouts from your Town Center (or Hunting Cabins you've already discovered) and have them scout around the map for the cabins.

The secondary benefit to this approach is that it enables you to pick up some of the many Treasure Chests you'll find along the way, and your Scouts can kill any wildlife they encounter to add to the unique Rus bounty system. With this system you earn Gold for every animal killed, and when you reach certain thresholds, you'll gain significant benefits to your economy.

The five cabins themselves are somewhat randomly placed, but they can often be found near **Positions C-I**. If there's wildlife near a cabin, kill it with your Scouts so that the Villagers can gather Food, otherwise build a Lumber Camp and have the Villagers gather Wood instead. Only once you've been around the map, found all of the cabins and have all of the chests should you rebuild the destroyed sections of Palisade Wall to complete this objective.

You can mouse over the bounty icon on your HUD to see your current bounty total and which tier of benefits you're on.

Objective 3

Expand Moscow

Through all of the hunting and cabin discovery you've been doing, you should already have more than enough Food and Gold to build the **Kremlin** Landmark straight away now. Produce some more Villagers to speed up the construction, and then after completing the Kremlin, build a Market and an Archery Range at the positions indicated in the game.

5

Objective 4

Build up Defenses Before the Mongols Attack

From this point there's some urgency, because after around eight minutes, the Mongols will attack. Start by building Wooden Fortresses in the indicated places around your base, and have your Archery Range start producing Archers until you have at least 20 of them. Research the **Hardened Spearmen** upgrade at your Barracks and have it start producing Spearmen. Once the Wooden Fortresses are complete, task those Villagers with building two more Barracks and Archery Ranges outside of your base to speed up unit production, and then a Blacksmith inside it to research **Bloomery** and **Fitted Leatherwork**. When the Deer around your Hunting Cabins runs out, build some Farms nearby instead so that you can still gather Food.

By placing your military production buildings outside of your base you can get reinforcements into the battle much faster, and they act as a buffer between enemies and your base.

Objective 5

Defend the Mongol Attack

Keep producing Spearmen and Archers throughout the Mongol attacks so that you always have superior numbers, and try to keep your army together unless you absolutely have to split it up and have the units to do so. Your Villagers should be done with construction now, so have them garrison inside the Wooden Fortresses for some extra defense. If you start getting pressured around the outside of your base, fall back inside and regroup. The Mongols attack in the manner shown above and the mission is complete as soon as you successfully defend against the final wave.

Mongol Attack Waves

#	Unit	Direction
1	Horsemen & Mangudai	North-East
2	Spearmen	North-East
3	Spearmen	North
4	Mangudai	North-West
5	Mangudai	North

1375

City to State

Tribute

Moscow walked a dangerous line. While Prince Dmitry paid tribute to the Golden Horde, he quietly forged alliances to challenge it.

As Moscow's territory grew, it owed more and more tribute to the Golden Horde. Prince Dmitry would need a constant flow of taxes from his allies in order to appease the khan.

Rewards

- City to State
- Forts & Kremlins
- Ushkuinniki

Objective 1

Pay the Mongols

This mission takes place in the same area as the previous mission, so you should already be familiar with its general layout. Some time has passed, however, and your base area is a lot more built up, and there are new Trade Posts scattered around the map. The Mongols require a tribute of Gold to be paid roughly every eight minutes for the duration of this mission, and because there are no natural sources of Gold, everything will have to be earned either through trade or hunting.

The tribute can be made by simply clicking on the Players & Tribute button on the top right of the HUD, and then selecting Gold. If the time expires and you haven't paid the tribute, a large Mongol army will invade and the mission will fail. Always have one eye on the timer, but don't actually pay them until the time is low so that you have more time to build up your economic and military forces.

Produce a small group of Scouts to explore the map and collect Treasure Chests while hunting Deer and Wolves to add to your bounty benefits.

Objective 2

Collect Taxes From Neighboring Settlements

Start by sending both of your Traders to Trade Post Columna at **Position A**, and then begin production of eight more Traders from the Market, along with constant Villagers from the Town Center. You'll also have five Villagers already gathering Wood, but they're doing so at two locations; move them all to one of the Lumber Camps and build a Wooden Fortress next to it for additional protection and Wood income. Two more Villagers are standing next to your

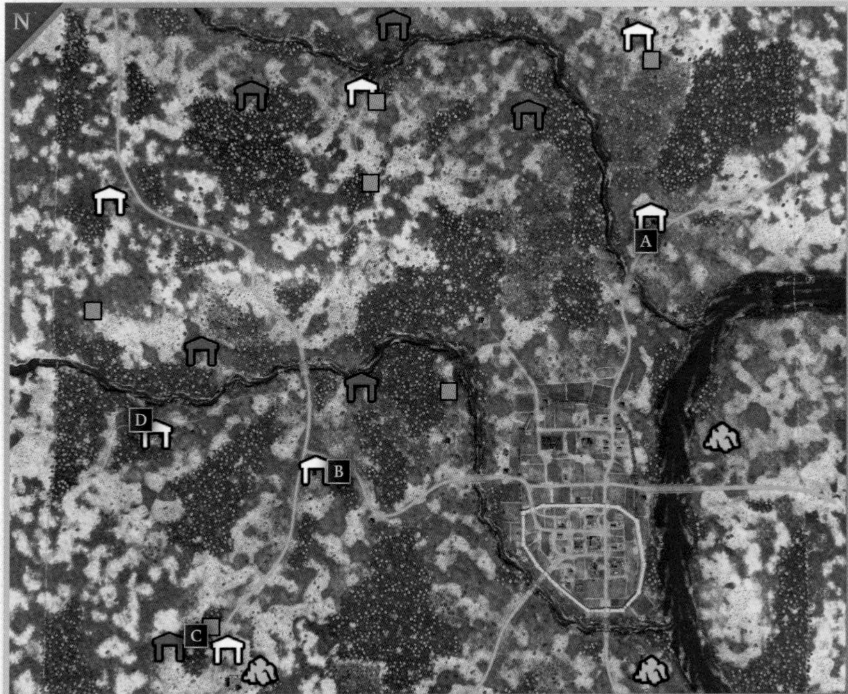

Moscow and the Mongols: 1322

On the long, dusty road to the court of the Mongol Khan, Prince Yuri of Moscow lay in the dirt—robbed, destitute, and desperate. His rival had stolen the rich offering of silver that Yuri meant to present to his Mongol overlord—a tribute that was overdue. The silver had been Yuri's last hope of keeping power over the Rus lands within Moscow. But the brother of his great rival, the prince of Tver, had robbed Yuri of his entire treasury. Yuri fled home. And the Khan stripped him of the title of Grand Prince of the region, giving it instead to Tver. Yuri wanted his power back. Three years later, he traveled with an even larger haul of silver to the Khan's court. Surely, now, the Khan would see Yuri's value and reinstate him as Grand Prince... He never had the chance to find out. The prince of Tver ambushed Yuri—and killed him. Years later, after Moscow finally wrested the grand princely title away from Tver, they remembered the lesson of Yuri's fate: To pay generous tribute to the Khan was to keep an unrivalled grip on power.

– Illuminated History

Town Center—send them to that same Lumber Camp. While moving your Villagers around, have your military buildings start producing Spearmen and Archers to defend against bandit attacks. Make your first payment to the Mongols once you've accumulated enough Gold.

Objective 3

Buy Settlements to Expand Moscow

Keep improving your economy and military by making sure you have around 20 Villagers on Food and 15 on Wood, and build two more Barracks and Archery Ranges to speed up your military unit production. You also already have a Blacksmith, so research **Bloomery** and **Fitted Leatherwork** to improve your Spearmen. Expanding Moscow's influence requires you to buy the Trade Posts around the map, but any new trade routes you establish are likely to come under attack from bandits from six different camps (indicated with the red settlement icons on the map).

You can search out and destroy the bandit camps, but that requires a force of around 50 units for a comfortable victory, and should only be attempted when you can do it without compromising your defense.

In order to be able to purchase a Trade Post you need to have earned at least 750 Gold from it through Trade, and then there's an additional fee of 500 Gold on top. Purchased Trade Posts turn into Town Centers and automatically generate Gold; once you buy one, your Traders will need to trade with a different location. To complete the mission you need to purchase four settlements while maintaining your tribute payments to the Mongols, which will also go up by 200 Gold every subsequent payment after the first two.

To protect those Trade Posts from bandit attacks you should build additional military production buildings near them and leave groups of units there. You should have completed enough trade and have sufficient Gold by this point to buy Colunma; purchase it, and then start sending all of your Traders to Troitskoy at **Position B**. You can keep track of your progress towards being able to purchase a Trade Post in the Players & Tribute menu, and for Troitskoy you'll need roughly two round trips with 10 Traders to make it purchasable.

The easiest approach to take for purchasing the four settlements is to focus on one side of the map and one Trade Post at a time, because that makes defending them a lot simpler. With that in mind, after purchasing Troitskoy, have your Traders go to Clin at **Position C** for your next purchase, and Pereslaw at **Position D** for your final one to complete the mission.

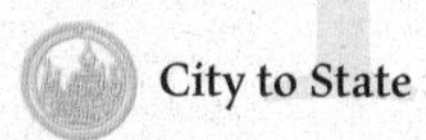

1380

City to State

The Battle of Kulikovo

Bolstered by allies, Prince Dmitry set out with an audacious goal: to defeat the Horde in battle.

Prince Dmitry and his allies prepared to make a historic challenge—the Rus would take the fight to the Mongol army. It would be victory or death.

Rewards

- Saint Dmitry Donskoy
- Swords & Sabers
- The Battle of Kulikovo

Objective 1

Prepare to Fight the Mongol Horde.

There's no economy management in this mission, so your success will be determined purely by how well you can position and control your army. There's also no time constraint at the moment so you're free to explore at your leisure. Start by moving your forces up to the nearby village, where a band of fresh recruits will join your army, and then continue up to **Position A** to gain another group.

While your Scouts are across the river picking up chests, take them on a quick detour up to **Position B**, where you'll find a hidden village with more soldiers willing to join Dmitry's cause. This village also has a Blacksmith that you can use; if you've been picking up all of the chests so far, you should have enough Gold to be able to research the **Decrabonization** and **Insulated Helm** technologies

While Dmitry and the rest of your army are busy recruiting, have your Scouts go around the map picking up all of the Treasure Chests; the resources they contain will allow you to acquire some invaluable upgrades.

now. Have that new group of units meet back up with your main army at **Position C**, where Dmitry will deliver the battle orders to a large group of allied soldiers.

The battle plan requires you to have your forces establish blockades at three key fords **(Positions D, E, and F)** along a river on the opposite side of the map, so start marching in that direction. The Mongols will attack the fords at the same time, but one location will face a heavier attack than the others. Watch for the red Threat Arrow to locate the ford that will be facing the strong attack and move Dmitry's army in to support. Once the allied armies and your own are in position, the Mongol horde will launch its attack.

Objective 2

Repel the Mongol Horde

The Mongol attack consists of 10 waves, and there are a couple of golden rules to follow to ensure a smooth defense. You should always let the allied army engage the opponents first to minimize your losses, and if there are archers in the enemy group, always send your cavalry after them straight away. Keep looking for the Threat Arrow to know where to send your army, but also keep an eye on the allied forces; if it looks like one ford is in trouble, don't hesitate to send some units to reinforce them. After the first wave, allied Villagers will construct some defensive buildings for you near the hill at **Position G**, just in case you get pushed back.

While repelling the Mongol horde, the healing from your Warrior Monks between attacks is more important than the buffs they provide during them, so put them on Stand Ground slightly back from your other units to ensure they stay alive.

The allied armies will retreat back to the hill at **Position G** after the third wave of attacks, at which time another group of reinforcements will also join; regroup with everyone at that position. Redistribute the reinforcements between your three armies to shore them up for the following waves. After wave four you'll get the ability to signal a group of allied cavalry to attack from the flank, and while it starts off quite small, more units get added to it over time. Wave seven is the most challenging wave to defeat, so try and save them for that wave unless absolutely necessary.

In wave six the Mongols will bring Springalds with them, so make sure to send a few melee units to attack them before they deal too much damage to your units. Wave seven has far more enemy units than any of the previous waves, and a number of deadly Mangonels. Now is the time to signal the cavalry reinforcements and let them deal with the enemy group from **Position D**, while the rest of your army fights off the other two groups. The allied cavalry will join your army once it arrives, so you can direct it as needed.

The allied forces will fall back again to some newly constructed defensive buildings at **Position H** after wave seven; have your army, and another fresh battalion of reinforcements that joins you, regroup there. The next two waves also have Springalds in them, so make sure you take them out quickly. Wave 10 has a number of Mangonels again, so they need to be your priority targets or else they can decimate your army—as soon as this final wave is defeated, the mission is complete.

Dmitry's Healing ability can prove invaluable for keeping your units alive during some of the tougher waves.

A design concept example for the city of Smolensk, showing the effects of including particular city features. It demonstrates that urban layouts are never evenly distributed. It includes a few different examples of this idea, such as concentrations of buildings being placed by roads and institutions, and fields and green areas typically working best near the edges of the city. It also suggests adding bodies of water to increase visual interest and aid in navigation.

Planning the Campaigns

"Another mission with unusual gameplay came from my research into medieval Russian history. In this period, the Rus principalities were subjugated under the Mongol empire and had to pay vast quantities of silver in tribute to the khan of the Golden Horde. At stake was the security of each principality (Mongol retribution would be swift for those who failed to pay) and the title of Grand Prince, which was assigned by the khan to one of the rival Rus princes based on his competence and ability to deliver tribute.

From this scenario came the "Tribute" mission in the Rise of Moscow campaign. In this mission, the player experiences the pressure that Prince Dmitry was under – of having to quickly develop their economy, pay their taxes, and prepare for a Mongol reprisal in the event of missing a payment. It can be a real scramble, which is hopefully a fair reflection of events at the time."

– Lauren Wood
Principal Designer, Narrative, Relic

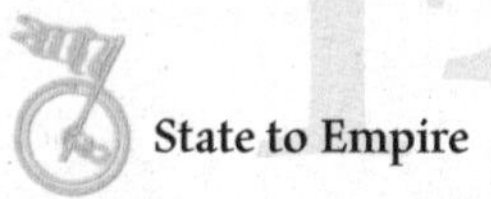

1382

State to Empire

Hold Against the Horde

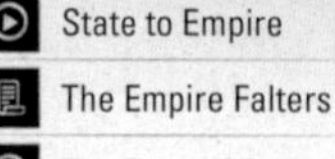

Rewards

- State to Empire
- The Empire Falters
- The Face of Battle

Retribution was coming to Dmitry. Moscow's stone walls would face their most arduous test yet: the full force of a khan enraged.

Dmitry Donskoy had angered the Golden Horde. Thirsty for revenge, Tokhtamysh Khan descended on the capital. Moscow would pay for its defiance.

Objective 1

Prepare for Mongol Retribution

For this mission you return once again to the city of Moscow, and are now tasked with defending it against an imminent Mongol attack. From the moment the mission starts you'll have five minutes to prepare yourself for the attack, so there's no time to waste. Your initial goal should be to reach Age III as quickly as possible so that you can take advantage of the additional upgrades that become available, and that means you'll need resources. You already have quite a few Villagers gathering resources when you start the mission, but you should start producing more at your Town Center to speed things up. Build Farms near your Town Center for Food, and send the other Villagers out to where your Lumber and Mining Camps are.

Villager Resource Distribution	Food	Wood	Gold	Stone
No. of Villagers	20	20	--	8

If you need reinforcements quickly, click the Players & Tribute button to call upon the aid of the trade settlements from the Tribute mission. By recruiting them, however, you'll lose the gold being generated by that settlement, so use it only as a last resort.

There's no natural Gold available on the map, so you're going to have to rely on other sources to get the required amount to construct an Age III Landmark. Moscow has grown and incorporated vassals of their own and the capital now gains Gold in the form of taxes. Open the Tribute & Reinforcements panel in the top right corner to see how much gold the vassals provide every minute. These allies can also provide an immediate group of reinforcements, but when requesting these units, the settlement will no longer provide Gold to Moscow. You can also sell resources at the Market to get Gold. The **High Trade House** is a good choice of Landmark because the extra Gold it generates will be very useful; when you have the required resources, build it at **Position A** where the majority of your Villagers gathering Wood are located. Your next building should be an Arsenal, and then start making the following upgrades as quickly as you can afford them.

Recommended Upgrades			
Archery Range	Veteran Archer		
Barracks	Veteran Spearman		
Blacksmith	Decarbonization	Insulated Helm	Military Academy
Arsenal	Balanced Projectiles	Silk Bowstrings	Wedge Rivets

Your starting army, which includes a number of ranged infantry units atop the Stone Walls, should be enough to repel the first couple of waves once the Mongols commence their attack, but you should build two more Barracks and Archery Ranges and have them produce Spearmen and Archers to bolster your numbers. A decent sized band of Knights is also very useful to have, because you can use them to attack the Mangonels that the Mongols will bring with them, and your overall goal should be to produce military units until you hit the 200 capacity.

Build additional houses in the inner section of the city so that when some of the outlying ones get destroyed, you can still keep producing military units as needed.

To better fortify the inner city you're going to need a lot of Stone, so make sure you have plenty of Villagers mining it. With that Stone you should build additional Stone Wall Towers at various points along the wall, and build Keeps at **Positions B**, **C**, and **D**. The wooden defenses around the outskirts won't last long against the Mongol army, so don't spend resources upgrading them, but your Stone defenses should all be upgraded with **Springald Emplacements**. When the fighting starts, bring in your Villagers and garrison them inside the Keeps for extra firepower.

You'll see a progress bar start to fill under the objective on the HUD once the attacks begin—this represents how long you'll have to hold off against the constant waves of Mongols. The waves get progressively stronger, and will eventually start bringing siege engines

Don't worry too much if you lose some of the outlying buildings, only the inner section behind the Stone Walls is important to secure.

with them to crack open your walls. While Springalds don't pose much of a threat to your walls, Mangonels can easily fire over them to destroy your buildings, and Trebuchets have no problem destroying the walls themselves.

Because the enemy waves tend to be quite large, you'll need to keep your army equally strong to defeat them, which means you should only split it into two groups and constantly move them around to attack the most dangerous targets. Once the more dangerous siege units start appearing, they should always take precedence over anything else. If population capacity isn't an issue, you might want to consider building a Siege Workshop and producing Mangonels of your own to take up defensive positions inside the city.

Objective 2

Hold the City While the Citizens Escape

Your victory for surviving until the progress bar is full is quite short-lived, because the Mongols will now make one final push to destroy the city, and this time they're bringing everything they've got. There is nothing you can do in the face of such overwhelming odds, so your only job now is to try and hold the line while the citizens of the city flee to safety.

Another progress bar will start filling that indicates the amount of citizens that have safely escaped, and you'll need to hold out until it is full. It takes a little while for the army to reach your walls, so take the time to build more Stone Wall Towers and reinforce your army, and then focus all of your units onto taking out the enemy siege engines until the mission is complete.

In case the Mongols come close to your Stone Walls, archers are a good choice to keep them away.

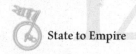

Fall of the Novgorod Republic

While Moscow bowed to the khan, not all Rus bowed to Moscow. The Republic of Novgorod would defend its independence to the last chime of its symbolic council bell.

Rewards

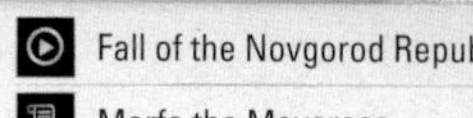

- Fall of the Novgorod Republic
- Marfa the Mayoress

Ivan III aspired to unify all the Rus territories under Moscow's control. But the independent republic of Novgorod would not submit without a fight.

Objective 1

Conquer the outlying towns

After the crushing defeat at the hands of the Mongols in the previous mission, you now pick up the story nearly a century later when Moscow is again ascendant. Start by moving your army to the nearby town of Kuklino at **Position A** and defeat the local militia to take control of the town. Try not to destroy any buildings in the process, because they'll all become yours once you gain control.

When the town is yours, a number of Villagers will join you and automatically begin gathering Food and Wood. You'll also have two more that are idle; use those Villagers to build a Siege Workshop and have it produce a Mangonel to use in your assault on Soltsy. Push forward with your army until your Mangonel is within striking range of the gate leading to Soltsy, and then have it attack the gate. Once the gate is down, go slow, and use your army to lure the enemy units back to your Mangonel so that it does the bulk of the work, because there are a lot of enemies to clear before the town is yours.

If you switch your Mangonel to Incendiary Ammo it can destroy the gate and other buildings much faster.

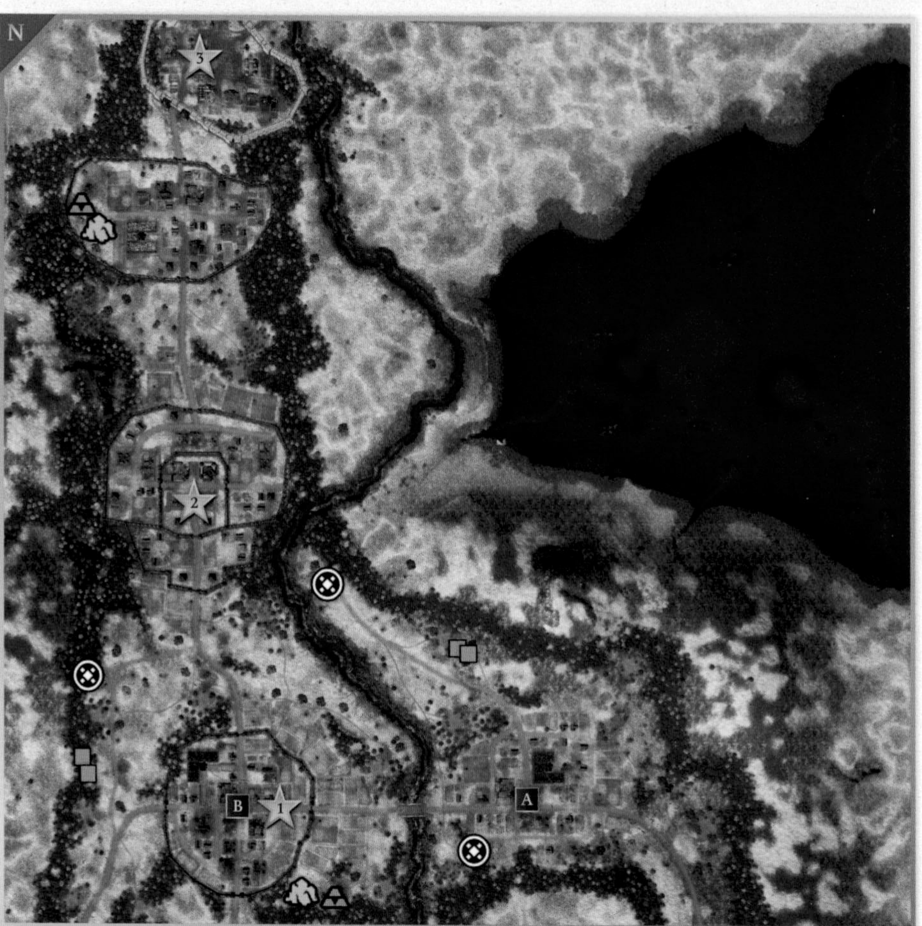

Accessibility

"There is certainly a lot more work that can be done to improve accessibility in the games industry. It's great to see that many gaming companies are now on board, supporting the initiative and placing more focus on accessibility in games. On Age of Empires IV, we chose to first focus on readability, navigation, and accessibility of key inputs.

Focusing on readability means that as we're designing the UI, we need to ensure that it meets a certain standard of contrast, that text and subtitles are able to scale up or down as needed, and that we don't just use colour to convey meaning but also utilize patterns/symbols alongside colour.

Focusing on navigation, in the context of supporting screen readers with UI Narration, means that as we design the layout and information structure of the UI, we need to ensure that the navigation of each UI element is positioned and placed intentionally in a logical way."

*– **Euphemia Wong***
Senior Designer, UX Lead, Relic

Objective 2

Eliminate the People's Militia

The key to breaking through the militia camp and on to Novgorod is having a large number of siege engines and a solid economic foundation to upgrade your units. After capturing both of the initial towns you'll only have to fend off periodic small raiding parties from the militia camp, so take some time to prepare for your next main assault.

Gold is scarce in this mission, with only one Gold Vein available and no ability to build a Market, so you need to spend it wisely. Have the bulk of your Villagers mine for Gold until it runs out, and then distribute them between Food and Wood; in total you'll want 30 Villagers on Wood and 20 on Food. To facilitate the production of your siege engines, build the **High Armory** Landmark in Soltsy to advance to Age IV, and then build two Siege Workshops near it to take advantage of the reduced production time.

You can generate additional Gold by building Hunting Cabins around the map, and by having one of your Warrior Monks capture the Sacred Sites.

Most of your Gold should go towards the construction of siege engines and upgrades for them and your infantry. While you're researching those upgrades, start producing the Archers and Spearmen that will form the backbone of your army (30+ of each), along with at least three more Mangonels and a pair of Traction Trebuchets.

As soon as your upgrades have been researched and your army produced, it's time to launch your attack on the militia base. There are a lot of units inside the base, so the best approach is to methodically advance and let your siege units decimate them, and only use your other units as a defensive barrier to protect the siege engines. After defeating all of the militiamen, the camp will no longer pose a threat.

Objective 3

Conquer Novgorod

Before launching your attack on Novgorod, take some time to build your forces back up by using some of your Villagers to establish your own forward base in the ruins of the former militia camp. Depending on your losses, build either one or two of all of the military production buildings, and it's worth adding a Keep near the front of the camp for some additional defense if you have the Stone.

Build back up to roughly the same strength as when you attacked the military camp, but this time have some additional Trebuchets with you because the inner part of Novgorod has Stone Walls that you'll need to knock down. As soon as you're ready, attack Novgorod in the same methodical manner as you did with the military camp, and keep advancing until you destroy the Veche Bell at the Town Center in the inner part of the city to complete the mission.

On the road to Novgorod, you'll encounter bigger militia groups so it's crucial to have enough units ready.

5

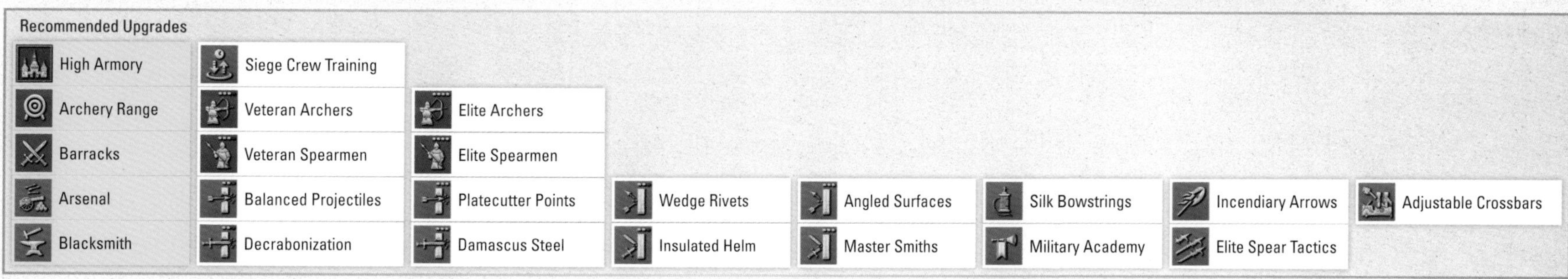

Recommended Upgrades

High Armory	Siege Crew Training						
Archery Range	Veteran Archers	Elite Archers					
Barracks	Veteran Spearmen	Elite Spearmen					
Arsenal	Balanced Projectiles	Platecutter Points	Wedge Rivets	Angled Surfaces	Silk Bowstrings	Incendiary Arrows	Adjustable Crossbars
Blacksmith	Decrabonization	Damascus Steel	Insulated Helm	Master Smiths	Military Academy	Elite Spear Tactics	

Church and State: 1480

The Abbot Joseph wrote of the grand prince of Moscow: "God has put you on His throne in His own stead." For the Muscovite prince, this divine sanction granted him total power. And in return, he would protect the church. In an effort to quash resistance to this move, the church took actions to bolster Moscow's divine position. It made saints of the prince's ancestors. It granted biblical significance to Moscow's military victories and claimed they were aided by saintly interventions. Ivan the Great was likened to Moses, leading the chosen people against the new pharaoh of the Horde. And Moscow was called the 'New Jerusalem'. As a symbol of his ultimate power, Ivan the Great became known as the 'Lord of all Rus', and later as the 'tsar'—a title usually reserved for the caesar of Rome or the khan of the Horde. Moscow's intentions were clear: to draw all power to its centre under the authority of God. Together, church and state would set their sights on both territorial and spiritual victory... as they continued to resist the infidel Mongol yoke.

– Illuminated History

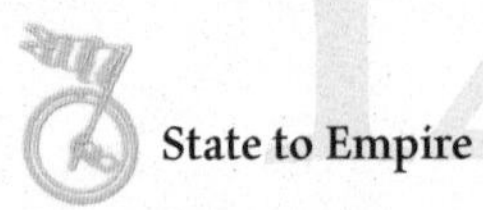

Great Stand on the Ugra River

Rewards

- Great Stand on the Ugra River
- The Cannon Yard
- The Harvest

In a show of strength, the Rus would stare down their conquerors in a resolute stand for independence.

As the Mongol army once again marched to punish Moscow, Ivan III chose his position to make a stand against the weakening power of the Horde. He would hold the line at the Ugra River.

Objective 1

Prepare for the Mongols

***Warning:** Do NOT step into or build on the fords at this time. The objective will complete and you'll end up with significantly less time to build up. You should also never cross the ford entirely, because an almost unstoppable Mongol ambush is all that you'll find there.*

The Mongol army is on the cusp of launching another huge attack, and you only have a short time in which to prepare your defenses and repel them at two key fords **(Position A and B)** crossing the nearby Ugra river. Getting to Age IV for the advanced units and upgrades will make your defensive stand a lot easier, so gathering enough resources to accomplish that should be your first goal.

You start with a number of Villagers already gathering most resources—to speed them up, locate them and build their respective drop-off building close by and have the six idle Villagers mine Gold. Start producing Villagers from your starting Town Center and have them build Farms nearby for Food, and when you have enough Stone, build a second Town Center at **Position C** and have that produce Villagers to work at the Gold Vein.

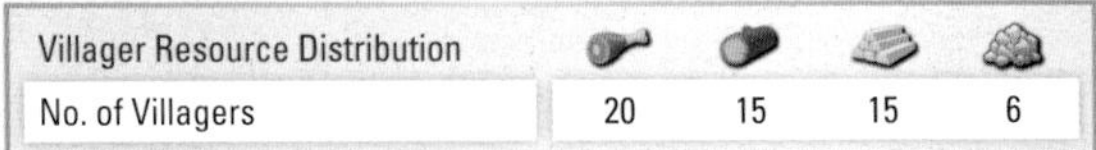

Villager Resource Distribution				
No. of Villagers	20	15	15	6

As soon as you have sufficient resources, build the **Spasskaya Tower** Age IV Landmark at **Position D** to help aid with defense at the southern ford. Ranged units and siege engines should be your focus for military units—to facilitate their production, build a second Archery Range and a Siege Workshop and have them start producing powerful Crossbowmen and Mangonels. You'll want to have a strong presence at each of the fords, so fill the numbers with some cheap Spearmen to help take down any enemy Battering Rams.

When there's around 90 seconds left, have some of your Villagers build a Stone Wall across the ford at **Position B**, and bring your army down to defend them. The initial raid is quite small so your starting army should be enough to defend your Villagers while they work. Once the wall is complete, build a gate and Stone Wall Towers along it. As soon as the raiding party in that area is defeated, move your army to **Position A** and ready them for an attack there. When the southern defenses have been built, have those Villagers build two more Archery Ranges nearby, and then build the same fortifications at the other ford. Make those Archery Ranges produce Crossbowmen, and set the rally point as the top of your walls so they get straight into position.

You need to keep units within the blue circles at the ford to count as defending it, so any defensive structures you build should placed along the edge of the circle to give your other units enough room to stand inside.

Objective 2

Maintain Superiority Over the Fords

The Mongols will continuously attack for this next stage of the mission, and you'll need to keep more units in the indicated areas than the Mongols for the duration of the objective. Keep increasing your defensive presence at each of the fords, including positioning the Mangonels you constructed behind your walls so that they can fire over them at enemy units. If you're running low on Stone for construction, sell some of your other resources for Gold, and use that Gold to buy Stone. Now is also the time to start making some upgrades.

Your units should be focused on bolstering the numbers on the fords and repelling any attackers; if your Town Center is destroyed, the mission will fail. If you need reinforcements at one of the fords quickly, remember to make use of Ivan's special **Production** ability, which lets him dramatically increase unit production speed for 15 seconds at buildings he's near.

When there's roughly six minutes left you'll get an optional objective to intercept a group of Mongol reinforcements that have come to join the battle. If you leave them alone, you'll have to contend with a more dangerous attack when the Mongols make a big push at around the two minute mark. But, if your defenses are strong enough, there's no need to weaken them by taking units away from your walls to engage those reinforcements now. Keep defending until the time expires, at which point the Mongols will fall back to their encampment, and it will be time to switch to offense.

The bars underneath the objective on your HUD indicate your relative strength in terms of unit presence at each of the fords. Aim to keep them as high as possible; if the Mongol's sense weakness, they will attack.

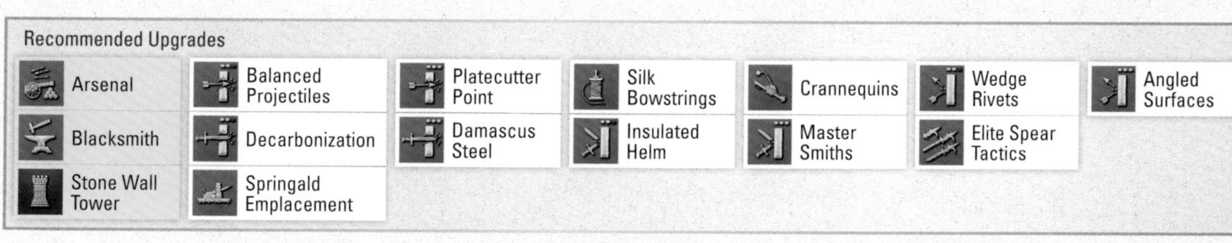

Recommended Upgrades

Arsenal	Balanced Projectiles	Platecutter Point	Silk Bowstrings	Crannequins	Wedge Rivets	Angled Surfaces
Blacksmith	Decarbonization	Damascus Steel	Insulated Helm	Master Smiths	Elite Spear Tactics	
Stone Wall Tower	Springald Emplacement					

Objective 3

Destroy the Mongol Encampment

There are no time concerns for this stage of the mission, and there will be no more attacks from the Mongols. Consolidate your forces near the ford at **Position B**, and then build them back up until you're at the population capacity. Include some Knights this time, because they'll be helpful in the assault on the encampment, and build a University and make some final upgrades.

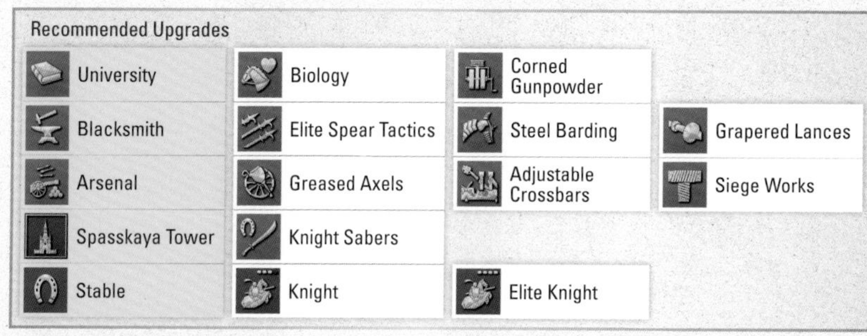

Recommended Upgrades

University	Biology	Corned Gunpowder	
Blacksmith	Elite Spear Tactics	Steel Barding	Grapered Lances
Arsenal	Greased Axels	Adjustable Crossbars	Siege Works
Spasskaya Tower	Knight Sabers		
Stable	Knight	Elite Knight	

Between all of the powerful Crossbowmen you've been amassing, Mangonels, and now Knights to go with your Spearmen, your army should be strong enough to deal with anything at the Mongol encampment. You only need to destroy the enemy Town Center at **Position E** to claim victory, so the ford at **Position B** is the ideal place to commence your attack from because it's much closer. When you're ready, march everything you have into the Mongol encampment, and use your Knights to quickly take out any enemy Mangonels that you come across. Don't stop advancing until the Town Center is destroyed and victory is yours.

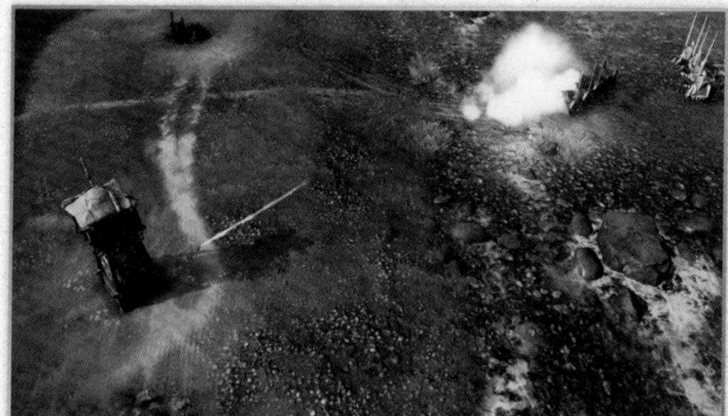

*If you feel brave enough and have enough resources and time ready, you can research **Chemistry** and produce Cannons to take out buildings. This will make destroying the Mongol Town Center much easier.*

The Reign of Elena: 1533 - 1538

Aged twenty-eight and at the height of her reign, Elena, the regent of Muscovy, fell sick with a sudden and grave illness. Succumbing to mercury poisoning, she died, leaving her son—the future Ivan the Terrible—to make sense of her murder. Ivan was eight years old. Elena was the beloved wife of Grand Prince Vasily III. On his death bed, Vasily transferred his power to Elena—a move that angered the elite families of Muscovy. They opposed her very presence: she was foreign, young... and female. Elite women were kept under strict seclusion, hidden from sight and away from the court. But Elena would not be pushed aside and allow her young son's throne to be usurped. She quickly stamped out treasonous plots, imprisoning and even executing her rivals. Despite fierce opposition, Elena was a diplomatic success. She negotiated treaties, built a wall around Moscow and unified the Rus currency. But her achievements would further rile the elite families... and lead to her demise. Elena's killer would remain a secret to history, but her legacy—and her death—would echo far into the future.

– Illuminated History

1514

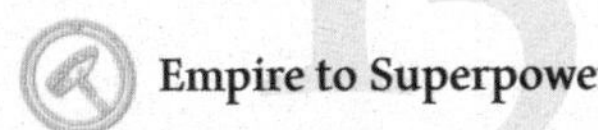

Moscow versus Lithuania

Rewards

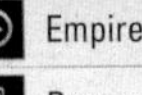

- Empire to Superpower
- Prosperity and Power

With the might of a strong Moscow behind him, Vasily III laid siege to the great Lithuanian fortress of Smolensk.

Ivan III's heir, Vasily III, picked up his father's fight to reclaim and unite the Rus lands. His next target was the fortified Lithuanian city of Smolensk.

Objective 1

Capture the Villages Surrounding Smolensk

Your first objective in this mission is to capture three nearby villages at **Positions A**, **B**, and **C**, each of which will become yours once you've defeated the enemy units defending it, so try to avoid destroying any buildings. Each of the villages focuses on the production of certain types of military unit, so as you gain control over them, you'll also gain the ability to produce those units. Head to Vyazma at **Position A** first, but leave your cavalry behind because you'll want them to be fresh for the upcoming battles. There's only a small militia guarding this village, so your infantry can easily defeat them.

This mission features more Treasure Chests than perhaps on any other map in the game, so make sure you pick them up after clearing each of the villages and while you move around the map.

Once the village is yours, have the two idle Villagers build a Lumber Camp near the other Villagers gathering Wood, and then start producing Villagers from the Town Center and have them build a Mining Camp to work the Gold Veins just outside of the village. Aim for about 10 Villagers on Gold, and while you're here, have the Barracks produce 10 Spearmen to stay in defense, as well as Men-at-Arms to join your main army.

Set your sights on Roslavl at **Position B** now, and this time bring all of your military units to ensure a smooth victory. After securing this village, start producing Villagers again, and then you should have enough resources to build a Landmark and advance to Age IV—build the **High Armory** outside the village at **Position D**. Once that's done, construct two Siege Workshops next to it, and then put those Villagers to work mining one of the nearby Gold Veins;

ideally you'll want 20 Villagers mining Gold in total at this point. Start producing Magonels at your Siege Workshops until you have four of them.

Produce some Knights from the Stables in Roslavl to stay behind in defense of the area, and then march your army towards Yelnya at **Position C** and capture the final village. Have the idle Villagers you get upon capturing Yelnya build Farms, and then produce another three Villagers there to do the same. You should now have 20 Villagers on Food, 5 on Wood, and 20 on Gold as you move into the next phase.

Objective 2

Cut off the Supplies into Smolensk to Stop Attacks From the City

Warning: *You will fail the mission if you lose the Town Centers at each of the villages you just captured, so leaving units behind to defend them is extremely important.*

Lithuanian Traders will constantly send supplies to Smolensk during this phase of the mission, and each time one makes it there successfully, a progress bar will fill; once it's full, they'll launch an attack. You'll also get an optional objective to secure access to another village—Krasny at **Position E**—which nets you some powerful Cannons. One of the main trade routes goes along the road at **Position F**, which means you basically have to go past Krasny to get there, so you may as well take the short detour. Before you do either thing, however, you should take some time to build up your army and upgrade any of the units you're using to their Elite versions.

Recommendary Army	Obj.2	Obj.3
Man-at-Arms	25	40
Crossbowman	25	40
Knight	15	15
Warrior Monk	2	5
Mangonel	4	6
Traction Trebuchet	2	2
Cannon	0	4

When your army's prepared, move them towards **Position E**, and then leave around 15 of your military units and siege engines there to assault Krasny while the rest of your army marches towards **Position F** to intercept the enemy Traders along that route. The attacks from Smolensk are frequent and feature highly upgraded units, so you need to put an end to them as quickly as possible.

Building one or two Keeps and garrisoning Villagers inside at each of the three initial villages can help considerably with their defense, to the point where you shouldn't need to leave behind many additional military units for much of the mission.

Leave some units behind at this crossroads to kill the Traders as they appear, and then move the bulk of your army back down to **Position A** and regroup. If you haven't already done so, build a Blacksmith and Arsenal now, and research upgrades at them and at the University in Krasny. Build your army back up to full strength, and then take them to **Position G** to blockade the second trade route.

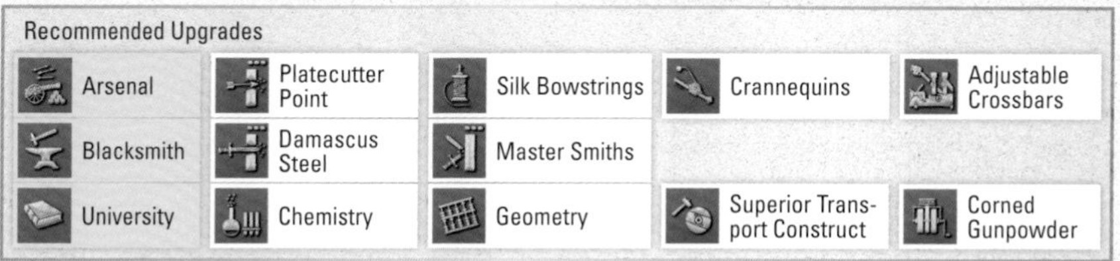

Recommended Upgrades				
Arsenal	Platecutter Point	Silk Bowstrings	Crannequins	Adjustable Crossbars
Blacksmith	Damascus Steel	Master Smiths		
University	Chemistry	Geometry	Superior Transport Construct	Corned Gunpowder

Objective 3

Breach Smolensk's Walls

With both trade routes cut off, you no longer have to worry about the constant attacks so you can spend some time to rebuild and consolidate your forces before assaulting Smolensk. There are a lot of enemy units and siege engines inside, so you'll want the biggest army you can muster. Use your Cannons and Trebuchets to destroy buildings when you begin your attack, and your Mangonels and infantry to protect your siege units against enemy attacks.

Objective 4

Capture Smolensk

Inside the city you will be met by a large number of troops and siege weapons. If the enemy brings in siege engines, have your cavalry quickly flank around to destroy them before they can decimate your infantry. Your goal now is to secure the city by defeating every enemy unit, so keep up the the attacks with your infantry and bombardments with your Mangonels until the city is yours.

The Cannons you find when completing the optional Objective are useful to break and raze Smolensk's walls and buildings.

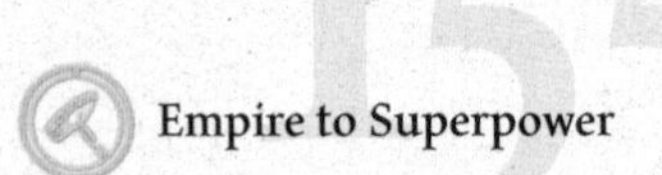

The Siege of Kazan

Tsar Ivan IV held the clenched fist of absolute power over his own people. Now he looked to claim new lands from a defiant enemy.

Ivan IV's ambitions lay far beyond Muscovy's borders. He brought the Rus war machine to the east of his domain and took aim at the Tatar Khanate of Kazan.

Rewards

- Ivan the Terrible
- Steltsy
- The Legacy of Muscovy
- The Siege of Kazan

Objective 1

Secure a Foothold

There are a lot of heavy defenses between your army and Kazan, so you're going to need to establish a significantly sized economic and military production operation, and that's going to require a base. March your army along the road, collecting the Treasure Chests and killing the animals along the way. Eventually you'll come to a small Tatar settlement that happens to be in a good spot for you; defeat every enemy unit and destroy every building to secure the area for your forces.

*Using Ivan IV's **Gunpowder Reload Speed** ability in conjunction with your Musketeers is a potent combination, and can go a long way to minimizing your losses in the early battles of this mission.*

With the area now yours, Ivan will call in a group of Villagers he had waiting nearby with supplies to begin construction. During the next phase of the mission you'll be attacked by Mongol forces crossing the fords at **Positions A** and **B**,

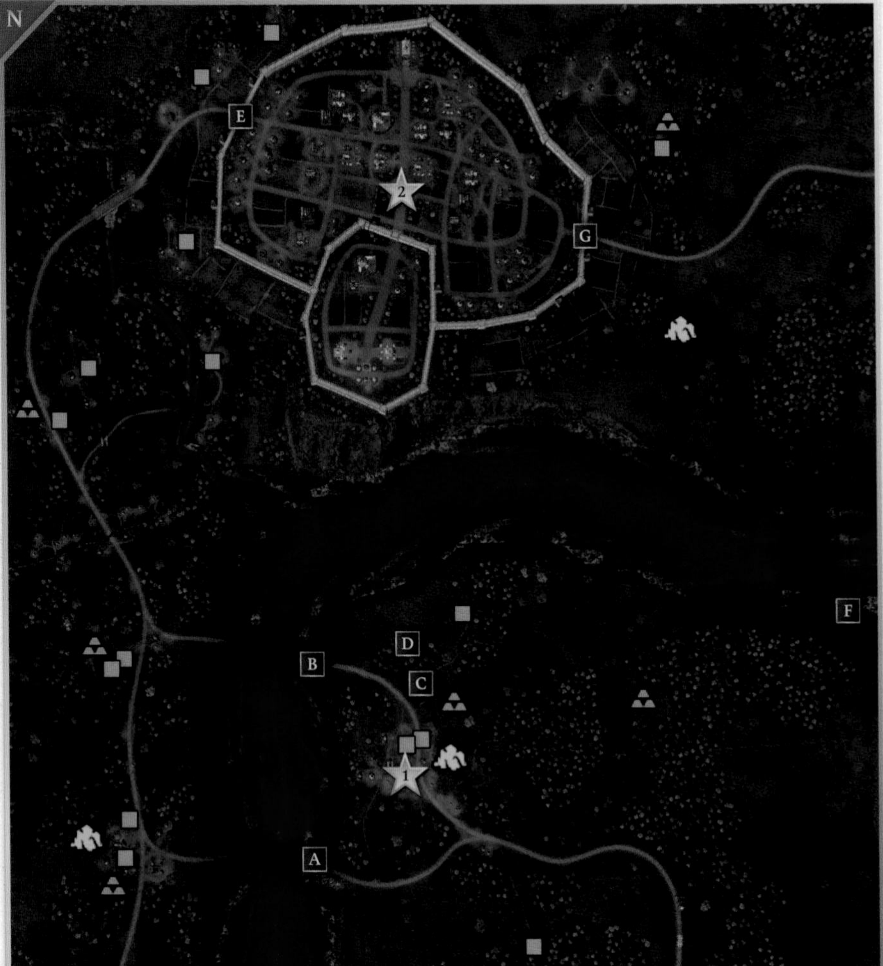

Fear and Control: 1530-1584

The reign of Ivan the Terrible was marked by fear and the absolute power of the tsar. Fearing that treachery was festering in the realm, Ivan dispatched his private police to hunt down anyone who opposed him. The tsar demanded total loyalty—on pain of death. Ivan's fixation with betrayal was firmly instilled from childhood. Orphaned at a young age, the future tsar was raised with a firm hand by courtiers who squabbled over control of Muscovy. Seeing back-stabbing all around him, Ivan grew into a paranoid ruler. To ensure that only his sons would inherit the throne, he used his private police to eliminate the claims of his relatives. By arrest, intimidation and even murder, he secured succession for his direct heirs—but this would have disastrous consequences for Muscovy. After the deaths of Ivan and his sons, no legitimate heirs remained. The centuries-long dynasty came to an end. Ivan's fearsome reign had undone the work of his ancestors. And their vision of a unified Rus nation gave way to chaos.

– Illuminated History

so the Tatar settlement would be a very difficult to defend location for your base. You still want to take advantage of the nearby resources, so with just a small adjustment you can make things much easier for yourself.

To speed up your economic growth, use some of your starting resources to build two Town Centers: one at **Position C** between the Gold Vein and the forest, and one at **Position D** near the Deer. In this configuration you won't have to move your army around quite so much to defend against the two attacking groups. One of the main issues you have is that you're already over the population capacity before you even do anything, so you'll need to build at least seven Houses to start producing units. The enemy attacks will commence at any moment, and while your starting army is fairly strong, they're going to need help. The biggest addition you can make at this time is something that can quickly deal with groups of units, so build a Siege Workshop and have it produce a Magonel.

Objective 2

Besiege Kazan

At this point you're a long way from being able to assault Kazan, so for now you have to sit back and defend against the constant raiding groups crossing the river. Put all of your starting Villagers to work gathering Food, and then have both of your Town Centers produce more Villagers and put them on Wood initially.

Villager Resource Distribution				
No. of Villagers	20	25	15	--

The recommended army composition for this mission is Archers and Spearmen backed up by strong siege engines like Mangonels and Cannons—for quick production, build at least three Barracks and three Archery Ranges. Destroying the two camps on the opposite side of the river to stop the constant raids should be your top priority, so while defending, try to build up an army of at least 40 units and a couple of Mangonels that you can attack with, while also leaving behind a similar force to defend. While you're producing those units, Build a University, Blacksmith and Arsenal to start making some upgrades.

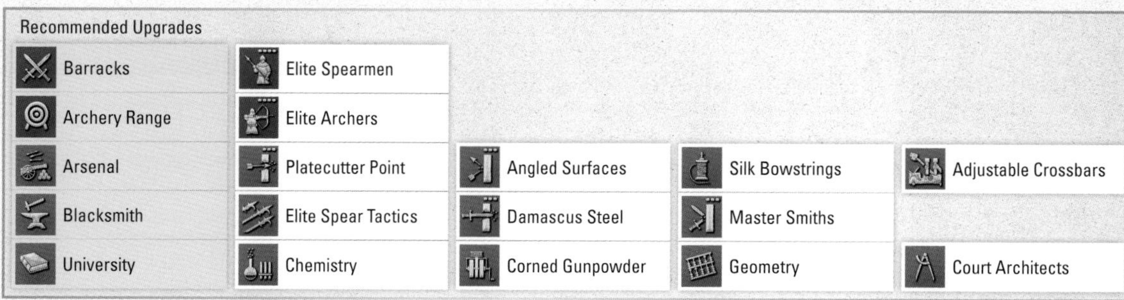

Recommended Upgrades				
Barracks	Elite Spearmen			
Archery Range	Elite Archers			
Arsenal	Platecutter Point	Angled Surfaces	Silk Bowstrings	Adjustable Crossbars
Blacksmith	Elite Spear Tactics	Damascus Steel	Master Smiths	
University	Chemistry	Corned Gunpowder	Geometry	Court Architects

As soon as you have a sufficiently strong offensive and defensive army, cross the ford at **Position A** and destroy the lower camp with your offensive army. Next, converge both of your military groups on the second enemy camp on the opposite side of the ford at **Position B**. You will still have to contend with small enemy groups coming from the blockade close to the second camp, but the might of your combined army should easily be able to defeat them.

Not only do you put an end to the constant raids on your base by destroying both enemy camps, you also secure two more Gold Veins and a Stone Outcropping, giving you a lot more resource gathering opportunities.

Your sights should now be firmly set on Kazan itself, so build up your army until you have at least 120 infantry, six Mangonels and four Cannons, and then you need only make the choice of which approach to take. As always, there are pros and cons to both options. Taking the northern route to **Position E** means you'll have to fight through a lot of enemy defenses to reach Kazan, but once you get there, you won't have to worry about any more enemy attacks, so it's much safer overall.

The eastern route can be accessed via the ford at **Position F**, after which you'll have a straight shot at Kazan's walls at **Position G** because there are no additional defenses. The drawback to this approach is that you'll still have to contend with attacks on your base from the enemies along the other route, so you'll need to leave behind a defensive army and manage battles on two fronts. If you go this route, it's worth setting up some defensive structures such as Keeps with garrisoned units and Stone Walls with ranged infantry on top near the fords close to your base.

Regardless of your approach, when you reach the walls, use your Cannons to destroy the Stone Wall Towers, and then move your Mangonels in to attack the enemy units on top of the walls while your Cannons work on the walls themselves. Your infantry's only job is to protect those siege engines from the incoming swarms of enemy units. After breaching the outer walls, take a bit of time to destroy the enemy's military production in the outer part of the city so that you don't have to contend with any reinforcements.

After breaking through the outer wall, you'll then have to break into a secure inner section that is also defended by Stone Wall Towers—take your time, and make full use of your Cannons to break through safely. Keep producing and sending in reinforcements so that you can keep attacking, and make sure you're near full strength before entering the inner part of the city. Within those walls are the extremely deadly elite guard of the Khan, and you need to kill all of them to complete the mission. Have your infantry form a wall in front of your Mangonels and make them keep bombarding until the last of the Khan's guard is defeated, and the ultimate victory is yours.

CHAPTER

Behind the Scenes

The Hands on History films that bookmark the game's campaign missions add an unexpected deal of richness and insight for players to discover. Unexpected, because nothing like these films has ever been seen before on such a scale in an RTS game; these films feature an expertly blended mix of historical education and entertainment that only an experienced and passionate team of filmmakers and broadcasters could put together. This chapter takes a closer look at them, along with an in-depth interview with digital artist Craig Mullins, whose evocative artwork has long been a hallmark of the Age of Empires franchise.

The Making of the Hands on History Films

The following section of the book was written by Mike Loades, who wrote and directed the majority of the Hands on History films. It begins with an essay in which he describes how the films came about, and then features detailed commentary on each film. Captions are provided by Noble Smith, Narrative Director at World's Edge.

Among other innovations, Age of Empires IV has the added bonus of 27 short (around three-minutes each) documentary films, which we are calling Hands on History. They can be accessed at certain stages of playing the game. As the title suggests, these are very much "doing" films, where experts get their hands on either the weapons or the tools of a particular culture and show how they were used, how they worked or how they were made. A signature element to all the films is their striking visual imagery and the passion of the experts sharing their insights.

I wrote, produced and directed a great many of these films (19 of the 27) and had a hand in the development of others. It all began for me when I met up in San Francisco with Bonnie Jean Mah, who was then the Narrative Lead at Relic (now the Franchise Narrative Director at The Coalition) and Bill Locke, a seasoned Executive Producer and Head of History at Lion Television in the UK. Both Bill and Bonnie were there for a conference and I lived nearby at the time. It was unsurprising to me that Relic had picked Lion, and Bill in particular, to produce these films. The technical spec was exacting and Lion had the experience and the creative flair to deliver. As a freelancer, I had worked with Bill and Lion for more than two decades on numerous projects, including some related to the video games industry. I was thrilled when he invited me to be part of this team.

At that first meeting Bonnie enthused us with her ideas for the films and we all hit it off, as if we had been working together for years. The ideas just flowed and bounced. Later I was to learn that there was another major creative force behind the scenes—Noble Smith, the Narrative Director at Microsoft. Once I started working on outlines for possible films (I did around 40 of these) and subsequently started writing the draft scripts, the notes and the feedback from Noble started to appear. This was always constructive and thoughtful and it always made the films better. I was excited to be part of such a top-notch team.

At Lion, the team was equally superb. It always feels like going home, when I walk into the Lion offices. As well as ordering the Hands on History films from Lion, Relic had also commissioned the Critical Path films. These were directed by Stuart Elliott—a brilliantly talented British television director, who I'd also worked with before. Stu was key to conceptualizing the style of both the Critical Path films and the Hands on History films. Also, because it was just not humanly possible for me to direct all the HoH films within our relatively tight delivery schedule, Stu took on the directing for eight of them.

Cameras

Cameras help us see the world (and past worlds) in ways that we cannot see unaided with the human eye. Giant macro-lenses—we used some pretty spectacular ones—allow us to see super-enlarged details. Drones—our drone pilots performed some pretty cool flying—give us the bird's-eye view the big picture. Time-lapse—yes we used that too—speeds thing up and gives a lot of story in an instant. However the big payoff is always the slow-motion shots, especially with action and effects. Seeing the spitting flames of a gunpowder-fuelled incendiary arrow as it is drawn back in the bow or cascades of sparks flying when an armourer's hammer strikes red-hot metal make your jaw drop at 1,000 fps and all the beauty and the power of a galloping warhorse is magnified many times over, when seen in ultra-slow-motion. We also had some rather unusual testing effects that we needed to capture in slow motion.

In order to hold up against the high-end graphics of the game, we were required to film in 4k HDR. The camera best suited to capturing extreme slow-motion to these specifications is the Phantom Flex. It is an extraordinary camera that gives sequences a very distinctive 'look'. However it is astronomically expensive to hire and, because it was designed for use in scientific laboratories, not out in the field, its knobs and dials are not entirely 'user-friendly' when

Editing the Films

"When we first pitched the idea of the Hands on History videos, people were a little dubious about making documentary style films for an RTS game. But after everyone saw the first completed video in all its glory, we knew we had embarked on a narrative path that was truly exciting and game changing for the Age franchise.

It was incredibly fun and inspiring to work on the Hands on History films. The review/editing process was fairly simple and highly collaborative between teams in London, Redmond and Vancouver. Lion Television would upload rough cuts to the ReviewStudio application, where The World's Edge and Relic creative teams could review them as shared files, and scrub through the video making notes that were automatically marked on the timecode. You can draw on still frames to illustrate a point (this came in handy when figuring out how to show the various functioning parts of a trebuchet using graphic overlays). The Lion crew, along with Mike Loades, Bonnie Jean Mah, and the wizards at Compost Creative, brought so much inventive firepower to these stories. They made history come to life."

—**Noble Smith**
Franchise Narrative Director, World's Edge

From top to bottom, images from the filming of the Hands on History films Campaign Life, and Falcons and Hawks.

shooting on location. Moreover the Phantom devours data with the appetite of NASA's Mission Control; data-wrangling to keep pace with the day's shooting schedule was always a race against the clock—or, in most cases, the fading light of the evening sun.

Presenters

All our presenters had to be hands-on and doing. We sought out authentic personalities with either direct knowledge of the subject matter or those with related experience, who could engage with other experts to learn about how something was done. We didn't want presenters who would teach and preach but rather ones who could talk while they were engaged in their tasks, looking up from time to time, to speak one-on-one with the game's fans.

Although for many, this was their first time in front of professional cameras, we asked them to speak to Age of Empires players straight down the barrel of the lens. Old-fashioned television-style interviews, where the expert speaks to an unseen person off-camera, were out. That approach doesn't have the sincerity, the authenticity or the contemporary feel that we were looking for. Most people today are used to speaking directly to a camera, even if it is the camera on their phone. Anything else would have seemed out-of-date. Even so, speaking into the lens of a professional camera is still quite difficult for a lot of folks to pull off in a natural manner, so we had to scout around very carefully to find the right people. In many cases they also had to be at the top of their game with some extreme action skills.

We ended up with a real mixture of people; all with quite different personalities. They all had one thing in common—a passion and fascination for the topic they were talking about. However the most important part of our presenter's job description was to have fun—and they did!

Locations

Where possible, we sought locations that evoked atmosphere and which rooted the films in an appropriate world. We filmed at Caerphilly Castle in Wales, Warwick Castle in England and at Czersk Castle in Poland. We made a trilogy of films at the enchanting Guédelon Castle project in France.

Peacock feathers were one of the preferred kinds of feathers used for fletching—the stabilizing flights on an arrow's shaft. English longbows were made of yew wood.

At Guédelon, near Auxerre, teams of traditional craftspeople have been busy since 1997 building, from scratch, a full-size replica of a typical 13th-century castle. Once completed it will have six towers, a great hall and high walls enclosing more than an acre of land. The outer walls are surrounded by an enormous dry moat. It already looks very impressive; it is already usable and it resembles how many castles would have looked during the Middle Ages—new, strong and not yet quite finished. The workers use only 100% authentic materials and the authentic tools and building techniques of the period. Among them are expert stonemasons, carpenters, tilers, plasterers, blacksmiths and other specialists. Great blocks of stone are quarried on the site and transported by horse-and-cart to where they are worked into shape by the masons. Finished stones are then winched to the upper levels as the walls grow higher and higher. The mechanisms for this are wooden medieval-style cranes, powered by giant treadwheels, which the workers walk in like hamsters. Every detail is accurate. As well as showing the scale and the detail of the building project, the Guédelon films range from looking at the very basic functions of castle sanitation to the rather more surprising elements of a castle's elaborate decoration.

Crews also went to Cosmeston Medieval Village in Wales and to the Weald and Downland Open Air Museum in West Sussex. Both locations offered an authentic backdrop of medieval style buildings. Green fields (with no electricity pylons, telegraph poles or modern building in sight) in both Poland and the UK, reverberated to the thunder of galloping hooves for several films. One team went to China, whilst

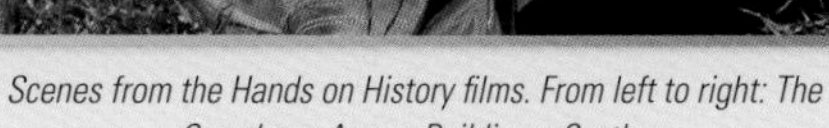

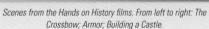

Scenes from the Hands on History films. From left to right: The Crossbow; Armor; Building a Castle.

my team filmed some scenes about the Mongols in a field in Northern California. Logistics and schedules play a huge part in selecting what can be done where and when. Many of our experts had extremely busy timetables and only a narrow window of a day or two when they could fit us in. We wanted the best people for the job, so we adjusted our plans to make it all work.

Short Films but not Small Films

The first HoH film that I directed was about the Chevauchée — a tactic in the Hundred Years War of raiding the enemy's civilian population to both weaken resistance and provoke a battle. Although the main thread of the film is learning how to make and shoot authentic medieval incendiary arrows, I wanted to set this in context. For that I needed an image of a medieval village on fire. Understandably the very nice people at our chosen replica medieval village (Cosmeston) did not want us to burn down their buildings. In order to get the illusion of the village on fire and to see the raiders' horses wheeling behind the flames, I ordered a long bonfire to be laid in a field in front of the village, so that we could film through the flames, with the village behind. The bonfire had to be long enough that we could get different camera angles, whilst still keeping the flames in shot. This required a massive truck-load of firewood to be delivered, creating a fire that was nearly as long as a city bus, about half as wide and standing waist high. When lit, it roared and crackled magnificently. In addition to the bonfire, we had archers with incendiary arrows, horses with riders carrying flaming torches, as well as chickens and pigs to populate the village. There was a policy of not creating sequences that required acting, but that didn't mean we didn't want dramatic images. We did and we certainly got some on this shoot.

Background Issues

Although our presenters remained in modern dress (it made them more relatable) we used setting with an appropriate period and cultural mood. Where possible we tried to keep these looking as naturally authentic as possible. Drone shots always offer the most challenging problems in this regard. When on location, a film crew has a lot of vehicles as well as equipment and baggage lying on the ground. However much you plan in advance, as soon as the drone goes up there is an immediate scramble to move everything to the other side of the field (and then back again). I remember one occasion when this was happening and someone, in the 'hurry, hurry alarm' of such manouevres reversed over the drone, standing by in its case. Hearts stopped but on inspection it was mostly the case that was damaged and a little bit of the housing on the drone that had broken. Fortunately the drone still worked and we got the shot.

Poland offered several great locations for the 'Rise of Moscow' films, locations which had an Eastern European feel. One of these was the majestic, late 14th-century Czersk Castle. For a film about the Streltsy, I had found the ideal spot for Gordon Summers to demonstrate how an arquebus worked but there was one snag—it had a portable toilet in the distant background. I asked if there was any way we could disguise it. "Don't worry, I'll move it" cried one of our intrepid, make-it-happen crew, as he raced towards the offending object. As he rocked the lightweight plastic cubicle energetically to-and-fro, there was a panicked cry from within. The unfortunate occupant was another of our crew! I think he's just about forgiven us.

Jeopardy

The more expensive a day's filming, the more pressure there is to come home with the goods. Normally, issues of weather, performance and the idiosyncrasies of the very expensive Phantom camera are enough to strain any director's stress levels. However many of our HoH shoots had an additional challenge—the jeopardy of special effects or stunts that hadn't been tried on camera before. We frequently attempted action sequences for the very first time, with no guarantee that they would work. Concepts from bathtub to field usually have some kind of testing phase in between but we didn't always have that luxury.

I imagined most of these shots as visual metaphors to convey the power of a particular weapon system and also to produce an effect that would read well on the Phantom slow-motion camera. For instance, for the Warhorse film, in order to illustrate the shock of an armoured knight striking with his lance in an impact charge, I asked my old friend Dr. Tobias Capwell (a formidable jouster as well as a renowned

armour scholar) to ride at a concrete paving slab fixed to a wooden post, using a very solid, sharp pointed lance that he would drive home with the full power of his spirited, galloping warhorse. I knew he had both the courage and the skill but what I didn't know for certain was whether the slab would shatter on impact or whether the rider would be unseated. Toby was wearing his full armour, which can also work as an effective crash cage, and so he was unfazed at the prospect of either outcome.

Similarly when I needed Andy Deane (from The Royal Armouries in the UK) to demonstrate the function of the hook attached to the head of a Mongol heavy-cavalryman's lance, I concocted another new stunt. I had Andy gallop at a weighty sack of potatoes mounted on what looked like a giant bird-table and, as he passed, attempt to hook them to the ground as if they were an enemy rider. I didn't know if he'd pull the potatoes off or if he would be the one who ended up on the ground but I did know that he'd give it his all. Of course he always had the option to let go of his lance.

For another of the films in the Mongol series, expert bow-maker Lukas Novotny built us a giant siege crossbow that had three powerful bows, all connected to each other. Such devices are to be found in manuscript drawings from the period. In theory such a contraption should be an enormously powerful weapon– but how powerful? I dreamed up various target tests, including shooting it at a seasoned oak wine barrel—a piece of wood of extreme hardness and toughness. It was also very thick and we had no idea what the result would be. In the Streltsy film for The Rise of Moscow series, I had ordered an extremely thick leather bag, packed with wood shavings, for Gordon Summers to slice open—in glorious slow-motion—with his giant, and keenly sharpened, bardiche axe. The bag was swinging from a gallows and we were running out of daylight. Gordon gave a mighty swing…

Working with animals also brings extra jeopardy. They don't always understand what you want. For instance, for the falconry film I wanted to get a head-on, super-slow-motion shot of a goshawk banking through dense woodland—it is a low-flying specialist, quite distinct from high-flying falcons. The flightpath had to be exactly right for the light. The Phantom camera needs lots of light and that is a scarce commodity in woodland. We found a spot that might work and the falconers set up a clever device. It was an electric winch that pulled a lure (a pad with a piece of meat on it) on a wire, along the ground at very high speed. We had several

A close up of the recreation of the giant crossbow from the Hands on History film Multiple Bow Crossbow.

goes. Sometimes the hawk beat the winch and got the pad before the end of the flight; sometimes she was just out of frame, changing her line slightly on her approach. There were many other shots to get that day, so every time we decided to set it up again, we had to look at the sun and gamble if we had the time. Two fingers above the horizon—ok just one more go. It would be a great shot if we could get it…

Horses of course are a little more predictable than hawks but anyone who rides will tell you that they are always full of surprises. Horse-archery is one of the more difficult things that you can attempt on a horse (you can't hold the reins, when you are shooting a bow!) It also happens to be my own personal passion. Modern-day horse-archers, however, ride mostly along a track cordoned off with rope barriers, so that the horses will run straight. They also do this one person at a time. It is all very orderly. In order to give an impression of military horse-archers for a film in the Rise of Moscow series, I wanted to show a squadron of horse-archers, all riding and shooting together, sweeping in from both flanks. It was a very tall order. In Poland, which has a very vibrant horse-archery culture today, we filmed a dozen expert horse-archers on some very good horses attempting just that!

It was ambitious, a lot could have gone wrong, but that has been the essence of making these films—aiming high, delivering high-end production values and designing original imagery to feed our imaginations and discover fresh insights into the past. Age of Empires is an immersive experience; an experience that draws in smart, thoughtful players who delight in facts and detail. These films, we hope, add a little colour and a little zest to that detail.

Crossbow

Presenters **Gordon Summers and Andy Deane**

The pre-eminent missile weapon of the Norman era was the crossbow. Longbows existed but were predominantly a hunter's weapon. From 1100 to 1250, crossbows dominated both battlefield and siege warfare. They were the weapons of commoners and kings. Compared to the longbow, crossbows required less training, their ammunition was relatively inexpensive and the shooter could hold the crossbow at full span for a sustained period, waiting for the optimal moment to take the shot. This was especially useful in sieges and at sea.

The bow part of a crossbow is called a lath. At first all crossbows had a wooden lath. As with the longbow, the best wood for this was yew. Even so, these early wooden bows had nowhere near the power that eventually became possible with steel laths in the 15th century. These early wooden crossbows had (by later standards) a relatively modest punch, for use at fairly close range. The lath had to be quite long to be capable of any force at all. Keep in mind that a longbow was drawn back to behind the ear; whereas a crossbow is only drawn back little more than a hand's breadth.

At first, crossbows were spanned by a loader laying on his back and bracing his feet against the lath, while he pulled on the string. An early improvement was the introduction of the stirrup (a metal arch fitted to the front end). The shooter could remain standing, place his foot in the stirrup and push down as he drew the string back. It was quicker and it paved the way for the next development. By 1200, the crossbowman was wearing a heavy-duty belt with an iron claw (hook) hanging from the front. He hooked the string over the claw and then pushed down with his foot in the stirrup. This was less of a strain on the back and enabled him to use a slightly stronger bow.

In future centuries new spanning devices were developed—the cord-and-pulley, the gaffle, the windlass and the cranequin. All gave a power advantage, allowing heavier draw-weight bows. However none of these made an appearance before the 14th century. Until then it was the belt-and-claw system only. There was one improvement, however. Around 1200 the composite crossbow lath was developed. This not only enabled crossbows of higher draw-weight but it also allowed the bow part to be much, much shorter in length, making it more manageable. Composite laths were made from a matrix of wood, horn and sinew, held together by special glues. They were covered in leather or bark to protect from the elements. Naturally composite bows were a lot more expensive than wooden bows, so they never entirely replaced them. Wooden-lath crossbows continued in service throughout the period. In defending a siege, the crossbowman could wait in safety, with his weapon loaded, before a brief exposure while he took his shot. In the age of castles, the crossbow was king.

The Pavise

"The French crossbowmen unit (arbalétrier) in Age IV did not originally have a deployable pavise—the long shields used by the arbalétrier to protect his entire body as he reloaded and shot his dart. But after seeing pavises demonstrated in the Hands on History film, we decided to add this shield functionality to the units. It's a cool and unique ability akin to the deployable palings for the English Longbowmen. This is a great example of the HoH videos influencing game design."

—**Noble Smith**
Franchise Narrative Director, World's Edge

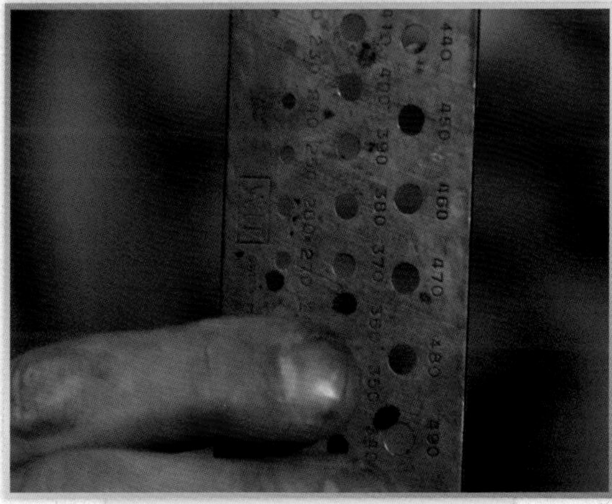

Above image: *A modern gauge used to pull wire for the making of mail rings.*

Mail-making

Presenters **Francesca Levey and Nick Checksfield**

Mail was the universal armor for the Norman period. It is correctly called mail, NOT chainmail—that is a mistaken Victorian term. A chain is single links in a line. Mail is an intricate web of interlocked rings. For the wearer it was a comfortable and flexible defence—a sheet of iron that moved like fabric. As the film shows, the first stage is to make wire. A drawing block has multiple tapered holes—each smaller than the next. An iron rod is pulled through successive holes stretching it into longer, thinner wire. The wire is then coiled until it looks like a spring. This is then cut, releasing lots of small open rings.

Next the rings are hammered flat, the ends overlapped and a small hole punched through the overlap section. The mail is then assembled into a garment—a coif for the head, or a shirt for the body or chausses for the legs. By altering the arrangement of the rings at key points—such as elbows, armpits, necks or knees—the garment can be shaped with incredible precision; tailored to fit a person perfectly. Well-fitted mail shouldn't bag or hang loose anywhere. A fighting man doesn't want to carry a single link more than he has to.

Each link of mail is closed by hammering a tiny iron rivet through the overlapping holes. It is painstaking and fiddly work but it makes the finished product extremely strong. The ratio of rings that linked through each single ring could be increased (5:1 was the standard) to create double-mail or triple-mail. These sections, favoured for areas such as the throat, were both more expensive and heavier but they gave better protection. Carefully judged heat treatment could also increase the hardness of the links, making them more resistant to sword cuts and other weapon strikes. High-end mail was 'proofed' by the maker. One test was to stab it with a dagger!

Mail was not worn on its own, but over a padded garment called an aketon and, later, a gambeson. High status knights could have their mail embellished with rows of brass rings. These either decorated the edges or formed intricate patterns within the main body of the piece. Mail could be cleaned by rolling it in a barrel of sand. Mail was valuable and often passed from father to son. One significant advantage it had over plate armor was that it could be altered—it could easily be made to fit another person or adjusted if the owner put on weight!

Falconry

Narration only

A knight's occupation was war but his passion was to hunt, and the hunting he loved most of all was to hunt with birds-of-prey. Falcons and hawks were prized gifts that kings, princes and nobles gave to each other. The very first panels of the Bayeux tapestry show King Harold taking falcons to Normandy on his visit to Duke William. Falcons (also known as longwings) have pointed wings and hunt by flying high and hovering. Then they 'stoop', that is dive-bomb from the sky, by folding their wings and dropping at incredible speed. Hawks (also known as broadwings) have shorter, broader wings. They hunt by giving pursuit from a tree branch or directly from the falconer's fist. The flying styles are very different, each suited to different terrain.

In training, birds are "flown to the lure"—a leather pad with a morsel of meat on it. Attached to a line, this is swung around the falconer's head and the bird performs spectacular aerial displays of flying and diving as it tries to catch the pad. Falcons hunt by sight and their eyesight is highly developed. So much so that they can become agitated with too much visual stimulus. Leather hoods are placed on their heads to trick them into thinking it is dark and they sit there quietly and peacefully—they've been "hood-winked." Keeping birds quiet is obviously essential when carrying them on horseback. When flying falcons in open country, the nobility rode out on their horses, so that they could follow the chase by galloping after a bird in full pursuit and be close by to witness it seize its prey. It was an aristocratic sport.

Birds-of-prey were symbols of Norman power—the lords of the sky for the lords of the land. One manifestation of Norman power was the seizure of vast areas of common land as exclusive hunting grounds for the nobility. Hunting was outlawed for the common man in these areas. Norman hunting laws announced that they not only claimed ownership of the territory and the people but that they also owned the wild animals that lived in the forests, fields, heaths and moors. They had dominion over it all.

A drone shot of Guédelon castle in Burgundy, France. Nearly all of the footage shot for the Hands on History and Campaign videos is original for Age of Empires IV.

Building a Castle

Presenter **Sarah Preston**

At Guédelon in France, they are building a full-size replica of a 13th-century castle from the ground up, using only traditional tools, methods and materials. Our crews visited this spectacular location to get the insider know-how from the people who are doing the work. Guédelon inspires with extraordinary images. For the Normans, castles were primarily weapons of conquest; they controlled the land. A network of castles provided safe bases for military garrisons that could ride out on daily patrols to deter or quell any local trouble. Built to be secure against attack, these large, imposing buildings dominated the medieval landscape.

Generally built on higher ground, in order to both see and be seen, castles were an imposing signal of Norman power. They were also the focal point of local communities and where the nobility lived, in both luxury and security. That security was paramount and, although their first castles were constructed from wood, the Normans soon became pioneers, in Europe, for building castles from stone.

Castles had to be reasonable proof against attack from over, under and through the walls. The curtain walls had to be high, making it easier to defend against escalade—men with ladders going over the top. Walls had to be broader at the base and have deep foundations to make them harder to undermine. Most importantly, walls had to be thick and strong to resist an unrelenting barrage of large stones hurled from massive trebuchets.

In order to absorb impact from stone missiles, curtain walls were given some elasticity by a clever construction technique that sandwiched a thick layer of rubble in between inner and outer walls of geometrically precise facing stones. The infill, making use of the odd shapes and sizes from the offcuts of quarried stone, was embedded in a special mortar, making the walls resilient, as well as formidably wide.

Each of the outside stones was fashioned to an exact size and shape by an army of skilled masons. It was also incised with mason's marks. These symbols, on every single stone, showed which way it should face, gave its depth in inches marked by Roman numerals (easier to carve) and also bore a mark that identified the man who had cut the stone—a system of quality control. Building a castle was a job of precision civil engineering. The genius of Norman architects and the expertise of Norman masons has weathered the test of time, as many of these glorious building still stand today.

Garderobe

Presenter **Sarah Preston**

Medieval people were not as dirty and unhygienic as popular culture would lead you to believe. Although the notion is not without some foundation, it is a highly exaggerated meme that helps modern people feel superior. They cleaned their teeth—using sticks of marshmallow, a woody, fibrous plant whose stems could be pounded to make a decent toothbrush. They had bathtubs and soap. Of course not everyone was as well-scrubbed as the next person but that is equally true today! Nevertheless the sanitation arrangements in castles left much to be desired by present-day standards. The latrine was called a garderobe. Garderobe is a French word, which, like the English term wardrobe, meant a place to keep clothes. The reason it acquired this nickname is because people literally hung their finest clothes in there. It was believed that the ammonia fumes from urine killed clothes mites.

The Garderobe Hands on History film is a web exclusive available on the Age of Empires homepage. ageofempires.com

In construction, the garderobe was a small room built into and overhanging the castle walls. It had a stone bench with a hole in the centre connecting to a chute that ejected human waste to the moat below. In the case of a dry moat, this just piled up at the base of the wall and had to be shoveled and carted away from time to time.

The interior walls of the garderobe were lime-washed. Lime-wash was made from limestone that had been crushed, burned, and mixed with water to make a paste.

This was then further diluted with water before application. Not only did the limewash make the garderobe look hygienically white, it also had some beneficial scientific properties. Lime's high pH level worked against bacteria and other microorganisms and its chemical composition was also helpful in reducing odours. Even so a castle's garderobe could still be an unpleasantly smelly place. To make the experience more fragrant, medieval people carried pomanders—a blend of sweet-smelling spices rolled into a wax ball—which they held directly to their noses for instant aromatic relief.

Moss, large fresh leaves or handfuls of sheep's wool were typical of the natural products used for cleaning posteriors after evacuation. More noble bottoms, however, might be washed from a dish of scented water and then patted dry with soft pads of muslin cloth.

Illuminated Manuscripts

Presenter **Patricia Lovett**

Before the invention of printing in the 15th-century, books were created and copied (many times over) by hand. Clerks and monks spent long hours, quill in hand, to make the knowledge of the world available to the ruling classes, to the few who could read. Knowledge represented power.

It could take years to create a full manuscript and these were consequently expensive and valuable items. To proclaim their worth and to entertain their patrons, manuscripts were most often adorned with painted decoration; a mixture of abstract patterns, images from daily life and allegorical scenes. Such manuscripts were richly colourful; using bright pigments. The illustrations, being on the inside pages of a closed book, have been fully protected from light over the centuries and, as a consequence, their vibrance has survived to this day. Moreover they were painted on treated animal skins (parchment or vellum), materials that preserve remarkably well over time.

Parchment is made from sheepskin and vellum is made from calfskin. Whilst vellum was perfectly useful for some manuscripts, parchment was compulsory for use in legal and state documents. If you try to make an alteration on a parchment document, it will show—the skin delaminates. Whereas you can scratch out a mistake on a piece of vellum and cover it up with virtually no tell-tale evidence.

The reason the finer books were known as 'illuminated' manuscripts was not on account of their bright colours but because of the extensive use of gold. Pages included a lavish application of gold leaf, which when seen in flickering candlelight, reflected the warm glow of the candles. This was the illumination they saw and it shimmered as if the book itself was producing the light—a metaphor for the knowledge within. In order to amplify the reflective properties of the gold, the leaf was laid over little mounds so that, like a diamond, the light hit it at various angles to make it sparkle. These raised areas were created with gesso, a substance made from rabbit-hide glue and chalk. As the gold leaf is applied over the sticky gesso, it is polished to its ultimate gleaming brightness with a special tool, having a smooth stone at its tip. This 'burnished' gold delivered a thrilling effect. It not only reflected the value of the manuscript, it also reflected the value of the person who owned it.

Medieval Paints

Presenter **Sarah Preston**

Medieval people loved colour. The medieval world was full of colour—bright, often gaudy, vibrant colour. It was not the drab, de-saturated, grey world that is portrayed in films. Kaleidoscopic rainbows of coloured light shone through stained-glass windows. Medieval art shows us people, of all classes, wearing highly colourful clothing. Furniture, objects and buildings were painted. Few organic materials—such as wood or textiles—survive from the period. However when they do, they reveal traces of strong colour that has long since faded. Castles were covered in plaster and painted with elaborate decoration on the inside. All this has washed away (once the roof goes, time and weather do their worst) and we are left with the sterile stone skeletons of these once opulent fortress dwellings. Our perceptions of the medieval world are distorted, when we only see it in shades of grey. By contrast, we are the grey ones.

At Guédelon in France, they have been building an authentic replica of a 13th-century castle from scratch. In this film Sarah Preston, an expert on the craft techniques of the period, demonstrates how medieval paint was made and uses it to decorate an interior wall of one of the rooms at Guédelon. She shows how pigments could be mined from the castles own building material. In this case it is sandstone with a high iron oxide content. This produces ores that contain ochre; a bright yellow earth pigment. The ore is crushed and pounded to make a fine powder, which is then put in a solution with water and sieved to remove larger particles. The ochre particles are finer and remain in the solution, which is then left to dry, creating a cake of raw colour.

Pounded to powder once more, the yellow pigment is then heated. At different temperatures the pigment transforms into a wide spectrum of different hues—browns, reds, oranges and purples. This palette of pigments is then turned into paint by mixing with raw eggs and tree sap. Other pigments, of course, could be produced from either different mineral sources or plant sources.

Interior castle walls were decorated in several ways. Some walls had plain colour, others had 1/3 or 2/3 of plain colour and the rest painted with intricate, repeating patterns. In important rooms such as the great hall, artists painted murals of delicate foliage or of scenes representing daily life. Castles were not just military citadels, they were also where the nobility lived. Here they displayed their wealth and status with luxurious furnishings, decorations and colour.

A close up of Hilary Merrill's custom belt quiver in a scene from the Hands on History film Horse-archers.

Horse-archers

Presenter **Hilary Merrill**

The armies of Moscow were predominantly cavalry armies. They fought with lances, sabres, javelins and bows. The enemies of Moscow, from the Golden Horde to the Tatar Khanate, also fought with sabres, lances, javelins and bows. Horse-archers were extremely versatile troops, who could switch weapons in an instant, according to the needs of the immediate tactical situation. For the initial attack, the weapon of choice was the bow. This was a composite recurve bow, made from horn, sinew, wood and glue. There are a lot of trade-offs in bow design and every culture produced its own distinctive styles. One advantage of a composite recurve bow is that it could be made shorter than an equivalently powered wooden bow and shorter bows were more manageable on horseback.

Moscow's horse-archers rode faster horses than the Mongol horses of the Golden Horde. Moscow's horses needed more maintenance and logistical support on long campaigns, but this was no problem for the regular border patrols, working from a fortified base, who kept Moscow safe. Horse-archers could deploy quickly and strike swiftly.

As they galloped towards the enemy, horse-archers loosed arrow after arrow in the hope of breaking formations. The secret to being able to shoot bursts of arrows was the techniques they developed for rapid re-loading (a process called 'nocking'). In the film Hilary Merrill of the California Centaurs, a professional horse-archery instructor, shows how it is done. A key element of these techniques is the horse-archer's use of a special ring, worn on the thumb of the string-hand.

In battle horse-archers had to be able to shoot at many angles; forwards, to the side and behind. They also had to be ambidextrous and shoot the bow both right- and left-handed. In the swirling confusion of a cavalry skirmish, an enemy could be coming at you from any direction. A common tactic, when feigning retreat, was to turn in the saddle and shoot behind as they rode away to regroup. This has become known as the 'Parthian shot' but the tactic was in use long before the Parthians so famously used it at the Battle of Carrhae (53 BCE). Another shot was the jarmaki, in which the archer drew the bowstring behind his head. It is reminiscent of the pool shot, in which the player holds the cue behind his back. In both instances the action permits shots at awkward angles, which could not otherwise be achieved.

Riding in formations and controlling horses at speed, whilst not holding the reins, required an extraordinarily high level of skill and training for both archers and horses, not to mention the additional weapon skills that horse-archers developed with lance, sword, javelin and bow. Horse-archers were elite troops.

Top image: Melting lead to make cast lead balls. ***Middle image:*** *The matchlock firing mechanism.* ***Bottom image:*** *The bardiche axe (a gun rest and weapon) is slung over the shoulder of one of the presenters from the Hands on History film Streltsy.*

Streltsy

Presenter **Gordon Summers**

In 1550 Tsar Ivan (IV) the Terrible created a corps of marksmen known as the Streltsy. Streltsy means 'shooters'. Their principal weapon was the arquebus—a smoothbore, long-barreled gun, fired from the shoulder, which was the forerunner of the musket. Although the Streltsy are most famed for their significant role in leading the advance of Ivan's army at the Battle of Kazan (1552), arquebus-men had existed in Moscow's armies for some time before. Individual Boyars (landed nobility) had frequently included detachments of arquebus-men in their feudal militia.

By the time of the Siege of Kazan, around 3,000 Streltsy had been recruited. 1,000 of them, 'chosen-men', formed Ivan's elite personal infantry guard. By the end of the century there were as many as 40,000 Streltsy in the Tsar's army. They were the nucleus of what was to become a full-time Muscovite army, replacing the system of feudal levies. The pay for this new professional army was extremely low. However, they received other compensations. Streltsy, and their families, lived in purpose-built settlements (slobody), created by the state and received stipends of bread and money from the state treasury. In addition some Streltsy were given grants of land, which they were permitted to farm.

In this film, Gordon Summers demonstrates how an arquebus works. From loading, to priming, to shooting; it was an elaborate and relatively lengthy process. Even for an expert it took considerable time compared to the instantaneous shots available with modern firearms. Another aspect of arquebus use was that, because the barrel was enormously long and heavy, it required a forked rest stuck into the ground to steady it for aiming. Setting it in its rest was just one more stage that took time.

Consequently, slow-loading arquebus-men were extremely vulnerable to a cavalry charge. However the Streltsy had an ingenious solution. They carried a massive bardiche axe, which doubled as a gun rest and as a weapon of last resort. The bardiche axe had a distinctively long, broad and heavyweight blade with a sweeping curve. It was a devastating slicer with the terrible power to cut down a charging horse. A Streltsy rested the barrel of his gun onto a ledge on his axe in order to steady his aim but, if after he had fired his shot, the cavalry were upon him, he could seize his bardiche in an instant. He also carried a sabre for skirmishes with other infantry.

One of the great advantages of the arquebus over its predecessor, the crossbow (which remained in use by some units), was the low cost and ready supply of ammunition. A sequence in the film shows just how quickly troops could produce lead balls. This was a relatively unskilled operation and, sitting by a campfire on the eve of a battle, individual Streltsy could produce enough ammunition for their needs the following day.

Forts and Kremlins

Presenter **Sarah Preston**

Kremlin is a Russian word meaning a 'fortress within a city'. The principal building material for medieval kremlins was the same as it was for frontier forts in the United States—logs. The dense forests growing to the north of Moscow were not only a natural defence against enemy invasions; they also offered a plentiful supply of lumber. Moscow had vulnerability on the broad, open steppe to the south, which was the natural terrain of marauding Mongol cavalry. The southern border had to be protected and Moscow did this with a network of wooden forts and kremlins.

Robust timber walls were built by joining logs horizontally on top of one another and creating a box construction around a core of rammed earth. This earth infill, which cushioned a great deal of impact force, made the walls especially strong against trebuchets. There was an ingenious way of locking the logs together; a system that allowed for pre-fabricated logs to be sent, by cart, sled or river, to a location under threat and a new fort to be erected in great haste.

Our wonderful castle expert from Guédelon in France, Sarah Preston, came to see replicas of this construction in Poland. To help her explain the clever jointing system, we recruited some expert historical woodworkers from Belarus.

Fine fellows with keen axes. Naturally many of our team were Polish, the key camera crew were German (a top team that I have worked with on several occasions) and there was myself and the Lion team from the UK. Unfortunately our Belarus axemen spoke neither English, Polish, German nor French. Together we had run out of languages, so I set up the shot with the universal language of mime. Two woodworkers were to enter in the background, carrying a long, heavy log on their shoulders, while Sarah introduced the piece in the foreground. 'Roll cameras. Action'. All was going well until I realized that the woodworkers were literally miming the action as I had showed it to them—they had a hand by their shoulders, one man behind the other, but they were not carrying the log!

Early forts had no towers, other than a gatehouse. However in the 13th-century it started to become common to build a tower, usually of red brick, within the wooden compound. Brick was used because it was more available than stone in many areas.

Even so the walls themselves continued to be constructed of timber until well into the 15th century.

Timber fortifications were often quite elaborate. One ingenious system for halting attackers, if they managed to get through the main gate, was the zakhab. This was a double wall arrangement, which forced the attackers down a corridor before they could reach a second gate for entry into the kremlin. Holes in the walls allowed the defenders to harass the enemy as they passed through.

Swords and Sabres

Presenters **Gordon Summers and Andy Deane**

There were two powerful cultural influences that shaped the development of arms and armor during the Rise of Moscow. Its geographical position meant that it was able to draw on the best traditions of both the East and the West. Sometimes this resulted in a fusion of styles, at others there were parallel tracks.

Moscow's armies relied heavily on cavalry but infantry are essential to hold ground. For this they required tough men with strong swords. The sword favoured by many of Moscow's infantry would have been equally familiar to knights and men-at-arms in France and England and other parts of Western Europe. It had a broad, double-edged blade with a simple cross-guard and a heavy circular pommel. It is what we call today an 'arming sword' or a 'knightly sword'. The popular term 'broadsword' is incorrect as many other sword types from other time-periods also had broad blades and broadsword was not a term in use at the time.

With its weighty pommel, the arming sword balanced perfectly and although it could deliver weighty blows, it was far from being a heavy sword. Both edges, and the point, could be used in a fluid system of fighting that required great agility. By the 14th-century, owing to technological improvements in iron manufacture, swords like this could also be made with much longer blades. These were called longswords and they were used with a two-handed grip. Not only did they deliver greater force, longswords allowed for the development of ever more sophisticated martial arts techniques. For all their cavalry dash, the old ways of standing firm, fighting hand-to-hand with swords, also remained part of the Muscovite way.

By contrast Moscow's cavalry favoured the shishka, a type of saber with a distinctively sweeping curve. Curved blades are better for cutting—they deliver slice to the blow. Even with a curved blade, the angle of the hilt results in the point being in direct line with the arm. It punctures just as effectively as it scythes.

When light cavalry is sent in to break up formations, it needs to keep momentum—that is cavalry's strength. It was a question of 'one cut' and onto the next; it was all about speed and movement. In most situations the shishka was a single strike weapon, using the speed and height of the horse for extra impact. Lightweight and razor sharp, the shishka cut swathes through Moscow's enemies.

The Face of Battle

Presenter **Dr Tobias Capwell**

Both the armies of Moscow and those of the Golden Horde were dominated by archers. Blizzards of arrows blew across their battlefields. Most vulnerable of all to arrows was the face and, by the early 13th-century, those who could afford

The Rus Mask

"We were so inspired by the Hands on History film The Face of Battle that we decided to make the hero unit Dmitry Donskoy (from the Rise of Moscow campaign) wear a version of this Rus mask. Years after this video was in the can, when we were working with artist Craig Mullins on the civilization art pieces, we asked him to feature this masked hero unit for the Rus image. So, the magnificent painting of the golden Rus knight (that appears on P.426) was initially inspired by Polish armorer Adam Mazier's stunning creation."

—Noble Smith
Franchise Narrative Director, World's Edge

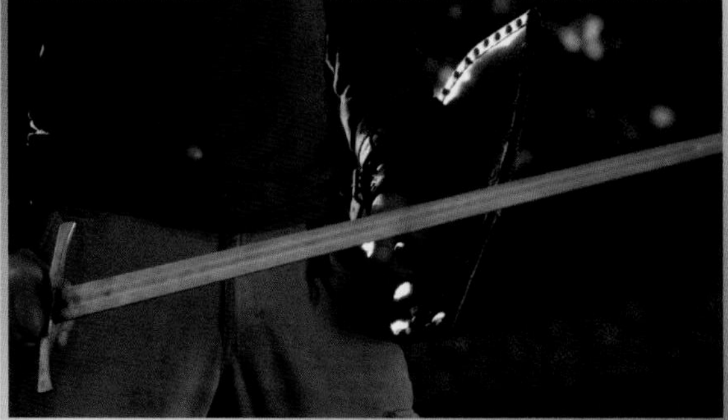

it were wearing elaborate face protection. In some cases this was a steel nose protector with an aventail of padded mail that came right up to the eyes. Such defences were effective and also presented a chilling, featureless face to the enemy. However there was another kind of armored face-mask—the anthropomorphic visor.

Forged in steel, these extraordinary pieces of armor had been influenced by a long-standing Eastern tradition of making visors as a sculptural representation of the human face. These masks covered the entire face and attached to the helmet at the top with a hinge. They had elaborate features, often with a cruelly smiling mouth.

Adam Mazier is a modern-day armorer in Poland who is a master at making these masks. At his forge he demonstrated how it was done; hammering a red-hot sheet of steel into an unflinching, resolute and stern human expression. There is astonishing artistry in his work and it is compelling to watch.

Also in Poland, though at a different location, we filmed some riders riding through the woods in anthropomorphic masks. The effect was eerie. Facing these compassionless human faces in battle would be as chilling as facing an army of robots. This was psychological warfare forged in cold steel.

To make these visors, an amourer had to have the skill and the eye of a sculptor. In fact, an anthropomorphic visor was sometimes made as an exact representation of the wearer's face. For a passing moment, I thought it might be an amusing in-joke to field an entire troop of a dozen riders all wearing my face. However common sense and budgets prevailed.

From the outset, I had wanted Dr. Tobias Capwell to be the presenter of this film but his schedule did not synchronize with our trip to Poland. Consequently I filmed him back in England, on Wimbledon Common, after we had captured the footage of Mazier at his anvil and the riders in the woodland. It all joins up remarkably well.

Not only was the anthropomorphic helmet a practical piece of equipment, not only was it psychologically intimidating to the enemy, it was also a mask to hide behind. Shielded by these visors a man could disguise his fear and, by doing so, be brave.

Chevauchée

Presenter **Patricia Gonsalves**

The chevauchée was a tactic used extensively by English armies when on campaign in France. It was a raiding campaign that swept through an enemy's territory, causing terrible destruction to the civilian population. The French word for horse (cheval) can be seen in the stem of the word and chevauchée might be loosely translated as a 'raid on horseback'. Certainly it was done swiftly; chevauchées often consisted of surprise attacks by skirmishing troops ahead of the main army.

Crops were burned, villages destroyed, houses and churches were pillaged, people were killed and terrorized. There was considerable brutality, and often atrocity. Edward III's troops, in an assault led by his archers, stormed the town of Caen in July 1346. Rampaging through the streets in a frenzy of indiscriminate slaughter, the fighting culminated in over 5,000 killed and most of the town being razed to the ground

The purpose of wreaking such havoc was to weaken the enemy economically by destroying his food supplies and seizing his wealth. Moreover it created discontent and wavering loyalty amongst his vassals—'why was their king not protecting them'? A chevauchée was also intended to provoke an adversary into pitched battle at a place and time of the invader's choosing. An army on campaign overseas had limited time and supplies before it needed to head back to its ships. There was theoretically an option for a King of France to avoid the cost and risk of a set-piece battle altogether and simply let the English exhaust their supplies before they had to head home. The provocations of a chevauchée made such a course of action unthinkable.

Fire was the principle weapon of a chevauchée. Burning fields and buildings could be seen for many miles around, spreading the terror of the raiders far and wide. In this film, Patricia Gonsalves went to meet Mark Stretton, a shooter of heavy warbows and a man with the secret of how medieval incendiary arrows were made. Using recipes from genuine medieval sources (hint: they include gunpowder and brandy) he manufactures some working examples, which they both

You can read more about incendiary weapons and medieval bows of all kinds in Mike Loades's fascinating and comprehensive book War Bows from Osprey Publishing.

Left image: *The warhorse is covered by a fabric bard and wears a chanfron (head armor) of plate.* ***Middle image:*** *A strong and fast destrier sans armor.* ***Right image:*** *A recreation of an early wrought-iron bombard banded with staves.*

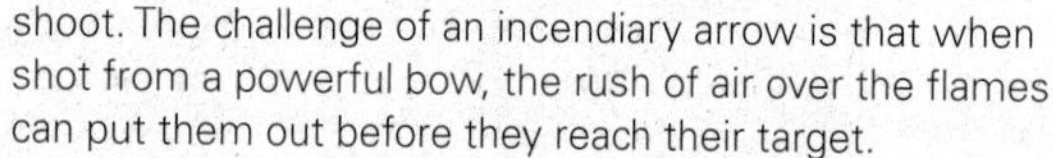

shoot. The challenge of an incendiary arrow is that when shot from a powerful bow, the rush of air over the flames can put them out before they reach their target.

The further an army goes into enemy territory without supply lines, the more vulnerable it becomes. Chevauchées were effective but they had to be managed carefully. The Great Chevauchée of 1373 saw an English army march over 550 miles from Calais to Bordeaux. Although it caused terrible destruction to French-held lands, the raiders lost a third of their men.

Warhorse

Presenter **Dr Tobias Capwell**

A knight's warhorse was his most prized possession. Warhorses were carefully bred and they required both special training and a higher level of riding skill. A knight had to fight from his warhorse, so it needed to spin, move sideways and backwards as instantly as a man could on foot.

The horses themselves were also trained to fight. They were stallions—powerful and aggressive. In a tight press they could rear and come down on an assailant pounding with their front hooves. Warhorses also performed a manoeuvre, called a capriole, in which they leapt vertically into the air before extending their hind legs in a double-barreled power kick. If a knight got surrounded by a group of infantry, a move like this might scatter them enough for him to make his getaway. Horses were immensely vulnerable on the battlefield—they were large targets. Consequently valuable warhorses weren't entirely unprotected—they wore specially designed horse armor.

For our film, we needed the right types of horses and also ones that had been trained in the appropriate way. We were very fortunate in having Dominic Sewell of Historic Equitation bring his superlative warhorses along. Warhorses had to be trained to face situations that would scare normal horses. Dominic has worked with desensitization techniques on his horses, so that they do not flinch when a lance is lowered or a sword is swung. They are unperturbed by the sound of clattering armor or the shouts of angry men. Most importantly a warhorse will charge where his rider asks him, even smashing into a mass of infantry.

The primary function of the mounted knight was the impact charge with the lance. Warhorses had immense muscle power that they collected under their haunches—power to deliver a shuddering impact. It was a terrifying and formidable force. There was no better person to demonstrate this power than veteran jouster Dr. Tobias Capwell, who also happens to be a world-renowned medieval scholar and the curator of Arms and Armor at The Wallace Collection, in London. Toby donned his armor, mounted his warhorse and charged at a slab of concrete fixed to a very solid wooden post. We wanted an image to show the forces at work when a knight uses the weight and speed of his horse to drive home his weapon and we filmed it in slow motion.

Chivalrous knights were by definition horse warriors. That was their heritage and their identity; that was how they saw themselves. However during the 100-years-war, the English began to dismount their knights to fight on foot. These tactics were successful, even against larger numbers. The French continued the old ways for a long time but, eventually, they too began to dismount their knights for battle more and more. Nevertheless, the knight on a proud and fierce warhorse remains one of the most enduring symbols of the medieval era.

Medieval Guns

Presenter **Dr. Sally Herriott**

The first sounds of gunfire at a major European battle were heard at the Battle of Crécy (1346) at the very beginning of the 100-Years-War. They came from English guns. By the last decades of this long, drawn-out conflict, gunpowder weapons had developed into several types and were in widespread use, especially by French and Burgundian armies.

For siege warfare there was the bombard. This was a short-barrelled, large calibre gun that could send massive gun-stones crashing into town and castle walls with great force. Bombards gradually replaced the trebuchet; being far easier to transport, quicker to operate and delivering their wall-breaking stones with a roar and a jet of flame that also struck terror into the besieged populations.

Bombards were set up on fixed wooden trestles but longer-barrelled 15th century canon could be moved about on wheeled gun carriages. So too could the lighter multi-barrelled gun called a ribauldequin. This had long, slender barrels assembled in a horizontal row. It was fired from a single fuse and the barrels each detonated in rapid succession. The action was not quickly repeatable—in fact it took quite a long time to reload—but the scattergun fury of a blast from a ribauldequin was extremely effective as an anti-personnel weapon against both formed infantry and cavalry. Horses in particular could be greatly panicked by it.

At the battle of Castillon (1453) Lord Talbot, Earl of Shrewsbury, led the English army. He had previously been captured by Joan of Arc. On his release he had given his word (parole) that he would not bear arms against France again.

Corned gunpowder, which is an upgrade in Age IV via the University (campaign only), increases the potency of the elements (charcoal, potassium nitrate and sulfur). These ingredients were dampened, and then dried and broken up into clumps. Wetting the compounds not only made them combine more effectively, but gunpowder was safer to process this way and less likely to explode.

He led the army in battle but, good to his word, he wore no armor and carried no weapons. He rode on a white horse at the head of his troops. He was 67 years old. He was cut down in the crossfire of French guns. It is uncertain if these were ribauldequins, or canon or even handheld guns. Handheld guns, such as the hackbut (an early form of the arquebus) had also begun to see more widespread use. In all probability it was a combination of all of these. Castillon was the last land battle of the 100-years-war. The age of gunpowder had truly arrived.

Campaign Life

Presenter **Dr Robert W. Jones**

Life on campaign could be tough, involving long marches through dangerous enemy territory and always at the mercy of the elements. When English kings took their armies to France, they mostly billeted the troops in towns and villages. Sometimes the locals would be paid; more often they were turfed out of their homes forcibly in order to give a tired and hungry army, rest, shelter and food. A loud banging on the door might mean that you were going to have to give up your bed to an archer and sleep with the livestock.

Armies also made camp, particularly if they were besieging a town—an undertaking that could take months. A medieval military camp was like a small town. In addition to streets of tents, known as pavilions, in which knights slept, there were kitchens and repair shops (armor required regular maintenance), stables and feedstores and numerous other supply depots. An army on the march was a significant economic opportunity for small traders and a second army of camp followers followed the main column to set up stalls, selling goods and services, at the campsite. English soldiers were reasonably well paid by the standards of the day and anything they picked up from looting on the way added to their disposable income.

Tents, cooking pots, armor, secondary weapons (shields for instance) and food supplies all had to be transported on slow-moving wagons. It has been estimated that Edward III took in excess of one million arrows on the Crécy campaign—that is around 100 wagonloads, just for arrows! Logistics were a major issue and for a typical medieval army there would be many hundreds of wagons and pack-animals following in a baggage train that stretched for miles. The only way to be sure of fresh meat was to bring it with you on the hoof. A legion of herdsmen with their livestock followed the baggage train.

Living conditions for most were rugged; recognizable to ordinary troops across the ages. However for knights and nobles, life on campaign could be a luxury experience. They had large, roomy pavilions, which were fitted out with every conceivable home comfort. As well as fine silk hangings and soft linens for their beds, a significant amount of furniture was carried on the baggage train. An inventory of Edward III's Crécy campaign tells us, among other things, that that he brought with him two portable thrones, 98 pairs of shoes and 100 chamber pots! All of this came at a cost—the cost of mobility. Although skirmishing troops could range far

ahead, the main army had to remain reasonably close to its baggage train; the army's crucial life-support system that also needed guarding.

Arrowmaking

Presenter **Patricia Gonsalves**

English armies relied heavily on the mass use of longbow archers during the 100-year-war. This necessitated considerable logistical organization to ensure they had adequate arrow supplies. Medieval arrows were, compared to the musket balls that superseded them, extremely expensive pieces of ammunition. That was because they were skilled-labour intensive and required multiple materials. A person who makes arrows is called a fletcher. In this film, Patricia Gonsalves, a professional archer, met up with John Potter, a fletcher who makes medieval war arrows, using only traditional tools, methods and materials, to discover just how complex these arrows were

First, seasoned staves were split into 'blanks'—square lengths having the rough diameter of an arrow. These were then worked to rough shape, using different types of plane. Shafts were given a taper towards the back, making them more aerodynamic and also shaped to be round in cross-section. Throughout this process, shafts had to be checked constantly with a gauge to ensure that the diameters were consistent. Shafts were then smoothed to a fine finish using dogfish skin (medieval sandpaper) and oiled.

In the next phase, a slot is sawn at one end to receive a thin sliver of horn. This will act as reinforcement to the 'nock' (the slot that fits over the bowstring). Without such reinforcement the power of a heavy warbow might shatter the arrow on release. After gluing it in place, the nock is sawn at 90 degrees to this horn insert. A file is then used to shape the whole nock assembly into a rounded profile.

In order to prepare feathers for the fletchings (these stabilize the arrow in flight), goose feathers were clamped between two boards and the stiff quill part was shaved with a sharp knife. Feathers were applied with glue, aligning by eye alone, to the shaft. They had to be further secured by binding them with silk thread. Only then were they trimmed to shape. A compound of glue, beeswax and copper sulphate was painted on the shaft between the fletchings to deter feather mites. Batches of arrows were stored in barrels for military shipment.

Quality arrows, in the quantity needed for warfare, were not something that an archer could put together in the camp on the eve of a battle. Wagonloads of arrows were taken on campaign in quantities of a million and more. These were made in England and shipped to France. A commander never knew if the battle he was fighting was going to be the last of the campaign. He always had to be mindful that there may yet be more fighting and to ration arrow supplies accordingly.

Armor

Presenters **Dr Tobias Capwell and Fred Ryall**

From the mid 13th-century, it became possible to manufacture relatively large plates of iron. This was a new development, producing plates large enough to be domed into protective elements for the knees, elbows and shoulders. Over time, larger plates were created and 'plate armor' gradually increased to the point where it eventually covered a knight from head-to-toe.

Plate armor defends in three ways: curved surfaces deflect the force of a strike, the enhanced hardness of the metal counters penetration and the thickness of the plates both absorbs the shock of impact and makes it harder to penetrate.

Thickness, of course, translates into weight. Plate armor was worn by knights; fighting men, who had to be able to move with martial vigour. As much as they needed protection in the thick of battle, they didn't want anything that would hamper their movement. An armored knight should still be able to mount his horse unaided. Trade-offs had to be made. Armor was at its thickest over vital areas such as

Shrewsbury

"I was born in Shrewsbury, a historic market town in Shropshire, England, near the Welsh border. I learned a remarkable story about Shrewsbury's place in the history books from the Medieval Surgery video in Age of Empires IV! I have learned other things about my country and places I've lived from our games, and that's truly special."

—Emma Bridle
Director of Customer Voice, World's Edge

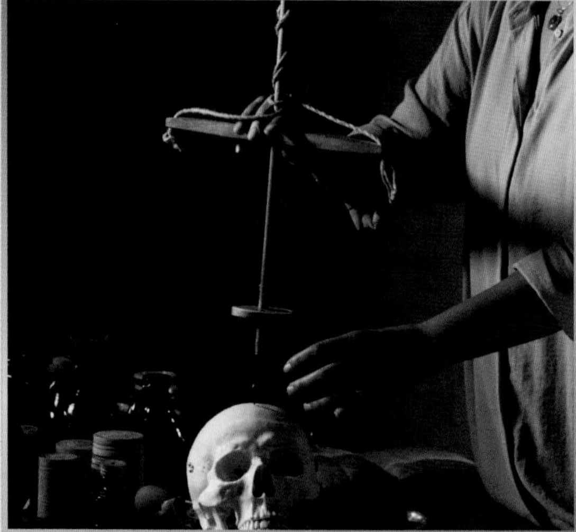

the chest and head but plates were significantly thinner, therefore lighter, over arms and legs, which were required to move quickly. Preserving stamina was also a factor in needing to keep plate armor as light as possible, whilst still offering good protection.

Not all plate armor was equal. There was a tremendous variation in quality, according to cost. Only the wealthiest knights could afford the very best, case-hardened steel armor from the best armorers in Europe. Germany and Italy were notably famous supply centres. All armor reduced the risk of mortal injury—it was a question of stacking the odds in the armored man's favour. Armor of reasonable proof against the weapons of the day was available, but not to everyone. In this film we also took a look at the brigandine—a typical armor for ordinary soldiers at this period. The brigandine offered good, though not excellent protection. It was relatively inexpensive and it was flexible, making it ideal for troops such as archers.

Plate armor was not just a defence system; the armored knight was a weapon in his own right. In close combat, a knight in full plate armor could throw himself into the thick of the fray with reasonable impunity. In his armor he had powerful mass for collision impact and, as well as his sword, mace or axe, he could use his armored elbows, knees and fists to strike an opponent with force. Armor was a defence; armor was a weapon and armor was also an expression of a knight's power and prestige. Plate armor transformed its wearer into a walking work of art. The armored knight was magnificent.

Medieval Surgery

Presenter **Dr. Saleyha Ahsan**

In this film, Emergency Medical Doctor, Dr Saleyha Ahsan, takes a look at an array of medical instruments that would have been available to the barber-surgeons attending the wounded after a medieval battle. She also reminds us that all these flesh-cutting, bone-sawing, crania-drilling devices were for use before the invention of anaesthetics. Undoubtedly there was terrible suffering. As wells as the brutality of surgery without pain relief, the horrors of battlefield wounds were compounded by the ever-present risk of infection. However there were notable successes. One such concerned the future Henry V of England.

When he was only 16-years-old, the young Prince Henry fought at the Battle of Shrewsbury (1403) and was wounded in the face by an arrow. According to his surgeon, John

Bradmore, the arrow entered his left check just above the eye-tooth and lodged 'in the back part of the bone of the head six inches deep'. Whilst continuing to ride into the fray, Prince Henry pulled out the arrowshaft, leaving the head embedded in his skull.

The most common form of helm for knights at that time was the houndskull bascinet. Its style of long-snouted visor was an especially good defence against arrows. It is therefore probable that he had lifted his visor, perhaps to issue commands in the flanking manoeuvre he was leading at the time. Even so, the power of longbows was such that a direct hit would have driven clean through the skull. What seems plausible, and which helps to explain the angle of entry, is that the arrow had ricocheted from the armor of someone close by. This would still have entered with tremendous speed and force, as was evidenced by the depth of the wound, just not as forcefully as a direct hit.

Either way, the problem subsequently was how to extract the arrowhead. If left, a fatal infection would have set in. John Bradmore designed an ingenious device for the purpose. He made a pair of tongs that, when inserted into the arrowhead's socket, screwed apart till they gripped its walls from the inside and the arrowhead could be pulled free. Before that, where the fleshy part of the face had closed over the entry wound, Bradmore had to widen it, over the course of several days, by inserting larger and larger "tents of the pith of old elder, dried well and sewed well in a clean linen cloth". These were soaked in rose honey, which contains natural antibiotics. The wound was cleansed with "a squirtillo of white wine" and dressed with a poultice of breadcrumbs, honey, barley and turpentine. Miraculously it healed completely within three weeks.

The massive counterweight trebuchet replica is one of the highlights of a visit to Warwick Castle in Warwickshire, England.

Trebuchet

Presenter **Dr Shini Somara**

A trebuchet is a large siege engine used for hurling rocks. Used in siege warfare, it sent heavy stone missiles crashing into the walls of fortifications to knock them down. Alternatively, it threw fireballs over the walls to start a conflagration within. At the Siege of Caffa (1346) trebuchets threw diseased carcasses into the town. This is thought by some historians to have been the source of the Black Death, which eventually killed more than half the population of Europe.

Constructed from heavy timbers, trebuchets consisted of a giant beam pivoting on a frame. At the rear end of the beam was a sling that held and propelled the missile. You can think of a trebuchet as a giant mechanical sling. The front end of the beam extended 2/3 in front of the pivot point, acting as a lever. There were two ways to operate this lever. The earliest trebuchets, first developed in Ancient China, were traction trebuchets. 'Tract-' is a Latin stem that means pulling (as in tractor). Traction trebuchets were operated by a team of men; all pulling together on ropes. Some featured as many as a hundred ropes.

An improvement to this was the counterweight trebuchet, developed towards the end of the 12th-century. This substituted the men on ropes with a counterweight in the form of a hopper of rocks. Apart from requiring far less manpower, the counterweight trebuchet had the advantage that range could be adjusted very precisely, simply by adding or removing stones from the hopper.

In order to winch the hopper into an elevated position, men walked in giant treadwheels, winding a rope around a central axle to pull the beam to vertical. Locked into place it required only a single person to pull on a rope to release the mechanism and let the counterweight fall. Creaking and groaning, the sling end of the beam swung upwards. At exactly the correct angle, one end of the sling slipped off a specially shaped hook and sent the missile flying.

For aim to be reliable, ammunition had to be consistent, in weight, size and shape. Stones were fashioned uniformly by chisel and hammer. As well as changing the weight in the hopper, range could also be calibrated by altering the length of the sling. To keep the sling in alignment with the beam, it travelled in a wooden channel for the first part of the throw. This channel could be moved a little to the left or right in order to line up the shot. Very small movements of the channel translated into significant distances at the end of the projectile's trajectory.

The team filmed the spectacular giant counterweight trebuchet replica at Warwick Castle in the UK. Its phenomenal power is clear to see in the film. Warwick Castle is a medieval site surrounded by other historic buildings. The channel of its trebuchet is locked into a fixed position. Adjusting it by so much as a finger's width would have risked unfortunate consequences.

The Yam

Presenter **Chris Yung**

The vast Mongol Empire was created by sword and fire; by arrowstorms, rage and terror. However it was sustained by systems, by rules and by bureaucracy. Information was power. Getting information from one end of the empire to the other at remarkable speed was the job of The Yam—the famed Mongol postal system, established by Ghengis Khan around 1200.

This system depended on relays of messengers stationed at regular intervals throughout the empire. Some were as close as 15 miles apart and a few were as far as 40 miles apart. Mongol armies moved quickly, so army intelligence had to move even faster. Once an area was subdued, it was essential to receive instant notice of any trouble brewing. Information and intelligence were everything. Yam couriers were so fast they were known as 'arrow messengers'.

Another name for The Yam was the Örtöö—it means 'checkpoint.' As identification at checkpoints riders wore a medallion—the paiza. These were sometimes made of wood, sometimes of metal. An inscription showed the status of the person sending the message. Yam stations accommodated traveling officials, senior military men, and foreign dignitaries. Diplomats were issued with a paiza as a diplomatic passport and the Mongols sent and received diplomatic missions from all over the known world.

Couriers reaching postal stations would be provided with food, water, and accommodation in addition to spare horses. Relay stations had corrals of livestock to ensure plentiful food. Tens of thousands of horses were constantly being shuttled from relay to relay. Hard galloping, day after day, was tough on the body. To support both the spine and the internal organs, messengers wore a tight wrap of cloth around their core. On top of that was either a second sash or broad leather belt. This was hung with small bells to alert the Yam stations that a messenger was approaching. It was important for his relay horse to be saddled and ready the instant he arrived.

Merchants also used the system. The Yam had pack animals as well as messenger horses. Either ox-carts or pack-mules carried goods for profitable trade, as well as for the all-essential tribute from vassal States. A universal currency further facilitated trade throughout the Empire. In addition to the silver coinage in use, Ghengis Khan introduced paper currency. This was backed by its value in silk, rather than gold.

A replica of a Mongolian signal arrow. Wind rushes through the holes and creates a whistling noise, alerting warriors to perform prearranged tactical maneuvers.

Although horses were the backbone of the system, the Yam also used boats along rivers. By the end of 13th C in China, it has been estimated that the Yam had: 1,400 postal stations; 50,000 horses; 6,700 mules; 1,400 oxen; 400 carts and 6,000 boats.

The Yam was a rapid communication system that, by means of organized relay stations, incorporated a rapid messenger service, a goods delivery service, a trading currency, diplomatic immunity and safe travel. It was the glue that held the Mongol Empire together.

War Drums and Signal Arrows

Presenter **Justin Ma**

Mongol armies used sophisticated battlefield tactics. They could encircle an enemy or attack from the flanks. Most famously they employed a frontal manouevre called the tulmugha. For this, horse-archers assembled to the right and left of the enemy line. Alternate squadrons then swept across the front of the line, each switching their start positions with each pass. An attack like this required co-ordination (it also required the archers to be ambidextrous). Battlefields are places of tremendous noise and confusion, so how did Mongol generals control their armies? How did they order attacks and withdrawals?

Visual signals, using flags and standards on tall poles were important devices for showing direction but it was large gongs and thunderous war drums that called troops to look in the direction of the banners. The Mongol war-drum was called the guangu. It was often massive and mounted on a cart. In these circumstances it was set up so that the faces of the drum were upright. Drummers stood and beat it rhythmically with their arms raised above their head. One first hand account describes a drummer striking "as hard as his strength and breath allow him to do."

It was an athletic performance, generating a sound that urged warriors to action.

Filming in the golden light of an early California morning, our ensemble of drummers beat out rousing rhythms that stirred the whole crew and which, we were told, could be heard from a very long way away. These were ancient sounds and rhythms that set the blood pumping and that would undoubtedly give courage to a man needing to ride into danger. Making a guest musical appearance with our drummers, was Justin Ma on the gong. Justin is an internationally respected authority on Asian archery and its history. He was there primarily to shoot signal arrows for us. As the founder of the Bay Area Asian Archery group, he also brought along many of its members to shoot volleys.

A useful method for a commander to communicate with his generals at different points of the battlefield was to send them a message tied to a signal arrow. These were blunt arrows with a whistling head that announced their arrival. Messages could be shot in relays along the line for considerable distances and the messages attached could convey quite complicated commands. A signal arrow was faster than a runner and faster even than a horse.

Used in conjunction, war drums and signal arrows, together with flags and banners, provided a complex and versatile battlefield signaling system. However once an attack was launched, it was the sound of the drums that rolled over the battlefield spreading dread amongst an enemy and inspiring young Mongol warriors to acts of reckless heroism. It was the sound of Mongol thunder and it was to be feared.

Building the Mongol Bow

Presenter **Lukas Novotny**

The Mongols were famed for the prowess of both their horse-archers and their infantry archers. Their bows were what are known today as 'composite recurve bows'. 'Composite' refers to the fact that a combination of different materials was used in their construction and 'recurve' to their geometry—both elements combined to make a powerful spring.

Composite recurve bows of different shapes and sizes occur in several other cultures, each with their own unique regional style. However the basic elements were the same for all these bows. The materials included a wooden core—the skeleton of the bow—which was jointed so that it could be fashioned with very strong curves. Curves that bend away from the archer are called reflex and the ones that curl towards the archer are called deflex. When you have both reflex and deflex it is called a recurve bow.

Supporting this extreme geometry were laminations of two vital materials—sinew and horn. Sinew—the dried and shredded tendons of animals such as cattle or deer—was layered on the back of the bow (the part that faces away from the archer). These fibres were especially strong in tension. They aided the spring of the bow and also prevented it all breaking apart; they acted as tendons. Strips of water-buffalo horn were laid on the belly (inside surface) of the bow. These stored considerable energy in compression—they were the muscles of the bow.

By far the most important ingredient, without which this technology would not be possible, was the glue. The best glue derived from the swim bladder of the sturgeon, a fish found in the rivers of Central Asia. Glue was said to be the blood of the bow. It had to withstand tremendous stresses. Even when dry, it had to remain flexible and not brittle. This clever glue technology was the secret of composite bows. Both the recurve geometry and the composite materials worked together to make the limbs of the bow spring forwards more quickly on release—far faster than was possible with a simple wooden bow. The faster the limbs return, the faster the string moves and so the bow propels the arrow with greater force.

Bowmaker Lukas Novotny and Asian archery authority Justin Ma load their replica of the Mongolian multiple bow crossbow.

In this film world-renowned champion horse-archer and composite bow maker, Lukas Novotny, shows Justin Ma, an internationally recognized expert on Chinese and Mongolian archery, the intricate process of how these bows were made, and he recruits Justin to help him with some of the messier steps. Lukas also demonstrated some horse archery and because we filmed these scenes near where I lived at the time in California, he is using my horse!

Multiple Bow Crossbow

Presenters **Lukas Novotny and Justin Ma**

Mongol armies were famed for their fast-moving horse-archers and their mighty heavy cavalry. What it is perhaps less well known is that they were also supremely adept at siege warfare. They were masters at building and using trebuchets and the great wagons in their baggage trains were capable of transporting a lot of heavy equipment over vast distances. This was a versatile army that could wage war in many ways.

Aside from trebuchets, the Mongols also experimented with other siege weapons, recruiting Chinese engineers to design and build all manner of ingenious devices for them. Giant siege crossbows, which could also be used on the battlefield, were a particular favourite. In the Wu Jing Zong—a military manual from the Song Dynasty, written in the 11th century—there are some remarkable examples. Some of these giant crossbows have two bows linked in parallel, doubling the force of the shot. What is even more surprising is an illustration of a crossbow with three bows. Most intriguingly, two of the bows are facing forward but the third one faces backwards. No examples of such a device exist archaeologically. However we wanted to find out if such a contraption could possibly work.

The obvious man to build it was Lukas Novotny, an expert bowmaker. Justin Ma, an authority on Asian archery, managed to source a copy of the Wu Jing Zong, which he brought along to discuss the designs with Lukas. My small contribution was that I already had a good replica of a Han dynasty cast-bronze crossbow trigger mechanism. Lukas built the stock and fitted it with bows and with my trigger. The question was how could all the bows be linked to work together.

As Lukas explained, the reversed bow helps, like a lever, to draw the paired forward-facing bows when cranking them back but when the crossbow is shot the reversed bow would act to put the brakes on, slowing the whole thing down. 'The only way it would work is with pulleys and I see no pulleys' Lukas said. Fortunately Justin, fluent in Chinese, had done his homework and he had found a text entry on a different page (associated with the double-bow version), which referred to the use of a 'rope and axle' (literal translation). "That means pulleys—they definitely had pulleys", Justin exclaimed.

"That changes everything," chimed a relieved Lukas. "Now we can build something because with a pulley we can reverse the direction of pull. Now we have a force multiplier that can harness the power of all three bows". Unless you have a master's degree in engineering, you may have to watch the film to understand fully how it all works but once you see it, it is obvious. You'll also have to watch the film to see how well it performed. It was a 'heart in your mouth' sort of a day.

Mongol Heavy Cavalry

Presenter **Andy Deane**

By definition, heavy cavalry are shock troops; heavily armored horsemen who smashed into an enemy to break up his formations. In addition to squadrons of lighter cavalry, such as horse-archers, the Mongol army had a high percentage of heavy cavalry. The heavy cavalry also carried bows, which they shot as they advanced but, instead of shooting and turning from the enemy, they then sheathed their bows, slipped their lances from their shoulders and went piling into an enemy.

On-Location Filming

"Taking crews around the world to film the cultures we represent and the locations we tell stories about is such a unique and amazing thing. Learning more about the lives of the peoples who came before us from manuscripts to mail making brings this period to life like nothing else I've seen in a game."

—Emma Bridle
Director of Customer Voice, World's Edge

In order to give themselves reasonable protection when making such direct contact, the Mongol Heavy Cavalry were fully armored—even their horses could be armored. The type of armor they used is called lamellar armor. In this film, Andy Deane from the Royal Armories in the UK shows us some examples and explains its ingenious construction. The scales for lamellar armor could be made from either metal or thick leather (this was treated to make it tougher). Lamellar armor had a number of advantages for the Mongol cavalryman. It was extremely flexible and reasonably lightweight, allowing him to use a full range of weapons, including the bow. Another advantage was that it was easy to repair, something that could be accomplished by relatively unskilled hands back at camp.

The first contact of an impact charge was most often made with a lance, using the speed and weight of a galloping horse to drive home its skewering point. After that first strike, the cavalryman could find himself vulnerably deep amongst the ranks of his foe. In such circumstances, he had ready recourse to sword and mace but for the Mongol heavy cavalryman, there was still one option left with his lance. It had a hook, close to its head. John of Plano Caprini, who wrote the History of the Mongols (Ystoria Mongalorum) during the 1240s, was especially impressed by the Mongol use of hooked lances to unseat opponents during cavalry actions. There is also an account of a battle in 1231 where a Korean general was plucked from his saddle by a hooked lance.

In mêlée situations every Mongol was expert with the sword. However, the favored weapon for hand-to-hand fighting from horseback was the mace—a brutal, no-nonsense, metal-headed club. Some Mongol warriors carried a 'great mace'. The great mace was a longer-hafted version that was used with a double-handed grip. As Andy demonstrates in the film, riding in at full pelt and rising in his stirrups to bring the weight of the mace down onto his target with two hands, a strike with the great mace from horseback had a terrifying and intimidating power.

Mongol Music

Presenters **Nature G and Uljmuren De**

This film is dedicated to the memory of one of its presenters, Nature G, who died in 2019. At the age of 29, he was tragically young. We filmed with him and his band co-member Uljmuren De in the summer of 2018. As well as being a creative force, Nature was a deep, thoughtful and gentle man. It was a privilege to meet him and work with him.

Nature Ganganbaigal, known to his many fans as Nature G, founded the 'nomadic folk metal' band Tengger Cavalry in

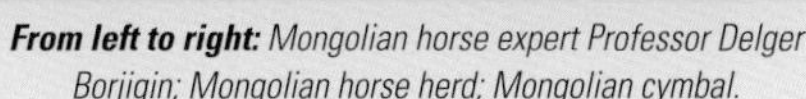

***From left to right:** Mongolian horse expert Professor Delger Borjigin; Mongolian horse herd; Mongolian cymbal.*

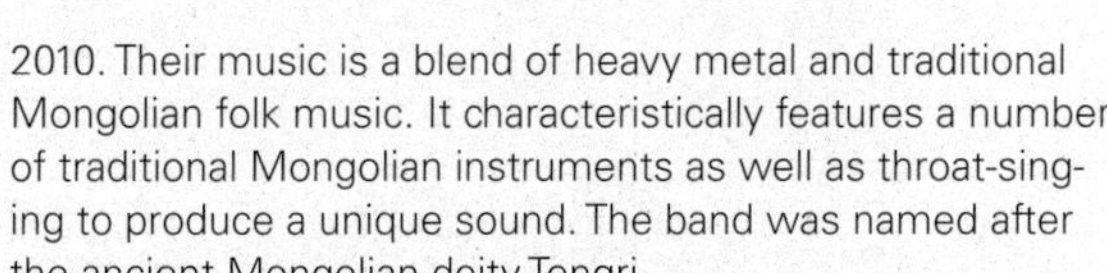

2010. Their music is a blend of heavy metal and traditional Mongolian folk music. It characteristically features a number of traditional Mongolian instruments as well as throat-singing to produce a unique sound. The band was named after the ancient Mongolian deity Tengri.

For the film they left their electric guitars at home and brought only their traditional instruments along. In addition to these, we were treated to virtuoso performances of throat-singing. Both Nature and Uljmuren are passionate about the music of their Mongol heritage and they speak about it both knowledgeably and poetically.

Music was a principal way in which a unifying cultural identity could be preserved amongst a nomadic people. Kublai Khan was especially interested in the instruments of the Mongol Empire. In 1264 he had musical instruments collected from all the provinces. When he moved the State capital to Beijing in the 14th-century, he established a great state orchestra there. Many of the themes of Mongolian music were centered on horses and incorporated sounds and rhythms that imitated the sounds of a horse. The morin khuur, known as the horse-head fiddle, features a carving of a horse's head and its strings were made from horsehair. It remains a symbol of Mongolian national identity, recognized by UNESCO as an object of cultural heritage.

Although the sounds of the morin khuur are hypnotic, throat-singing is undoubtedly the most distinctive aspect of Mongolian music. When you walk in the mountains or the snowlands, in the forests or the grasslands, you can hear the thunder of galloping hooves or a rushing river from far away. You can hear the wind. In a natural soundscape it is not just one pitch, it is different pitches and that is what throat-singing evokes. Traditional Mongol music is the music of the natural world. Mongol lived in harmony with the natural world—that was their freedom.

Mongol Horses

Presenter **Professor Delger Borjigin**

One of several reasons that the Mongols were feared was because large armies had the reputation of appearing from seemingly nowhere. Mongol horses had several natural advantages that made these surprise attacks possible. They were stocky, native ponies that were extremely hardy. This meant that they could survive on sparse and rough grazing, avoiding the need to bring feed for the horses on the march. Other armies, using different types of horses, were slowed on campaign because they had to keep pace with slow wagon trains, hauling the hay and the oats to feed their mounts. Mongol horses lived entirely on whatever they could find on the trail. Also their tough hooves didn't need horseshoes. They were low maintenance.

Each warrior had a string of horses (5 or 6) that followed each other. Moreover an order from Ghengis Khan forbade horses to wear bridles on the march. This meant that the horses could graze naturally whilst on the move—each one stopping to graze for a few moments and then catch up with the others. The whole army never, ever stopped moving. Mongol warriors slept in the saddle and changed horses frequently by leaping from one saddle to the other, not wasting time to set their feet on the ground. It was this relentless, constant day and night, stop-for-nothing advance, which so often caught enemies by surprise. Nobody expected an army to cover that much ground that quickly.

When crossing rivers, the Mongols swam across with their horses, packing their clothes into an oiled leather bag to keep them dry—nothing slowed them. Mongol horses also have a distinctive way of moving that made them fast travellers. They have a natural 5th gait. Most horses have four gaits—walk, trot, canter and gallop. Mongol horses had an additional very, very fast walk, called in English an amble. The horses can keep it up hour after hour, covering considerably more ground in a day than a horse that walks, trots and canters, each for short periods. This 5th gait is also exceptionally comfortable and non-fatiguing for the rider, leaving him with far more stamina and fighting energy at the end of a long ride.

On the battlefield, Mongol horse weren't as fast as taller grain-fed horses but they were swift enough; they also had another advantage. Mongol horses lived semi-wild in natural herds, not in pens or stables. Herds respond to a predator with flight but stampeding horses never bump into each other—unlike a panicked crowd of humans. This enhanced spatial awareness and co-operation found in wild horse herds is called synchrony and it had an application on the battlefield. For horse-archers in particular, who are using both hands to shoot their bows, there is a great benefit in a squadron of horses staying together, without collision, perhaps following a single leader to direct their attack. Shaggy little ponies they may be but Mongol horses were a key factor in Mongol military success.

The Art of Craig Mullins

This section presents a very special look at the series of artworks that Craig Mullins created for Age of Empires IV. For over 30 years, Craig has been a leading pioneer of digital art and illustration, working in the form since the earliest days of Photoshop 1.0. He worked at Industrial Light & Magic in the 1990s before becoming a full time freelance artist, and has since produced art for a long list of major movie and videogame franchises. In addition to an interview about the Age of Empires images, Craig has provided some drafts and sketches, which are presented alongside some commentary by the artist himself.

Can you describe a typical day during your work on the Age of Empires IV project for us?
My schedule is a little bit strange. I think a lot of people are regimented into workdays, then evenings, then weekend then more workdays. I have a more 24/7 schedule, where I mix everything in like a stir-fry, where I'm constantly working, I'm constantly playing and I'm always getting up—I never work for more than an hour at a time, otherwise my concentration goes away. If I'm having problems on a certain thing I'll go out in the yard and hit golf balls around. So in my typical work day I try not have anything that I really have to do at a particular time, because I may not be in the frame of mind to do that thing, so I'll do what I'm in the mood for. I find that work goes a lot easier that way.

How much time do you dedicate to each of the AoE IV pieces in total? Did any particular image take longer to complete?
I would say around 50 hours each, some of them less, some of them more. The huge poster key art image (shown on pages 2-3 of this book) took a long, long time. We went through so many different iterations of it, and I kept on repainting the characters over and over. That's kind of typical of the way that I work. Most people think about starting an image that then becomes more and more refined as it goes

"These were the original ideas that I sent to Han [Randhawa] when we were first discussing the series. You can see between numbers six and seven, that's where I tried the idea of each character being different, but having them be in the exact same pose. It would have been exactly the same composition with the same shapes over and over. Then Han very simply said, "you see number three, I like that one!" It had a wide angle lens and was very heroic, so that's where we headed. I knew Han was right, that we need to show the civilizations in a heroic way, so using that lower angle is something you just have to do."

"Playing with the textures on this one was so much fun. The swooshes and the architecture motif at the bottom cover up a lot of nice stuff going on in the ground. Trying to render the elephant's armor to make it look real was very difficult. I don't think I ever quite got the golden stuff on the side quite right. I was happy with the red flag above the elephant, though. There's actually pure white underneath it—there's one layer of think paint over it, and some of the white pokes through. That's another technique from Leyendecker, where he would paint strokes but deliberately leave white in between them to create a stylized specularity. It reads like specularity because the white underneath is absolutely flat. For something to read as specular there has to be an absence of texture—the darkest darks and the brightest brights need to be completely flat."

on, and the last fifty per cent of working on it is dealing with smaller and smaller details. But I find that if I take what I've learned from working about half way through it, and put that back into starting over again, then when I come back to that fifty per cent point it'll be much further head and it'll be much more solid. The ideas will be much clearer. So I'm using the experience that I'm gaining to go through the process from beginning to end as many times as time will allow. That means I repaint a head, for example, probably ten or twenty times, as opposed to doing it just once, and then painting eyebrows for the remainder of the time that I have. This is because I really think that God lives in the gesture as opposed to the details.

"The Delhi Sultanate was probably the only one where I started without an obvious need for a strong central figure—I guess everyone is in love with the elephants, so it made sense for the elephant to be the main figure here. I really like this one. The more I go back and look at the drafts, the more I think we should have just used some of them. They're really more evocative to me than some of the finals images."

"In the end I just wasn't happy with this one and decided to go back and put more architecture in it. Something about the sky just wasn't working for me."

How do you go about preparing to start a piece? We'd really like to hear about your process of historical research for pieces like these.

I try to start by imaging a scenario that might not be obvious. When you think of "Mongol warrior," you don't really think of the image of a girl riding down a hillside in deep snow—it's not something you'd ordinarily come up with. But a lot of it is just sketching, and being very open to anything that might come out of it. I'm very creative procedurally in how I work. As Bob Ross might say, I'm very open to happy accidents. Something will happen and the painting talks back to me and suggests something further, and soon I'm starting over again on an even better idea. It can just start out by me trying to get as familiar as I can with the characters and their overall shapes, just doing very simple—almost caricature-like—drawings of what the characters are. For example with a Mongol warrior, the shape of the hat they would wear and how it turns under, and how it would look from different angles, or the clothes she'd have on, or the shape of her head—is it round or more boxy? So I'm just exploring to see how simple I can make things. That makes it easier to compose with and turn it around in space.

Usually, in doing all of this playing around, ideas come out of it. It's like when writers talk

"I totally changed the background after the first drafts of this one. The original landscape was something I just made up, and—not being God or a geologist—it shows. The credibility of the landforms wasn't there. So that's why I changed to something based in reality, and I eventually found this place in Scotland that worked well for it."

about when a characters get developed to a point where it starts talking back—they'll write a line and the character will tell them, "Well I wouldn't say that, dummy." So it does kind of come alive a bit.

At what stage of Age of Empires IV's development did you begin work on the art pieces? Did you see much of the game before starting?
I'd gotten to see almost nothing of the game. The game engine in its alpha stage isn't easily accessed. It's not like the old days when you could just download an executable and fire it up. I probably should have tried to get access, but I don't think it really occurred to me. In general, I try to stay away from games as much as I can these days. I got sucked into Left 4 Dead in 200 and became a competitive player, which took up all my time. From that point on I said, "no more games." Sometimes I think, "I'm just going to fire it up to see what the graphics look like," but now I don't even let myself install it. My dad also got semi-addicted to Age of Empires III. He played it for two hours every night for about five years.

Seeing more of the game early on could have helped, but it could also have maybe limited what I did. I remember way back, one of the first game artworks I ever made was for a universe expansion of Bungie's Marathon. It wasn't a high definition game, so I had to imagine how it would look like if it was real. And that's also how I approached Age of Empires IV, but the AoE series is based on real people, so I started out from that standpoint as opposed to starting out from the game.

"This sketch was the first try at the English archer, and Han [Randhawa] wrote back and said, "I'm not feeling it. It looks like a person in cosplay out in someone's back yard on a random Saturday." You can really see that this reads like an English archer—it's basically the same thing as the next sketch, but there's actually such a difference in the shapes and it gives the whole thing a very different expression."

"Another battle is in how much detail to show in the shadow—looking at this figure, and the shadow beneath his right arm... How dark should that be? The shadows lower in the body are being cast onto darker materials, so they're definitely darker. But I could have gone a lot denser with some of the shadow areas, and then the shapes would become stronger. But you lose the feeling of light, because you don't have light coming into those shadows. The lighter you make the shadows, the more you reduce the graphic read of the image, in exchange for much richer detail in the shadows. So it's a tight balance that goes back and forth."

"This one has a very brutal head and I tried to emphasize the roundness of it by making the lighting on that sphere quite classical, but completely interrupted by the whole structure of the eye. Keeping it really simple is essential, because there's two different materials and colors here, but the actual form is uninterrupted—keeping it so simple gives it a strength. I think a lesser way of working would be to render all the little folds in the skin and all the highlights on the mail, and lose that sphere in the process. In the next full draft I think it lost that shape and form that is so apparent in the sketch, but in the final version I think I got it back. The way I treated the hair, I think you can feel the head underneath it."

"This was the initial sketch for the Chinese. The shapes here that make the character heroic are all a bit caricatured, and in fact all of these pieces have an aspect of caricature. No human male can ever really have those proportions. You can see in these sketches how bold everything is, and getting those readable shapes first is everything. Part of finishing an image is avoiding rendering things to the point where that graphic read goes away."

It's not at all common to commission eight or nine pieces of highly detailed key art for a game. How did it come to be decided to create a unique piece for each of the eight civilizations?

Microsoft was happy with what I did on the main key art, which was the first image I worked on for Age of Empires IV, and they wanted to use me more. They wanted as many assets as they could get from me, and I was happy to do them. And well, there were just a lot of civilizations, so it made sense.

What do you feel ties these pieces together and makes them consistent?

I was after variety above all else. I wanted them to look different. They needed to fit with the previous work I'd done for Age of Empires. So they had to be lush, nineteenth century, romantic, with overripe fantasy textures... So those are really the elements they share that bring them all together. But I was really trying to make each one different.

You've said in interviews that you no longer want to work long hours to hit tight deadlines. Is that something you've been able to get away from in recent years?

Yeah it has been. Microsoft were very generous with the terms, and that included the time I would have. I probably had too much time, because I didn't jump into it really, really quickly. I had such ambition for the series of images—I really wanted to make something of the level that you would see in a Paris salon. I researched what goes into those paintings, and not only would it not be only one single artist, but they would have a whole studio working on them, hiring models and doing sketches. They would work on one image full time for a year. I'm trying to do things out of my head in much less time. So I think my ambition was way too high, and I think the paintings could have come out better if I had been realistic with the time and budgeted it better.

Even though it seemed like a ton of time, these are really involved images. Some of them I repainted entirely from scratch. I'd spend a month painting it and then just start over, much to the surprise of Han [Randhawa], the Art Director at World's Edge. The painting always came out better for it, and I think all the final paintings would come out much better still if I were to start over on all them now. I understand them better now, I know where I screwed up and how to solve certain things better. But time runs out, and at some point you have to just say, "it's done."

Was anything different about working on these pieces compared to working on previous Age of Empires games?

The first Age of Empires game I worked on was Age of Empires III, and that was for Ensemble Studios, not through Microsoft, though the terms were still very generous. Then at some point that changed, and advertising agencies got involved and for a while it was a disaster. The wanted me to collage some photos together, and I was asking, "why hire me to do this?" But that's what they wanted, so I did it. Since then it's been nothing like that, though. Working on the Definitive Editions and now Age of Empires IV, it's been amazing. Everyone I've worked with has been great, and they've protected me from all internal wrangling. It's just been fantastic.

"These black and white studies were done in a wonderful program called HeavyPaint, which is an excellent tool for setting limitations that make you a much stronger artist. There's no nonsense that you can hide behind—it's just drawing and shape."

"I really struggled with this one to avoid the same old tropes. And when I got some feedback, they said he looked evil, when they wanted it to look heroic, but badass. They wanted it to look "wise, but like he could carve a hole through you." I backed off a little to make him a bit less sinister, but when it's bottom-lit like this it's actually hard not to look sinister. We did need something to set the character apart, so that's why I made his mortar very prominent, and also its light source is very strong, to help differentiate him, making him more than just some guy in a cape and shoulder armor."

"Most of the time you're taught to paint going from very large shapes to small shapes. This was an attempt to do a drawing first and then fill in the shapes—not paint from large to small, but stay small the whole time. Digital art is so completely plastic that you can change anything at any time, and that can lead to a lack of consideration at the very beginning. This is one of the reasons why I like to get half way through and then start over again. Sometimes you can take the painting you have and just paint over it, but sometimes it's so noisy that you can't really see the bigger shapes as they should be. So this little sketch is to me a way of subverting everything that I do normally. I tried to do the opposite and see what happened."

"This is one that I really spent a lot of time on. I repainted her face at least a dozen times trying to get it just exactly right. I actually kind of ran out time with the horse. I tried to get the feeling of reflectivity in the horse, and there's something off about the lens on it compared to the rider; something in the perspective is not perfectly correct—there are two different lenses working here—but I'm not an expert on horse anatomy at all. So it was difficult to paint horses in unusual angles being lit by a complex environment. To me that horse looks awful and I'd like to have worked on it more, but I put all my time into the girl, and the bow and her torso."

"This image is another example of removing the requirement of including architecture allowing for a much more interesting image. When I think about, "how could I have included yurts in this image?" it becomes obvious how limiting the idea really was. There is something I like a lot more about this sketch than the final image—it's just a lot less restrained."

"This one gave me problems. It was a bit less designed for the vertical crop than the others, and it uses a very, very long lens. The pieces weren't designed from the start to have the building overlays—those were a compromise between Han and myself. The original idea was to always have a unit alongside some architecture. But I was trying to make them in a somewhat more naturalistic, "you are there" kind of way, and the idea that these characters are all in heroic poses right in front of architecture that represents their culture wasn't just clichéd, but it greatly reduced the possibility of composition. The architectural overlays gave me a lot more freedom to compose and move things around, and it meant I could use much less architecture in the actual images."

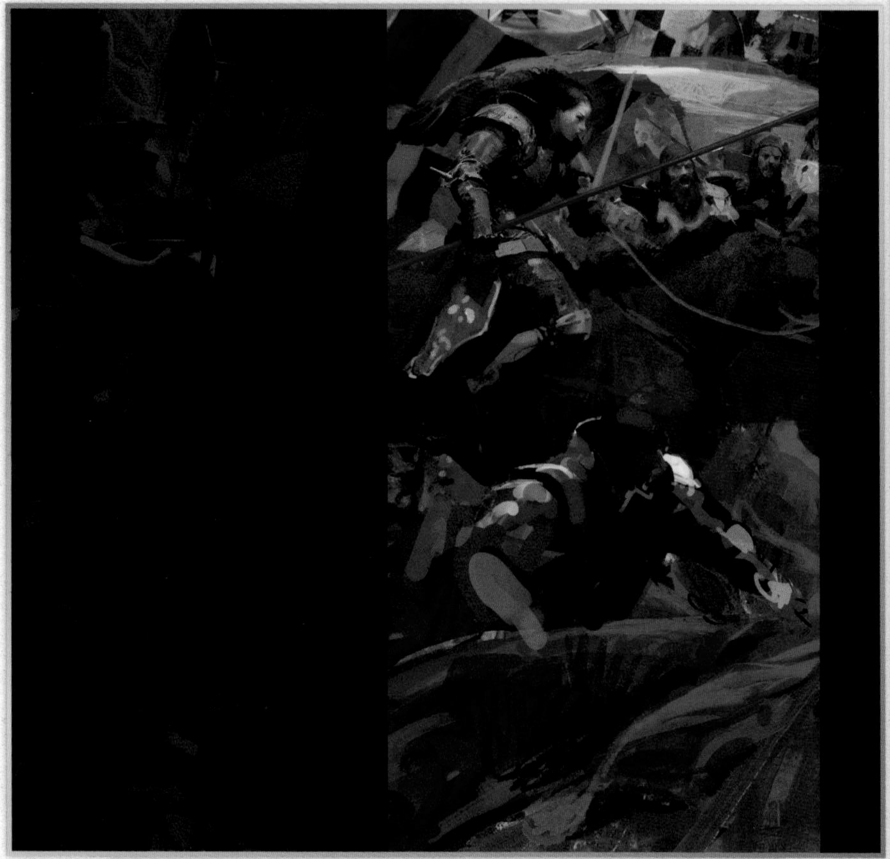

"This is an earlier stage of the final image. I'm much happier with this painting than the one I ended up with. Noble [Smith] wanted the [Jeanne D'Arc] character's hair to match the in-game version and the key art, and for some reason I just could not paint that head properly. The head in the draft version looks far better to me—it looks more credible because it's being pulled back. You can really see the roundness and youth of her head through the forms, and there's an intense eye socket. So to me the shapes are much more intriguing and forceful than the mop of hair coming over the front."

How free are you to choose the subject matter of each Age of Empires IV image you work on? What kind of guidelines do you usually work to and how much back and forth is there with World's Edge during the process?
They were completely open to anything. I could pretty much do anything that I wanted. The one limitation was that they sent me some screenshots of some units to work from. Though that wasn't even a real limitation, it was more of a small problem, because even at high resolution, the camera isn't very close to the units so it can't resolve much detail. A mounted Chinese warrior was probably 100 pixels high at most, so I couldn't really tell what was going on. There was also some concept art I could look at, but the game had already changed quite a bit since that was made.

The characters in the game are designed with very high contrast silhouettes so that it's clear what and where they are. So on the one hand I wanted to make illustrations that players could look at and say, "those are my English Longbowmen, or my archers." But on the other hand, rendering them out realistically in those bright colors might come with the danger of making them look clownish. But Han and Noble [Smith, Narrative Director at World's Edge] were very understanding about me changing costumes. As long as it was historically reasonable then they were fine with it, even though it didn't always match the in-game characters.

Do you have a particular favorite image from the eight-civilization series?
It's not easy to pick one, but I probably worked hardest on the English archer. I cast shadows from the arrow onto the sleeve, and gave the extensor and the outside of the arm a lot of definition to give motion to the pull of the bowstring. I carefully designed the folds in the tunic. It's realistic and well rendered but also all the folds and shapes are very designed. I was looking at it kind of like [J.C.] Leyendecker, who would make all these design decisions, but I'm painting it straight from my head, so it was very complex work, and at times incredibly difficult to do.

"This study of Jeanne D'Arc was based on a photograph of a statue and modified heavily, all done in Photoshop. I knew I wasn't going to a full piece from this, so it was just to get my head around what the character could maybe be, and playing with the idea that she could look a little bit beaten up."

"This is an earlier version of the final Holy Roman Empire painting. It's using a very dark armor, which I really prefer to the shiny chrome armor of the final version. I also really like the brutality of the forms here and the strength of the stance."

"At first I tried something without any armor. Both Han and Noble thought he looked a little bit too "fancy", or that the outfit was a bit too much like cosplay. So they asked for armor to make him look more serious, and I changed it."

Is there any other videogame artwork, or artist who works primarily on videogames, that you particularly admire?

I love Yoji Shinkawa and the Metal Gear Solid artwork especially. I've seen so much art from games that I love, but I'm not really into games as much these days so I don't follow everything. So much of the work that is done now is kind of painting over 3D models, and I always appreciate the stuff that doesn't do that as much—I like stuff that has more of a personal draw to it. I always do admire the design work, though.

You've created some highly polished promotional artworks in the past, including some truly iconic ones for series such as Age of Empires and Halo. How do you feel about the way that videogame "key art" has evolved over the years?

That is a really good question—I could speak for an hour on this, but I think that digital art and the software that has been developed is extremely powerful and time-saving. And that leads to things getting done quickly, but with more and more homogenization, so I'm seeing more of the software and less of the artist. And I'm not at all saying, "enough 3D and photo-bashing, let's all get back to drawing with pencil and paper." But I see people doing things with software for which it was never designed—that's exactly what happened with Photoshop, which was initially designed for photo manipulation. That's how I started working with it, doing what would later become known as photo-bashing. It just wasn't designed for drawing and painting.

Of course there's going to people—with software like zBrush and Unreal Engine—there are probably young people out there that will be using these tools in ways their designers never envisioned. I'm not bemoaning the fact that there's really powerful stuff out there. I guess I have more of a problem with it when those tools are used as a shortcut to doing hard work. I've probably drawn hundreds of thousands of heads in my life, but if every time I had to draw one I had instead gone and got a photograph and put it over a 3D model, then that's one more instance where I didn't draw it and didn't develop as an artist. So to some extent I think it's dulling the sharp edge that concept artists need to have. I actually think more comic book artists should be hired to design key arts. A lot of the designs that you see in comics are way cooler and often much less generic than the highly polished and rendered stuff that we see a lot of today. Comic artists are drawing every single day with pencil and paper, and you see their personality and development coming through, and to me that's very attractive. That's not to say that 3D should be outlawed by the artistic police—there will be plenty of artists that do use it in very artistic ways that I don't think we've even really begun to see yet.

You seem equally at home with sci-fi, fantasy and purely realistic/historical settings. Do you have a true preference of genre, and if so, why?

I never really break things down by genre. I find that if I don't apply those artificial distinctions from genre, then they can kind of mix in my head a little easier, and maybe lead to more interesting results. If you have a person with a sword, it can be from a thousand years ago or a thousand years in the future, but it doesn't have to be immediately obvious which of those it is.

You've mentioned before that you'd like to get back into using traditional materials in your work. Have you been able to do that, and if so, in what way?

I still draw all the time. I have a plastic box with a clipboard on top that contractors use, and that goes everywhere with me. If I have even 30 seconds I'll be drawing. But actually sitting down to do a physical painting, that's something I just haven't been able to find the time to do in the past few years.

"The application of the paint here is a little finicky, maybe a little over-rendered. I don't know how accurate the shiny chrome armor actually is, but it's almost certainly closer to how the armor would have been than the drafts were."

I have experimented with going in and out of analog and digital in the same piece, and using both to their advantage. Maybe it's just because I'm lazy and don't want to waddle over to the scanner again and again, but in the end I always find a way to get the result I want digitally. Sometimes a limitation can be really quite creative, and sometimes simpler tools can force you to find a better solution. For example, an entire Photoshop painting where you're only using a round brush—some would say all the custom brushes are far superior to the round brush and you have to use them—but I don't see it as a limitation, and sometimes just using the simplest tools is the best. Looking at it like that, going between analog and digital multiple times just adds a whole lot of complexity to it, bringing you away from what matters, which is your understanding of the form and shape and how light works. Doing a lot with textures, custom brushes or scanning in textures and so on, just seems to be secondary to me at this point, though there was a time when I was definitely playing a lot with that.

Can you tell us about your digital art equipment and environment? Do you work primarily in Photoshop with a Wacom tablet, for example? Are there any other programs or devices that you enjoy using or feel have certain advantages?

I work on a Windows PC. I was on a Mac from 1982 until 2001, and I moved over to PC in 2001 and just haven't looked back. With a PC, I can get a machine configured exactly the way I want it at exactly the price I want. I do love OSX and the core of Unix underneath it, though—I'd love to have that on a fully configurable PC.

"These are early sketches that show more examples of trying to think graphically. At this point I didn't even know the Abbasid Dynasty would ride camels. Once I knew that, it gave me a chance to really differentiate it and avoid all the images being the same."

"Camels are hard to paint. They're bizarre in their forms and colors, and how their fur can be thick or thin—some are almost bald and some are like Llamas. The concept art for the Abbasid Dynasty always featured their soldiers in these bright blue costumes, so this is one piece where I really tried with the costumes and the colors to make them very similar to the in-game units—I tried to do that sometimes, when it really made sense."

Left Page: *"This one was a draft done entirely in Rebelle, and I think it really shows. There's some very natural-style painting that you can't do in Photoshop."*

"This was a fairly quick study of a head—not for any particular civilization—that mixed Photoshop and Rebelle."

I use a standard Wacom Intuos tablet. The good folks at Wacom were kind enough to send me a Cintiq, and I tried to get used to it, but in the end I couldn't. I found that my hand being constantly backlit by something that was bright and moving gave me serious headaches. The eye having to constantly adjust to the contrast, and the hand covering some of the image—and also that I'd having to wear reading glasses while working—all combined to distract me. I now use a 40-inch 4K monitor that I sit four feet away from, so the reading glasses aren't an issue and it's much better for my eyes.

As far as software goes, yes I do use Photoshop, but I'm trying my best to move away from it. Mostly because I think Adobe has kind of abandoned the development of Photoshop as a professional painting tool. So I think there are other programs that are blowing by it as far as painting goes. One of them is even open source—Krita—and I think it's a brilliant program and I'd love to support it. I think they only have around five developers working on it now. They set out 15 years ago to very specifically make a program for digital painting, and they have absolutely succeeded in that. I love it and I've used it quite a bit in the Age of Empires work alongside Photoshop. Photoshop is still very much out in front in terms of speed, though. The brush management system is much improved, but for my purposes it hasn't changed otherwise since CS6.

Another program I like a lot is Rebelle, a watercolor simulation program made by a very talented developer. It simulates watercolor beautifully and it does weird, unexpected things, in the same way that watercolor does. You can see quite a bit of this in the watercolors visible in the background of the Abbasid Dynasty piece.

Finally, is there anything from your own experiences that might benefit artists who are starting out today?
Having worked at ILM for a short period, the influence of the other artists there was like a tornado sucking me in, and after a while I knew that I had to go off and do my own thing, and develop my own way of doing things. It was a real gamble, though; I may have suffered from the lack of the speed of learning you get from being around so many other talented artists—you really do benefit from that. I had a period where I was getting bored with what I was doing, and I would have given anything to be like the hot new artist, the one where everyone says, "oh my god, look what they can do!" But in the end you realize that you have to do what you do, and it is special. You might be tired of it and you might not think it's going anywhere, but the rest of the world may not see it that way at all, so you have continue to develop it on its own line. So don't try to be anyone else—you can't—you're you. I have a much better time with my work when I look at it that way, as opposed to looking at other super talented artists and going, "holy crap I'll never be able to do that."

"When I look at these drafts in reduced and compressed form, I like them even more. The finished ones can sometimes look noisy, while the sketches look much stronger. Looking at them at full resolution on a 4K monitor, the finished ones do look nice, but there's a lot to be said for how graphic these drafts are."

"I was happy with the way the horse came out in this piece. The angle and the lighting—a point source—are much simpler than in the Mongols piece, and there's no extreme motion. Those are all multipliers of complexity. Here the anatomy is static and I can exaggerate it, because it's a powerful warhorse, so it's much easier to pull off, and I think the overall silhouette says "horse" in a much more credible way than in the Mongols one."

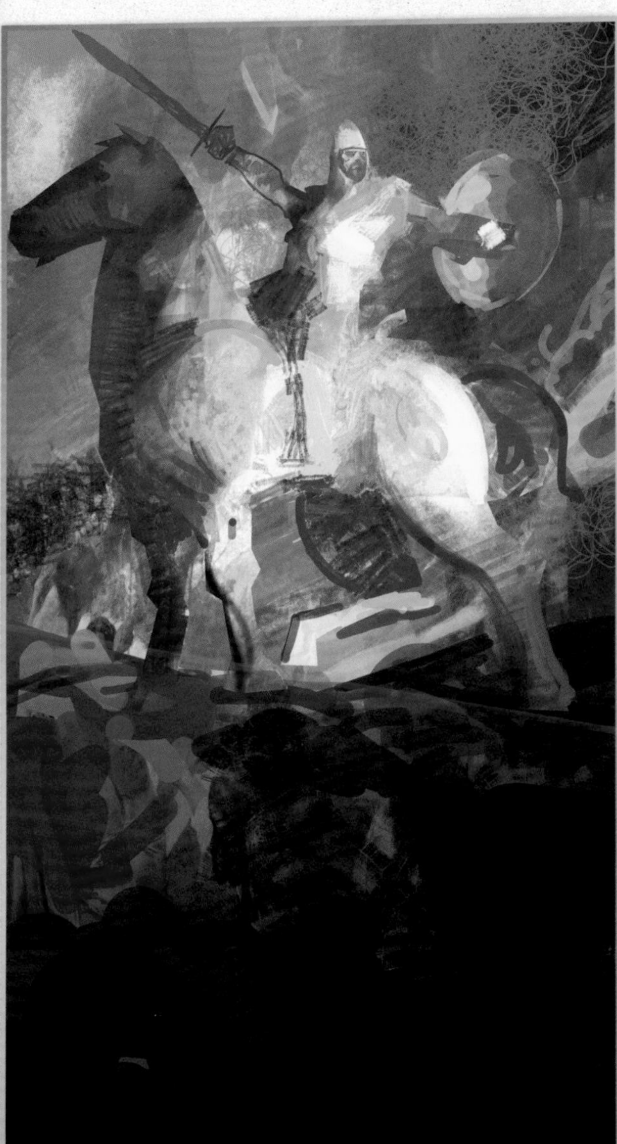

"The vertical crop was part of the idea from the very beginning. Most of the work went into that vertical slice and the outside parts could be very loose. I think the idea came from Han Randhawa—he wanted the stripe to always be in the same place, which made the series much harder to work on. It's an unusual aspect ratio and it encourages you to place a character in it around knee height, so you're looking up their nostrils, over and over again. I thought that if we couldn't get around that, then maybe we could incorporate it, and just have all of them be the same view but with a different character in exactly the same pose, on purpose. Putting them all together like that could have made the point very clearly, but in the end we decided to do them all differently.

At the start they sent me a template with the eight vertical crops, and said, "this is what it has to be." So I didn't even worry about the wings too much for quite a while, I thought I'd figure what goes in them later. Then, later on, I had boxed myself in to some nasty corners, and that's when I started composing the entire landscape images."

Visual Direction

This short section is home to an essay provided by Art Director at Relic Entertainment, Zach Schläppi. Zach provides some insight into the process and thinking that characterized the development of Age of Empires IV's visuals, and examines the kind of questions they asked along the way.

Nearly four years ago we were approached by Microsoft to develop the next game for the "Age of Empires" franchise. Imagine our excitement at the opportunity to refresh the "look and feel" of a revered twenty-year-old RTS phenomenon!

Just what is the visual brand of Age of Empires? From Age's first to most recent title the franchise has made significant technical jumps from isometric tile maps and sprites to fully realized 3D environments, lighting, atmosphere, and a free orbiting camera. This amount of technical change has shifted the look and feel of the game to a certain extent. However, Age's one enduring theme is its historical visual tone: History is colorful, celebratory, and epic. We captured the essence of Age through memorable battles, extraordinary campaigns, and the fun "what if" fantasy mash-up of pitting different civilizations from different regions and eras against each other in multiplayer's various procedural terrain and ocean maps.

So how did we update the visuals so that Age feels fresh for new fans without alienating current ones? We kept the core "celebratory history" tone and added another popular Middle Ages trope of the to play against: the "Dark" Ages.

We have the early 14th century Tuscan scholar Francesco Petrarca to thank for giving us the term "Dark Ages". We enjoy even popularizing this era in a more overcast, grim, and primitive environment. Ask anyone on the planet what they see and feel when they think "Middle Ages", and no doubt they will often describe it as such; even though more recent academic research reveals the "Dark Ages" as a far more colorful and brighter era. This is exactly how we start the player: a town center, jewel-like as if torn from the cover of a coffee-table book, a vibrant oasis surrounded by a menacing wilderness, of "darkness and dense gloom".

Why is gold and Medieval illustration such a prevalent motif in our presentation design? Gold is one of the most iconic resource mechanics in Age as well as one of history's most enduring universal currencies among nearly all civilizations. Likewise, the precious metal has fueled growth in both business, culture, and expansion as well as in conflict, defense, innovation—and destruction.

Our primary inspiration is Medieval illuminated manuscripts. These are illustrated texts that covered, among other things, religion, inventory and chronology of rulers and daily life, grandly embellished with color and gold leaf. These artifacts can be commonly found among many civilizations, regardless of region or religion. We took the gold-leaf imagery and overlayed it upon important in-game events, such as aging up, construction, victory and defeat; the F/X and UI and even included it in our historical mini-documentaries.

This concept painting was annotated by Zach to illustrate how different stages of environmental development should naturally transition. It flows from the hinterlands to the left to the urbanized, crowded town on the far right.

Jonathan Lai & Zach Schläppi
Environmental Proggression Example
Concept Artwork

Stuart Ng
Environment and Mood Exploration
Concept Artwork

This is our nod to augmented reality, an outline of our past that behaves in a molten state, evoking both spilt blood and brushed ink coursing along a path, illuminating, erratic, expanding like empires and time. Despite the countless hours of technical direction, asset polish, production management, motion capture, audio engineering, and special effects tuning, our intention is to ensure this intimate and imperfect shared narrative of humanity was prevalent throughout the game.

Technically, the art direction of Age was also an exercise in strategic visual self-control. Because the pace and intensity of a real-time-strategy session can quickly tax a player's visual attention we had to prioritize readability with conveyability. How do we harmonize the visual tone and design of Age with gameplay while still maintaining a familiar and fresh presentation?

We help the player's eye by curating the amount of detail the silhouette, color, texture, and saturation in each environment. The intent is to reinforce the most important visual reads for easy and rapid identification under duress—using the terrain to an advantage, assessing enemies' settlements, or making difficult choices along sprawling battlefields. The shape and size of buildings and characters are the most stylized elements in the game. Primary and secondary reads, like helmets, shoulders, shields and weapons, along with rooftops, banners, decorative motifs, landscaping and building footprints are oversized and exaggerated to reinforce readability and classification. The franchise's saturate color legacy is maintained, albeit restricted to the most critical gameplay. Characters are the most saturate and brightest, followed by UI/UX, while terrain becomes the most neutral toned canvas by comparison.

Regardless of the 4K resolution and physically based rendering technology, Age is not a photorealistic franchise. Hyper resolution can work against complex real-time-strategy environments: detail is important, but too much—or the wrong amount—quickly exhausts the eyes and proves harder to discern the important information from the noise during gameplay. This graphic stylization avoids any unnecessary detail that could inadvertently become an interference and instead provides a point of visual rest for the player to convey clearer movement and identification. The detail that is revealed in structures, foliage, water and terrain is mostly expressed through hue variation leaving the style to feel richer and more painterly without feeling cartoonish.

The question we always ask is, what do we want the player to feel when they return from school or work at the end of the day, sitting in front of their television, monitor or surface? They want to feel transported to a fantasy of their making. We aim to show the player a rich and colorful cinematic tapestry of an era worthy of spending time with. We visually reward those who enjoy building and defending as well those who enjoy conquering and destroying. Age of Empires: IV is both a generous nod to Microsoft's colorful franchise, as well as a visual celebration of Relic's creative gameplay. We are proud to offer our players a range of choices that both entertain as well as enrich; whether it is watching compelling short historical documentaries, stepping into history in our campaigns, or assembling a civilization dream team. Maybe it's just looking over the shoulder of a player, watching them push against the landscape of "darkness and dense gloom" acting—as Petrarch envisioned for his era—as a harbinger of light, progressing to what will eventually become the Renaissance.

Enjoy and wololo!

—Zach Schläppi
Art Director, Relic Entertainment

Index

This index is provided to make the book a little easier to use as a reference guide. If you're looking for details on particular units, buildings or technologies, you'll find their most relevant pages listed here in alphabetical order.

Civilizations

Buildings

Technologies

Units

Credits & Thanks

Created and published by

FUTUREPRESS

Verlag & Marketing GmbH
Mansteinstr. 52, 20253 Hamburg, Germany

Managing Directors **Frank Glaser**
Jörg Kraut

Editor-in-chief **Wil Murray**

Creative Director **Jörg Kraut**

Senior Editor **Bruce Byrne**

Authors **Clemens Kabas**
Rosanna Klein
Bebe Lees
Florian Zametzer

Layout **Jörg Kraut**
Wil Murray

Stay in touch **future-press.com**
facebook/futurepress
@futurepress

Thanks to our friends & families

Ryan Payton, Jonathan Gagné, Charley K. Ziegler, Wayne Norwood, Hirofumi Yamada, Anwar Hassan, David Waybright and Björn Hammarstroem.

Ania Smok, Annette & Patrick Byrne, Kathleen & Patrick Murray, Ulrike, Jim & Caitlin Murray, Grit, Jil & Emmie Preuss, Lea, Alex & Katja Glaser.

Additional thanks

AussieDrongo, Brisolyn, True, TheViper, WinstonWaffles, HarrisonC

A special thank you to Relic Entertainment, World's Edge, and all internal and external partner studios and groups, and the Community Council that brought Age of Empires IV to life, and as a result, helped fill the pages of the Companion Book you now hold in your hands.

General Companion Book Support

World's Edge

Shannon Loftis (VP, Studio Manager)
Michael Mann (Executive Producer)
Noble Smith (Franchise Narrative Director)
Han Randhawa (Senior Art Director)
Adam Isgreen (Franchise Creative Director)
Christopher Rubyor (Design Director)
Todd Masten (Audio Director)
Maja Persson (Principal Lead Producer)
Betsy Aoki (Senior Producer)
Yasemin Kuyumcu (Senior Producer)
Savannah Harrison (Senior Producer)
Emma Bridle (Director of Customer Voice)
Joe Homes (Community Manager)
Tim Fritz (Lead Producer)

Microsoft

Saro Balbhadruni (Program Manager, Localization)
Jeff Nelson (Age IV Quality Lead)
Shon Damron (Senior PR Manager)
Brandon Wells (Senior Product Marketing Manager)

Relic Entertainment

Greg Wilson (Executive Producer)
Eliot Hong (Senior Community Manager)
David Phan (Principal Producer)
Sam Sayer (Producer)
Barry McDougall (Principal Artist, Presentation Lead)
Philippe Boulle (Principal Designer, Narrative Lead)
Zach Schläppi (Principal Artist, Art Director)
Brent Breedveld (Principal Animator, Animation Director)
Lin Gardiner (Principal Designer, Music Lead)
Bryan Rennie (Principal Audio Designer, Audio Director)
Eric Wrobel (Senior Designer, Balance Lead)
Zak Robinson (Senior Designer, Balance)
Colin Hamilton (Designer, Balance)
Taylor Fales (Senior Designer, Balance Lead)
Dan Pool (Senior Designer, Speech Lead)
Nick Bedell (Senior Sound Designer)
Kristina Wiik (Senior Designer, Narrative)
Lauren Wood (Principal Designer, Narrative)
Stuart Ng (Senior Concept Artist)
Kevin Lam (Concept Artist)
Michael Conkin (Senior Designer, Ritual & Retention Lead)
Katherine Magnaval (Designer, Ritual & Retention)
Euphemia Wong (Senior Designer, UX Lead)
Nick Taylor (Designer, Maps Lead)

ISBN-13: 978-3-86-993110-4